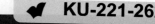
Table of Contents

Glossary

Glossary

achievement motivation   according to David McClelland, the drive to strive for success.

acquiescence response set   a bias in which people are more likely to agree than disagree with anything that is asked of them.

act frequency approach   assessing personality by examining the frequency with which a person performs certain observable actions.

agape   according to Rollo May, a type of unselfish love characterized by devotion to the welfare of others.

aggregation   according to Seymour Epstein, the averaging of behaviors across situations (or over time), to improve the reliability of behavior assessments.

aggression drive   Alfred Adler's concept that an individual is driven to lash out against the inability to achieve or master something, as a reaction to perceived helplessness.

aggressive personality   according to Karen Horney, a neurotic trend to see most others as being hostile, to believe that only the most competent and cunning survive, and to behave hatefully and hostilely toward others in order to maintain a feeling of control and power.

aggressive style   according to Karen Horney, a mode of adapting to the world used by those who believe in fighting to get by.

Agreeableness (Big Five)   the personality dimension that includes friendliness, cooperation, and warmth; people low in this dimension are cold, quarrelsome, and unkind.

Alzheimer's disease   a disease of the brain's cerebral cortex, primarily affecting elderly people, that causes altered behavior and memory loss.

American Dilemma   Gunnar Myrdal's term for the paradoxical idea that slavery was allowed and endorsed despite the claim that the United States was founded on the principle that all men are created equal.

American paradox   the contemporary situation where we have material abundance co-occurring with social recession and psychological depression.

anal stage   Freud's stage of psychosexual development around age two during which children are toilet trained.

androgen   the class of sex hormones typically considered the "male" hormone.

androgenized females   genetically female individuals who were prenatally exposed to excessive levels of androgens and are born with either masculine or ambiguous external genitalia.

androgyny   the consolidation of both female and male traits.

anima   according to Carl Jung, the archetype representing the female element of a man.

animus   according to Carl Jung, the archetype representing the male element of a woman.

anterograde amnesia   the inability to form new conscious memories.

antisocial personality disorder   a personality disorder in which an individual is excessively impulsive, violates the rules of society, and lacks anxiety or guilt for his or her behavior.

anxiety   a state of intense apprehension or uncertainty, resulting from the anticipation of a threatening event or challenge, either external or internal; the ego's job is to protect against anxiety, but its failures lead to psychological problems.

anxious-ambivalent lovers   according to Phillip Shaver, people who have a romantic attachment style in which they want to get close but are insecure with the relationship.

approach–approach conflict   a term used by Dollard and Miller to describe a conflict in which a person is drawn to two equally attractive choices.

approach–avoidance conflict   a term used by Dollard and Miller to describe a conflict between primary and secondary drives that occurs when a punishment results in the conditioning of a fear response to a drive.

archetypes   in Carl Jung's neo–analytic theory, emotional symbols that are common to all people and have been formed since the beginning of time.

attachment   the close bond that forms shortly after birth between an infant and the mother (or other caregiver).

attention-deficit/hyperactivity disorder (ADHD)   a disorder in which a person has atypical attentional processes.

attribution theories   theories that examine the ways in which individuals draw inferences about other people's behavior.

authentic love   according to Rollo May, a type of love that incorporates all other types of love.

authoritarian personality   a person with antidemocratic tendencies; such a person tends to be narrow-minded, rigid, defensive, and tends to show prejudice against minority groups.

authoritarian personality type   according to Erich Fromm, a person who has a cruel penchant for exerting power over others, abusing them, and taking their possessions; such a personality characteristic may result from a particularly negative relationship with one's parents.

avoidance–avoidance conflict   a term used by Dollard and Miller to describe a conflict in which a person is faced with two equally undesirable choices.

avoidant lovers   according to Phillip Shaver, people who have a romantic attachment style in which they feel uncomfortable being close to others or having others close to them and have trouble trusting and being trusted by others.

Barnum effect   the tendency to believe in the accuracy of vague generalities about one's personality.

B-love   *see* being love.

basic anxiety   according to Karen Horney, a child's fear of being alone, helpless, and insecure that arises from problems with one's parents.

behavior potential   a term used by Julian Rotter to describe the likelihood that a particular behavior will occur in a specific situation.

behavioral genomics   the study of how genes affect behavior.

behavioral signature   according to Walter Mischel, the set of situation–behavior relationships that are typical of an individual and that contribute to the apparent consistency of an individual's personality.

behaviorism   the learning approach to psychology introduced by John Watson that emphasizes the study of observable behavior.

being love   according to Abraham Maslow, love that is unselfish and cares for the needs of others; a person who is involved in being love is more self-actualized and helps his or her partner toward self-actualization.

being-in-the-world   the existential idea that the self cannot exist without a world and the world cannot exist without a person or being to perceive it.

Bem Sex Role Inventory   a measure designed by Sandra Bem to classify individuals as masculine, feminine, androgynous, or undifferentiated (low in both masculinity and femininity).

Big Five   the trait approach to personality that is supported by a great deal of research and suggests personality can be captured in five dimensions: Extroversion, Agreeableness, Conscientiousness, Neuroticism, and Openness.

biological determinism   the belief that an individual's personality is completely determined by biological factors (and especially by genetic factors).

bipolar disorder (also called manic-depression)   a disorder in which an individual swings regularly between bouts of wildly enthusiastic energy and bouts of hopeless depression.

bisexuality   sexual attraction to both men and women.

borderline personality disorder   combination of impulsive, self-destructive behavior, fragile self-identity, and moody, stormy relationships.

broaden-and-build model   proposes that experiences of positive emotions, such as joy, interest, pride, contentment, and love can broaden people's modes of thinking and responding, bringing more possible actions to mind.

brotherly love   according to Fromm, the type of love that involves loving all of humankind and that reunites isolated individuals with one another.

cardinal dispositions   a term used by Gordon Allport to describe personal dispositions that exert an overwhelming influence on behavior.

Cartesian dualism   the concept proposed by René Descartes that there is a separation of the mind and body.

case study design   a research method that involves an in-depth analysis of a single individual.

castration anxiety   according to Sigmund Freud, an unconscious fear of castration that results from a boy's struggle to deal with his love for his mother while knowing that he cannot overcome his father.

categorization   the perceptual process by which highly complex ensembles of information are filtered into a small number of identifiable and familiar objects and entities.

central dispositions   a term used by Gordon Allport to describe the several personal dispositions around which personality is organized.

choleric   a personality type based on the ancient Greek humors discussed by Hippocrates and Galen in which one is angry against the arbitrary controls of one's life and has generally poor interpersonal relations.

chumship   Harry Stack Sullivan's idea, derived from the sociological concept of the social self, that a preadolescent's chums serve as a social mirror for forming his or her identity.

circumplex model   an arrangement of two basic dimensions of social interaction that shows the circular pattern of the combined characteristics.

classical conditioning   the concept that after the repeated pairing of an unconditioned stimulus that elicits an unconditioned response and a neutral stimulus, the previously neutral stimulus can come to elicit the same response as the unconditioned stimulus.

cognitive complexity   the extent to which a person comprehends, utilizes, and is comfortable with a greater number of distinctions or separate elements into which an entity or event is analyzed, and the extent to which the person can integrate these elements by drawing connections or relationships among them.

cognitive intervention   teaching people to change their thought processes.

cognitive simplicity   according to George Kelly, the tendency for some people to fail to make distinctions among other people and to perceive other people as similar to one another.

cognitive style   an individual's distinctive, enduring way of dealing with everyday tasks of perception and problem solving.

collective unconscious   according to Carl Jung, the component of the mind that contains a deeper level of unconsciousness made up of archetypes that are common across all people.

common traits   the term used by Gordon Allport to describe organizing structures that people in a population share.

competencies   according to Walter Mischel, a person's abilities and knowledge.

complex   a group of emotionally charged thoughts, feelings, and ideas that are related to a particular theme.

Conscientiousness (Big Five)   the personality dimension that includes dependability, cautiousness, organization, and responsibility; people low in this dimension are impulsive, careless, disorderly, and undependable.

construct validity   the extent to which a test truly measures a theoretical construct.

contemporaneous causation   Kurt Lewin's concept that behavior is caused at the moment of its occurrence by all the influences that are present in the individual at that moment.

content validity   the extent to which a test is measuring the domain it is supposed to be measuring.

control group   a comparison group that provides a standard by which to evaluate a theory or technique.

controllability of causality   according to Bernard Weiner, the perception that events are due either to controllable factors or to influences beyond an individual's control.

convergent validation   the extent to which an assessment is related to what it should be related to.

corpus callosum   the fibers that connect the two brain hemispheres.

correlation coefficient   a mathematical index of the degree of agreement or association between two measures.

3

correlational studies studies in which the degree of relationship between two variables (or among multiple variables) is assessed.

criterion-related validation the extent to which an assessment predicts outcome criteria that were produced by different assessment methods.

critical period the point during development when an organism is optimally ready to learn a particular response pattern.

cultural effects the shared behaviors and customs learned from the institutions in society.

cultural imperialism the extending of one's own cultural approaches over those of another culture or subculture.

cumulative continuity the tendency of personality to remain stable over time through consistency of interpretations, environments, and reactions.

D-love *see* deficiency love.

deductive approach an approach to psychology in which the conclusions follow logically from the premises or assumptions.

defense mechanisms in psychoanalytic theory, the processes that distort reality to protect the ego.

defensive pessimism the approach of anticipating a poorer outcome, thus reducing anxiety and actually improving performance in a risky situation.

deficiency love according to Abraham Maslow, love that is selfish and needy.

deficiency needs according to Abraham Maslow, needs that are essential for survival including physiological, safety, belonging, love, and esteem needs.

delay of gratification a specific aspect of self-control that occurs when an individual chooses to forgo an immediate reinforcer in order to wait for a later, better reinforcer.

demographic information information relevant to population statistics such as age, cultural group, place of birth, religion, and the like.

demon archetype according to Carl Jung, the archetype that embodies cruelty and evil.

denial a defense mechanism in which one refuses to acknowledge anxiety-provoking stimuli.

Despised Self Karen Horney's concept of the part of personality consisting of perceptions of our inferiority and shortcomings, often based on others' negative evaluations of us and our resulting helplessness.

dialect regional variations in phonology, vocabulary, and syntactic forms.

dialectical humanism Erich Fromm's approach to personality, which tries to reconcile the biological, driven side of human beings and the pressures of societal structure by focusing on the belief that people can rise above or transcend these forces and become spontaneous, creative, and loving.

dialectical tension concept used by Mihaly Csikszentmihalyi for the idea that creative people tend to have traits that are seemingly contradictory but that play a role in their creativity.

diathesis the often hereditary predisposition of the body to disease or disorder.

diathesis-stress model model of disease that suggests that although a predisposition to illness exists because of genetics or upbringing, the illness itself will not appear unless or until it is elicited by the environment.

discriminant validation the extent to which an assessment is not related to what it should not be related to.

discrimination the concept that a conditioned response will not occur for all possible stimuli, indicating that an animal can learn to tell the difference between different stimuli.

disease-prone personality personality characteristics associated with an increased likelihood of becoming ill.

displacement a defense mechanism in which the target of one's unconscious fears or desires is shifted away from the true cause.

document analysis a method of assessing personality by applying personality theories to the study of diaries, letters, and other personal records.

ectomorph according to W. H. Sheldon, a somatotype describing slender bookworm types of people.

effect size a statistical index of the magnitude of a measured effect, capturing how much difference a variable makes.

ego in psychoanalytic theory, the personality structure that develops to deal with the real world; in neo-analytic theory, this term refers to the individuality of a person that is the central core of personality; and specifically for Carl Jung, it is the aspect of personality that is conscious and embodies the sense of self.

ego crises in Erik Erikson's theory of identity, each of the series of eight "crises" (conflicts or choices) that must be resolved, in sequence, for optimal psychological development.

ego development an individual's level of psychological maturity.

ego-resilient a term used to describe people who are calm, socially at ease, insightful, and not anxious.

egoistic dominance according to Whiting and Edwards, trying to control the behavior of others in order to meet one's own needs.

electrodermal measures measures that monitor the electrical activity of the skin with electrodes.

electroencephalogram (EEG) a measurement of electrical brainwave activity using electrodes attached to the outside of the skull.

emic approach an approach that is culture-specific, focusing on a single culture on its own terms.

emotion knowledge the ability to recognize and interpret emotions in the self and others.

emotional intelligence the set of emotional abilities specific to dealing with other people.

encoding strategies according to Walter Mischel, the schemas and mechanisms one uses to process and encode information.

endomorph according to W. H. Sheldon, a somatotype describing overweight, good-natured types of people.

environmental press the push of the situation emphasized in Henry Murray's approach to personality; it is a directional force on a person that arises from other people and events in the environment.

eros according to Rollo May, a type of procreative love that is experiential and savoring.

erotic love according to Fromm, the type of love that is directed toward a single individual; it is a short-lived intimacy that satisfies sexual needs and alleviates anxiety.

error variance variations of a measurement that are the result of irrelevant, chance fluctuations.

estrogen   the class of sex hormones typically considered the "female" hormone.

ethnic bias   a type of bias in which a test fails to take into account the relevant culture or subculture of the person being tested.

ethnic group   a group whose membership is based primarily on shared cultural habits or customs.

ethnocentrism   evaluating others from one's own cultural point of view.

ethology   the study of animal behavior patterns in natural environments.

etic approach   an approach that is cross-cultural, searching for generalities across cultures.

eugenics   the movement begun by Francis Galton that encouraged preserving or purifying the gene pool of the elite in order to improve human blood lines.

evolution   the theory in which individual characteristics that enable the organism to pass on genes to offspring become more prevalent in the population over generations.

evolutionary personality theory   an area of study applying biological evolutionary theory to human personality.

existentialism   an area of philosophy concerned with the meaning of human existence.

expectancies   according to Mischel, a personality variable encompassing a person's outcome expectancies and self-efficacy expectancies.

experience sampling method of assessment   a method in which participants record their current activity or thought processes when they are paged by the experimenter at various intervals during the day.

experiencing person   in Carl Rogers's phenomenological view, important issues are defined by each person for himself or herself in the context of the total range of things the person experiences.

explanatory style   a set of cognitive personality variables that captures a person's habitual means of interpreting events in his or her life.

explicit memory   a memory that can be consciously recalled or recognized.

expressive behavior   behavior that involves the emotional well-being of one's social or family group; contrasts with instrumental behavior.

expressive style   a term used to describe nonverbal social skills such as vocal characteristics, facial expressions, body gestures, and movements.

external locus of control   according to Julian Rotter, the belief that things outside of the individual determine whether desired outcomes occur.

extinction   the process by which the frequency of the organism's producing a response gradually decreases when the response behavior is no longer followed by the reinforcement.

Extroversion (Big Five)   the personality dimension that includes enthusiasm, dominance, and sociability; people low on this dimension are considered introverted.

extroversion (Eysenck)   in Hans Eysenck's biologically based theory, the term is used to describe the characteristic of being generally sociable, active, and outgoing; extroverts are thought to have a relatively lower level of brain arousal and thus tend to seek stimulation.

extroversion (Jung)   a term used by Carl Jung to describe the directing of the libido, or psychic energy, toward things in the external world.

F-scale   a scale developed at the University of California, Berkeley, to measure a person's proneness to being rigid and authoritarian.

facet   within the Big Five trait approach, the component characteristics (also sometimes called subfactors) that underlie each of the Big Five factors.

factor analysis   a statistical technique in which correlations among a number of simple scales are reduced to a few basic dimensions.

femininity   the qualities associated with being a woman.

fictional goals   according to Alfred Adler, strivings for self-improvement that vary from person to person but that reflect an individual's view of perfection.

field dependence   the extent to which an individual's problem solving is influenced by salient but irrelevant aspects of the context in which the problem occurs.

field independence   the extent to which an individual's problem solving is *not* influenced by salient but irrelevant aspects of the context in which the problem occurs.

field theory   Kurt Lewin's approach to personality, suggesting that behavior is determined by complex interactions among a person's internal psychological structure, the forces of the external environment, and the structural relationships between the person and the environment.

fixed interval reinforcement schedule   a pattern of reinforcement occurring after a regular interval of time

fixed ratio reinforcement schedule   a pattern of reinforcement occurring after a regular number of responses by the organism.

forced-choice recognition   a procedure in which a person studies a word list and then chooses which word appeared on the list from pairs of words.

free association   a method used in psychoanalysis in which an individual reports everything that comes into awareness.

free recall   a procedure in which a person studies a word list and then reports as many words as he or she can remember from the list.

Freudian slip   a psychological error in speaking or writing that reveals something about the person's unconscious.

frustration-aggression hypothesis   the theory that aggression is the result of blocking, or frustrating, a person's efforts to attain a goal.

functionalism   the approach to psychology that declares that behavior and thought evolve as a result of their functionality for survival.

functionally autonomous   a term used by Gordon Allport to describe the idea that in adulthood many motives and tendencies become independent of their origins in childhood and that finding out where such tendencies originated is, therefore, not important.

functionally equivalent   Gordon Allport's concept that many behaviors of individuals are similar in their meaning because the individuals tend to view many situations and stimuli in the same way; for Allport, the trait is the internal structure that causes this regularity.

Gemeinschaftsgefuhl   community feeling: Adler's term for a person's level of social interest.

gender roles   social roles based on gender.

gender schema theory   the theory that argues that our culture and gender-role socialization provide us with gender schemas.

gender schemas organized mental structures that delineate our understanding of the abilities of, appropriate behavior of, and appropriate situations for males and females.

gender typed describes an individual whose conception of self and of others is unusually strongly organized around gender schemas.

generalization the tendency for similar stimuli to evoke the same response.

generalized expectancy according to Julian Rotter, expectancies that are related to a group of situations.

genetic sex whether an individual has XX chromosomes (female) or XY chromosomes (male).

genital stage Freudian stage of psychosexual development beginning at adolescence in which attention is turned toward heterosexual relations.

gestalt a German word for pattern or configuration.

Gestalt psychology an approach to psychology that emphasizes the integrative and active nature of perception and thought suggesting that the whole may be greater than the sum of its parts.

habit hierarchy in social learning theory, a learned hierarchy of likelihoods that a person will produce particular responses in particular situations.

habits in learning theory, simple associations between a stimulus and a response.

hemispheric activity the level of activity within one cerebral hemisphere (left or right).

hero archetype according to Carl Jung, the archetype that represents a strong and good force that does battle with the enemy in order to rescue another from harm.

human genome project an effort to identify each of the thousands of genes in our chromosomes.

human potential movement an existential-humanistic movement in which people are encouraged to realize their inner potentials through small group meetings, self-disclosure, and introspection.

humanism a philosophical movement that emphasizes the personal worth of the individual and the importance of human values.

hydraulic displacement model Sigmund Freud's concept that suggests that unacceptable impulses build up like steam in a boiler and must be released.

hypermnesia a situation in which a later attempt to remember something yields information that was not reportable on an earlier attempt to remember.

hypnosis a process by which a person is induced into a trance state where action is partially under the control of another person.

hysteria a term used for various forms of mental illness for which no organic cause could be found and which could sometimes be cured by psychological and social influences.

I-It monologue a phrase used by philosopher Martin Buber to describe a utilitarian relationship in which a person uses others but does not value them for themselves.

I-Thou dialogue a phrase used by philosopher Martin Buber to describe a direct, mutual relationship in which each individual confirms the other person as being of unique value.

id in psychoanalytic theory, the undifferentiated, unsocialized core of personality that contains the basic psychic energy and motivations.

Ideal Self Karen Horney's concept of the self that we view as perfection and hope to achieve, as molded by perceived inadequacies.

identity crisis a term proposed by Erik Erikson to describe uncertainty about one's abilities, associations, and future goals.

identity formation the process of developing one's individual personality and concept of one's self.

idiographic involved in the study of individual cases.

idiolect each individual's own unique version of his or her native language.

illusion of individuality according to Harry Stack Sullivan, the idea that a person has a single, fixed personality is just an illusion.

immature love according to Fromm, the type of love in which the taking of love overwhelms the giving of love.

implicit memory a memory that is not consciously recalled but that nevertheless influences behavior or thoughts.

implicit personality theory a type of biasing tendency for people, perhaps erroneously, to see certain traits as going together and to perceive consistencies when viewing the personalities of others.

imprinting a term used by ethologists to describe a type of learning that occurs at a particular early point in an organism's life and cannot be changed later on.

Individual Psychology Alfred Adler's theory of personality that stresses the unique motivations of individuals and the importance of each person's perceived niche in society.

inductive approach an approach to psychology in which observations are systematically collected and concepts are developed based on what the data reveal.

infantile amnesia the phenomenon of adults being unable to remember what happened to them before age three or four.

inferiority complex according to Alfred Adler, an individual's exaggerated feelings of personal incompetence that result from an overwhelming sense of helplessness or some experience that leaves him or her powerless.

instrumental behavior behavior that is oriented to objectives that are task-focused and beyond our interpersonal system; contrasts with expressive behavior.

internal consistency reliability degree of consistency between subparts or equivalent parts of a test.

internal locus of control according to Julian Rotter, the generalized expectancy that an individual's own actions lead to desired outcomes.

interpersonal theory of psychiatry Harry Stack Sullivan's approach to personality that focuses on the recurring social situations faced by an individual.

intimacy motive the need to share oneself with others in intimate ways as studied by Dan P. McAdams.

Introversion (Big Five) this term is used to describe those who are low on the personality dimension of Extroversion; people who are introverted tend to be shy, submissive, retiring, and quiet.

introversion (Eysenck) In Hans Eysenck's biologically based theory the term is used to describes characteristic of being generally quiet, reserved, and thoughtful, introverts are thought to have a relatively higher level of brain arousal, which causes them to shy away from stimulating social environments.

introversion (Jung) a term used by Carl Jung to describe the directing of the libido, or psychic energy, toward things in the internal world.

item intercorrelation the extent to which test items are related to one another.

Item Response Theory (IRT) a mathematical approach to choosing test items in which the probability of a positive response to an item is determined by the person's estimated position on the underlying trait being measured, as well as by characteristics of the item.

Judgment–Perception scale subclassification of the Myers-Briggs Type Indicator that reflects whether a person is oriented toward evaluating or perceiving things.

kin selection the idea that increasing the likelihood for the family members of an individual to survive increases the likelihood that the individual's genes will be carried on to the next generation even if the individual did not reproduce him- or herself.

L-data the term used by R. B. Cattell to describe data gathered about a person's life from school records or similar sources.

latency period according to Sigmund Freud, the period from age 5 to age 11 in which no important psychosexual developments take place and during which sexual urges are not directly expressed but instead are channeled into other activities.

latent content the part of dreams or other aspects of psychological experience that underlies the conscious portion and reveals hidden meaning.

Law of Effect Edward Thorndike's concept that the consequence of a behavior will either strengthen or weaken the behavior; that is, when a response follows a stimulus and results in satisfaction for the organism, this strengthens the connection between stimulus and response; however, if the response results in discomfort or pain, the connection is weakened.

learned helplessness the term used by Martin Seligman to describe a situation in which repeated exposure to unavoidable punishment leads an organism to accept later punishment even when it *is* avoidable.

learned optimism the term used by Martin Seligman to describe an optimistic style that people can be trained to achieve.

learning style the characteristic way in which an individual approaches a task or skill to be learned.

libido in Sigmund Freud's psychoanalytic theory, the sexual energy that underlies psychological tension; in Carl Jung's neo-analytic theory, the term is used to describe a general psychic energy that is not necessarily sexual in nature.

life-course approach approach to personality by Avshalom Caspi that emphasizes that patterns of behavior change as a function of age, culture, social groups, life events, ad so forth, as well as because of internal drives, motives, and traits.

life space in Kurt Lewin's theory, all the internal and external forces that act on an individual.

life tasks a term used by Nancy Cantor to describe age-determined issues on which people are currently concentrating.

linguistic relativity the idea of Benjamin Lee Whorf and Edward Sapir that claims that our interpretation of the world is to a large extent dependent on the linguistic system by which we classify it.

locus of causality according to Bernard Weiner, the perception that situations are caused either by some internal factor within an individual or by external situational issues.

locus of control in Julian Rotter's theory, the variable that measures the extent to which an individual habitually attributes outcomes to factors internal to the self versus external to the self.

longitudinal study according to Jack Block, the close, comprehensive, systematic, objective, sustained study of individuals over significant portions of the life span.

love tasks according to Alfred Adler, the fundamental social issue of finding a suitable life partner.

lysergic acid diethylamide (LSD) hallucinogenic drug derived from a fungus that evokes dreamlike changes in perception and thought.

manifest content the part of dreams or other aspects of psychological experience that is remembered and consciously considered.

masculine protest according to Alfred Adler, an individual's attempt to be competent and independent rather than merely an outgrowth of his or her parents.

masculinity the qualities associated with being a man.

maternal instinct according to the functional school of psychology, an inborn emotional tendency toward nurturance that is triggered by contact with a helpless infant.

mature love according to Fromm, the type of love in which each partner cares for the other, feels responsibility to the other, and gives love freely.

melancholic a personality type based on the ancient Greek humors discussed by Hippocrates and Galen in which one is brooding, sad, and depressive.

Ménière's disease an inner-ear disorder that can produce disabling dizziness, nausea, and auditory disturbances.

mesomorph according to W. H. Sheldon, a somatotype describing muscular, large-boned, athletic types of people.

meta-analysis a statistical technique for combining the results of multiple research studies.

Minnesota Multiphasic Personality Inventory (MMPI) a comprehensive, self-report personality test that is focused on assessing psychopathology.

mirror neurons brain cells that react (fire) in the same way both when a person (or animal) acts and when that person (or animal) sees another person act in the same way.

mother archetype according to Carl Jung, the archetype that embodies generativity and fertility.

motherly love according to Fromm, the type of love that is completely one-sided and unequal, in which the mother gives love and asks for nothing, and from which a child acquires a sense of security and stability.

motives internal psychobiological forces that induce behavior towards a goal or push for expression.

multiple intelligences Howard Gardner's theory that claims that all human beings have at least seven different ways of knowing about the world and that people differ from one another in the relative strengths of each of these seven ways.

multitrait-multimethod perspective the use of multiple assessment methods and various traits in order to determine test validity.

Myers-Briggs Type Indicator a widely used instrument that attempts to measure introversion and extroversion and several other subclassifications as defined by Carl Jung.

narcissistic personality disorder a disorder in which one feels powerless and dependent yet appears to be authoritative and self-aggrandizing.

narrative approach Dan P. McAdams's approach to personality that involves studying motivations through biographies in order to understand the full life context of the whole person.

natural selection the process by which certain adaptive characteristics emerge over generations.

need term used by Henry Murray to describe a readiness to respond in a certain way under given conditions.

need for achievement (n Ach) according to Henry Murray, the need to succeed on tasks that are set out by society.

need for affiliation (n Aff) according to Henry Murray, the need to draw near to and win the affection of others.

need for exhibition (n Exh) according to Henry Murray, the need to show one's self before others and to entertain, amuse, shock, and excite others.

need for power (n Power) according to Henry Murray, the need to seek positions and offices in which one can exert control over others.

negative reinforcement an aversive event that ends if a behavior is performed, making it more likely for that behavior to be performed in the future.

neo-analytic approach the approach to personality psychology that is concerned with the individual's sense of self (ego) as the core of personality.

neurotic need in Karen Horney's approach, a need that is a dominant focus for a neurotic individual.

neurotic trend In Karen Horney's approach, a strategy or pattern of interaction that becomes the predominant mode by which a neurotic individual defends against anxiety.

Neuroticism (Big Five) the personality dimension that includes nervousness, tension, and anxiety; people low in this dimension are emotionally stable, calm, and contented.

neuroticism (Eysenck) one of Hans Eysenck's three biologically-oriented personality dimensions; it includes emotional instability and apprehensiveness.

neurotransmitter a chemical used by nerves to communicate.

nomothetic seeking to formulate laws.

nondeterministic the idea that it is an oversimplification to view people as controlled by fixed physical laws.

nonshared environmental variance features of the environment that children raised in the same home experience differently.

normal symbiotic according to Margaret Mahler, the forming of ties between a child and mother in which the child develops empathy and the sense of being a separate but loving person.

nuclear quality Gordon Allport's term for describing personal dispositions in terms of a person's unique goals, motives, or styles.

object relations theories The approach to personality that focuses on the objects of psychic drives and the importance of relations with other individuals in defining ourselves.

objective assessment measurement that is not dependent on the individual making the assessment.

observational learning learning by an individual that occurs by watching others perform the behavior, with the individual neither performing the behavior nor being directly rewarded or punished for the behavior.

occupational tasks according to Alfred Adler, a fundamental social issue in which one must choose and pursue a career that makes one feel worthwhile.

Oedipus complex a term used by Sigmund Freud to describe a boy's sexual feelings for his mother and rivalries with his father.

Openness (Big Five) the personality dimension that includes imagination, wit, originality, and creativity; people low on this dimension are shallow, plain, and simple.

operant conditioning the changing of a behavior by manipulating its consequences.

oral stage Freudian stage of psychosexual development before age one, when infants are driven to satisfy their drives of hunger and thirst.

organ inferiority Alfred Adler's concept that everyone is born with some physical weakness at which point incapacity and disease are most likely to take place, but the body attempts to make up for the deficiency in another area.

organismic a term sometimes used to describe theories that focus on the development that comes from inside the growing organism and that assume a natural unfolding, or life course, for each organism.

outcome expectancy the expected consequence of a behavior that is the most significant influence on whether or not an individual will reproduce an observed behavior, in the view of Albert Bandura; also, the extent to which an individual expects his or her performance to have a positive result.

partial reinforcement a reward that occurs after some, but not all, occurrences of a behavior.

passive style according to Karen Horney, a mode of adapting to the world used by those who believe that they can get along best by being compliant.

patterns the basic underlying mechanisms of personality that dynamically direct activity and remain relatively stable.

peak experiences according to Abraham Maslow, powerful, meaningful experiences in which people seem to transcend the self, be at one with the world, and feel completely self-fulfilled; Mihaly Csikszentmihalyi describes them as the "flow" that comes with total involvement in an activity.

penis envy a term used by Sigmund Freud to describe the phenomenon in which a girl develops feelings of inferiority and jealousy over her lack of a penis.

perfection striving according to Alfred Adler, an individual's attempt to reach fictional goals by eliminating his or her perceived flaws.

persona archetype according to Carl Jung, the archetype representing the socially acceptable front that is presented to others.

personal construct theory the approach to personality proposed by George Kelly that emphasizes the idea that people actively endeavor to construe or understand the world and construct their own theories about human behavior.

personal disposition a term used by Gordon Allport to describe a trait that is peculiar to an individual.

Personal Orientation Inventory (POI) a self-report questionnaire that asks people to classify themselves on a number of dimensions for the various characteristics of self-actualization or mental health.

personal projects   a term used by Brian Little to describe tasks that people are currently working on that motivate them on a daily basis.

personal strivings   a term used by Robert Emmons to describe abstract, overarching goals that may be satisfied by a number of different behaviors.

personal unconscious   according to Carl Jung, the component of the mind that contains thoughts and feelings that are not currently a part of conscious awareness.

personality disorder   deep-rooted, ongoing pattern of behavior that impairs the person's functioning and well-being.

personality psychology   the scientific study of the psychological forces that make people uniquely themselves.

Personality Research Form (PRF)   a self-report test that assesses needs by forced responses to short, standardized items.

personality test   a standardized stimulus that evokes different responses in different individuals and assesses these differences.

personological system   Henry Murray's term for his theory of personality that emphasizes the richness of the life of each person and the dynamic nature of the individual as a complex organism responding to a specific environment.

phallic stage   Freudian stage of psychosexual development around age four in which a child's sexual energy is focused on the genitals.

phenomenological   the concept that people's perceptions or subjective realities are considered valid data for investigation.

philia   according to Rollo May, a type of brotherly love or liking.

phlegmatic   a personality type based on the ancient Greek humors discussed by Hippocrates and Galen in which one is apathetic and conforming on the outside but tense and distraught on the inside.

phobia   an excessive or incapacitating fear.

plans   according to Mischel, a personality variable encompassing our intentions for our actions.

pleasure principle   the operating principle of the id to satisfy pleasure and reduce inner tension.

positive psychology   the movement in modern psychology to focus on positive attributes rather than on pathology.

positivism   the philosophical view of the world that focuses on the laws that govern the behavior of objects in the world.

posttraumatic stress   anxiety, nightmares, and flashbacks that result when the conscious mind cannot deal with overwhelmingly disturbing memories.

primary drive   a fundamental innate motivator of behavior, specifically hunger, thirst, sex, or pain.

primary reinforcement   according to Dollard and Miller, an event that reduces a primary drive.

principle of reinforcement   the theory that the frequency of a behavior depends on its consequences or the types of outcomes that follow it.

projection   a defense mechanism in which anxiety-arousing impulses are externalized by placing them onto others.

projective test   an assessment technique that attempts to study personality through use of a relatively unstructured stimulus, task, or situation.

prolactin   the hormone that causes lactation.

proprium   Gordon Allport's term for the core of personality that defines who one is; Allport believed that the proprium has a biological counterpart.

prospective design   using early measures to predict later outcomes.

Prozac   a drug that blocks reabsorption of the neurotransmitter serotonin in the brain and thus elevates moods and alters emotional reaction patterns.

psyche   the essence of the human mind or spirit or soul; in Carl Jung's theory, personality as the dynamic sum of its parts.

psychoanalysis   Sigmund Freud's approach to understanding human behavior; also, Freud's psychotherapeutic techniques.

psychoanalytic   Sigmund Freud's basic approach to understanding personality.

psychological situation   according to Julian Rotter, the individual's unique combination of potential behaviors and the value of these behaviors to the individual.

psychopharmacology   the study of the role of drugs and other toxic substances in causing and treating psychiatric disturbance.

psychosomatic medicine   treatment based on the idea that the mind affects the body—that mental health affects physical health.

psychosurgery   operating on the brain in an attempt to repair personality problems.

psychotherapeutic interview   an interview in which a client talks about the important or troubling parts of his or her life.

psychoticism (Eysenck)   this dimension includes a tendency toward psychopathology, involving impulsivity and cruelty, tough-mindedness, and shrewdness.

punishment   an unpleasant consequence to a behavior that decreases the likelihood of performing the behavior in the future.

Q-data   the term used by R. B. Cattell to describe data gathered from self-reports and questionnaires.

Q-sort   a method of personality assessment in which a person is given a stack of cards naming various characteristics and is asked to sort them into piles.

race   large groupings based upon physical characteristics, such as skin color, eye shape, or height, tied to geographical origin.

radical determinism   the belief that all human behavior is caused and that humans have no free will.

rationalization   a defense mechanism in which post-hoc logical explanations are given for behaviors that were actually driven by internal unconscious motives.

reaction formation   a defense mechanism that pushes away threatening impulses by overemphasizing the opposite in one's thoughts and actions.

readiness   the extent to which individuals are likely to respond appropriately in a given situation, as a function of their prior experiences with that situation.

Real Self   Karen Horney's concept of the inner core of personality that we perceive about ourselves, including our potential for self-realization.

reality principle   in Freudian psychoanalytic theory, the operating force of the ego to solve real problems.

regression   a defense mechanism in which one returns to earlier, safer stages of one's life in order to escape present threats.

reinforcement   an event that strengthens a behavior and increases the likelihood of repeating the behavior in the future.

reinforcement schedules   the frequency and the interval of reinforcement that may be based on time or responses.

reinforcement value the extent to which an individual values the expected reinforcement of an action.

rejection sensitivity a personality variable capturing the extent to which an individual is overly sensitive to cues that he or she is being rejected by another.

relative self the philosophical idea that there is no underlying self but that the true self is composed merely of masks.

reliability the consistency of scores that are expected to be the same.

repression a defense mechanism that pushes threatening thoughts into the unconscious.

response set a bias responding to test items that is unrelated to the personality characteristic being measured.

Rogerian therapy the client-oriented psychotherapy developed by Carl Rogers in which the therapist tends to be supportive, nondirective, and empathetic, and gives unconditional positive regard.

Role Construct Repertory Test an assessment instrument designed by George Kelly to evoke a person's own personal construct system by making comparisons among triads of important people in the life of the person being assessed.

romantic attachment styles according to Phillip Shaver, one's style of adult romantic relationships, which is modeled on and reflects the nature of one's childhood attachment relationships to the parents or caregivers.

ruling type according to Alfred Adler, a type of person who proceeds for his or her own gain without consideration of others.

salutogenesis Aaron Antonovsky's theory of how people stay healthy; according to this approach, the world must not necessarily be controlled or ordered for the healthy individual, but the individual must have a sense of coherence.

sanguine a personality type based on the ancient Greek humors discussed by Hippocrates and Galen in which one is hopeful and cheerful.

schema a cognitive structure that organizes knowledge and expectations about one's environment.

schizophrenia a condition whose symptoms include distorted reality, odd emotional reactions, and sometimes paranoia and/or delusions.

scientific inference the use of systematically gathered evidence to test theories.

script a schema that guides behavior in social situations.

secondary drives in social learning theory, drives that are learned by association with the satisfaction of primary drives.

secondary reinforcement according to Dollard and Miller, a conditioned reinforcement; a previously neutral stimulus that becomes a reinforcer following its pairing with a primary reinforcer.

secure lovers according to Phillip Shaver, people who have a romantic attachment style in which they easily form close relationships with others and let others be close to them.

self-actualization the innate process by which one tends to grow spiritually and realize one's potential.

self-efficacy an expectancy or belief about how competently one will be able to enact a behavior in a particular situation.

self-monitoring Mark Snyder's concept of self-observation and self-control guided by situational cues about the social appropriateness of behavior.

self-presentation a term used by Mark Snyder to describe doing what is socially expected.

self-regulation monitoring one's own behavior as a result of one's internal processes of goals, planning, and self-reinforcement.

self-system according to Albert Bandura, the set of cognitive processes by which a person perceives, evaluates, and regulates his or her own behavior so that it is appropriate to the environment and effective in achieving goals.

Sensation–Intuition scale subclassification of the Myers-Briggs Type Indicator that reflects whether a person is more prone to realism or imagination.

sensation seeking a tendency to seek out highly stimulating activities and novelty.

sense of coherence a person's confidence that the world is understandable, manageable, and meaningful.

SES gradient a phenomenon in public health in which the higher a person's socioeconomic status, the lower is that person's risk of getting sick and dying prematurely.

sex according to Rollo May, a form of love consisting of lust and tension release.

shadow archetype according to Carl Jung, the archetype representing the dark and unacceptable side of personality.

shaping the process in which undifferentiated operant behaviors are gradually changed or shaped into a desired behavior pattern by the reinforcement of successive approximations, so that the behavior more and more resembles the target behavior.

sick role a set of societal expectations about how a person should behave when ill.

situated social cognition social-cognitive processes that change with changes in the situation.

Skinner box an enclosure in which an experimenter can shape the behavior of an animal by controlling reinforcement and accurately measuring the responses of the animal.

Social Darwinism the idea that societies and cultures naturally compete for survival of the fittest.

social desirability response set a bias in which people are likely to want to present themselves in a favorable light or to try to please the experimenter or test administrator.

social engineering control of environmental contingencies to influence individual behavior.

social intelligence the idea that individuals differ in their level of mastery of the particular cluster of knowledge and skills that are relevant to interpersonal situations.

social learning theory a theory that proposes that habits are built up in terms of a hierarchy of secondary drives.

social roles gender roles and many other roles pertaining to work and family life that involve expectations applied to a category of people.

social roles theory Alice Eagly's theory that the social behaviors that differ between the sexes are embedded in social roles; that is, the different roles in which men and women find themselves specify their behaviors.

social self George Herbert Mead's idea that who we are and how we think of ourselves arise from our interactions with those around us. Also, having an identity in a social world.

societal tasks according to Alfred Adler, a fundamental social issue in which one must create friendships and social networks.

sociobiology the study of the influence of evolutionary biology on individual responses regarding social matters.

socioeconomic status (SES) a measurement of one's level of education and income.

somatopsychic effect   disease or genetic predispositions to illness that affect personality.

somatotypology   W. H. Sheldon's theory relating body type to personality characteristics.

specific expectancy   according to Julian Rotter, the expectancy that a reward will follow a behavior in a particular situation.

stability of causality   according to Bernard Weiner, the perception that the causes of occurrences are either long-lasting across time or of the moment and changing across time.

stereotype   a schema or belief about the personality traits that tend to be characteristic of members of some group.

stereotype threat   the threat that others' judgments or one's own actions will negatively stereotype an individual.

strategies   according to Walter Mischel, individual differences in the meanings people give to stimuli and reinforcement that are learned during experiences with situations and their rewards.

structured interview   a systematic interview in which the interviewer follows a definite plan so that similar types of information are elicited from each interviewee.

subjective assessment   measurement that relies on interpretation by the individual making the assessment.

subjective well-being   what individuals think of their own level of happiness or their quality of life.

sublimation   a defense mechanism in which dangerous urges are transformed into positive, socially acceptable motivations.

superego   in Freudian psychoanalytic theory, the personality structure that develops to internalize societal rules and guide goal-seeking behavior toward socially acceptable pursuits.

superiority complex   according to Alfred Adler, an exaggerated arrogance that an individual develops in order to overcome an inferiority complex.

survival of the fittest   the concept that species evolve because those individuals who cannot compete well in the environments in which they live tend to be less successful in growing up and producing offspring.

symbiotic psychotic   according to Margaret Mahler, the forming of emotional ties that are so strong that a child is unable to form a sense of self.

System of Multicultural Pluralistic Assessment (SOMPA)   a system developed by Jane Mercer that assumes that test results cannot be divorced from the culture and focuses on comparisons among individuals within a cultural group rather than between cultural groups.

systematic desensitization   gradually extinguishing a phobia by causing the feared stimulus to become dissociated from the fear response.

systems   according to Henry Murray, sets of dynamic influences with feedback.

T-data   the term used by R. B. Cattell to describe data gathered from placing a person in a controlled test situation and noting or rating responses.

teleology   the idea that there is a grand design or purpose to one's life.

temperament   stable individual differences in emotional reactivity.

test–retest reliability   the degree of consistency between the results of the same test taken on different occasions.

testosterone   a sex hormone, the most common of the androgens typically considered the male sex hormone.

thanatos   according to Freud, the drive toward self-destructive behavior or death.

thema   according to Henry Murray, a combination of needs and presses typical for the individual.

Thematic Apperception Test (TAT)   a projective test in which a participant is asked to make up a story (including what will happen in the future) about a picture that is presented.

Thinking-Feeling scale   subclassification of the Myers-Briggs Type Indicator that reflects whether a person is logical and objective or personal and subjective.

trait   according to Gordon Allport, a generalized neuropsychic structure or core tendency that underlies behavior across time and situations.

trait approach   use of a limited set of adjectives or adjective dimensions to describe and scale individuals.

tropism   the tendency to seek out specific types of environments.

Turing Test   a standard test by which to judge whether a computer can adequately simulate a human; in this test, first proposed by Alan Turing, a human judge interacts with two hidden others and tries to decide which is the human and which is the computer.

Turner's syndrome   an anomaly in which an individual is born with only a single X chromosome; such a person has female external genitals but no ovaries.

Type A behavior pattern/Type A personality   a tense, competitive style that is especially likely to be associated with coronary heart disease.

Type T theory   Frank H. Farley's theory that suggests a psychobiological need for stimulation due to an internal arousal deficit; Type T stands for "Thrill Seeking."

types   a theoretical approach to personality in which people are divided into discrete categories or classes as opposed to being placed along a continuum.

typology   a categorical scheme in which a person is a member of only one of a small set of groups.

unconscious   the portion of the mind that is not accessible to conscious thought.

validity   the extent to which a test measures what it is supposed to be measuring.

vicarious learning   learning achieved by watching the experiences of another person.

withdrawn style   according to Karen Horney, a mode of adapting to the world used by those who believe that it is best not to engage emotionally at all.

zero acquaintance   observation and judgment of someone with whom one has never interacted.

What Is Personality?

Chang and Eng were attached twins, joined above the waist through a small connection of tissue near the sternum. Born in 1811 in Siam (now Thailand), they made famous the term "Siamese twins," although the more scientific term "conjoined twins" is now used. Conjoined twins develop when a dividing (twinning) embryo suddenly stops dividing before the process is complete, thus leaving a pair of attached identical twins.

Chang and Eng always attracted a lot of people who were curious to see their condition. After their father died when they were eight years old, they moved to the United States and toured with exhibitions to support themselves. Chang and Eng were often observed and interviewed. They were said to get along very well with each other, each "knowing" the other one's feelings (as many twins similarly report). Each eventually married, established separate households and alternated visits with their spouses, and fathered a number of children. They lived in North Carolina and were well liked in their community.

© Hulton Archive/Getty Images

Both twins were bright and hard-working, yet they also developed different reaction patterns, with Chang being more irritable and experiencing more stress. Eng, in contrast, was an avid reader. Later in life, Chang started drinking and suffered a stroke. Eventually, Chang died, and of course Eng died a few hours later.

Chang and Eng obviously had a great deal in common—genes and environment—yet they each developed a unique personality, as do other conjoined twins (Smith, 1988). Where does individuality come from, and how does it change and develop? What psychological forces made Chang who he was and Eng who he was? As we will see in this text, the assumptions we make about the origins and meanings of individual differences have striking implications for how we understand and treat others and how we structure our communities and societies. This text explores what psychologists theorize and know about personality.

M ost basically, personality psychology asks the question, *What does it mean to be a person?* In other words, How are we unique as individuals? What is the nature of the self? Personality psychologists answer these fascinating questions through systematic observations about how and why individuals behave as they do. Personality psychologists tend to avoid abstract philosophical or religious musings and focus instead on the thoughts, feelings, and behaviors of real people. Personality is generally *not* studied in terms of nonpsychological concepts such as profits and losses, souls and spirits, or molecules and electromagnetism. Personality is a subfield of psychology.

Personality Psychology
The scientific study of the psychological forces that make people uniquely themselves

Personality psychology can be defined as the scientific study of the psychological forces that make people uniquely themselves. To be comprehensive, we can say that personality has eight key aspects, which together help us understand the complex nature of the individual. First, the individual is affected by *unconscious aspects,* forces that are not in moment-to-moment awareness. For example, we might say or do things to others that our parents used to say or do to us, without recognizing that we are motivated by a desire to resemble our parents. Second, the individual is affected by so-called *ego forces* that provide a sense of identity or "self." For example, we often strive to maintain a sense of mastery and consistency in our behavior. Third, a person is a *biological being,* with a unique genetic, physical, physiological, and temperamental nature. The human species has evolved over millions of years, yet each of us is a unique biological system. Fourth, people are *conditioned* and *shaped* by the experiences and environments that surround them. That is, our surroundings sometimes train us to respond in certain ways, and we grow up in varying cultures. Culture is a key aspect of who we are.

Fifth, people have a *cognitive dimension,* thinking about and actively interpreting the world around them. Different people construe the happenings around them in different ways. Sixth, an individual is a collection of specific *traits, skills,* and *predispositions.* There is no denying that each of us has certain specific abilities and inclinations. Seventh, human beings have a *spiritual dimension* to their lives, which ennobles them and prompts them to ponder the meaning of their existence. People are much more than robots programmed by computers. They seek happiness and self-fulfillment. Eighth, and finally, the individual's nature is an ongoing *interaction* between the person and the particular environment. Taken together, these eight aspects help us define and understand personality.

Personality and Science

Modern personality psychologists are scientific in the sense that they attempt to use methods of **scientific inference** (using systematically gathered evidence) to test theories. A person might be able to learn a great deal about personality by reading about Raskolnikov in Dostoyevsky's novel *Crime and Punishment,* or by seeing *Hamlet* at a Shakespeare festival. Indeed, it has been argued that Shakespeare invented personality as we have come to recognize it (Bloom, 1998). Such insights are not scientific, however, until they have been tested in a systematic way, using validated methods. As we will show, scientific methods have yielded insights into personality that are not available to a keen novelist or philosopher.

Should you use astrologers and other such stargazers in assessing personality? Or, why not go to the nearest carnival and have your personality read from the lines in the palms of your hands? Perhaps you should turn to physiognomy—the art of face reading—to evaluate others. Should you make personality inferences about people who have large foreheads? No, such approaches do not work. All of these techniques are generally invalid; they are wrong or vague as often as they are right. However, through an understanding of personality psychology—classic theories and modern research—meaningful answers about personality *are* available.

Some scientists believe that rigorous study of personality must become mathematical and involve numbers—for instance, statistics such as *correlations.* A **correlation coefficient** is a mathematical index of the degree of agreement (or association) between two measures. For example, height and weight are positively correlated: in most (but not all) cases, the taller a person is, the more the person weighs. Extroversion and shyness are negatively (inversely) correlated: Knowing that a person scores high on a test of extroversion lets us predict that the person will not often act in a shy manner. In the example shown in Figure 1, there is a negative correlation between a person's degree of introversion and the number of friends that person has on Facebook. Such statistics help us quantify relationships.

Correlations tell us about associations, but not about causal relationships. For example, if we learn that stout people tend to be jolly, that positive correlation does not tell us why the relationship exists. Is there some underlying predisposition that makes certain people tend to eat a lot and also be happy? Does plentiful food and extra weight make a person feel happier? Do happy people not worry about their looks and so gain weight? Do plump people hide an inner loneliness by pretending to be jolly? Do other people assume that portly people are jolly and therefore approach them in a kidding way, thereby making them more jolly? What are the causal relationships? There has, in fact, been some scientific research on whether the stout are more jolly, but no clear conclusions can yet be drawn, although obesity may

Scientific Inference
The use of systematically gathered evidence to test theories

Correlation Coefficient
A mathematical index of the degree of agreement or association between two measures

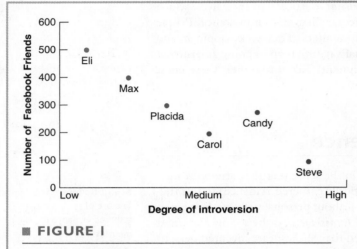

■ **FIGURE I**

Correlation Between Facebook Friends
and Introversion.

These data show a negative (inverse) correlation between introversion and an aspect of social networks: the more introverted the subject, the fewer the friends, generally speaking.

Note, however, that Candy is quite introverted but still has an average number of Facebook friends. Such statistics are used to evaluate the validity of both the measure and the construct of introversion.

What might explain this sort of correlation? It might be that Steve is introverted, hesitates to approach others, and so is rarely friended. Or, it might be that he has few friends because his computer is always breaking, and so he loses social contacts, becomes lonely, and turns more introverted. Or, it might be that Steve has a thyroid disorder, looks overweight, and therefore keeps to himself and becomes introverted and something of a loner; but if his thyroid condition were corrected, both his extroversion and his number of friends would increase. The true causal links affect what types of interventions would be successful but usually cannot be judged from simply knowing the correlation.

be a risk factor for depression (Roberts, Strawbridge, Deleger, & Kaplan, 2002, Roberts, Deleger, Strawbridge, & Kaplan, 2003). Thus, the scientific study of personality helps us untangle these webs of associations.

Although statistics such as correlations can indeed be extremely helpful, they are only tools to be used to help uncover the truth. Here we present various sorts of systematic analyses in addition to correlational analyses, including case studies (intensive focus on an individual), cross-cultural comparisons, and research into biological structures. By piecing together insights from these and other sources, we can gain a deep and valid understanding of personality.

Is a person outgoing or even domineering? Preoccupied with sexual attraction and sexual fulfillment? Does he or she have very good or very poor work habits? Insecurities that seem to arise from childhood experiences? High goals but doubts about ability to achieve them? Personality psychology provides the tools to begin to understand why people are the way they are.

Where Do Personality Theories Come From?

Many personality theories have arisen from the careful observations and deep introspection of insightful thinkers. For example, Sigmund Freud spent many hours analyzing his own dreams, which revealed to him the extent of the conflicts and urges hidden within. He had first noticed the power of repressed sexual urges in his patients, and he developed this idea into a comprehensive theory of the human psyche. Working from his assumptions about the struggle with sexual urges, Freud elaborated his theory to account for the many problems he saw in his medical practice and then to broader conflicts in society. The analysis develops from fundamental postulates about the nature of the mind. This is mostly a **deductive approach** to personality, in that the conclusions follow logically from the premises or assumptions. In deduction, we use our knowledge of basic psychological "laws" or principles in order to understand each particular person.

Deductive Approach
An approach to psychology in which the conclusions follow logically from the premises or assumptions

Second, some personality theories arise directly out of systematic empirical research. For example, we might be interested in knowing which basic dimensions or traits (such as extroversion) are essential to understanding personality. By collecting many trait-relevant observations on many people, we can get a sense of which traits are fundamental and which are less important, vague, or redundant. We can gather lots of systematic data from many people and continuously revise our conclusions as new data are gathered. This is an **inductive approach** to personality because concepts are developed based on what carefully collected observations reveal. Induction works from the data up to the theory. A schematic diagram of these processes is shown in Figure 2.

Inductive Approach
An approach to psychology in which observations are systematically collected and concepts are developed based on what the data reveal

A third source of personality theories involves analogies and concepts borrowed from related disciplines. For example, much progress is currently being made on understanding the structure and function of the human brain. Several types of brain scans are being used. Functional magnetic resonance imaging (fMRI) scans, for example, use magnetic fields, and computerized tomography (CT) scans use X-rays to obtain detailed pictures of the living brain. Positron emission tomography (PET) scans can show ongoing brain activity by tracing where radioactive glucose is being channeled as people think and respond. These techniques are often applied to people with abnormal personalities—such as schizophrenics and those with brain damage—to search for reasons for their disorders. Certain models of personality become

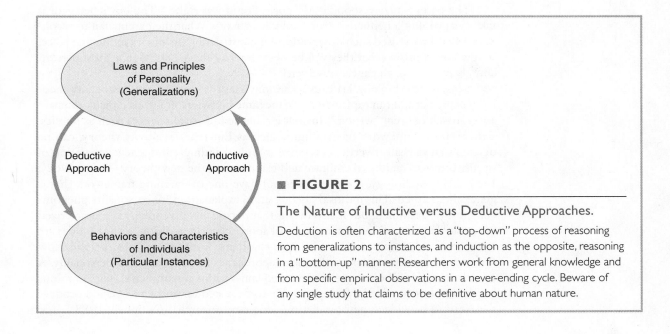

■ **FIGURE 2**

The Nature of Inductive versus Deductive Approaches.

Deduction is often characterized as a "top-down" process of reasoning from generalizations to instances, and induction as the opposite, reasoning in a "bottom-up" manner. Researchers work from general knowledge and from specific empirical observations in a never-ending cycle. Beware of any single study that claims to be definitive about human nature.

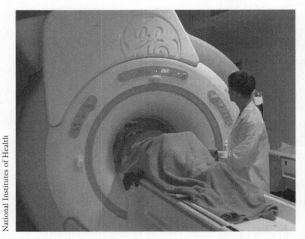

National Institutes of Health

■ As we learn more about brain structure and function through modern technologies such as functional magnetic resonance imaging (fMRI), we achieve a better understanding of the biological contributions to personality.

implausible if they are inconsistent with what we know about the structure and function of the brain. On the other hand, pictures of the brain can suggest new ways to explore its psychological organization.

Anthropologists have provided basic information both about human evolution and about differences between cultures. Some characteristics of humans, such as our social nature, exist across time and space; people tend to live together in groups—family groups and cultural groups. On the other hand, some aspects, such as the degree of emphasis on individuality, tend to vary dramatically across cultures. For example, Americans tend to celebrate individual achievement and individual freedoms, but Japanese value harmony and the avoidance of personal distinction. Any successful approach to personality must take into account such anthropological facts.

In practice, almost all personality theories involve some elements of all these approaches. All theories develop in part by deduction, in part by induction, and in part by analogy. Occasionally, an interesting misunderstanding arises from a failure to recognize this fact. For example, a basic tenet of Freudian theory is that little boys are motivated to "get rid" of their fathers and "marry" their mothers. The resolution of this conflict is said to have a direct effect on adult personality. Interesting predictions about personality can be deduced from this tenet or assumption. What is fascinating is that often young parents who have taken a course in personality psychology are amazed to see their four-year-old son march into their bedroom and attempt to climb into bed and order the father out!

The parents may respond, "My gosh, Freud was right!" The boy's behavior is taken as proof of a deduction from Freudian theory. What the parents fail to recognize is that Freud used such observations in constructing his theory in the first place, so it is not surprising that they will be observed by others. (Freud, like most personality theorists, was an expert observer.)

This line of thinking leads us to an important point: Various personality theories will predict and can explain many of the same behaviors. It is thus difficult to prove an approach entirely "wrong." In well-established physical sciences such as physics, a theoretical framework or paradigm, such as Einstein's relativity theory, can be devised that radically overthrows previous understandings, and a new generation of scientists moves rapidly to embrace and elaborate on the new theory (Kuhn, 1962). Personality psychology, however, does not have one overarching framework that is generally accepted. This means that competing explanations for personality phenomena must be examined, but it also means that personality psychology is characterized by an intellectually stimulating set of rival approaches. In addition, some theories are more applicable to certain domains than to others. For these reasons, we will show the strengths and weaknesses of various approaches in understanding personality. A sound theory will be comprehensive (explain various phenomena), parsimonious (explain things concisely), falsifiable (able to be tested for correctness), and productive (lead to new ideas, new predictions, and new research) (Campbell, 1988).

Preview of the Perspectives

Almost everyone has heard of Sigmund Freud's theories, and you might have heard that Freud says that in dreams the following objects may be symbolic of a penis: hammers, rifles, daggers, umbrellas, neckties (long objects peculiar to men), snakes, and many other objects. They are all phallic symbols. You might also have heard that the vagina may be dreamt of as a path through the brush, or as a garden, as in a dream in which a young woman asks a gardener if some branches could be transplanted to her garden. Taken out of context, such assertions may seem senseless, yet Freud greatly influenced twentieth-century thought. We will attempt to show why Freudian theory has had such a tremendous impact.

Many other personality theorists and researchers are quite well known, but the best and most modern understanding of personality comes from a synthesis of psychological research on such matters as the nature of the self, psychobiology, learning theories, trait theories, existential approaches, and social psychology. As a taste of what lies ahead, here is an introduction to the concepts and the psychologists we will be investigating. Major features of the perspectives to be covered are presented in Table 1.

Overview of the Eight Perspectives

We will examine the psychoanalytic aspects of personality, with a focus on the unconscious. Interestingly, study of the unconscious has once again become a significant area of ongoing research in psychology. It is now clear that the brain has complex, hidden subsystems, just as Freud postulated. We focus on the ego or "self" aspects of personality, tracing notions of the self from Alfred Adler's work

■ **TABLE 1** The Eight Basic Aspects of Personality

Perspective	Key Strength
Psychoanalytic	Attention to unconscious influences; importance of sexual drives even in nonsexual spheres
Neo-Analytic/Ego	Emphasis on the self as it struggles to cope with emotions and drives on the inside and the demands of others on the outside
Biological	Focus on tendencies and limits imposed by biological inheritance; easily combined with most other approaches
Behaviorist	Emphasis on a more scientific analysis of the learning experiences that shape personality
Cognitive	Emphasis on active nature of human thought; uses modern knowledge from cognitive psychology
Trait	Focus on good individual assessment techniques
Humanistic/Existential	Appreciation of the spiritual nature of a person; emphasizes struggles for self-fulfillment and dignity
Interactionist	Understanding that we are different selves in different situations

on inferiority complexes right up to modern theorizing about multiple selves. Theories of how and why we have a sense of "self" continue to fascinate psychologists (Dweck, Higgins, & Grant-Pillow, 2003).

Just as people come in different sizes, shapes, and colors, so too do people differ somewhat in their biological systems. We study the biological aspects of personality. An individual's characteristic emotional and motivational nature, generally known as temperament, is strongly influenced by multiple biological factors. Such matters have attracted the attention of leading scientists since the time of Charles Darwin. Today, new developments in evolutionary theory and in understanding human genetics are being applied to personality psychology.

Behaviorist and learning aspects of personality are considered. Starting with the work of radical behaviorist B. F. Skinner, we examine the extent to which personality can be "found" in the external environment. We analyze the cognitive aspects of personality, with a focus on people's consistencies in perceiving and interpreting the world around them. As we will see, cognitive approaches are increasingly joined with social psychology into social-cognitive approaches to personality, such as Albert Bandura's notions of the importance of self-efficacy. We also focus on trait aspects of personality. In the mid-twentieth century, the Harvard psychologist Gordon Allport almost single-handedly developed intriguing trait approaches that have dominated this area ever since, although there has been a recent resurgence of scientific interest in trait approaches. Today, notions of five basic trait dimensions provide a common currency for thinking about personality traits.

Humanistic and existential aspects of personality focus on freedom and self-fulfillment. Starting with the influential work of Carl Rogers, we examine what seems to make humans uniquely human. Further, what makes people happy and fulfilled? Person–situation interactionist aspects, which form the most modern personality approach, are explained later.

Are Personality Aspects Really Separable?

Is it best to divide the field of personality by aspects? All brilliant personality theorists necessarily include more than one aspect of personality in their writings. For example, Freud had many biological notions in his theories, and he certainly appreciated the major role played by socialization forces. Similarly, B. F. Skinner, the ultimate behaviorist, well understood the tremendous influence of other people in our lives, despite his research focus on the conditioning of laboratory animals. Our goal is not to place sophisticated theories into narrow pigeonholes, but rather to provide an in-depth examination of different sorts of significant insights into the nature of personality.

Which personality perspective is right? Are people governed by traits or hormones or unconscious motives or nobility of spirit? This is a different question from "Which personality *theory* is right?" or "Which *hypothesis* is true?" Theories and hypotheses are testable and, by their nature, can be proven wrong; that is, they are falsifiable. We will examine many such theories and hypotheses later in this text and show which aspects are wrong or doubtful. But the question here is "Which personality *perspective* is correct?" This question is easy to answer: All eight are right in that they all provide some important psychological insight into what it means to be a person. In other words, we can benefit from learning about the strengths (and the weaknesses) of all eight perspectives.

This answer is not an evasion or a dodge. Human nature is tremendously complex and needs to be examined from multiple perspectives. In fact, it is a weak strategy to rely too much on one approach and ignore the valuable insights provided by other perspectives and scientific research. Each of these perspectives adds richness to our understanding of personality. On the other hand, it is inappropriate to perpetuate notions that are not supported by concrete evidence.

A Brief History of Personality Psychology

A number of scientific and philosophical forces that converged early in the twentieth century made possible the birth of personality psychology. Sigmund Freud, very conscious of these new beginnings, deliberately published one of his major books, *The Interpretation of Dreams,* in the year 1900 (rather than in 1899). By the 1930s, modern personality theory was taking shape. Personality psychology is only about a century old, but its roots go back through human history. The time line shows the approximate sequence of important milestones in the history of personality psychology and their relationship in time to important world events.

Theater and Self-Presentation

Some roots of personality psychology can be traced to the theater. Theophrastus, a pupil of Aristotle, is one of the earliest known creators of character sketches—brief descriptions of a type of person that can be recognized across time and place—such as someone who is cheap or tidy or lazy or boorish (Allport, 1961). Ancient Greek and Roman actors wore masks to emphasize that they were playing characters different from themselves. This indicated a fascination with the true (unmasked) nature of the individual. By Shakespeare's time, the masks were mostly gone, but there was a tremendous delight with the roles people played. In *As You Like It,* Shakespeare observed that "All the world's a stage, and all the men and women merely players" (act III, scene 7). By this time it was clear that the role of jealous king or spurned lover could be occupied (played) in similar ways by different people, because everyone recognizes and understands the basic archetypal characters.

Is there really something fixed beneath the surface of the parts people play in their lives? In the twentieth century, theater took another imaginative step as playwrights such as Luigi Pirandello (1867–1936) toyed with the idea that characters could step outside the action of their plays. For example, a player could move totally off the stage (or out of the movie set) and comment on the drama. Suddenly, the character seems to take on a reality of its own—and reality becomes a series of illusions. At the same time, social philosophers began considering the idea of a **relative self:** that is, there is no underlying self beneath an outward-facing mask, but rather the "true" self is comprised merely of masks (Hare & Blumberg, 1988; G. H. Mead, 1968). In other words, these twentieth-century musings challenged the idea that there is any core self or personality to be discovered.

All these theatrical notions have subsequently been addressed in personality psychology, especially in understanding the importance of the social situation. They have

Relative Self
The philosophical idea that there is no underlying self but that the true self is composed merely of masks

also influenced existential and humanistic psychologists who have speculated about what it means to be a human being. But where theater gives momentary insight, personality psychology seeks lasting and universal scientific principles.

Religion

Other aspects of personality psychology can be traced to religious ideas. Western religious traditions (Judaism, Christianity, Islam) assert that humankind was created in God's image and from the beginning has faced temptation and moral struggle. People

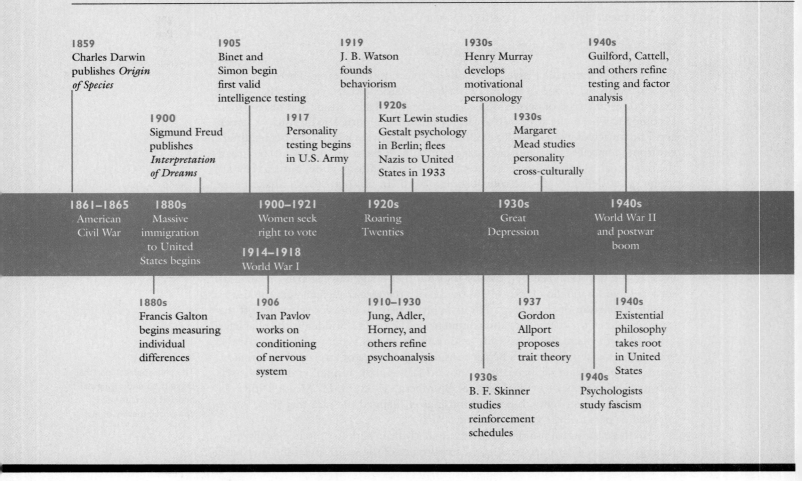

TIME LINE

Developments in the Field of Personality Psychology

The major developments in the field of personality psychology can be seen here in historical relation to one another and in relation to their broader societal and cultural contexts.

1859
Charles Darwin publishes *Origin of Species*

1900
Sigmund Freud publishes *Interpretation of Dreams*

1905
Binet and Simon begin first valid intelligence testing

1917
Personality testing begins in U.S. Army

1919
J. B. Watson founds behaviorism

1920s
Kurt Lewin studies Gestalt psychology in Berlin; flees Nazis to United States in 1933

1930s
Henry Murray develops motivational personology

1930s
Margaret Mead studies personality cross-culturally

1940s
Guilford, Cattell, and others refine testing and factor analysis

1861–1865
American Civil War

1880s
Massive immigration to United States begins

1900–1921
Women seek right to vote

1914–1918
World War I

1920s
Roaring Twenties

1930s
Great Depression

1940s
World War II and postwar boom

1880s
Francis Galton begins measuring individual differences

1906
Ivan Pavlov works on conditioning of nervous system

1910–1930
Jung, Adler, Horney, and others refine psychoanalysis

1937
Gordon Allport proposes trait theory

1940s
Existential philosophy takes root in United States

1930s
B. F. Skinner studies reinforcement schedules

1940s
Psychologists study fascism

fulfill a divine purpose and struggle for good and against evil. In this tradition, people's nature is primarily spiritual—a spirit inhabits the body while it is on earth. These conceptions discourage a scientific analysis of personality because they may regard people not as part of nature but rather as part of the divine order; but many modern theologians try to integrate scientific understandings into more traditional views, and many personality theorists drew on religious wisdom about humanity.

Eastern philosophies and religions emphasize self-awareness and spiritual self-fulfillment. These Eastern concerns with consciousness, self-fulfillment, and the human spirit came to play an important role in certain aspects of modern personality

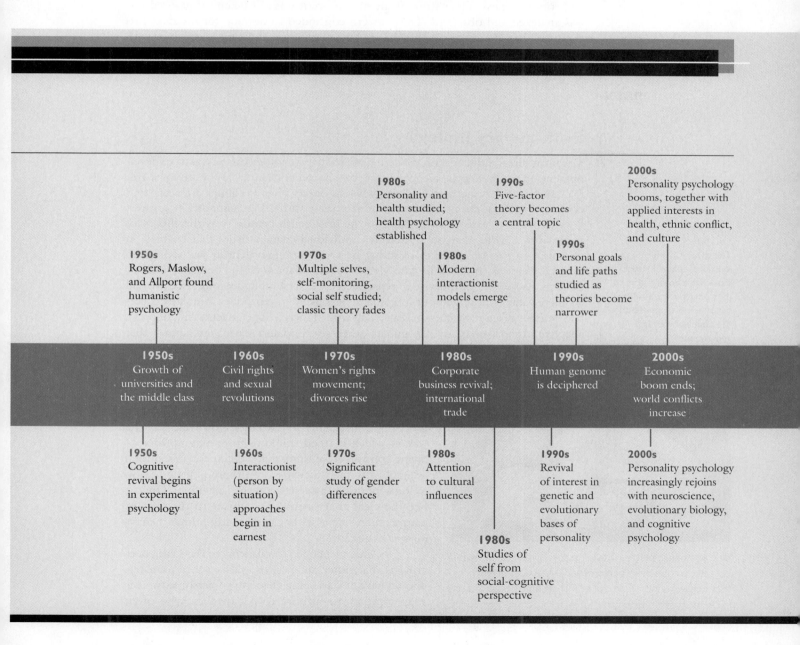

1950s
Rogers, Maslow, and Allport found humanistic psychology

1970s
Multiple selves, self-monitoring, social self studied; classic theory fades

1980s
Personality and health studied; health psychology established

1980s
Modern interactionist models emerge

1990s
Five-factor theory becomes a central topic

1990s
Personal goals and life paths studied as theories become narrower

2000s
Personality psychology booms, together with applied interests in health, ethnic conflict, and culture

1950s
Growth of universities and the middle class

1960s
Civil rights and sexual revolutions

1970s
Women's rights movement; divorces rise

1980s
Corporate business revival; international trade

1990s
Human genome is deciphered

2000s
Economic boom ends; world conflicts increase

1950s
Cognitive revival begins in experimental psychology

1960s
Interactionist (person by situation) approaches begin in earnest

1970s
Significant study of gender differences

1980s
Attention to cultural influences

1980s
Studies of self from social-cognitive perspective

1990s
Revival of interest in genetic and evolutionary bases of personality

2000s
Personality psychology increasingly rejoins with neuroscience, evolutionary biology, and cognitive psychology

theory, most clearly seen in the work of humanistic and existential psychologists such as Abraham Maslow. Eastern thought also influenced such seminal personality psychologists as C. G. Jung. Most university research in personality today is, however, more in the arena of modern, positivistic science and less concerned with spiritual matters.

Religious influences on Western conceptions of human nature began eroding during the Renaissance, especially during the seventeenth century. In the writings of philosophers Descartes, Spinoza, and Leibniz and their followers in the 1600s, we see debates about mind and body, emotion and motivation, and perception and consciousness. The nature of the human spirit was not taken for granted but was analyzed and observed. This concern continued to develop for the next two centuries. In modern personality theory, these influences show up as concerns with the integration and unity of the individual personality. They are also seen in attempts to integrate biological with psychological knowledge—join the mind with the body.

Evolutionary Biology

The most direct influences on modern personality psychology can be traced to developments in the biological sciences during the nineteenth century. Why are some animals such as tigers aggressive loners, whereas others such as chimps are social and cooperative? What characteristics do humans share with other animals? The greatest development in biological thinking in the nineteenth century was the theory of **evolution.** Charles Darwin argued that individual characteristics that enabled an organism to pass on genes to offspring become more prevalent in the population over generations. Individuals who were not well adapted to the demands of their environment would not survive to reproduce. So, for example, a strong sex drive had adaptive value—those without it would be less likely to reproduce. Similarly, a certain amount of aggressiveness and a certain type of social cooperativeness might prove adaptive. Animals that could dominate others for food and mates, and animals that could cooperate with others to secure their safety, would survive and pass on their genes. This focus on function—that is, the utility of behavior—has remained an important aspect of our thinking about personality.

Evolution
The theory in which individual characteristics that enable an organism to pass on genes to offspring become more prevalent in the population over generations

© Fotolia

■ Even though pets can't take personality tests, their owners can describe their "personalities"—the ways in which they behave as individuals rather than as simply dogs or cats.

The key contribution of Darwinian evolutionary theory to personality psychology, however, was the way in which it freed thinking from assumptions of divine control. If we think that a divine force is in total control of human activity, then there is little reason to look for other influences on the individual. Once it became clear that people are subject to the laws of nature, then scientists began to study human behavior systematically.

One little-mentioned corollary of the Darwinian doctrine is that other animals, especially other primates, should have at least some elements of personality. This may come as no surprise to pet owners, who often describe the personalities of their dogs, cats, and horses. But personality psychologists conducted little research on animal personality until quite recently. Obviously, we cannot ask animals to introspect about their inner minds, but it may be the case that research on animal personality will help us think in new ways about assessing and conceptualizing human personality (Gosling, 2008). For example, a primate such as a chimpanzee will dramatically change behavior patterns if it rises to the top of the

Classic to **Current**

Animal Personality

Personality psychology began to develop in the late nineteenth century, after Charles Darwin published his theory of evolution. Darwin revolutionized conceptions of human nature by proposing that all species, including humans, evolved over the millennia, as those organisms who were the most fit for their environments were able to survive and reproduce. For many years, the main impact of this work on personality psychology was that it freed scientists to think of human nature with a scientific approach. For example, Sigmund Freud (who studied evolution in medical school) was able to propose evolved instincts that are hidden below the conscious mind, and Gordon Allport was able to postulate biological subsystems that are somehow manifested in common personality traits. We will see that evolutionary theory has many implications for personality psychology (and many dangers of misuse). But as an example of how classic theories can come to shape current personality research, consider animal personality.

Many of us like to speak of dogs, cats, and even fish as being friendly, aggressive, clever, empathetic, and so on. But is this just anthropomorphizing, in which we are being silly in viewing pets as having human traits? Modern personality research lets us begin to answer such questions in a scientific way. For example, since animals generally cannot offer self-reports or self-conceptions, studies of animal personality have turned to using trait ratings (judgments) made by humans. Fortunately, personality research has shown researchers how to make reliable ratings (that are replicable) and how to make valid ratings (that focus on the trait of interest and not on others). Animals can also be subjected to experimental tests to code how they respond when facing a particular situation (such as competition for food). It turns out that

judges do agree in their ratings of animal personality, especially for certain basic dimensions (Gosling, 2001, 2008).

Which traits are commonly and reliably rated in animal studies? One analysis reviewed 19 studies of personality factors in various nonhuman species (chimpanzees, gorillas, monkeys, hyenas, dogs, cats, donkeys, pigs, rats, guppies, and octopuses) in terms of basic dimensions commonly used in human studies of personality. The results reveal that the basic dimensions of Extroversion, Neuroticism (anxiety), and Agreeableness show the strongest cross-species generality (Gosling & John, 1999). (And, as in people, extroversion is easiest to rate reliably.) Further, extroverted, sociable animals do seem to have better and more frequent interactions with their peers. In fact, such chimps are the happiest chimps (as rated by their zookeepers), especially if they are the dominant chimps (King & Landau, 2003). So, it may indeed make scientific sense to speak of your dog as being outgoing, calm, and friendly, and a neighbor's dog as being timid, neurotic, and untrustworthy (Gosling, Kwan, & John, 2003).

As an additional note, we cannot resist mentioning that along with Dr. Gosling, other eminent scholars in this area are named Brian Hare, Robin Fox, Max Wolf, and Lionel Tiger.

FURTHER READING

Gosling, S. D. (2001). From mice to men: What can we learn about personality from animal research? *Psychological Bulletin, 127,* 45–86.

Gosling, S. D. (2008). Personality in non-human animals. *Social and Personality Psychology Compass, 2,* 985–1001.

Gosling, S. D., Kwan, V. S. Y., & John, O. P. (2003). A dog's got personality: A cross-species comparative approach to personality judgments in dogs and humans. *Journal of Personality and Social Psychology, 85,* 1161–1169.

status hierarchy, thus illustrating the important interaction of basic individual characteristics with the social environment (de Waal, 2001b). Furthermore, zoo employees' ratings of chimps' personalities are clearly associated with the chimps' behavior patterns (Pederson, King, & Landau, 2005). These matters are taken up in the Animal Personality box. This box is the first in the series of Classic to Current boxes, which illustrate how classic theoretical notions in personality psychology have led to modern empirical research.

Testing

Attention! The purpose of this examination is to see how well you can remember, think, and carry out what you are told to do. We are not looking for crazy people. The aim is to help find out what you are best fitted to do in the army.

So began the instructions for a test that was administered to over one million young American men, as the United States entered World War I in 1917 (Yerkes, 1921). Americans had a job to do and thought they could do it better if they measured people just as they measured machinery. This practical "can-do" approach of American psychology brought a distinctive perspective to the study of individual differences.

Much psychological research on personality has been supported by wartime strategies for combat or peacetime efforts for the national defense. Even today the U.S. armed forces employ hundreds of psychologists to conduct research and testing on uniformed personnel. Back in 1917, the army was mostly concerned with weeding out so-called imbeciles, but they also looked for tendencies of applicants to collapse under stress. For example, one inventory asked recruits, "Do you feel like jumping off when you are on high places?" (Woodworth, 1919). It is this type of questionnaire that contributed to the development of modern personality tests.

The army tests were developed under the influence of psychologists Lewis Terman of Stanford and Robert Yerkes of Harvard, who were primarily interested in intelligence testing. This was the first mass use of mental tests. The psychologists hailed the great success of their testing. They imagined many future uses for the tests, such as the mass screening of school students to find those who would become the future elite of society. Unfortunately, this testing also set the stage for the use of biased tests to discriminate unfairly against those groups least favored by the test-givers. For example, the "smartest" immigrants were found to be those from northern Europe (whose culture was most in tune with the American tests). And those with darker skin, who were already the victims of rampant

■ World War I saw the first large-scale use of psychological testing for purposes of screening out so-called undesirables from elite roles and assigning inductees to units that were appropriate to their individual profiles.

© Bettmann/CORBIS

SHARPEN YOUR THINKING · Current Controversy

Who Should Have the Rights of a Person?

In recent years, animal rights activists have begun to argue that animals, especially those that are highly intelligent, should be given many of the same rights as humans. While not claiming that gorillas or dolphins are human, these activists argue that such animals have a level of understanding and sentience (feelings and consciousness) that merits granting them expanded rights of self-determination. In parallel, personality researchers and primatologists have begun demonstrating that the happiness and the personality of animals such as chimpanzees can be reliably rated by humans (de Waal, 1996; King & Landau, 2003). On what basis should a society determine what privileges and restrictions should be accorded nonhuman animals? Substantial intelligence and skill at interacting with humans is required for a dog to function as a service animal for a person with disabilities or to work as a police dog. If a dog can be deployed in that way, is there any reason not to do so? How far should our animal-protection laws go—is outlawing maltreatment enough, or should the laws require good treatment? Do microbrained animals like ants or dust mites also have some set of rights, and are they different from the rights of a chimp? How about a virus, or a plant? Personality psychology helps us think about what it means to be a person, and how we are similar to or different from other creatures.

educational and social discrimination, were certified as inferior by tests not in tune with their cultural ways of thinking.

Intelligence and creative abilities are often separated from personality in the belief that they are more like "skills" such as physical strength than they are like "traits" such as extroversion. However, to the extent that intellectual abilities are central to an individual's psychological makeup, they should be considered part of personality. On practical grounds, the vast information available on intelligence cannot be fully integrated into our analysis of personality. We do, however, include certain relevant pieces.

Knowledge of testing and measurement, applied to personality by such psychometricians as J. P. Guilford (Guilford, 1940), soon combined with insights emerging from clinical (therapeutic) work and with approaches evolving in experimental psychology to form the basis of modern personality theory and research.

Modern Theory

Modern personality theory began to take formal shape in the 1930s. It was heavily influenced by the work of three men—Gordon Allport, Kurt Lewin, and Henry Murray. Allport, who was broadly trained in philosophy and the classics, devoted his attention to the uniqueness and dignity of the individual. Allport defined personality as "the dynamic organization within the individual of those psychophysical systems that determine his unique adjustment to his environment" (Allport, 1937). Building on the work of psychologist–philosopher William James, he rejected the idea of trying to break down personality into basic components (such as sensation or innate drives) and instead looked for the underlying organization of each person's uniqueness.

Kurt Lewin came out of the Gestalt tradition in Europe. The Gestalt psychologists emphasized the integrative and active nature of perception and thought, suggesting that the whole may be greater than the sum of its parts. For example, the Gestalt pioneer Wolfgang Kohler gives the example of trying to memorize a list of pairs of nouns, such as *lake–sugar, boot–plate,* and *girl–kangaroo.* Kohler notes that these words are not normally associated with each other, but the pairings may be easily learned. The Gestalt explanation is as follows: "When I read those words I can imagine, as a series of strange pictures, how a lump of sugar dissolves in a lake, how a boot rests on a plate, how a girl feeds a kangaroo. If this happens during the reading of the series, I experience in imagination a number of well-organized, though quite unusual, wholes" (Kohler, 1947). This emphasis on the whole picture that a person imagines when encountering a situation had a tremendous influence on Lewin, and subsequently on personality and social psychology.

Lewin's approach, like Allport's, was dynamic, as he looked for systems that underlie observable behavior. Lewin drew attention to "the momentary condition of the individual and the structure of the psychological situation" (Lewin, 1935). In other words, Lewin emphasized that the forces affecting a person change from time to time and from situation to situation. Modern personality theories have adopted these emphases on understanding the current state of a person in a particular situation.

The third main sculptor of modern personality theory was Henry Murray. Murray attempted to integrate clinical issues (problems of real patients) with theory and assessment issues. Importantly, he believed in a comprehensive orientation, including longitudinal research—studying the same people over time. Murray took a broad approach to personality, defining it as the "branch of psychology which principally concerns itself with the study of human lives and the factors which influence their course, [and] which investigates individual differences" (Murray, 1938). He emphasized the integrated, dynamic nature of the individual as a complex organism responding to a specific environment, as well as the importance of needs and motivations.

In short, Allport, Lewin, Murray, and their associates set the stage for modern personality theory by emphasizing that the whole human being should be the focus of study, not parts of the being and not collections of organisms. Each person at each moment in each situation is a unique collection of related psychological forces that together determine the individual's responses. In other words, a successful approach cannot ignore the integrity of the individual or the various forces—conscious and unconscious, biological and social—operating at a given moment. This is the modern view of personality.

Lurking in opposition to these developing ideas were the new learning theories of Clark Hull and his associates at Yale, and the behaviorist theories of B. F. Skinner and his associates at Harvard. This opposition eventually led to a stimulating tension, which helped refine modern notions of human nature.

Also influential in the 1930s—though probably not as influential on personality psychology as it should have been—was the startling work of anthropologist Margaret Mead. In her book *Sex and Temperament in Three Primitive Societies,* Mead showed that masculinity was not necessarily associated with aggressiveness and femininity was not necessarily associated with cooperativeness. Rather, personality was heavily influenced by culture. According to Mead (1935/1963),

We have now considered in detail the approved personalities of each sex among . . . primitive peoples. We found the Arapesh—both men and women— displaying a personality that, out of our historically limited preoccupations, we would call maternal in its parental aspects, and feminine in its sexual aspects. We found men, as well as women, trained to be cooperative, unaggressive, responsive to the needs and demands of others. We found no idea that sex was a powerful driving force for men or for women. In marked contrast to these attitudes, we found among the Mundugumor that both men and women developed as ruthless, aggressive, positively sexed individuals, with maternal cherishing aspects of personality at a minimum.

Mead's work unequivocally demonstrated that personality should not be studied in only one culture or one context. She also shattered many myths about the nature of man as compared to the nature of woman, as well as ideas of innate and unchangeable sexual aggressiveness. American psychology has often overlooked the importance of culture in shaping people's lives (Betancourt & Lopez, 1993), and Mead's lesson was long ignored by personality researchers. We have tried to be especially sensitive to cultural issues; it is good science to do so.

Some Basic Issues: The Unconscious, the Self, Uniqueness, Gender, Situations, and Culture

Certain issues in the study of personality psychology reappear at different times and in different theories; they are fundamental to understanding personality.

What Is the Unconscious?

You may have noticed that some male friends or relatives are attracted to and marry women who are similar to their own mothers. Of course, most men do not consciously set out to find wives who are like their mothers. At times, though, we seem to be influenced by internal forces of which we are unaware or we may feel inner urges or feelings that we do not understand. On the other hand, it is generally believed that people are responsible for their own actions. Except for the insane, we expect that people know what they are doing and why they are doing it; they act consciously. So we face the dilemma of conscious versus unconscious determinants of behavior. Personality psychology struggles to understand how and to what extent unconscious forces play a role in human behavior.

What Is the Self?

Why are TV celebrities especially likely to be narcissistic, tending to be vain, exhibitionistic and arrogant (Young & Pinsky, 2006)? Carl Jung (1933) said that the "meeting of two personalities is like the contact of two chemical substances; if there is any reaction, both are transformed". Should we think of the self as a complex chemical substance or (as Jung also sometimes said) as a spirit? How important are social influences on the self, such as parental deprivation or excessive praise from others? Is the self really more like a set of perceptions about the characteristics of "me," which attempts to fulfill its human potential (Rogers, 1961)? Is the sense of self merely an inconsequential epiphenomenon or secondary perception arising from other forces (such as biological drives) that really matter? What is the core of who we are? All these questions are legitimate issues in personality psychology.

Does Each Individual Require a Unique Approach?

Nomothetic
Seeking to formulate laws

Idiographic
Involved in the study of individual cases

To what extent can we apply general methods to all people? Or is it possible, even necessary, to use a unique approach to the special qualities of each individual? Science, by its nature, searches for universal laws. It is therefore often **nomothetic,** which means that it seeks to formulate laws (from the Greek *nomos*, which means law, and *thetic*, to lay down). However, Gordon Allport strongly argued that a key aspect of the study of personality must focus on the individual and thus be **idiographic**—involved with the study of individual cases (from *idio*, Greek for private, personal, distinct). Certainly it makes sense to use intensive biographical analysis to understand a person, but each person's biography is different. So how can we generalize? This dilemma remains a significant challenge. Many years ago, Allport complained that most introductory psychology textbooks threw in (half-heartedly) a chapter on personality, usually at the tail end, that ignored or failed to capture the vital, dynamic individuality of each human being. Researchers were so concerned with being scientific that they ignored the most interesting (but complex) aspects of personality. This problem is still with us today.

Are There Differences between Men and Women?

What are the differences between men and women, and where do they come from? The most basic sex differences are of course the anatomical ones, and they are clearly determined by our genes, before we are born. But what are we to make of the various psychological differences between men and women that appear in our society? Why do men often seem more aggressive, dominant, antisocial, and better at performing mathematical and spatial tasks? Why are women generally more socially connected, more prone to depression, and more nurturant? Who has the greater sex drive, and who controls sexual encounters, and why? Such fascinating issues are basic to the study of personality and have been addressed by almost all personality theorists. Although we offer no simple answers to these questions, we do offer a sophisticated and reasoned consideration of the relevant issues.

The Person versus the Situation

Since the very beginnings of modern personality theory earlier in the past century, it has been well recognized that there are inconsistencies in every individual's behavior (Woodworth, 1934). An individual who acts extroverted one day may act introverted the next in a different situation. Furthermore, it has been established since the 1920s that some individuals are much more self-consistent than others (Hartshorne & May, 1928). For example, some children almost always behave honestly but others vary quite a bit.

If extroverted people can act like introverts, or if honest people can behave dishonestly, what sense does it make to talk about personality? And how do we take into account the fact that everyone is influenced, at least in part, by situation?

To What Extent Is Personality Culturally Determined?

The poet Walt Whitman (1871) wrote, "It is native personality, and that alone, that endows a man to stand before presidents or generals, or in any distinguished collection, with *aplomb*—and *not* culture, or any knowledge or intellect whatever". This statement summarizes the position that personality is innate—that we are born with a certain temperament and character that is permanent.

Of course, there is also good reason to believe that children are affected by the environments and cultures in which they grow up. As we will see, although the nature–nurture relationship is tremendously complex, many answers are now available. We do not have to equivocate and assert that personality is partly innate and partly culturally determined. Instead, we will ascertain which parts of personality are relatively fixed and which are more changeable.

Is Personality a Useful Concept?

Is personality a useful scientific concept for understanding human behavior, or is it merely an illusion, a misunderstanding of causality? Most of us have probably received cards from close friends with flattering messages such as:

> *It's not your name or background*
> *Or great things that you've done.*
> *It's not your help that makes you*
> *The best friend that I've found*
> *It's not your smarts I count on,*
> *Though you're nice and honest, too.*
> *It's what you are that makes you*
> *A very special friend.*

Such verses assume that there is some inner essence that makes us who we are. Unfortunately, such notions of "personhood" are vague and misleading. For example, lovers are often shocked to discover that their partner, whose essence they knew so well, actually had a criminal side, or an adulterous side, or an aggressive side. Further, efforts to capture this inner core generally prove scientifically fruitless. People are complex creatures, and it is important to avoid simplistic illusions or wishful thinking about a personality.

Does this mean that the scientific study of personality should be abandoned? Absolutely not. As we will show, the multiple scientific techniques used to study and understand personality are among the most sophisticated to be found in any science.

In addition to these basic issues of personality psychology, there are many topical questions of interest in modern personality research. Most current researchers are not constructing new grand theories of personality, but rather are working to answer applied questions such as the role played by personality in physical health and sickness, and in marriage and divorce. Is there a disease-prone and a self-healing personality? Do certain personalities make good lovers or good marriage partners? The answers to such questions, addressed later in this text, are quite complex.

Personality in Context

Authoritarian Personality
A person with antidemocratic tendencies; such a person tends to be narrowminded, rigid, defensive, and tends to show prejudice against minority groups

During the 1930s and 1940s, American psychologists were investigating the **authoritarian personality,** an excessively masculine, cold, and domineering personality that tended to become a fascist and to persecute members of the out-group. At the same time, fascist (Nazi) German psychologists were investigating the anti-type—people who were likely to be weak, liberal, artsy, and effeminate (Brown, 1965). What Americans called rigidity, the Germans called stability. What the Germans called eccentricity, Americans called individuality. What the Germans called perversion, the Americans called esthetic sensitivity. Without doubt, the Nazis were fantastically destructive murderers while the Americans of that era were striving to promote freedom and security. Still, it is interesting to see the ways in which observations about personality could be strongly influenced by the cultural contexts in which they occurred.

Today, most personality research has a distinct flavor of Western culture in general and mainstream American culture in particular. The unique viewpoints of Asian, Latin, African, and Native American cultures are too often overlooked. For example, in North American society, individuals who want to "do things their own way" and who challenge the conventional expectations of their companies or the government usually would be positively viewed as assertive and independent (and possibly even heroic). But in Japanese society the same behavior would be viewed as rude, uncooperative, selfish, and antisocial. In other words, our explanations of human behavior are dependent on our cultures, and therefore some amount of bias is inevitable.

We try to pay attention to the cultural context of personality theory and research, often by focusing on the theorists' own lives as an illustration. Critiques of ideas should not become ad hominem arguments; that is, we must evaluate the quality of theory and research on its own terms, rather than in terms of the theorist who proposed it. Just because many of Sigmund Freud's patients were middle-class Jewish European women at the turn of the past century does not mean that his insights are not applicable to others. Nevertheless, explanations are more likely to be valid if they take into account the contexts in which the theories arise.

Finally, let us do a little demonstration. Suppose we tell you that people with the following characteristics are likely to develop significant personality problems in later life:

These people often have feelings of loneliness and sometimes question their self-worth. They wish they were more popular. They regularly have sexual thoughts and sexual dreams about certain special others. They wish that they had better bodies. They are sometimes unsure about who they are and why they are alive.

In fact, this is phony information. But such a description would characterize many college students. That is, many college students would feel that this description applies to them as individuals (and that therefore they are prone to personality problems)

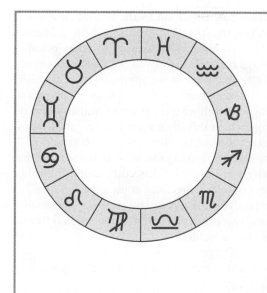

■ **FIGURE 3**

The Zodiac Signs, and "Prophetic" Message, of a Horoscope.

Are people who believe in astrology more likely to accept generalized personality descriptions of themselves than are skeptics? One study confirmed that astrology believers are indeed especially susceptible to the Barnum effect, but almost everyone finds personal meaning in vague generalities to some degree (Glick, Gottesman, & Jolton, 1989).

even though the profile is ridiculously general, as in the example in Figure 3. This tendency to believe in the accuracy of vague generalities about one's personality is sometimes termed the **Barnum effect** (Snyder, Shenkel, & Lowery, 1977; first shown by Ulrich, Stachnik, & Stainton, 1963). This demonstration illustrates the care that is required to ensure that personality theories and assessments are specific and have been scientifically validated. Personality is a fascinating field but it is one that is subject to abuse and distortion if the utmost care is not taken by those who evaluate theories.

On the other hand, there is societal value in attempting to understand the uniqueness of each person. Blaise Pascal (1670/1961), the great French philosopher and mathematician, wrote in *Pensées,* "The more intelligence one has, the more people one finds original. Commonplace people see no difference between men" (I.7). Modern psychobiology confirms Pascal's assertion, and in this text, we show the great value of understanding each individual, each in his or her own context.

Barnum Effect
The tendency to believe in the accuracy of vague generalities about one's personality

Summary and Conclusion

Personality psychology asks the questions, What does it mean to be a person? How are we unique as individuals? What is the nature of the self?

Personality psychology answers these questions in terms of systematic observations about how and why individuals behave as they do, with a focus on the thoughts, feelings, and behaviors of real people. Personality psychology can be defined as the scientific study of the psychological forces that make people uniquely themselves. To be comprehensive, we can say that personality has eight key aspects, which together help us understand the very complex nature of the individual.

Personality psychologists attempt to use methods of scientific inference to test theories. Techniques range from the most formal mathematical assessment of traits and abilities to the careful, rich examination of a single individual's thoughts, feelings, and behaviors. Why does a certain 18-year-old high school senior seem consumed by intrusive thoughts and sexual fantasies? Is it hormones? repressed sexual drives? the influence of the surroundings? past experiences and conditioning? an existential crisis? combinations of these and other personal influences? A thorough understanding of personality involves a firm grasp of the meaning, validity, and implications of these various perspectives.

Personality theories arise from various sources. They come from careful observation and from deep introspection; from systematic measurement and from statistical analyses; from biological brain scans and from studies of mental illness; from anthropology and sociology and economics and philosophy. Theorists apply these sundry insights to a psychological understanding of the individual.

Some of the roots of personality psychology can be traced back to the theater. Other aspects derive from religion, and from Eastern and Western philosophical traditions. Darwinian evolutionary biology had a profound influence on personality psychology, an influence that is currently enjoying a resurgence. Breakthroughs in personality testing and intelligence testing helped shape both the theories and the methods of modern personality psychology, although the significant effects of culture on test scores were often ignored.

Modern personality theory began to take formal shape in the 1930s, thanks to the pioneering work of three men—Gordon Allport, Kurt Lewin, and Henry Murray. Allport (1937) defined personality as "the dynamic organization within the individual of those psychophysical systems that determine his unique adjustment to his environment". Lewin's approach was also dynamic, as he looked for systems that underlie observable behavior. Lewin (1935) drew attention to "the momentary condition of the individual and the structure of the psychological situation". Murray believed in a comprehensive orientation that included longitudinal research—studying the same people over time. He took a very broad approach to personality, defining it as the "branch of psychology which principally concerns itself with the study of human lives and the factors which influence their course, [and] which investigates individual differences" (Murray, 1938. Contemporaneously, Margaret Mead demonstrated that personality was heavily influenced by culture, but her work was not fully appreciated at the time.

Certain basic issues in the study of personality appear and reappear at different times and in different theories. These include

What is the importance of the unconscious?

What is the self?

To what extent can our approaches be nomothetic (concerned with universal laws) as opposed to idiographic (studying individual cases)?

What are the differences between men and women, and where do they come from?

Which affects behavior more—the person or the situation?

To what extent is personality culturally determined?

Is personality a useful scientific concept or merely a convenient illusion?

In sum, personality psychology addresses some of the most interesting yet complex questions involved in understanding what it means to be a human being. As Gordon Allport put it, all books on personality psychology are at the same time books on the philosophy of what is a person.

■ Key Theorists

Gordon Allport	Kurt Lewin	Henry Murray

■ Key Concepts and Terms

personality psychology	Darwinian evolutionary theory
deductive versus inductive approach to personality	nomothetic science versus idiographic science
eight perspectives on personality	Barnum effect

How Is Personality Studied and Assessed?

When we took our two young sons to Disneyland, they came across a 7-foot-tall pirate who looked very much like the evil Captain Hook. The pirate was mingling with the crowd, shaking hands (and hook) with passersby. Although a great admirer of pirates, and a veteran of innumerable viewings of *Peter Pan*, our older son recognized Hook, backed away from him, and stood behind his mother. Our younger son, in dramatic contrast, marched right up to the pirate, smiled, and shook hands.

We had just stumbled on a new sort of personality test—a standardized stimulus that provokes reactions and assesses revealing individual differences. We could call it the Pirate Test for Children. We could bring other children up to the pirate and see how they respond. As personality tests go, this test is not a bad start, but it is not complete. Like any test of personality, it has certain strengths in capturing the characteristic it seeks to measure and certain weaknesses or limitations that make it incomplete or flawed.

Courtesy: Everett Collection

From Chapter 2 of *Personality: Classic Theories and Modern Research*, Fifth Edition. Howard S. Friedman, Miriam W. Schustack. Copyright © 2012 by Pearson Education, Inc. Published by Pearson Allyn & Bacon. All rights reserved.

Objective Assessment
Measurement that is not dependent on the individual making the assessment

Subjective Assessment
Measurement that relies on interpretation by the individual making the assessment

The Pirate Test, like many other personality measures, is not very objective in yielding a test score. In an arithmetic test or a high-jump test, the results are objective scores: a percentage of correct answers or a jump height in inches. Some personality tests similarly entail **objective assessment,** in which the measurement is not dependent on a judgment by the individual making the assessment. Such tests may ask the test-taker to find an embedded figure in a complex drawing or to push a button as soon as a familiar tone is heard. Clear measures emerge from such tests; in these examples, it is the percentage of embedded figures uncovered and the reaction time (to the familiar tone) in seconds. But the Pirate Test depends on observers to interpret how the child is reacting. Then again, our Pirate Test allows for an experienced observer of children to form detailed, rich impressions—that is, it allows for subjective assessment.

Subjective assessment—measurement that relies on interpretation—has complementary strengths and weaknesses. The problems revolve around the fact that different observers may make different judgments, and such judgments are fallible. This challenge is not unique to psychology. In many arenas of human endeavor, the subjective judgment of an expert plays an important role. For example, consider judgments of art. Poor Vincent van Gogh and many other now-famous impressionist painters had trouble selling their paintings over a century ago. A panel of observers assembled from the mainstream existing culture or from the street would have rejected many impressionist works as not "real art." A panel of observers may disagree in their opinions; and even if they agree, their judgment may be questionable.

On the other hand, a group of experts can often see through the complexities of a rich phenomenon and gain wonderful insights. The same is true for personality psychology. Insightful clinicians, observing a child interact with Captain Hook, might notice a reaction pattern that points to a significant maladjustment or suggests a childhood trauma or perhaps indicates certain tremendous strength of adaptive personality. Many commonly used personality tests thus incorporate a subjective element. In personality assessment, we must walk the line between being so objective that our information is sterile and being so subjective that our observation is idiosyncratic and our inference is unscientific. Fortunately, there are many guidelines and techniques that promote meaningful and scientific assessment of personality (e.g. Aiken, 1999).

© Erich Lessing/ Art Resource, NY

■ Observers may agree among themselves about the quality of a work of art (that is, be reliable in their judgment) but have questionable validity. Many paintings by Vincent van Gogh were considered virtually worthless in his day but now are highly valued, bringing millions of dollars when sold at auction. Observers' judgments of personality similarly may have questionable validity on certain dimensions.

Measuring Personality

When asked to name leaders high in charisma, people usually name such figures as John F. Kennedy, Martin Luther King Jr., Ronald Reagan, Mahatma Gandhi, Franklin Roosevelt, Winston Churchill, and Malcolm X. These leaders were able to attract and inspire large numbers of followers. But we meet people every day who show a kind of personal charisma—people who are attractive, influential, expressive, and who are often the center of attention. In fact, in a seminar class or other small group, there is usually considerable agreement among the members as to which one of them is the most charismatic.

How can we assess whether someone is especially expressive and likely to be an influential emotional leader in a group? How can we identify such people so that we can go on to study in more detail the notion of charisma, in terms of both the charismatic persons themselves and their social influence processes? Could we construct a simple charisma test? One simple measure of personal charisma is called the Affective Communication Test, or ACT (Friedman, Prince, Riggio, & DiMatteo, 1980). The ACT is shown in Table 1. You can take this test now: Rate the extent to which each statement is true of you, using a scale from –4 to 4, where –4 means "not at all true of me," and 4 means "very true of me." You will learn more about this simple test and how to score it later in this chapter.

© AP Images

■ Many people attribute the success and fame of charismatic public figures such as the late President John F. Kennedy to their charm and personal appeal rather than to their policies.

Reliability

If you were to step on a bathroom scale (to measure your weight) every half-hour during the course of an afternoon, you would expect your weight to be about the same each time. The term **reliability** refers to the consistency of scores that are expected to be the same. A reliable scale is consistent. If the scale showed your weight changing from 150 pounds to 140 to 160 to 120 over the course of a single afternoon, you would throw out the scale as unreliable.

Of course, you might find slight differences in measured weight as the spring in the scale changes slightly due to changes in room humidity or repeated usage. Such random variations produce what is called the **error variance** or error of measurement—variations that are caused by irrelevant, chance fluctuations. The best scales are highly reliable; they give consistent measurement. In assessing charisma, we would expect that a person who scores as very charismatic on Monday would not score as uncharismatic on Tuesday. Reliability also implicitly contains the idea of precision. You would not be satisfied with a bathroom scale that tells you that you weigh "over 100 pounds."

Reliability
The consistency of scores that are expected to be the same

Error Variance
Variations of a measurement that are the result of irrelevant, chance fluctuations

Internal Consistency Reliability

The reliability of a personality test is usually determined in two ways. First, the degree of consistency is measured by seeing whether subparts or equivalent parts of a test yield the same results. For example, we might split a paper-and-pencil test in half and then figure the split-half reliability by finding the correlation between the two halves (when the test is given to a number of people). We would expect the halves of the test to be highly correlated; for example, the person who scored highest on the first half of the test should also score very high on the second half. This is termed **internal consistency reliability.** In the ACT measure of charisma, scores on the various items tend to be similar, though not identical.

Internal consistency is often measured by a statistic called Cronbach's coefficient alpha. We can think of alpha as the average of all the possible split-half correlation

Internal Consistency Reliability
Degree of consistency between subparts or equivalent parts of a test

■ TABLE 1   The Affective Communication Test

Please Read These Instructions Carefully.   Below you will find a series of statements indicating an attitude or behavior that might be true as it applies to you or might not be true of you. Your task is to read carefully each statement and circle the number between minus 4 (−4) and plus 4 (4) that best indicates your answer. The more negative your answer, the more you believe the statement is false as it applies to you. The more positive your answer, the more you believe the statement is true of you.

Example:

*I feel very happy when I see pretty flowers.	Not at all true of me	−4 −3 −2 −1 0 1 2 3 4	Very true of me

Circling 2 would indicate that you feel somewhat happy when you see flowers but not as much as if you had circled number 4. If you had circled −4, this would mean that the opposite is true—that you feel very unhappy when you see flowers.

There are no right or wrong answers. Please circle only one number on each scale. Read each statement carefully and indicate an answer for every one.

1. *When I hear good dance music, I can hardly keep still.	Not at all true of me	−4 −3 −2 −1 0 1 2 3 4	Very true of me
2. *My laugh is soft and subdued.	Not at all true of me	−4 −3 −2 −1 0 1 2 3 4	Very true of me
3. *I can easily express emotion over the telephone.	Not at all true of me	−4 −3 −2 −1 0 1 2 3 4	Very true of me
4. *I often touch friends during conversations.	Not at all true of me	−4 −3 −2 −1 0 1 2 3 4	Very true of me
5. *I dislike being watched by a large group of people.	Not at all true of me	−4 −3 −2 −1 0 1 2 3 4	Very true of me
6. *I usually have a neutral facial expression.	Not at all true of me	−4 −3 −2 −1 0 1 2 3 4	Very true of me
7. *People tell me that I would make a good actor or actress.	Not at all true of me	−4 −3 −2 −1 0 1 2 3 4	Very true of me
8. *I like to remain unnoticed in a crowd.	Not at all true of me	−4 −3 −2 −1 0 1 2 3 4	Very true of me
9. *I am shy among strangers.	Not at all true of me	−4 −3 −2 −1 0 1 2 3 4	Very true of me
10. *I am able to give a seductive glance if I want to.	Not at all true of me	−4 −3 −2 −1 0 1 2 3 4	Very true of me
11. *I am terrible at pantomime as in games like charades.	Not at all true of me	−4 −3 −2 −1 0 1 2 3 4	Very true of me
12. *At small parties I am the center of attention.	Not at all true of me	−4 −3 −2 −1 0 1 2 3 4	Very true of me
13. *I show that I like someone by hugging or touching that person.	Not at all true of me	−4 −3 −2 −1 0 1 2 3 4	Very true of me

coefficients. Measurement becomes more consistent and stable as we take repeated relevant measures (Rosenthal & Rosnow, 1991). In statistical terms, this means that internal consistency is a function of the number of items and their degree of correlation. In constructing a personality test, we want to add relevant items until the total score becomes very stable. But we don't want to add so many items that the test becomes unwieldy or boring. In tests that are to be widely employed, the coefficient of internal consistency reliability generally should be about .80.

Sometimes the consistency issue applies to our expert observers. In the case of our new Pirate Test, we would like our observers to agree in their judgments. Usually about 12 observers are sufficient to achieve consistency.

Test–Retest Reliability

The second measure of reliability involves the instrument's degree of consistency on different occasions. That is, people who are expressive people or conscientious people on Monday should score similarly on Thursday. In developing the ACT, researchers measured the same people twice, two months apart. This notion of temporal stability is termed **test–retest reliability.** The test–retest reliability of the ACT is about .90. Over short periods of time, ACT scores remain about the same, although there is some error of measurement. When internal consistency reliability and test–retest reliability are high, we know we are measuring something real—we have a reliable personality test.

Of course, we want to be able to take into account that people may change over time. Our biological systems mature and age, we are shaped by experiences, we gain insights into ourselves and others, and the situations we face change over time. So it makes sense that personality might change as well. This is not a problem for measuring weight—we are all too aware that our weight fluctuates as we diet or overeat. But personality by definition is assumed to be fairly stable. All this leaves us with a significant theoretical and measurement challenge: How can we have a reliable (stable) assessment of personality if personality may change?

There are two sorts of sophisticated answers to this challenge. First, as Allport repeatedly emphasized, personality consists of **patterns** that dynamically direct activity. Although a person's particular activities and daily responses may change, the basic underlying patterns remain relatively stable. In fact, the temporal (time) dimension should be included in many studies of personality; that is, we should ascertain the individual's patterns of response over time (Larsen, 1989). Consistent patterns often emerge. For example, if a person with bipolar disorder cycles between being manic and being depressive, this is not a reliability problem if we consider the personality to be manic-depressive. If we did not examine patterns over time, however, we might conclude (erroneously) that our measurement is unreliable—first the person seemed manic and then depressive.

The second answer to the challenge of personality change is to allow that personality may change over the long term (or after a major trauma) and to expect personality stability only over shorter periods of perhaps several years. For example, it would be useful to have a reliable measurement of extroversion at age 16 if identifying that trait helped us understand the person's behavior in college and young adulthood. If the person then became introverted after many years, that would not necessarily be a problem for reliability. In fact, it might be an interesting phenomenon in its own right: Why do some extroverts become more introverted? Studying

Test-Retest Reliability
The degree of consistency between the results of the same test taken on different occasions

Patterns
The basic underlying mechanisms of personality that dynamically direct activity and remain relatively stable

Classic to **Current**

The TAT

When Sigmund Freud and his psychoanalytic colleagues discovered the unconscious, they faced a troubling challenge for their research. Unconscious motivations are, by definition, not accessible to conscious thought processes. They are hidden. So, of course, we cannot expect a person to be able to tell us directly about these unconscious motivations. Freud relied mostly on free association explorations during therapeutic interviews, and on dream analysis. His followers, however, sought out additional methods.

Projective tests allow a person to "project" his or her own inner motivations onto the assessor's test. They thus gather insights into thoughts and feelings that are outside the test-taker's awareness. One of the most commonly used projective tests is the Thematic Apperception Test, or TAT, developed by Henry Murray and Christiana Morgan. The assessor or clinician tells the participant to make up a story about a picture that will be presented, including a prediction of what will happen next in the story. The assessor then holds up the first picture (for example, a picture of a young woman grabbing the shoulders of a young man), which can bring out various psychological associations relevant to the test-taker's own life. The TAT thus attempts to see how a person places order on a vague stimulus. The TAT is heavily used by psychodynamically oriented clinicians as a key tool into important issues of inner personality and motivation.

Unfortunately, the TAT has long been beset by controversy, and these disputes continue. Psychologist Scott Lilienfeld and his colleagues carefully reviewed the research evidence and raised serious questions about the validity of the TAT and related tests, especially in terms of how they are often used (Lilienfeld, Wood, & Garb, 2000). One issue is that there are several standardized TAT scoring systems in use, and many clinicians simply prefer to rely on their own clinical impressions. A second issue concerns discrepancies between TAT results and self-report scales; is the discrepancy a problem of validity, or is it an expected result of the discrepancy between conscious and unconscious motivation? Overall, the scientific disputes revolve around issues of reliability and validity—that is, is a

person's score approximately the same when he or she is tested again, at a later time or by a different examiner? And is a person's score associated with and confirmed by other indicators, and is it predictive of certain outcomes? There are still no absolute answers to these questions.

The crux of the controversy often comes down to the purpose of the TAT test (Dawes, 1998; Woike, 2001). If a client in psychotherapy is experiencing chronic anxiety, and if the TAT can provide the clinician and client with insights into experiences or conflicts that might be causing the anxiety, then the test is valuable, even if it is sometimes in error. If, however, the purpose is to evaluate someone's suitability to be a teacher or to provide courtroom testimony against someone accused of child abuse, then any errors resulting from weak reliability and validity would have very serious consequences. Further, if projective tests like the TAT are given to large numbers of healthy people as some sort of screening, and if they are interpreted by clinicians who are accustomed to treating people with mental problems, weak validity may allow a tendency to "overpathologize"—that is, to see healthy people as disturbed.

For the student of personality, such issues are also important in a practical way, as you may encounter such a controversy about testing in the workplace, in the courtroom, or in a doctor's office. With some understanding of how personality assessments are constructed, their strengths and limits, the purposes for which they are best used, and the theories on which they are based, you may make a more intelligent judgment about whether the assessment is appropriate and sound for the specific context in which it is being used.

FURTHER READING

Dawes, R. M. (1998). Standards for psychotherapy. In H. S. Friedman (Ed.), *Encyclopedia of mental health* (Vol. 3, pp. 589–597). San Diego, CA: Academic Press.

Lilienfeld, S. O., Wood, J. M., & Garb, H. N. (2000). The scientific status of projective techniques. *Psychological Science in the Public Interest, 1*, 27–66.

Woike, B. (2001). Working with free response data: Let's not give up hope. *Psychological Inquiry, 12*, 157–159.

and measuring personality always involve these sorts of trade-offs. Measuring conscious biological systems (people) is not like measuring physical quantities like height and weight. People grow and change, and even their basic patterns of responding may change.

Construct Validity

Suppose we went to a shopping mall and stood on a scale every hour all afternoon and kept getting the same, reliable result; the scale, one of those electronic devices with a computer voice, keeps announcing "11, 11, 11." That seems like a funny weight. It turns out that the scale is specially designed for shoe stores and it is really using pressure to measure the length of our feet (and intoning our shoe size, very reliably). Is the test measuring what it is supposed to be measuring? What is it measuring? This is the issue of **validity.**

> **Validity**
> The extent to which a test measures what it is supposed to be measuring

The most important (and complex) aspect of validity is **construct validity.** Construct validity refers to the extent to which a test truly measures a theoretical construct. For example, is the ACT really measuring personal charisma, or is it perhaps measuring friendliness or nurturance?

> **Construct Validity**
> The extent to which a test truly measures a theoretical construct

Construct validity is ascertained by seeing if the assessments predict behaviors and reactions implied (theoretically) by the construct. Charismatic people should do more than score high on a paper-and-pencil measure. They should engage in certain charismatic activities, and they should show a certain pattern of responses on other measures. For example, they should be more extroverted than introverted. Construct validation is an ongoing process and involves showing that (1) the assessment is related to what it should theoretically be related to—this is called **convergent validation;** and (2) the assessment is not related to what it should not be related to—this is called **discriminant validation** (Campbell & Fiske, 1959; Campbell, 1960). If the ACT is related to extroversion scales (as it should be), then that is evidence for convergent validity. If the ACT were related to intelligence (as it should not be), then that would be evidence that it is lacking in discriminant validity.

> **Convergent Validation**
> The extent to which an assessment is related to what it should be related to
>
> **Discriminant Validation**
> The extent to which an assessment is not related to what it should not be related to

Ultimately, construct validation is a process closely tied to theory development. Only a theory can tell us what our personality construct should and should not relate to. Theory development in the social sciences is notoriously complex. Theories are a function of many assumptions and many hard-to-measure entities. Paradoxically, the theory informs the assessment and the assessment in turn informs the theory. We begin with certain ideas about personality, and as we measure personality, we refine our theories. This is why assessment is a recurring theme in any course on personality. For example, the ACT originally set out to measure nonverbal expressiveness, but as more was learned, it became clear that the ACT was a good measure of personal charisma. For example, the number one Toyota salesperson in the United States scored very high on the ACT.

What if we created a brief new paper-and-pencil intelligence test that correlated well with other paper-and-pencil intelligence tests, but we never bothered to see whether scores were related to real-world problem-solving ability? To demonstrate our test's validity, we must also show that our test relates to the outcome criteria in the expected ways, using different assessment methods. This is sometimes termed **criterion-related validation**—whether our measure predicts to outcome criteria. For example, the ACT predicts who is likely to be a leader, just as it should. Because

> **Criterion-Related Validation**
> The extent to which an assessment predicts outcome criteria that were produced by different assessment methods

Multitrait-Multimethod Perspective
The use of multiple assessment methods and various traits in order to determine test validity

Content Validity
The extent to which a test is measuring the domain it is supposed to be measuring

proper test validation involves assessing various traits and utilizing multiple assessment methods, the validation approach is termed a **multitrait-multimethod perspective** (Campbell & Fiske, 1959).

Content Validity

Content validity refers to whether a test is measuring the domain that it is supposed to be measuring. For example, a test might seem to be measuring creative ability but might in fact be measuring only artistic ability and ignoring musical ability, writing ability, and other aspects of creative ability. In gathering items for the ACT, we collected a wide range of characteristics that seemed relevant to having a highly expressive style. Unreliable items and ambiguous items were discarded, but the final scale includes items about nonverbal expressions (such as touching and laughing and facial expression), about acting, about social relations (such as behavior at parties), and about interpersonal expressive communication (such as giving a seductive glance). The ACT tries to capture many of the content dimensions of personal charisma.

Item Selection

Which items are best for a personality test? Obviously, items should be clear, relevant, and relatively simple, if at all possible. Beyond that, the choice depends a lot on assumptions about the nature of personality; assessment should not proceed in the absence of theory. The mathematical assumptions underlying the construction of reliable and valid personality tests can become quite complicated. There are psychologists who spend their entire careers working on the best ways to design and score assessments. For example, we have already noted that lengthening an assessment generally improves its reliability and validity (up to a certain point), but at added expense. Although efforts are made to select the best items and reject poor items, defining *best* in this context is not so simple.

Item Intercorrelation
The extent to which test items are related to one another

One desirable quality of a test item is that it should discriminate among test-takers; an item is useless if everyone answers it the same way. So generally speaking, each item in an assessment should divide the group of test-takers into roughly two groups. Also relevant, however, is that all the items should be intercorrelated (or related to one another); each item is measuring some aspect of the overall construct. This **item intercorrelation** in turn affects the discriminability issue—too high an intercorrelation merely provides redundant information. The total scores on the assessment should also have the proper distribution. That is, we need to be able to assess a full range of people. The ACT, for example, should measure the few who are extremely charismatic, the few who are extremely uncharismatic, and the many who are in between.

Item Response Theory (IRT)
A mathematical approach to choosing test items in which the probability of a positive response to an item is determined by the person's estimated position on the underlying trait being measured, as well as by characteristics of the item

One particular mathematical approach to choosing the best items has undergone a lot of development in recent years. It is termed **Item Response Theory (IRT).** Using item response mathematical techniques, we can examine the probability of a positive response on a particular item, given the person's overall position on the underlying trait being measured by the test (as estimated by the other answers). Some items might perform differently for men than for women (that is, be diagnostic only for one gender) and thus would be considered biased items. A description of the mathematics of IRT can be found in technical books and articles on personality assessment (Flannery, Reise, & Widaman, 1995).

Bias

One of the thorniest issues in personality assessment involves the potential for bias in measures and assessments. We consider the issue of bias throughout this text, but here we will describe three such sources of bias: response sets, ethnic bias, and gender bias.

Response Sets

In scoring the ACT, items 2, 5, 6, 8, 9, and 11 (Table 1) are worded in the reverse direction. Agreeing with these items indicates a lack of expressiveness. Reverse wording is done to combat an **acquiescence response set.** Some people simply are more likely than others to agree with anything you ask them. **Response sets** are biases, unrelated to the personality characteristic being measured. So, in addressing the acquiescence response set, it is important to include items that are worded in the reverse direction. Before scoring the ACT, you must reverse the responses to these items.

An especially difficult challenge is posed by a **social desirability response set.** Many people want to present themselves in a favorable light or respond to please the experimenter or test administrator. Few people will agree truthfully with a statement like "I have thought about molesting young children." On the other hand, someone who wanted to pretend to be mentally ill might untruthfully agree with such a statement. One way to try to deal with social desirability response sets is to present items of equal desirability and ask the test-taker to choose between the two.

Similarly, sometimes people give purely random answers to a multiple-choice personality test. Perhaps they cannot read very well, or they are trying to subvert a study (being conducted by a researcher they dislike), or they are tired of filling out forms as part of a psychology class experiment. Some tests therefore have lie scales, which include items like "I have walked on the moon (yes/no)." Such items help pick out the liars (but may mess up when testing that rare astronaut).

Even a cleverly designed personality assessment is subject to various sources of distortion or bias. You could easily distort your score by lying on the ACT. It is therefore valuable for the personality psychologist to employ multiple means of assessment, as we describe later in this chapter. On the other hand, assessments can have some bias and still be of value. Most established personality assessments have at least a fair to good degree of validity; they yield worthwhile information on most people in most circumstances.

The norms of the ACT are shown in Table 2. To compute your ACT score, first add 5 points to each item (to eliminate negative numbers). Then, reverse the scores for the six reversed items (items 2, 5, 6, 8, 9, and 11), so that a 1 becomes a 9, a 2 becomes an 8, and so on. Finally, add all the item scores.

Ethnic Bias

When our children were reacting to Captain Hook at Disneyland, another child was having a very different reaction. Evidently from Asia, this puzzled little boy did not seem to know who or what Captain Hook was all about.

Acquiescence Response Set
A bias in which people are more likely to agree than disagree with anything that is asked of them

Response Set
A bias responding to test items that is unrelated to the personality characteristic being measured

Social Desirability Response Set
A bias in which people are likely to want to present themselves in a favorable light or to try to please the experimenter or test administrator

■ **TABLE 2**   Norms for the ACT Scale

Overall mean	71.3
Overall median	71.2
Overall mode	68.0
Minimum score obtained	25.0
Maximum score obtained	116.0
Standard deviation	15.7
Mean for females	72.7
Mean for males	69.5

Note: Based on a tested population of 600 college students.

Ethnic Bias
A type of bias in which a test fails to take into account the relevant culture or subculture of the person being tested

Our Pirate Test for Children might have been inappropriate for this little boy because it makes certain assumptions about the knowledge and background of the "test-taker." Like many tests, this test is culturally biased and should therefore be used only with a certain subset of the population.

Although all tests rely on a set of assumptions and thus might be called biased, the tests are not necessarily bad or worthless. Rather, they must be properly used and interpreted in order to be valid. A man who took multiple wives, beat his children, and regularly sacrificed animals in religious rites would be evaluated quite differently today than he would have been in earlier times (when such behaviors were common). Personality assessment has meaning only in context. We should become sensitive to the context of all our assessments.

As noted, one of the most common types of test bias is **ethnic bias.** All too often, tests fail to take into account the relevant culture or subculture of the person being tested; theories and measures developed in one culture are improperly applied to another culture. For example, well-socialized Asian Americans are often raised to behave with cooperation, humility, and modesty, whereas equally well-socialized Italian American children are often expected to be assertive, outgoing, and expressive. Of course, it is true that both subcultures usually produce well-adjusted, successful adults. It would be an assessment mistake to label the average Asian American child as "excessively shy," or to label the average Italian American child as "especially aggressive." On the other hand, it might prove helpful to compare an Asian American child who seems painfully shy with other Asian Americans; and it might prove similarly informative to compare an Italian American child who is experiencing difficulties with friends with other children raised in the same subculture.

Sometimes bias causes a cultural strength to be perceived as a weakness. For example, Hispanic American children have sometimes been viewed as lacking in achievement motivation (viewed as a deficit), when in fact they have been raised to be more cooperative with their peers (which is often a strength).

It can be difficult to notice ethnic prejudice in our own theories and assessments, so let us consider an example from the 1800s. For much of the nineteenth century, criminal personality was seen as an innate characteristic, fixed at birth (Gould, 1981). Crime was considered to be the result not of an abusive childhood, peer pressure, lack of opportunity, lack of education, or social stress; rather it was the result of having a criminal nature. Not surprisingly, people who were not part of the dominant mainstream culture were especially likely to be so labeled. Such blind prejudices have a long and sordid history in American culture, in which African Americans have often been labeled as having an innate criminal nature. Ironically, during the decades of American slavery, the slaves were seen by their masters as obviously having a docile, slave-like personality (except when they tried to escape; then they were seen as innately criminal).

It is difficult to emphasize how subtle and yet how ingrained in our society are such biases. Personality psychology too often studies samples of convenience—one's patients, one's students, one's neighbors, one's children—and too rarely makes a systematic attempt to ascertain whether conclusions apply to other peoples, in other places, in other times.

Gender Bias

Let us say we are developing a new test of extroversion, and preliminary results with our scale show that women score higher than men. What do we do? Do we throw out those items on which women score higher, thus "equalizing" the scores? We might do this if we had a strong theoretical reason to assume that men and women are equally extroverted. Usually, however, we have no such theoretical reason; we merely have prejudices. We adjust the test scores to fit our prejudices. A second common type of test bias is gender bias.

Consider a problem often diagnosed in women: a self-defeating personality (Tavris, 1992). Many popular theories and associated assessments attempt to document and explain why many American women are unhappy, frustrated, and overly trusting, and are often stuck in miserable marriages and dead-end jobs. Tests can demonstrate that these women are masochistic, codependent, love too much, want too much, are addicted to men, or are simply basically depressive. Less frequently is the focus turned to the environment—toward abusive husbands, job discrimination, or lack of equal educational opportunity.

Consider also gender-related expectations for a healthy personality. If a woman scores as highly nurturant toward children, highly cooperative toward others, horrified by violence, fearful of mice, very concerned with her looks, and enchanted by crocheting, baking, and decorating, this woman will usually be scored as mentally healthy. But what if a man showed the exact same pattern?

Even well-designed personality tests are tools, and like other tools they may be properly used or blatantly misused. For example, although tests may be dangerous when they carelessly assert dramatic personality differences among ethnic groups, they may be helpful in examining personality differences *within* ethnic groups (say, among Asian Americans). Furthermore, testing may uncover interesting group differences that should be followed up by other research techniques. Thus we should not ban tests because they might be biased, just as we should not ban tools because they may be misused. Rather, we should learn the limits of our assessments. These matters are considered further in the section later in this chapter on the ethics of personality testing.

One of the great triumphs of personality testing of the past century has been the development of many different types of personality tests. When properly used, all of these tests have something to contribute to our understanding of the complexity of what it means to be human. In the remainder of this chapter, we describe the various types of personality tests.

Varieties of Personality Measures

There are theoretical reasons and methodological reasons for having different types of personality tests. On theoretical grounds, it is apparent that certain tests are more or less appropriate for measuring the aspect of personality under consideration. For example, it does not make sense to ask people to report about their unconscious motivations; by definition, such motivations cannot be consciously grasped and reported.

On methodological grounds, it is important to have various ways of measuring personality because each suffers from inherent biases. For example, interviews can probe more deeply and reactively into a person's inner thoughts and feelings than can a standardized questionnaire. On the other hand, observations of behavior or the analysis of a person's expressive style are often best at capturing what a person actually does. The weaknesses in one assessment technique can be compensated for by other techniques, thus helping us achieve a more complete understanding of personality. Table 3 lists the major types of personality measures, along with examples of each type.

Self-Report Tests

The most common personality tests are, like the ACT measure of charisma, dependent on the test-takers' self-reports. Such tests are easy and inexpensive to administer and are often objective, but their validity must be carefully evaluated.

Minnesota Multiphasic Personality Inventory (MMPI)
A comprehensive, self-report personality test that is focused on assessing psychopathology

One comprehensive self-report personality test is the **Minnesota Multiphasic Personality Inventory (MMPI).** Responding to about 500 statements, the test-taker answers either "true," "false," or "cannot say." The MMPI was created using criterion-related item selection. That is, the selected items distinguished between a target group such as depressed people and a normal control group. It was thus focused on assessing psychopathology (mental illness). The inventory was revised in 1989 (to the MMPI-2) in an attempt to eliminate outdated terms and to create norms from a sample that better represents the population of the United States (Butcher, 1990). A further revision (the MMPI-2-RF released in 2008) has distinct subscales and is more helpful in forecasting psychological problems, such as a tendency toward being aggressive and abusive.

You might encounter the MMPI if you apply for certain types of jobs that demand strong emotional stability (such as police work), or if a psychiatrist or psychologist is trying to understand why you suffer from pain of unknown origin. But because the test was constructed with criterion-related item selection (seeing empirically which items distinguish impaired from normal groups of people) and contains questions about sex and other private bodily feelings and habits, it is now unlikely to be used in general employment screening. Companies got tired of being sued for invasions of privacy.

■ **TABLE 3** Types of Personality Measures

Type of Test	Examples
Self-report tests	Minnesota Multiphasic Personality Inventory (MMPI); Affective Communication Test (ACT); Millon Clinical Multiaxial Inventory; NEO-PI; Personality Research Form (PRF); Myers-Briggs Type Indicator (MBTI)
Q-sort tests	Self-concept; self-esteem; family relations
Ratings and judgments by others	Ratings by parents, teachers, friends, spouse; judgments by psychologists
Biological measures	Reaction time; skin conductance; electroencephalogram (EEG); positron emission tomography (PET) scan, magnetic resonance imagery (MRI), functional MRI (fMRI); postmortem analyses; hormonal and neurotransmitter levels; chromosomal and gene analyses
Behavioral observations	Experience sampling; judgments by videotape coders
Interviews	Type A structured interview; Kinsey sexual interview; clinical (psychiatric) intake interview
Expressive behavior	Speech rate; gaze patterns; posture; gesture; gait; interpersonal distance
Document analysis	Psychobiography; dream diaries
Projective tests	Draw-A-Person; Rorschach Inkblot; Thematic Apperception Test (TAT)
Demographics and lifestyle	Age; cultural group; sexual orientation; political affiliation

Enhancing the individual scale scores, MMPIs are often evaluated using a profile that graphs the *pattern* of scale scores. For example, some people score very high on the three MMPI scales called hypochondriasis (complains of physical symptoms), depression (feels depressed), and hysteria (turns psychological problems into physical problems); these people are especially interesting to researchers in behavioral medicine because this triad often describes patients who report being in chronic pain. High scorers on these three scales are more likely to overuse medical facilities and to benefit from psychological treatment that accompanies their medical treatment.

In this tradition of using personality tests to help therapists design treatments, the Millon Clinical Multiaxial Inventory is a thorough attempt to assess personality disorders (Craig, 1993; Millon, 1997). For example, it helps in diagnosing clinical syndromes, such as alcohol dependency, and personality patterns, such as the so-called passive-aggressive, in which people hide their aggressiveness through a phony pleasantness (talking sweetly to the spouse but refusing sexual relations).

There are several excellent, modern personality inventories that attempt to measure basic dimensions of personality in normal adults. One of these, the NEO Personality Inventory (NEO-PI), is built around the idea of five basic dimensions of personality (Costa & McCrae, 1992a, 1992b). This approach to measuring personality relies

Factor Analysis
A statistical technique in which correlations among a number of simple scales are reduced to a few basic dimensions

Personality Research Form (PRF)
A self-report test that assesses needs by forced responses to short, standardized items

Q-sort
A method of personality assessment in which a person is given a stack of cards naming various characteristics and is asked to sort them into piles

heavily on the statistical technique termed **factor analysis.** Factor analysis starts with the correlations among a number of simple scales and then reduces this information to a few basic dimensions. For example, notions about being outgoing, active, warm, talkative, energetic, sociable, and so on are captured in the factor called Extroversion. Primarily descriptive, the factors must then be explained by a theory. The five basic dimensions of personality are Conscientiousness, Extroversion, Agreeableness, Neuroticism, and Openness.

A complementary approach to self-report scales is taken by the **Personality Research Form (PRF)** (Jackson & Messick, 1967). The PRF starts out with an attempt to measure the basic needs and motivations proposed by Henry Murray (1938). The test is thus driven by theory but was developed using correlational techniques. Another self-report assessment based directly on personality theory is the Myers-Briggs Type Indicator, or MBTI (Myers, 1962; Hammer, 1996), which was built on Carl Jung's Type theory. Personality assessment always struggles with this tension between inductive approaches that begin with lots of data and deductive approaches that begin with a compelling theory. As we will see, both approaches have proved helpful.

With the proliferation of electronic devices like iPhones, self-report assessments can now be done electronically, sampling the person at different times or in different situations. This flexibility means that it is becoming more feasible to assess personality stability and change over time and to see how personality combines with particular situations to affect feelings and behaviors.

Q-Sort Tests

An interesting method for collecting self-reports that is more active than questionnaires is the **Q-sort.** In the Q-sort, a person is given a stack of cards naming various characteristics and asked to sort them into piles on a dimension such as least characteristic to most characteristic of oneself. A card might say "Is basically anxious" or "Is thoughtful." By telling the test-taker how many piles to make and how many cards to put in each pile, the examiner can ensure that the self-reports form a desired statistical distribution. (If a normal curve is approximated, then this is called a *forced normal distribution.*) Note that the test-takers make comparisons among their own characteristics but do not compare themselves to other people.

A peculiar advantage of the Q-sort is that the items (characteristics) being sorted can be held constant while the context can be changed. For example, after sorting (describing) himself, a man might be asked to use the same Q-sort cards to describe his wife, or the way he was as a child, or the way he ideally would like to be. Comparisons among the Q-sorts might be quite revealing about the person's approach to the characteristics under study (Ozer, 1993).

Q-sorts can also be used to code behavior in structured situations (Funder, Furr, & Colvin, 2000). For example, a male student's behavior might be observed (either in person or on videotape) in a situation in which he meets a female student and compared to a situation in which he meets a male student. The observer can describe the behaviors by choosing the appropriate cards from a set of dozens of basic behaviors such as "seems likable," "acts irritated," "speaks fluently," and so on. The choices can then be sorted from most characteristic and relevant to least so. Such methods illustrate a modern attempt to capture more objective behavioral data in studying personality.

Ratings and Judgments by Others

In 1921, Lewis Terman began a study of over 1,500 bright young boys and girls in California schools. Terman, who developed the Stanford-Binet intelligence test, was interested in seeing how very bright children grew up. Would they turn out to be odd, unsociable nerds? high achievers? persuasive leaders? To explore these matters, Terman (1921) undertook a lifelong study of these children—examining not only their high intelligence, but also their personality and social skills.

Reliable and valid self-report personality tests had not yet been developed. Fortunately, Terman had a brilliant idea, an idea that should be followed more often in personality research today. Terman collected various sorts of other information about these children. For example, during the 1921–1922 school year, Terman had parents and teachers rate the youngsters (who were about 11 years old) on a number of dimensions, including the following:

prudence/forethought	conscientiousness
freedom from vanity	truthfulness

Together, these ratings clearly formed an excellent scale of conscientiousness/social dependability. It is very reasonable to expect that parents and teachers can discern whether an 11-year-old child is conscientious and socially dependable. It turns out that these ratings *are* reliable; for example, the coefficient alpha for these four ratings is .76. It also turns out that these ratings are valid; they predict well many other behaviors that we would expect of such children. Most interesting, however, is that these conscientiousness/dependability ratings (from 1922) turn out to be a good predictor of longevity across the life span! Children rated as more conscientious live significantly longer than those rated as low on this scale (Friedman et al., 1993). The effect is comparable in degree to well-known biological markers of health such as cholesterol level. Obviously, something important about the individual is being measured by these parent and teacher ratings that are derived from their answers to questionnaires like the one shown in Figure 1. In short, the judgments of knowledgeable others can sometimes be an exceedingly effective way to assess personality.

The use of ratings implies that others can make valid judgments of one's personality. Can they? There is indeed much evidence that this is true, including many systematic studies of the personality assessments that others—friends, acquaintances, and even strangers—can make (Funder & Colvin, 1991; Funder & Dobroth, 1987; Funder & Sneed, 1993; Kenny, Horner, Kashy, & Chu, 1992). For example, judgments of teachers' overall nonverbal style, made by viewing them on tape for segments of less than 30 seconds (observing "thin slices of behavior"), were able to tell something about how the teachers would be evaluated by others (Ambady & Rosenthal, 1993). In other words, our initial impressions of another on certain dimensions like extroversion can sometimes be quite accurate (Holleran, Mehl, & Levitt, 2009).

Traits such as extroversion are comparatively easy to judge because they involve relations with others; these activities are readily observable. Collection of observations from friends and family often can be facilitated with use of the Internet (Vazire, 2006). Other aspects of personality such as hidden internal conflicts are of course more difficult to observe, although even these sometimes "leak out" through nonverbal cues such as hand gestures. Expressive cues are further considered later in this chapter.

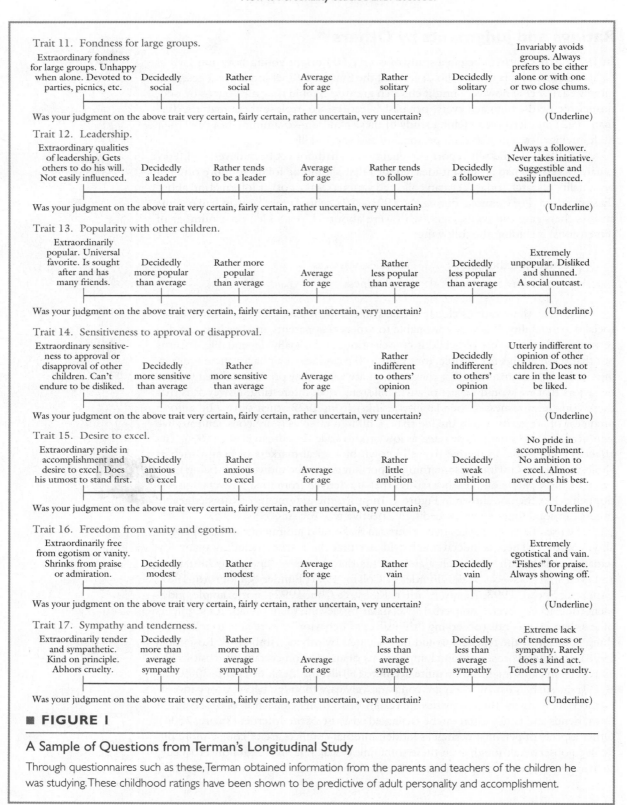

Trait 11. Fondness for large groups.

Extraordinary fondness for large groups. Unhappy when alone. Devoted to parties, picnics, etc. | Decidedly social | Rather social | Average for age | Rather solitary | Decidedly solitary | Invariably avoids groups. Always prefers to be either alone or with one or two close chums.

Was your judgment on the above trait very certain, fairly certain, rather uncertain, very uncertain?   (Underline)

Trait 12. Leadership.

Extraordinary qualities of leadership. Gets others to do his will. Not easily influenced. | Decidedly a leader | Rather tends to be a leader | Average for age | Rather tends to follow | Decidedly a follower | Always a follower. Never takes initiative. Suggestible and easily influenced.

Was your judgment on the above trait very certain, fairly certain, rather uncertain, very uncertain?   (Underline)

Trait 13. Popularity with other children.

Extraordinarily popular. Universal favorite. Is sought after and has many friends. | Decidedly more popular than average | Rather more popular than average | Average for age | Rather less popular than average | Decidedly less popular than average | Extremely unpopular. Disliked and shunned. A social outcast.

Was your judgment on the above trait very certain, fairly certain, rather uncertain, very uncertain?   (Underline)

Trait 14. Sensitiveness to approval or disapproval.

Extraordinary sensitiveness to approval or disapproval of other children. Can't endure to be disliked. | Decidedly more sensitive than average | Rather more sensitive than average | Average for age | Rather indifferent to others' opinion | Decidedly indifferent to others' opinion | Utterly indifferent to opinion of other children. Does not care in the least to be liked.

Was your judgment on the above trait very certain, fairly certain, rather uncertain, very uncertain?   (Underline)

Trait 15. Desire to excel.

Extraordinary pride in accomplishment and desire to excel. Does his utmost to stand first. | Decidedly anxious to excel | Rather anxious to excel | Average for age | Rather little ambition | Decidedly weak ambition | No pride in accomplishment. No ambition to excel. Almost never does his best.

Was your judgment on the above trait very certain, fairly certain, rather uncertain, very uncertain?   (Underline)

Trait 16. Freedom from vanity and egotism.

Extraordinarily free from egotism or vanity. Shrinks from praise or admiration. | Decidedly modest | Rather modest | Average for age | Rather vain | Decidedly vain | Extremely egotistical and vain. "Fishes" for praise. Always showing off.

Was your judgment on the above trait very certain, fairly certain, rather uncertain, very uncertain?   (Underline)

Trait 17. Sympathy and tenderness.

Extraordinarily tender and sympathetic. Kind on principle. Abhors cruelty. | Decidedly more than average sympathy | Rather more than average sympathy | Average for age | Rather less than average sympathy | Decidedly less than average sympathy | Extreme lack of tenderness or sympathy. Rarely does a kind act. Tendency to cruelty.

Was your judgment on the above trait very certain, fairly certain, rather uncertain, very uncertain?   (Underline)

■ FIGURE I

A Sample of Questions from Terman's Longitudinal Study

Through questionnaires such as these, Terman obtained information from the parents and teachers of the children he was studying. These childhood ratings have been shown to be predictive of adult personality and accomplishment.

Biological Measures

In the 1800s, the writings of Franz Joseph Gall led thousands of people to attempt to assess personality by feeling the position and shapes of bumps on people's skulls. This practice was called *phrenology* (DeGiustino, 1975). The idea was that different psychological characteristics are represented in the brain (a reasonable idea) and that highly developed abilities or deficits show up in skull distortions. As more and more was learned about brain function, of course, this inference about skull shape was shown to be ridiculous. The brain's response depends on its networks of nerve cells (neurons), not on the peculiarities of the skull. Even so, the basic idea of phrenology has influenced subsequent thinking about biological assessment of personality.

Modern biological assessments of personality are based on the assumption that the nervous system (including the brain's network of neurons) is the key. So assessments may try to measure nervous-system–related behaviors such as reaction time or skin conductance (sweating), but such attempts have often been disappointing. More exciting are current attempts that focus on the nervous system by aiming directly at the brain. In fact, some of the greatest progress of recent years on assessing individual differences has come from new biological measures (Blascovich, 2000; Cacioppo, Berntson, Sheridan, & McClintock, 2000; Kircher et al., 2000). The brain is specialized into distinct areas (nuclei), and methods exist that attempt to correlate individual differences in personality with activity in these specialized regions (Schwartz et al., 2010).

A classical method used to study neuronal activity within the neocortex (higher level functioning) involves measuring evoked potential on **electroencephalograms (EEGs).** EEGs measure electrical potentials at the scalp that are caused by large populations of neurons becoming active simultaneously. An advantage of EEG is that a large piece of fixed laboratory equipment is not necessary (only external electrodes on the scalp are used), thus allowing more flexibility in research. For example, evoked potentials—brain waves measured by EEG after presentation of a stimulus—can show something about how the brain is responding from moment to moment (Cacioppo, Crites, Berntson, & Coles, 1993).

Positron emission tomography (PET) scanning is a useful technique that shows brain activity by recording the brain's use of radioactive glucose. Because nerve cells use glucose to make energy when they are active, the areas that light up on a PET scan while a person is completing a task represent areas of the brain that are involved in the processing of the task. That is, we can watch brain activity while people think or cope, or compare levels of brain activity across individuals. For example, one study found that neuroticism was negatively correlated with glucose metabolism in the prefrontal cortex of the brain during rest (Kim, Hwang, Park, & Kim, 2008). The output of a PET scan is shown in Figure 2. It is possible that systematic individual differences in thought processes can be revealed by this technique (Blascovich, 2000; Freitas-Ferrari et al., 2010).

Photo courtesy of Science Museum of Minnesota

■ The practice of phrenology (precise skull measurement) was a sincere, if misguided, attempt to apply scientific tools to personality measurement. This elaborate electromechanical device, patented as the "Psycograph," may well have been very reliable in determining the contours of the skull, despite the absence of validity.

Electroencephalogram (EEG)

A measurement of electrical brainwave activity using electrodes attached to the outside of the skull

■ FIGURE 2

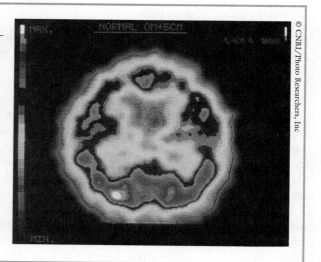

© CNRI/Photo Researchers, Inc

PET Scan of a Normal Brain during REM (Rapid Eye Movement) Sleep

PET images of the brain record the activity level of brain areas while the person performs a specific task. Researchers get useful information both about usual patterns of brain activity and about how that pattern is changed by various brain disorders. Individual differences in brain activity can be measured and correlated with other measures of personality. In this image, the lightest color represents the brain areas with the highest level of metabolic activity. This image looks horizontally at the brain of a normal 20-year-old, with the left of the image showing the left side of the brain (nose on top).

Functional magnetic resonance imaging (fMRI) assesses brain activity by measuring changes in oxygenated blood flow, as blood flow will be directed to regions of the brain where activity is highest. Although this technique can show which areas of the brain are involved in particular emotional reactions of an individual, it can be challenging to then interpret what this means, until science understands much more about brain processes (Lieberman & Cunningham, 2009). Hormone levels are another promising biological measure. Certain aspects of the bases of personality are undoubtedly tied to hormones. For example, people deficient in the thyroid hormone thyroxin may act sluggishly or become depressed. Perhaps the clearest example of hormone effects involves the sex hormones testosterone and the estrogens. These hormones certainly influence and change the personality of adolescents at puberty. However, even in rats there is no simple correspondence between hormones and behavior. For example, the sexual activity of castrated rats is partly affected by their previous experiences and the eliciting stimuli around them (Whalen, Geary, & Johnson, 1990), as well as by their hormone level. It is an oversimplification to say that testosterone causes sexual activity, even in rats. The relationships in humans are far more complex. Although it is important to avoid jumping to silly, simplistic conclusions about hormones and personality, it is true that gross deficiencies or excesses of certain hormones, which can be detected through blood assays, can have a profound effect on personality (Kuepper et al., 2010).

In the cases of certain diseases, biological assessment may again provide valuable information about personality—in this case, an abnormal personality. For example, mania or lethargy caused by a tumor on the thyroid gland may be detected by a thyroid function test. Mild brain poisoning (such as by mercury or lead poisoning) can be detected by blood screenings. Schizophrenia-like symptoms can be a result of various sorts of poisons.

Certain major genetic conditions such as Down syndrome, which has effects on intelligence and personality, can be spotted easily in a chromosome analysis. (In Down syndrome there is a trisomy, or extra strand, on chromosome 21.) Current genetic research may increasingly use gene-chip analysis, in which a collection of

DNA sequences (genes) are rapidly compared to a biological extract (perhaps some brain tissue) to see which of the genes is present in the sample extract. An overview of biological measures of personality is presented in Table 4.

Behavioral Observations

Francis Galton, a nineteenth-century British scientist, pioneered many approaches to understanding individual differences, including techniques of behavioral observation. In his anthropometric laboratory, Galton (1907) collected all sorts of physical measurements of people, and he then began studying their reactions in controlled situations. For example, Galton's whistle elicited subjects' reactions to high pitches, and his instruments measured the strength of their grasps. He suggested using a pressure gauge hidden under people's chairs to measure their degree of "inclination," and he used his sextant to measure unobtrusively the dimensions of "bounteous" women.

■ English scientist Sir Francis Galton (1822–1911) was focused on measuring individual differences on many variables, using ingenious instruments of his own design.

Brilliant as he was, Galton was also clearly influenced by the prevailing attitudes of his time and social class; for example, he spoke in racist terms about "the highest Caucasian" and "the lowest savage." Many outstanding personality researchers during the past century were similarly blinded by the racist prejudices that pervaded their intellectual environments.

In the 1920s, after slugging dozens of home runs, Babe Ruth was tested (in a lab) by psychologists on his reaction time and on the steadiness of his hands. Not surprisingly, he did very well (Fuchs, 1998). In the modern study of personality, behavioral observation can be as simple as counting people's experiences (such as how many times they stutter or scratch themselves, or how many drinks they consume). Or it may become quite complex, as researchers attempt to understand the individual's interactions with others. (Videotapes may be employed here.) In a more fine-grained analysis, facial expressions of emotion can be finely and validly observed and coded (Ekman, Friesen, & Hager, 2002).

The availability of cell phones and electronic pagers has allowed more complete sampling of behavior. When the participant is called or texted, he or she makes a notation about current activity or thoughts (Stone, Kessler, & Haythornthwaite, 1991). This is sometimes termed the **experience sampling method of assessment.** (It is amazing how many college students daydream about sexual activity.) Use of behavioral observation assumes that present behavior is a reliable and valid predictor of future behavior. When an adequate sample of present behavior is collected, this assumption generally does prove true.

Experience Sampling Method of Assessment A method in which participants record their current activity or thought processes when they are paged by the experimenter at various intervals during the day

Interviews

A seemingly obvious way to find out about someone's personality is to conduct an interview. The classic interview in psychology is the psychotherapeutic interview, in which the client (patient) talks about important or troubling parts of his or her life. In psychoanalysis, the patient does indeed often lie on a couch.

■ TABLE 4 Biological/Neuroscience Measures of Individual Differences

Measure	Description
Skin conductance, heart rate, blood pressure	Reflect activity of the autonomic nervous system; often are too broad to be useful measures of personality.
PET (positron emission tomography)	Uses radioactively tagged molecules to probe brain function, such as radioactive glucose to examine changes in energy metabolism associated with activity. Other compounds can also be tagged radioactively and used to examine brain processes. But metabolic changes may be slow and delayed.
fMRI (functional magnetic resonance imaging)	Uses very large magnetic fields to probe the movements of molecules. fMRI takes advantage of differences in the properties of oxygenated and deoxygenated hemoglobin, thus yielding a signal that is related to brain activity (neural activity uses oxygen and increases blood flow).
EEG (electroencephalogram)	Measures electrical potentials at the scalp that are caused by large populations of neurons becoming active simultaneously. The P300 wave occurs in response to novel stimuli and may prove useful in studying differences in reactions to novelty.
MEG (magnetoencephalography)	Similar to EEG, but instead of recording electrical potentials, it records the magnetic fields that result from the electric currents in the brain.
Neurochemical assays	Chemical analyses for the presence of certain neurotransmitters, transmitter metabolites, or hormones. The sites of assay can be in the cerebrospinal fluid or in the blood. In animal studies, assays can be directly in the brain by microdialysis.
Postmortem analysis	Examines individual differences in anatomy (both gross and cellular) and in the numbers and locations of neuroreceptors (after death) using immunohistochemistry or histological staining.
Candidate gene studies	Searches for specific genes that correlate with specific personalities, although multiple genes likely contribute to any personality trait. With the successful unraveling of the human genome, this biological approach is likely to gain prominence in the years ahead.

The validity of an assessment interview is difficult to ascertain. Certainly there are many reasons why some people may be unwilling or unable to talk about their deepest thoughts, feelings, and motivations. One way the validity of a **psychotherapeutic interview** can be judged is by the results of the therapy. Presumably, an interview diagnosis that results in a clearly effective treatment is more likely to be correct than a diagnosis that results in a failed treatment. Many other factors of course enter in. Still, interviews often prove quite valuable assessment tools.

In the 1940s and 1950s, Alfred Kinsey (Kinsey, Pomeroy, & Martin, 1948) used interviews to probe human sexuality. By building a sense of trust with those he

Psychotherapeutic Interview
An interview in which a client talks about the important or troubling parts of his or her life

interviewed, Kinsey was able to elicit disclosures that those people would never have committed to paper. Kinsey also knew how to ask leading questions and how to pursue a line of questioning doggedly until sensitive information was revealed. Interviews can be quite loose and subjective, but a skilled interviewer may uncover startling information not available by any other means. For example, many of Kinsey's participants eventually told him about their hidden homosexual experiences, their sexual relations with animals, and their extramarital affairs.

In recent years, assessment interviews have tended to become more systematic or structured. Rather than follow the interviewee's meanderings, the interviewer follows a definite plan. In this way, it is hoped that similar types of information can be elicited from each interviewee and the assessment can become more valid. One of the best-studied **structured interviews** is the one used to assess the Type A behavior pattern.

In the 1950s, two cardiologists proposed that certain people—characterized by a tense, competitive style—are especially likely to develop coronary heart disease. They termed these people (mostly men) "Type A." A standardized interview has proven quite reliable in assessing Type A personality. In the Type A structured interview, the interviewer asks a series of challenging questions (Chesney & Rosenman, 1985). Many of these questions concern competitive situations with others: "What do you do when you are stuck on the highway behind a slow driver?" Interestingly, Type A is diagnosed based on both the verbal and the nonverbal responses to such questions. A driver who answers angrily with rapid words, loud voice, and clenched teeth, "I would cuss out the slow-poke," would probably be viewed as Type A. The most extreme example of a Type A man we ever interviewed was asked whether he played games in order to win. He shouted back, "I play to kill!"

Assessing the Type A pattern also raises the issue of Types versus Traits, a long-standing puzzle in personality theory. A **typology** is a categorical scheme in which people are in either one group or another. For example, being male or female is a Type. Everyone is either one or the other, with rare exceptions. However, what about masculinity—having psychological characteristics (like aggressiveness) typically ascribed to males? This is not a Type but a Trait because people (both males and females) can be more or less masculine. Trait approaches are much more common than Type approaches in personality research today.

In general, interviews have the significant disadvantage of being subject to bias by the behaviors of the interviewer. An interviewer who expects a client (or a patient or an applicant or a student) to be "troubled" can often draw out those expected behaviors from the interviewee. Further, as with self-report questionnaires, the interviewer can best retrieve information that the interviewee knows and is willing to reveal. On the other hand, as noted, a good interviewer can probe dynamically for facts and feelings that are difficult to find any other way.

Expressive Behavior

In the case of the Type A structured interview, personality assessment is based partly on the verbal responses but partly on the nonverbal vocal responses such as the loudness and rate of speech. Nonverbal cues of **expressive style** are in fact an interesting way of assessing personality, even by themselves. The modern study of expressive style and personality got a big push in the 1930s from the work of Gordon Allport and P. E. Vernon (1933).

Structured Interview
A systematic interview in which the interviewer follows a definite plan so that similar types of information are elicited from each interviewee

Typology
A categorical scheme in which a person is a member of only one of a small set of groups

Expressive Style
A term used to describe nonverbal social skills such as vocal characteristics, facial expressions, body gestures, and movements

© Mark Mainz/Getty Images

©Larry Marano/Getty Images

■ Some people have extraordinary expressive skills, which allow them to portray different characters successfully; they can adopt widely varying emotions, demeanors, postures, and styles. Expressiveness is an important aspect of personality and a key element of charisma.

Often, the way people do things is more informative than what they do. Some people talk loudly, some softly; some smile a lot and are very expressive, but some look angry or depressed. We can often recognize a phone caller by the way she says "Hello," and we can often recognize our friends by their gaits as they move across campus. Expression, particularly emotional expression, seems closely tied to dynamic, motivational aspects of personality. (Note that observation of expressive style, although considered a part of "behavioral observation," has its own distinct flavor.)

Expressive style is an excellent way to assess personal charisma—more valid, but also more demanding of the examiner than a self-report questionnaire like the ACT. For example, charismatic people show fewer nervous, body-focused type gestures, and they tend to have more fluent, inspiring speech. In fact, they tend to attract the attention and interest of strangers.

Like other measures, expressive style is often biased by cultural factors. For example, people from the American South tend to speak more slowly, in a southern drawl. It would be a mistake to equate this slow speech with the speech of a New Yorker who speaks slowly; for the New Yorker the unusual (slow) speech is probably revealing of personality, but for the southerner the slow speech is reflective of regional culture. Or, consider differences in gaze—people's patterns of looking. White Americans in a conversation tend to look at their partners while listening but look away while speaking; African Americans do relatively more looking while talking and relatively less looking while listening (LaFrance & Mayo, 1976). If these cultural norms are not taken into account, then errors in personality assessment will occur. For example, a White person might assess a Black person as less cooperative than he really is.

Some nontraditional assessors like fortune-tellers probably often rely on expressive style in making their judgments. For example, imagine that an overweight young woman gingerly approaches a fortune-teller and asks him about her future in a soft,

terrifying environments imaginable, Anne was still strongly focused on many of the normal concerns of the preadolescent and adolescent—her physical appearance, her independence from her parents, her developing identity, and her sexuality.

Many insightful biographers rely on the paper trail left by historical figures. Of course, there are reasons why documents such as love letters or employment applications or autobiographies may not be honest disclosures of thoughts and feelings, but the pattern of such documents may nevertheless prove revealing. Document analysis is especially useful when the goal is to understand the psychological richness of a particular individual's life. These successes are usually psychobiographical studies of complex individuals about whom we have abundant information from other sources. For example, exceptional insights come from Erik Erikson's works *Young Man Luther* (1958) (a study of Martin Luther) and *Gandhi's Truth* (on Mahatma Gandhi). Another more limited study analyzed the language used by then New York mayor Rudy Giuliani in his press conferences after the terrorist attacks of 2001; changes in his linguistic style were taken as evidence of changes in his personality under stress (Pennebaker & Lay, 2002). In short, personal writings and musings are very helpful when our assessments can be confirmed by other sources of information.

Projective Tests

When a child has gone through a traumatic experience such as sexual abuse, a gory traffic accident, or violence similar to that found on a battlefield (as in civil war or cult violence), psychologists and psychiatrists are often called in to assess the effects on the child's long-term functioning. A commonly used assessment technique in these situations is to ask the child to draw a picture or a series of pictures.

The use of pictures as part of psychological assessment dates back to the 1920s. The idea is that the child (or adult) may be willing to draw certain things that are too uncomfortable to say. Or, it is thought that pictures may sometimes reveal things that are even outside consciousness, such as unconscious motivations. If a child draws a picture of a father with a tremendously large penis, or without facial features, or surrounded by snakes, the drawing may indicate a psychological problem.

Draw-a-person assessment techniques are subjective. (Attempts to make them objective by finding firm links between particular features of pictures and particular aspects of personality have been unsuccessful.) Their utility thus depends on the skill of the interpreter, who is usually a therapist. But as noted, pictures do allow for potentially rich insights into the "artist." An example of this test is shown in Figure 5.

Assessment techniques that attempt to study personality through use of a relatively unstructured stimulus, task, or situation are termed **projective tests** because they allow a person to "project" his or her own inner motivations onto the assessor's test. In addition to drawing a picture, projective tests include telling a story, completing a sentence, or doing word associations. Projective tests seemed especially valuable to proponents of psychoanalytic theories because the theories are based on unconscious motivations and projective tests attempt to capture such motivations.

A century ago, a Swiss psychiatrist named Hermann Rorschach began showing inkblots to his patients and asking for descriptions. The Rorschach has since become one of the most widely used projective tests. An example of the type of inkblot used for the test is shown in Figure 6. Like other projective tests, the Rorschach presents

Projective Test
An assessment technique that attempts to study personality through use of a relatively unstructured stimulus, task, or situation

59

■ FIGURE 5

A Child's Response to the Draw-a-Person Test

Projective tests allow the test-taker substantial control over the content of the response. This picture was drawn by a nine-year-old child who was given a pen and paper and asked to "Draw a person." Some psychologists believe that we can gain insight into the child's personality by analyzing the characteristics of the picture he or she draws.

vague and ambiguous stimuli and notes a person's responses (Exner, 1986). As a person views and responds to a series of 10 inkblots, the Rorschach examiner records what is said and later notes whether the person is looking at the whole inkblot or parts, "seeing" an object in motion, reacting to shading, and so on. The examiner may then follow up with questions such as "Where in this picture was it that you said you saw a bouncing ball?"

Because people are often unaware of factors motivating their behavior, exploring such motivations is no easy matter but is essential if behavior is to be understood. Projective tests, by using vague tasks or stimuli and then gauging the participant's emotional or motivational response, attempt to get at deep personal styles in viewing the world. Our Pirate Test for Children has some projective aspects, as pirates may evoke dramatic responses in kids, and there is no obviously correct way to respond. For example, a child who lets out a lusty pirate scream when he meets Captain Hook,

■ FIGURE 6

A Rorschach-Type Inkblot

The Rorschach test asks the examinee to describe each of a series of inkblot images. Because the images are ambiguous, the person is thought to project his or her inner conflicts and motives in the description, which is then interpreted by a trained psychologist sitting with the examinee. Leonardo da Vinci (1452–1519) used a similar technique to understand his pupils and their art.

and who often marches around at home with a sword and bandanna of his own, might be correctly assumed to have an aggressive aspect to his personality.

The Rorschach shares a significant problem with all projective tests, namely scoring. The examiner's personal interpretations might give us some interesting insights to follow up, but there would be no reliability. That is, different examiners or even the same examiner at different times might come up with a different interpretation (score). This problem might be addressed by training scorers in a standardized scoring system; for example, people who see a grayish scene in most inkblots might be labeled as depressed. Unfortunately, research using the Rorschach has not found it to be highly valid (Wood, Nezworski, Lilienfeld, & Garb, 2003), but it is still potentially useful, especially for gaining clinical insights (Exner, 1986; Peterson, 1978).

One of the most commonly used projective tests is the **Thematic Apperception Test, or TAT** (Bellak, 1993). In administering the TAT, the assessor simply tells the participant to make up a story about a picture that will be presented, including a prediction of what will happen next. The assessor then holds up the first picture (which may be of a young boy contemplating a violin). Sometimes the assessor writes down the story; sometimes the participants write down the stories themselves. The TAT thus attempts to see how a person places order on a vague stimulus. For example, if the participant decides that the boy is distressed because he has just dropped the violin down the stairs and is afraid his father will beat him, the assessor may begin to look for clues of latent aggression.

Some projective-like tests try to measure strength of associations between an individual's implicit concepts by administering challenging cognitive tasks to perform and then seeing which tasks are done more quickly or with fewer errors. For example, the Implicit Association Test (IAT; Greenwald et al., 2002) may ask a person to sort stimuli representing four concepts (e.g., good, bad, fat, or thin) into only two response categories; presumably, closely related concepts are more quickly sorted. (For example, it might take longer to sort a stimulus person who is fat into the combined category "fat or good," thus suggesting you hold an implicit belief that being fat is bad.) Still, the basic idea is that the test can detect things about the mind that cannot be reported through conscious self-examination.

Projective tests, like all personality tests, make assumptions about the nature of personality and about behavior. Projective tests generally assume that there are deep, basic motivational patterns and that these patterns show up in how we respond to perceptual stimuli. Tests like the TAT were seen as especially valuable by Henry Murray because his theory of personality was based on the idea of unconscious needs struggling to be realized (Smith, 1992).

Thematic Apperception Test (TAT)
A projective test in which a participant is asked to make up a story (including what will happen in the future) about a picture that is presented

Demographics and Lifestyle

It is not that unusual to hear someone say, "I can't stand a Capricorn, but I'm really attracted to an Aries." The speaker is relying on astrology—using celestial bodies and the signs of the zodiac (an imaginary belt of the heavens)—for clues about personality. Astrology began well over 2,500 years ago, when many ancient peoples believed their fate was written in the stars. Today, astrology usually charts the positions of celestial bodies at the time of a person's birth in an attempt to predict the person's characteristics and fate.

■ Singer and film star Jennifer Lopez had her roots in a Puerto Rican family in the Bronx. A success as the highest paid Latina actress ever, J Lo also has had several albums and singles at the top of the music charts, and has been honored as the most influential Hispanic entertainer in America. Her arrest and jailing after a nightclub brawl in 1999 was followed by a broken engagement and a failed marriage that seem mismatched to the rest of her image. Can we understand the contradictions in her life by putting her individual personality characteristics into the context of the cultural environments of rappers, media pressure, and Hollywood?

Demographic Information
Information relevant to population statistics such as age, cultural group, place of birth, religion, and the like

It is not impossible that celestial happenings influence human behavior; for example, the moon affects the tides, solar radiation affects magnetic fields on earth, and the earth's position affects the weather. But astrology has relied mostly on superstition and faith rather than on any rigorous scientific analysis. It has no known scientific validity. The stubborn popularity of astrology reminds us of the willingness of many people to accept almost any explanation of personality.

Nevertheless, in attempting to understand an individual, it is generally helpful to ascertain various sorts of **demographic information**—age, cultural place of birth, religion, family size, and so on. All such information relevant to population statistics helps provide a framework for better understanding the individual. The assessment of a 22-year-old should generally be different in its conduct and interpretation than the assessment of an 80-year-old. But, by itself, demographic information can be misleading, as in the case of twin brothers who share all the demographic characteristics but have different personalities.

To gain a good understanding of an individual, we need to know the person's cultural milieu and cultural identity. This is especially true if the culture is outside the mainstream. For example, the Black Panthers, who emerged from the civil rights movement of the 1960s, were often seen by the dominant culture as troubled and aggressive rebels, even though the Panthers were rarely violent and were heavily involved in social programs benefiting their communities. Similarly, gay men and lesbians in the United States are increasingly influenced by gay culture, especially in large cities like San Francisco, Los Angeles, and New York. A gay individual's unusual (nonmainstream) pattern of behavior might erroneously be attributed to his or her personality if the relevant culture were not taken into account.

These demographic and cultural groupings are not psychological and so do not fit smoothly into most personality theories. On the other hand, personality psychologists too often overlook such societal influences. For example, the fact that there were so many communists in Russia in the 1920s, and so many hippies in California in the 1960s, and so many divorces in the United States in the 1970s are best explained in terms of social and societal factors rather than through notions that the individuals involved had communist personalities, or rebellious personalities, or divorce-prone personalities.

Is There One Best Method of Assessment?

Which personality assessments are best? The answer depends in part on the person, the assessor, and the purpose of the assessment. For example, if we are interested in seeing which aspects of personality predict coronary heart disease, then we should strive to refine and utilize assessment techniques that do indeed accurately and usefully predict heart disease; if we are interested in unconscious motives behind aggression, we should use projective tests or behavioral observations rather than self-report personality tests; and so on. Most important is that we retain a strong focus on continuously evaluating validity. Some of the advantages and limitations of common personality measures are shown in Table 5.

The validities of almost all personality assessment techniques are threatened by the overgeneralization phenomenon of the Barnum effect—the tendency of individuals and clinicians to readily accept vague personality descriptions as though they were valid and specific (Cash, Mikulka, & Brown, 1989; Prince & Guastello, 1990). The best assessments reveal what is special or different about the person being

■ TABLE 5   Advantages and Limits of Personality Measures

Type of Test	Advantages and Limits
Self-report tests	Straightforward to standardize, easy to administer, reliable, capture views of self well; but limited in richness, easy to fake, depend on self-knowledge.
Q-sort	More active (more respondent involvement) than questionnaires, can yield ranking of characteristics, and same items can be used to rate different targets; but same limits as self-report tests.
Ratings by others	Provide a perspective not biased by the self-reports of the individual, and clearly reveal "visible" traits; can be used to rate children (or animals); but invalid to the extent that raters (others) lack knowledge or are biased.
Biological	Can reveal individual reactions without relying on self-report or rater judgment, but can be difficult and expensive to use; relation between biological substrates and complex behavior patterns not often simple.
Behavioral observations	Capture what the individual actually does, but can be hard to interpret as personality or may be unrepresentative of whole range of a person's behavior.
Interviews	Can probe deeply and can use follow-up questions, very flexible; but can be biased by the interviewer or respondent, expensive, and time-consuming.
Expressive behavior	Captures actual unique behavioral style, including subtleties and emotions; but can be difficult to capture, code, and interpret.
Document analysis	Can be used to assess an individual across time (if writings are continuously available), can be quite detailed and objective, and can be used even for deceased persons; but may show only certain aspects of the person, may not be completely honest, and may not be available from important times or events.
Projective tests	One of the few ways to go below the surface and assess aspects that the person may not be able to self-report, may yield insights for further study; but often have significant problems of reliability and validity.
Demographics and lifestyle	Shows the framework and grouping in which the individual functions (age, gender, occupation, culture); but by itself can tell little about the individual person.

assessed. Overall, it is almost always best to use multiple methods. This way, the inherent weaknesses of each method are minimized and important characteristics or traits will repeatedly emerge (Westen & Rosenthal, 2003). With various measurement methods simultaneously applied to various characteristics, we can "triangulate" in on valid personality constructs.

How Not to Test Personality

It is amazing to see how much time and money some people spend attempting to assess personality in ways that are marginally valid at best. Many are simply frauds or fantasies. As noted, one of the oldest and silliest methods is astrology, learning about your personality from the stars. Many newspapers still print astrological charts, proffering vague advice such as "Your fortune is near." They are about as valuable as fortune cookies, except they do not taste as good.

Then there are the assessment methods used in carnivals, private parlors, or bogus religions. Traditionally, these have included palm-reading and numerology, but today they may extend to pseudo-high-tech nonsense such as hair analysis or computer-interpreted voice analysis.

More problematic are assessment techniques that involve aspects of expressive style; they are problematic because expressive style (especially emotional style) *can* be a valid indicator of personality. One of these dubious techniques is graphology, or handwriting analysis. Handwriting analyses are often sold to businesses as a means of screening potential employees. Although there is no decent evidence to justify the detailed assessments offered by graphologists, it is probably the case that some information is revealed by a person's handwriting (see Figure 7). For example, male handwriting is probably often distinguishable from female writing; old, infirm handwriting is distinguishable from younger, healthy writing; and perhaps a few other dimensions are usually discernible. But such information is even more obvious in an interview! It is a long way from such mundane observations to absurd pronouncements like, "The way she crosses her *ts* indicates that she will not persevere in her work."

It is not the case that graphology could not in principle tell us something about personality. Rather we should ask ourselves, What is the theory underlying graphology? Is this consistent with what we know about human biology and human behavior? What are the reliability studies? What are the validity studies? Has the evidence been confirmed by independent scientific work? In other words, have all the usual standards been applied? In the case of handwriting analysis, they have not. One of the prime advantages of the in-depth study of personality is that it leaves us better prepared to make such determinations throughout our lives.

■ **FIGURE 7**

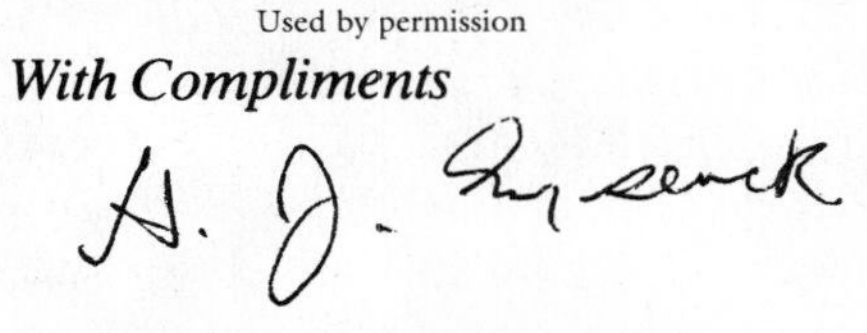

Used by permission

With Compliments

The Signature of Hans Eysenck

Do you think you can tell from this signature whether this psychologist was an introvert or an extrovert? (Used by permission.)

The Design of Research

How do personality psychologists go about choosing research designs with which to explore personality? Personality research is usually not a straight linear process, going from hypothesis to final proof. Rather, there is frequent backtracking and circling around as ideas are tested and refined. Still, there is a certain logical progression of inference that can be said to underlie the research process. The basic elements are case studies, correlational studies, and experimental studies.

Case Studies

Let us assume that we want to understand the interpersonal power and influence of a charismatic leader like the Rev. Martin Luther King Jr. What is special about the charismatic personality? We might first turn to an in-depth study of such individuals. We might examine interviews to see how he thought about himself and others. We could examine his documents, such as his speeches, writings, and educational work. We could collect judgments from those who knew him, both casually and in-depth. We could analyze the expressive behavior of his gestures and voice tones. We might look at his reactions under challenge, his interactions with subordinates and superiors, his relations with women, his politics, and his lifestyle. This flexible, in-depth study illustrates the advantages of the **case study design.**

Such case studies are generally the way we gather ideas and hypotheses about personality, but these hypotheses need further systematic study to become scientific. Case studies cannot be easily generalized to other people. And case studies do not tell us much about causal relationships.

Case Study Design
A research method that involves an in-depth analysis of a single individual

Correlational Studies

In **correlational studies,** we assess the degree of relationship between two variables, and then among more variables. For example, we might gather a sample of leaders, both charismatic and uncharismatic, and ascertain whether charisma is associated with being extroverted (and enjoying being around people). We might be able to see if charisma is associated with having dynamic gestures and an expressive voice. We then would see if the expressive style is associated with extroversion. In other words, we would gather a series of associations among variables, and measure which ones are associated with (or not associated with) which others. We would first use correlation coefficients and then factor analyses (analyses of sets of correlations; by taking into account the overlap or shared variance, factor analysis mathematically consolidates information from a set of intercorrelated variables).

Correlations, however, do not tell us anything about the causal direction of the associations. For example, they do not tell us if people motivated to be successful leaders begin using expressive gestures, or if people with expressive gestures are chosen to be leaders, or if both leadership and gestures are the result of some underlying third variable such as a biological tendency to be active and seek stimulation. To understand more about the causal patterns, we need to turn to experimental and quasi-experimental research designs.

Correlational Studies
Studies in which the degree of relationship between two variables (or among multiple variables) is assessed

SHARPEN YOUR THINKING Current Controversy

Can There Be Ethical Use of Unethically Produced Data?

As the scientific community has become highly sensitized to the issue of research ethics, scientific groups and governments have developed standards that regulate how researchers treat research participants and how the resulting data may be used. Safeguards are in place at multiple points in the cycle of experimentation to prevent the implementation of studies that violate current ethical standards (although admittedly these safeguards are far from perfect). When the infamous Tuskegee Syphilis study on African Americans was begun in the 1930s, some researchers appear to have believed that the benefit of learning about the natural course of the disease (syphilis) when left untreated outweighed any potential harm to the participants from withholding treatment. Of course, current views of that project reflect a very different perspective, especially because the participants were not fully informed. Having subjected the participants to unacceptable harm, should all the data on the course of the disease in a population of several hundred men be discarded, even if the data might otherwise be useful?

The U.S. and Canadian governments were involved in a decades-long program in the mid-twentieth century testing the effects of administering the hallucinogen LSD and other psychoactive drugs to ordinary citizens without their knowledge or consent. At least some of these unwitting research participants suffered serious permanent impairment or even death as a result. At the time, the researchers believed that the goal of developing another Cold War covert weapon justified the risk to the participants. Should the unethical way in which data were collected require us to disregard any useful information about the drugs that may have been gained?

One position is that data collected by unethical methods must be thrown out as tainted, regardless of any benefit that might potentially have resulted. The alternative view is that the harm (or risk of harm) was deplorable, but any possible good should be salvaged by using any results that may be relevant. While many ethics authorities line up behind the "fatal taint" view, there are recent examples of a less absolute position gaining ground.

Consider the complexity of using human embryonic stem cells, which provide hope of curing disease. In harvesting these cells from human embryos, the embryos are necessarily destroyed. Once the stem cells have been isolated and specially treated, they can be cultured to produce a continuing cell line. Many people believe that this line of research is promising and worthwhile, while many others believe that it is unethical to destroy human embryos for any purpose. The U.S. government under President George W. Bush took a middle-ground position on this issue in 2001. It prohibited the use of federal funds to create new stem cell lines, under the belief that destructive use of an embryo is morally unacceptable (even for an embryo produced in the laboratory and not usable for implantation). But, under the same order, stem cell lines that were in existence as of the date of the regulation could continue to be cultured and used in federally funded experimentation. In this view, the potential benefits of embryonic stem cell research are seen as not great enough to outweigh the harm of further destructive stem cell harvesting, but great enough to allow the use of stem cell lines already derived through such harvesting. Others, however, believed that the unused embryos were going to be discarded in any case, and that it would be unethical not to use them in an attempt to help people with serious diseases. More recently, research has progressed on developing stem cells from adult cells, which sidesteps many of the ethical concerns.

While the possible ethical lapses involved in personality research tend to be on a smaller scale than these life-and-death examples, the research community still needs to decide what to do with data that were collected without adequate informed consent, or when participants were not free to discontinue their participation without penalty.

Experimental Studies

The most straightforward way to arrive at a valid causal inference is to design a true experiment (Campbell & Stanley, 1963). In a true experimental design, people are randomly assigned to either a treatment group (which will receive the treatment being tested) or a **control group** (which will provide a standard for comparison), and then the two groups are compared. For example, say we want to see whether teaching people expressive gestures will make them charismatic. We could do the following: We take a group of people and we randomly assign half of them to take instruction on expressive gesturing, while the control group people take instruction on an irrelevant topic like how to swim the crawl stroke. Then we follow up all the people and see if those who had gesture instruction and experience are more likely to become (or be perceived as) charismatic. (The determination of "more likely" is done statistically.) If so, we have a good idea that the intervention caused the effect.

Because of random assignment to conditions, an experimental design protects us from the possibility that the treatment group and the control group differed initially in some unknown way. But even in such an experimental design, there can be problems of inference. First, we do not know if the finding can be generalized to others who have different characteristics from those studied. Second, and relatedly, we do not know which moderating factors may be important; for example, our intervention may work very well for older people but poorly for younger people. Third, there could have been problems (biases) in the ways our elegant design was carried out; that is, there could have been experimenter errors. Finally, we do not really know how other interventions would work, nor which is best.

A true experiment has these various limitations, but the conclusions drawn are superior to those based solely on case studies or correlations, especially if they build on solid correlational work. In medicine, such true experiments are usually termed "randomized clinical trials." In personality psychology, they are usually called "experimental methods."

Unfortunately, in most personality research, we are limited in the extent to which we can use random assignment. We cannot easily randomly assign 10,000 teenagers to have five years of gesture instruction, assign 10,000 other teenagers to a control group, and then see which group produces more charismatic adult leaders. So, we rely on quasi-experimental research or naturally occurring experiments to see what influences and components increase the likelihood that a charismatic leader will emerge. For example, we might compare teenagers from coed high schools to those from single-sex high schools. As an exercise, see if you can think of examples of the types of evidence that would be useful to gather in understanding the origins and components of charisma.

Control Group
A comparison group that provides a standard by which to evaluate a theory or technique

The Ethics of Personality Testing

The first psychological tests of any substantial validity are a little over a century old. Alfred Binet pioneered valid intelligence testing in Paris at the end of the nineteenth century. His goal was a noble one: His tests could be used to find students who were really quite bright but who had been mislabeled "stupid" as a result of problems such

TIME LINE

The History of Personality Assessment

The major developments in the field of personality assessment can be seen here in historical relation to one another and in relation to their broader societal and cultural contexts.

Developments in Personality Assessment		Societal and Scientific Context
Little systematic effort to measure personality	before 1800	Humans are seen primarily in religious or philosophical terms
Francis Galton, cousin of Darwin, sets up labs to measure individual differences	1880s	Increasing attention to evolution and individual variation
Mental testing begins, focusing on intelligence, but unsuccessful until the work of Alfred Binet	1890–1910	Period of heavy immigration to the United States; mathematical statistics receive increasing attention
Robert Yerkes, Lewis Terman, et al. work with the U.S. Army to select and screen soldiers; efforts lead to further mass testing	1910–1920	Increasing technology and industrialization; large technical armies; World War I 1914–1918
Studies of individual values and vocational interests begin; biological temperament draws interest	1920s–1930s	Economic boom and bust; progress in mathematical statistics
Allport and others list traits; statistical analyses of traits follow development of new statistical techniques; neo-analysts begin using projective tests	1930s	Fascism and impending world war; economic depression, propaganda; growth of large corporations
Studies of authoritarianism and ethnocentrism take hold, often measured in multiple ways	1940s	Intellectual reactions against fascism
Interviews are used by Kinsey to study sexuality and by market researchers to study purchasing; emerging ideas of cognitive psychology lead to cognitive assessments	1940s–1960s	New roles for women, work, and social relations; economic boom with huge new middle class; baby boom; marketing becomes scientific
Expressive style assessed as nonverbal communication regains attention	1970s–1980s	Decline of behaviorism; emphasis on communication in relationships and families; rise of television in politics
Trait measures return to fore as factor theories take hold; life stories regain prominence	1990s	Better understandings of the individual in the workplace
Increased use of computer-based and Internet-based testing	2000s	Increased globalization, rise of virtual social networking

as hearing or language impairment. In other words, Binet aimed to help those who had been overlooked by society (Binet & Simon, 1916).

The same sorts of arguments for testing apply to people with other psychological or relationship problems. In order to help people with problems, an accurate diagnosis of their problems and their strengths is useful. Thus, fair and valid testing can be beneficial to everyone. There is always a danger that test results will be wrong due to various limitations. Inaccurate testing will be a major problem if testing is being done to identify people who are less "worthy." In this case, an error or bias is especially tragic.

The Mismeasure of Man, by paleontologist Stephen Jay Gould (1981, 1996) describes the sorry saga of scientific racism. Focusing on intelligence, Gould tells how even the most eminent scientists were blinded by their prejudices while believing they were engaged in purely scientific assessment. For example, in the mid-nineteenth century, the respected physician Paul Broca used skull size (craniometry) to "prove" that men are smarter than women and Caucasians are smarter than Africans. Broca, like many well-intentioned scientists who followed him in the twentieth century, was probably not conscious of the distortions in his data. He was simply biased by his powerful preexisting beliefs. Undoubtedly, such biases also afflict modern personality testing, but without the benefit of hindsight, they are difficult to uncover.

Unfortunately, just as the first intelligence tests were quickly corrupted to search for "morons" and "idiots," psychological assessment is sometimes used today for purposes of discrimination and persecution. For example, tests might be legitimately designed to screen job applicants. But such a test easily could be biased (intentionally or unintentionally) against those from traditionally less-employed groups. It is as if medical diagnosis were being used, not to help in successful medical treatment, but rather to decide who should be shunned as "diseased."

Because of the abuses of assessments, some have argued that testing should be outlawed. This is an extreme reaction. It is like saying that we should outlaw science because scientific developments have led to the creation of terrible weapons. Or that we should outlaw surgery because many people die on the operating table. The real problem is that some personality tests are poorly constructed, improperly used, and wrongly employed. The solution is to ensure that educated people are well versed in understanding the valid uses and the severe limits of personality tests.

Summary and Conclusion

Personality tests involve standardized encounters that provoke and assess revealing individual differences in reactions. Objective tests include measures that are easily quantified and defined, but they may miss more subtle aspects of personality. Subjective tests rely on interpretations by observers or test-givers, but they may result in disagreements about interpretations. The best assessment relies on multiple measures to paint a picture of the individual.

Personality tests should be reliable. Reliability refers to the consistency of scores; people should receive similar scores on the same test on different occasions because personality is assumed to be relatively stable. (Personality may change, however, in the long run or in response to traumatic events.) Internal consistency reliability examines the subparts of a personality test. Test–retest reliability compares the scores on different occasions, usually several weeks apart.

Is a test measuring what it is supposed to be measuring? What is it measuring? These are issues of validity. The most important aspect of validity is construct validity. Construct validity is ascertained by seeing if the assessment predicts behaviors and reactions implied (theoretically) by the construct. Is an assessment related to the things to which it is supposed to be related? If so, it has convergent validity. On the other hand, the assessment should be distinguishable; that is, it should not be related to theoretically irrelevant constructs. This is termed discriminant validity. Content validity refers to whether a test is measuring the domain that it is supposed to be measuring.

One desirable quality of a test item is that it should differentiate among test-takers. Items should also be intercorrelated (i.e., related to one another) because each item is measuring some aspect of the overall construct. Finally, the items should produce a useful distribution so that the test is able to assess a full range of individuals.

Response sets are biases, unrelated to the personality characteristic being measured. People with an acquiescence response set are more likely than others to agree with anything you ask them. An especially difficult challenge is posed by a social desirability response set. That is, many people are likely to want to present themselves in a favorable light or to try to please the experimenter or test administrator. Although all tests rely to some degree on a set of assumptions and thus might be called biased, the tests are not necessarily worthless. Rather, they must be properly constructed, used, and interpreted to be valid.

A common type of test bias is ethnic bias. Tests often fail to take into account the relevant culture or subculture of the person being tested, and theories and measures developed in one culture are improperly applied to another culture. For example, Hispanic American children have sometimes been viewed as lacking in achievement motivation when in fact they have intentionally been raised to be more cooperative with their peers. Personality psychology too often studies samples of convenience—patients, students, neighbors—and too infrequently makes a systematic attempt to ascertain whether conclusions apply to other people, in other places, at other times.

Gender bias is also a prevalent type of test bias. Tests may demonstrate "problems" with women without turning the focus to the environment—toward

husbands, job discrimination, or lack of equal educational opportunity.

One of the great triumphs of personality testing of the past century is that many different types of valid personality tests have been developed. Many important personality assessments do not rely on self-report. The use of ratings by others shows that friends, acquaintances, and even strangers can make valid judgments of personality. Modern biological assessments of personality are based on the assumption that the nervous system is key. Exciting current assessment attempts in this area focus on the brain, measuring evoked potential on electroencephalograms (EEGs), and glucose metabolism (using positron emission tomography, or PET). Behavioral observation such as counting people's experiences or behaviors is another technique that has proved valuable. An experimenter who calls or pages the person to make a diary notation about current activity or thought processes is employing the experience sampling method of assessment.

The classic interview in psychology is the psychotherapeutic interview, in which the client talks about important or troubling parts of his or her life. In recent years, assessment interviews have tended to become more systematic or structured. In the case of the Type A structured interview, personality assessment is based partly on the verbal responses and partly on the nonverbal vocal responses, such as the volume and rate of speech. Nonverbal cues of expressive style are in fact an interesting and underutilized way of assessing personality. For example, expressive style is an excellent way to assess personal charisma. In contrast, letters and diaries (which contain no nonverbal cues) can be a fine source of information for the study of personality change because they provide data from multiple points in time.

Projective tests such as the Rorschach present an unstructured stimulus and allow a person to "project" his or her own inner motivations onto the assessor's test. They include drawing a picture, telling a story, completing a sentence, or doing word associations. The main drawback of projective tests is the problem of scoring. The examiner's personal interpretations may give us some interesting insights to follow up, but there is no reliability. That is, different examiners or even the same examiner at a later time might come up with a different interpretation. This problem can be partially addressed by training scorers in a standardized scoring scheme.

Finally, if we are to gain an accurate understanding of an individual, we need to know the person's cultural milieu and cultural identity. This is especially true if the culture is outside the mainstream. For example, silly attempts have been made to assess personality in African Americans without sufficient attempts to understand African American culture.

Personality testing can be and has been incorrectly employed. Because of the abuses of assessments, some have argued that testing should be banned. But the real problem is that some personality tests are poorly constructed, improperly used, or wrongly employed for political ends or other agendas. The solution is for people to achieve a good understanding of the valid uses and the severe limits of personality tests in the context of personality theories.

■ Key Concepts and Terms

objective assessment versus subjective assessment
reliability
construct validity
response set
bias
self-report tests
Q-sort tests
ratings and judgments by others
biological measures
behavioral observations

experience sampling method of assessment
psychotherapeutic interview
structured interview
expressive behavior
document analysis
projective tests
demographics and lifestyle information
case study design
correlational study
experimental study

Psychoanalytic Aspects of Personality

From Chapter 3 of *Personality: Classic Theories and Modern Research*, Fifth Edition. Howard S. Friedman, Miriam W. Schustack. Copyright © 2012 by Pearson Education, Inc. Published by Pearson Allyn & Bacon. All rights reserved.

Psychoanalytic Aspects of Personality

© Mary Evans /SIGMUND FREUD COPYRIGHTS/The Image Works

© Bettmann/CORBIS

In 1882, Dr. Sigmund Freud fell in love with a slender young woman named Martha Bernays. Unfortunately for Freud, he had neither the money nor the social status for an immediate marriage, and his sexual urges could not be gratified. Consistent with the times and their Austrian-Jewish culture, Freud and Martha, then in their 20s, would not engage in premarital sexual relations. They had to wait four long years until marriage, during which time Freud, a very perceptive young scientist, thought deeply and often about the pressures that his sexual longings put on other aspects of his life. Ten years later, in the 1890s, Freud began developing his psychosexual theories of the human psyche.

Freud's mother (shown with him in the photo on the top) was the third wife of his father, Jacob Freud, who was 20 years her elder. She was quite attractive, and the young Freud, as well as others, adored her. Freud later recalled the impression it made when he, as a young child, once saw his mother nude. He incorporated love and thwarted-love relations into the foundations of his theories.

When Freud was two and a half years old, family complications arose: His mother gave birth to his sister, raising his wonder about human reproduction and provoking deep concerns of sibling rivalry in the highly intelligent little Sigmund. Further complicating the picture was the fact that Freud's two adult half-brothers (from his father's previous marriage) lived nearby and seemed quite attached to his young mother. Why did his half-brothers flirt with his mother? In later years, Freud well remembered the tangle of erotic relationships of his childhood (Gay, 1988; Jones, 1953).

Although Freud was Jewish and his wife, Martha, was raised as an orthodox Jew, he was passionately against religion and refused to let Martha fully practice. He was quite defensive about the topic despite the fact that anti-Semitism was a significant factor in the lives of all European Jews, much as skin color is a significant factor in the lives of present-day African Americans. Trained as a physician, Freud was primarily a biologist—a biologist swept up in the writings and influences of Charles Darwin. Darwin had recently revolutionized scientific thought by proposing that people were highly intelligent animals, but animals nonetheless—biological creatures. Freud himself spent many years early in his career studying the biological evolution of fish. It is important to understand this aspect of Freud's work: He saw himself as a biologist, a scientist, endeavoring (with all his abilities) to understand the biological structures and laws underlying psychological responses (Bernstein, 1976; Freud, 1966b; Gay, 1988; Jones, 1953).

T his discussion of the early life of Sigmund Freud has hinted that childhood experiences, repressed erotic feelings, and unconscious conflicts can affect adult behavior. This type of analysis seems perfectly reasonable to most modern-day college students, but it was actually quite rare before the beginning of the twentieth century. The naturalness of a Freudian interpretation of personality gives elegant testimony to the success and influence of many of the ideas of a Freudian, **psychoanalytic** approach to personality.

Psychoanalytic
Sigmund Freud's basic approach to understanding personality

Freud visited the United States in 1909 at the invitation of G. Stanley Hall, the influential child psychologist, then president of Clark University. Freud was accompanied by Carl Jung (then in his early 30s; Freud was in his 50s). Neither man was yet well known, but their ideas about unconscious sexuality were intriguing to those Americans who read about them. They were visited at Clark by many influential psychologists, including William James, the Harvard philosopher–psychologist who was one of the founders of American psychology. Freud, although anxious before such a distinguished audience, did a fine job of presenting his ideas. This was the beginning of the significant spread of psychoanalytic ideas in North America. Freud's work is now the most heavily cited in all of psychology, and it is extensively referenced in many of the humanities as well.

Sigmund Freud is sometimes treated as a historical curiosity because some of his ideas have been disproven by modern research in biology and psychology. This attitude is a misreading of Freud's impact, and it may lead the field to overlook the insights that psychoanalytic theory can add to our understanding of personality. In this chapter we show how Freud's startling ideas are alive and highly influential even today. We also examine important limits and failures of the psychoanalytic approach.

Basic Psychoanalytic Concepts

As his young medical career began to develop, Sigmund Freud became more and more interested in neurology and psychiatry. Needing to develop clinical medical skills that could earn him money, he began paying less attention to research in biology and directed more efforts at problems plaguing patients. In 1885, Freud went to Paris to study with the famous neuropathologist J. M. Charcot.

Charcot was studying **hysteria**. Although hysteria is uncommon today, it was quite a problem just over a century ago. It is almost accurate to say it was a fashionable disease. Many people, especially young women, would be afflicted with various forms of paralysis for which no organic cause could be found. Sometimes, almost miraculously, they could be cured by psychological and social influences. For example, Charcot and Pierre Janet (Janet, 1907) successfully used **hypnosis** to cure hysteria. The idea behind the therapy was that, unbeknownst to the patient, psychological forces in the mind were causing physical ailments. By unlocking the inner psychological tension, the outer body could be liberated.

The Unconscious and Therapeutic Techniques

Freud began employing hypnosis but eventually found it inadequate to treat many of his patients. So Freud, influenced by his fellow physician and physiologist Josef Breuer, began experimenting, moving from hypnosis and other forms of intense suggestion to techniques of **free association**—spontaneous, free-flowing associations of ideas and feelings; and finally he moved to dreams (Breuer & Freud, 1957). It became more and more apparent to Freud that most patients were not consciously in touch with the inner conflicts that caused their observable mental and physical problems. But dreams might provide a key to unlock their inner secrets.

Dreams have been interpreted since biblical times, and even before. They were often seen as prophecies or divine revelations. But to Freud, the evolutionary biologist, dreams were a product of the individual's psyche. He saw dreams as pieces of and hints about the **unconscious**—that portion of the mind inaccessible to usual, conscious thought (Freud, 1913).

Freud called dreams the "royal road" to understanding the unconscious. Let us say that you repeatedly dream that you are chasing your boss up the stairs. You run faster and faster and become more and more frustrated but never reach the peak. Freud interpreted such activity as representing sexual intercourse, but intercourse that is never consummated. Why might one have such a dream? Because it might be too threatening, psychologically speaking, to admit to such thoughts. It might be threatening to one's marriage or to one's self-concept or to one's sense of morality to admit to such constant lustful urges. The urge is therefore turned into a non-threatening symbol—running up flights of stairs.

Hysteria
A term used for various forms of mental illness for which no organic cause could be found and which could sometimes be cured by psychological and social influences

Hypnosis
A process by which a person is induced into a trance state where action is partially under the control of another person

Free Association
A method used in psychoanalysis in which an individual reports everything that comes into awareness

Unconscious
The portion of the mind that is not accessible to conscious thought

Courtesy of the National Library of Medicine

■ Jean-Martin Charcot is shown here demonstrating the case of a woman suffering from hysteria. A copy of this same picture is shown hanging above the couch in Freud's study in the photo on the next page.

In dreams, almost any phallus-like object—from a clarinet to an umbrella—could represent a penis, that is, be a phallic symbol. And any enclosed space such as a private, walled courtyard, or a fur pocket, or a box could represent female genitalia. However, Freud, a great cigar smoker, is said to have commented that sometimes a cigar is just a cigar. (By the way, Freud's smoking was his ultimate undoing; he died of cancer of the mouth and jaw in 1939.)

But what about people who do indeed dream about having sexual intercourse with their boss or their coworker? Why isn't their sexual motivation hidden? Among Freud's patients, their problem was often some inner conflict or tension. This was especially true in the straight-laced Victorian society of the late nineteenth century, in which sexual matters were scandalous. Explicit lustful dreams were rarely encountered in patients; and if they were, they were interpreted as representing some other, even deeper, hidden conflict. It would be fascinating to hear what Freud would say about today's open, let-it-all-hang-out sexuality. Might he say that ours is still not really a sexually open and relaxed society?

According to psychoanalytic theory, dreams, and indeed most aspects of psychological experience, are said to have two levels of content—**manifest content** and **latent content**. The manifest content is what a person remembers and consciously considers. The latent content is the underlying hidden meaning. We might say that dreams are similar to icebergs—a little piece floats above the surface but much more is hidden underneath. This is the hallmark of the psychoanalytic approach to personality: The idea is that what we see on the surface (what is manifest) is only a partial representation of the vastness that is lying underneath (what is latent). The implication of this for understanding personality is that any assessment tools or tests that rely on people's conscious replies or self-reports are necessarily incomplete; they capture only the manifest content. The unconscious can manifest itself symbolically in a dream.

A vicious circle (or tautology) sometimes results from a psychoanalytic explanation of personality. Let us say, for example, that a young woman's severe nervous cough, squint, and partial paralysis are attributed to an unconscious conflict about her sexual abuse. In psychotherapy, the issue is gradually brought to light and thoroughly explored, its emotional energy diffused. Yet the patient still suffers from many nervous or hysterical problems. Do we therefore conclude that the psychoanalytic explanation was totally wrong? No, the psychoanalyst may search for even deeper, more

Manifest Content
The part of dreams or other aspects of psychological experience that is remembered and consciously considered

Latent Content
The part of dreams or other aspects of psychological experience that underlies the conscious portion and reveals hidden meaning

■ Sigmund Freud's study in Vienna. His patients would recline on the couch and let their free associations flow.

hidden aspects of the problem. There is thus no logical or scientific means of evaluating the explanation. Another way of stating this problem is to say that psychoanalytic investigations *rarely have a control group;* that is, there is no comparison or standard by which to carefully evaluate the theory or the therapy. In the movie *Annie Hall,* actor/director Woody Allen's character (Alvy) tells Annie that he has been seeing a psychoanalyst "just for fifteen years." When Annie is amazed, Alvy replies that he will give it one more year and then go to Lourdes (the center of faith healing in France). The comparison of psychoanalysis to religious miracle cures is an apt one in reflecting the criticism that Freud's ideas sometimes are not subjected to the same critical, scientific scrutiny as are other psychological theories.

Today, most laypersons believe that dreams contain meaningful information (Morewedge & Norton, 2009). For example, many individuals planning to travel report that they would be much more worried if they dreamed about a plane crash than if they received warning from the government about an increased risk of a terrorist attack. Because people's interpretations of dreams and free associations affect how they will act, it is important to understand whether, when, and how unconscious processes are truly relevant to daily life.

The Structure of the Mind

All personality theories agree that human beings, like other animals, are born with a set of instincts and motivations. Most basically, newborns will cry in response to painful stimulation and will suck milk until they are satiated. At birth, the inner motivating forces have obviously not yet been shaped by the external world. They are basic and unsocialized. Freud referred to this undifferentiated core of personality using a term that is translated as **id** (which is Latin for *it*). In German, the phrase Freud used was *das es,* literally *the it*. The id contains the basic psychic energy and motivations, often termed instincts or impulses. The id operates according to the demands of the **pleasure principle**. That is, the id strives solely to satisfy its desires and thereby reduce inner tension. For example, the baby is driven to suck, obtain pleasure, and relax. The need for food leads to a drive to suck and obtain relief.

Id
In psychoanalytic theory, the undifferentiated, unsocialized core of personality that contains the basic psychic energy and motivations

Pleasure Principle
The operating principle of the id to satisfy pleasure and reduce inner tension

However, even infants must face reality. There is a real world out there—tired mothers, dirty diapers, cold bedrooms—that soon must be responded to. The personality structure that develops to deal with the real world Freud termed the **ego**, or literally, the *I* (*ego* is the Latin word for *I*—Freud used the German term *das ich*, literally *the I*). The ego operates according to the **reality principle**; it must solve real problems. Wishing for a breast or a cuddle does not bring it about. One must plan and act, constrained by the real world. Infants soon learn to exaggerate their crying in order to bring their mothers.

Throughout life the pleasure-seeking id constantly struggles with the reality-checking ego. Individuals never outgrow the id, but most adults keep it under control. In some people, though, pleasure-seeking dominates inappropriately or too often; gratification becomes a core aspect of their adult personality. A graphic representation of the role of the id is shown in Figure 1.

There is still another set of problems. The young child cannot simply learn the most realistic ways of satisfying inner drives. We cannot be totally self-centered. Rather, we are forcefully shaped by our parents and the rest of society to follow moral rules. The personality structure that emerges to internalize these societal rules is termed the **superego**. Literally, Freud thought of it as the *Over-I* (he called it *Über-Ich,* meaning *above the I* in German) because it ruled over the ego or *I*. The superego is similar to a conscience, but goes further. We can think about what our conscience, our internal set of ethical guidelines, is telling us to do, but parts of the superego are unconscious. That is, we are not always aware of the internalized moral forces that press on and constrain our individual actions.

When the ego and especially the superego do not do their job properly, elements of the id may slip out and be seen. Consider the case of the anatomy professor quoted

Ego
In psychoanalytic theory, the personality structure that develops to deal with the real world; in neo-analytic theory, this term refers to the individuality of a person that is the central core of personality; and specifically for Carl Jung, it is the aspect of personality that is conscious and embodies the sense of self

Reality Principle
In Freudian psychoanalytic theory, the operating force of the ego to solve real problems

Superego
In Freudian psychoanalytic theory, the personality structure that develops to internalize societal rules and guide goal-seeking behavior toward socially acceptable pursuits

■ FIGURE I

The Psychoanalytic View of the Structure of the Mind

The ego (represented here by the town hall) and the superego (represented here by the church) both have their roots and foundations in the id (represented here by the sea), just as this volcanic island arises out of, and is surrounded by, water.

by Freud (1924a) who says, "In the case of the female genital, in spite of the tempting, I mean the attempted . . . " (p. 38). Freud deems the linguistic explanations of such slips inadequate and blames the error on unconscious urges. It is not simply a problem with speech; a much deeper motivation is being revealed. Such psychological errors in speaking or writing have come to be called **Freudian slips**. (Technically, mistakes that reveal the unconscious are termed *parapraxes*, Greek for *alongside the action*.) Temporarily forgetting your friend's name is not seen in terms of a learning theory of memory or in light of simple fatigue, but rather is seen as evidence of an unconscious conflict with this friend. Similarly, if a young woman fingers or taps her engagement ring while she talks to an attractive new acquaintance, this action is indicative of an unconscious concern regarding her relationship with her fiancé.

Freudian Slip
A psychological error in speaking or writing that reveals something about the person's unconscious

A Freudian slip may even have occurred during the writing of this text, when the simple omission of the letter *n* made quite a difference in one draft. In preparing an outline of the differences between men and women, a student assistant meant to write that "it is evolutionarily important for men to have as many sexual contacts as possible, in order to perpetuate their genes." But this (female) assistant wrote, much to her embarrassment, that "it is evolutionarily important for *me* to have as many sexual contacts as possible." Needless to say, others who saw this sentence found it quite amusing.

Freud admits that slips of the tongue or pen are more common when a person is tired or distracted but argues that at such times our defenses are down and, with less resistance, unconscious impulses can more easily surface. Freud was an extremely perceptive and acute observer who was not satisfied with superficial explanations of personality. The fact that a leading antitobacco activist is named Randolph Smoak would not surprise him—Freud looked for meaning in even the most minor connections, thoughts, and behaviors.

We now know quite a bit about the structure and function of the human brain, but 100 years ago, Freud and his colleagues knew very little. We now know that the brain is clearly *not* divided into id, ego, and superego compartments. But there are indeed various levels and structures in the human brain. Some are more primitive and are similar to those found in primitive animals. Other brain structures seem evolved to produce emotion and motivation, and the upper cortical layers contain complex networks of nerves that allow for higher levels of human intelligence and self-control. Freud was correct in concluding that certain parts of the mind are not subject to conscious awareness.

It is an interesting exercise to keep track of your verbal and written slips and your dreams for a while. You can best remember dreams by keeping a pen and paper next to your pillow; lie still after awakening (with your eyes closed), trying to recall your dreams; write down as much as you can remember. (The process gets easier with practice.) After several weeks, search for common themes and try to relate these themes to your worries, conflicts, and friends and family. This exercise may or may not provoke insights, but it will provide a taste of the kind of self-analysis that Freud worked on for many years. For example, in one modern study college students were asked to write in their journals before going to bed. They were instructed to choose someone they knew, and then either to write about that person directly or to write about something else while

Why Does It Matter?

Freud and his followers pioneered the idea that the mind has both rational and irrational, and biological and societal components, and that these elements are often hidden, in conflict beneath the surface. Although he got many of the details wrong, Freud's theories opened new approaches to human nature and psychotherapy, and they showed us that such matters could be systematically studied.

© Jupiter Images

■ When the World Trade Center towers were attacked and destroyed by terrorists, some psychologists speculated (on news shows) that one of the reasons for this choice of target was that the towers were phallic symbols, so their destruction would not only wound but also emasculate the United States. Such comments were generally met with smirks by newscasters. Yet one of the hijackers who piloted the jet into the tower left behind a will. It said, "I don't want women to go to my funeral or later to my grave. And I don't want any pregnant women to come and say goodbye." In understanding the complexities of motivation, the psychoanalytic approach emphasizes the role that sexual dysfunction and abnormal sexual relationships, thoughts, and desires play in the hidden recesses of our minds.

suppressing thoughts about that person. The next morning they recorded their dreams, which were studied by the experimenters. It turned out that bedtime suppression increased the amount of dreaming about the target person more than did thinking about the target person (Wegner, Wenzlaff, & Kozak, 2004).

Psychosexual Development

Freud saw the psychological world as a series of opposing tensions, such as tension between selfishness and society, and inner tensions that strive for relief. Underlying these tensions, he argued, was the sexual energy, or **libido (the Latin word for desire or lust)**. This psychic energy is the basis of drive or motivation.

Prior to Freud's attempt to put sexuality into a scientific framework, sexual urges and sexual behavior outside of marriage were not considered healthy or normal. Furthermore, in the late nineteenth century, several physicians and scientists, including Richard von Krafft-Ebing (1886/1965) and Havelock Ellis (1913; 1899/1936), began writing books exploring human sexuality and sexual deviancy. Freud was intrigued with the wide variety of sexual experiences he read about and encountered in his own patients. Why would some people want to have sexual relations with children, with corpses, with barnyard animals, with whips and chains, with shoes, in groups, in front of observers, obsessively, and so on? Freud, playing scientist rather than moralist or judge, tried to discover why sexual energy could be directed in so many ways.

Oral Stage

Infants are driven to satisfy their drives of hunger and thirst, and they turn to their mother's breast or bottle for this satisfaction, as well as for the security and pleasure

Libido
In Sigmund Freud's psychoanalytic theory, the sexual energy that underlies psychological tension; in Carl Jung's neo-analytic theory, the term is used to describe a general psychic energy that is not necessarily sexual in nature

Oral Stage
Freudian stage of psychosexual development before age one, when infants are driven to satisfy their drives of hunger and thirst

© Shutterstock

A two-year-old who takes great pleasure in feces expulsion and becomes fixated at this stage may develop a personality pattern of creativity and open expression—letting it all hang out.

that comes from nursing. At some point (usually at about age one in American society), the baby must stop sucking and be weaned. This creates a conflict between the desire to remain in a state of dependent security and the biological and psychological necessity of being weaned ("growing up"). It is one instance of the conflict between the id and the ego. Some babies easily resolve this conflict and redirect their psychosexual energy (libido) toward other challenges. But some children have difficulty with this transition, perhaps being moved to solid food before they are ready. According to psychoanalytic theory, such children remain concerned with being mothered and taken care of, and keeping their mouths full of desired substances. In technical terms, they are said to be fixated at the **oral stage**.

As their personality develops, individuals fixated at the oral stage remain preoccupied with issues of dependency, attachment, and "intake" of interesting substances and perhaps even interesting ideas. The fixation is the framework for their development. As adults, they may derive pleasure from biting, chewing, sucking hard candy, eating, or smoking cigarettes. They analogously derive psychological pleasure from talking, being close (perhaps too close) to others, and constantly seeking knowledge. Modern research confirms the importance of this early sense of security. The mother's responsiveness is one of the best predictors of infants' patterns of attachment and later social adjustment (Johnson, Dweck, & Chen, 2007; Pederson et al., 1990; Sroufe & Fleeson, 1986).

Anal Stage

If someone today were called an anal character type, it might be seen as an insult or as some pop psychology label. This is because the context and flavor of Freud's ideas have largely been lost. Freud used an important event of early childhood as an explanation of deep patterns that underlie later personality.

All one-year-olds in Western cultures use diapers but almost all three-year-olds use toilets. Sometime around age two, a child has to be toilet-trained. Although most people do not remember their own toilet training, most parents remember all too well the difficulty they faced in training their children.

The two-year-old, following the urges of the id, takes pleasure in the relief—the tension reduction—of defecating. The parents, however, want to control when and where the child urinates and defecates. In other words, the parents want society's proscription against unbridled defecation represented in the child's superego.

Some children readily learn such self-control, and this becomes a healthy aspect of their personality. Others overlearn it; they take pleasure in holding in their feces in order to maintain some control over their parents. They deliver their feces only when they are good and ready. (Some children's holding back feces becomes such a significant threat to their health that they must be given laxatives.) Still other children fight the attempts to regulate their urination and defecation, trying to maintain total freedom of action. Psychoanalytic theory sees these patterns as carrying on throughout life (A. Freud, 1981; S. Freud, 1908; Fromm, 1947).

As adults, such people who remain fixated at the **anal stage** may take great satisfaction in a large bowel movement. Psychologically, people fixated at the anal stage may like bathroom humor or making messes—including messes of other people's lives. Or they may be overly concerned with neatness, parsimony, order, and organization. That is, severe toilet training may lead to a great pleasure in control over feces that (theoretically) manifests itself in adulthood in obstinacy ("I'll go when I want") and stinginess ("I'll keep it for myself"). Although this simple mechanism has not been confirmed by empirical research, and although psychoanalysis is not the best treatment for people with obsessive-compulsive disorders, the idea that such early emotional patterns and conflicts can have enormous influence on personality development has generally been accepted.

As noted, anal retentive people (who overlearned retaining their feces) may grow up to be excessively stingy. Such people are also often passive-aggressive. For example, they may not do anything overtly nasty but attack passively, such as by giving you the silent treatment. This parallels the childhood holding in of the feces—"I didn't do anything overtly wrong, Mommy; no poopy mess."

Is focusing on toilet training the best way to understand a stingy or passive-aggressive adult? If we believe that a pattern learned successfully in childhood is reapplied in assorted versions throughout one's life, then this approach often makes sense. If, however, we maintain that a fixation of libido at the anal stage is a direct physiological cause of the adult behavior patterns, then we have gone well beyond what is supported by current theory and research.

In general, attempts to link adult personality directly to breast-feeding and weaning, or to age and type of toilet training, have proved unsuccessful. In extreme circumstances, a very traumatic experience in toilet training could set a pattern that persists throughout life. But for most people, their early experiences, taken in isolation, do not have simple, direct effects on later personality. Many of the clusters of characteristics are valid, however. As Freud noted, and modern research confirms, being neat, stubborn, and stingy do seem to be related characteristics; and perhaps such patterns may result from a set of pressures that some parents and some aspects of society apply to certain children (Fisher & Greenberg, 1996; Lewis, 1996).

Phallic Stage

Around age 4, the child enters the **phallic stage**, in which sexual energy is focused on the genitals. Children may explore their genitals and masturbate, but open masturbation is not socially acceptable (and certainly was absolutely taboo in Freud's society). In many families, private masturbation is also forbidden by parents, who

© Hans Namuth/Photo Researchers, Inc.

■ Jackson Pollock (1912–1956) claimed that the inspiration for his artwork was his unconscious. He was a pioneer of unorthodox ways of using paint, often abandoning the brush to drip or pour or throw liquid paint directly onto a canvas on the ground or on the floor. Describing his process of creating a painting, he claimed to be *in* the painting as it developed, and not conscious of his own actions as he created it.

Anal Stage
Freud's stage of psychosexual development around age two during which children are toilet trained

Phallic Stage
Freudian stage of psychosexual development around age four in which a child's sexual energy is focused on the genitals

may threaten their children with dire consequences. Children also focus now on the differences between boys and girls. By age 6, most children have a good sense of their gender identity. Central to this stage of Freudian theory is the Oedipus complex.

Oedipus Complex

In the first decade of the twentieth century, psychoanalytic ideas developed rapidly and flourished. A particularly influential case study was that of Little Hans, the subject of Freud's "Analysis of a Phobia in a Five-Year-Old Boy" (1909/1967).

Phobia
An excessive or incapacitating fear

Little Hans was the son of one of Freud's friends and admirers. The boy suffered from a **phobia**—an excessive or incapacitating fear. In Hans's case it was a fear of horses. (These were the days before automobiles.) He was afraid horses would bite him, to the point that he became afraid of going outdoors.

Different theories explain such a phobia in different ways. Freud's explanation was in terms of unconscious sexual conflict. He noted that Hans's father had a large mustache and was a large and powerful man; likewise, horses wear a muzzle across their faces and are large and powerful. Just as symbols are important in dreams, Freud viewed horses as a symbol in Hans's mind of his father. But why was Hans unconsciously so afraid of his father?

Freud noted that Hans, like many little boys, was very concerned with penises—his penis, his father's penis, a horse's large penis. Hans was also concerned with those people (like his sister) without penises. Hans had been threatened for playing with his penis. Freud concluded that Hans was struggling to deal with his intense love for his mother, coupled with the knowledge that he could not overcome his powerful father. His horse phobia resulted from this struggle. This unconscious fear is termed **castration anxiety**. Hans feared that his father would take revenge and castrate him, thus making him like his sister.

Castration Anxiety
According to Sigmund Freud, an unconscious fear of castration that results from a boy's struggle to deal with his love for his mother while knowing that he cannot overcome his father

In Greek legend, Oedipus, king of Thebes, unwittingly kills his father and marries his mother. Similar legends of patricide have occurred throughout history in many cultures. Freud was very well-read in classic literature and believed such legends and stories were not mere amusements; rather, they captured the fundamentals of human nature. Freud thus took the term **Oedipus complex** to describe a boy's sexual feelings for his mother and rivalries with his father. These feelings of a young boy, and his psychological defenses against threatening thoughts and feelings, are critically important because they form the basic reaction patterns that are used throughout life; that is, they form personality.

Oedipus Complex
A term used by Sigmund Freud to describe a boy's sexual feelings for his mother and rivalries with his father

A 5-year-old boy cannot kill his father and marry his mother. To resolve the unconscious tension between fear and erotic desire, a successfully developing boy turns to identification with his father. He assumes manly characteristics and tries to be like his father. In addition to diminishing the danger of castration, this identification allows the little boy to vicariously "obtain" his mother—that is, through his father.

Penis Envy

What about girls? Freud believed that little girls become quite upset when they recognize that they do not have a penis as do boys and men. This is not an unreasonable assumption in times or places where boys are granted much higher status than girls. A little girl, wondering why she is less worthy, might look to the only observable physical difference, her lack of a penis. Note also that given Freud's

■ Little Hans had an excessive fear of horses, which Freud viewed as Hans's displaced fear that he would be castrated by his powerful father (who had in common with the horse a large, muscular body, a large penis, and a hairy muzzle).

elevation of sexuality as *the* shaper of personality, it makes sense that little girls would be quite concerned about their lack of easily visible genitals. According to this thinking, girls develop feelings of inferiority and jealousy, a phenomenon termed **penis envy**.

Like boys, girls first develop a sexual attachment to their mothers. However, because her mother has allowed her to be born without a penis or perhaps (she thinks) has cut off her penis, the girl transfers her love to her father, in an attempt to capture a penis. Here, Freud points to the conflicting feelings of a little girl who of course loves her mother but responds to the affections and strengths of her father. This idea would not be controversial except for the sexual undercurrents that Freud attaches to these relations. (The girl's conflict is sometimes termed by others as the "Electra complex," after the maiden in Greek mythology who convinced her brother Orestes to murder their mother Clytemnestra; but Freud himself did not like this term.)

Just as a boy cannot marry his mother, a girl cannot marry her father. So, in Freud's view of normal development, a girl decides that although she cannot have a penis, she can have a baby when she grows up, thereby becoming complete. In other words, for Freud the development of a girl's personality builds on early psychosexual feelings surrounding her genital identity. It follows that a healthy adult woman should want to find a good man like her father and produce a baby.

It is not uncommon for us to know men who seem to be seeking girlfriends who are like their mothers, or who are the exact opposite of their mothers. We also know females who are seeking boyfriends like their fathers, or the opposite of their fathers. All of these motivations are directly derivable from psychoanalytic theory. Various sorts of modern-day evidence confirm that

Penis Envy
A term used by Sigmund Freud to describe the phenomenon in which a girl develops feelings of inferiority and jealousy over her lack of a penis

Why Does It Matter?

Freud's theory of psychosexual development is a stage theory, meaning that normal adjustment involves resolving one set of childhood challenges and moving on to face and resolve the next set of challenges. What about an adult who cannot form a normal intimate relationship with a partner or who, for example, is a pedophile? Pedophilia is a disorder in which an adult derives primary sexual satisfaction from prepubertal children, such as by asking 5-year-old girls to remove their clothes. Why does this occur and where should we look for a therapeutic treatment? From a Freudian psychoanalytic framework, the disorder derives from an unsuccessful navigation through psychosexual stages in one's own childhood. This is in contrast to other explanations involving such issues as abnormal learning and conditioning, a biological problem with brain development, lack of moral education, poor role models.

many aspects and problems of courtship and marriage revolve around issues related to the partners' parents and other early relations, though not always in the ways Freud predicted (Andersen, Reznik, & Glassman, 2005). Adults may replay unresolved conflicts from their childhoods (Snyder, Wills, & Grady-Fletcher, 1991; Sullivan & Christensen, 1998).

Latency Period

Latency Period
According to Sigmund Freud, the period from age 5 to age 11 in which no important psychosexual developments take place and during which sexual urges are not directly expressed but instead are channeled into other activities

It is clear to any observer that sexual drives become a significant influence at puberty. But what about the period between resolution of the Oedipus complex (around age 5) and puberty (around age 11)? Freud did not note any important psychosexual developments during this time, and so he called it a **latency period**. During this period, because it is usually not possible for sexual urges to be directly expressed, sexual energies are channeled into such activities as going to school and making friends.

The fact that Freudian theory has little to say about the grade school years reveals a significant weakness of the whole approach. These years are the time when a child learns to make friends, to become a leader or follower, to cooperate with teachers and other authorities, and to develop study and work habits. Such matters are not easily explained in terms of unconscious motivations and sexual drives. To understand such matters, we need to understand more about self-concept and about traits and abilities, issues.

Although Freud did not know it, it turns out that this is by no means a dormant period of biological development. In the years before puberty (between ages 6 and 11), the adrenal glands are maturing, and there is a growth spurt coupled with changes in adrenal-stimulated hormones. It is not unusual for there to be sexual attraction in the fourth grade, well before the individuals reach sexual maturity (McClintock & Herdt, 1996).

Genital Stage

Genital Stage
Freudian stage of psychosexual development beginning at adolescence in which attention is turned toward heterosexual relations

If a person makes it through the many challenges of early childhood with enough sexual energy still available (that is, without strong fixations), then there will supposedly

■ The worldwide fascination with the legends of Dracula, in which a vampire-person bites and sucks the blood of an innocent victim, thereby binding them in a shared pollution, can be seen as a surface manifestation of unconscious concerns about sex, aggression, and related deep, dark forces.

be a fairly well-adjusted life, dominated by the **genital stage**. In other words, Freud thought that if a person was not trapped or hung up along the way, then adolescence marks the beginning of an adult life of normal sexual relations, marriage, and child-rearing.

Freud was correct in proposing that deviant experiences in childhood can produce personal idiosyncrasies or personality problems in adulthood. Indeed, this assumption is the basis of much modern-day psychotherapy, in which the early environment is seen as setting the pattern for later life (Horowitz, 1998). It seems, however, that Freud was off track in assuming that it is childhood sexual urges that suddenly spring to life in adolescence. It is now clear that striking hormonal changes occur at puberty, and the adolescent struggles to become independent. Many conflicts occur at puberty, but they do not seem closely tied to the psychosexual development of infants and toddlers. Further, it is now much clearer that there are many issues of adult sexuality and adult behavior that must be considered on their own terms, rather than in the context of one overarching psychoanalytic psychosexual model.

In the genital stage, attention is supposed to turn away from masturbation and toward heterosexual relations. Any deviation (for example, remaining single, remaining childless, homosexuality, or other sexual behaviors) is considered a flaw, unnatural. In this regard, Freud was clearly wrong. Cultural and biological research indicates that varying mating patterns, masturbation, homosexuality, and a wide variety of sexual activities are found in psychologically healthy, productive, well-adjusted people. One may have religious, moral, practical, or cultural reasons for discouraging various forms of adult sexuality, but there is no scientific or biological reason for such prejudice (Kaplan, 1983; Masters & Johnson, 1966). Freud made this mistake, and many other well-intentioned people make the same mistake today.

Freud was a physician and his theories arose from treating patients. By definition, his patients had problems or else they would not have been seeking his specialized care. Thus Freudian theory is based on a medical model of pathology, therapy, and cure. This is an odd way to construct a general psychological theory; as you might suspect, it is apt to overemphasize pathology. Indeed, this is a significant criticism of Freudian theory: It tends to focus on the deviance and the problems in human development and therefore tends to view too many behaviors and reactions as sick or inappropriate or conflict-based. There are many other important motivations and experiences that shape human personality. Nevertheless, much recent research confirms the predictive value, and perhaps the causal influences, of temperament and personality during the first few years of life.

Why Does It Matter?

Research confirms that the processes of temperamental adjustment of children are reliably related to their personalities and social behaviors in young adulthood (Caspi, 2000). Or, as poet William Wordsworth put it, "the child is father of the man."

Male Versus Female

With his focus on sexuality as a key force in human nature, it is not surprising that Freud's theories quite often dealt with the penis. In theorizing about women, it seemed logical to examine the implications of the absence of a penis.

Freud noted the significance of minimizing the importance of a girl's clitoris. Even in today's vastly more open societies, girls are often not taught the name for their clitoris and are rarely taught to examine it or stimulate it. A self-focus on the clitoris might diminish the importance of men to women's sexual experience, and indeed, today it is generally the most feminist women who emphasize clitoral education. Seen in this light, it is understandable that Freud would propose that the mature sexual development of a girl involves shifting pleasure-seeking to the vagina. Freud therefore postulated a "vaginal orgasm," which is psychologically and biologically superior to a "clitoral orgasm." A vaginal orgasm supposedly results from "natural" stimulation by a penis, whereas a clitoral orgasm could result from "artificial" stimulation.

Modern research on human sexual response by Masters and Johnson (1966) and others has not confirmed such different types of orgasms, although different muscles may be more or less active as a function of where the stimulation occurs. An orgasm is an orgasm. Freud's speculations, as developed by his followers, have led to much distress for women, as many women have been treated by therapists for not having the "correct" vaginal orgasm. This is another example of Freud having good ideas but poor data. It makes sense (then and now) to view a mature person as one who can achieve sexual satisfaction in a deep relationship with a partner. But it does not make sense to postulate biologically different female orgasms. (In fact, penile stimulation of the vagina sometimes stimulates the clitoris.)

Freud, like many others of the late-nineteenth-century Western culture, viewed men as inherently superior to women. His theories thus focused on male behavior as the norm and female behavior as a deviation. One of Freud's arguments was that women have an unconscious desire for suffering (and receive unconscious pleasure from suffering). Freud had observed many women trapped in uncomfortable or abusive relations with men, and yet they stayed in such relations and explained to him why they preferred such relations. Freud had uncovered the extreme limits to which people will go in order to rationalize their life situation. Freud's female patients were trapped in such relations because women of the time had few opportunities for social, educational, or economic attainment on their own. Freud saw such women as masochistic. Today, such women are more likely to be viewed as brainwashed, self-defeating, or victimized. Viewing women as victims, however, was virtually impossible for men of Freud's time because all societal institutions—religious, political, educational, judicial, familial—saw women as subservient and subordinate to men.

In this area, as in many others, Freud achieved a basic insight the implications of which were distorted by those who came later. Boys and girls do indeed show different patterns of development. As women's rights have come to be recognized, the value and importance of the "female" tendencies are increasingly appreciated. Most psychologists today, including feminist psychologists, agree that there are vast differences in the psychosocial tendencies of men and women. But the implications of these differences are now often reversed. Women's emotionality and family orientation are now seen as healthy nurturance and cooperativeness, whereas men's toughness and independence are seen as aggressiveness and lack of relatedness.

Feminist writers of the 1970s and 1980s often condemned the sexist aspects of "Freudianism," the pseudo-religion into which psychoanalysis developed in some circles. They noted that Freud was merely a diagnostician for what feminism purports to cure, and that psychoanalysis itself became the disease it purports to cure (Firestone, 1970; Millett, 1974). In 1972, Congresswoman Pat Schroeder, asked about being both a mother *and* an accomplished career person remarked, "I have a brain and a uterus, and I use both" (Pogrebin, 1983, p. 121). Such discussions led modern thought in new directions, as the various biological and cultural influences on male and female development were examined in great detail.

Defense Mechanisms

Challenges from the outer environment and from our inner urges threaten us with **anxiety**. These might be conflicts with those close to us or threats to our self-esteem (embarrassment, guilt, self-disappointment, etc.). The ego, governed by the reality principle, tries to deal realistically with the environment. However, sometimes we must distort reality to protect ourselves against the painful or threatening impulses arising from the id. The processes that the ego uses to distort reality to protect itself are called **defense mechanisms**. Some of the most interesting and influential insights from Freud's psychoanalytic approach concern defense mechanisms (Freud, 1942).

Repression

A while ago, a retired man went on trial for murdering an 8-year-old girl. Surprisingly, the murder had taken place two decades earlier. Why was the man accused only now? The new evidence was the sudden testimony of the man's 29-year-old daughter. She reported that an old memory suddenly flashed into her consciousness after more than two decades. She now recalled that when she was 8, she saw her father molest and then bludgeon to death her young classmate. According to Freud, **repression** is the ego defense mechanism that pushes threatening thoughts back into the unconscious.

Could such an important memory be repressed for 21 years? Can we believe that it is accurately remembered when it bursts into consciousness decades later? Could each of us be harboring such hidden memories?

Interesting evidence along these lines is provided by what has come to be called **posttraumatic stress** (posttraumatic stress disorder, PTSD). After the Vietnam War, it was noticed that many thousands of U.S. veterans began experiencing anxiety, nightmares and sleep difficulties, and failed marriages (Jaycox & Foa, 1998). The only clue to their troubles was that some of the veterans reported daytime flashbacks to combat experiences, which they persistently tried to avoid thinking about. It seemed, as Freud postulated, that the conscious mind could not face overwhelmingly stressful and grisly memories, in this case of burned, maimed bodies and butchered children. More recently, as many as one in six American soldiers returning from Iraq or Afghanistan suffered from PTSD.

Combat veterans with posttraumatic stress disorder are more likely to withhold their general emotional responses (Roemer, Litz, Orsillo, & Wagner, 2001). Voluntary self-disclosure groups with other veterans and psychotherapy focused on discussing the traumatic event have proved helpful as treatment (as Freud suggested). Note that if the veteran knows that his or her problems are the result of combat experience, then the defense is not repression because it is not unconscious. However, in

Anxiety
A state of intense apprehension or uncertainty, resulting from the anticipation of a threatening event or challenge, either external or internal; the ego's job is to protect against anxiety, but its failures lead to psychological problems

Defense Mechanisms
In psychoanalytic theory, the processes that distort reality to protect the ego

Repression
A defense mechanism that pushes threatening thoughts into the unconscious

Posttraumatic Stress
Anxiety, nightmares, and flashbacks that result when the conscious mind cannot deal with overwhelmingly disturbing memories

■ George Franklin Sr. was tried and convicted of murder on the basis of his adult daughter's testimony that she had recently recovered her memory of watching him molest and kill her playmate 20 years earlier. Was this a true memory, long repressed because of the daughter's fear and horror, that rose to consciousness? (The verdict was later overturned.)

many cases, people who have faced early traumas overcome the initial shock and seem to go on with their lives, but the hidden memories pursue and plague them. Such cases seem to validate the existence of repression.

In line with Freud's concern with repressed sexuality, another area in which repression is often discussed in today's practice of psychology is incest. Freudian theory maintains that sexual assault by one's father or mother would be so psychologically distressing that it might very well be repressed. Freud himself, however, claimed that most such parent–child sexual activity was imagined rather than real (Masson, 1984). (Some feminists accuse Freud of succumbing to his sexist orientation in denying the common assaults on little girls.) These matters currently draw a lot of attention in courtrooms (Crews, 1996; Loftus & Ketcham, 1991). Grown children may sue their parents for alleged abuse that occurred many years before. Interestingly, a general population study in St. Louis found that people most likely to be suffering from posttraumatic stress disorder were men who were combat veterans and women who were the victims of physical assault (Helzer, Robins, & McEvoy, 1987).

If there is no objective evidence of abuse other than the child's formerly repressed memory, a very unfortunate legal situation results. The alleged victim, who may now be a 22-year-old woman with anxiety disorders, accuses her father or a neighbor of incest or molestation or perhaps other crimes. The defendant, presumed innocent under the law, who is perhaps a 55-year-old married man, is forced to defend himself against allegations that scandalous activities took place many years before.

By the way, in the case described earlier of the father accused of murder, he was indeed convicted of murder on the evidence of his daughter's repressed memory. He was, however, released from prison after a federal appeals court overturned the conviction. His daughter remains convinced of his guilt. (These issues are considered further in the Self-Understanding box.)

To further complicate matters, well-meaning psychotherapists can sometimes plant the idea of abuse in the client's memory. For example, if a college age woman seeks therapy because she is depressed, has nightmares, and cannot relate well to men, the therapist might say, "Were you ever sexually abused as a child? Such abuse, even at an early age, can produce symptoms like yours." This comment might get the client thinking that she might have been abused. She may then search her memory for evidence or clues. In the current social climate, in which many women trace their problems to early sexual abuse, the woman may convince herself that she was indeed molested. Modern research on memory clearly demonstrates that false memories can sometimes be "implanted," either intentionally or accidentally, just as preferences for certain styles of clothing or certain political beliefs can be induced through subtle social influence. We can come to believe stories and recall experiences that in reality never happened (Appelbaum, Uyehara, & Elin, 1997; Loftus & Davis, 2006; Loftus & Ketcham, 1991).

On the other side of the coin is the unavoidable question of the prevalence of child molestation, incest, and other forms of abuse (Alexander et al., 2005; Herman, 1992; Koss & Harvey, 1991). When Freud began exploring the childhoods of his patients, he found that a surprising number of them seemed to be struggling with sexual conflicts, traceable to childhood molestation. This was quite shocking in the prudish times in which Freud lived, but Freud persisted with this line of exploration. Indeed, the attention he drew to the influence of sexuality on personality is one of Freud's major and lasting contributions. However, as we have noted, Freud either could not or did not want to believe that so much sexual abuse of children was occurring. So, in Freudian theory, most sexual conflict is thought to be imagined; children become fearful that their father will harm their genitals but, he contended, the danger is only in their imaginations. Modern population surveys do indicate, however, that many more people (especially females) are molested than was commonly thought.

Reaction Formation

Religious evangelists who preach on television can reach millions of viewers with their expressions of holiness and their urgings for people to follow religious gospel. It must be an interesting experience to talk passionately about deeply personal religious feelings in front of such a large public. What motivates such pastors (sometimes referred to as televangelists)? In most cases it seems that these preachers have a sincere, overwhelming desire to help other people achieve spiritual rewards. Psychoanalytic theory, however, suggests a very different sort of explanation.

Jim Bakker ran an extremely popular televised ministry; he seemed to epitomize righteousness and convinced millions of viewers to send him money to do the Lord's work. It eventually turned out that Bakker was engaging in a number of unethical, illegal, and immoral activities, both financially and sexually. When caught, he collapsed in tears and was eventually sent to prison. Jimmy Swaggart was another well-known television minister who ranted and railed against sexual immorality. He

■ Prominent evangelical preacher Ted Haggard, who led a megachurch he had founded, and headed the National Association of Evangelicals, was forced to step down from both positions after a male prostitute claimed that Haggard had been a paying customer of his for years and that Haggard also used illegal drugs. The prostitute claims he came forward when he did because Haggard was supporting a state constitutional amendment to ban gay marriage. Haggard confessed to his congregation that "There is a part of my life that is so repulsive and dark that I've been warring against it all of my adult life" (O'Driscoll, 2006).

Self-Understanding

Repressed Memories of Sexual Abuse?

The late Joseph Cardinal Bernardin of Chicago was publicly scandalized when he was accused by a man named Steven Cook of sexually molesting Cook 17 years earlier. The Catholic priest heatedly denied the charges, but Cook claimed to have remembered the molestation after reportedly being treated by a hypnotherapist. Later, after further psychological and legal investigation, Cook recanted and admitted he was mistaken to accuse the cardinal. He had misremembered. In many such cases, it may be that the therapist, wittingly or unwittingly, is the source of the "memories."

About the same time, television comedian Roseanne Barr was in the news claiming that she had been sexually molested by her father; her parents vigorously denied the charges. Similar cases have appeared involving thousands of people (usually women). A woman who is currently having psychological or sexual problems seeks psychotherapy. During therapy, the problems are traced to childhood sexual abuse, the memory of which has been repressed. Should these accusations be believed? Are the memories accurate? How can one evaluate one's old "memories?"

There is no simple answer to this question because two established phenomena are in conflict. Ironically, both of these phenomena were a focus of Freud's work. First, it is known that memories can indeed be separated from painful feelings in the mind. A traumatic experience can produce emotional distress such as sleeplessness, nightmares, and anxieties, while the conscious mind refuses to think about the horrific image. Second, it is known that people are suggestible; they can distort their memories and can be influenced by their therapists. Often, memory cannot be trusted.

Complex childhood memories are generally not eidetic—they are not like photographs. A child who was repeatedly molested between the ages of 3 and 5 would, as an adult, have memories that were influenced by all the subsequent events in her life. Thus we should be suspicious when a distressed adult suddenly begins blaming all her problems on her early childhood, without confirming evidence. Clear memories of such an ongoing molestation are unlikely to reappear suddenly out of the deepest unconscious. An innocent person, even a cardinal, could be smeared. On the other hand, an alarming number of children are indeed molested, even by clergy, as evidenced by the recent large-scale revelations of child abuse by Catholic priests.

A memory of a single, shocking scene, however, may indeed be repressed in a form that can be almost wholly retrieved. Someone, child or adult, witnessing a bloody murder, or a mutilation, or even an extremely embarrassing social misstep, might carry that memory for many years, hidden from awareness.

© AP Images/Angelo Scipioni

■ The late Joseph Cardinal Bernardin was accused of sexual abuse in a "recovered memory" case. The accuser later withdrew his accusations, disclaiming the memories.

resigned from his church after being photographed with a New Orleans prostitute. He, too, tearfully confessed and his ministry collapsed. Later in California, he was cited for three traffic violations while riding with a woman who reported being—guess what?—a prostitute.

According to psychoanalytic theory, the base, inner drives of such people (the id forces) are pushing them to engage in behaviors—various sexual acts, greed, deception—that are incompatible with their religious beliefs. Their sense of self is thus severely threatened, and the self (the ego) distorts these unconscious urges and turns them into their opposites. So, instead of acting out their sexual desires, such people may instead preach vehemently against sexual "sins."

Reaction formation is the process of pushing away threatening impulses by overemphasizing the opposite in one's thoughts and actions. Reaction formation is a controversial notion because it suggests that many apparently "moral" people are really struggling desperately with their own immorality. Are some ministers acting pious because they really feel devilish and unholy? Are people who proudly refuse to serve alcohol in their homes really motivated by their own inner desires to let go and get drunk? Are gay-bashers in fact unconsciously threatened about their own possible latent homosexual impulses?

Reaction formation is a fascinating idea that has rarely been systematically evaluated by modern personality research, although there are always many individuals whose stories provide vivid anecdotal evidence (see Table 1). Occasionally, when it is studied, support does indeed emerge. For example, one study of self-identified heterosexuals compared homophobic men (those who had very negative feelings toward gay men) to nonhomophobic men in terms of how aroused they became

Why Does It Matter?

Many current issues of guilt and innocence, abuse and justice, depend on an understanding of the phenomenon that Freud termed *repression*. There are as yet no simple answers. There is no litmus test we can use to decide if a thought that suddenly appears is a genuine long-repressed memory or a false inference resulting from suggestion or other influence processes. Only a careful analysis of the evidence in each particular case, coupled with an intelligent, state-of-the-art understanding of how the mind works, can rightfully be employed. This is a clear example of how the study of personality psychology can prove very important for people's daily lives. Repression has remained a key concept in psychology, relevant to our relations with others and to our general physical health (Blatt, Cornell, & Eshkol, 1993; Emmons, 1992; Loftus & Davis, 2006).

Reaction Formation
A defense mechanism that pushes away threatening impulses by overemphasizing the opposite in one's thoughts and actions

■ U.S. Congressman Gary Condit, a Democrat who promoted a "family values" agenda, grew up in the Bible Belt as the son of a Baptist minister. An evangelical Christian, he cosponsored legislation to post the Ten Commandments in public buildings, and he publicly scolded former President Clinton for withholding information about his affair with Monica Lewinsky. It became clear, after the mysterious disappearance of a young woman who was an intern in Washington, that Condit had been having an affair with her (and possibly with other women as well), and he did not immediately cooperate with authorities investigating her disappearance. The incident ended his political career. Are men like Condit puzzling or very understandable?

■ **TABLE 1**   Real-Life Examples of Reaction Formation

Roy Cohn, special counsel to Sen. Joseph McCarthy during the "Red Scare" of the 1940s to 1950s, avidly pursued what McCarthy and his committee called "communists and queers" in the government and military. Cohn was widely believed to be gay and died of AIDS (although he claimed to the end that he did not have AIDS).

William Bennett, prominent conservative, former U.S. secretary of education and first U.S. "drug czar," wrote a widely read book titled *The Book of Virtues,* full of pious advice on how to live a moral life. He was revealed as a high-stakes casino gambler who had lost millions of dollars betting. One columnist labeled him "The Bookie of Virtues."

John Terry Dolan, founder of the National Conservative Political Action Committee, attacked employment rights and adoption rights for gays and lesbians. He made a deathbed confession that he was gay and died in his 30s of AIDS.

Edward Schrock, a Virginia congressman who publicly supported a proposed constitutional amendment banning gay marriage, had to resign his office when he was exposed as being gay himself.

Congressman Robert Bauman, a notable opponent of gay rights in any form and known for trying to deny all public benefits to gay people, was arrested in a gay bar soliciting a 16-year-old boy.

James West, former Washington state senator and mayor of Spokane, was known for his strong antigay positions. He was forced to resign after he was caught in a sting operation by the local newspaper: West propositioned a decoy posing as a 17-year-old boy on a gay website, and when West went to meet his "date," he found newspaper reporters instead. There are further allegations that, as a Boy Scout leader, West molested much younger boys (under age 12). Among the legislation that West had sponsored was a bill to bar gays and lesbians from working in schools or daycare centers.

Mark Foley, a prominent Florida congressman, was best known for his interest in protecting children, adolescents, and young adults. He sponsored the "Foley Amendment" to allow campuses to reveal the names of students who commit violent crimes; he helped pass a law that allows youth organizations access to FBI fingerprint information on their adult leaders; he strengthened sex offender laws to protect children; and he tried to pass legislation banning sexually suggestive images of teens to protect them from pedophiles. He resigned after revelations of sexually explicit messages exchanged with underage boys serving as congressional pages, which brought forward further accusations of sexual exploitation of boys over many years. He then came out to live in an openly gay relationship with a long-time (adult) partner.

Larry Craig, Idaho senator and staunch conservative, was arrested for lewd behavior in an airport men's room. Several men came forward after that incident to claim that Craig had solicited or engaged in homosexual activity with them. Craig denied any homosexual behavior. He did not resign immediately, but was forced to decline to run for reelection.

Eliot Spitzer, governor of New York, had earned a national reputation fighting white-collar crime, and was often referred to as "Mr. Clean." He was widely quoted saying, "I have always stated that I want ethics and integrity to be the hallmarks of my administration." He had been active in the prosecution of money-laundering via wire transfer by criminal enterprises and had prosecuted several prostitution rings in his career. Spitzer resigned as governor after it was revealed that he had repeatedly engaged the services of high-priced prostitutes. He was caught because of bank reporting of his suspicious wire transfers of funds, which were traced as being paid to an illegal offshore front company for an "escort service."

■ **TABLE I**   Real-Life Examples of Reaction Formation
South Carolina governor Mark Sanford was known for conservative views on preserving traditional marriage and for his opposition to government spending. He was shown on national television sanctimoniously scolding Bill Clinton for undermining public trust by lying to officials and for violating the sacred oath of marriage. Sanford was discovered with his mistress in Argentina (with state funds paying his travel), after telling his wife and his staff that he was hiking the Appalachian trail alone.
Richard Barrett was a well-known White Supremacist leader and virulently anti-gay. He was murdered in his home—and the confessed killer was a young African American man who claims that he stabbed Barrett when Barrett propositioned him for sex.
George A. Rekers, a psychologist and ordained Baptist minister, had been an officer of an organization that purports to "cure" homosexuality through therapy. He had once been hired by the state of Florida as a witness in support of the state's proposed ban on adoption by gay couples. On a trip to Europe, he hired a young man to accompany him and carry his luggage—finding the assistant through a gay-sex website and allegedly getting daily nude massages from his young travel companion.
Indiana Representative Mark Souder made abstinence education one of his main issues in office, along with his advocacy of preserving traditional marriage and fighting "the assault on American values." He characterized the abstinence education approach as "teaching morality" to prevent teen sex. He distributed a video showing one of his female staffers interviewing him about his tireless efforts to promote abstinence. He was forced to resign when an affair with a staff member was discovered—and his mistress turns out to have been the interviewer.

when viewing very erotic videos of heterosexual and homosexual couples. Only the homophobic men showed an increase in penile erection when viewing the male homosexual stimuli (Adams, Wright, & Lohr, 1996).

Denial

When a tragedy has occurred, it is sometimes the job of police officers or other public servants to visit homes in their city and inform parents that their child has been killed in an accident or a homicide. Sometimes, the response of the parent is simple: "No, that can't be. I'm on my way now to pick up my child at school." The parent absolutely denies the terrible fact. Similarly, a teenage girl in the advanced stages of an unwanted pregnancy may deny, to herself and to others, that she is pregnant, despite strong evidence to the contrary.

When terrorists destroyed the World Trade Center in New York in 2001, killing over 3,000 civilians, many of the victims were vaporized by the extreme temperatures of the burning jet fuel, or were crushed by the collapsing skyscrapers. Their bodies thus were "missing," and relatives and friends began a fruitless search from one hospital to another, looking for them. When, days later, reporters began asking these bereaved relatives if they had lost hope of finding their loved ones, the most common answer was a calm response that they still had confidence that they would be successful, and everything would turn out fine. It was too much to believe, too much for the human mind to grasp, that one's young, vital spouse, sibling, or child could be obliterated in an instant.

Research on response to physical pain and injury reveals a similar phenomenon. For example, one worker slipped and put a screwdriver through his hand. He did not feel any pain until he looked down at what he had done and saw the blood; then the truth began to "sink in." Soldiers injured in battle or even football players injured on the field often do not feel the pain of their injury until many hours later. The mind has a means of keeping its own sensations out of conscious awareness.

Denial
A defense mechanism in which one refuses to acknowledge anxiety-provoking stimuli

Denial, simply refusing to acknowledge anxiety-provoking stimuli, is a common defense mechanism (Baumeister, Dale, & Sommer, 1998). Although it is usually seen in adults in conditions of severe stress or pain, people will also sometimes distort some aspects of a situation, say, telling their friends that a terrible fight with their spouse was really just a lover's quarrel. In such instances, they lie to themselves. Like repression, denial is a mechanism that has been subject to some active attention by researchers studying stress, coping, and health (Fernandez & Turk, 1995).

Projection

Projection
A defense mechanism in which anxiety-arousing impulses are externalized by placing them onto others

Projection is a defense mechanism in which anxiety-arousing impulses are externalized by placing them, or projecting them, onto others. A person's inner threats are attributed to those around him or her.

Consider an extremist politician on the rampage against people involved in premarital sex, against children born out of wedlock, gay people, and sex education teachers in the schools, claiming, "Those subversive pinkos are wrecking our moral fabric!" Is this politician a noble and moral prophet bringing a better life to all, or a disturbed personality, hung up on sexuality and afraid of the surging id forces within? Freud was willing to apply his theories to major issues in society, such as the causes of prejudice and war.

In some ways, the true motivations of our extremist politicians (or anyone) cannot be scientifically proven. This is one of the weaknesses of this aspect of Freudian theory, and of psychoanalytic theory in general. For example, the traditional Freudian sources of "proof," namely, further disclosures during psychotherapy and improvement in psychological functioning after disclosure or therapy, can easily be the result of other factors. And if the maladaptive patterns continue after psychotherapy, it may be claimed that the unconscious urges are even more deeply hidden; this finding is unprovable. On the other hand, if a politician shows certain accompanying behaviors, then a psychosexual dysfunction seems more likely. In the extreme, if we find that a married politician who is always talking about family values turns out to have a long-time secret lover, then we may rightly wonder if that politician was struggling with his libido using reaction formation (doing the opposite of one's urges) and projection (placing one's urges onto others). This would be confirmed if the politician showed other signs of instability. Other examples are more subtle.

Consider the case of a female community activist who attends school board meetings to ensure that children are not taught about sexuality and birth control in the public schools. She argues that sexuality and contraception are a matter for the family to discuss at home (or in church). If this is really her motivation, then this woman should be able to provide the relevant information to her children; she should be very comfortable with and knowledgeable about such matters as the erection of the penis, the lubrication of the vagina, orgasms, and so on; sexual problems such as premature ejaculation; and sexually transmitted diseases like AIDS and chlamydia. This could be ascertained in private adult discussion. If the woman can intelligently discuss such matters, then a Freudian interpretation does not seem applicable. If, however, the woman turns bright red, becomes extremely hostile, or brings up irrelevant matters when basic facts about human sexuality are discussed, then a Freudian would be confident about the motivation for the woman's behaviors.

An analogous kind of analysis could be applied to a liberal politician or activist who seemed especially concerned with ideas of free love or the public expression of erotic art. Freud's perspective would allow an observer to ascertain whether this is a rational and logical set of beliefs, or an irrational adaptation to uncontrolled, instinctual sexual forces. Discussion and research on defensive projection has remained a fascinating topic throughout this century, with at least some support found for Freud's views (Allport, 1954; Newman, Duff, & Baumeister, 1997; Vaillant, 1986).

There is evidence that people who are less comfortable with ambiguity and uncertainty are more likely to hold conservative views while people who have less need for order and closure are more liberal (Jost, 2006; Jost, Glaser, Kruglanski, & Sulloway, 2003). This does not necessarily mean that one set of views is less rational; some conservatives and some liberals make illogical decisions. Rather, it suggests that we tend to hold some political views that fit well with deep-seated aspects of our personalities.

Many modern studies have documented the existence of unconscious prejudices, especially racial prejudices (Greenwald et al., 2002). For example, one experiment presented participants with a series of African American and White faces, paired with either a positive or negative adjective. Whites with an unconscious prejudice against African Americans should have this prejudice primed by seeing the African American face. The participants' job was to press a key quickly to indicate whether the presented word was positive or negative. Response latency (reaction time) to the negative words paired with an African American face should thus indicate unconscious prejudice. In fact, the results did show that this measure of individual differences in prejudice predicted whether an African American confederate (of the experimenters) later viewed the participants as friendly and positive when she debriefed them about the study (Fazio, Jackson, Dunton, & Williams, 1995).

Displacement

Remember that in the case of Little Hans, the boy was afraid that a horse would bite or step on him, but in actuality he feared that his big, strong father would castrate him. This is an example of **displacement**. Displacement is the shifting of the target of one's unconscious fears or desires.

A classic example of displacement is the case of a man who, when he is humiliated by his boss, goes home and beats his children and kicks the dog. Such an example is an interesting one because there are other theoretically interesting alternative explanations. Displacing the anger to the dog implies that the unacceptable feelings of wanting to kill one's boss are released, more acceptably, on the poor canine. This is a **hydraulic displacement model** that is typical of Freudian explanations. Pressure builds up like steam in a boiler and must be released. Other, non-Freudian explanations would focus more on the situation that releases the aggressive action, or on

Displacement
A defense mechanism in which the target of one's unconscious fears or desires is shifted away from the true cause

Hydraulic Displacement Model
Sigmund Freud's concept that suggests that unacceptable impulses build up like steam in a boiler and must be released

previous learning history, or on the man's aggressiveness, or on his sense of self and sense of purpose. The explanation is important because there are different implications for preventing the aggression (Melburg & Tedeschi, 1989; Neubauer, 1994). According to the hydraulic displacement explanation, some release valve must be found for the bottled-up aggressive impulses triggered by frustration and humiliation.

Overall, there is good research evidence in support of the phenomenon of displaced aggression (Marcus-Newhall, Pedersen, Carlson, & Miller, 2000). Furthermore, the more similar the target is to the provocateur, the more displaced aggression occurs.

Sublimation

Sublimation is the transforming of dangerous urges into positive, socially acceptable motivations (Loewald, 1988). For example, anal retentive impulses based on the holding back of feces might lead to a desire to control and order the lives of everyone at home and at work. Through sublimation, these drives might be transformed to a desire to organize children's activities or to clean up the local riverfront.

Artistic endeavors are often attributed to sublimation. In a psychohistorical analysis of Leonardo da Vinci, Freud (1947) argued that Leonardo's genius arose from his sublimation of sexual energies into a passion for scientific creativity and discovery. Of course, innate talent was also necessary; not everyone with sublimated sexual energies can become a Leonardo. Freud did a similar analysis of Michelangelo.

Freud viewed society as a means to turn sexual energy away from sexual ends and toward societal goals. According to this view, society fears nothing more than that sexual urges may return to their original goal—sexual fulfillment. It can be argued that modern society provides an ongoing test of Freud's theory. Since Freud's prudish time, a sexual revolution and a dramatic sexual liberation have occurred. As people become more and more sexually liberated, psychoanalysis predicts that art, creativity, and even civilization itself will suffer and eventually disintegrate.

Regression

In **regression** we return to earlier, safer stages of our lives. This defense mechanism is most easily seen in children. A recently weaned child may try to return to the bottle or breast. A child who was already toilet trained may begin having "accidents" when a new baby arrives. A threatened child beginning school may begin acting like a toddler. In particular, there may be regression to the stage at which there was previously a fixation.

In adults, regression is more difficult to document. Classic examples include an anxious adult who begins whimpering like a child, looking for maternal care. Or a distraught man may try to curl up to his wife's breast, or a stressed woman may climb into her husband's lap. An adult under stress may seek out the comfort foods of childhood. The regression defense reminds us that psychoanalytic theory is a stage theory: psychosexual development proceeds along fixed, well-delineated steps.

© The Granger Collection, New York

■ Freud analyzed the Italian artist Michelangelo (1475–1564) from archival materials. Freud determined that Michelangelo was a repressed homosexual dominated by his mother, who sublimated his sexual energies into great creativity as a sculptor, painter, architect, and poet. This is Michelangelo's statue of the biblical giant-slayer, David.

Sublimation
A defense mechanism in which dangerous urges are transformed into positive, socially acceptable motivations

Regression
A defense mechanism in which one returns to earlier, safer stages of one's life in order to escape present threats

Rationalization

In the film *The Big Chill* (1983), one character asserts that there is nothing more important than sex. His friend replies, "Oh yeah? Ever gone a week without a rationalization?" **Rationalization** is a mechanism involving post hoc (after the fact) logical explanations for behaviors that were actually driven by internal unconscious motives. Psychoanalysis well recognizes that the explanations we give for our behavior are not necessarily even remotely related to the true causes. Rather than admit that we moved across the country to be near a sexy lover, we may explain (not only to others, but to ourselves) that we were looking for better job opportunities or new challenges. The dangers of rationalization (leading to illogical behavior) have also been emphasized by many other approaches to personality; however, if the defense is not seen as a protection against threatening urges from the unconscious, then it is not a psychoanalytic defense mechanism.

One interesting empirical study of psychoanalytic defense mechanisms has been conducted on a sample of middle-aged and older men who have been followed since they were in junior high school (Vaillant, Bond, & Vaillant, 1986). Descriptions of how these men responded to challenges in their lives were converted into a defense mechanism framework. This work suggests that defensive style is an enduring aspect of personality. The maturity of the defenses, including rationalization, was also found to be associated with independently measured indexes of the men's psychological maturity—better overall mental health. Another study found that people who are politically conservative are generally happier than those who are politically liberal, in part because conservatives are much less bothered by the facts of income inequality—that some of their neighbors are poor (Napier & Jost, 2008). In other words, conservatives may be less emotionally troubled by inequality and so are able to come up with less egalitarian policies, whereas liberals feel emotionally conflicted and so propose higher taxes on the wealthy. According to this argument, neither side truly understands that its policies are rationalizations that arise from hidden emotions.

In a more experimental approach, one fascinating study investigated circumstances in which romantic partners may be unconsciously motivated to make mistakes when judging each other's thoughts and feelings (Simpson, Ickes, & Blackstone, 1995). First, male and female members of 82 dating couples completed questionnaires that assessed the closeness of their relationship and their thoughts or insecurities about its permanence. Next, they sat together and viewed a series of slides, during which the male partner rated prospective female dates according to their physical attractiveness and sexual appeal, and the female partner rated prospective male dates. The stimulus slides showed either very attractive or unattractive potential dates. While they then discussed these choices, the couples were videotaped.

Later, the male and female partners independently viewed the videotape of their discussion in separate rooms, indicating at what points during the interaction they experienced a thought or feeling, what it was, and whether it was positive or negative. Following this, each partner was asked to view the interaction again and was asked to infer what her or his partner had been thinking or feeling at each point. It turned out that dating partners who were close, who were insecure about their relationship, and who viewed highly attractive (i.e., threatening) opposite-sex persons

Rationalization
A defense mechanism in which post-hoc logical explanations are given for behaviors that were actually driven by internal unconscious motives

■ Although the role of psychodynamic, psychosexual forces in human nature is given relatively little attention in modern research in personality, illustrations of the power of these complex forces appear regularly in the news. Consider the case of John G. Schmitz (left photo), an ultraconservative state legislator from California known for strongly espousing family values and for fiercely opposing sex education in the schools. Yet his career ended in scandal when it was discovered that he had a pregnant mistress. Even more interesting, Senator Schmitz was the father of Mary Kay LeTourneau. In 1997, LeTourneau, a 35-year-old married teacher, was convicted of having a sexual affair (and having a child) with a 13-year-old boy in her school. Her own son was only a year younger. She became pregnant again by the teenage boy after her release from prison and was sent back to prison to serve a long term. Upon completion of the second prison term, she once again reunited with the young man (who had turned 21 by then), and married him (right photo).

displayed the least empathic accuracy when they tried to infer each other's actual thoughts and feelings from the videotape. In other words, their abilities to understand their partner's feelings were impaired when there was a threat to their relationship. At some level, they did not want to know the truth about what their partner thought or felt about an attractive potential rival. This study is a good example of how modern personality researchers try to use experiments to explore concepts first proposed by Freud.

Cross-Cultural Issues

Freud explored the unconscious in exquisite detail, but he was relatively unconcerned with possible cultural variations. Although interested in applying psychoanalysis to understanding culture, he believed the same basic psychodynamic forces underlay all cultures, especially the dynamics surrounding the Oedipus complex.

Totem and Taboo, Freud (1912/1952) traced the origin of civilization to the time when brothers came together and murdered the primal father of the tribe, co-opting his power and his wives. Freud thought that this would leave traces in all civilizations in the form of cultural taboos, such as the taboo against incest. Similarly, religion was seen as arising from psychodynamic forces; he did not consider that religion may have created certain psychodynamic forces.

Freud also engaged in psychobiography; in fact, Freud and his colleagues founded this field of inquiry. When he turned his attention to Leonardo da Vinci, Freud analyzed him from archival materials as a repressed homosexual who was dominated by his mother and who sublimated his sexual energies. And again, Freud proceeded to assume that the phenomena he had uncovered were universal. The psychoanalytic principles derived in nineteenth-century Austria could be directly applied to understanding the life of a man in fifteenth-century Italy.

It is known that Germans have stricter child-punishing habits than Americans. Can we therefore infer that the outcome is an inherently rigid German personality (Rippl & Boehnke, 1995)? Analogously, are Americans innovative scientists (winning many Nobel prizes) because they are raised in a more liberal, child-centered society and grow up with an independent personality? Do Japanese schools, with their emphasis on uniformity, produce adults with a personality suited to cooperative work in large, impersonal conglomerates? Although such generalization may at first appear clever, there is a serious logical error in drawing such conclusions. Why attribute such adult behaviors to a culturally induced personality when the culture itself serves as an obvious explanation? Germans drink a lot of beer, but there is no reason to postulate a German beer-drinking personality; they simply live in a culture in which drinking beer is popular. Would we say that Jews have a bagel-and-lox–prone personality? Or that Italians have a pasta-prone personality? It makes much more sense to say that people in a certain culture learn common behaviors from their families and friends. These behaviors are not a result of their personalities; if they moved to a new place with new friends, their behaviors would change. Habits are not personality.

Nevertheless, in order to test such notions of personality and culture, anthropologists turned to projective tests like the Rorschach. They reasoned that such tests (which used inkblot pictures and so were not language-specific) would be applicable (valid) in all cultures. Unfortunately, these cross-cultural studies were plagued by serious methodological flaws and false assumptions (Lindzey, 1961). Most basically, the search for basic, deep-seated personality traits that characterized a culture, using projective measures, was inherently biased. Researchers had preconceived notions of the expected cultural personality, used measures that had not been adapted for and validated in different cultures, and often did not select truly representative samples of people to study. Furthermore, if invalid projective clinical measures of psychopathology are used in cross-cultural research, the whole foreign culture may wind up (and sometimes did wind up) labeled as pathological.

Culturally based personality patterns have not yet been well documented. With newer research techniques that are more sensitive to the unique features of each culture, the prospects for viable cross-cultural research on personality are great (Benet-Martínez & Oishi, 2008; Segall, Dasen, Berry, & Poortinga, 1990).

Major Contributions and Limitations of Freudian Psychoanalysis

Before the twentieth century, before the work of Sigmund Freud, there was no personality psychology. Certainly there were explanations for individual differences. Major theologians saw human behavior as determined by divine influence, by an all-powerful God who controlled or inspired everything. Mechanical medical models saw people as influenced by internal fluids. But there was no *psychology* of human personality and behavior until Freud, following Darwin's example, asked about the reasons for—the functions of—the human mind. And there was no psychotherapy.

Freud further revolutionized psychology with his emphasis on sexuality as a prime element of personality. Ask any young man or woman with bubbling hormones whether sexuality is a significant influence on his or her behavior—whether getting dates is important—and you will hear no dispute. Freud's breakthrough was to extend this idea of dynamic motivation to children—the idea of infantile sexuality—and to generalize it to a pervasive motivational force.

Freud thus stressed the importance of early childhood experiences on adult personality. This assumption has been almost completely accepted in scientific circles as well as popular culture. Few now doubt that neglectful or abusive treatment of young

Famous

Personalities

Lorena Bobbitt

It was just another day in the life of Lorena Bobbitt. Her husband, John Wayne Bobbitt, came home late and made crude sexual advances toward her. This time, she denied him because he was drunk. But, despite her refusal, he overpowered her 5'2" frame and raped her. At 4 A.M., Lorena took the kitchen carving knife to her slumbering husband's penis and dismembered him. She then put the penis, with ice, into a Ziploc bag and held it as she drove around the city. Finally, she discarded it from the window of her car and continued driving, toward the house of a friend.

Lorena was a 24-year-old manicurist who, until that night, appeared to live an average and uneventful life. What could have triggered her to commit such an aggressive act? According to Lorena's later accounts, John had abused her emotionally, physically, and sexually throughout their marriage. She was sometimes beaten, forced to have anal intercourse, and even coerced into having an abortion.

Another complaint was that he never, ever waited for her to come to orgasm. But if this had been going on for four years, what was different about this particular night?

Lorena said that after she was assaulted that evening, she began to have flashbacks about all the other times her husband had terrorized her. She said that she then lost her grip on reality and was not in control at the time she attacked her husband. Twenty-six-year-old John denied abusing his wife, although he did admit to having extramarital affairs. Was Lorena simply getting revenge for his unfaithfulness and making sure that he would never be able to cheat on her again? What might Freud have to say about all of this?

According to psychoanalytic theory, there was more going on here than meets the eye: Lorena's behavior was likely attributable to unconscious motives influenced by her internal sexual conflicts. Lorena was not necessarily a total victim because, Freudians argue, many women have an unconscious desire for suffering (as evidenced by the many battered women who stay in abusive relationships). A more likely explanation is that the problem was Lorena's inability to control her id, which was seeking to relieve her libidinal tensions.

children—especially sexual abuse—can produce devastating impacts throughout their lives. Freud also argued that the essence of personality was formed by age five. This idea too has been widely accepted. The importance of the early years to later life is little challenged, although Freud's developmental approach has been extended throughout the life span by others.

Because people are not generally aware of their inner drives and conflicts, Freud was led to explore and develop another influential contribution—the idea of the *unconscious*. The reality of Freudian slips and the potential of dream analysis are widely accepted. This in turn led to the exploration of different structures of the mind. Freud also showed that mental illness was on a continuum with physical illness and could be approached in a scientific manner. Anyone who seeks psychological counseling owes a debt to Freud. Modern brain research and cognitive psychology confirm many of Freud's observations but disconfirm his postulated structures, which were based on a primitive understanding of the brain.

Because it views behavior as a function of inner conflicts, the psychoanalytic approach is a pessimistic and deterministic view of personality. It is also oriented toward understanding pathology. (See the Famous Personalities box below.) To counteract these emphases, many theorists originally trained in **psychoanalysis** have moved to existential and humanistic approaches. Freud's reliance on a hydraulic model of psychic energy was also exaggerated. Modern researchers give more attention to brain structure and cognitive approaches.

Psychoanalysis
Sigmund Freud's approach to understanding human behavior; also, Freud's psychotherapeutic techniques

In simple Freudian terms, Lorena was suffering from penis envy, which most girls suffer but few act on directly. If Lorena had been able to give birth to her baby, this might have been avoided. Giving birth is one of the ways in which the ego tries to satisfy the female desire for feelings of strength and self-worth that men have by virtue of their male anatomy. Instead, she was compelled by her husband to abort her child, and perhaps therefore she was still seeking to recapture the penis that was denied her at birth. These feelings of desire help explain why she carefully preserved the organ in a Ziploc bag with ice—it was valuable to her.

What is highly unusual in this case is that Lorena actually acted directly on her concerns about her man's penis. According to Freudian theory, such conflicts are unconscious and so usually show up in other ways.

Lorena claimed that she "just wanted him to disappear," and it is interesting that her way of removing him from her life was to remove his penis, causing him to be, in a Freudian view, a worthless and inferior man. The vengeful blow also indirectly enabled her to obtain a penis of her own.

Lorena was tried but acquitted because her impulses were believed to be irresistible. The jury found that she couldn't have prevented herself from doing this act. So in a sense, modern society accepts the idea of overpowering unconscious motivation. Freud might have said that Lorena's ego and superego both failed to control her inner drives, and her id won in its battle for what it wanted most. In fact, Freudian theory has been the subject of many hot disputes about legal theory. In the eyes of the law, if we are sometimes controlled by our ids, how can we be held responsible for our actions?

The Bobbitt case is a good example from which to launch a discussion of the strengths and weaknesses of Freud's theories. On the one hand, it is virtually impossible ever to uncover Lorena's true motivations in a straightforward scientific manner. On the other hand, the tremendous fascination with this case around the world hints that something very basic to human behavior—some deep, dark secret—has been tapped, just as the doctor from Vienna would have predicted.

Psychoanalytic approaches to personality are generally difficult to evaluate as scientific theories. They often are not disconfirmable because there is always another postulated hidden mechanism ready to explain any observations. Controlled studies are rarely employed. This is unfortunate because their absence causes many modern researchers to ignore valuable insights Freud provided. We try to point out the value and the weaknesses of each approach to personality. Psychoanalytic theory may be flawed but it is hardly useless.

Some modern psychoanalysts revere Freud almost as the author of a bible; psychoanalysis has some faddish, unscientific aspects, and many "adherents." Is it fair to blame Freud for his followers' quirks? When Freud set out to study personality and the unconscious, he saw his work as a temporary approximation of how the brain worked. But in some cases, psychoanalytic theory was interpreted as a theory of the physical structure of the brain, with disastrous results. **Psychosurgery**—operating on the brain in an attempt to repair personality problems—has a long and horrific history. In the 1940s, the prefrontal lobotomy was the technique of choice. The surgeons would drill holes into the skull, insert a dull knife, and slice the brain lobes until the patient (who was under only local anesthesia) seemed totally disoriented. The purpose of the surgery was to cut the nerve connections between the higher centers of the brain and the lower "seats" of animal instincts (such as the thalamus), consistent with psychoanalytic theory. If the patient survived the operation as more than a vegetable, he or she often did indeed act less abusively and aggressively than before the surgery. Of course, there are other explanations for the effects of the surgery than those that involve literally cutting unconscious drives.

Psychosurgery
Operating on the brain in an attempt to repair personality problems

Freud was trained as a neurologist and a biological scientist. We could speculate that if he were alive today, he would be a neuroscientist. So, in many ways it is unfair to dismiss vast aspects of Freud's work because some of his assumptions have proved to be wrong. On the other hand, Freud liked being the center of attention and did not take kindly to criticism. His position as the founder and undisputed master of the psychoanalytic approach encouraged much of the unscientific meandering that has been launched in his name.

Freud postulated fundamental, psychoanalytically based differences between men and women. Because little girls do not pass through the Oedipus

CHANGING Personality

What are the implications of psychoanalytic approaches for changing one's personality? At the most basic level, the psychoanalytic view is pessimistic and deterministic, saying that the individual is controlled by inner drives and conflicts. Yet Dr. Freud and his followers treated patients in an often-successful effort to make them feel and function better. According to these views, there are two good ways to improve your personality (beyond years of therapy): First, gain insights into your hidden underlying motivations by keeping track of your slips of the tongue, your dreams, and your unusual hobbies and relationship patterns. For example, notice and then try to figure out why you are so fascinated with automobiles or princesses. Second, capitalize on your unconscious thought processes by welcoming your hunches and feelings of intuition, and "sleeping on" your choices before making a decision. For example, when trying to decide whether to join a new organization, stop analyzing the pros and cons for a few days, and let the inner recesses of your mind work through your deeper inclinations.

complex, Freud asserted that they do not develop a strong moral character; this radical idea has of course been thoroughly discredited. On the contrary, most women do develop a strong sense of guilt, are usually the caretakers of the weak, are empathic, and have a high concern with justice (Block, 1984; Eagly, 1987; Friedan, 1963; Hall, 1990; Tangney & Fischer, 1995; Tangney, Wagner, Hill-Barlow, & Marschall, 1996).

Finally, a key criticism of psychoanalysis is that Freud was relatively unconcerned with interpersonal relations or with the individual's identity and adaptation throughout life. These issues were taken up later by the neo-analysts and the ego psychoanalysts.

Modern Developments from Experimental Psychology

In recent decades, many of Freud's ideas have resurfaced in more mainstream psychology, although somewhat transformed (Dijksterhuis & Nordgren, 2006). For instance, Freud's ideas were tremendously influential in shaping humanistic approaches to personality. As human cognition developed into a strong and rigorous area of study, researchers from within this domain came upon their own need to consider unconscious processes (Hassin, Uleman, & Bargh, 2005). Freud's impact has resurfaced in modern cognitive psychology (Cohen & Schooler, 1997), and despite the fact that the methodologies, approaches, and goals of cognitive psychology are vastly different from those of psychoanalysis, the cognitivists have found themselves looking at many of the same aspects of human behavior that interested Freud.

Before being banished by behaviorism, in the very early years of psychology's development, even the most rigorous experimentalists saw the need to posit internal processes that occurred outside the scope of awareness. Hermann von Helmholtz (1866/1925), a nineteenth-century pioneer in the study of human perception, claimed that visual perception required unconscious inferences to be made. Consider the following example of unconscious sensation. Most people do not fall out of bed each night. Yet in a state of deep sleep, you wouldn't know if someone slipped into your room, looked at you, and walked out. We keep ourselves in bed, but we are unaware of surrounding events. In the morning, we do not remember the times that we almost fell out of bed but caught ourselves in time. This simple example suggests that some sensory systems are constantly at work, even when we are not aware of them. On the other hand, someone hospitalized in a coma or on drugs may indeed fall out of bed; hospital beds have guard rails to prevent such accidents. Thus there must be different types of being unaware or "unconscious." Modern research has followed up on many of Freud's ideas about unconscious processes, although not always in the ways he expected.

Unconscious Emotion and Motivation

Is there any evidence that part of the mind, full of emotional forces, exists outside consciousness? The idea of unconscious motivation is clearly supported by research on emotion, which indicates that emotional-motivational states such as anger can exist independently of thought. Some of this research relies on brain studies that reveal

SHARPEN YOUR THINKING   Current Controversy

Are People Responsible for Actions Outside Their Awareness?

Modern legal systems rely heavily on the concepts of intent (what a person meant to do) and knowledge (what a person knew at the time an event occurred) in evaluating the legal consequences of the person's action. For example, if an automobile hits and kills a pedestrian, the driver may face a variety of possible charges, ranging from no charges up through first-degree murder. The determining factors involve both situational and psychological components. If the driver had no intention to harm the pedestrian, could not have known that the pedestrian would cross the path of the car, was driving appropriately for conditions at the time of the event, and responded appropriately (e.g., braking or swerving to avoid hitting the pedestrian), then the driver would normally not be charged with a crime. A different set of factors would lead to the most serious criminal charges: If the driver had intended to kill the pedestrian, and if the act had been coolly premeditated rather than committed in the heat of rage, then the driver would probably be charged with first-degree murder.

What role should a person's state of consciousness play in the determination of which type of crime, if any, was committed? Suppose the driver was a young man who harbored unconscious hatred of his stepfather, which was suspected by his psychiatrist. If the stepson had the desire to kill his stepfather, but was not consciously aware of that desire, does that change how the stepson should be charged if he kills his stepfather by running him over? Should there be any role in the legal system for including unconscious desires as part of the assessment of intent?

Suppose a young woman was in the late stages of pregnancy, but was in denial about it and did not believe she was pregnant. If she smoked crack cocaine or injected herself with heroin, and her baby was then born addicted, should she be liable not only for her own illegal drug use, but also for child abuse or child neglect for exposing the baby to drugs? In many jurisdictions, there are serious legal consequences for using drugs during pregnancy that exceed the normal consequences for drug use at other times. If the woman had known that she was pregnant, she would be guilty of the additional crime. If she didn't believe she was pregnant despite ample evidence, then what should be her responsibility?

If state of consciousness should have any role to play in determining criminal liability, what methods would be appropriate to use to assess a person's state of consciousness? How can a court determine whether there was conscious or unconscious intent, and how should unconscious intent be interpreted differently from conscious intent? Is it possible to reliably determine whether an intent was conscious? Should people be held responsible for the unconscious motives that may influence their behavior?

distinct neurological systems (Panksepp, 1991). In other words, through the course of evolution, nerve circuits have developed in the human brain that are relatively independent of higher cortical functions involving thinking. These circuits can fire even if not triggered by a higher level (cortical) thought (Winkielman & Berridge, 2004).

Other research on certain emotions reveals that they are innate, universal, neuronally tied to facial expressions, and able to be induced independently of thought (cognition). Sometimes we correctly feel things or learn things without any conscious effort; that is, our intuitions are often valid since they come from parts of the brain that are not under conscious control (Dijksterhuis & Nordgren, 2006; Wilson, 2002). All of this research is consistent with the Freudian notion that we can experience internal emotion and motivation that we do not cognitively understand or appreciate. Freud could not have known the precise biological structures that comprise the brain, but many of his guesses were on the mark (Izard, 1992).

Illusion of Free Will

A cornerstone of Freud's approach is that we do things out of unconscious motivation, not free will. For example, say we intend to (want to) get up and get something to eat, and we do so. Is this action a response to our will, or might it be that our action is caused by unconscious forces, but we explain or rationalize it as something we wanted to do? Studies in neurology (measuring brain waves) and in experimental psychology (which manipulate the causal attributions we make) suggest that we often misunderstand these causal relations in our bodies. What if our brain shows activity before we decide to take action and our conscious intention to act is actually an afterthought—a thought that develops as our brain has begun directing our body to take action? In fact, there is evidence that just such a sequence sometimes occurs (Berns, McClure, Pagnoni, & Montague, 2001; Wegner, 2002; Wegner & Erskine, 2003).

Relatedly, schizophrenics who hear voices in their heads usually think someone is talking to them—perhaps God, the devil, or a dead relative; that is, they understand the voices as coming from outside themselves. It is too troubling to believe that one does not understand what is inside one's own head. But an observer knows that the "voices" are really coming from a disturbance inside the schizophrenic's brain. In an analogous way, it may be that we all do not really understand what is motivating us, and we explain away our actions by attributing them to our desires and intentions. Other examples involve strong survival drives, such as when we eat a quart of ice cream after consciously "intending" to go on a diet, or when we become sexually attracted and behave in ways that others deem irrational (but which we can certainly "explain"). In other words, the questions of free will and unconscious motivation are now a topic of modern research for those studying the brain and behavior. It remains to be seen whether and when the conscious mind exercises free will.

Hypermnesia

When sitting and talking with a childhood friend, we described an experience we enjoyed together long ago—making ice cream sundaes. Suddenly, our friend's memories came flooding back, as she recalled various related experiences that she had not remembered in thirty years. **Hypermnesia** (literally, *excess memory*) refers to a situation in which a later attempt to remember something yields information that was not reportable on an earlier attempt to remember. A central phenomenon in the psychoanalytic literature, hypermnesia has its counterpart in modern-day cognitive psychology research (e.g., Madigan & O'Hara, 1992).

Hypermnesia
A situation in which a later attempt to remember something yields information that was not reportable on an earlier attempt to remember

In general, human memory tends to fade over time as the original event becomes more distant. The characteristic finding in memory experiments is that people show the best memory for an event when they are questioned immediately following its occurrence, and that their memory declines (at first rapidly, and then more slowly) as time passes. A traditional explanation from stimulus–response psychology ("learning theory") is that the memory or association extinguishes or disappears over time; it is eroded away. That, however, is not the whole story of human remembering. Many factors other than the simple passage of time have now been shown to be important determinants of what can be reported.

In psychoanalysis, free association is used as a key method of uncovering memories that are initially not accessible to the patient's consciousness. After years in analysis, people often do report previously "forgotten" (unreported) material: traumatic events from their childhoods or evil wishes and terrifying thoughts from their pasts. These recovered memories are viewed within psychoanalysis as the fruit of the joint efforts of patient and therapist to overcome the defense mechanisms that initially succeeded in keeping the memories repressed. There are two basic questions that a skeptic (or a modern-day cognitive psychologist) would ask: First, are these memories veridical; that is, did these past events, wishes, and thoughts that the patient now reports really occur? Second, did these memories just now rise to consciousness, having earlier been inaccessible, or is it rather that the analyst and the analytic environment help evoke the report of the memories?

In psychoanalysis, the difficult task of verifying childhood memories is usually not even attempted. But, from the perspective of understanding human memory, it is a critically important issue. In everyday life, people often report vivid memories that turn out to be inaccurate in light of objective factual information. For example, an eyewitness to a crime is certain she recognizes a suspect, who later turns out to have been out of the country; a student reports a vivid memory of being in Spanish class when he heard about the explosion of the *Challenger* shuttle, but his transcript shows that he didn't take Spanish that year; and so on (Harsch & Neisser, 1989). Sometimes people are quite confident in their false memories, and their later behavior is affected (Conway, 1996; Loftus, 2004; Pezdek & Banks, 1996).

The second critical question—whether the information is newly remembered versus newly reported—is one that has been explored in the memory experiment. One robust finding is that different methods of probing a subject's memory for an event yield different amounts of information recalled (Baddeley, 1990). For example, suppose two groups of subjects study a word list. Subjects in one group are then given blank sheets of paper and asked to write down as many words from the list as they can remember (a procedure known as **free recall**). The other group is given pairs of words and asked which word from each pair appeared on the list (a procedure called **forced-choice recognition**). Not surprisingly, subjects' reports are more accurate in the forced-choice condition; it is easier to correctly select the studied word from a presented pair than it is to generate it without any external cues. Does this mean that the strength or accuracy of the underlying memories differed between the groups? Given that the groups were not differentiated until the time of testing, it can only be the method of testing that causes the apparent difference in memory. The availability or accessibility of a memory can be increased by providing appropriate cues, hints, and probes (Tulving & Osler, 1968). In the psychoanalytic setting, directed questioning by the therapist or talking about events related to the previously unavailable memory may allow or prompt its retrieval. In this way, cognitive psychology has validated this aspect of psychoanalytic remembering (Erdelyi, 1996, 2006).

Can hypnosis help? Should police interrogators use hypnotists to help elicit longrepressed memories of criminal molestation? Early in his development of psychoanalysis, Freud and his colleague Josef Breuer used hypnosis—intensive suggestion by the therapist—to attempt to access hidden memories in their patients. In modern experimental psychology research, this enhanced memory under hypnosis would be termed "hypnotic hypermnesia" (Kihlstrom, 1998). Lab experiments demonstrate that hypnotic hypermnesia does sometimes appear—hypnosis is sometimes effective in increasing reported memory—but it is not any more effective than other memory-enhancing effects such as using relevant cues to elicit the memory. In fact, hypnosis

Free Recall
A procedure in which a person studies a word list and then reports as many words as he or she can remember from the list

Forced-Choice Recognition
A procedure in which a person studies a word list and then chooses which word appeared on the list from pairs of words

Classic to Current

Are Psychoanalytic Insights Still Useful?

Sigmund Freud and his associates developed the basic ideas of the psychoanalytic approach a century ago. Has modern personality research made these ideas as extinct as the dinosaurs, ready to be dumped in the pile of fossilized intellect? Or are these ideas, like those of Charles Darwin, still a vibrant force in modern science? The answer is some of each.

In a paper called "The Scientific Legacy of Sigmund Freud: Toward a Psychodynamically Informed Psychological Science," Drew Westen (1998) argues that psychoanalytic insights are alive and well. Although many of Freud's specific postulates have been surpassed by findings in modern biology and neuroscience, many of Freud's insights and issues remain current. Reports of his intellectual demise are premature. To be fair, we need to consider the evolution of psychoanalytic insights and not rely solely on the precise formulations that Freud first offered.

Freud's most central insight was that much of mental life—including thoughts, feelings, and motives—is unconscious. In other words, people sometimes do things for reasons that they themselves do not understand. Westen points out that the psychological unconscious is now an important topic in personality psychology, cognitive psychology, and cognitive neuroscience, as scientists endeavor to understand how parts of the brain sometimes process and respond to sensation and information without direct involvement of the self-conscious higher processes of the neocortex. As we have noted, there is implicit perception, implicit memory, and implicit motivation. We sometimes "see" things without consciously knowing that we are seeing them, we sometimes learn and remember things without consciously knowing how or that we have learned them, and we sometimes act for reasons hidden deep inside our complex motivational systems. For example, we sometimes handicap or enhance our performance for reasons of which we are not conscious.

Second, much modern research documents that people can have and act on unconscious feelings, such as when they are subtly hostile or defensive toward members of ethnic minority groups or other out-groups. Strained interpersonal relations between groups are often the result. Psychoanalytic clinicians have long been willing to pay attention to signs of hidden emotion, by observing nonverbal behavior (such as facial expressions, shifting posture) and verbal behavior (such as nervous shifts in topic, disorganization in narratives). As Freud proposed, such inner conflicts are usually a sign of defense mechanisms, a basic psychodynamic construct. For example, experimental studies that make people more aware of their mortality (such as by having them complete a mortality relevant questionnaire or placing signs of a funeral home nearby) often lead them to respond defensively, although they have no awareness of the feelings that are affecting these responses or the effects on their behavior. This is postulated to be a death anxiety (Strachan, Pyszczynski, Greenberg, & Solomon, 2001). Or people may bolster their own self-esteem by derogating out-groups (but not know why they are doing so). As we have seen in this chapter, a considerable body of evidence has documented links between early experiences such as abuse, neglect, and family disruptions in childhood and later interpersonal problems and personality disorders, outside of awareness.

Although some of Freud's ideas, such as his views about the inferiorities of women, were undoubtedly biased by the milieu of his times, many of Freud's insights are reflected in the most modern psychological research.

FURTHER READING

Strachan, E., Pyszczynski, T., Greenberg, J., & Solomon, S. (2001). Coping with the inevitability of death: Terror management and mismanagement. In C. R. Snyder (Ed.), *Coping with stress: Effective people and processes* (pp. 114–136). New York: Oxford University Press.

Westen, D. (1998). The scientific legacy of Sigmund Freud: Toward a psychodynamically informed psychological science. *Psychological Bulletin, 124*, 333–371.

seems somewhat less effective (Kihlstrom & Barnhardt, 1993); in other words, experimental research supports the superiority of free association and related exploratory and cueing processes over hypnosis. Freud was correct in abandoning hypnosis early in the development of psychoanalysis.

Infantile Amnesia

Infantile Amnesia
The phenomenon of adults being unable to remember what happened to them before age three or four

According to Freud, most human motivation arises from desires in early childhood that are unacceptable in adult society, such as a boy's desire for intimate relations with his mother. We have seen that adult neuroses are viewed as the result of repressed internal conflicts. In support of this idea, Freud insightfully noted that most adults cannot remember much from their early years (although they can remember quite a bit from their elementary school years)—a phenomenon termed **infantile amnesia**. This observation that adults and older children do not remember much of what happened to them before age three or four has been confirmed in a number of studies (Pillemer & White, 1989). Yet young children certainly do a tremendous amount of learning during these years, and they seem to have good memories at the time (Oakes, Ross-Sheehy, & Luck, 2006). A three-year-old can do a remarkable job of describing last week's visit to the zoo. Are these memories later repressed?

As with much of Freud's work, the phenomenon is accepted but the explanation has changed. One problem with Freud's idea is that his theory explains only why threatening early memories are forgotten, yet practically all early memories are forgotten, not merely the traumatic ones. So recent attention has been focused more on the cognitive structure of memory. Perhaps young children have a brain that is too immature and disorganized for long-term memory (Richmond & Nelson, 2007). But research indicates that even young children have at least some well-organized memories that are similar to those of adults (Bauer, 2007; Nelson, 1993). In one study, memories of preschool classmates tested by a direct, explicit method (pick out your classmates from among these photos) were quite poor. But other measures that did not require reporting who was a classmate showed that the classmates were, at some level, familiar (Newcombe, Drummey, Fox, Lie, & Ottinger-Alberts, 2000). The memories exist, but we do not have easy access to the memories for explicit reporting.

It may be the case that young children have not yet developed the ability to think about their own history or the ability to share their memories with others in conventional ways. For example, older children may talk about how lucky they were to go on a favorite vacation and thus practice (rehearse) the memory and incorporate it into an idea of how they think about themselves (Nelson, 1993). Then the event is much easier to remember. Note also that this explanation is linked to the idea of forming an identity, which is precisely what Freud asserted. Although the reasons why we forget our earliest and most important years are still being studied, Freud was asking a significant question.

Memory

The direct study of human memory provides many good examples of how cognitive descriptions intersect with psychoanalytic ones. The verbal learning approach—learning word lists—has generated thousands of published experiments about how subjects' later memory for the studied words is affected by the ways in which the materials are presented. Two phenomena repeatedly noticed in this research are relevant to a cognitive reinterpretation of Freudian ideas. First, what is remembered about an event is not identical to the event itself, but rather is a personalized, interpreted, internalized representation of that event. Two people who are exposed to what is overtly the same event will not necessarily have identical memories of that event.

Instead, every person experiences every event from a unique, individual perspective that depends on that person's needs, goals, assumptions, and other experiences, both at the moment the event is experienced as well as before the event occurred.

The more complex the original information is, the more variability there will be in what is remembered. A complex story engenders more varied recollections than does a simple word list. In other words, memory is an integration or blend of information about the actual event and a person's expectations and beliefs (Bartlett, 1932; Owens, Bower, & Black, 1979). Such findings verify Freud's notions that extraneous factors distort memories, but the emphasis in modern research is more on the complex structures of the mind and less on defenses against unwanted thoughts.

Even this individualized memory is not one single, crystallized entity that must be either present or absent in the person who experienced the event, but rather it is a complex, multifaceted, constantly changing representation. What is reported about the event (even whether anything at all is reported) varies tremendously with the circumstances under which that memory is probed. Memories that can be shown by various means to "be there" might not be reported by a subject who is questioned at a different time or by a different method or experiencing a different mental state (see Figure 2). In modern jargon, a memory might be available but not always accessible. These findings are relevant to a Freudian view because they exemplify a methodologically rigorous approach to aspects of consciousness and the unconscious that are central to Freud's work. In psychoanalysis, the therapist will encourage repeated attempts to remember important early memories, to remember the context of the events (such as the house where they occurred), the people who were involved, and the feelings that were present. All of these strategies are consistent with what modern research shows is helpful in remembering (e.g., Williams & Hollan, 1982). Most people going through such therapy report achieving a clearer understanding of important influences in their lives that they had never considered before. There is even some neuroscience evidence for repression. Using functional magnetic resonance imaging (fMRI) to study neural systems involved in keeping unwanted memories out of awareness, researchers found increased dorsolateral prefrontal activation and

■ FIGURE 2

Sleepwalking and Sleepeating as Unconscious Processes

Sleeping pills such as Ambien can release a primitive motivation to eat, causing some patients to sleepwalk into their kitchens and eat huge portions of food. In the morning they do not remember anything but may wonder about the peanut butter smudges on their pillows (Saul, 2007).

TIME LINE

The History of Psychoanalytic Approaches to Personality

The major developments in the psychoanalytic approach can be seen here in historical relation to one another and in relation to their broader societal and cultural contexts.

Developments in Psychoanalytic Aspects of Personality		Societal and Scientific Context
Little attempt to plumb the unconscious, except for some exorcism	before 1800	Humans are seen primarily in religious or philosophical terms
Charcot and Janet study hysteria and hypnosis, visited by Freud	1800s	Increasing attention to evolution and brain function; comparisons between humans and other animals
Freud develops notions id, ego, superego, repressed sexuality (libido), and dream analysis	1890–1910	Period of industrial and technological change; Victorian era with patriarchal families, respectability, and religious conformity
Neo-analysts begin break with Freud, disputes about drives and defense mechanisms, death instinct proposed	1910–1930	Increasing technology and industrialization, large technical armies, World War I 1914–1918, rise of behaviorism in American psychology
Freud flees Nazis in Austria and dies in England	1930s	Economic depression, social unrest, propaganda; psychiatry grows in United States
Psychoanalytic thought influences various theories of drives, motivation, attachment, conflict, amnesia, illness, and more	1920s–1940s	Freud's ideas appear in art, literature, films, medicine, comedy, and throughout Western culture
Classic (orthodox) psychoanalytic approaches separate from mainstream personality psychology	1950s–1960s	Psychoanalysis becomes more of a clinical and medical tool, of less direct interest to personality researchers
Modern experimental and cognitive psychology and linguistics offer new explanations for Freudian phenomena	1960s–1990s	Great advances in brain sciences; progress in assessments and in developmental psychology
Freudian ideas reinterpreted in light of modern knowledge	2000s–	Brain imaging in science; complexities of social pathologies recognized

reduced hippocampal activation; that is, there is neuroscience evidence for "motivated forgetting" (Anderson et al., 2004). All of this is consistent with Freud's basic point that a great deal of what constitutes personality lies beneath the surface of conscious awareness.

Although cognitive psychology uses different terminology, many of Freud's notions about the existence and importance of the unconscious are mirrored in modern cognitive approaches. For example, experiments have been able to demonstrate remembering without awareness. We typically think of memory as **explicit memory**—we can recall or recognize something. But there is also **implicit memory**—we might change how we think or behave as a result of some experience that we do not consciously recall (Schacter, 1987, 1992). People frequently "forget" (that is, fail to show evidence of any explicit memory for) a prior experience like solving a puzzle or learning a new motor skill, but at the same time they show in their skill at actually performing the task that they have practiced it before. In other words, the person being studied cannot consciously remember some event that the experimenter knows has occurred because it happened within the setting of the experiment, and that the subject was clearly conscious of at the time it occurred. But at a later time, although the subject cannot consciously remember having had that experience, she or he still performs the task better than a novice presented with the task for the first time. This dissociation between explicit and implicit memory demonstrates that experiences that are not consciously remembered can still influence our behavior, including our behavior toward others (Chartrand, Maddux, & Lakin, 2005).

Amnesia

Interesting cognitive research on the entire phenomenon of memory without awareness has focused not on ordinary people but on patients with a form of amnesia in which no new conscious memories can be successfully retrieved even minutes after an experience has occurred. You could have a long conversation with such a person, then leave the room and return five minutes later—and the amnesic will claim never to have seen you before! What is fascinating about these patients, though, is that they can learn new skills. For example, one such patient with **anterograde amnesia** was given repeated practice over many days in solving a complex maze. Over time, his skill at tracing out the correct path through the maze improved, just as it would in a person with normal memory. What is interesting is that even as he became extremely proficient in performing the task, he claimed each day that he had never before so much as seen the maze (Milner, 1962). His performance clearly showed the influence of experiences for which he had no reportable memory.

Memory research on such amnesic patients focuses on exposing them to many categories of experiences (such as learning new motor skills, hearing new songs, meeting new people, reading new facts, and the like), and looking for principles that differentiate the kinds of experiences that can be reported as "remembered" from the kinds of experiences that influence performance even though they are not "remembered." In this research, one prominent finding has been that the ability to report experiences as consciously remembered does not coincide with the extent to which those "forgotten" experiences influence behavior (Graf, Mandler, & Squire, 1984; Warrington & Weiskrantz, 1978). That is, there is strong evidence for a dissociation between the conscious memories of amnesic patients and those events that have actually influenced them. To the extent that this finding is applicable beyond the clinical population, it implies that many experiences that influence our ongoing psychological lives are not readily available to consciousness, just as Freud suggested. Modern research also finds evidence for the idea that there are different systems

Explicit Memory
A memory that can be consciously recalled or recognized

Implicit Memory
A memory that is not consciously recalled but that nevertheless influences behavior or thoughts

Anterograde Amnesia
The inability to form new conscious memories

operating independently in the brain, outside conscious awareness, and with occasional communication between systems (Kihlstrom & Glisky, 1998).

As noted, Freud thought that repressed beliefs, feelings, and desires show up as errors in speaking (or writing) that distort what the person consciously intended to say. A perspective from experimental *psycholinguistics* (the study of the psychology of

■ **TABLE 2** Reinterpreting Slips of the Tongue (and Pen)

What Was Said	Psychoanalytic Interpretation	Psycholinguistic or Written Explanation
Gentlemen, I take notice that a full quorum of members is present and herewith declare the sitting closed.	The speaker consciously intended to open the meeting, but unconsciously wished for it not to proceed. (*This is Freud's own interpretation of this example.*)	The terms *open* and *closed* are closely associated semantically; the unintended word *closed* was highly activated by the intention to say *open*.
I have a snore neck …	The problem of the sore neck is unconsciously believed by the speaker to somehow be related to sleeping.	*Sore* is changed to *snore* due to phonological anticipation: the *n* sound that will be uttered in *neck* is moved to the preceding word *sore*. Error made more likely because it forms a real word.
I'm allergic to lasses … glasses.	Speaker reveals his fear and distaste toward females or has an unconscious association between a pair of round eyeglasses and female breasts.	Consonant cluster *gl* is reduced. May be caused by perseveration of the initial sound of the previous stressed syllable (*LER* in *allergic*).
I worry about testes all week …	The student is unconsciously worried about his sexual identity. He may fear infertility or be worried that he got his girlfriend pregnant.	*Tests* and *testes* are almost identically spelled, differing only by the presence of an *e* (which is often silent in that position).
Magellan was the first man to circumcise the globe.	The student has severe castration anxiety.	In searching for the correct word in his mental lexicon, the student is seeking an uncommon verb that begins with the prefix *circum-*. When he finds one, he utters it.
[The industrial revolution brought] a mechanical raper that could do the work of ten men in half the time.	The student views rape as a common avenue by which male sexuality is expressed.	In writing an unfamiliar word for an unfamiliar concept, the cognitive effort required makes error more likely. In this situation, the first letter *e* is accidentally dropped (from *reaper*). The resulting error forms a legitimate word, making it less likely that the writer will notice the error.

Sources: Examples are taken from Hansen (1983), Freud (1917), Jaeger (1992), and Dell (1995).

language) explains the same errors without mentioning psychodynamic mechanisms. Some examples are shown in Table 2. Further, Freud viewed the unconscious as the repository for the libido—the most threatening, most sexually charged, most socially unacceptable, most irrational drives. Cognitive psychologists view the unconscious

Evaluating the Perspectives

Advantages and Limits of the Psychoanalytic Approach

- **Quick Analogy**
  - Humans as a bundle of sexual and aggressive drives constrained by civilization.

- **Advantages**
  - Emphasizes the effects of patterns established early in life on personality development.
  - Attempts to understand unconscious forces.
  - Considers basic motivational drives of sex and aggression.
  - Considers defense mechanisms as an essential aspect of personality.
  - Assumes multiple levels are operating in the brain.

- **Limits**
  - Pessimistic overemphasis on early experiences and destructive inner urges.
  - Relatively unconcerned with interpersonal relations or with the individual's identity and adaptation throughout life.
  - Difficult to test empirically.
  - Many ideas about structure have been discredited by more modern research on the brain.
  - Assumes any deviation from heterosexual relations is pathological.
  - Focuses on male behavior as the norm and female behavior as a deviation.

- **View of Free Will**
  - Behavior is determined by inner drives and conflicts.

- **Common Assessment Techniques**
  - Psychotherapy, free association, dream analysis.

- **Implications for Therapy**
  - Because personality problems are the result of deep inner conflicts, real change must come through long-term, insight-oriented psychotherapy, in which you explore your inner self through hypnosis, free association, or dream analysis, guided by your highly paid psychotherapist. Traditional psychoanalytic psychotherapy can last years, but newer shorter-term, insight-oriented psychotherapies try to create a therapeutic alliance between practitioner and client in which the client is guided toward meaningful insights.

much more benignly as a collection of information (memories, concepts, processes) currently outside the limited scope of conscious awareness, either because it is irrelevant, because it is too weakly represented to be called forth, or because it is by its nature represented in a manner incompatible with conscious awareness. For example:

- You might not consciously be aware of your memories of your first teenage date as you currently go about dating or hoping to date. Is this because those memories are not relevant to your current focus of attention or because there is some unresolved sexual urge?

- You might not be readily able to recall the names of all the second-grade teachers in your elementary school on request, although you knew them all when you were in second grade. Is this because those memories are too weakly represented to be easily accessed without proper cueing or because you were sexually molested at about that time?

- You can't explain why you intensely dislike the taste of olives, or how you even identify the taste of olives. Can this process never be brought into consciousness, or do you have repressed feelings about testicles?

In the cognitive view of the unconscious, there is no active process of protection from the potentially painful and harmful contents of the unconscious (Kihlstrom, 1987). It remains to be seen whether Freud was overgeneralizing and overinterpreting his observations about unconscious processes and memory, or whether modern psychologists tend to overlook a phenomenon of great importance.

Summary and Conclusion

Although Sigmund Freud is sometimes treated as a historical curiosity by laboratory-oriented modern personality researchers, a misreading of Freud's impact may lead one to overlook the numerous insights that psychoanalytic theory can add to our understanding of personality. Many of Freud's startling ideas have been disproved or superseded by modern research in biology and psychology, but many others are alive and highly influential even today (Westen, 1998). This chapter points out the significant intellectual contributions but also notes the limits and failures of the psychoanalytic approach.

Early in his career, Freud began to develop his theories of the importance of the unconscious, initially using hypnosis to tap this area of the mind but soon moving on to free association and dream analysis.

Freud believed that dreams and other thoughts are made up of images that are readily accessible to recall (or manifest) but that these images are often symbolic of unconscious issues and tensions (that is, they have latent meaning).

As Freud listened to the dreams and problems of his patients—and as he remembered his own childhood—he developed the theories of the structure of the psyche and of psychosexual development for which he is well known today. According to Freudian theory, individuals have a core being, called the *id*, which is the most primitive part of the psyche and which is motivated to obtain pleasure. At the next level is the *ego*, whose goal is to find practical ways to satisfy the needs of the id. Finally, the *superego*, which is similar in concept to the conscience but includes an unconscious aspect, internalizes societal norms and guides our goal-seeking behaviors toward socially acceptable pursuits.

Freud's psychosexual theory of development proposed that individuals encounter stages in their developmental trajectories in which certain goals are most important. He further posited that if the conflict associated with a particular stage were not resolved, the individual would become *fixated* at that stage. The first stage (*oral stage*) is a period during which drives to satisfy hunger and thirst are of paramount importance; individuals who become fixated here are overly concerned with issues of dependency and consumption. The second stage (*anal stage*) deals with the relief of defecating and issues of doing so at socially appropriate times; individuals fixated at this stage may be passive-aggressive or excessively neat or sloppy. During the third stage (*phallic stage*) the focus is on the genitals, and it is during this time that boys are postulated to face an *Oedipus complex* (whereas girls experience an *Electra complex*), resolved through identification with a parent. The fourth stage is relatively longer than the first three stages and is termed the *latency stage* because sexual energies are not visible but are channeled into more academic and friendship pursuits. The successful resolution of the last stage (the *genital stage*) is indicated by a healthy adult heterosexual relationship, loving marriage, and the rearing of a family. The idea that the patterns of resolution of such childhood conflicts can greatly influence adult personality has generally been accepted, but many of the specific predictions have not been strongly supported or have been proven to be too closely tied to Freud's times, culture, and biases.

Freud also developed complex but influential theories of defense mechanisms—the mind's attempts to distort reality to make life more palatable and less threatening. One key defense mechanism is *repression*, or the ability to relegate painful memories to the unconscious. Posttraumatic stress disorders and repressed memories of sexual abuse, issues often seen in today's headlines, are direct applications of this idea of repression. In *reaction formation*, if a person has urges that go against his or her own fundamental beliefs, these urges may be transformed into their opposite form and that opposing urge may then be acted on. A related mechanism is that of *sublimation*, the transformation of dangerous urges into altruistic or otherwise useful and socially desirable motivations. *Denial*, another defense mechanism, is the inability (or refusal) of the mind to acknowledge some undesirable reality; in cases in which the truth cannot be completely denied, portions of it may be distorted. *Projection* occurs when anxiety-provoking impulses are attributed to someone else, rather than being claimed by the individual who generated them. *Displacement* occurs when threatening feelings are transferred to something or someone other than their true cause; the new target is generally more manageable and less threatening than the original target. In *regression*, individuals "go back in time" to a safer and happier period in their lives, to escape present threats. Although regression may be seen in early childhood, it is difficult to substantiate in adults. Finally, and perhaps most common, is the defense mechanism of *rationalization*—assigning logical explanations to behaviors and events that were originally motivated by unconscious motives.

Freud's ideas continue to draw significant criticism, perhaps most wittily conveyed by the novelist Vladimir Nabokov who said, "Let the credulous and the vulgar continue to believe that all mental woes can be cured by a daily application of old Greek myths to their private parts" (Nabokov, 1973). Although Freudian theory is sometimes denounced as primitive, it should be remembered that Freud's ideas were bold and innovative, fostering many important later developments in theory and research. In addition to the extensive current psychoanalytic theory and practice that grew directly out of the work of Freud, Freudian theory can be used as a basis to begin exploring many current topics in psychology. For example, *hypermnesia*, the phenomenon in which a later attempt to remember something yields information that was not reportable on an earlier attempt to remember, has taken a central place in modern psychology research, as the remembering of supposedly early memories involving child abuse is studied. Likewise, *infantile amnesia*, the phenomenon that people generally do not remember things from infancy and very early childhood, is of great interest to those studying child development and language. Studies of implicit memory, also popular today, are derived from Freudian ideas about the unconscious, even though modern research techniques and theories are based on much new knowledge. Finally, although Freud's preoccupation with human sexuality and the id are nowadays viewed as an over emphasis, it remains to be seen whether Freud overinterpreted his observations or whether modern psychologists are missing phenomena of great consequence.

■ Key Theorist

Sigmund Freud

■ Key Concepts and Terms

unconscious
manifest content versus latent content
structure of the psyche—id, ego, superego
pleasure principle versus reality principle
psychosexual theory of development
libido
Oedipus complex
castration anxiety

penis envy
defense mechanisms
hydraulic displacement model
hypermnesia
infantile amnesia
explicit memory versus implicit memory

Neo-Analytic and Ego Aspects of Personality: Identity

© Kevin Mazur/WireImage/Getty Images

What happens to the personality of young music stars or Hollywood actors, who move from a struggle for recognition to suddenly being surrounded by fans, reporters, photographers, and an entourage of admirers and hangers-on? Do they believe that they deserve their new-found status? Can they trust their new celebrity friends? Will they rely on values from youth or move to adopt the fast-living, exciting lifestyle of their new surroundings?

What about a college student who is studying to be a doctor, but

From Chapter 4 of *Personality: Classic Theories and Modern Research*, Fifth Edition. Howard S. Friedman, Miriam W. Schustack. Copyright © 2012 by Pearson Education, Inc. Published by Pearson Allyn & Bacon. All rights reserved.

sometimes cannot sleep nights, kept awake by worries about her career choice? She does well in her premed studies, but she is the first in her family to head toward medicine. She has left behind her high school friends, and sometimes she is not sure about who she is and what she should do. She resents the sexist comments made by her male classmates about "ugly women doctors." We would understand if she were said to be having an "identity crisis."

How does this compare to someone who struggles to relate to peers—who is overly concerned with how his self-image compares to the status of others? This young adult is always trying to outdo others, but still feels inferior. Could it be that this pattern of responding originated in unresolved conflicts from his or her childhood?

I n puberty and young adulthood, individuals face sexual maturity (and the ability to act on sexual urges), a break with the continuity of childhood, and a great concern with how they are seen by others. The psychoanalyst Erik Erikson (1950) described these psychosocial events as a stage of development, which often shows itself in such well-known teenage phenomena as cliques and puppy love. If this stage of life is successfully negotiated, the teenager can go on to the next stage— mature adulthood—capable of true intimacy.

The term "complex" was coined by C. G. Jung to refer to repressed drives that affect later behavior (as in Freud's Oedipus complex). But the word was soon applied by psychoanalyst Alfred Adler to refer to a child's struggle to repress and thereby overcome feelings of being small and powerless. For example, a young boy might feel himself to be inferior in everything from athletic ability (compared to his older brother) to penis size (compared to his father), and an intrapsychic struggle to cope with these matters would inevitably ensue. Adler called this complex the "inferiority complex," the same term that is now in common usage.

What is significant about Adler's notion is that it involves comparisons and rivalries with other people. For Adler, *social* interest is a primary source of motivation. The internal drives emphasized by Freud are complemented by external pressures, especially those arising from relationships.

Neo-Analytic Approach
The approach to personality psychology that is concerned with the individual's sense of self (ego) as the core of personality

Although Sigmund Freud believed that people are dominated by their instincts (id), major thinkers working in the Freudian tradition soon recognized and argued for the importance of the feelings of self (ego) that arise throughout life from our interactions and conflicts with others. The term "ego" as used by these individuals is not quite the same as the Freudian ego. Here, the idea of the ego is broader, defining the core individuality of the person. Because these theorists start from psychoanalysis but expand it in new directions, this approach is often called **neo-analytic** (that is, the "new analysis"). Furthermore, in the latter half of the twentieth century, these ego approaches allowed the development of theories of the self that ever more completely discard Freudian notions of the id but still emphasize motivations and social interactions (Brenner, 1994). All these approaches are less biological, more social, and thus more optimistic than Freud's approach. They are the subject of this chapter.

Carl G. Jung and Selfhood

History abounds with stories in which the crown prince or successor has a bitter falling out with the king or the board chair. Take, for example, the biblical account of Absalom's treason against his father, King David. Even if you are not familiar with the story, you can probably correctly guess many of its components. You might guess that King David was a wise and good ruler who tried to do what was right. You might also guess (correctly) that Absalom was a spoiled and greedy son who became so enchanted with the idea of having power and riches that he was willing to betray his own father in order to obtain these things for himself.

Why is it that such themes spring so easily to mind? Why is such a scenario so easy to imagine? Carl Jung believed that we are preprogrammed to see and accept certain truths not only because of our own past experiences but also because of the cumulative past experiences of our ancestors. The story of David and Absalom has repeated itself over and over again through the centuries. But not all of the stories are so extreme. The next time you are flipping through TV channels, look at the lineup on many of the talk shows: children feuding with parents and stepparents, employees sniping in bitter antagonism against their bosses, and "followers" denouncing their gurus and stepping out to become leaders and champions of their own causes. This pattern was also true of Freud and Jung, with Carl Jung (Freud's "crown prince") providing the key initial break with Freudian orthodoxy.

Background to Jung's Approach

Jung's Childhood

Carl Gustav Jung was born in July 1875, in Kesswil, Switzerland. He grew up in a religious home; his father, the Reverend Paul Jung, was a country minister, and his mother, Emilie, was a minister's daughter. Jung's theories of personality were unique, and their roots can be traced to thoughts and experiences from his childhood. In particular, two childhood themes would later become the basis for his theory of personality.

The first was his belief that he was, in fact, two different personalities: he was both (1) the child that he outwardly appeared to be and (2) a wise and cultured gentleman of the previous century. Jung was an introverted and withdrawn child who spent much time alone, in solitary play and contemplation. He would often sit on a large stone in his garden and focus on two ideas: that he was a boy sitting on a stone and that he was a stone being sat upon by a boy. His ability to take the perspective of the rock gave him the idea that he might actually have more than one form of being. This notion seemed to solidify when the father of a friend chastised him for a misdeed. As he was being scolded, he suddenly felt indignant that this man should be treating *him* in such a way. *He* was an important and distinguished person who should be respected and admired. At the same time, he was aware that he was also a naughty child, presently being reprimanded by an adult.

The second key theme from Jung's childhood was that the visions and dreams he often experienced were not unimportant coincidences, but instead were valuable communications of information from the realm of the paranormal. This idea would later form the basis for his concept of the collective unconscious. Around the age of

10, Jung carved for himself a small wooden mannequin, carefully dressed it in homemade attire, and hid it, along with a small painted stone, in the attic of his house. Thinking of this mannequin and stone hidden away secretly together was pleasurable for Jung and somehow had the ability to calm him when he became distressed. He would also write coded messages on little scrolls of paper, to be tucked away with the mannequin—a sort of furtive library for its pleasure (Jung, 1961a).

Beginnings of Jung's Theory

It wasn't until years later, while doing research for a book, that Jung read about prehistoric "soul stones" (located near Arlesheim) and ancient monumental statue-gods. As he read, he easily formed a mental picture of the stones and statues because they were very similar to his painted stone and mannequin of childhood. He had never before seen pictures of these objects, nor had he read about them (he checked his father's library to be sure), yet he had created them for himself as a young child! These occurrences indicated to him that there were certain psychic elements that are common from generation to generation, passed through an unconscious channel.

Jung studied medicine at the University of Basel, and it was here that he became interested in psychiatry. He graduated in 1900, the same year that Freud's *Interpretation of Dreams* was published. Jung read in 1906 began a correspondence with Freud. The two quickly became mutual admirers, and by April 1907, it was clear that Freud had chosen Jung as his protégé to carry on the psychoanalytic tradition (Brome, 1981).

Although things went smoothly for a time, Jung believed that the goals and motivations of individuals were just as important in determining their life courses as were their sexual urges. He had come to believe in the existence of universal archetypes (emotional symbols), which he recognized over and over in his conversations with patients. While Freud believed that personality was largely fixed by middle childhood, Jung preferred to look at personality in terms of its goals and future orientation. Eventually, the rift between these two pillars of psychological thought grew to the extent that a parting of ways seemed the only answer. They went their separate

■ Carl Jung's (1875–1961) analytic psychology was less sexually focused, more historically oriented, and more attuned to the spiritual and supernatural than Freud's psychoanalytic psychology. Jung was very open to alternative ideas. When he conducted a psychoanalysis of Christiana Morgan, an upper-class "free spirit" (who served as a kind of erotic muse), he was so taken that he came to view her as the quintessential "anima" (the feminine spirit), and he encouraged her to engage in a scandalous affair with Harvard personologist Henry Murray (with whom she helped develop the TAT) (Douglas, 1993; Robinson, 1992).

© The Granger Collection, New York

directions in 1913, after which Jung withdrew to the privacy of his home for a period of solitude and introspection that lasted for several years. During this time, he searched himself deeply, getting to know the individual components of his psyche. He put intensive effort into keeping a private journal, later called "The Red Book," in which he wrote in multiple languages using beautiful calligraphy and drew the elaborate, colorful images that had appeared to him in dreams and visions. (Although the journal was seen by very few people during Jung's lifetime and was locked in a Swiss bank vault upon his death, his heirs eventually decided years later that the book was an important part of Jung's legacy and allowed a facsimile edition to be published [Jung, 2009].) When his period of focused self-examination ended, Jung was firmer than ever in his belief that the basic tenets of his theory were universally valid. To distinguish his theory from that of Freudian psychoanalytic theory, he called it *analytic psychology.*

Jung's Analytic Psychology

According to Jungian theory, the mind or **psyche** is divided into three parts: (1) the conscious ego, (2) the personal unconscious, and (3) the collective unconscious.

The Conscious Ego

Jung's **ego** is quite similar in scope and meaning to Freud's. It is the aspect of personality that is conscious, and it embodies the sense of self. (Jung believed that this personal identity, or ego, developed around age four.)

The Personal Unconscious

Jung's second component of the mind, the **personal unconscious**, contains thoughts and feelings that are not currently part of conscious awareness. Thoughts from the personal unconscious can be accessed, however. The personal unconscious contains thoughts and urges that are simply unimportant at present as well as those that have been actively repressed because of their ego-threatening nature. For example, when you are in psychology class you are not thinking about last night's date (we hope). That information has not been repressed; it's just not relevant at the moment. The person sitting next to you might harbor deep resentment and animosity toward a sibling because of extensive past rivalries and yet belong to a family in which love for family is of paramount importance. This individual might repress these resentments because they threaten her ability to view herself as a "good" person. Both of these thoughts and urges are considered to be part of the personal unconscious by Jung. Jung also saw the personal unconscious as containing both past (retrospective) and future (prospective) material. This grew from the observation that many of his patients experienced dreams that were related to future issues and events. It is not that they "see" the future, but rather they sense things that are likely to happen. Further, the personal unconscious serves to *compensate* (balance) conscious attitudes and ideas. That is, if a person's conscious views are very one-sided, the personal unconscious may accentuate the opposing viewpoint through dreams or other means, in an attempt to restore some sort of equilibrium (Jung, 1961b, 1990). (Happiness would lose its meaning if it were not balanced by sadness.) Modern research confirms that there are such automatic mental processes outside of conscious attention that influence how

Psyche
The essence of the human mind or spirit or soul; in Carl Jung's theory, personality as the dynamic sum of its parts

Ego
In psychoanalytic theory, the personality structure that develops to deal with the real world; in neo-analytic theory, this term refers to the individuality of a person that is the central core of personality; and specifically for Carl Jung, it is the aspect of personality that is conscious and embodies the sense of self

Personal Unconscious
According to Carl Jung, the component of the mind that contains thoughts and feelings that are not currently a part of conscious awareness

we react to others in particular situations and how we pursue our goals (Bargh & Williams, 2006). For example, if we have been thinking about our friends or we are in a good mood, we are more likely to behave altruistically.

The Collective Unconscious

Collective Unconscious
According to Carl Jung, the component of the mind that contains a deeper level of unconsciousness made up of archetypes that are common across all people

Archetypes
In Carl Jung's neo-analytic theory, emotional symbols that are common to all people and have been formed since the beginning of time

Animus
According to Carl Jung, the archetype representing the male element of a woman

Anima
According to Carl Jung, the archetype representing the female element of a man

Persona Archetype
According to Carl Jung, the archetype representing the socially acceptable front that is presented to others

Did you ever have the feeling of déjà vu—that you have previously experienced something that you, in actuality, have not seen before? The third component of the psyche was termed the **collective unconscious** by Jung. Perhaps the most controversial, it comprises a deeper level of unconsciousness and is made up of powerful emotional symbols called **archetypes**. These images are common to all people and have been formed from the beginnings of human time (that is, they are "transpersonal" rather than personal or individual). These archetypes are derived from the emotional reactions of our ancestors to continually repeating events, such as the rising and setting of the sun, the changing of the seasons, and repeating interpersonal relationships such as mother–child. The presence of such archetypes or emotional patterns predisposes us to react in predictable ways to common, recurring stimuli. Jung described many different archetypes, including the hero, the wise old man, the trickster, and the shadow, all of which clearly appear in popular movies such as the *Star Wars* films (with the wise old Obi-Wan Kenobi, the demonic Darth Vader, the hero Luke, and so on). The following are descriptions of some of his best-known archetypes (see also Table 1).

ANIMUS AND ANIMA.   Two important archetypes are the **animus** (the male element of a woman) and the **anima** (the female element of a man). The animus archetype implies that each woman has a masculine side and a corresponding innate knowledge of what it means to be male; the anima archetype implies that a feminine side and therefore a knowledge of what it means to be female resides in every man.

PERSONA AND SHADOW.   These two opposing archetypes represent the differences between our outward appearances and our inner selves. The **persona archetype** (Latin for "mask") represents the socially acceptable front that we present to others. Although each persona, when viewed outwardly, is idiosyncratic, the archetype itself is an idealized picture of what people should be; it is modified by each individual's

■ TABLE 1 Jung's Archetypes and Modern Symbols	
Archetype	**Examples**
Magician (or Trickster)	Sorcerer, wizard, clairvoyant
Child-God	Elf, leprechaun
Mother	Wise grandmother, virgin Mary
Hero	King, savior, champion
Demon	Satan, anti-Christ, vampire
Shadow	"The dark side," evil twin
Persona	Mask, social façade, actor

unique efforts to achieve this goal. In contrast, the **shadow archetype** is the dark and unacceptable side of personality—the shameful desires and motives that we would rather not admit. These negative impulses lead to socially unacceptable thoughts and actions, much as the unchecked desires of Freud's id might instigate outrageous behavior.

MOTHER.   The **mother archetype** generally embodies generativity and fertility. It may be evoked by an actual mother-figure (for instance, one's own mother or grandmother) or a figurative one (for example, the church). Additionally, the mother archetype may be either good or evil, or perhaps both, much as real mothers have the potential to be.

HERO AND DEMON.   The **hero archetype** describes a strong and good force that does battle with the enemy in order to rescue another from harm. The opposite of the hero is the **demon archetype**, which embodies cruelty and evil. In our example of David and Absalom, King David would represent the hero, whereas his ungrateful son would be the demon.

Jung's beliefs about the collective unconscious and its archetypes, although intriguing, should not be accepted without thoughtful skepticism. Modern scientific psychology doubts the existence of the collective unconscious, at least in the sense of *memories* in the brain that resulted from the experiences of our ancestors. However, a more complex version of Jung's idea probably does have some validity. For example, all infants and young children throughout the world are fascinated by animals, but also are predisposed to fear snakes (LoBue & DeLoache, 2010) (see Figure 1).

Throughout time people seem to struggle with the same issues over and over. For example, for thousands of years war has been waged in the name of gods, and even today this continues. Another issue that every generation wrestles with is gender differences: What are the differences and how important are they? Our Western society has progressed far from the days early in the twentieth century when women could not attend college, could not vote, and were considered to be the property of their husbands. But despite this greater equality, society is still interested in *differences*.

Shadow Archetype
According to Carl Jung, the archetype representing the dark and unacceptable side of personality

Mother Archetype
According to Carl Jung, the archetype that embodies generativity and fertility

Hero Archetype
According to Carl Jung, the archetype that represents a strong and good force that does battle with the enemy in order to rescue another from harm

Demon Archetype
According to Carl Jung, the archetype that embodies cruelty and evil

Dave King/© Dorling Kindersley Media Library

■ **FIGURE I**

Fear of Snakes.

Evidence ranging from Eve's encounter in the Book of Genesis to modern experimental research in primatology and experimental psychology (Shibasaki & Kawai, 2009) suggests that humans share an evolved fear of snakes. People are quick to notice snakes, very quickly learn to fear snakes, and can react to snake stimuli outside of conscious awareness (Ohman & Mineka, 2003). Such findings may indicate that the human brain has a form of "collective unconscious."

Why Does It Matter?

Why does it matter whether there is a collective unconscious common to everyone and full of primordial (ancient, primeval) ideas? To the extent the idea is valid, it helps us understand universal mythologies, explains commonalities in literatures, provides a basis for gut-level empathy, and gives a basis for numerous intuitive realizations. But if the idea of a collective unconscious is invalid, then common or universal themes and ideas must somehow emerge from the combination of more primitive instincts with the general structures of societies.

Why do we continue to be interested in topics like gender differences and finding the "true God" or the "right religion"? Perhaps because, on some level, Jung was right. It seems that we as people share certain interests, certain passions, in a way that borders on instinct. These sorts of questionings and strivings are part of what it means to be human. For Jung, a successful life involves a process of *self-realization*, through which a person integrates archetypes from the unconscious into a more fully developed self. Some of the more modern theories try to be more "objective" in their data, at the expense of ignoring these deep and fundamental questions. To avoid that mistake, we try to show the strengths *and* weaknesses of the various approaches to personality.

Complexes

Complex

A group of emotionally charged thoughts, feelings, and ideas that are related to a particular theme

For Jung, a **complex** is a group of emotionally charged feelings, thoughts, and ideas that are all related to a particular theme (for instance, an adolescent celebrity's inferiority feelings). The strength of any given complex is determined by its libido, or "value." Note that Jung's definition of libido differs from Freud's in that it describes a general psychic energy that is not necessarily sexual in nature.

Jung substantiated his claims of the existence of complexes with his word-association test. He presented his clients with a list of words (see Table 2), arranged in what he believed was an optimal ordering scheme, and the clients

■ **TABLE 2**   Some Stimulus Words for Jung's Word-Association Test

head	blue	frog	to wash
green	lamp	to part	cow
water	to sin	hunger	friend
to sing	bread	white	happiness
death	rich	child	lie
ship	to prick	pencil	narrow
to pay	pity	sad	brother
window	yellow	plum	to fear
friendly	mountain	to marry	stork

Instructions: After each word is read to you, respond immediately with the first word that comes to your mind.

Interpretation: First, for each word, note if you answered immediately or experienced a delay. Then, list the words for which you experienced a response delay, gave a very unusual response, gave a long or multiple-word response, or showed some emotion. Finally, see if you can find a theme in these special words. Jung thought that this theme provided a peek into your unconscious.

Source: Adapted from Jung (1910).

were to respond to each word with the word that most quickly occurred to them. Jung and his colleagues would measure the amount of time it took a client to respond (delays indicating an abnormality or conflict of some kind), rate of respiration, galvanic skin response, and memory on retest. In this way he identified certain words that produced emotional arousal, and with prodding, these words could often be used to uncover the nature of the complex. Interestingly, similar (but more sophisticated) methods are used today in cognitive psychology. Jung believed that personality is made up of opposing forces that continually pull against one another, thus establishing (in the healthy person) some measure of equilibrium. He eventually concluded, however, that the word-association test by itself was not able to discriminate properly between feelings related to imagined stimuli and feelings related to actual occurrences, and he abandoned the method.

Functions and Attitudes

Jung posited four *functions* of the mind: (1) sensing ("Is something there?"); (2) thinking ("What is it that is there?"); (3) feeling ("What is it worth?"); and (4) intuiting ("Where did it come from and where is it going?"). Thinking and feeling were termed rational by Jung because they involve judgment and reasoning. In contrast, sensing and intuition he called irrational because conscious reasoning is virtually absent from these processes. Although all of these functions exist in every individual, one of them normally dominates.

In addition to these four functions, Jung described two major *attitudes:* **extroversion** and **introversion**. These terms are in wide use today but are generally understood as being opposite poles of the same dimension, rather than two separate and opposing constructs as Jung thought of them. And, analogously to functions, extroversion and introversion both exist in every individual, but one is usually dominant. Extroverts direct their libido (psychic energy) toward things in the external world, whereas introverts are more inwardly focused. The combination of these two attitudes with the four functions yields eight possible personality types (Jung, 1924). Take, for example, a person whose dominant function is feeling and whose dominant attitude is extroversion; the "feeling" tendencies of the person would be directed outward. That is, in general, the person would make friends readily, would tend to be loud, and would be easily swayed by the emotional feelings of others. If, however, the predominant attitude was introversion, the feeling tendencies of the person would be channeled into introspection and a preoccupation with inner experiences that might be interpreted as cold indifference and, ironically, a *lack of feeling* by observers. Thus, you can see that any dominant function may take on a very different flavor when paired with one or the other of the two attitudes, yielding eight very different categories or types of personalities. This typology forms the basis for one well-known personality inventory—the Myers-Briggs Type Indicator.

Most significantly, it was Jung who challenged Freud and broke new conceptual ground about motivation and the ego, allowing other approaches to flourish. Further, Jung's willingness to concern himself with more mystical and spiritual aspects of personality had an important influence on existential-humanistic approaches. Like Freud, Jung was one of the intellectual giants of the early twentieth century, sweeping away medieval cobwebs

Extroversion (Jung)
A term used by Carl Jung to describe the directing of the libido, or psychic energy, toward things in the external world

Introversion (Jung)
A term used by Carl Jung to describe the directing of the libido, or psychic energy, toward things in the internal world

of ideas that had been passed down for generations and opening up new ways of thinking about what it means to be a person. However, Jung was more a philosopher than a scientist.

Alfred Adler—The Inferiority Complex and the Importance of Society

A while back, the U.S. attorney general commented on the importance of being an advocate for children's rights, stating that "working with dropouts at 12 and 13 is too late—they'd already formed inferiority complexes" (Liu & Cohn, 1993). As noted earlier, Carl Jung coined the idea of complexes, but the *inferiority* complex is Alfred Adler's contribution.

Born in Vienna in February 1870, Alfred Adler was a frail child and, in fact, came close to death on several occasions. He suffered from rickets, which often forced him to play the role of observer to his siblings' games. During his fifth year he contracted such a severe case of pneumonia that the family doctor gave up hope of his recovery (fortunately, his parents sought a second opinion). He was run over in the street, not once, but twice—the trauma being extensive enough to cause him to lose consciousness (Orgler, 1963). These flirtations with death and the knowledge of his own fragility left him feeling powerless and fearful. He determined to become a physician in order to learn to defeat death.

Adler studied medicine at the University of Vienna (and although Freud lectured at the university while Adler was there, the two did not meet then), graduated in 1895, and started his own practice soon thereafter. He was married two years later to Raissa Epstein; two of their four children later went on to become psychologists.

Adler's Differences with Freudian Theory

In 1902, Adler was one of those invited to attend some small, casual seminars with Freud. Although his views were somewhat different from those of the Freudian psychoanalysts, he remained a member of the group for a number of years. But by 1911, the disagreements between Freud and Adler had become heated and emotionally intense; Adler resigned from his position as president of the Vienna Psychoanalytic Society (as the group had come to be called) and ended all contact with it. The debates with the domineering Freud and other members of the group had, however, helped Adler think through his own emerging theory of personality. He soon started his own society, called the Society for Free Psychoanalysis (later changed to the Society for Individual Psychology).

One of the central ways in which Adler's views differed from those of Freud was the emphasis each placed on the origin of motivation. For Freud, the prime motivators were pleasure (remember that the id operates on the so-called pleasure principle) and sexuality. For Adler, human motivations were much more complex.

■ Alfred Adler (1870–1937). Many of Adler's theoretical constructs (inferiority complex, organ inferiority, masculine protest) echo his personal experiences as a sickly child.

Adler's Individual Psychology

Adler called his theory **Individual Psychology** (1959) because he firmly believed in the unique motivations of individuals and the importance of each person's perceived niche in society. Like Jung, he firmly proclaimed the importance of the teleological aspects, or goal-directedness, of human nature. Another major, and related, difference in their philosophies was that Adler, much more concerned than Freud with social conditions, saw the need to take preventive measures to avoid disturbances in personality.

Striving for Superiority

For Adler (1930), a central core of personality is the striving for superiority. When people have an overwhelming sense of helplessness or experience some event that leaves them powerless, they are likely to feel inferior. If these feelings become pervasive, an **inferiority complex** may develop. An inferiority complex takes normal feelings of incompetence and exaggerates them, making the individual feel as if it is impossible to achieve goals and therefore hopeless to try. Take the case of David, who has never done very well in school. He's not a terrible student, but beside the honor-roll records and academic accomplishments of his two siblings, his record looks paltry. Over time, he has developed an inferiority complex—an uncomfortable sense of being dull, even inferior to his brother and sister.

An individual struggling to overcome such a complex might fabricate a **superiority complex** as a way of maintaining a sense of self-worth, and in fact this is what David has done. If you were to meet him for the first time, you wouldn't guess that there was an "inferior" bone in his body. He appears to have a very high opinion of himself—always bragging and quick to argue that his solution to a problem is the right one. If you look a bit deeper, though, you see that this exaggerated arrogance is really an overcompensation for what David believes he lacks; he has developed a superiority complex as a way of counteracting the inferiority he feels. He is trying to convince others and himself that he is valuable after all. Unfortunately for David, superiority complexes are usually perceived as obnoxious by others, and he is therefore likely to be treated with reserve or even distaste when he exhibits his overbearing attitude. This rejection in turn might increase his inner feelings of worthlessness, leading to even more aggressive compensation—and a maddening spiral has begun. As the satirist Ambrose Bierce put it in *The Devil's Dictionary* (1911), an egotist is "A person of low taste, more interested in himself than in me."

The Evolution of Adler's Theory

Adler's theory underwent a series of changes as his thoughts about human motivations changed. The first concept he described was that of **organ inferiority**—the idea that everyone is born with some physical weakness. It is at this "weak link," says Adler, that incapacity or disease is most likely to take root, and so the body attempts to make up for the deficiency in another area. He contended that these infirmities (and perhaps more important, individual *reactions* to them) were important motivators of people's life choices.

A short time later, Adler added the concept of the **aggression drive** to his model. He believed that drives could be either directly effective or reversed into

Individual Psychology
Alfred Adler's theory of personality that stresses the unique motivations of individuals and the importance of each person's perceived niche in society

Inferiority Complex
According to Alfred Adler, an individual's exaggerated feelings of personal incompetence that result from an overwhelming sense of helplessness or some experience that leaves him or her powerless

Superiority Complex
According to Alfred Adler, an exaggerated arrogance that an individual develops in order to overcome an inferiority complex

Organ Inferiority
Alfred Adler's concept that everyone is born with some physical weakness at which point incapacity and disease are most likely to take place, but the body attempts to make up for the deficiency in another area

Aggression Drive
Alfred Adler's concept that an individual is driven to lash out against the inability to achieve or master something, as a reaction to perceived helplessness

SHARPEN YOUR THINKING   Current Controversy

The Theorist's Life or the Theorist's Theory?

The theorist himself or herself is presented as a topic of interest because it is tempting to speculate about the relationship between aspects of the theory and aspects of the theorist's personality. In scientific domains beyond psychology, this approach would not usually be feasible. Is looking at the theorist as part of the theory a helpful approach? Does it provide a view of the theory that would not otherwise be available? Is it an invasion of the theorist's privacy? Is it too speculative to provide solid evidence?

Sometimes the characteristics and experiences of the theorist had an acknowledged role to play in the development of the theory. For example, in discussing Jung's notion of the collective unconscious, we point out his childhood experiences of perceiving himself with dual identities and his creation of a wooden talisman and painted stones. Jung himself had identified these early experiences as contributing to his later views on the commonality across time and culture of people's underlying understanding of the world, thus the connection

between theorist and theory is an important part of the creation and evolution of the theory.

Is it equally sound, though, when the connections between theory and the theorist's personal experiences and characteristics are made by external observers? In our treatment of Alfred Adler, for example, we point out the possible connection between his own frailty and poor health as a child and his promulgation of the theoretical construct of "organ inferiority." Does knowing that Adler himself was sickly and disabled change the way you think about that aspect of his theory? Should it?

When are the personality and life experiences of the theorist relevant to understanding and evaluating the theory? How deeply into the theorist's personal life do we have the privilege to delve? Is it nosiness or valid scientific curiosity that drives the writers of secondary sources to the theorist's personal life? Should we be looking as broadly and deeply as possible at the theorist's life and worldview, or should we understand and evaluate theories purely on their own merit?

---

an opposite drive (similar to a Freudian defense mechanism). Aggression was particularly important to Adler because he believed it was a reaction to perceived helplessness or inferiority—a lashing out against the inability to achieve or master something.

Adler's next step was what he termed the **masculine protest**. He did not mean, however, that only boys experienced this phenomenon. During that period in history, it was culturally and socially acceptable to use the words *femininity* and *masculinity* as metaphors for inferiority and superiority. Adler believed that all children, by virtue of their relatively powerless and dependent position in the social order, were markedly feminine and that both boys and girls experience this masculine protest, in an effort to become independent from and eventually equal to the adults and people of power in their little worlds. Masculine protest is an individual's attempt to be competent and independent—autonomous, rather than merely an outgrowth of one's parents. Sometimes, striving for superiority can be healthy, if it involves a positive assertiveness. This search for autonomy and for a sense of control and efficacy was later incorporated into the theories of many other personality psychologists (White, 1959).

A key concept for Adler was **perfection striving**. He believed that people, unless neurotically bound to an inferiority complex, often spend their lives trying to meet their **fictional goals**—imagined future achievements. (This is sometimes termed "fictional finalism.") These goals vary from person to person, reflecting what each

Masculine Protest
According to Alfred Adler, an individual's attempt to be competent and independent rather than merely an outgrowth of his or her parents

Perfection Striving
According to Alfred Adler, an individual's attempt to reach fictional goals by eliminating his or her perceived flaws

Fictional Goals
According to Alfred Adler, strivings for self-improvement that vary from person to person but that reflect an individual's view of perfection

person sees as perfection and requiring the elimination of their perceived flaws. The belief in the reality of such fictional goals is sometimes called an "as if" philosophy. For example, one of Cleo's fictional goals is to have a "perfect career." She envisions herself sailing through school with good grades, completing a prestigious internship, and being invited to join an international company with a pleasant working environment, enviable pay, and a chance to travel. Of course, she will also be very successful and efficient in her job, pleasing all of her superiors and amazing them with her great talent. In reality, Cleo is not "sailing" through school; she is working very hard to maintain her high GPA. It remains to be seen whether she will get a prestigious internship or just a run-of-the-mill job and whether she will climb the corporate ladder or be a bench player. But having these fictional goals gives her focus and motivation, and envisioning her sparkling future is its own small reward. If she set her sights lower, it is likely that she would never achieve any of these dreams.

Adler was very concerned with individuals' perceptions of social responsibility and their social understanding. Building on Freud's attention to love and work, Adler identified three fundamental social issues that he believed everyone must address: (1) **occupational tasks**—choosing and pursuing a career that makes one feel worthwhile; (2) **societal tasks**—creating friendships and social networks; and (3) **love tasks**—finding a suitable life-partner. He also believed that the three were intertwined; that is, experiences in any one arena would have influences on the other two.

The Role of Birth Order

By focusing on social structure and making astute observations (both of others and of his own childhood), Adler came to believe in the importance of birth order in determining personality characteristics. *First-born children* live for a time as the favored child because they are "only children." They later must learn to deal with the fact that they are not the sole focus and that parental attention must be shared with the other sibling(s). This rather rude awakening may create the tendency for independence and striving to regain status, or the first-born may become a socially oriented pseudo-parent, helping to nurture siblings and others. *Second-born children* are born into a situation of rivalry and competition. (In the animated movie *Antz*, the ant named "Z," voiced by Woody Allen, complains that "It's hard being the middle child of five million.") Adler himself felt a great sense of rivalry with his older brother, and his inability to compete on a physical level because of his ill health led to subsequent feelings of inferiority. Although this may be useful in that it pushes the second child toward greater achievements, repeated failures have the potential to be quite damaging to the self-esteem. *Last-born children* are usually more pampered than any of the others. They will remain forever the "baby of the family." Adler believed that the overabundance of sibling role models might lead this child to feel overly pressured to succeed in all areas, and the likely inability to do so might result in a lazy and defeatist attitude.

These ideas about birth order and personality (which actually derived in part from the earlier work of Francis Galton) have generated a tremendous amount of research; among the many findings, first-borns are indeed more likely to go to college and to achieve success as scientists (Simonton, 1994). But later-borns may be more likely to be creative, rebellious, revolutionary, or avant-garde. The book *Born to Rebel* (Sulloway, 1996) proposes that revolutions in science, religion, politics, and social movements are very disproportionately driven by later-borns. On the basis of

Occupational Tasks
According to Alfred Adler, a fundamental social issue in which one must choose and pursue a career that makes one feel worthwhile

Societal Tasks
According to Alfred Adler, a fundamental social issue in which one must create friendships and social networks

Love Tasks
According to Alfred Adler, the fundamental social issue of finding a suitable life partner

a broad review of the biographies of 6,000 people prominent in Western history, Sulloway concludes that while first-borns show a pattern of high achievement, they are overwhelmingly less likely than later-borns to propose or support revolutionary viewpoints.

Sulloway points to the dynamics of the family—in which first-born children adopt survival strategies different from those of their later-born siblings—to explain this effect of birth order on the propensity to foment dissent and accept radical ideas. Charles Darwin himself is a classic example of a later-born revolutionary: The data on which Darwin based his theory of evolution in 1837 were broadly available to scientists of his era, but it took the rebelliousness of a later-born to recognize that the data required a heretical rethinking of the accepted doctrine of divine design. Note that, for Sulloway's approach as well as Adler's, it is not the birth order position per se that is important, but rather the motivations it creates. Adler thus paved the way for many future motivational psychologists.

Birth order studies do not usually separate the effects of biological birth order from the effects of rearing order. For example, if the first-born child dies at birth, then the second-born child is the oldest sibling. Or, if a first-born child is adopted into a family that already has children, this new child is biologically first-born but reared as a later-born. There are known biological differences between pregnancies (e.g., the uterus is smaller during the first pregnancy, the hormonal environment is different, the nursing breasts may be different, and so on). Future research therefore should pay more attention to disentangling what happens when the biological birth order is different from the rearing order (Beer & Horn, 2000). Nevertheless, there is good evidence that first-borns are more achievement-oriented and more conscientious than later-borns (Paulhus, Trapnell, & Chen, 1999; Healy & Ellis, 2007).

Adler's Personality Typology

Adler cast his ideas into the classic Greek notion of temperamental humors underlying personality. According to these ancient ideas, a predominance of yellow bile was indicative of an irritable (**choleric**) temperament; a predominance of blood was believed to result in a cheerful (**sanguine**) temperament; black bile resulted in a brooding (**melancholic**) temperament; and phlegm resulted in a lethargic (**phlegmatic**) temperament. To this basic pattern, Adler added his ideas about varying levels of social interest (termed **Gemeinschaftsgefuhl** in German, or "community feeling"), as well as a consideration of activity level.

As Table 3 shows, Adler renamed the four components of his typology: (1) Ruling-Dominant (aggressive and domineering), (2) Getting-Leaning (takes from others; somewhat passive), (3) Avoiding (conquers problems by running away), and (4) Socially Useful (meets problems realistically; is cooperative and caring). This orientation was thought to grow out of early experiences. Adler wrote that a body that is ill-suited to its environment will be felt by the mind as a burden. Children who have suffered from such "imperfect organs" are challenged to try to overcome their limits, either in an active way that is not social (becoming domineering), in an active way that is social (cooperation), in a passive way that is not social (taking what others dish out), or in a passive way that is depressed (running away from problems). For many children with physical or intellectual disabilities, the mind becomes overburdened and they become self-centered (egoistic). The road to physical and mental health involves

Choleric
A personality type based on the ancient Greek humors discussed by Hippocrates and Galen in which one is angry against the arbitrary controls of one's life and has generally poor interpersonal relations

Sanguine
A personality type based on the ancient Greek humors discussed by Hippocrates and Galen in which one is hopeful and cheerful

Melancholic
A personality type based on the ancient Greek humors discussed by Hippocrates and Galen in which one is brooding, sad, and depressive

Phlegmatic
A personality type based on the ancient Greek humors discussed by Hippocrates and Galen in which one is apathetic and conforming on the outside but tense and distraught on the inside

Gemeinschaftsgefuhl
Community feeling: Adler's term for a person's level of social interest

Greek Humors	Greek Types	Social Interest	Activity	Adler's Types
Yellow bile	Choleric	Low	High	Ruling-Dominant
Phlegm	Phlegmatic	Low	Low	Getting-Leaning
Black bile	Melancholic	Very low	Low	Avoiding
Blood	Sanguine	High	High	Socially Useful

■ **TABLE 3**   A Comparison of Adler's Typology with Classical Greek Typology

overcoming this self-centeredness. As with most grand theories, it has proved very difficult to establish a simple, empirical validation of this typology.

Some of Adler's conceptions concerning the great importance of social situations were further developed by Harry Stack Sullivan. Adler also paved the way for thinkers like Erich Fromm, who accepted both the basic, biologically driven side of personality and the severe societal restraints on personality, but who also tried to reconcile these forces with ideas of creativity, love, and freedom. Perhaps Adler's greatest gift to personality psychology was his insistence on the positive and goal-oriented nature of humanity. He leaves us with a picture of people striving to overcome their weaknesses and to function productively—in other words, people contributing to society.

Karen Horney—Culture and Feminism

When a bright, ambitious girl named Karen Danielson was growing up in Hamburg, Germany, at the end of the nineteenth century, she faced many personal and social challenges. Her father, a sea captain, had lost his first wife after having four children. He remarried the attractive and sophisticated Clotilde, who was 18 years his junior. They had a son, and four years later, a daughter—Karen. Karen thus grew up in a world of stepsiblings who never fully accepted the new family additions (Horney, 1980; Quinn, 1987).

Her father, 50 years old when she was born, was a stern and very religious man. He based his beliefs about the inferiority of women on his interpretations of the Bible, and he ruled his family with a firm hand. Although he was more openly affectionate with Karen's brother Berndt, he nonetheless did care for Karen. He sometimes brought her gifts from far-off lands and even allowed her to accompany him on several trips aboard his ship. Thus Karen grew up with conflicting feelings toward her father: She admired him, yet she felt less loved by him than she would have liked. She and her mother were quite close, however.

Although Karen was not unattractive, she believed that she was homely, and early on she determined that if she could not be pretty, at least she could be intelligent. She loved school and became an excellent student. By the time she was 12, she had decided to become a physician, a choice that did not please her father. But with Karen, Berndt, and Clotilde all urging him, he finally agreed to provide the tuition money for Karen to attend a premedical school.

In society at large, relations between the sexes were in turmoil at this time. Women were clamoring for more rights and educational opportunities. Karen was one of the first women to be allowed to attend advanced high school (the German gymnasium). Medical schools were also just opening their doors to women. In 1906, Karen began her medical training in Freiburg, Germany. It was during this time that she met Oskar Horney (pronounced *Horn*-eye), and the two quickly developed a strong friendship. They married in 1909, and by 1910, their first child was on the way. This was a stressful year of many changes for Karen. She was newly married and pregnant. She was undergoing psychoanalysis with Karl Abraham, a disciple of Freud, to ready herself for the practice of psychiatry. And, to top it all off, her mother died shortly before Karen's own child was born.

Karen and Oskar had three children in all, and each of the daughters later remembered that their mother was somewhat detached from them during childhood.

Famous **Personalities**

Hugh Grant's Ego

It was 1:30 in the morning. A man was driving home from a late dinner in Los Angeles. Cruising in his white BMW down Sunset Strip, he saw a woman walking. He stopped and gave her $45, she got in the car, and they parked along a side street. While they were in the back seat, a police car pulled up; the officer investigated and immediately arrested the pair. It would have been a typical night in LA, except that the man in the mug shot was actor Hugh Grant.

A major celebrity at the time, Grant had already starred in a string of very successful movies. Not only was his acting career peaking in both England and the United States, but his personal life was set to climax as well; he was engaged to his girlfriend of many years, actress/supermodel Elizabeth Hurley. Why, then, would this 34-year-old man with movie-star looks and a gorgeous fiancée risk his image by employing a street prostitute?

For Grant, Stella Thompson (alias "Divine Brown") was reportedly the image of his sexual fantasies. She was dark, sensual, and illegal. A fantasy, she may have symbolized something that Grant, growing up, felt he could not have. As a youth he was raised by a mother who was an English schoolteacher; as a young man he went on to Oxford for his degree. Grant was probably restricted and guided by socially conservative values. Grant admitted he had grown up desiring something he could not have, or rather someone, or a type of someone. This was superbly illustrated by his recollection that he'd always had crushes on cheerleaders, with Catholic cheerleaders being his favorites.

Psychoanalysts might remark that Grant grew up with an inner conflict between his id, which desired forbidden fantasies, and his superego, which (usually) restrained him from this forbidden fruit. He was unable to negotiate a complete compromise between id and superego because there is no way to have these forbidden girls in a socially and morally acceptable manner. But as Grant achieved more and more success, id,

Although part of this was no doubt intentional, an effort to foster independence (something both Karen and Oskar firmly believed in), there was also a lack of warmth and interest in her style of child-rearing. This is particularly interesting in light of Karen's own feelings of neglect during childhood and her later theories of the role of parental indifference in fostering neuroses.

In the early 1920s, Karen and her husband began to drift apart. Then, tragedy struck. In 1923, Oskar's financial investments went sour, and with inflation running rampant, his salary was no longer enough to keep the family from bankruptcy. In addition, he suffered a severe case of meningitis, which left him weak and frail. It was also during this year that Karen lost her beloved brother Berndt to a lung infection. Both Karen and her husband sank into depression, and by 1926, it was clear that their marriage would not survive. Karen and the three daughters moved to a place of their own that very year, but Karen and Oskar's divorce was not final until 1939.

Karen Horney's ideas were in some ways similar to Adler's. Horney believed, as did Adler, that one of the most important discoveries a child makes is that of his or her own helplessness and that it is the ensuing struggle to gain individuality and control that molds much of the self. She believed strongly in the importance of self-realization and growth for each individual. And she was much more focused on the

already in the pattern of getting everything, came to exert greater influence. Further, Grant had not had any recent behavior-related problems, so perhaps his super-ego was off guard; society's restraints were not salient to him.

But, from the neo-analytic perspective, his problem was with ego. Many successful popular actors develop ego problems. Rather than working through challenges toward maturity and wisdom, they wallow in the false and superficial adulation of an adoring public that sees their image but not their true selves. Grant himself commented in an interview that "The fake esteem you get from being in the public eye feels like self-worth, but actually your own powers to produce it shut down" (MacSweeney, 2007). Grant's ego was unable to resist the power of the archetypal temptress embodied by Divine Brown.

Grant once stated in an interview that he really hates acting, and wishes he had chosen what he considers a more creative path, such as writing. But he feared he lacked the self-discipline to take on such a task

(although he subsequently did begin to write a novel). And, after his public break-up with Elizabeth Hurley, his subsequent relationships were not lasting. This dissatisfaction with both career and love fits in with the notion of a deficiency of ego.

Driving down Sunset Boulevard, Hugh was tempted by that old desire to have what was morally and socially unacceptable—that off-limits yet sexually appealing woman. He had the money, he was great, he was loved by everyone, so why not? With a well-developed ego testing reality and telling him that this indulgence was irrational, untrue to his fiancée, illegal, dangerous, and "nuts," he would have kept on driving.

Psychoanalytic theory would argue that this whole fiasco was traceable to one of Grant's early id desires that was repressed by the superego. But the neo-analysts focus more on his ego—his sense of who he was and what he should be doing. Grant had everything and was accustomed to getting what he wanted. Why stop?

© Bettmann/CORBIS

■ Karen Horney (1885–1952) modified Freudian psychoanalysis to show the social and cultural influences on personality, rejecting Freud's emphasis on innate sexuality and the penis. Her feminist perspective countered the patriarchal Freudian view.

Basic Anxiety
According to Karen Horney, a child's fear of being alone, helpless, and insecure that arises from problems with one's parents

Passive Style
According to Karen Horney, a mode of adapting to the world used by those who believe that they can get along best by being compliant

Aggressive Style
According to Karen Horney, a mode of adapting to the world used by those who believe in fighting to get by

Withdrawn Style
According to Karen Horney, a mode of adapting to the world used by those who believe that it is best not to engage emotionally at all

social world and social motivations than were the Freudians (who focused almost exclusively on sexual drives). In 1932, Horney emigrated from Berlin to the United States. This tremendous cultural change further opened her eyes to the influences of society on the individual's development.

Rejection of Penis Envy

Freud's analysis of women was built around the concept of penis envy. Horney rejected the notion that women felt their genitals were inferior, yet her careful observation revealed that women often *did* feel inferior to men. Freud, making the same observation, explained it in terms of an anatomy-based cause—lack of a penis. Horney, however, argued that women's feelings of inferiority stemmed from the ways they are raised in society and from an overemphasis on securing the love of a man. She believed that when women were raised in environments in which "masculinity" was defined as strong, brave, competent, and free, and "femininity" as inferior, delicate, weak, and submissive, then women would of course come to see themselves as subordinate and to therefore desire "masculine" things as a way to gain power. But she did not agree with Freud that it was a penis that women wanted; rather, they wanted the autonomy and control that they associated with maleness. She also postulated that men are unconsciously envious of some feminine qualities, such as the ability to bear children.

Basic Anxiety

Because children are powerless—unable simply to go out into the world and claim their rightful place—they must repress any feelings of hostility and anger toward the powerful adults in their worlds and instead strive to please these adults as a means of getting their needs met. Horney thus replaced Freud's biological emphasis with the idea of basic anxiety. **Basic anxiety** is a child's fear of being alone, helpless, and insecure. It arises from problems in the child's relations with his or her parents, such as lack of warmth, stability, respect, or involvement. Eventually, Horney believed, the basic anxiety could be directed at virtually everyone, in which case the internal turmoil would be focused outward, on the world in general. Thus, although Horney accepted Freud's basic psychoanalytic notion that people are driven by unconscious, irrational motives that develop in childhood, she saw these motives as arising from social conflicts within the family and larger conflicts within the society (Horney, 1968, 1987, 1991).

In reaction to basic anxiety, individuals were hypothesized to settle into one primary mode of adapting to the world. Those who believe that they can get along best by being compliant adopt the **passive style;** those who believe in fighting to get by adopt the **aggressive style;** and those who feel that it's best not to engage emotionally at all adopt the **withdrawn style**. These ideas are of much more than simple historical interest; they form a widely accepted framework for understanding good child-rearing. Much of the modern-day concern with providing warm, respectful family environments for children derives from such neo-analytic theorizing about the role of society in taming biological instincts.

136

The Self

Neo-analysts focus on identity and sense of self. In analyzing neurotics, Horney described different aspects of self. First, there is the **Real Self,** the inner core of personality that we perceive about ourselves, including our potential for self-realization; this core is damaged by parental neglect and indifference. This parental neglect can produce the **Despised Self,** consisting of perceptions of inferiority and shortcomings, often based on others' negative evaluations of us and our resulting feelings of helplessness. Perhaps most important, Horney identified the **Ideal Self**—what one views as perfection and hopes to achieve, as molded by perceived inadequacies. In describing the Ideal Self, Horney referred to what she called the "tyranny of the should," which is the litany of things we should have done differently, and with which we torment ourselves. The Ideal Self is a composite of all of these "shoulds." For Horney, the goal of psychoanalysis was not to help someone achieve his or her Ideal Self, but rather to enable the person to accept his or her Real Self. Someone who is alienated from his or her Real Self becomes neurotic and develops an interpersonal coping strategy to "solve" the conflict.

Real Self
Karen Horney's concept of the inner core of personality that we perceive about ourselves, including our potential for self-realization

Despised Self
Karen Horney's concept of the part of personality consisting of perceptions of our inferiority and shortcomings, often based on others' negative evaluations of us and our resulting helplessness

Neurotic Coping Strategies

Horney then proposed a series of strategies used by neurotics to cope with other people. The first of these approaches she referred to as "Moving Toward" people—that is, always attempting to make others happy, to gain love, and to secure the approval and affection of others. Horney believed that individuals employing this coping strategy are overidentifying with a Despised Self and are therefore seeing themselves as unworthy of love. Their actions to gain love are attempts, on the one hand, to disguise what they believe to be true of themselves and, on the other, to make others believe that they are worthy of affection. For example, women raised by alcoholic parents may have learned to obtain self-esteem by conforming to exploitive demands; as adults, these women may seek out exploitive men and devote themselves to attempting to make the men happy and thereby win their approval (Lyon & Greenberg, 1991). In popular jargon, this disturbed pattern of relationships is sometimes referred to as *codependency.*

Horney called the second approach "Moving Against" people—that is, striving for power, recognition, and the admiration of others. Horney believed that these individuals, instead of overidentifying with the Despised Self, are overidentifying with the Ideal Self. They have come to believe that all the things that they wished they were are true, and their strivings for recognition and power are an effort to reaffirm for themselves the truth of this illusion.

A third approach was called "Moving Away" from people—that is, the withdrawal of any emotional investment from interpersonal relationships, in an effort to avoid being hurt in those relationships. Horney believed that these individuals want to overcome the Despised Self, and yet they feel incapable of ever becoming the Ideal Self. They see themselves, in their present state, as unworthy of the love and attention of others, and yet they feel unable to achieve anything greater. Thus, to avoid the unpleasant contrast—the gap—between these two aspects of self, they hide behind independence and solitude.

© AP Images/Damian Dovarganes

■ If you neurotically overidentify with the Ideal Self and believe you are so terrific, you are at risk for misery. Recently, in fact, it has been argued that many people born from the 1970s to the 1990s have been so heavily praised and told that they could "do anything and succeed at everything" that they are narcissistic (selfish and with excessive self-regard), and thus often anxious, depressed, and miserable (Twenge, 2006).

■ **TABLE 4** Karen Horney's 10 Neurotic Needs

Moving Toward	
• Affection and approval	constantly seeking to please others
• A domineering partner	excessive dependence
Moving Against	
• Power	need for controlling others and despising weakness
• Exploitation	fear of being exploited but not of exploiting
• Recognition and prestige	seeking ever higher status
• Admiration	seeking compliments, even if undeserved
• Ambition and achievement	wanting to be the best, as a result of inner insecurity
Moving Away	
• Self-sufficiency	never committing to others
• Perfection	attempting to be flawless
• Narrow limits	being content with having little, and thus submitting to others

According to Horney, neurotic people irrationally and compulsively focus on one or more of these needs in all their social interactions, but can never be satisfied (Horney, 1942).

Ideal Self
Karen Horney's concept of the self that we view as perfection and hope to achieve, as molded by perceived inadequacies

Neurotic Trend
In Karen Horney's approach, a strategy or pattern of interaction that becomes the predominant mode by which a neurotic individual defends against anxiety

Neurotic Need
In Karen Horney's approach, a need that is a dominant focus for a neurotic individual

Horney believed that psychologically healthy people use a mixture of all three of these self-protective approaches to resolve conflicts. For a neurotic, though, a single strategy will be pervasive, dominating the personality. Horney refers to this unhealthy focus on a single coping strategy as a **neurotic trend**. She enumerated 10 specific defenses against anxiety, which have become known as the 10 **neurotic needs**. They are listed in Table 4, grouped by the neurotic coping strategy (neurotic trend) with which they are associated.

Horney's Impact on Psychoanalytic Thinking

In sum, Karen Horney helped move psychoanalytic thinking about personality away from purely biological, anatomical, and individualistic emphases. While she accepted the significance of unconscious motives developed in childhood, Horney emphasized the importance of a warm, stable family, as well as the impact of the larger society and culture. Furthermore, just as Horney struggled with society's obstacles to women's achievement in her own life, she rejected the idea that women's nature makes them inherently weak and submissive. She saw the influences of the family and the culture on each person, and she insisted that people could strive to overcome their unconscious demons. She emphasized the distress of the "tyranny of the shoulds"—the neurotic internal demands for perfection. She wrote that psychoanalysis is not the only way to resolve inner conflicts: that "life itself" is a very effective therapist (Horney, 1945).

Despite Horney's efforts, psychoanalysis remained heavily male-centered and paternalistic. As feminist Germaine Greer (1971) quipped, "Freud is the father of psychoanalysis. It had no mother".

Bridges to More Modern Conceptions: Anna Freud and Heinz Hartmann

Anna Freud was born in December 1895 to Sigmund and Martha Freud—parents who had previously decided that they would have no more children. Perhaps Anna grew up feeling that she had to strive especially hard to earn their affection and admiration. In childhood and adolescence, she was shy and quiet but attached to her father (Young-Bruehl, 1988). When she was in her early 20s, she underwent psychoanalysis (including by her father) and subsequently became a part of the Vienna Psychoanalytic Society.

In 1922, she presented her first paper to the society, and in 1923, she entered the practice of psychoanalysis, with no formal credentials in psychology or medicine. This was also the year that her father's cancer of the jaw was diagnosed. The ensuing surgeries brought about a host of complications and perhaps further fueled her own passionate work to extend her father's theories.

In contrast with her father, Sigmund, who attempted to uncover childhood from the adult patient's perspective, Anna Freud worked directly with child patients. She adapted psychoanalytic techniques to the special needs of children, as necessitated by their different verbal skills and attention spans. For the next half-century, Anna Freud applied psychoanalytic theory to children and teens. Although she never strayed far from traditional psychoanalytic thought, she nonetheless began to build the bridge that later neo-Freudians would cross, by lending credibility to the direct study of the ego. She brought the ego more clearly into focus with her emphasis on the influence of the social environment, yet she maintained the ego's links to the id and superego. She also moved psychoanalytic thinking slightly away from determinism; that is, although she certainly did not renounce the importance of the id forces or the superego constraints, she endowed the human ego with a bit of proactive, independent functioning which later theorists were able to expand on (A. Freud, 1942).

© The Granger Collection, New York

■ Anna Freud (1895–1982) is shown here at age 17 with her father, Sigmund, during a family vacation in 1913. She was caretaker for her father until his death, and a faithful disciple of the psychoanalytic approach. Her work focused on applying psychoanalytic approaches to treating children and teenagers.

Heinz Hartmann (1894–1970) has sometimes been called the founder of ego psychology. Like Anna Freud, Hartmann worked within a classical Freudian framework, while expanding Freud's conception of the ego to deal with the pressures of the real, external world. Hartmann did not believe the ego was under the control of the id, but he also did not see it as completely autonomous. Rather, he believed that the id and ego worked in a compensatory fashion, each regulating the other. Because Hartmann accepted the idea that the "job" of the ego was to help a person function within the world, he had to modify the traditional Freudian concept of the individual as a purely tension-reduction and pleasure-seeking organism. Instead, he saw that the ego was often able to direct a person to do things that in the long run were self-preserving but in the short term were unpleasant. The ego not only defended against libidinous urges, but also functioned independently to cope with society's demands (Hartmann, 1958).

Object Relations Theories: A Conceptual Link Between Self-Identity and Social Identity

Overall, as psychoanalytic approaches to personality continued to develop, it became clearer and clearer that attention should be expanded away from the individual's inner psyche and toward relations with other people. In other words, the essence of a person cannot be known without understanding that person's relations with significant others. These approaches are sometimes called **object relations theories**, because the term "object relations" is used in this context to refer to the mental representation of significant others. That is, the child learns about self and others primarily through interactions with other people.

There is quite a bit of overlap in theories among object relations psychologists, ego psychologists, and neo-analytic psychologists; it is rare that a theorist limits her or his theorizing strictly to one area. However, object relations theorists particularly focus on the importance of relations with other individuals in defining personality, and they believe that the self is socially constructed as a function of specific interpersonal interactions, rather than something that emerges naturally through biological development (Kernberg, 1984). (See the Self-Understanding box.)

Margaret Mahler and Symbiosis

The child psychiatrist Margaret Mahler worked with children with emotional and behavioral disorders. She observed that certain children seemed unable to form emotional ties with other human beings (notably their mothers), and in this way they shut themselves off from the world. **Symbiotic psychotic** children, on the other hand, formed emotional ties that were so strong that the child was unable to form a sense of self—that is, he or she had no autonomous being. In general, we face a struggle between a need for autonomy and a longing to surrender to and become one with a close other.

Object Relations Theories
The approach to personality that focuses on the objects of psychic drives and the importance of relations with other individuals in defining ourselves

Symbiotic Psychotic
According to Margaret Mahler, the forming of emotional ties that are so strong that a child is unable to form a sense of self

Mahler believed that forming healthy ties with the mother was of utmost importance to psychological health and that children who did so were **normal symbiotic** children. They developed empathy and a sense of being a separate but loving person. Like Anna Freud and Heinz Hartmann, Mahler placed increasing importance on the individual's potential for mastery of his or her world and on the creation of a healthy ego. But most especially, Mahler (1979) added the importance of effective mothering skills for the development of an emotionally healthy child. This notion is commonly accepted today.

As object relations theory developed, it broadened out and moved away from mechanistic views. For example, Otto Kernberg (1984), like Mahler, argued that from birth on, it is our emotional relations with significant others that matter most. We learn about ourselves, we learn about our significant others (called "objects" in object relations theory), and we learn the nature of the basic emotional ties (such as love, mistrust, etc.). These experiences or representations then consolidate into an integrated self, which is the "I" or ego. Interestingly, as we shall see, such broad views of the socially constructed self were simultaneously developed in the sociological side of social and personality psychology.

Modern work studying nonhuman primates tends to confirm these ideas. For example, one project studied certain rhesus monkeys who are biologically prone to show impulsive and inappropriately aggressive responses to mildly stressful situations. It was found that aggressive and other unhealthy patterns were especially likely among monkeys who experienced insecure early relationships with their mothers during infancy, but not in monkeys who had secure attachments with their mothers (Suomi, 2003).

Melanie Klein, Heinz Kohut, and the Relational Perspective

The Vienna-born British psychiatrist Melanie Klein (1882–1960) also worked closely with children and focused on how children come to think about and represent others (in their own minds). Klein was a developer of "play therapy," in common use today. For example, children grieving over the death of a parent or an assault on their bodies might today be treated at a grieving center, where they work out their unconscious feelings and conflicts while playing with toys or crafts, much as an adult might do through dream analysis or free association. Would you recommend such treatment to the child of a friend or to a child in your family who is facing grief? Answering such questions is facilitated when we understand the origins of and theories underlying such treatments.

Taking Freud's ideas in new directions, Klein (1975) examined such early patterns as the infant's reaction to the removal of the mother's breast after nursing. The breast is the infant's first source of satisfaction, and when it is removed, the infant in some sense blames the mother. Thus we both love and hate those closest to us. This conflict is resolved when the infant comes to understand that the mother's love is not simply her breast. There is a differentiation and a deeper comprehension. This early development of the understanding of other people sets the pattern for future relations with others.

In recent years, the ideas of Melanie Klein have been extended by modern ego (object relations) theorists such as Stephen Mitchell (2000) to what has been called

Normal Symbiotic
According to Margaret Mahler, the forming of ties between a child and mother in which the child develops empathy and the sense of being a separate but loving person

Self-Understanding

Ego Assessment

Ego approaches to personality focus on the conscious self—who we think we are—as a central aspect of the individual. For insight into ego assessment, we present three exercises; each exemplifies a different ego psychology approach to this issue.

I. What Do Your "Fictional Goals" Reveal?
   a. What are the three main goals (your strivings for self-improvement) in your life right now?
   b. What do these fictional goals tell you about yourself?
   c. What do they tell you about your perceived weaknesses, or perhaps even weaknesses that you haven't admitted to yourself?
   d. How might these fictional goals help shape your life in the future?
   e. Will changing your goals do anything to change your identity?

II. An Exercise to Think Critically about Ego Approaches

   This exercise requires a partner who knows you. First, in private, each of you writes five short (one-sentence) self-descriptions. These descriptions may be general or specific; the important thing is that they attempt to capture the essence of *who you are*. Now, take a moment to think about your partner, and then each of you writes five short (one-sentence) descriptions of the other person. When you have done this, compare lists.

   How well did your partner describe you? How well did you describe your partner? If there are inconsistencies (and most pairs will have some), do these say anything about the differences between your social and personal self? Do you define yourself in terms of social roles? in terms of goals? Does knowing how others see you cause you to redefine yourself in any way?

III. Dream Analysis

   We all dream every night, although many of us forget our dreams. Keep a notebook and a pencil next to your bed, and keep a dim night-light on. When you wake up during a dream at night or early in the morning, keep your eyes closed for a moment and focus on remembering your dream. Then open your eyes and quickly write what you remember. (You should get better at recalling details over the course of a couple of weeks.)

   Look over your dreams for recurring themes or motivations. Then compare these to goals and themes and motivations in your daily life. For example, is there anger or conflict in your dreams that corresponds to some ongoing anger or conflict in your daily life? a concern with failure? a focus on love? Are any of Jung's archetypes represented?

   If you do this, say, every December for several years, you can look for changes over time in your motivations and identity.

the *relational perspective* in psychoanalysis. These developments are attempts to discover how the initial patterns and representations of self–other relations that we construct as infants and children go on to influence our self-concepts and social relations throughout various challenges of later life. If there has not been a stable basis, then psychopathology may later result. Identity may fail to develop normally without appropriate early experiences (see Figure 2). For example, a stalker, who is obsessed with "love" of a celebrity, might be understood in terms of a failure to develop a normal differentiation of self-identity, love relations, and understanding the perspective of another. These views also give more attention to the effects of *culture* on identity as well as on gender and sexual discrimination; Freud was not uncovering universal truths (Chodorow, 1999a). Such approaches are more clinical, more humanistic, and more philosophical than the more experimental, empirical approaches of mainstream modern personality psychology, but they deal with the same issues of the social nature of the self.

Psychoanalyst Heinz Kohut (1971) likewise argued that a key problem for many anxious people is the fear of the loss of an important love object (most often the parent). He worked with patients who had a **narcissistic personality disorder**, meaning that they felt powerless and dependent yet projected bravado and self-aggrandizement. He believed that the problems of these patients stemmed from a lack of acceptance on the part of their parents, which resulted in an inability on the part of the patients to fully accept themselves. He found that by playing the part of the therapist–parent he could often reverse this process and enable his patients to develop a healthy self-concept.

Narcissistic Personality Disorder
A disorder in which one feels powerless and dependent yet appears to be authoritative and self-aggrandizing

As an example, let's look at Philip, a 24-year-old who is seeking treatment for very low self-esteem. His self-concept is so completely wrapped up in what others think of him that he can barely make decisions on his own; he constantly worries about what people are going to think. At the same time, this insecurity makes him feel entitled to special attention. His therapist, using Kohut's framework, has determined that Philip experienced a traumatic event involving one of his parents (probably his mother) before he was old enough to have fully made the distinction between "mother" and "self." As part of Philip's treatment the therapist will utilize *idealizing transference;* that is, Philip will come to see the therapist as the parental love-object. The therapist-qua-parent can then help Philip develop an internal

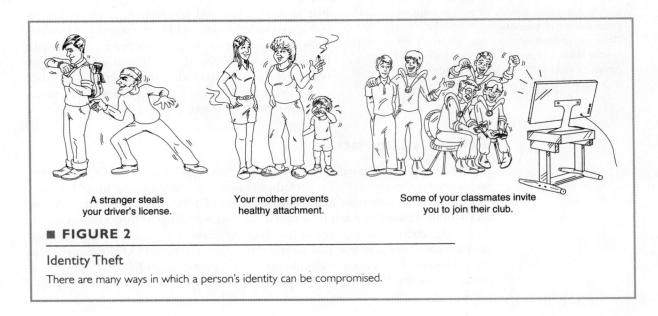

A stranger steals your driver's license.

Your mother prevents healthy attachment.

Some of your classmates invite you to join their club.

■ **FIGURE 2**

Identity Theft

There are many ways in which a person's identity can be compromised.

system for maintaining self-esteem, rather than depending on others for that esteem. Kohut was a bridge between Freudian psychoanalysis and the more optimistic and ego-based approaches of many humanistic psychologists.

The Contributions of Object Relations Approaches

Object relations theorists began to view the ego as a much more *independent* entity, and they brought to the forefront the importance of human individualization and mastery. A series of brilliant thinkers took Freudian theory (which had shattered previous ideas about human nature) and developed it so that it could deal with emerging insights into what it means to have a social self—an identity in a social world. Many of these neo-analytic ideas—of inferiority complexes, of psychic archetypes, of strivings for mastery, of sibling rivalries, of basic anxieties and the importance of mother–infant relations, of the differentiation of identity, and many more—permeate our modern notions of child-rearing, families, and human nature. These ideas are now found in literature, politics, education, and the arts. A wise student of personality will recognize these now-common assumptions in everyday life and will have some idea of their origins and history.

CHANGING Personality

A big issue facing many people—especially narcissistic, self-centered people—is the temptation to leave their partner (significant other) and begin an affair with someone else. Break-up rates and divorce rates are sky-high. What are the implications of neo-analytic approaches for changing personality to prevent such problems? Because adult actions are seen as arising from unconscious patterns developed in childhood, a first step would be to come to a better understanding of the strengths and the flaws in your parents' marriage. Did your father cheat on your mother, either physically or emotionally, and can you develop a more mature understanding of their failings? A second step would be to learn to recognize the current social situations that tend to evoke these hidden feelings in you, such as noticing when you are starting to feel abandoned, disrespected, or isolated (cf. Hunyady, Josephs, & Jost, 2008). For example, are you especially distressed and jealous when your partner must be out at social dinners or business meetings without you? Once you understand these deeper themes of conflict in your social relations, you may be able to avoid repeating many of the same mistakes that your parents made.

Erik Erikson—Life-Span Identity and Identity Crises

Just as Adler expanded psychoanalytic theorizing to include social influence, and Horney altered its conceptions of women, Erik Erikson moved psychoanalytic thought beyond childhood. For Erikson, adulthood was not simply a reaction to childhood experiences, but rather a *continuing* developmental process that was influenced by its own previous stages.

Erikson's Life Path

Born in Frankfurt, Germany, in 1902, young Erik was unsure of his life's direction as he grew to maturity. Erik's stepfather (whom Erik thought was his father) was Jewish. (His Scandinavian birth father abandoned Erik's mother before Erik was born.) Erik's blond hair and blue eyes made him feel different from the rest of the family. At school he was viewed as Jewish by his classmates, yet at Jewish gatherings he was viewed as a non-Jew. Not surprisingly, he felt as if he didn't belong anywhere.

His stepfather, Theodor Homburger, was a physician, and as Erik grew up, it became clear that the kindly man hoped that Erik would follow in his footsteps. Erik, however, wanted to make his own way in life—to be different. He went to art school and became a wandering artist, but he still wasn't completely happy. He enjoyed his art and the freedom from social responsibility that it afforded him, yet he yearned to devote himself to something truly meaningful. There seemed to be no occupation that could fill both of these conflicting needs.

As time went on, Erik became fascinated with child development, and met Anna Freud and the rest of the Vienna circle. Erik greatly respected Sigmund and Anna Freud and saw psychoanalysis as a field that might allow him to be productive without having to go through all the traditional steps to success (that is, without going to medical school). He underwent psychoanalytic training with Anna Freud, and with only this and a Montessori diploma, he managed to become one of the most influential psychologists of the twentieth century (Coles, 1970).

During the Nazis' rise to power in Germany in 1933, Erik and his wife emigrated to Boston. When he became an American citizen, he thought carefully about who he was and who he wanted to be. He changed his name from Erik Homburger to Erik H. Erikson. It is interesting that he chose to reiterate his first name with his last—perhaps hinting at what he had found his own "identity" to be. For a while he worked with Henry Murray, who was also concerned with personality changes across the life span. Erikson then developed his own theory about personality development from a life-span perspective. An outline of his stage theory of personality development is shown in Table 5.

> ### Why Does It Matter?
>
> These developments in the lifelong importance of a child's thoughts about relations with parents set the stage for many forms of cognitive psychotherapy that are in use today. Many psychological disorders are seen to involve a poorly structured ego (mistrust, narcissism, lack of empathy) and are addressed as the therapist helps the client change thoughts and behaviors to improve relations with friends and family.

Identity Formation and Ego Crises

According to Freud, identity was fixed in childhood—formed by age five or six. Erikson renounced this notion, arguing that **identity formation** is a lifelong process. In part, Erikson was rejecting European notions that personality is fixed and life is determined; instead, he adopted the more American philosophical view that individuals

Identity Formation
The process of developing one's individual personality and concept of one's self

■ TABLE 5   Erik Erikson's Stage Theory

Ego Crisis	Freud's Stage	Ego Skill Gained	Age
Trust versus Mistrust	Oral	Hope	Infancy
Autonomy versus Shame and Doubt	Anal	Will	Early childhood
Initiative versus Guilt	Phallic	Purpose	Early to mid-childhood
Industry versus Inferiority	Latency	Competence	Mid- to late childhood
Identity versus Role Confusion	Genital	Loyalty	Teenage years
Intimacy versus Isolation	None	Love	Early adulthood
Generativity versus Stagnation	None	Caring	Middle adulthood
Ego Integrity versus Despair	None	Wisdom	Late adulthood

■ The child's first ego crisis occurs in infancy, when the child must come to believe that the environment can be trusted to satisfy his or her needs

could and did undergo significant change. This view also implies that the individual must take some personal responsibility for his or her life.

According to Erikson, personality (actually, Erikson focused on *identity*) develops through a series of eight stages as life unfolds (Erikson, 1963, 1978). The outcome of each stage (that is, the resultant personality) is dependent to some degree on the outcome of the previous stage, and successful negotiation of each of the **ego crises** is essential for optimal growth. He used as his basis Freud's stages of psychosexual development, and indeed his first five stages reflect ego crises that are tied to Freud's stages.

Trust versus Mistrust

The first ego crisis Erikson termed "Trust versus Mistrust." During this stage (at about the same time period as Freud's oral stage), the infant is struggling to achieve successful nursing, peaceful warmth, and comfortable excretion. If the environment provided by the mother satisfies the infant's needs, the child develops a sense of trust and hope. However, disruptions at this stage can produce feelings of mistrust and abandonment. An infant whose mother does not respond reliably to its hungry cries or who is rarely held is likely to experience feelings of insecurity and suspicion of the environment—the world cannot be trusted. If this ego crisis is never resolved, the individual may have difficulties establishing trust with others throughout life, always convinced that other people are trying to take advantage of him or her in business dealings, or that friends cannot be confided in.

Ego Crises

In Erik Erikson's theory of identity, each of the series of eight "crises" (conflicts or choices) that must be resolved, in sequence, for optimal psychological development

Autonomy versus Shame and Doubt

The second ego crisis Erikson termed "Autonomy versus Shame and Doubt." During this time (corresponding approximately with Freud's anal stage), the young child is learning that she or he has control over her or his own body. Parents should ideally guide the child, teaching her or him to control impulses, but not in an overly harsh manner. Successful negotiation of this stage results in a child who knows the difference between right and wrong, and who is willing and able to choose "right" most of the time. Overly controlling and punitive parenting results in feelings of "I'm always bad . . . I don't know how to be successful" on the part of the child.

Initiative versus Guilt

Erikson termed the third stage (which corresponds with Freud's phallic stage) "Initiative versus Guilt." The child enters this stage knowing that he or she is an independent and autonomous person, but not much else. It is during this period that the child learns how to plan and carry out actions, as well as how to get along with peers. Unsuccessful negotiation of this stage results in a child who may be able to envision possibilities but is too fearful to pursue them. If such feelings are not resolved, an individual emerges in later years who cannot take initiative or make decisions, whose self-confidence is low, and who has little will to achieve. Much research confirms that

■ According to Erikson's theory, identity and role concerns of the teen years define the primary crisis of this developmental stage.

children from dysfunctional families have later problems with self-esteem (Kernis, Brown, & Brody, 2000).

Industry versus Inferiority

The fourth stage was termed "Industry versus Inferiority" (similar to Freud's latency stage). At this time, the child learns to derive pleasure and satisfaction from the completion of tasks—academic tasks in particular. Successful completion of this stage yields a child who can solve problems and who takes pride in accomplishments. On the other hand, a child who does not master this stage feels inferior, as if he or she were incapable of reaching positive solutions and unable to achieve what peers are accomplishing.

Identity versus Role Confusion

The fifth ego crisis (corresponding roughly to Freud's genital stage) is the most famous and influential of Erikson's stages: "Identity versus Role Confusion." At this

■ Drew Barrymore was a highly successful child actress, from a family with several generations of successful stage and film actors. She had a major role in the movie *E.T. the Extraterrestrial*, and that success at age six was followed by a life of television appearances, premieres, and parties. By age nine, she was drinking; the next year, she began smoking marijuana and later taking cocaine. Her career was going well during that period, but her life was not. Her problems during that period could be seen as her failure to successfully navigate Erikson's stage of identity versus role confusion. As a rising Hollywood star, her public identity was being constructed by agents, directors, and movie-studio publicists rather than by normal adolescent exploration and self-reflection. The pressures and demands of the image created for her may have prevented her from developing her own identity during this stage. Following multiple attempts at rehab, she emerged from this challenging period and made the difficult transition from "former child actress" to a successful adult career as an actress and film producer.

stage, the adolescent experiments with different roles, while trying to integrate identities from previous stages. For instance, the child is both son (or daughter), student, friend, and possibly sibling. How do these fit together into a cohesive whole? To complicate matters, at the same time adolescents are trying to figure out who they are and who they want to become, society is beginning to allow them more freedom in the areas of friendships and careers. Successful completion of this stage results in a person who has a clear and multifaceted sense of self—one who has managed to integrate many roles into a single "identity" that is his or her own. Erikson traced the self-consciousness and embarrassment of the teenage years to an identity confusion—an uncertainty about one's abilities, associations, and future goals. He termed this confusion an **identity crisis**. A failure to successfully work through this ego crisis results in an individual with a perpetual identity crisis: someone who is not sure who she or he is, and who continually struggles to find out.

Identity Crisis
A term proposed by Erik Erikson to describe uncertainty about one's abilities, associations, and future goals

© AP Images/Daniel Hulshizer

■ Jennifer Capriati made her debut as a tennis prodigy at age 13, but took a leave from the professional circuit at age 17 as a result of her inability to cope with the stress of competing as an adult when she was a young teenager. Following this, the Women's Tennis Association ruled that no girl could play in a major tournament before age 16, an implicit acknowledgment of the importance of psychological development, not merely athletic skill, in determining who is ready to be a professional player. Capriati made a successful comeback, though, and at age 25 had fought her way back up to the #2 rank among players on the women's circuit.

Intimacy versus Isolation

The sixth stage (it is here that Freud's stages end and Erikson breaks totally new ground) was termed "Intimacy versus Isolation." During this time period, young adults are learning to interact on a deeper level with others. They are allowing others to get to know this newfound "self" in an intimate way. The goal in this stage is for the individual to find companionship with similar others, specifically to develop a love relationship. The inability to create strong social ties without losing oneself in the process results in isolation and loneliness instead of love and fulfillment. Such a person may be unable to form intimate relationships at all, either becoming a "loner" or striking up plenty of superficial relationships.

For example, Ann seems popular and some of her classmates are envious of her apparent social ease. She always has a date and is usually surrounded by people. Despite this, she feels lonely inside. Nobody knows the real Ann, and she can't seem to get close enough to anyone to let them see what she's like; she's afraid nobody will like her true self. In contrast, Jill lives her life in a much quieter way. She's not disliked, but neither is she terribly popular. She has quite a few acquaintances, but only two close girlfriends. Her friendships with these two, however, are deep and satisfying. In addition, she is dating someone she cares for; they have been going out for nearly a year, and she feels close to him, almost as if they have known each other all their lives. Although to the casual observer Jill might appear to be more isolated than Ann, she has actually dealt much more effectively with the Intimacy versus Isolation ego crisis than has Ann.

Generativity versus Stagnation

Erikson termed his seventh stage "Generativity versus Stagnation." It is at this stage that the individual comes to value a giving of self to others. This often takes the form of bearing and raising children, but it is also reflected in other activities such as community service. The idea is to give something back to the world, to do something to ensure the success of future generations. You probably know people who, having achieved many of their material goals, have set new goals for themselves—goals that embody helping others. For example, some successful artists and celebrities donate time and money to charitable causes or become spokespersons for organizations they see as important. The inability to take this generative perspective results in a feeling that life is worthless and boring. This individual may be achieving worldly goals, but underneath the overt success, life seems meaningless.

Ego Integrity versus Despair

The eighth and final stage of ego development Erikson termed "Ego Integrity versus Despair." In this stage of old age, the individual derives wisdom from life experiences and can look back on life and see meaning, order, and integrity. Reflections are pleasant, and present pursuits are in keeping with the integrated life goals the person has pursued for years. Psychosocial failure at this stage means a sense of despair: I have not accomplished what I would have liked to in life, and it is now too late to do anything about it.

■ Erik Erikson is himself a good example of the positive resolution of the final stage of ego development. In old age, he exemplified wisdom and integration.

Resolving the Ego Crises

Erikson emphasized a *balanced* outcome as optimal for each of these eight ego crises; this characteristic of his theory is often oversimplified and misunderstood. At the first stage, the goal is for the child to develop trust, yet it would not be good for the child to be totally gullible and naïve. An overemphasis on trust might lead to just as many problems as an overemphasis on mistrust. Instead, the individual at this stage must learn the ability to trust, and should perhaps have trust as a first inclination, but should nonetheless maintain the ability to be skeptical and self-preserving when necessary. The same is true for each of the stages. At each stage, one of the two features should prevail, but true maturity includes rather than excludes the other pole.

Erikson (1969) not only drew attention to personality changes throughout the life span, but he also emphasized the importance of culture and society. He studied history and anthropology, and he profiled such famous men as Martin Luther (the leader of the Protestant Reformation) and Mahatma Gandhi. These personality profiles provide elegant examples of Erikson's theories in action. His life-span approach, combining as it did both positive and negative potentials, is more realistic for looking at ordinary human growth (as opposed to focusing only on human problems). Neo-analytic ego psychologists like Erikson keep their eyes on the goal of understanding what it means to be an individual in a social world, even though this is not an easy task. As poet Alan Watts (1961) put it, "Trying to define yourself is like trying to bite your own teeth".

When we talked to him in his later years, Erikson seemed to be living out his own theories. He was wise and mature, but still reading, writing, and learning. He died in 1994 at the age of 91.

Modern Approaches to Identity

The modern ego psychologists are usually not much concerned about tracing adult motivations back to childhood traumas. Their view is expressed by Holden Caulfield (J. D. Salinger's adolescent antihero in *Catcher in the Rye*, 1951): "The first thing you'll probably want to know is where I was born, and what my lousy childhood was like, and how my parents were occupied and all before they had me, and all that David Copperfield kind of crap, but I don't feel like going into it". Instead, modern ego psychologists focus on the present: Who are we today? What defines us? What influences us? What do we hope to become? and, How do our aims for the future help us to create our present identities?

Personal and Social Identity

Instead of attempting to determine whether identity is more accurately conceptualized as an internal and personal construct (as a traditional ego psychologist might argue) or an external, socially defined construct (a pure social psychologist's view), psychologist Jonathan Cheek posits that some people might best be defined by the personal view and others by the social view (Briggs & Cheek, 1988; Cheek, 1989). That is, for some individuals, the most important part of "self" might be who they are in relation to others—for example, popularity and the way one acts and the impressions one makes when meeting other people. For other individuals, however, the social roles may be less important, and "self" is best described with introspection: "I am someone who believes in making a kinder world" or "I am very creative." Other aspects of the self are a communal/collective identity (e.g., religion, ethnicity) and a relational identity (e.g., having mutually satisfying personal relationships). In a questionnaire of aspects of identity, Cheek and his colleagues present individuals with a list of entries such as "my thoughts and ideas" or "my attractiveness to other people" and ask participants to rate each item's importance to their sense of self. The goal is to better understand what people are like inside; that is, what is their internal scheme for organizing their various social and personal roles?

A related approach to understanding the extent to which a person has a more social or more personal identity is Mark Snyder's concept of self-monitoring. **Self-monitoring** involves self-observation and self-control guided by situational cues to the social appropriateness of behavior. Someone who is high on self-monitoring is willing and able to engage in **self-presentation**—doing what is socially expected. The former president (and actor) Ronald Reagan was very willing and able to present himself; in fact, he was known as the Great Communicator. But low self-monitors are often not aware of social expectations or are unwilling or unable to act according to social expectations, and they may be more inward-looking and reflective; that is, there tends to be a *dispositional orientation* in low self-monitors, but a *situational orientation* in high self-monitors.

Snyder (1987) and other modern theorists are thus turning to a **functionalist** approach for explaining personality, asking What is the function or purpose of certain behavior? They see (1) what people want, (2) why they want it, and (3) how they try to get it as important for defining who people are. Snyder looks at the environments in which people choose to put themselves. This is important because our

Self-Monitoring
Mark Snyder's concept of self-observation and self-control guided by situational cues about the social appropriateness of behavior

Self-Presentation
A term used by Mark Snyder to describe doing what is socially expected

Functionalism
The approach to psychology that declares that behavior and thought evolve as a result of their functionality for survival

Classic to **Current**

Putting Feelings into Words

Ego psychologists are primarily concerned with the feelings that arise throughout life from our challenging interactions and conflicts with others. Their focus shifts away from the Freudian preoccupation with the primitive forces of the id, and it instead examines the jealousies, anxieties, strivings, and neuroses that arise from disrupted interpersonal relations with significant others. A healthy ego or sense of self can cope with challenges in a more rational and productive way, and will not be beset by irrational emotional triggers of rivalry, powerlessness, mistrust, insecurity, self-hatred, narcissism, lack of autonomy, and other failings of the neurotic personality.

These neo-analytic and ego ideas—of inferiority complexes, of strivings for mastery, of sibling rivalries, of basic anxieties, of the differentiation of identity, and many more—permeate our modern notions of child-rearing, families, and human nature. Yet the challenge of appropriate coping remains major and unresolved. We do not yet well understand how to think about coping with stress after a molestation, a significant taunting, a betrayal, or a random terrorist attack. What we do know suggests that somehow coming to terms with these imbalances or discrepancies in our sense of self (ego) seems to make things somewhat better. Thus, we visit friends or therapists or support groups to talk about what has happened to us and about any destructive interpersonal patterns we have developed. Attaching words and a meaning to our distress often seems to be the first important step on the road to recovery. Why might this be?

An interesting current approach to these classic questions of self is being pursued by the psychologist James Pennebaker. Pennebaker asks such questions as: What are the causes and effects of disclosing emotional topics to others? and What are the features of language that predict changes in health and well-being?

Professor Pennebaker first showed, just as the neo-analysts had concluded from their clinical experiences, that there are health benefits of narrative. Writing about important personal experiences in an emotional way for as little as 15 minutes over the course of three days brings about improvements in one's mental and physical health (Pennebaker & Seagal, 1999; Pennebaker & Chung, 2007). Formation of a narrative, and thus organizing complex emotional experiences, is critical in resolving inner emotional conflict. For example, traumas that are not disclosed to others are linked to higher rates of illness (Pennebaker & Keough, 1999).

More recently, he has taken this research into an exploration of the role of language itself in facilitating these processes. Pennebaker and his colleagues have gathered large numbers of writing samples from various people in various conditions. Analyses of the text samples indicate that particular patterns of word use can be used to characterize personality and also to predict health (Pennebaker & Graybeal, 2001; Stirman & Pennebaker, 2001). For example, in an analysis of 300 poems from nine suicidal poets (aged 30 to 58 at death) and nine nonsuicidal poets, the writings of suicidal poets contained more words pertaining to the individual self and fewer words pertaining to the collective (others) than did those of nonsuicidal poets. That is, suicidal individuals are more detached from others and are preoccupied with self; this is revealed in their use of language and presumably dominates their thoughts. Thus, language itself may be a key missing link between our emotional-motivational conflicts and a more rational and adaptive healthy coping.

FURTHER READING

Pennebaker, J. W., & Chung, C. K. (2007). Expressive writing, emotional upheavals, and health. In H. S. Friedman, & R. C. Silver, (Eds.), *Foundations of health psychology* (pp. 263–284). New York: Oxford University Press.

Pennebaker, J. W., & Graybeal, A. (2001). Patterns of natural language use: Disclosure, personality, and social integration. *Current Directions in Psychological Science, 10*(3), 90–93.

Pennebaker, J. W., & Keough, K. A. (1999). Revealing, organizing, and reorganizing the self in response to stress and emotion. In R. J. Contrada & R. D. Ashmore (Eds.), *Self, social identity, and physical health: Interdisciplinary explorations* (pp. 101–121). New York: Oxford University Press.

Pennebaker, J. W., & Seagal, J. D. (1999). Forming a story: The health benefits of narrative. *Journal of Clinical Psychology, 55*(10), 1243–1254.

Stirman, S. W., & Pennebaker, J. W. (2001). Word use in the poetry of suicidal and nonsuicidal poets. *Psychosomatic Medicine, 63*(4), 517–522.

environments help determine our behaviors, and even our thoughts, thus shaping our identities. In order to say something about what kind of person you are, Snyder would want to see what kinds of people you spend time with, what kinds of hobbies you enjoy, and so on. Because these are choices over which you have much control, they say a lot about who you are and how you view yourself and interpret others (Snyder & Klein, 2005). For example, who will volunteer to help people living with AIDS (Omoto & Snyder, 1995)? A motivation to help that fulfills a need of one's personality is one key predictor. This type of analysis is a modern update of neo-analytic concerns with social motivation and social identity, but without the underlying Freudian assumptions. On the other hand, these modern approaches are much more modest in the scope of what they can explain.

The Role of Goals and Life Tasks

Personal Projects
A term used by Brian Little to describe tasks that people are currently working on that motivate them on a daily basis

A related way that modern researchers are helping define identity functionally is by asking people what their personal goals are—what they find important. For instance, the phrase **personal projects** refers to goals or activities that people are currently working on (Little, Salmela-Aro, & Phillips, 2007). There are big projects, like "becoming a physician," and little projects, like "not biting my fingernails." These personal projects are specific tasks that motivate people on a daily basis. For example, they affect differences in how individuals think about and act each day to maintain their health (Peterman & Lecci, 2007). Robert Emmons (1986, 1992) describes more abstract goals as "personal strivings" (for instance, "impress my friends") that may be satisfied by a number of different behaviors. For example, you could probably impress your friends by getting all As, by driving a fancy car, or by being a good conversationalist. Therefore, **personal strivings** are overarching goals that include, and make functionally equivalent, lots of smaller goals and behaviors. However, our social identities can shape motives, goals, and behaviors without our being aware of these influences, consistent with the unconscious forces postulated by neo-analytic theories (Devos & Banaji, 2003).

Personal Strivings
A term used by Robert Emmons to describe abstract, overarching goals that may be satisfied by a number of different behaviors

Psychologist Nancy Cantor (1994) focuses on what she calls **life tasks**. These are age-determined issues on which people are currently concentrating. Cantor gets down to the nuts and bolts: What do college students think about their dating relationships? What do they say about them? What do they do about them? For example, following their past ego development, some individuals seek to build a union with a special other and some do the opposite—work to maintain their independence. Some people reveal their innermost secrets, whereas others want to keep some things (such as a diary) completely theirs alone.

Life Tasks
A term used by Nancy Cantor to describe age-determined issues on which people are currently concentrating

This work is in the framework established by Erik Erikson, in that an individual's tasks are defined to a large extent by the stage of life. For example, a three-year-old is unlikely to have "finishing high school" as a goal, but this is an important and normal life task for a 16-year-old. Similarly, young adults should ideally learn who they are—they should have identity as a goal—before attempting to form close and lasting bonds with partners, as in marriage. However, whereas grand theorists such as Adler and Erikson coupled in-depth study of certain individuals with wide-ranging theoretical observations about social conditions, modern personality researchers are much more likely to collect systematic, comprehensive data on a group of people sampled from the relevant population. Cantor, like most modern researchers in personality, also heavily emphasizes the importance of situational influences on the individual.

TIME LINE

The History of Neo-Analytic and Ego Approaches to Personality

The major developments in the neo-analytic and ego approach can be seen here in historical relation to one another and in relation to their broader societal and cultural contexts.

Neo-Analytic and Ego Aspects: Identity		Societal and Scientific Context
People are thought to derive their identity mostly from their position in life (woman, lord, minister)	before 1800	Humans are seen primarily in religious or philosophical terms; children often are not differentiated from adults
Scholars in Europe gathered around Freud begin considering expansion of his ideas beyond libido	1880s–1900	Increasing attention to evolution and reproduction; comparisons between humans and other animal groups
Neo-analysts begin break with Freud; disputes about drives and defense mechanisms; Jung proposes collective unconscious	1910–1930	Increasing technology and industrialization; anthropological discoveries about cross-cultural similarities and differences
Adler and Horney shift focus to the child's social world; object relations theories develop	1920s–1940s	Victorian era with patriarchal families gives way to women's suffragist movements; child psychiatry develops
Erikson and others shift identity study to consider the full life span	1940s–1960s	People live longer lives, with more choices; traditional sex roles and work roles break down
Modern theorists focus directly on identity, in terms of life tasks, self-monitoring, self-presentation, and attachments	1960s–1980s	Increasing individual freedom and pursuit of goals; less formal social structure and increased mobility and education
Goals and motivations attract new interest	1990s–2000s	Schools, corporations, sports teams look to increase performance

Evaluating the Perspectives

Advantages and Limits of the Ego (Neo-Analytic) Approach

■ Quick Analogy

- Humans as conscious actors and strivers.

■ Advantages

- Emphasizes the self as it struggles to cope with emotions and drives on the inside and the demands of others on the outside.
- Emphasizes the importance of the positive and goal-oriented nature of humanity.
- Acknowledges the impact of other individuals, society, and culture on personality.
- Attempts to explain the structure of the healthy and unhealthy psyche.
- Assumes development continues throughout the life cycle.

■ Limits

- Relatively unconcerned with biology and fixed personality structures.
- Very difficult to test empirically.
- Sometimes a hodgepodge of different ideas from different traditions.
- Sometimes relies on abstract or vague concepts.

■ View of Free Will

- Though personality is largely determined by unconscious forces, individuals do have the ability to overcome these.

■ Common Assessment Techniques

- Varies from free association to situational and autobiographical study with an emphasis on self-concept.

■ Implications for Therapy

- As with psychoanalytic therapy, insight into inner motivations is key, but because the ego is central, there is less concern with unconscious motivation. So, for example, you could work with a therapist to understand your constant bragging to friends or your fear of getting close to a lover in terms of early fears of abandonment, insecurity, mistrust, and feelings of inferiority. You may come to see your faulty patterns of relations with peers as derived from poor patterns of relations with your parents or siblings or early teachers.

Possible Selves and the Search for a Meaningful Life

The ideas of Karen Horney and the neo-analysts about the ideal self and "shoulds" and the ideas of the object relations theorists about multiple selves have reappeared in modern personality research, but with a much more cognitive thrust: These modern theorists agree that we imagine ourselves in different roles and states, but this is seen as a more rational, cognitive process rather than one rooted in deeper emotional conflicts (Markus & Ruvolo, 1989). The psychologist E. Tory Higgins writes about the actual self (the current self-concept), an ideal self (hopes, wishes, or aspirations), and the ought self (beliefs about one's duties). Discrepancies between actual and ideal selves result in chronic disappointment and dissatisfaction. Discrepancies between one's actual and ought selves lead to guilt and anxiety over failure in one's responsibilities (Higgins, 1999; Higgins & Spiegel, 2004). Emotion and motivation may arise out of these discrepancies. For example, if you are pursuing ever-greater rewards, you may become depressed, whereas if you are worrying about ever-greater responsibilities, you will become anxious and neurotic. If you can picture yourself becoming your ideal self and can imagine yourself getting there, your motivation to move in that direction is increased (Norman & Aron, 2003). And if your goals, identities, and traits are compatible, you naturally tend to be more satisfied (McGregor, McAdams, & Little, 2006). Such mini-theories do not attempt the psychological depth of the neo-analytic theories but rather look at motivation and self-regulation in particular spheres of daily life.

One study of college students asked seniors, "How have you changed since you entered college?" The students had previously been assessed upon entering college, so changes could be evaluated. Students who explained their personality changes in ways that included many positive feelings and reflective thought (such as about issues of justice) tended to become especially more emotionally mature during their college years (Lodi-Smith, Geise, Roberts, & Robins, 2009). As the ego psychologists like Erikson predicted, the developing narratives we tell about who we are seem to be an important core of our identity.

Roy Baumeister is another contemporary researcher who is trying to more fully explain what we mean by "self." Interestingly, he believes that much of human preoccupation with "finding oneself" is really a disguised search for a meaningful life, and that self-esteem is not a useful target (Baumeister, Campbell, Krueger, & Vohs, 2003; see Figure 3). In fact, efforts to bolster the self-esteem of poor students (a tactic often tried in schools) can backfire, making the students do even worse (Crocker & Knight, 2005; Forsyth, Lawrence, Burnette, & Baumeister, 2007). We all have a need to belong—a desire for interpersonal attachments (Baumeister & Leary, 1995). In fact, social exclusion—even being ignored by our friends during a simple game of catch—leads to perceiving life as much less meaningful (Stillman et al., 2009).

Baumeister points out that life is constantly changing (our communities, our goals, our jobs, our friends), and yet the meaning we would like to attribute to life is a constant (our values). We want to find purpose and make a difference, as well as to justify actions, and to feel self-esteem. This view of identity is more philosophical in nature than those of some of the other modern theorists we have noted. But it shares with them the concepts of identity creation and the functional importance of

■ FIGURE 3

Self-Esteem and Performance

Contrary to what many people believe, high self-esteem does not necessarily cause good academic performance or good job performance, nor does it necessarily lead to good social relations. Instead, people who achieve good performance feel good about themselves because of their accomplishments (Baumeister et al., 2003). This suggests that we should spend less time praising children in the abstract and more time with them teaching skills and rewarding accomplishment.

the ego. These modern theorists, without exception, argue that individuals continue to grow psychologically after childhood and that looking at people's goals and their strategies for achieving them provides valuable insights into their identities. (See the Evaluating the Perspectives Box.)

Summary and Conclusion

Although Sigmund Freud placed the ego between the struggles that pitted the id against the superego, he was more fascinated with the drives and the struggle and less concerned with the ego. Many of Freud's successors took up the cause of the ego, as they recognized that it was an important and independent force of the psyche, and not just a response to the id. The notion of the conscious "self"—who we think we are—remains a major element of modern conceptions of personality.

Carl Jung was interested in the deepest universal aspects of personality and expanded ideas of the unconscious to include emotionally charged images and quasi-instincts that seem characteristic of all generations. In particular, he was interested in beliefs that we all share and in how our many similarities develop. He developed conceptions of the collective unconscious and archetypes, and although these ideas are not accepted by contemporary personality theorists in their simple and literal sense, Jung's brilliant creativity in this area has opened doors for subsequent theorists, and this portion of his theory may in time be accepted in some more complex form. Another Jungian contribution—the concept of "complexes" (emotionally charged thoughts and feelings on a particular theme)—has been well accepted by the psychological community. Indeed, the term has made its way into our everyday language. Finally, Jung described personality as being comprised of competing forces, pulling against one another to reach equilibrium, best illustrated by the dimensions of extroversion (a tendency toward outward focus) and introversion (a tendency toward inward focus). These terms are also widely used today, although they are usually conceptualized as opposite poles of the same dimension.

Alfred Adler focused attention on the social world and its impact on ego or identity formation. Although some wits now joke that "My inferiority complex is worse than yours," we owe to Dr. Adler our current important conceptions of the inferiority complex (exaggerated feelings of personal incompetence) and the corresponding superiority complex (ego-protective feelings of grandeur). Adler's is an individual psychology that focuses on the uniqueness of individuals and the importance of how they perceive themselves. He believed that many personality problems could be avoided by using detailed knowledge about individuals to construct healthier social environments. Adler also developed a personality typology based loosely on ancient Greek notions of the bodily humors, but he is perhaps best known as someone who firmly believed in the positive, goal-oriented nature of humankind.

Karen Horney changed the way that psychoanalytic theory viewed women, putting aside Freudian beliefs about penis envy and replacing them with theories, based on her own observations, for the reasons why women often did feel inferior to men. She emphasized the social influences on women—their relative lack of opportunities—as determinants of these inferiority feelings. She also modified Freudian biological determinism with her concept of basic anxiety (the child's sense of helplessness and insecurity). Thus, she moved psychoanalytic thought away from its predominately deterministic view and toward a more inclusive and interactive interpretation.

Erik Erikson demonstrated that important developmental steps mark the individual's route through life. The first stages of his developmental theory of personality look similar to a neo-analytic version of Freud's psychosexual stages, but Erikson did not stop there. Instead of viewing adulthood primarily as a reaction to childhood experiences, he saw it as a continuing developmental process, with its own issues and conflicts. At each stage a certain ego crisis must be resolved, and successful resolution of each crisis enables healthy development at later stages, throughout life.

Modern personality approaches to identity are not so apt to offer sweeping generalizations about large classes of people. Just as the neo-analytic theorists revised Freudian theory to take into account the effects of society, of culture, of gender differences, and of development across the life span, modern identity theorists further focus on the unique personal and situational demands facing each individual in the ongoing struggle to maintain a sense of self—of who we are. Modern identity theorists often take a functional approach to personality; that is, they look at motivated behaviors and goals in order to understand the self that underlies them. Some researchers believe that day-to-day goals have the most impact on personality, whereas others believe that our far-reaching, abstract goals are more significant. Some place more importance on the ways individuals plan to reach their goals than on the goals themselves. But all of these researchers agree that it is useful to look at these building blocks of identity (goals, motives, strivings, desires) to understand more fully the person beneath.

Two questions will not be easily answered: Where is the ego? What constitutes an identity? We must agree first on what the definition of *identity* will be. Will it be global in nature, encompassing aspects of the individual as she or he relates to the world? Or will it be more internal, personal, and introspective? In either case, it is of the utmost importance that the self-directedness of the individual is not lost, for it is the ability of psychology to see and study this proactive nature that the neo-analysts have worked so hard to create.

■ Key Theorists

Carl Jung
Alfred Adler

Karen Horney
Erik Erikson

■ Key Concepts and Terms

personal unconscious versus collective
  unconscious
archetypes
Jung's four functions of the mind
extroversion versus introversion
Individual Psychology
inferiority complex
superiority complex
organ inferiority

aggression drive
Adler's personality typology
basic anxiety
object relations theories
symbiotic psychotic versus normal symbiotic
Erikson's stages of identity formation
identity crisis
self-monitoring
self-presentation

Biological Aspects of Personality

In 1953 James D. Watson and Francis Crick discovered that DNA was structured as a double helix. Dr. Watson, shown here holding a DNA model, won a Nobel prize for his role in that research. In 2007 Watson (then aged 79) was handed a computer drive holding his individual fully sequenced genome. Watson promptly made the information public, becoming the first person to do so. With open genetic sequencing, Watson says, "Instead of asking a child to shape up, we'll stop having unrealistic expectations" (Begley, 2007. In other words, he claims that who we are is there in our genes. Soon after, however, Watson was forced to resign from

© Frank Boellman/Photo Researchers, Inc.

his prestigious research lab after making controversial remarks about the genetic inferiority of Africans.

This biological view of personality would not be surprising to most parents. Ask any parent why his or her children behave differently from each other and he or she will tell you that the kids were born that way. Research in child psychology, however, has tended to focus on the environmental influences on personality. Families are bombarded with advice on how to raise a productive, contented, well-adjusted member of society. Books about childcare have generated great interest, as parents strive to take an active role in helping their children grow up to be wonderful, accomplished individuals.

This emphasis on the environment is due in part to cultural belief in opportunities for self-improvement. A person's place in life is not fixed at birth. We like to believe that almost any child, with enough motivation and the proper upbringing, can go on to achieve almost anything he or she desires. These beliefs go back to the Enlightenment of the seventeenth and eighteenth centuries and its philosophical musings about the potential for glorious accomplishments by free men, which influenced the thinking of the American Revolution against the British in 1776. For example, the seventeenth-century English philosopher John Locke (1690/1964) wrote that the human mind is a blank slate—*tabula rasa*—at birth. With the right upbringing, anyone could become a person of distinction.

There is no doubt that the dream of self-fulfillment through proper rearing and hard work does indeed come true in many cases. There is also no doubt, however, that biological factors, starting with one's genes, affect a person's characteristic responses. A person is *not* born a blank slate that is then written on by the environment; rather, people start with certain inherent predispositions and abilities. Instead of arguing about the relative effects of heredity versus effects of the environment, it is more productive to try to understand the effects of human biology on human personality, without understating, overstating, or misstating the impacts of heredity.

Direct Genetic Effects

In the middle of the nineteenth century, Charles Darwin turned the life sciences upside down by arguing that people evolved directly from more primitive species. We are cousins of chimps and apes. This idea was so radical that Darwin spent much effort arguing points such as the similarity of human bones, nerves, and muscles to those of other primates. Such close anatomical relations were not accepted at the time.

Natural Selection and Functionalism

Darwin (1859) points out that each person is different from every other person. Some of these differentiating characteristics help the individual survive—that is, reproduce and pass on her or his genes to offspring. The process by which certain adaptive individual characteristics emerge over generations is known as **natural selection**. For example, in a dangerous environment full of predators, those individuals who are large or tough or fast or smart or able to organize defenses are most likely to survive. In a Darwinian analysis, attention is thus drawn to the *function* of a characteristic (such as speed or intelligence or sociability) in survival.

But which characteristic is the most important? In the predatory environment, was it the speed or the intelligence of the individual, or organizational abilities, or camouflage techniques that made the difference to survival? Or perhaps it was something else altogether. This is a major difficulty with developing the details of a Darwinian approach: It is hard to know what were the precise selection pressures that shaped human evolution over millions of years. This problem plagues the modern application of Darwin's ideas to individual differences—sometimes called **evolutionary personality theory** (Buss, 2003; Simpson & Kenrick, 1997). Individual differences and motivations are seen as due to either alternative adaptive strategies or to random variation, but it is difficult to determine the precise causes. Still, it is clear that many of our individual tendencies are "in our bones" or, more accurately, in our genes.

Natural Selection
The process by which certain adaptive characteristics emerge over generations

Evolutionary Personality Theory
An area of study applying biological evolutionary theory to human personality

Angelman Syndrome: Genes and Personality

Consider this example. Can you imagine an excessively happy child, one who is always filled with glee and good humor? In fact, such a condition is one of the signs of a rare genetic disorder called *Angelman syndrome*. Such children are usually also especially attractive and friendly. Sound good? Unfortunately, they also suffer mental retardation, sleep very little, and walk with a jerky movement, sort of like a puppet.

Angelman syndrome is a biological disorder caused by a defect on chromosome 15 (Zori, Hendrickson, Woolven, & Whidden, 1992). Human cells have 23 pairs of chromosomes, with half of each pair contributed by each parent. The chromosomes contain the genes, which control the body's manufacture of proteins. Genes affect development in many ways, including structural development (how our brains and bodies grow) and physiological development (how our hormones and general metabolism function).

Another example is Williams syndrome, a rare disorder characterized by physical and developmental problems including an excessively social personality, as well as limited spatial skills and intellectual ability (Bellugi & St. George, 2001; Bellugi, Järvinen-Pasley, & Doyle, 2007). Persons with Williams syndrome, who are missing about two dozen genes on chromosome 7, love music, and are about the friendliest and most sociable people you can meet. Extreme cases like these syndromes demonstrate that genetic factors can dramatically influence personality. Although genes *can* dramatically influence personality in unusual cases,

Photo courtesy of the Angelman Syndrome Foundation, Inc., reprinted by permission of Lisa and Luis Franco

■ This child has Angelman syndrome. The parent support group refers to the afflicted children as "Angels," both in honor of Dr. Angelman (who first identified the disorder) and in recognition of the children's generally sweet and sunny dispositions.

questions remain about the *extent* to which genes affect personality in normal development, and *which* aspects they shape (DiLalla, 1998).

Behavioral Genomics

Behavioral Genomics
The study of how genes affect behavior

The human genome is the complete set of genes, located on the 23 pairs of chromosomes, that define the biological human being. In the year 2000, the human genome was mostly "unraveled," in the sense that the genes were mapped; that is, genes were marked on the DNA strands. The functions or roles of each gene are far from understood, but this genetic map holds the potential for better understanding personality by discovering the biological instructions given by each of our genes. The study of how genes affect behavior is called **behavioral genomics** (Plomin & Crabbe, 2000).

More traditionally, the field called behavioral genetics has endeavored to understand how individual differences in biology affect behavior. As we will see, some of these studies analyze twins adopted or separated at birth to compare nature and nurture (sometimes called "quantitative genetics"). Other studies examined the products and correlates of a specific gene (sometimes called "molecular genetics"). Now, however, with behavioral genomics, we can begin to examine the complex matter of how our genes, evolved from variation and natural selection, function together with each other and the environment to influence behavior. This examination reveals fascinating insights into what it means to be a person. It also raises many important ethical issues.

It is easy to assume that a strong sex drive has survival value; individuals with no interest in sexual relations are usually unlikely to pass their genes on to offspring. Yet people vary markedly in their sex drives (libidos). It is also probably safe to assume that love and fear and anger have a genetic basis. They are universal and eternal. Unfortunately, this knowledge does not help us much in explaining the variations from person to person. To do that, we have to find stable individual differences in biological responsiveness. The remainder of this chapter explores such differences.

Genetic Effects through Temperament

Ivan Pavlov, the Russian physiologist who discovered classical conditioning in the salivation responses of dogs, was also very interested in differences in individuals' nervous systems (Pavlov, 1927). His investigations focused on an animal's orientation responses to new stimuli. Pavlov knew that the organism must respond appropriately for the organism to orient adaptively to the environment. For example, the organism must have the correct sensitivity to detect food or danger, but an overreaction to stimuli would leave the organism overwhelmed or unable to discriminate appropriately. We need to respond when danger is near but not to respond as if everything is a danger.

Temperament
Stable individual differences in emotional reactivity

At birth, certain temperamental and sensitivity differences among babies are apparent. The term **temperament** is used to refer to stable individual differences in emotional reactivity. For example, some babies are cuddly, quiet, and may sleep soundly much of the day. Others are exceptionally active, or respond poorly to

■ Differences in temperament are visible in the way children respond to their environments. Some children are shy, like the late Princess Diana (left), and hold back from interaction; others, like this daredevil on his bicycle, seek out opportunities for new experiences.

cuddling, and drive their parents to exasperation. Longitudinal developmental studies begun in the 1920s suggest that at least some of this reactivity remains stable over time as the children mature. On a physiological level, people exhibit different nervous system responses to unpleasant stimuli, and these individual response patterns likewise remain stable over time (Kagan, Snidman, & Arcus, 1995; see also Conley, 1984; Goldsmith, 1989; Schwartz et al., 2010). (See the Self-Understanding box.)

Activity, Emotionality, Sociability, Impulsivity

Temperament is easy to see in other animals. It is well known that many animals such as dogs and roosters can be bred to be fiercer and more aggressive or gentler and more cooperative. In the human domain, however, children's counselors and psychologists are often surprised to notice that so-called problem children, youngsters who are especially aggressive or hyperactive, sometimes come from very stable, warm families; their parents complain (often correctly) that the kids were born that way. So, as the limits of simple environmental explanations become apparent, there has been increasing attention to theories and research on temperament.

Although there are differing accounts and models of temperament, most agree on the following four basic aspects of temperament (Buss & Plomin, 1984; Fox, Henderson, Marshall, Nichols, & Ghera, 2005; Rothbart, 1981; Thomas, Chess, & Korn, 1982). First, there is an *activity* dimension. Some children are almost always in vigorous motion while others are more passive. Second, there is an *emotionality* dimension. Some children are easily aroused to anger or fear or other emotions, whereas other children are calmer. Third, there is a dimension of *sociability*. Sociable children approach and enjoy others. Fourth, there is an *aggressive/impulsive* dimension, which characterizes the extent to which children are aggressive and cold rather than conscientious and friendly.

Decisions about scientific models and dimensions of temperament are usually based on data that come from observing, counting, and coding certain behaviors in children. For example, parents might record how many times a child cries in a given day. Or the child's reactions to meeting strangers might be systematically observed. Depending on the behavior recorded, the coding criteria, the task used, the coders,

Self-Understanding

What Is Your Biological Temperament?

Although the best ways to assess biological aspects of personality will eventually incorporate direct biological assessments (such as measurement of hormone release, heart rate reactivity, and PET scans of the brain), we can often get a sense of our temperaments by looking for certain themes that we see in ourselves or that others see in us.

I. Introversion–Extroversion
   a. Do you prefer being in crowds and at parties or spending time by yourself?
   b. Do you hate or fear public speaking? Does it give you a pounding heart?
   c. Do you seek out roller coasters, parachute jumps, exotic travel?

II. Emotionality
   a. Were you a fearful child?
   b. Are you easily aroused to anger (hot-tempered)?
   c. Do you have mood swings, from very high to very low?

III. Activity
   a. As a child, were you always in motion?
   b. Are you more passive? restful? lethargic?
   c. Do you hate to sit around?

IV. Aggression/Impulsivity
   a. As a child, were you more of a bully or more of a peacemaker?
   b. Do you win conviviality awards or cold-shoulder awards?
   c. Do you tend to make and follow plans, or do you rush off in new directions?

V. Other Drives
   a. Do you have a very high sex drive?
   b. Do you have a large appetite for food and/or drink?
   c. Do you resemble one of your parents in a drive or ability that has always seemed to be natural and special rather than trained or learned (such as artistic or musical talent, athletic ability, high intelligence)?
   d. Do you have a deficit in some biological ability that has led you to overdevelop a compensating ability?

Remember that biological factors combine with the other aspects of personality in complex ways to produce adult patterns of behavior.

the situation, the subculture, and similar factors, somewhat different results on basic temperament will emerge.

Eysenck's Model of Nervous System Temperament

The best way to clear up these discrepancies about basic temperaments would be to find the actual biological substrates of these observable patterns of emotional reactivity. That is, it would be helpful to track the nervous system and hormonal changes that accompany stable patterns of reactivity. Perhaps several patterns of physiological responsiveness could be identified.

Interesting research on the effects of biological temperament on personality was inspired by the work of the late British psychologist Hans Eysenck, particularly in the area of introversion–extroversion. Introverts are generally quiet, reserved, and thoughtful. Extroverts are active, sociable, and outgoing. Most people fall somewhere in between. The introversion–extroversion dimension thus combines elements of the activity dimension with the sociability dimension of temperament. Although notions of introversion–extroversion appear in many personality theories, Eysenck ties the dimension directly to the central nervous system.

The basic idea is that extroverts have a relatively low level of brain arousal, and so they seek stimulation. They want to get things "pumped up." Introverts, on the other hand, are thought to have a higher level of central nervous system arousal, and so they tend to shy away from stimulating social environments. In particular, Eysenck points to the part of the brain known as the ascending reticular activating system (Eysenck, 1967). There is as yet, however, little empirical evidence that this brain system is directly related to personality. The argument has also been extended by Eysenck and others to a neuroticism–emotionality dimension, with the point being that stable people are said to have a well-modulated nervous system, whereas neurotic people have a very reactive nervous system, which promotes emotional instability. The validity of this intriguing model is also still unknown (Gale, 1983; Zawadzki & Strelau, 2010).

There are many problems in trying to test a nervous system–based theory of temperament, which Eysenck himself acknowledged (Eysenck, 1990). First, it is difficult to define and measure nervous "arousal"; there is no impartial gauge like a thermometer and no single response like a fever. Second, many problems arise from the fact that the human body is a system that attempts to maintain equilibrium; responses rise and fall, varying in baseline, intensity, and duration.

There is, however, assorted evidence that extroverts do indeed differ physiologically from introverts (Corr, 2008; Pickering & Gray, 1999; Stelmack & Pivik, 1996). Some of this corroboration comes from studies using electrodermal measures—monitoring the electrical activity of the skin with electrodes. Other support comes from brain scans. There is also evidence that, as predicted, introverts are slower to habituate to (get used to) sensory stimuli such as unusual tones that are played (Crider & Lunn, 1971; Zuckerman, 1999). Stimulation bothers them. In colloquial terms, it "gets on their nerves." Overall, extroverts generally show less brain arousal at rest than introverts do. Although this approach is promising, it is likely that a more complex model of brain arousal and temperament needs to be developed, one that does not rely on only one aspect of nervous arousal (Eysenck, 1990; Gale, 1983; Pickering & Gray, 1999).

Approach and Inhibition: Gray's Reinforcement Sensitivity Theory

An extension of the physiological, brain-based model of personality to incorporate findings from modern neuroscience comes from Jeffrey Gray and colleagues (Kumari, Ffytche, Williams, & Gray, 2004; Leue & Beauducel, 2008; Pickering & Gray, 1999). This approach again begins with Pavlov's classic notion that animals' nervous systems have evolved to orient them to attractions and dangers, but also emphasizes the notion of the importance of reward or punishment for appropriate/inappropriate behaviors. In other words, observation *and* learning are key to survival.

This approach therefore postulates two relevant biological systems. The first is the *behavioral inhibition system (BIS)*. This system provides the orienting response to novel situations and also responds to things that are punishing. If this system is sensitive, then you are prone to anxiety, always alert and worrying that something bad will happen. Second, there is the *behavioral activation system* (sometimes called the *behavioral approach system*, or *BAS*), which regulates our response to rewards. It is how we learn to enjoy rewarding activities like good food and friends. If this physiological system is overly active, then you are impulsive and constantly seeking rewards. There is evidence that persons with an active behavioral approach system are more prone to drug addiction and overeating (Davis et al., 2007; Franken, Muris, & Georgieva, 2006).

This conception fits the observation that impulsive people are mostly shaped by rewards, whereas anxious, obsessive people are mostly concerned with avoiding unknown situations and punishment. Would you go away on a weekend ski trip with a blind date? A person with an active biological approach system will be pulled by the potential for many rewards. A person controlled by a strong behavioral inhibition system, however, will shy away, worrying about everything from embarrassment to injury to sexually transmitted diseases.

Sensation Seeking and Addiction-Proneness

A related nervous system approach to personality focuses directly on **sensation seeking** (Joseph, Liu, Jiang, Lynam, & Kelly, 2009; Zuckerman, 1999, 2007). Think about people who are always on the lookout for a new challenge or a new high. Sensation seekers have a consistent tendency to seek out highly stimulating activities, such as sky-diving, and they are also attracted to the unknown. Sensation seekers, however, have no consistent preference as to whether they enjoy being around others. Thus, they are not simply extroverts. But this theory similarly proposes that sensation seekers may have a low level of natural (internal biological) activation and so seek arousal from the environment. Consistent with Pavlov's original notions, sensation seekers seem

Photo by Michelle Buckham, Arrowtown, New Zealand

■ Some individuals are more likely than others to seek out exciting (and potentially dangerous) activities. Possibly, they are seeking arousal from the environment to compensate for their lower levels of internal biological activation.

to have a strong, nervous system–based, orienting response. They seem biologically primed to seek out and engage their environments.

Understanding such natural inclinations depends on knowledge about the workings of the brain and the nerves, including **neurotransmitters**—the chemicals nerves use to communicate. One likely possibility involves the neurotransmitter dopamine, with evidence of genetic differences in dopamine availability and regulation (Klein et al., 2007; Zuckerman & Kuhlman, 2000). For example, why might sensation-seeking individuals be drawn to cocaine? Cocaine is a psychomotor stimulant that is an especially widespread and dangerous drug. Cocaine prevents the reabsorption of the neurotransmitter dopamine by binding to the dopamine uptake transporter, hence inhibiting dopamine reuptake and leaving more dopamine in the synapse (Bloom & Kupfer, 1995). When dopamine concentrations therefore rise (and nerve activity increases) due to cocaine, emotional highs are initially (and artificially) created. But the brain is severely disrupted as dopamine levels later crash.

It is likely that some people have natural defects or disease-caused weaknesses in their dopamine systems, and such people may be especially susceptible to cocaine addiction. Even in initially healthy people, chronic cocaine use tends to produce symptoms of paranoia, as the brain tries to adapt to the high dopamine levels. A nervous system–based model of individual differences in susceptibility to drug addiction is shown in Figure 1.

The neurotransmitter serotonin also is related to impulsivity (Carver, Johnson, & Joormann, 2008; Cyders & Smith, 2008). For example, there is an inverse correlation between impulsivity and serotonin levels in vervet monkeys (Fairbanks, Melega, Jorgensen, & Kaplan, 2001). Furthermore, the monkeys' impulsivity can be dramatically altered by giving them the drug fluoxetine (**Prozac**), which blocks the reabsorption of serotonin in the brain, thus enhancing mood. By the way, how do you tell if a vervet monkey is impulsive? (It will not take a Rorschach test.) In the case of captive monkeys, you bring an intruder monkey to the edge of the subject monkey's territory. Then you code responses. Impulsive monkeys recklessly rush the intruder, sniff it, and attempt to touch it (Fairbanks, 2001). Their cautious, unimpulsive peers, on the other hand, stay back and observe the monkey intruder for a while.

There are also larger structural differences. The human brain has two distinct halves—a left and a right hemisphere. One promising method of addressing biological differences in personality focuses on individual differences in **hemispheric activity**; that is, relative differences in activation between the right and left cerebral hemispheres in the brain (Biondi et al., 1993; Davidson & Fox, 1989; Maxwell & Davidson, 2007).

How is all this relevant to personality? The idea is that relatively greater activation of the right hemisphere is associated with greater reactions of fear and distress to a stressful situation; that is, individuals who have a relatively more active right hemisphere are more likely to overreact to a negative stimulus.

Sensation Seeking
A tendency to seek out highly stimulating activities and novelty

Neurotransmitter
A chemical used by nerves to communicate

Prozac
A drug that blocks reabsorption of the neurotransmitter serotonin in the brain and thus elevates moods and alters emotional reaction patterns

Hemispheric Activity
The level of activity within one cerebral hemisphere (left or right)

Why Does It Matter?

In addition to helping understand susceptibility to addiction, knowledge of biological influences on individual differences can help in uncovering the best treatments for depression. For example, brain-derived neurotrophic factor (BDNF) is an important substance involved in the health and growth of nerve cells and is relevant to depression. Variations (polymorphisms) in the gene that influences BDNF production are being studied to understand optimal drug treatments. There is evidence that certain variations are not responsive to fluoxetine (Prozac). For depressed people with such a genetic variation, Prozac may not work, and the psychiatrist may want to look instead to other antidepressant drugs. In other words, with genetic testing, doctors may have to rely less on trial-and-error therapeutics for people with serious mood disorders and instead could target prescriptions at the likely problem for a particular individual (Chen et al., 2006).

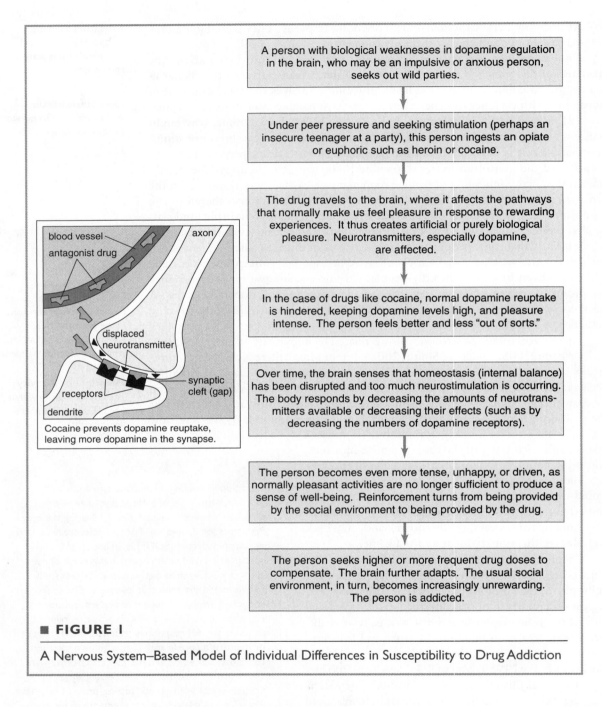

A person with biological weaknesses in dopamine regulation in the brain, who may be an impulsive or anxious person, seeks out wild parties.

Under peer pressure and seeking stimulation (perhaps an insecure teenager at a party), this person ingests an opiate or euphoric such as heroin or cocaine.

The drug travels to the brain, where it affects the pathways that normally make us feel pleasure in response to rewarding experiences. It thus creates artificial or purely biological pleasure. Neurotransmitters, especially dopamine, are affected.

In the case of drugs like cocaine, normal dopamine reuptake is hindered, keeping dopamine levels high, and pleasure intense. The person feels better and less "out of sorts."

Over time, the brain senses that homeostasis (internal balance) has been disrupted and too much neurostimulation is occurring. The body responds by decreasing the amounts of neurotransmitters available or decreasing their effects (such as by decreasing the numbers of dopamine receptors).

The person becomes even more tense, unhappy, or driven, as normally pleasant activities are no longer sufficient to produce a sense of well-being. Reinforcement turns from being provided by the social environment to being provided by the drug.

The person seeks higher or more frequent drug doses to compensate. The brain further adapts. The usual social environment, in turn, becomes increasingly unrewarding. The person is addicted.

blood vessel

antagonist drug

axon

displaced neurotransmitter

receptors

dendrite

synaptic cleft (gap)

Cocaine prevents dopamine reuptake, leaving more dopamine in the synapse.

■ FIGURE 1

A Nervous System–Based Model of Individual Differences in Susceptibility to Drug Addiction

All in all, if certain aspects of personality are indeed based on biologically induced temperament, then we should expect to see such differences in all cultures. Indeed, the introversion–extroversion dimension does seem to appear worldwide (Eysenck, 1990). Also of interest, studies of brain development and brain activity reveal that the brain reaches its maximum number of synaptic connections and its greatest metabolic activity around age 3 or 4, thus supporting the psychoanalytic observation that the basis of personality is formed by around this age. The brain does, however, continue to alter its organization to some extent throughout life.

TIME LINE

The History of Biological Approaches to Personality

The major developments in the biological approach can be seen here in historical relation to one another and in relation to their broader societal and cultural contexts.

Developments in Biological Aspects		Societal and Scientific Context
Charles Darwin publishes *On the Origin of Species by Means of Natural Selection*, the first formal statement about evolution (1859)	1850s–1880s	Biology adopts evolutionary paradigm
Francis Galton studies families and twins, beginning the biological study of individual differences, and he launches the eugenics movement	1860s–1890s	Development of the field of genetics, but Social Darwinism misappropriates ideas to provide a pseudoscientific basis for fascism
Studies of temperament and individual constitution begin, focused on body types and emotional patterns	1940s–1960s	Psychology is dominated by behaviorist and other nonbiological approaches; fascism is defeated and democracy spreads throughout the West
Hans Eysenck proposes brain-based model of personality	1960s–1970s	Hormones, temperament, and brain neurotransmitters begin to receive significant attention
Studies of effects on the brain of drug abuse, pollution, and genetic diseases begin in earnest	1980s	Fields of environmental toxicology and psychopharmacology develop
Evolutionary personality psychology takes root, as evolved predispositions toward sex, love, hate, jealousy, and aggression are studied	1990s	More sophisticated views of genetics and evolution develop, as the complex interactions of biology and behavior are uncovered
Personality psychology begins serious study of the genetic bases of individual behavioral patterns	2000s–	Human genome is unraveled, new ethical challenges arise

Twins as a Source of Data

We should be able to detect systematic biological influences on personality by studying twins. Twin research is indeed now one of the most active areas of research in the study of the biological aspects of personality, with many intriguing studies comparing identical twins to fraternal twins. Identical twins share the same genetic makeup (share 100 percent of their DNA), but fraternal twins (who develop from separate fertilized eggs) have a comparable genetic overlap to ordinary brothers and sisters (sharing 50 percent of their DNA). On various key dimensions—including emotional stability, conscientiousness, intelligence, and extroversion—identical twins are indeed more similar than fraternal twins (Bouchard & McGue, 2003; Heath, Eaves, & Martin, 1989; Rose, Koskenvuo, Kaprio, Sarna, & Langinvainio, 1988; see also Loehlin, 1992).

Does this prove a biological basis? Not necessarily, because identical twins may be treated more similarly than fraternal twins. Identical twins look more alike, and their parents may dress them alike, and so on. Or identical twins may consciously try to act more similarly than fraternal twins. For these reasons, it is much more informative to compare twins who have been adopted and raised apart from each other.

Sir Francis Galton

In the latter half of the nineteenth century, the British scientist Sir Francis Galton began the study of genetic influences on personality (Galton, 1869). He was inspired by the work of his cousin Charles Darwin. Galton drew family trees of blood relatives of famous and eminent people. Sure enough, he found that eminence seemed to run in families. For example, a son might succeed his father as a professor at a university chair (professorship). Galton also noticed that among the lower classes in nineteenth-century Britain, hardly anyone achieved eminence.

Although one of the most brilliant and well-intentioned men of his time, in retrospect Galton was what we would today call a benign racist. He endeavored to be scientific, but he began from the supposition that upper-class Englishmen were a superior population. It is hardly surprising that the son of a wealthy, well-educated professor would be more likely to achieve prominence in a hierarchical society than would the son of poor, illiterate parents. To his credit (given the tenor of the times), Galton recognized this possibility, and he suggested that adopted children be studied, including adoptive twins. So it was Galton who began this type of study. But Galton did not worry that too much would come of such studies; he was convinced of his own natural superiority (and that of his relatives and friends).

© Thinkstock

■ Parents may draw attention to the similarity of identical twins by dressing them in the same clothing, providing matching hairstyles, and treating them identically. If identical twins are treated more similarly to each other than fraternal twins are, then we cannot conclude that greater similarity in personality among the identical twins is of purely genetic origin. So, psychologists have turned to studying twins raised apart.

It is curious that one seemingly obvious flaw in Galton's line of thinking did not jump out and destroy it—namely, the case of women. Female children of eminent British professors did not follow their fathers into professorships. Women were generally not even allowed access to the best schools. (In the United States, women could not graduate from top colleges like Yale or Princeton until the 1970s.) The same lack of access and resources, of course, applied to the lower classes—men as well as women—in Galton's Britain.

Interestingly, Galton also began the **eugenics** ("good birth" or "good genes") movement. He argued that eminent families should have lots of children, thus improving human blood lines. Unfortunately, this seemingly well-intentioned line of thinking contributed to the scientifically "justified" worldwide racism (even genocide) that tainted the twentieth century. (We return to this issue later in this chapter.) Biological theories of personality seem inextricably tied to social and political outcomes.

Eugenics
The movement begun by Francis Galton that encouraged preserving or purifying the gene pool of the elite in order to improve human blood lines

Minnesota Twin Study

Consider now the case of Jack and Oskar. Jack and Oskar are identical twins who were separated in infancy but brought together as adults. Oskar was raised in Germany by his Catholic maternal grandmother; Jack was raised outside Europe by his Jewish father. It turns out that these twin brothers share many traits and habits. They are both absentminded, like spicy foods, and most important for our purposes, have a domineering, angry sort of temperament.

As identical twins, Jack and Oskar have the same genes (i.e., are *monozygotic*—coming from a single zygote or fertilized egg). Given their disparate upbringings, their similarities are likely somehow due to their genetic endowments. No one has a problem with this argument in terms of Jack's and Oskar's striking physical resemblance. But direct genetic control of personality is less easy to swallow.

These identical twins and others raised apart from each other have been gathered in a study at the University of Minnesota (Bouchard, 1999; Bouchard, Lykken, McGue, & Segal, 1990). Such studies have found impressive similarities in personality between people who have the same genetic makeup. These similarities are less than those of identical twins raised together, thus showing the influence of the environmental upbringing. But the similarities of identical twins are greater than those of fraternal twins, who have overlapping but not identical genetic makeups (Pedersen, Plomin, McClearn, & Friberg, 1988; see also McCartney, Harris, & Bernieri, 1990).

The controversy arises as to *why* identical twins have such similar personalities. Is there a gene for being stingy and a gene for being optimistic? Probably not. But, as noted previously, there may very well be patterns of genes that affect our temperaments and our behavioral predispositions—for example, that make us more aggressive or more sensitive and cautious. When these innate tendencies encounter similar environmental pressures, they may often result in similar patterns of behavior—that

■ The case of identical twins separated at birth provides a potentially rich source of information about the roles of genetic and environmental factors in determining personality. These twins didn't even know of one another's existence until they met as adults and discovered striking parallels. Both had become fire captains, and both wore similar mustaches and glasses and had many of the same personality traits.

© Thomas Wanstall/ The Image Works

Classic to Current

It's Not Nature versus Nurture

Evolutionary personality theory attempts to root out individual behavior patterns in our evolutionary history. For example, throughout time, males who did not ensure that their mates remained faithful would have helped raise the children of another male. Their own characteristics thus would not survive, but those of the "jealous" males who watched their mates would have more survivable offspring. Thus, it could be argued that there was selection for genes associated with jealousy. Of course, this analysis assumes that we know what the selection factors (for survival) were at some time long ago. Some theorists might then make the further oversimplified assumption that "jealous" men have this "jealous" gene. Such theorists might scoff at the neoanalytic notions of the childhood (learned) bases of jealousy.

One problem with such a nature-versus-nurture analysis is that genes unfold and have their effects as a function of the environments they are in (Gottlieb, 2000). For example, the genes that control the development of the visual cortex of cats do not activate without visual stimulation. The genes that control the auditory system of mice do not activate without the proper acoustic stimulation. Even in fruit flies, the light–dark cycle is necessary for certain protein expression. Genes activate as a function of the environment, and we do not yet understand how or if this occurs with complex human emotions.

Perhaps more important, many characteristics that seem to be genetically determined are not really controlled simply or directly by genes. One interesting example of this involves attitudes, which are surely learned within a subculture and culture. An insightful study compared monozygotic (identical) and dizygotic (fraternal) twins on a wide range of attitudes. Looking at the twins' differences in various ways, this study found a "genetic basis" for certain attitudes (Olson, Vernon, Harris, & Jang, 2001). But this does not at all mean that we inherit a gene for a specific attitude.

In the example in which attitudes toward athleticism seemed to have a biological basis (in the twin comparisons), such attitudes were correlated with self-reported athletic ability. The findings likely indicate that individuals born with tendencies toward naturally good coordination and strength were more successful at sports, more understanding of sports, more involved in sports, and so developed more favorable attitudes toward sports. Similarly, attitudes toward intense experiences like loud music, big parties, and roller coaster rides showed a strong "genetic" basis in the comparisons among twins. This does not mean that we are born with a tendency regarding such attitudes (the "I like roller coasters gene"). Rather, this suggests that a complex biological tendency toward enjoying certain experiences can sometimes lead us to form corresponding attitudes. Seen in this light, it does not make much sense to make a simple, sharp separation between nature and nurture for many human behavior patterns.

FURTHER READING

Gottlieb, G. (2000). Environmental and behavioral influences on gene activity. *Current Directions in Psychological Science, 9*, 93–97.

Olson, J. M., Vernon, P. A., Harris, J. A., & Jang, K. L. (2001). The heritability of attitudes: A study of twins. *Journal of Personality and Social Psychology, 80*, 845–860.

is, similar personalities (Waller, Kojetin, Bouchard, & Lykken, 1990). For example, a cautious, unaggressive boy with a body that is sensitive to pain and stimulation may be unlikely to become a football tackle. This is not to say there is a gene for "sports interest," but there likely is a genetic influence on relevant responsiveness. The distinction is important because it implies that given the right circumstances, the cautious, sensitive, unaggressive boy might very well become a star football tackle.

Along these lines, one study compared monozygotic (identical) and dizygotic (fraternal) twins on a wide range of attitudes and found a "genetic basis" for certain attitudes (Olson et al., 2001). This does not at all mean that we inherit a gene for a specific attitude. (See the Classic to Current box.) Another study found that identical twins are more alike in whether they vote in elections than are fraternal twins (Fowler, Baker, & Dawes, 2008), but this doesn't mean that there is a gene called "tendency to vote." We won't know why such associations emerge until we understand much more about the complex biological bases of human social behavior and development, and how they are affected by specific environments.

There is an ongoing search for genes that might underlie certain aggressive or antisocial personalities. For example, following Galton's example, researchers constructed family trees of a group of aggressive men in the Netherlands (Morell, 1993). It is thought that a genetic defect prevents manufacture of an enzyme that breaks down certain neurotransmitters (technically a monoamine oxidase polymorphism). When faced with environmental challenge, these men are primed to "go off"—to overreact because their nervous systems are not being properly regulated. Note that if such a link does become firmly established, the gene itself does not directly cause the aggression. Rather, the gene affects an enzyme, which predisposes the body to react in certain ways; the actual reactions are then determined by the environment and by other aspects of the person. Further, as we shall see, there may be gene-influenced differences in parenting styles, or evoked bad parenting from an aggressive child (Moffitt, 2005).

Nurture and Nonshared Environmental Variance

Children of the same parents who are raised in the same family share both some biological endowment and much environmental influence, yet their personalities are often strikingly different (Saudino, 1997). To some extent, children in the same family have different experiences and are treated differently, but it is difficult to know precisely how and why (Baker & Daniels, 1990; Dunn & Plomin, 1990). Significantly, in moving from childhood to adulthood, the environmental effects on personality become more evident. There is an inverse correlation between personality similarity and age for both monozygotic and dizygotic twins: As twins get older, their personalities become more different (McCartney et al., 1990).

In a controversial book *The Nurture Assumption* (1999), author Judith Rich Harris argued that parents matter little but peers (classmates and friends) sometimes matter a lot. Harris began with the evidence that identical twins raised apart have similar personalities. She went on to note that different children raised by the same parents have different personalities; that many children from loving homes turn to drugs or violence; that adoptive children raised by the same parents have different personalities and so on, with more evidence showing the limits of parenting.

In some ways this analysis overstates its case. For example, on broader, complex traits (rather than specific biological abilities), children do tend to adopt their parents' religions, styles of interaction, political affiliations, and many attitudes and customs (Plomin, 2001; Segal, 1999). By pointing out the importance of peers, Harris does, however, illustrate the concept of **nonshared environmental variance**. Nonshared environmental variance includes those features of the environment that children raised in the same home experience differently (Turkheimer & Waldron, 2000). Most obviously, the first child in a family experiences the second child as a sibling, whereas the second child has the first child as a sibling. Their family environments thus include different members. But there are many other differences. Each sibling does not live in

Nonshared Environmental Variance Features of the environment that children raised in the same home experience differently

the other siblings' shoes, and their many minor daily experiences differ. As a child grows older, he or she begins choosing certain environments but is also exposed to more varied situations, and so some aspects of the genetic predispositions become more important while others become less important (Bergen, Gardner, & Kendler, 2007; Haworth, Dale, & Plomin, 2009a).

Getting back to the case of studies of identical twins raised apart, who often show similar personalities, many complex questions arise (Johnson, Turkheimer, Gottesman, & Bouchard, 2009). Were they placed into similar types of homes by adoption agencies? Did they learn about each other, perhaps through hearing about their twin? Do they try to act similarly upon being brought together, knowing they are twins? Did they tend to seek out similar environments? Perhaps most important, was the process of their similar personality development much more complex than a simple genetic model would assume?

So again, how much of personality is genetically determined? No simple answers are expected to be forthcoming in the near future. In fact, the question itself is too simplistic to be helpful in understanding individual differences. Biological predispositions interact with the eliciting circumstances of the environment and the influence of the environments we seek out (Bouchard, 1999, 2004; Reiss, 1997). Some

Famous Personalities

Born Athletes?: Venus and Serena Williams

Since the mid-1990s, the world of women's tennis has been shaken up by the rapid rise of two amazing players. Venus and Serena Williams, sisters born just 15 months apart, are in many respects an unlikely pair of tennis stars. They are strikingly different in many ways from most of their close competitors on the women's professional tennis circuit. They are African Americans from a disadvantaged background, champions in a sport characterized by its connection to genteel upper-class old-money society. They are flamboyant in their dress and style within a sport where restrained and decorous behavior—by both the players and their fans—is traditional. They did not participate fully in the junior tournaments that are the normal stepping-stone to the women's professional circuit, and they both turned pro at the early age of 14.

Their success has been phenomenal, though. When younger sister Serena won the U.S. Open championship in 1999, she was the first African American woman to win a Grand Slam title in over 40 years. Older sister Venus

has won Wimbledon several times and had her first U.S. Open victory in 2000. They have played against one another in the final match of a grand slam tournament many times, knowing that the title would stay in the family. They are willing and able to compete when they play against one another—but they form a well-coordinated team when they play doubles. Playing together, Serena and Venus have repeatedly won major doubles titles, as well as the Olympic gold medal for women's doubles. At different times, each sister has been ranked the number one women's player. Between them, they hold over a dozen Grand Slam wins in singles, and another dozen in doubles (playing as partners).

They show a strong resemblance to one another in many ways—unsurprising, perhaps, given their shared genetic background as full siblings. Both women are tall and muscular; they have similar facial features; and they both have the strength, speed, stamina, agility, and coordination that have allowed them to become world-class athletes. Plus, they have spent many years together in intensive training and on the competition circuit. But maybe you have never heard of Isha, Lyndrea, or the late Yetunde, half-sisters of Venus and Serena Williams. They were never involved in playing professional tennis or any other professional sport. They are genetically similar to Venus and Serena, so there

reviewers estimate that approximately 40 to 50 percent of the variance in personality characteristics is genetically influenced, but it is hard to understand what this number means (except in a mathematical sense in an adoptive twins study), since it is established that biology, socialization, and environment all are important to personality and behavior (Borkenau, Riemann, Angleitner, & Spinath, 2001). That is, genes set us on a path, but the ultimate directions we take are then heavily influenced by the people and circumstances we encounter. Further, there is substantial flexibility in the central nervous system, allowing for changes in brain development to occur as a result of environmental (nurture) experiences.

Schizophrenia, Bipolar Disorder, Depression

It is easy to overgeneralize the importance of genetics to personality. Consider the case of schizophrenia. **Schizophrenia** is a devastating condition in which a person loses touch with reality. Such people may have delusions, become paranoid, and generally talk or behave very strangely. Interestingly, up until the 1960s, most psychologists and psychiatrists believed that schizophrenia was caused by disturbed parenting. The evidence was that deviant children tended to have deviant parents.

Schizophrenia
A condition whose symptoms include distorted reality, odd emotional reactions, and sometimes paranoia and/or delusions

might be more to the success of Venus and Serena than their genes and their family environment. Of course, it could simply be the case that Venus and Serena inherited more of the traits that make for a successful athletic career than their older sisters did, but there is probably a stronger case to be made for the influence of specific experiences.

In fact, news reports claim that their father, Richard Williams, decided that his younger children would grow up to be tennis stars. As their manager and coach, he created their training regimen and exposed them from a very early age to the experiences that would allow his dream to come true. Of course, had the youngest girls not had the necessary athletic talent, intelligence, and temperament, their father's dream would never have come to fruition. But his planning, supervision, and support were also essential factors in their success—factors that differentiate Venus and Serena from their older sisters who were not given the same early training or subjected to the same pressures. Maybe the older sisters had the same athletic gifts as Venus and Serena, but lacked the appropriate environmental stimulation that would have allowed those gifts to develop. The abilities and predispositions of star athletes have a genetic component, but appropriate environmental factors are necessary as well. In a sense, great athletes are born, then they are made.

© Julian Finney/Getty Images

■ When two members of the same family are strikingly successful in the same domain, it is likely that both hereditary similarities and a common home environment are responsible. Venus and Serena Williams are sisters, world-class athletes, and tennis celebrities.

Why Does It Matter?

Simple genetic determinism of personality has been discredited but many people do not understand this; unfortunately, they look for straightforward explanations of abilities and behavior. The problem is that we may then invalidly and incorrectly give up on ourselves or others, thinking "why bother to practice hard, train thoroughly, or be devoted to a goal, since academic success, athletic ability, popularity, and success are all genetically fixed anyway?"

As the influence of biological abnormalities on markedly abnormal behavior became better understood, an intensive search began for biological causes of this disorder. Many studies have confirmed that schizophrenia tends to run in families (Schiffman & Walker, 1998). That is, if one has a schizophrenic parent, the odds of schizophrenia rise dramatically. They rise even further if one has a fraternal twin with this condition. Most important, if one has a schizophrenic identical twin, the odds approach 50–50 of developing this strange syndrome of distorted reality and odd emotional reactions. A correlation exists even if the twins are raised in different families (Gottesman, 1991; Gottesman & Moldin, 1998).

Because of these correlations, some have concluded that schizophrenia is a genetic disease. This is an imprecise deduction at best, as many of the identical twins of schizophrenics never develop the condition. (In comparison, the identical twin of someone with blue eyes always has blue eyes.) If schizophrenia is simply a direct result of defective genes, then the identical twins of schizophrenics should likewise have the condition. Furthermore, a careful analysis of the brains of identical twins casts doubt on this assertion of direct genetic causation. In this study, 15 sets of identical twins were studied; in each set, one twin had schizophrenia and the other was normal. As identical twins, the members of each pair had identical genetic makeup. However, using brain MRI scans and related techniques, scientists were able to show clear differences in their brain structure. The afflicted twin usually had larger fluid-filled ventricles, suggesting that some brain tissue was missing. The schizophrenic twins also had some signs of brain atrophy or developmental failure (Suddath, Christison, Torrey, & Casanova, 1990). Because identical genes would give identical instructions to the body for brain development, something else—some other factor—must be contributing to the schizophrenic brain development (or lack thereof). Faced with this puzzle, researchers now say that there is a "genetic predisposition" to schizophrenia; that is, certain genes make schizophrenia more likely, but they are not the sole, direct cause. What it really means is that genes play some role but we really don't know how the process works.

The same is true of many other genetic influences on personality. For example, the probability of a match—called *concordance*—of **bipolar disorder** (manic-depressive illness) is very high. If an individual swings regularly from wildly enthusiastic energy to hopelessly dark depression, then the identical twin is also very likely to suffer this disorder. The concordance is high (Suinn, 1995). Yet it is also well established that depression is a complex phenomenon, heavily influenced by the environment. It would be a serious mistake to think of it as solely biologically determined.

In fact, certain persons with a particular genetic makeup are especially likely to become depressed when exposed to significant stressful life events (Caspi et al., 2003). That is, depression can often be predicted by an interaction of a certain gene pattern and stressful challenges in life. Individuals who have the risky genes but live in a healthy environment are much less likely to develop depression. In another study of the interaction of genes and life challenges, researchers analyzed individual variation in a gene called the mu opioid receptor gene (OPRM1). This gene is

Bipolar disorder (also called manic-depression)
A disorder in which an individual swings regularly between bouts of wildly enthusiastic energy and bouts of hopeless depression

related to pain perception—both physical pain and the pain of social rejection. (Morphine affects this receptor.) The study found that individuals with this genetic variation were more sensitive to social rejection (that is, being excluded from a game of catch), and that this social pain could be seen (on fMRI brain imaging) in the region of the brain that generally processes physical pain (Way, Taylor, & Eisenberger, 2009). Thus, we should always remember to consider the influence of biological factors on personality in a broad context. This necessitates sophisticated thinking about biology and personality.

Sexual Identity and Homosexuality

People who are sexually attracted to members of their own gender have existed throughout history and in all societies around the world. In addition to engaging in nonnormative sexual practices, gay men and lesbians sometimes exhibit expressive behaviors that appear to indicate a homosexual orientation. Homosexuality or heterosexuality is clearly an important aspect of personality, one that a personality theory should be able to explain.

Freud, in a now-discredited analysis, regarded homosexuality as an illness, resulting from a disruption of normal psychosexual development. According to Freud, a normal child passes through psychosexual stages until his sexual urges can finally be directed, in a mature way, at an appropriate love object of the opposite gender. Most children pass through a stage in this process with a love of their own genitals—a self-focused, narcissistic love. But some children retain a focus on their own genitals as a love object: Some little boys do not grow to identify with their fathers but instead try to please their fathers and eventually look to find lovers with genitals like their own. That is, they become homosexual. This argument, although unsupported by research, did have a major impact on the practice of psychiatry. Not until 1974 did the American Psychiatric Association evaluate the scientific invalidity of the Freudian explanation and remove homosexuality from its handbook of mental illnesses, much to the relief of the thousands of well-functioning gay men and lesbians. In fact, much of the distress felt by this group can be traced to society's severe reactions against them (Herschberger, 1998).

Many gay men and lesbians report being attracted to members of their own gender even before having any sexual experiences. Many face societal persecution or discrimination; there is little reason to think that gay people actively choose to have these feelings and attractions. Because homosexual just seems to be the way some people are, interest has been drawn to possible biological bases. But because of the great societal stigma attached to homosexuality, research on homosexuality in humans is sparse, contradictory, or uninformative. Some research suggests that a homosexual predisposition is at least partly (but only partly) genetically determined (Bailey & Pillard, 1991, 1995; Buhrich, Bailey, & Martin, 1991). Homosexuality tends to run in families, and monozygotic twins are more likely than dizygotic twins to have the same sexual preference (Långström, Rahman, Carlström, & Lichtenstein, 2010). There is also some evidence that part of the brain's anterior hypothalamus, known to be related to sexual behavior, is significantly smaller in gay men (LeVay, 1991), and that the hypothalamus reacts differently to sexual smells in

Why Does It Matter?

Why some people are attracted to same-sex partners and how society should recognize long-term relationships between same-sex people have become controversial social and political issues. As scientific understanding of these matters increases and is distributed to the general public, societal awareness may better correspond to real issues and dissipate irrational fears (Herek, 2006). Personality psychology cannot solve legal and moral conflicts, but it can provide data that are relevant to reasoned discussions.

gay versus straight men (Savic, Berglund, & Lindström, 2005) and in lesbian versus straight women (Berglund, Lindström, & Savic, 2006). None of these factors alone proves that homosexuality has a genetic origin. But, taken in concert with the fact that homosexuality seems universal across time and culture, these findings are strongly suggestive of at least some biological origin for a tendency toward homosexuality.

On the other hand, the fact that the associations between genetic heritage and homosexuality are nowhere near perfect suggests that environmental factors often play an important role in this aspect of personality (Bailey, Dunne, & Martin, 2000). As we have seen with other biological predispositions, biological sexual orientation probably grows or matures in certain ways in certain contexts. It is also possible that some instances of homosexuality have nothing to do with genetics and are instead the result of conditioning or other experiences. Some gay people, especially those who reach puberty early, may be surrounded by friends of the same sex (most 11-year-old boys have only other boys as close friends); and so these boys may have their first sexual fantasies or early experiences with same-sex others (Storms, 1981). Such pleasurable experiences may then be sought in the future. This is a possible but unproven environmental basis for some homosexuality. The different perspectives on personality are not mutually exclusive; on the contrary, we need various approaches in order to understand fully the diversity of human behavior. This may not be satisfying to those who seek a simple, definitive explanation of complex behavior patterns, but it is a reflection of the state of our current understanding.

Photo courtesy of Jennifer Lin and Jeanne Fong

■ Although homosexuality appears to have some biological basis, gays—like all people—are heavily influenced by their cultures and upbringings. Many people in the gay and lesbian community are fighting for the right to civil marriage. The legal rights and responsibilities granted to spouses are one major goal, but symbolic recognition by society, including the opportunity to be a bride or a groom, is also a motivation. Here, marriage equality activists Jennifer Lin and Jeanne Fong attend a rally in support of same-sex marriage.

Exotic Becomes Erotic

Another approach that attempts to combine biology and socialization into explaining some cases of homosexuality or bisexuality is encapsulated in Daryl Bem's (1996) phrase "exotic becomes erotic." Simply stated, Bem proposes that inborn temperament influences young children to engage in gender-congruent (socially expected) behavior or not. For example, a little girl who likes to play quietly in a nurturing way will have girls as friends. But if she tends to prefer lots of rough and tumble ("tomboy") activities, then she will have many boys as friends. In this latter case, boys will seem common and ordinary.

What happens at adolescence? As the hormones of puberty hit, so do strong feelings and physiological arousal. Although most girls apply this arousal to exotic figures like music stars and movie actors and then even to those unfamiliar boys at her school, the tomboy already has lots of boys as friends and so she may see certain girls as exotic, and then as erotic. The opposite is true of certain boys; some of those who grow up with many female friends might become intrigued with boys. Although this theory has not yet been well tested, it does illustrate that there are various possible complex pathways to sexual attraction.

Reproductive Advantage

How can homosexuality have been selected through evolution, given that gay people usually have fewer biological children than heterosexuals? Why didn't tendencies toward homosexuality disappear long ago, since there does not seem to be much survival value inherent in this tendency?

One possibility involves what is called **kin selection** (Burnstein, Crandall, & Kitayama, 1994). If the nieces and nephews of gays and lesbians are especially likely to survive, then the genetic tendency toward homosexuality will also survive (because nieces and nephews share some genetic makeup with their gay aunt or uncle). Research on this hypothesis, however, has failed to support it (Bobrow & Bailey, 2001; Rahman & Hull, 2005), although gay men may be especially altruistic toward their nieces and nephews (Vasey & VanderLaan, 2010).

Or, perhaps the straight sisters of gay men are especially likely to have more children. This idea that the enhanced fitness of relatives is sometimes very important is termed *inclusive fitness*. (The Scottish physiologist Haldane is said to have dryly remarked that he would lay down his life for two brothers or eight cousins.) That is, such analyses shift attention away from the individual's survival and toward analysis of the whole population—population genetics.

Another possibility is that a genetic tendency toward gayness survives because it somehow confers a direct reproductive advantage to heterosexuals who carry it. What this might be is currently not known. Finally, there is the poorly understood phenomenon of **bisexuality**, namely sexual attraction to both men and women. Many people who engage in homosexual behavior also engage in heterosexual behavior, possibly as part of a greater or more undifferentiated interest in sexual matters. Some research suggests that bisexual men do not have the same strong genital arousal in response to both male and female sexual stimuli but rather have a more of a subjective interpretation of being so aroused (Rieger, Chivers, & Bailey, 2005). Bisexual women likewise often maintain sexual relationships with both men and women rather than becoming more lesbian over time (Diamond, 2008).

Sex Hormones and Experience

It may also be the case that some biological aspects of homosexuality result from early hormonal experiences and not genetics. For example, medical conditions or drugs in the mother may affect the child in the uterus or in early infancy (Persky, 1987). Indeed, many biological bases of personality result from early experiences rather

Kin Selection
The idea that increasing the likelihood for the family members of an individual to survive increases the likelihood that the individual's genes will be carried on to the next generation even if the individual did not reproduce him- or herself

Bisexuality
Sexual attraction to both men and women

CHANGING **Personality**

Because the biological perspective sees personality as heavily influenced by hormones and neurotransmitters, the most direct route for personality change is through pharmaceuticals. So, for example, to change the personality of men with abnormal and illegal sexual interests such as pedophilia (sexual attraction to children) or exhibitionism (flashing), we might turn to a drug like leuprolide acetate (Lupron). This drug acts on the pituitary gland at the base of the brain to dramatically reduce the blood levels of certain important sex hormones. As testosterone levels fall, so should sexual urges (Guay, 2009; Schober et al., 2005).

It turns out, however, that although leuprolide acetate does reduce sexual urges (as does castration), it is not by itself a cure for these sexual disorders termed paraphilias ("abnormal attractions"). Rather, severe sexual deviancy also depends on the individual's thoughts, his past learning experiences, the current environment, and often on unusual childhood experiences. Thus, multi-pronged treatments are often much more effective than a simple use of pharmaceutical medicines alone. And in some cases, learning and motivations are so deep-seated and habitual that strong biological intervention has no significant effect at all on the deviant behavior.

than from genes. The growth of the brain and the rest of the nervous system—a biological factor—is strongly influenced not only by genes but also by the environment.

Because unique results emerge when certain biological aspects of personality are combined with certain environments, the outcomes cannot be predicted by either the biology or the environment alone. For example, in a hard-driving autocratic family in which the father uses lots of punishment to raise his two sons, the inherently aggressive, outgoing son might grow up hard-driving and autocratic like his father, whereas the sensitive, emotional son might grow up kind and charitable, vowing never to behave like his cruel, loudmouthed father. If, however, the same two sons were raised by a very nurturing, democratic father, the results might almost reverse; the sensitive son might grow up more assertive while the aggressive son might channel his energies into helping others. In other words, there is an interaction effect. In mathematical terms, personality is a multiplicative function of the two influences, rather than an additive function. In analyzing the origins of sexual identity and gender-typed behavior, we cannot simply average together the biological influences and the environmental influences to predict personality; rather, we must analyze the uniqueness that results when the two combine.

Ménière's Disease
An inner-ear disorder that can produce disabling dizziness, nausea, and auditory disturbances

Mediated Effects of Biology

© Bridgeman-Giraudon/Art Resource, NY

■ Vincent van Gogh (shown here in self-portrait) cut off part of his own ear with a razor after a quarrel with Paul Gauguin and committed suicide shortly thereafter. His bizarre behavior may have been the result of the psychological effects of organic disease.

Vincent van Gogh, the brilliant impressionist painter, was long thought to be such an intense genius that he drove himself mad. Indeed, van Gogh often behaved oddly and even cut off his own ear (and then painted a self-portrait). He committed suicide in 1890. It now appears that van Gogh may have suffered not from a personality dysfunction, but from **Ménière's disease**, an inner-ear disorder that can produce disabling dizziness, nausea, and auditory disturbances (Arenberg, 1990). Illness can cause dramatic effects on our patterns of reactions, and toxic substances can also cause such changes.

Effects through Environmental Toxins: Poisoning

In *Alice in Wonderland*, Alice encounters the Mad Hatter. The phrase "mad as a hatter" has been in common use for over a century. It arose because hat makers in fact suffered brain damage as they worked with mercury in making felt hats (as described in the photo caption). It is now well documented that dramatic changes in personality can result from poisoning.

Today, mercury is commonly used in industry and agriculture and sometimes shows up in fish that lived in polluted waters. People who eat contaminated fish may start behaving strangely; ingestion of mercury is known to produce marked changes in personality, even today (Fagala & Wigg, 1992; O'Carroll, Masterton, Dougall, & Ebmeier, 1995). Because mercury is a component of dental amalgams (cavity fillings), there has been much speculation in recent years about possible subtle effects on physical and mental health. There is, however, no solid evidence that people are being inadvertently poisoned by their dentists.

Although acute mercury poisoning is relatively rare, heavy metal neurotoxicity (brain impairment) is still widespread. Today, a significant number of children suffer gradual brain damage traceable to lead poisoning. Many hundreds of thousands of children are exposed to potentially toxic levels of lead from old paint or plumbing fixtures, leaded gasoline, and other environmental sources. Lead poisons the child's developing nervous system, impairing cognitive function and producing deviant (often antisocial) behavior (Marcus, Fulton & Clarke, 2010; Needleman & Bellinger, 1991). Bone tests have shown Ludwig von Beethoven suffered from lead poisoning, perhaps the cause of his chronic irritability (and abdominal pain).

Many other metals, including manganese and cadmium, likely affect personality, although to an unknown degree (Hubbs-Tait, Nation, Krebs, & Bellinger, 2005; Kern, Stanwood, & Smith, 2010). People who mine manganese sometimes become compulsive fighters and later develop Parkinson's disease. Manganese also seems to affect some Pacific Islanders, whose volcanic soil is rich in this and other metals.

Effects through Physical Illness

A stable personality depends on a healthy, well-functioning brain. Diseases or toxins that affect brain function often affect personality (Grunberg, Klein, & Brown, 1998). Besides metals, there is a long list of toxic substances known to affect personality, but often it is not known whether the problem is triggered by toxins, microbes, or the body's own failings. **Alzheimer's disease** is a devastating ailment of the brain's cerebral cortex. Although it usually strikes only elderly people, its root cause is unknown. The early psychological manifestations of Alzheimer's are often quirks of behavior and some memory loss. As the disease progresses, alterations in personality are dramatic; the patients seem to lose their personalities altogether. These effects are often the most difficult to bear for the (grown) children of elderly people living with Alzheimer's. It is tragic to watch a parent lose his or her personality and become a stranger. The pain we experience in facing such changes demonstrates the great degree to which we do indeed love people for their personalities.

Strokes, which damage parts of the brain, also can have dramatic effects on personality. Often, a kind person who has a stroke becomes aggressive and uncooperative; sometimes the reverse occurs. It depends in part on which region of the brain is damaged. Many other medical conditions (such as temporal lobe epilepsy) and various surgical procedures also can produce biologically based changes in personality, but these are rarely studied by personality psychologists. For example, many people complain to doctors that their spouses' personalities became somehow "different" after they underwent coronary bypass surgery, but this phenomenon is not fully understood. One possibility is that the life-support

■ For *Alice's Adventures in Wonderland,* author Lewis Carroll and his illustrator Sir John Tenniel created the character of the "Mad Hatter" who exemplifies the nineteenth-century stereotype of the mentally unstable hat maker. Although the psychiatric symptoms of mercury poisoning even have their own name in the medical literature, "erythism," there are likely many other instances not yet recognized in which toxic chemicals in the environment alter aspects of behavior and personality.

Alzheimer's Disease
A disease of the brain's cerebral cortex, primarily affecting elderly people, that causes altered behavior and memory loss

and anesthesia procedures used in the operating room may damage small areas of the brain. It is interesting to speculate that a wide range of diseases may have poorly understood or subtle effects on personality. Just as diseases such as Alzheimer's and poisons such as lead were not understood for many years, there are undoubtedly many conditions and toxins that today affect personality, though they are unknown to us.

In Pick's disease (see Figure 2), as in Alzheimer's, there is brain deterioration, but there is often a dramatic change in a patient's sense of self, long before total incapacity. In particular, patients with deterioration in the brain's right frontal lobe (an area that is not related to language) may markedly change their beliefs and preferences (Miller, 2001; Perry & Miller, 2001). For example, one wealthy woman quickly discarded her designer clothes and switched from eating French cuisine to eating at Taco Bell. Physical illnesses, including such frontotemporal lobe dementias can thus give us important insights into the biological bases of personality (Goodkind, Gyurak, McCarthy, Miller, & Levenson, 2010), but it would be a big mistake to claim that the frontal lobe is the "ego."

Our understanding of such biological influences on personality has major implications for our beliefs about law and justice. One extreme position is that most criminal or evil acts are committed by people who couldn't help themselves; they are either compelled, or not restrained, by some disorder in their nervous system. Interestingly, although this position is often identified with a very liberal or left-wing political orientation, it is actually quite similar to the position that some people simply have "bad genes." This latter argument is usually made by conservative, right-wing politicians. Thus, ironically, both extreme political positions are often comfortable with the idea of **biological determinism** of personality.

The more difficult, complex position is the one that acknowledges that biological factors influence personality but still recognizes the individual's capacity to challenge and sometimes overcome these biological tendencies. In fact, we usually attribute the mantle of true heroism only to those noble people among us—such as Helen Keller or Vincent van Gogh—who can overcome the frailties inherent in their "nature."

Biological Determinism The belief that an individual's personality is completely determined by biological factors (and especially by genetic factors)

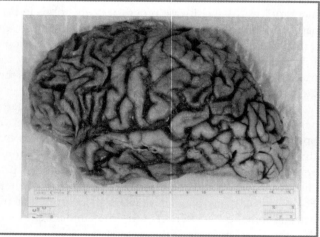

■ FIGURE 2

Brain of a Person with Pick's Disease

Pick's disease is a degenerative brain disease that can result in dramatic changes in one's sense of self. This brain shows atrophy (shrinkage) of the neocortex, where the convolutions (folds) of grey matter would normally fill the space. Patients with significant damage to their brain's right frontal lobe seem to lose their normal sense of self. For example, one lifelong political conservative suddenly became a radical animal-rights activist.

SHARPEN YOUR THINKING   Current Controversy

Postpartum Personality

Depression can be a consistent and stable feature of a person's psychological profile; complex interactions of biological, psychological, and environmental factors can be part of the development and persistence of this complex disorder (Ingram & Scher, 1998). But there is a specific subtype of depression that has a strikingly straightforward biological basis: postpartum depression. In the postpartum (literally, after birth) period, the woman who has just given birth is at very high risk for depressive illness. Although a difficult home situation and prior psychological problems increase the risk, these disorders are common even in women with no personal or family history of mental illness whose pregnancy was desired and planned (Seyfried & Marcus, 2003).

A very substantial portion of new mothers suffer a brief mood disorder called the "baby blues" (or the "maternity blues"): Within three to five days after the birth, the new mother experiences a period of one to three days of sadness, irritability, confusion, anxiety, crying spells, volatile mood, sleep disturbances, and changes in appetite as her hormones fluctuate dramatically (Hamilton, 1989; O'Hara, 1995). Fortunately, this mild disturbance fades quickly and without any treatment in most women.

More serious is postpartum depression, which is estimated to occur in over 10 percent of postpartum women. Postpartum depression is diagnosed on the basis of the same criterion used for depression in general (that is, the presence of at least five of nine specific symptoms), beginning soon after childbirth. Although most women recover with treatment, postpartum depression can have long-term negative consequences for the mother, her new baby, and the rest of the family.

The most serious postpartum disorder is postpartum psychosis, a rare but devastating illness. In this psychotic illness, women can be dangerously out of touch with reality, experiencing persistent disturbing thoughts, hallucinations, and delusions. These thoughts, hallucinations, and delusions often focus on suicide, the baby's death, or the mother and/or her baby being possessed by demons or having divine powers. In this psychotic state, some women go beyond fantasizing or hallucinating the death of their babies and commit infanticide. Should such an act be considered murder, and punished accordingly, or should the mother's mental state qualify her for an insanity defense?

When Andrea Yates drowned her five children in a bathtub six months after the birth of the youngest, she was charged with murder, convicted, and sentenced to life in prison. While Yates admitted that she had killed the children, she pled not guilty by reason of insanity. Her insanity defense did not succeed—the jury accepted that she was mentally ill at the time of the murders, but they were convinced that she knew that the murders were wrong, and thus she did not meet the legal criterion for the insanity defense. (Her conviction was later overturned due to an error made by an expert prosecution witness, and she was found not guilty by reason of insanity in her retrial and committed to a mental hospital.) Many Western countries (including Great Britain, Canada, Italy, and Australia) specifically allow a woman's postpartum depression to be used as a defense against charges of infanticide, but the United States does not.

Postpartum psychosis is closely tied to changes in hormonal and neurotransmitter function that occur in the period just after a woman gives birth. Should the strong biological basis of the disorder change the level of legal responsibility? Is infanticide by the mother a different crime from other infanticides? Is it different from any other form of killing by a person who is psychotic? If a society determines that infanticide committed by a psychotic mother is "special" in terms of its legal treatment, does that open the door to other biological states (such as menopause or premenstrual syndrome [PMS]) gaining special status? To what extent should legal treatment reflect what is known about biological states, and should the laws change as our biological understanding improves?

■ A drug, pramipexole, prescribed to treat Parkinson's disease, helps restore dopamine levels in the brain but can lead to compulsive gambling or hypersexuality.

istockphoto

Effects from Legal and Illegal Drugs

Many chemical effects are not accidental. Widely prescribed drugs such as tranquilizers (like Valium), sleeping pills (like Halcion), and various antidepressants (like Prozac) are known to have short-term and sometimes long-term effects on personality. Long-lasting, dramatic alterations in personality are thought to be quite rare, but they can occur with a single dose of a drug such as cocaine or LSD. The fact that dramatic changes occur at all should make us wonder about more widespread, subtle effects (Alessandri, Sullivan, Bendersky, & Lewis, 1995; McMahon & Richards, 1996).

Consider the case of chronic cocaine users. Cocaine tends to produce symptoms of paranoia. Users may become hypersensitive—to light, to noise, to other people. They may worry, become obsessed with details, and feel they are being persecuted. Cocaine addicts may become nervous and depressed. As noted, there is evidence that cocaine prevents the reabsorption of the neurotransmitter dopamine (the chemical that certain neurons use to communicate with each other). When dopamine concentrations rise after a cocaine hit, the initial effect is an emotional high; but brain activity is disrupted as dopamine levels later crash. It is likely that some people have natural or disease-caused defects or weaknesses in their dopamine systems, and so these individuals might be prone to paranoid personalities. They may also be especially susceptible to cocaine addiction. Some aspects of this sequence were illustrated in Figure 1, (addiction proneness). Similarly, it has long been noticed that people with Parkinson's disease seem to be stoic; since Parkinson's disease involves a defect in the dopamine system, it may be the case that this defect produces this aspect of personality (Menza, Forman, Goldstein, & Golbe, 1990). On the other hand, people with too much dopamine may develop compulsions (Driver-Dunckley, Samanta, & Stacy, 2003).

There is thus increasing interest in personality theories that might be constructed based on analyses of neurotransmitters. For example, researchers such as the psychiatrist C. R. Cloninger have focused on dopamine and sensation seeking; serotonin and impulsivity or conscientiousness; and norepinephrine as most relevant to alertness and reward seeking. But this field of neurotransmitter abnormality and personality is still in its infancy (Bond, 2001; Cloninger, 1998; Hariri, 2009). When legal (prescription) drugs are tested for their safety and efficacy, there is rarely if ever much comprehensive, in-depth tracking of effects on personality. We may hear about the murderer who blames her criminal behavior on her sleeping pills, but there is no regular monitoring of whether various medications increase the likelihood of divorce or child abuse or sociability. Given the vast numbers of people who consume potent legal and illegal drugs, it is surprising that so little is known.

Because drugs and poisons can have such major and dramatic influences on personality, a basic field of study called "personality toxicology" is in order. There should be experts who focus on the major and minor effects of environmental substances and toxins on human personality. Unfortunately, the study of personality is usually seen to be so far removed from the study of biochemistry that there is little intersection of the fields. (The reverse is also true: Could you imagine a biochemistry course having a major section on personality?) Some psychiatrists study the role of drugs and other toxic substances in causing and treating psychiatric disturbance—the field is called **psychopharmacology**—but this work has little to do with the mainstream study of personality.

The existence of many environmentally based biological influences on personality is another reason to be cautious about assuming hereditary causes of personality. That is, many correlations between biological functioning and personality may derive from a common environmental cause, not from heredity. For example, if the children of felt hat makers have a manic personality like their fathers', it is not their genes that are at fault, but rather the mercury that is coming into the home. Just because a disease runs in families does not mean it is genetic. Similarly, but less obviously, if high-strung people who are prone to heart attacks are found to have very reactive nervous systems, the link is not necessarily ascribable to their inherited constitutions.

Finally, note that someone trying to make policy recommendations for the prevention or treatment of smoking or alcoholism would be hard-pressed to come up with sensible recommendations without an understanding of the biochemical bases of personality. This is thus another way in which it is important to understand what it means to be a person.

Psychopharmacology
The study of the role of drugs and other toxic substances in causing and treating psychiatric disturbance

Effects from Creation of Environments

Crying infants can drive their parents into states of frustration and exasperation; the infant then lives in this frustrated, exasperated environment. That is, one way that biology can affect personality is by affecting the environments in which we find ourselves. Biological influences may cause us to wind up in certain situations, and these situations may then influence our personalities (Jaffee & Price, 2007; Rutter & Silberg, 2002; Scarr & McCartney, 1990).

Tropisms

Consider the case of a person who experiences a series of stressful life events such as loss of a loved one, a move, a new job, new friends (Plomin & Neiderhiser, 1992). Such stressful events are usually considered to be random intrusions of an unpredictable environment. In fact, there are stress scales that measure the amount of stress or challenge in a person's life.

But sometimes these events may not be totally outside the influence of the individual. Genetic or other biological characteristics may influence the likelihood that we will experience certain events. For example, people with an innate tendency toward being more aggressive might be more likely to experience divorce. Extroverts, seeking stimulation, might be more likely to experience job changes and other moves. Certain characteristics of the individual lead to certain experiences which in turn influence individual responding (Saudino, Pedersen, Lichtenstein, & McClearn, 1997). Similarly, people who are very active, strong, and athletic may seek out certain environments where sports are common and available; these environments then in turn may shape a "sports personality." In fact, sometimes the environment changes the genes, as when the nature of the mother's care affects the biology of her infant's brain (Champagne, 2009; Champagne & Mashoodh, 2009). The situation can affect the genome.

Just as phototropic plants move toward a source of light, some individuals grow toward more fulfilling and health-promoting spaces while other individuals remain subject to darker, health-threatening environments. These forces have been called **tropisms** (Friedman, 2000a). Some of these motivational forces originate in temperamental differences, which themselves derive from combinations of genetics, hormonal exposures, and early experiences. Other tropisms are more clearly environmental, as punishments and rewards push and pull certain children and adolescents toward certain life paths. But temperament is not independent of the environment. For example, sensitive, active infants and children may create disorganization, anxiety, or sleeplessness in their parents' lives, and the children then experience a very different family life than if they were calm, cooperative children. Similarly, neuroticism (tendency toward anxiety and depression) tends to predict that one will encounter negative life events (Magnus, Diener, Fujita, & Payot, 1993). That is, it is often *incorrect* to think of personality, located within the individual, as randomly encountering various stressful or unstressful events (Bolger & Zuckerman, 1995; McCartney et al., 1990; Van Heck, 1997).

Biological influences on the creation of environments can also function in even subtler and more complex ways. For example, consider the case of blindness. Various biological conditions lead children to be born blind or to lose their sight early in life. The lack of sight would naturally be expected to produce certain common personality characteristics. For example, blind children with a creative bent are obviously more likely to be drawn to activities that use nonvisual senses, such as hearing (music) or touch (sculpture). Blindness is easily identified. But imagine that two people are born to perceive the world in special but similar ways. Perhaps they have an excellent sense of smell or vision, or perhaps they have exceptional hand–eye coordination, or perhaps their minds tend to work in terms of images rather than of words (sort of like the difference between road symbols and signs). In such cases, the biological predisposition will lead to an attraction to certain environments or activities that will in turn sometimes have systematic influences on personality (Chipuer, Plomin, Pedersen, McClearn, & Nesselroade, 1993; Plomin & Nesselroade, 1990). For example, researchers have identified "supertasters" who have more receptors (taste buds) on their tongues and are three times as sensitive to bitterness than people of low taste sensitivity (Bartoshuk et al., 2001); such people may be especially unlikely to eat their vegetables. This phenomenon is shown in Figure 3. It might also be the case that children with fine artistic vision select a whole host of activities that helps shape their "artistic personality." Such processes are little studied.

Tropism

The tendency to seek out specific types of environments

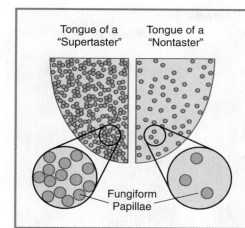

■ FIGURE 3

Tongue Papillae of Supertasters and Nontasters

You can test whether you are a supertaster by swabbing some blue food coloring on the tip of your tongue. Then place a looseleaf reinforcement on the dyed area to define the region to be counted. Your papillae will look like tiny mushrooms. If there are only a few of them in the ring, then you are a normal taster. If there are two dozen or more, you are a supertaster.

Do Looks Reveal Personality?:
Somatotypes and Beyond

In his play *Julius Caesar*, Shakespeare wrote, "Cassius has a lean and hungry look" (act I, scene 2). If Cassius were fatter, he presumably would be less dangerous. Do looks really reveal personality? Systematic study of this topic began with the work of the German psychiatrist Ernst Kretschmer (1925, 1934). Observing his patients, Kretschmer speculated about the association between physique and mental disorders. For example, he thought that schizophrenics were more likely to be slender people. W. H. Sheldon elaborated on this idea and applied it to normal people (Sheldon & Stevens, 1942). Sheldon measured people's proportions and their personalities and developed a theory of body types, or *somatotypes*.

Sheldon's **somatotypology** differentiates three body types: (1) **mesomorphs**— muscular, large-boned athletes; (2) **ectomorphs**—slender, bookworm types; and (3) **endomorphs**—roly-poly, and supposedly good-natured, types. Although Sheldon's work attracted a lot of attention, it was not supported by most research. We cannot gather important information about personality just by measuring belly size. The idea was undoubtedly too simplistic. Sheldon's work is thus sometimes noted in psychology books today as a historical curiosity. But could such an approach to body types have contained a kernel of truth? Could there be a physiological basis for the possible relations between physical characteristics and personality?

It could be the case that a certain type of physiology affects both personality and physical shape. For example, perhaps a nervous system that makes one shy and introverted is also a nervous system that keeps one thin. This might be because of a high metabolism or a hunger mechanism that is easily satiated. Social influences may also be involved. Consider the case of anorexia, a condition in which an otherwise healthy person eats less and less and becomes thinner and thinner (Mussell & Mitchell, 1998). For example, news reports indicated that actress Mary-Kate Olsen (of the Olsen twins) was treated for an eating disorder. An anorexic may even die of

Somatotypology
W. H. Sheldon's theory relating body type to personality characteristics

Mesomorph
According to W. H. Sheldon, a somatotype describing muscular, large-boned, athletic types of people

Ectomorph
According to W. H. Sheldon, a somatotype describing slender bookworm types of people

Endomorph
According to W. H. Sheldon, a somatotype describing overweight, good-natured types of people

187

 Actress Mary-Kate Olsen (right) was treated for an eating disorder but her fraternal twin sister Ashley does not have this problem, despite being exposed to similar career pressures. Can you suggest various scientific explanations that might account for this difference?

complications of the weight loss. Anorexics are usually very sensitive young women who are shy, are often hassled by their families (or fans), and feel out of control. In such cases, physical characteristics (being excessively thin) are good markers for personality (shy and sensitive).

It could be the case that dramatically changing one's physical characteristics—say, by gaining a lot of weight or becoming a serious body builder—might also change one's usual physiological reaction patterns. It is known that changing one's physical condition does indeed influence such bodily conditions as resting heartbeat, heartbeat change in response to challenge, cholesterol level, blood pressure, lung capacity and function, and similar physiological characteristics, any or all of which might indeed affect psychological responses. Personality may thus be affected.

It is undeniably the case that our physical characteristics can influence the reactions of others (Heatherton & Hebl, 1998). For example, if people such as teachers approach children who are thin and "intellectual-looking" with the belief that these children are likely to be good students, then they may make their own expectations come true. For this to be a significant influence on personality, people must share stereotypes about the personalities associated with physical characteristics, and indeed they do (Tucker, 1983). This line of thought is the subject of the next section.

Effects from Reactions of Others

The greatest environmental influence on psychological development is the reactions of the people around us. Our sense of identity depends to a large extent on how we are treated; if our parents and teachers and friends like us and expect great things from us, we are likely to form positive self-images. Unfortunately, the reverse is also true; undesirable physical characteristics can lead to unpleasant reactions, and to negative self-images.

Think about people's reactions to those of us who are either very short or tall. We tend to "look up to" tall people, but "look down on" short people. Tall may be exalted, lofty, and prominent, but short may be low, debased, and squat. For women, there are further restrictions because women are not expected to be taller than men. Of course these reactions are stereotypes, but they are so common and so strong that they often have a significant effect. This effect is in addition to the effects caused by creation of environments—the places and activities that tall and short people may seek out. For example, not all short guys are precluded from excelling in high school sports, but their peers may expect them to be less physically successful. These expectations can in turn affect personality.

Physical Attractiveness Stereotype

Research in social psychology has documented that many people expect physically attractive others to do good and to be good (Dion, 1972, 1973; Hatfield & Sprecher, 1986). This physical attractiveness stereotype has been summarized as our tendency to believe that "What is beautiful is good." Adults have higher expectations for attractive children, and most of us think that attractive people are more successful. What is the likely effect on personality? Not surprisingly, physically attractive people tend to be happier, although they may suffer more if they lose their attractiveness as they age. Here again, personality is partially a result of biology (physical attractiveness), but it is not a direct effect of genes; rather, it operates through reactions of others.

Similar processes apply to children who have a skin color, eye shape, or other ethnic sign that is different from the majority (Shelton & Sellers, 2000). There are more positive expectations for children with the culturally "desirable" characteristics. As we have seen, such negative expectations may be compounded and reinforced by biased testing of such children. The long-term results on personality are hard to assess, but they undoubtedly are substantial.

What happens when we put all these sorts of biological influences together? Well, we should find many arenas in which biological aspects of personality have a profound effect on social life. For example, consider the case of divorce. There is evidence that concordance for divorce is significantly higher in monozygotic twins than in dizygotic twins (McGue & Lykken, 1992); that is, if you have a twin and you are divorced, then your twin is more likely to get divorced if she or he is your identical twin than if she or he is your fraternal twin. Does this mean that divorce is genetically determined? Such an assertion is ridiculous; the likelihood of divorce varies dramatically as a function of upbringing, religion, income, culture, time period, and other environmental factors. However, identical twins may indeed share temperaments, abilities, sex drives, reactions from others (to their beauty, height, etc.), self-created marriage environments, health, and so on, involving the various factors we have discussed in this chapter. The result is a "genetically" correlated likelihood of divorce.

The history of the twentieth century shows us that many very smart people are willing to make many oversimplified and dangerous assumptions about the genetic basis of personality. There is something captivating about reducing the complex influences on personality to a simple (although invalid) explanation of genetic causation.

Sociobiology and Evolutionary Personality

Sociobiology

Sociobiology
The study of the influence of evolutionary biology on individual responses regarding social matters

The scientific study of the influence of evolutionary biology on an organism's responses regarding social matters defines the field called **sociobiology**. Sociobiologists study the reasons for (the functions of) the evolution of animal social behaviors, such as sexual fidelity. For example, various colors, scents, calls, or dances have been shown to have evolved as part of species' mating rituals or territorial defense or social organization. During mating season, males of various species (from deer to tropical fish) engage in ritualized duels for the most desirable mates.

Some species have evolved to be monogamous (at least for each breeding season), whereas in other species a dominant male has access to most of the females for mating. Although patterns sometimes break down in unusual circumstances, it is generally safe to say that many such patterns are "in the nature" of the particular species. These analyses work best with animals such as ants, fish, spiders, bees, and many birds, because many of these animals' behaviors are governed by instincts or fixed patterns of responding (Wilson, 1975).

Much more complex are attempts to apply these sorts of analyses to large-brained animals like humans, in a search for evolutionary personality theory. Here sociobiologists often must walk the fine line separating themselves from the ideas of social Darwinism and eugenics (see the following section "Social Darwinism and Eugenics"). The display of bright plumage is an integral part of the mating ritual of peacocks. Certain people also wear fancy clothes to attract mates, but it is obviously an oversimplification to assume that the same simple courtship mechanisms are applicable.

Attachment
The close bond that forms shortly after birth between an infant and the mother (or other caregiver)

Sociobiological-type analyses are commonly applied to human aggression, human courtship, and human family relations, since aggressive competition, mating, and raising of the young are a prime focus of evolutionary biologists studying organisms such as insects, fish, or birds. For example, in all human societies, a close bond, or **attachment**, develops shortly after birth between the infant and the caretaker (usually the mother). This is also true in nonhuman primates (and indeed in many mammals), and it certainly appears to have a biological basis. Using this approach, John Bowlby and Mary Ainsworth explain that infants have evolved to cling, gurgle, smile, and so on to attract the mother, while the mother in turn nurtures the infant (Ainsworth, 1979; Ainsworth & Bowlby, 1991; Bowlby, 1969). For example, reward-processing regions of mothers' brains light up (on fMRI scans) when they see photos of their infants (Strathearn, Li, Fonagy, & Montague, 2008). This strong attachment system helps ensure the survival of the infant, and thus helps ensure the passing on of the mother's genes. There is an evolutionary function that explains why babies are so cute.

Cinderella Effect

There is also a dark side. Consider the case of Cinderella, who was abused by her cruel stepmother. Cinderella and untold numbers of real children have been mistreated by their stepmothers or stepfathers. There is indeed evidence that one's stepchildren are, on average, treated worse than one's genetic children, and that this difference cannot be easily explained by social factors such as poverty level. Sociobiologists suggest that the Cinderella phenomenon results from natural selection, in which parents have evolved to give preference and protection to their biological children (Daly & Wilson, 1988a, 1988b, 1998, 2005a).

Such analyses can be provocative and intellectually stimulating when they help us think about innate tendencies on which human cultures have been built. For example, to what extent do societal taboos against incest and societal patterns of homicide and aggression have their roots in ancient pressures for survival (Daly & Wilson, 1988a, 1988b)? Perhaps families have an innate predisposition to defend themselves and their territories. Many evolutionary psychologists try to stick closely to the evidence, but such evolutionary analyses can turn foolish or dangerous if they ignore the tremendous influences of human learning and human culture on human behavior. It is certainly the case that aggression varies markedly as a function of cultural times and places. For example, even if relations with stepchildren are more likely to be conflict-prone due to evolutionary pressures (which is a reasonable hypothesis but not scientific fact), this does not mean that loving, wonderful relations with stepchildren do not occur. Many adoptive parents would give up their own lives for their adopted children. The speculations of sociobiologists can be twisted by politicians for their own ends. It is a difficult task to try to capture fully and scientifically the vastly diverse forces that shape personality (Petrinovich, 1995).

Evolution and Culture

As Darwinian thought took hold in the late nineteenth century, notions of "survival of the fittest" often led to the incorrect assumption that it is a "dog-eat-dog world" in which it is "every man for himself." Such an assumption is not implied by evolution, and it is not what Darwin proposed. Rather, it is clear that in complex species like primates, what evolves is a *capacity* for certain types of behavior in certain situations; but whether the behavior will occur depends on learning, and patterns of learning are shaped by culture (socially transmitted expectations and knowledge).

In many nonhuman primates, certainly in chimps and apes, knowledge and habits are acquired from others. Many animals have communication and social organizational "societies." For example, chimpanzees learn from others to wash bananas in jungle streams (de Waal, 2001a). So, we will never find a simple gene that leads directly to someone's being aggressive or cooperative. Rather, individuals vary in their capacities for a variety of tendencies, and which ones will be realized depends on the multiplicity of interacting forces that we describe in this text. Ironically, many times in the twentieth century, people made the mistake of thinking not only that the "fittest" individual is the one who can out-reproduce all others, but they assumed (wrongly) that the fittest culture is the one that can conquer all others. Biological issues in personality psychology should be examined in terms of how they are being interpreted for purposes of public policy.

■ Many nonhuman animals, such as the vervet monkeys shown here, communicate extensively with each other and have social organizations for cooperation. They may cooperate, for example, to watch for predators, gather food, groom one another, or fend off enemies. Since these behaviors are often learned from others within the group, and passed on to offspring, they represent a rudimentary form of culture. In nonhuman species as well as in humans, biological factors play an important role but have their influence within the broader environmental context of the life of the organism.

Personality and Public Policy

Survival of the Fittest
The concept that species evolve because those individuals who cannot compete well in the environments in which they live tend to be less successful in growing up and producing offspring

Darwin proposed that species evolve because those individuals who cannot compete well in the environments in which they live tend to be less successful in growing up and producing offspring. This notion of **survival of the fittest** is one of the most misunderstood and misused concepts in all of science.

Social Darwinism and Eugenics: Pseudoscience

This unfortunate expression—survival of the fittest—has sometimes been changed from a biological principle to a moral imperative and interpreted to mean that weak creatures and cultures *should not* survive. In fact, it has been used as a license to kill.

In America and elsewhere, importation of slaves from Africa began well before the time of Darwin. Asians, Native Americans, and other groups were similarly considered inherently inferior, well before Darwinian theory. For example, Euro-American societies believed that African Americans were by nature incapable of learning to read, so it was just as well that they were picking cotton. Just to be on the safe side, it was also illegal to try to teach a plantation slave to read.

Social Darwinism
The idea that societies and cultures naturally compete for survival of the fittest

What evolutionary theory did, however, was to provide a pseudoscientific justification for the oppression that was occurring. At the end of the nineteenth century, many leaders, including many intellectuals and scientists, were quick to adopt views of "genetic inferiority" for those thought inherently inferior. The worst distortion appeared in what later came to be known as **Social Darwinism** (Hofstadter, 1959). Applying evolutionary theory in a crude way to societies, Social Darwinism argued that not only individuals but societies and cultures naturally competed in a survival of the fittest. It followed therefore that it was biologically and morally just (and even imperative) that White people invade, conquer, and dominate other societies. After all, the Whites saw themselves as more "fit."

In various ways, such ideas, which amounted merely to prejudice against culturally different others, greatly affected American governmental policy. For example, American immigration laws passed in the early 1920s strictly limited immigration from "inferior" or "unfit" places such as eastern and southern Europe and Asia. (And not surprisingly given American history, Africans were considered the most unfit.) Sad to say, psychologists and other scientists of the time played an important role in providing flimsy justifications for the discrimination. Psychologists were involved in creating biased tests that "proved" that the undesirable cultures were indeed intellectually and morally subordinate (Gould, 1996).

Many psychologists, like many other intelligent people, were caught up in the bigoted ideas of their time, and they allowed their thinking and research to be distorted. Many wrote of the importance of preserving or purifying the gene pool of the elite. This eugenics movement advocated such steps as the forced sterilization of the poor. It is important for personality psychologists of today to be aware of this history, so that the chances of making similar mistakes can be diminished. In fact, as noted at the beginning of the chapter, James D. Watson, the codiscoverer of DNA, resigned from his position as director of a major research laboratory after casually offering an unfounded opinion that Black Africans were genetically less intelligent than other people. Watson was an expert on genetics but not on intelligence or behavior.

Culture, Nazis, and "Superior Races"

Many millions of people have been murdered in part because of a misunderstanding and misuse of the notion of biological influences on personality. In Europe early in the twentieth century, this was carried to its most awful extreme, as Adolf Hitler and a small band of ruthless fascists took over a German society that was willing to believe in a genetically superior "master race."

There is, of course, good evidence that people from different cultures differ systematically from each other, but there is little evidence that these differences are genetically based. When immigrants move to the United States from Asia or Africa or Europe or Latin America, their children for the most part become capitalistic, freedom-loving Americans, fond of baseball, Mickey Mouse, automobiles and open roads, American music, and so on; that is, the children of immigrants soon come to behave more like Americans than like the cultures of their parents and grandparents. People in Beijing behave differently from people in New York or Nairobi because of their culture.

Yet biological determinism of personality has its allure. Even educated people are attracted to the idea that "other" people are inherently inferior and therefore less deserving of freedom, success, and even life. In the case of Hitler and the Nazis, the inferior subhumans were Jews, Gypsies, homosexuals, and those with physical or mental disabilities. Many physicians helped lead the way to mass murder (Lifton, 1986). Although this subject is a complex one, it is important for students of personality to be knowledgeable about the common societal errors and biases about the nature of personality.

Evaluating the Perspectives

Advantages and Limits of the Biological Approach

■ Quick Analogy

- Humans as genes, brains, and hormones.

■ Advantages

- Emphasizes the tendencies and limits imposed by genetics, physical health, and bodily endowment on personality.
- Acknowledges the effects of biological influences on the reactions of others and on the environments that individuals choose.
- Can be combined with other approaches.

■ Limits

- Tends to minimize human potential for growth and change.
- Serious danger of misuse by politicians who oversimplify its findings.
- Uses biological concepts, which may not be most appropriate for psychological phenomena.
- Difficult to capture consciousness.

■ View of Free Will

- Behavior is determined by biological tendencies.

■ Common Assessment Techniques

- Neuroscience, heritability studies, physiological measures.

■ Implications for Therapy

- Since behavior is seen as resulting from evolved biological structures, genes, hormones, chemical imbalances, and environmental interactions with these structures, therapy is focused on biological interventions: psychotropic drugs such as Prozac or Valium for mental "illness," hormones for conditions such as PMS irritability, plastic surgery (or liposuction) for physical abnormalities, and antihistamines or cleaner environments for allergy- and toxin-related conditions. General health-promoting activities like exercise may prove helpful (such as in treating anxiety and depression). Eventually, gene therapies may be commonplace, with the attendant moral dangers.

The Human Genome: Racist Eugenics of the Future?

Biologists are hard at work on the **human genome project**, an effort to identify the functions of each of the 20,000 or so genes. The immediate goal is to develop treatments for inherited diseases such as muscular dystrophy. However, genes (or patterns of genes) that influence people's propensities to be aggressive or depressed, or intelligent or shy, and so on are increasingly being discovered. Should these genes be altered to make a "better" human being?

A subtle kind of genetic racism sometimes creeps into the thinking of researchers in this area. The argument goes as follows: Modern medicine is keeping alive people who otherwise would have died. Therefore, "survival of the fittest" is defunct, and the human genetic pool is deteriorating. Therefore, if we are to evolve, we must engage in genetic engineering to fix and preserve the healthy gene pool. By the way, who should be in charge of these efforts? Why, the geneticists of course.

The errors made by this argument are subtler but just as menacing as those made by the Social Darwinists. There is no evidence that the human gene pool is deteriorating. In fact, it is hard even to define what such a statement might mean. Certainly, physical characteristics of humans are improving rather than declining: People are taller, stronger, and longer-lived than ever before. In terms of mental or artistic abilities, it would be a dangerous lie even to hint that we have any idea about the genetic bases of such accomplishments. Musical, artistic, or scientific genius often arises in "unexpected" places—in descendants of serfs or slaves or laborers. Furthermore, we know very little about the human characteristics that have been selected for over the millennia; anyone who claims to know the precise selection pressures operating throughout evolutionary history should be challenged.

Going beyond these racist errors, the question still remains as to whether we should tinker with our genes to make a "better" person. Wouldn't it be nice if no one were genetically predisposed to be a criminal? Why not eliminate schoolyard bullies? How about even weeding out those people who are a stubborn pain in the neck? Answering these questions intelligently requires a good knowledge about what it means to be a person—in other words, it requires a good knowledge of personality psychology.

On the other hand, it is senseless to condemn genetic research, or to accuse all genetic scientists of being racist. Personality psychology tells us that individuals do indeed differ, and they differ in a number of ways and for a number of reasons. As we uncover more of the biological reasons for individual differences, we will need a society that has a more sophisticated understanding of what such findings imply and do not imply (Ehrlich & Feldman, 2007; Tooby, Cosmides, & Barrett, 2003).

If you or your relatives have some genetic disease or defect that makes life especially difficult, you would probably be very happy if science could repair the problem. But what about defects in your personality? We all have them. Would you like some scientist to "fix" you? How would you feel if your best friend or lover suddenly decided to undergo such repair work? For example, perhaps your lover thinks he or she is too sweet and sentimental and wants to be altered to become more sensible and pragmatic. Or maybe your child's teacher or doctor recommends "fixing" your child's unruly behavior. Such questions are now arriving on our doorsteps.

Human Genome Project
An effort to identify each of the thousands of genes in our chromosomes

Summary and Conclusion

Do relatively unchangeable biological characteristics such as genetic inheritance, the neuroendocrine system, bodily endowment, and physical health affect personality? Undoubtedly at times they do, and such influences should be carefully studied by the serious student of personality. Gordon Allport (1961) wrote decades ago that although psychology is the safest approach to follow in constructing the science of personality, "Someday the 'biological model' may catch up". Today, biology has indeed provided many insights into what it means to be a person. For the most part, these insights concern the outer parameters or limits of human responding.

Americans like to believe that almost any child who has enough motivation and the proper upbringing can go on to achieve almost anything she or he desires. Success can indeed come from hard work and proper "rearing," but there is also no doubt that biological factors affect a person's characteristic responses. A person is not born a blank slate, to then be written on by the environment; people start with certain inherent predispositions and abilities.

Charles Darwin turned the life sciences upside down by arguing that people evolved directly from more primitive species. In a Darwinian analysis, attention is drawn to the *function* of a characteristic (such as speed or intelligence) in survival. A prime difficulty of a Darwinian approach is that it is hard to know precisely which selection pressures worked to shape human evolution over millions of years. This problem plagues the modern application of Darwin's ideas—the field of evolutionary personality theory.

The term *temperament* is used to refer to stable individual differences in emotional reactivity. Four dimensions of temperament are usually isolated: (1) an activity dimension, (2) an emotionality dimension, (3) a sociability dimension, and (4) an aggressive/impulsive dimension. Eysenck's introversion–extroversion factor combines elements of the activity dimension and the sociability dimension of temperament. The basic idea is that extroverts have a relatively low level of brain arousal, and so they seek stimulation. Introverts, on the other hand, with a higher level of central nervous system arousal, tend to shy away from stimulating social environments.

Another promising method of addressing biological differences in personality focuses on individual differences in hemispheric activity—that is, relative differences in activation between the right and left cerebral hemispheres. Relatively greater activation of the right hemisphere is associated with greater reactions of fear and distress to a stressful situation; individuals who have a relatively more active right hemisphere are more likely to overreact to a negative stimulus.

Studies of twins have found impressive similarities in personality between people who have the same genetic makeup. The similarities of identical twins are greater than those of fraternal twins. But the similarity of twins raised apart is less than that of twins raised together, evidence of the influence of the environmental upbringing. There is thus much controversy about how much of personality is genetically determined. Interestingly, siblings (including twins) raised by the same parents often have personalities that are strikingly different, illustrating their experience of nonshared environmental variance such as having different friends. In moving from childhood to adulthood, the important environmental effects (and the interaction effects of genes and environments) on personality become especially evident. There is an inverse correlation between personality similarity and age for both monozygotic and dizygotic twins; as twins get older, their personalities become more different.

Dramatic changes in personality can result from poisoning and from certain illnesses, such as strokes. A stable personality depends on a healthy, well-functioning brain. It follows that diseases or toxins that affect brain function often affect personality. And the list of toxic substances and illnesses known to affect personality is a long one. Because drugs and poisons can have such major and dramatic influences on personality, there should be a basic field of study called "personality toxicology."

Our understanding of biological influences on personality has major implications for our beliefs about law and justice. One extreme position is that most criminal or evil acts are committed by people who couldn't help themselves—they have some disorder in their nervous system. Interestingly, although this position is often identified with a very liberal or left-wing political orientation, it is actually quite similar to the right-wing position that some people simply have "bad genes."

An intriguing way that biology can affect personality is by affecting the environments in which we find (or put) ourselves; that is, certain biological influences may cause us to wind up in certain situations, and these situations may then influence our personalities. For example, extroverts, seeking stimulation, might be more likely to experience job changes and other moves. Certain characteristics of the individual lead to certain experiences which in turn influence individual responding. Many aspects of personality are attributable to strictly social mechanisms—the expectations and reactions of others.

"Survival of the fittest" is one of the most misunderstood and misused concepts in all of science, as this unfortunate expression has sometimes been changed from a biological principle to a moral mandate that weak creatures *should not* survive. In fact, it has been used as a license to kill. Applying evolutionary theory in a crude way to societies, Social Darwinism argued that societies and cultures naturally compete for survival of the fittest. It followed that it was biologically and morally just (and even imperative) that some people invade, conquer, and dominate other societies. The eugenics movement advocated such steps as the forced sterilization of the poor.

There is a certain lure of biological determinism of personality. Even educated people are often attracted to the idea that "other" people are inherently inferior and therefore less deserving of freedom, success, and even life. In the case of Hitler and the Nazis, the inferior subhumans were Jews, Gypsies, homosexuals, and those with physical or mental disabilities. Going beyond these racist errors, the question still remains as to whether we should tinker with our genes to make a "better" person.

Unfortunately, it is very easy for people to accept stereotypes and to rationalize the inequities in the status quo. Until very recently, most men (and most women) "knew" that men were better suited by their nature to run governments, to manage property, to become scientists and artists, and to run businesses. It was thought to be women's nature—as the "weaker" sex—to stay home, manage households, and nurture children. Thus, it was perfectly logical that women were not allowed to attend the best colleges, to vote or hold office, to own property, and so on. Allowing women to do so was seen as "going against nature." Today's unfounded prejudices are of course more difficult for us to see (after all, they are prejudices). Should we be suspicious of those political leaders who play up the importance of genetic determinism and ignore the many other important aspects of personality? Given the sad history of misguided searches for "genetic purity," a deeper understanding of personality should be insisted upon.

■ Key Theorists

Charles Darwin	Francis Galton	David Buss
Ivan Pavlov	Robert Plomin	Martin Daly
Hans Eysenck		

■ Key Concepts and Terms

natural selection

behavioral genomics

introversion–extroversion dimension of temperament

sensation seeking

nonshared environmental variance

kin selection

survival of the fittest

sociobiology

human genome project

evolutionary personality theory

four basic aspects of temperament

nervous system arousal

neurotransmitters

eugenics

somatotypology

Social Darwinism

attachment

biological determinism

Behaviorist and Learning Aspects of Personality

A while back, a friend of ours came into a small fortune as the result of a successful business venture. Feeling happy, generous, and curious, he took a short taxicab ride and paid the $10 fare with a $100 bill. Carefully watching the unfolding expressions on the cabdriver's face, our friend said, "Keep the change," and went on his way. This cabdriver had never received such a lavish tip and was unlikely to receive another for a long time, if ever. Yet we can predict that this cabdriver may look for customers who resemble our friend, try to behave as he did when traveling

© Christolph Wilhelm/Getty Images

Courtesy of Melvin Bates

From Chapter 6 of *Personality: Classic Theories and Modern Research*, Fifth Edition. Howard S. Friedman, Miriam W. Schustack. Copyright © 2012 by Pearson Education, Inc. Published by Pearson Allyn & Bacon. All rights reserved.

with our friend, and in general drive his cab in the hopes of another such tip; and he may do so for a long time to come. In other words, the cabdriver is now acting in a consistent and relatively predictable manner thanks to receiving a significant reward from a patron. In a sense, this behavior is now part of his personality.

A large, unpredictable reward such as the cabdriver's tip is called a **partial reinforcement** by behaviorist psychologists. Experiments show that a reward that comes after some, but not all, occurrences of a behavior (i.e., is partial) is more powerful in influencing behavior than a reinforcement that is continuous. Just as a rat will press a lever or button dozens of times for an occasional food pellet, people will continue their activities for that occasional but highly rewarding slot machine jackpot, birdie golf shot, sexual liaison, A+ grade from a professor, or $100 tip. This chapter explains how certain reward structures in an environment can produce consistencies in an individual's behaviors—the behaviorist and learning aspects of personality.

Partial Reinforcement
A reward that occurs after some, but not all, occurrences of a behavior

ehaviorist approaches strike at the very heart of most other personality approaches, which rely on ideas of internal traits, tendencies, defenses, and motivations. Behaviorists reject such concepts; they see people as controlled absolutely by their environments. Much controversy has necessarily resulted. Poet W. H. Auden (1970) wrote,

> *Of course, Behaviorism "works." So does torture. Give me a no-nonsense, down-to-earth behaviorist, a few drugs, and simple electrical appliances, and in six months I will have him reciting the Athanasian Creed in public.*

As you will see, Auden's description is not an accurate one, but the controversial issues behaviorism raises about the nature of human beings are very real. This chapter considers the strengths and the weaknesses of behaviorist and learning approaches to personality.

The Classical Conditioning of Personality

A philosophical basis for the learning approach to personality was laid down by the English philosopher John Locke (1632–1704). Locke viewed an infant as a blank slate—*tabula rasa*—on whom the experiences of life would write their tale. This assumption does not preclude certain other approaches to personality, but it definitely elevates the great influence of the situation. However, as all psychology students know, it was the brilliant Russian physiologist Ivan Petrovitch Pavlov (1849–1936) who laid the foundation for modern learning approaches.

Conditioning a Response to a Stimulus

Studying digestion in dogs, Pavlov discovered the important principle called **classical conditioning.** He presented food (the unconditioned stimulus), which causes salivation in dogs (the unconditioned or automatic response), to a hungry dog, at the same time pairing it with something that normally did not cause salivation, such as a bell (a neutral stimulus). Pavlov found that if he paired the food presentation and bell a number of times, eventually merely the sound of the bell elicited salivation; that is, the conditioned stimulus (the bell) came to elicit a conditioned response (salivation). Similarly, people can be conditioned to salivate in response to the sound of a food chime on a ranch. Normally, of course, bells have nothing to do with salivation. But dogs and people can learn (i.e., be conditioned to) an automatic association.

Pavlov also noted that the conditioned response would occur in response to stimuli that were *similar* to the conditioned stimulus, indicating that there was **generalization** of the conditioning. However, the conditioned response would not occur for *all* possible similar stimuli, indicating that the animal also could learn to tell the difference between different stimuli; this is called **discrimination.** Thus, if the food followed a bell of only one tone and did not follow the ringing of a bell of other tones, the dog would discriminate this

■ Ringing the dinner bell can cause humans to salivate, a classically conditioned reaction virtually identical to what Pavlov observed in his laboratory dogs.

one tone, and the conditioned response would occur only in response to that particular relevant tone. Analogously, a young boy who is stung by bees and bitten by mosquitoes might become fearful of (be conditioned to react to) the buzzing of all insects (generalization). Or, on the other hand, if he sees that the flies and gnats buzzing around him do not cause any problems, he may learn to discriminate the buzzing of stinging insects from that of other flying insects.

Behavioral Patterns as a Result of Conditioning

Many behavioral reaction patterns are explainable by classical conditioning. Neutral stimuli associated with positive, enjoyable occurrences become "likes," but events or consequences associated with negative responses become "dislikes" (or worse). For example, a college student might learn to associate drinking at parties with having a pleasant, sociable time with friends. On the other hand, a woman date-raped at a party might develop a "personality" that fears college social events that involve alcohol.

Pavlov's constructs thus often provide a basis for explaining emotional aspects of personality. For example, why do some people have extreme fear reactions (phobias) to certain things while other persons do not? Many people are herpetaphobic and have extreme emotional reactions even to still pictures of snakes. This might be conditioned if a grandmother took her five-year-old granddaughter to the zoo and exhibited great anxiety in the child's presence when they approached the "snake house." This conditioning explanation of a phobia is very different from a biological explanation that relies on an evolved innate fear of snakes, or a psychoanalytic

Classical Conditioning
The concept that after the repeated pairing of an unconditioned stimulus that elicits an unconditioned response and a neutral stimulus, the previously neutral stimulus can come to elicit the same response as the unconditioned stimulus

Generalization
The tendency for similar stimuli to evoke the same response

Discrimination
The concept that a conditioned response will not occur for all possible stimuli, indicating that an animal can learn to tell the difference between different stimuli

explanation that sees snakes as symbolic of a threatening penis, or a neo-analytic explanation in which fear of snakes is part of our collective unconscious.

Extinction Processes

Extinction
The process by which the frequency of the organism's producing a response gradually decreases when the response behavior is no longer followed by the reinforcement

What happens if pairing of the conditioned and unconditioned stimulus stops? Then **extinction** may occur; that is, the conditioned response becomes less frequent—the association weakens—over time until it disappears. In other words, "personality" (pattern of response) changes. A rape victim who developed a fearful personality (afraid of going to parties, out on dates, or even going to shopping malls) could undergo a dramatic personality change for the better if she repeatedly experienced these events in the calm presence of a supportive friend. Unfortunately, people who have learned to fear certain things will often *avoid* them, thus not allowing their fear to extinguish.

Conditioning of Neurotic Behavior

But how does behaviorism explain a complex personality dimension like neuroticism? Pavlov, in fact, was able to condition a response similar to neurotic behavior in a dog. First, he associated food presentation with a circle but not with an ellipse, and the dog developed a conditioned response to the circle, discriminating it from the ellipse. Then Pavlov gradually increased the roundness of the ellipse so it approximated the circle. When the dog could no longer discriminate the circle from the ellipse, it began to exhibit neurotic behaviors (Pavlov, 1927). This hints that neuroticism may be a

Famous Personalities

John Travolta: Reinforcement of Stardom?

Like flashes in the dark, celebrities come and go. As overnight success stories whose careers are launched by the fuel of public appeal, these rockets become teen idols, figures of adolescent crushes, and objects of adult envy. With their stardom shining bright in the public eye, these sudden success stories often fizzle out just as quickly.

Film star John Travolta's career is a striking exception, but not in the way you might first think. First hitting the spotlight in the 1970s, Travolta's career skyrocketed with his performances in the blockbuster movies *Saturday Night Fever* and *Grease*. During that period, Travolta was considered by many to be the biggest box-office property around. After a brief period of stardom, though, Travolta was eclipsed. Still in his 20s, he became a "former movie star," accepting a few roles in mediocre movies and then turning down roles that were offered to him.

What makes Travolta's story different from the usual path of the has-been is that he made a successful comeback, and then later came back again! Decades after the roles that initially brought him stardom, and after more than a decade of near-invisibility, he resurfaced in 1994 with his on-screen reappearance in Quentin Tarantino's award-winning pop-culture film *Pulp Fiction*. That was the start of a second rise to stardom; further successful film roles followed in *Get Shorty, Face/Off*, and *The Thin Red Line*. He then did it again a decade later, with five films in 2004 and 2005, including *Be Cool*. Additional successful films followed, including a starring role in *Hairspray* (in drag), 2007's *Wild Hogs*, 2008's *Bolt* (where he sings with Miley Cyrus), 2009's *Old Dogs*, and 2010's *From Paris with Love*.

conditioned response, fostered by an environment that requires the individual to discriminate between events under conditions in which that judgment is almost impossible (Wolpe & Plaud, 1997). For example, some children find it impossible to predict the reactions of their unstable parents. If children are never sure whether to expect praise or punishment, they may feel frustrated, anxious, and depressed.

Pavlov was the son of a Russian Orthodox priest and intended to become a priest himself. However, as a young man, he read with fascination the recently published theories of Charles Darwin and turned to a career in science (Windholz, 1991). His studies of the function and control of salivation were firmly rooted in Darwin's ideas.

Complexities in Application of Conditioning Principles

Modern research suggests that classical conditioning is not as simple as Pavlov had hoped. For example, he assumed that conditioning principles were general rules that applied uniformly to all animals, but it is now known that different organisms are more easily conditioned to respond in certain ways to certain stimuli (Garcia & Koelling, 1966). Hungry dogs can be conditioned to salivate with a bell that is paired with the sight and smell of meat, but each species and even each individual has certain tendencies that facilitate or impair certain learning. For example, humans rely more on visual cues than smells, and different people have different perceptual and aesthetic inclinations. Yet classical conditioning remains a powerful explanation of response patterns, especially when there is a strong natural pairing of stimulus and automatic response. However, much more of our learned patterns of responses comes

Can Travolta's career (sudden stardom, rapid eclipse, reemergence to stardom) be understood by a behaviorist interpretation? One way to describe Travolta's early upward trajectory is that his behavior (in this case, his acting) was shaped through strong positive reinforcement (in the form of money, the "perks" of stardom, respect from his colleagues, and public admiration). In operant conditioning terms, the more closely his behavior resembled that of the ideal star, the more he was rewarded; the well-structured contingencies of Travolta's environment conditioned him to become a star.

Then what happened? Perhaps poor choices of roles led to the extinction of those behaviors that had propelled him to success. Perhaps, after not being reinforced for engaging in his "star" behavior—that is, after his failure in several movies—Travolta slid into a downward spiral of the extinction of his "star" behavior. Having not been reinforced for several movies he did take on, he may have been reluctant to accept new roles or unable to act

at top form. As he became less visible, he was less likely to be offered desirable new roles. The downward path may have become a spiral of negative reinforcement; by not taking on any new roles, he could avoid reexperiencing the scorn and bad reviews that his recent roles had brought.

How to account for his comeback through behaviorist principles? Perhaps Travolta's experiences out of the limelight (his more recent reinforcement history) had brought about a change in his responses to seeking or accepting a movie role. Perhaps the actions of the director of his comeback movies were especially successful in evoking Travolta's long-dormant behavior patterns from his days of stardom. Once these appropriate responses had been restimulated and reinforced, they became more likely to reappear in subsequent situations. In one sense Travolta was always Travolta, but in another sense he became a different actor in response to the different situations at different times in his life.

by experiencing or anticipating the consequences (effects) of our actions. This is the focus of behaviorist approaches to personality. (See the Famous Personalities box.)

The Origins of Behaviorist Approaches: Watson's Behaviorism

Around the turn of the last century, not only Freud but also many experimental philosopher–psychologists, such as Wilhelm Wundt, were studying psychology using subjective analyses of the human mind, asking people to introspect about their thoughts or to free associate to reveal unconscious processes. This approach was fraught with methodological difficulties. There was no way of validating or verifying the data and conclusions. How could we know if what people reported thinking was really a good representation of their psyche?

The Rejection of Introspection

Behaviorism
The learning approach to psychology introduced by John Watson that emphasizes the study of observable behavior

In response to the perceived limitations of introspectionism, **behaviorism**, the key learning approach in psychology, was founded by John B. Watson. Watson wanted to develop a rigorous science and thus completely rejected introspection. According to Watson, thoughts and feelings elicited through introspection are unobservable and unscientific.

Watson was born in Greenville, South Carolina, in 1878. His experiences led him to start graduate study in philosophy at the University of Chicago, but he soon switched to psychology and also studied neurology, physiology, and animal research. Interestingly, while doing his dissertation, Watson noticed that he had a dislike of using human subjects; he much preferred using animals. Watson believed that he could learn the same things by using animals that others claimed to learn by studying humans.

Watson was a professor at Johns Hopkins University from 1908 to 1919. His basic theories about studying observable behavior and disregarding introspection were laid out in 1914 in his book *Behavior*, and he and Rosalie Rayner wrote an important book about behaviorism in 1919 called *Psychology from the Standpoint of a Behaviorist*. In a sweeping critique, they condemned both introspectionists, who were studying consciousness, and psychoanalysts, who concentrated on the unconscious.

Applying Conditioning Principles to Little Albert: Conditioned Fear and Systematic Desensitization

Watson demonstrated the manner in which emotional responses are conditioned when he applied Pavlov's theory, developed through the study of animals, to the conditioning of little Albert, an 11-month-old boy (Watson & Rayner, 1920). They conditioned Albert to fear a rat, an animal that did not initially provoke a fear reaction in the baby. They repeatedly made a sudden loud noise (hitting a hammer against a steel bar—a noise that had severely frightened little Albert during pretesting) to startle the infant when the rat was presented, or when he reached for the rat with interest. Soon, the mere sight of the rat made him cry.

Generalization was also demonstrated as little Albert's conditioned fear generalized to other furry objects, including a rabbit, a dog, and a fur coat. Poor Albert even feared a Santa Claus mask. This study thus suggested that an emotional response that was conditioned to one stimulus could result in later emotional reaction to a variety of events/stimuli. It also demonstrated that any neutral stimulus might end up eliciting an emotion. Watson believed that this was how most of personality was formed. Confident that Freud's notions of the sexual basis of personality were ridiculous, he teased Freudians by maintaining that Albert's fear of fur would be interpreted by a psychoanalyst in terms of an early experience with pubic hair.

Watson and Rayner's approach was also used to countercondition the fear of rats, rabbit fur, feathers, and the like, in a little boy called Peter (Jones, 1924). Peter played with three other children while a fear-inducing rabbit was present; the fear was gradually extinguished by slowly bringing the rabbit closer and closer to the child while keeping him happy. This was one of the first documented cases of the use of what has come to be called **systematic desensitization.** Peter became desensitized to the rabbit; thus this aspect of his personality changed.

This deconditioning of phobias by treatment using systematic desensitization techniques is now a common and successful form of therapy (Choy, Fyer, & Lipsitz, 2007). This suggests that even highly emotional aspects of personality can disappear (be extinguished) over time. Recently, the technology that enables people to experience *virtual reality (VR)* has improved substantially both in terms of the quality of the experience created and the cost (in time and money) of creating the simulated environments. Current research is focusing on the use of VR therapy for phobias by applying the techniques of systematic desensitization using electronically simulated anxiety-provoking situations rather than imagined ones or actual ones (Wiederhold & Wiederhold, 2005). Positive results have been shown for a range of common phobias, including fear of spiders, heights, enclosed spaces, flying, and even post-traumatic stress (e.g., Emmelkamp et al., 2002; North, North, & Coble, 1998; Parsons & Rizzo, 2008; Riva et al., 2010). There are potentially many benefits to such an approach beyond reduced cost and higher effectiveness. People with

Systematic Desensitization
Gradually extinguishing a phobia by causing the feared stimulus to become dissociated from the fear response

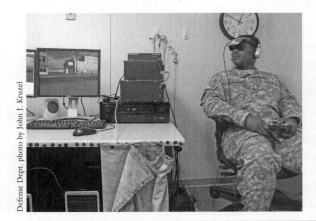

Defense Dept. photo by John J. Kruzel

■ When people suffer from phobias, they often can be successfully treated by desensitization training, which applies the principle of extinction. The fear response is "deconditioned" by pairing the experience of being calm and anxiety-free with successively closer approaches to the fear-inducing situation. This approach has been adapted to the treatment of PTSD (posttraumatic stress disorder). Military veterans suffering from PTSD are being treated with virtual reality exposure therapy specific to their individual combat experience (virtual Vietnam and virtual Iraq), with some success.

CHANGING Personality

The behaviorist approach to changing personality focuses on altering an undesirable behavior rather than finding out what caused it. A fundamental underlying assumption is that the cause of the problem is irrelevant (although the cause surely lies in the prior history of reinforcement)—the behavior itself is the issue. Merely apply the training tools to change the behavior, and the problem will be solved. In this perspective, an undesired behavior can be changed by learning a different behavior. Suppose you are a nail-biter, and that habit is creating problems of infected cuticles and embarrassment over unsightly hands. A behaviorist approach would be to train you to stop biting your nails, using a planned program of shaping via reinforcement. From many other perspectives, though, especially a psychodynamic one, fixing the symptom is not ultimately of value because the underlying problem will then just manifest itself in some other way. A traditional psychoanalyst would accept that the nail-biting could be stopped by conditioning, but would see such an effort as a distraction from the real goal of helping the nail-biter understand the inner conflicts that are causing self-destructive behavior. You could spend years in intensive psychoanalysis sessions to get at the root of the problem—or go for a few sessions of behavior therapy and stop the nail-biting.

phobias are more willing to enter a treatment program where they know that they won't have to confront the target of their phobia *in vivo*, but only a computer-generated simulacrum (Garcia-Palacios et al., 2001; Garcia-Palacios, Botella, Hoffman, & Fabregat, 2007).

Another early application of conditioning principles was to the treatment of bedwetting (Mowrer & Mowrer, 1938). An electrical device—a loud bell—awakens the child when the slightest wetness is detected. Such a treatment is effective for many children. Soon, the child learns to respond to the sensations before becoming wet. This approach contradicts the Freudian explanation of bedwetting as the result of a personality disorder resulting from being fixated at a stage of psychosexual development. The focus instead is on staying dry through the night as a skill that can be learned via conditioning from the outside rather than on bedwetting as a symptom of psychic distress on the inside. The application of behaviorist conditioning techniques to therapy developed into a field sometimes referred to as behavior modification or applied behavior analysis.

In 1920, Watson had an affair, divorced his wife, and married his student assistant. This scandalous act in the environment of the time (undoubtedly linked to poor moral conditioning in childhood) resulted in great social pressures, and he had to leave Johns Hopkins University. This disruption produced a major change of career for Watson. He applied his learning theories to the marketplace and became a successful consultant to business. He published another book, *Behaviorism*, in 1924, but his career as an experimental psychologist pretty much ended when he left the university. Watson died in 1958. Whatever happened to little Albert, conditioned to fear fur? He died later in childhood, leaving some psychologists forever wondering what kind of personality the adult Albert would have had.

In modern research, the effects of classical conditioning on personality provide an interesting way to think about the *initiation* of many habits and addictions, but patterns of behavior are maintained when they are rewarded. For example, smoking, drinking, and gambling may initially elicit an unconditioned positive response (of positive arousal, euphoria, excitement), but the persistence of the behaviors in the long run may be better explained as a consequence of the rewards they provide.

Watson (1924) took seriously the idea that a child was a blank slate. He boasted, "Give me a dozen healthy infants and my own specified world to bring them up in, and I'll guarantee to take any one at random and train him" to be anything, from a doctor or lawyer to a beggar or thief, regardless of his talents, color, inclinations, or whatever. In other words, Watson is proclaiming much more than a specific theory about personality; he is espousing a worldview in which the *environment* is key to understanding a person. Accordingly, if children are raised properly, they will behave properly, because their personalities are a function of the environment. This perspective is in marked contrast to the perspectives described in other chapters. It was Watson's assumptions that laid the basis for the work of B. F. Skinner.

The Radical Behaviorism of B. F. Skinner

Burrhus Frederick ("Fred") Skinner (1904–1990) was born in Susquehanna, Pennsylvania. His lawyer father and his mother followed a stringent morality. According to Skinner, he lived in a stable, loving home. His parents and grandparents taught him to respect the Puritan work ethic, virtues, and morals.

As a child, Skinner constructed machines (scooters, rafts, seesaws, slingshots, blow guns, steam cannons) and invented contraptions (among others, a flotation system to separate ripe from green berries), and these childhood interests may have been reflected later in his building and using laboratory equipment and machines (Hall, 1967). From his early years, he was also very interested in animals and their behavior; for example, he watched the trained pigeons at the fair.

Skinner would later say that he could trace his adult behaviors to his childhood reinforcements, not to "personality development" as described by personality theorists such as Freud and Jung. Skinner emphasized that who he was, his personality, was clearly the result of his **reinforcement** history as a child—the rewards and punishments he experienced. His life and personality, he claimed, were determined and controlled by environmental events.

When Skinner was studying literature at Hamilton College, a small liberal arts college, he sent some stories to the poet Robert Frost, who recommended he continue to write. After graduation he did spend a year trying to write but determined that he didn't have anything significant to say. (We might wonder why Robert Frost's positive reinforcement did not encourage him to keep trying. Was it the limited positive reinforcement he received? Did his behavior extinguish without further rewards?) He then spent six months in Greenwich Village during which time he read Pavlov's *Conditioned Reflexes* and some works by and about Watson. He was also influenced by the pioneering experimental psychologist Edward Thorndike, whose **Law of Effect** argued that the consequences of a behavior (i.e., the effect) will either strengthen or weaken that behavior. Learning initially comes about through trial and error. We learn to do those actions that bring us rewards or help us avoid pain.

Skinner decided to do graduate work in psychology at Harvard after determining that one needs to understand behavior (as a psychologist does), not just describe it (as a writer does). During graduate school, he concluded that the environment controls behavior: Environmental events, particularly the *consequences of behavior*, are responsible for most behavior. That being the case, Skinner reasoned, one must uncover the environmental conditions surrounding any behavior in order to understand the behavior. Skinner endeavored to explain behavior without having to refer to physiology or internal personality constructs. He took his Ph.D. in psychology from Harvard in 1931.

Reinforcement
An event that strengthens a behavior and increases the likelihood of repeating the behavior in the future

Law of Effect
Edward Thorndike's concept that the consequence of a behavior will either strengthen or weaken the behavior; that is, when a response follows a stimulus and results in satisfaction for the organism, this strengthens the connection between stimulus and response; however, if the response results in discomfort or pain, the connection is weakened

© Ken Heyman/Woodfin Camp & Associates

■ Skinner's behaviorist approach explicitly claimed that the principles of learning were common across all species. He used primarily pigeons (shown here) and rats—both are capable of making responses that are easily recorded mechanically (pecks on a key, pressing a bar, etc.). Here's an interesting question: Could pigeons be smarter than people when the contingencies of reinforcement are more important than reflective thought? One study investigated the "Monty Hall dilemma" (derived from the TV show, *Let's Make a Deal*). The contestant (or pigeon) tries to guess which of three doors conceals a desirable prize. After the choice is made (say Door 1), one of the *other* doors is opened (say Door 3), but it doesn't have the prize. The contestant then gets the option of remaining with their initial choice or switching to the other unopened door (Door 2). Most humans stay with their initial choice. But pigeons who have been put through this situation a number of times quickly learn to switch to the other unopened door. The correct move is to switch—it doubles your probability of winning—but most people don't learn this, even after multiple trials (Herbranson & Schroeder, 2010).

By the way, here's the explanation for the advantage of switching: When you pick Door 1, there is a 2/3 chance that the prize is behind one of the other two doors (and only a 1/3 chance that it is behind your door). When you learn that it is not behind Door 3, that means that there was a 2/3 chance that it was behind Door 2 (as there was still only the 1/3 chance that you had initially picked correctly). So you should switch your choice to Door 2. Most people cannot figure this out and so do much worse than the pigeons, who don't think too much and so have a smarter "personality."

Operant Conditioning as an Alternative Description of Personality

Operant Conditioning
The changing of a behavior by manipulating its consequences

Shaping
The process in which undifferentiated operant behaviors are gradually changed or shaped into a desired behavior pattern by the reinforcement of successive approximations, so that the behavior more and more resembles the target behavior

After Harvard, Skinner went to Minnesota, and then to Indiana for a short time, and finally returned to Harvard in 1948. He became sort of an animal trainer using his newly developed principles called **operant conditioning**. In operant conditioning, behavior is changed by its consequences; that is, Skinner manipulated the environment in such a way that he was able to train animals (rats, pigeons) to do things (such as playing badminton) that were far from their native behaviors. He did this by gradually **shaping** successive approximations to the desired behavior. Trained seals do not jump through hoops because of their personality but rather because they have been rewarded with fish for performing the behaviors desired by their trainers.

Skinner's theory of operant conditioning emphasized the study of overt, observable behavior, environmental conditions, and the process by which environmental events and circumstances determine behavior. Thus, the theory places its emphasis on the function of behavior (what it does) rather than the structure of personality. It is also a *deterministic* theory, in which there is no free will.

According to Skinner, the term "personality" is meaningless. There is no place for internal components of personality, psychical structures (id, ego, superego), traits, self-actualization, needs, or instincts. This strong rejection of "mentalism" in favor of directly observable behaviors has been an ongoing conflict between behaviorism and most other psychological theorizing (Uttal, 2000). The thing we know as personality is merely a group of responses to the environment, in Skinner's view. To Pavlov's ideas, Skinner added and developed the important notion that responses produced by the organism have environmental consequences; if the responses are rewarded, then they are more likely to appear again. Skinner argued that most behavior of a person or other organism is of this type and that it is these operant behaviors, taken together, that we call personality.

Skinner cleverly analyzed the behavior of a superstitious individual, without relying on any internal aspects of personality. How can we understand a person who wears lucky shoes to important exams, eats only peanut butter sandwiches before job interviews, and always wears a silver bracelet when going to a party to look for a date? Skinner would explain that if a person has experiences in which a behavior (like wearing one's shiny black shoes) coincides with getting an A on exams, especially on a few random occasions, the person continues that behavior because the reinforcement strengthens the performance of the behavior even though there is no causal connection. There is no need to propose a "superstitious personality."

Skinner found that any one animal's learning and behavior did *not* look like the average animal's behavior, emphasizing the individuality of environmental conditions and responses. He therefore stressed that we must apply the principles of learning to each organism individually. Thus, his was an idiographic (rather than nomothetic) approach. He did, however, look for general laws of learning that would apply equally to all organisms, human and nonhuman, underscoring a common process.

Of course, Skinner did not consider himself a personality psychologist. On the contrary, notions of internal, nonobservable psychological characteristics were anathema to him. He relied heavily on animal research, whereas other personality theorists studied the development of human personality as a uniquely human process. Skinner believed that the universal laws of behavior acquisition, resulting in what we know as personality, operate in the same manner in human and animal, maybe just more simply in nonhuman animals.

Noam Chomsky (1973), the linguist and political commentator, was one of many who detested the view of humanity propounded by Skinner:

Suppose that humans happen to be so constructed that they desire the opportunity for freely undertaken productive work. Suppose that they want to be free from the meddling of technocrats and commissars, bankers and tycoons, mad bombers who engage in psychological tests of will with peasants defending their homes, behavioral scientists who can't tell a pigeon from a poet, or anyone else who tries to wish freedom and dignity out of existence or beat them into oblivion.

Is it true that Skinner couldn't "tell a pigeon from a poet"? As we have noted, Skinner studied literature and loved to write. He did, however, view the consistencies in behavior of his laboratory pigeons and his Harvard colleagues as similar in principle. In person (especially in his later years), Skinner, contrary to reputation, generally acted as a polite and friendly gentleman.

Controlling the Reinforcement

Skinner Box

An enclosure in which an experimenter can shape the behavior of an animal by controlling reinforcement and accurately measuring the responses of the animal

Negative Reinforcement

An aversive event that ends if a behavior is performed, making it more likely for that behavior to be performed in the future

Because Skinner, like Watson, believed that a child (like a pigeon) was a function of the environment, he set out to design the best ways to raise children and even to structure whole communities. His inquiries led to the invention of what is sometimes called the **Skinner box** (although Skinner himself did not call it this and did not like others to use this designation). In this enclosure, termed the experimental chamber or operant chamber, the animal (or child) was segregated from all irrelevant environmental influences, except those under the control of the experimenter. For animals, the box contained either a lever (to be pressed by the rat) or a key (to be pecked by a pigeon). This lever or key, when pecked or pressed, triggered release of a food pellet (providing positive reinforcement) or stopped the administration of an aversive stimulus like a shock (providing **negative reinforcement**).

The reinforcement rate could be carefully calibrated and controlled, and the rate of pressing/pecking was registered by the device. Even the earliest of the boxes allowed accurate measurement of the response rate while the reinforcement rate and schedule were controlled. Partial reinforcement schedules, in which the reward was delivered intermittently, were generally found to be most effective at shaping behavior patterns. These techniques were later applied to the design of teaching machines and self-paced teaching regimens, in which students receive rewards as they master skills. As applied to a young child, this might be a sort of fancy playpen that provides structured feedback about how the world works. As applied to a corporation employee, it might be a salary bonus schedule tied to certain productivity or profit increases (Skinner, 1938).

Skinner's Behaviorist Utopia: *Walden Two*

But Skinner, like Freud and other influential theorists, also had a broad vision for the design of society. In his novel *Walden Two*, Skinner (1948) describes a utopian community that is behaviorally engineered, based on principles of operant conditioning. A benevolent government rewards (reinforces) positive, socially appropriate behavior. Walden Two is problem-free because only positive reinforcement is used; people always behave reliably and responsibly, and they are invariably very competent. There is no issue of freedom because Skinner believes free will is only an illusion.

In a sardonic move, Skinner carefully selected the title for his novel from the work of the nineteenth-century essayist Henry David Thoreau. Thoreau lived alone for two years in a cabin at Walden Pond in Massachusetts; the experience had been the inspiration for his classic *Walden*. Thoreau was an individualist who called for self-reliance and rejection of authority. The individual was seen as the source of freedom. In Skinner's Walden Two, there is no freedom, only perceived freedom, as the community engineers everyone's behavior.

Time magazine called *Walden Two* a "depressingly serious prescription for communal regimentation, as though the author had read Aldous Huxley's *Brave New World* and missed the

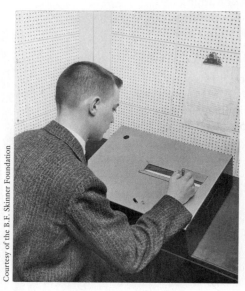

Courtesy of the B.F. Skinner Foundation

■ B. F. Skinner devised a "teaching machine" to administer controlled reinforcement to a human learner. It was used to help teach an undergraduate course at Harvard in the 1950s, establishing the "programmed instruction" approach to teaching.

point" ("Box–Reared Babies," 1954). Skinner, of course, had not missed the point. He well knew about fears that the government would assume control over self-destiny, but he himself did not fear this. Indeed, he did not worry at all because he believed that all behavior is determined anyway. Rather, he believed that a desirable utopian community could be designed by controlling the environment rather than leaving it unstructured.

Skinner formalized these ideas in his 1971 book *Beyond Freedom and Dignity*, a nonfiction treatise advocating a society like Walden Two. He proposed a behaviorally engineered society, using environmental control to shape human behavior—a technology of behavior in which environmental conditions are manipulated to shape human actions. Although Freud believed that horrible human problems could be traced to id forces and the death instinct, and although many biological psychologists believe that there is an evolved aggressive drive, Skinner believed that most such problems—including war and crime—are just human behaviors that can be shaped through learning. If society could reinforce better behaviors, they would supersede the maladaptive ones. Skinner's (1974) ideas stand in precise opposition to visions of individual freedom and self-fulfillment.

Skinner was willing to apply some of his principles to his own life. For example, he arose at the same time early each morning and sat at the same writing table to establish the habit of daily productive writing. He arranged a working and sleeping setup for himself in his basement, so that he could structure his environment to reinforce the desired

Courtesy of Juan Robinson

■ In the years immediately following the publication of Skinner's *Walden Two*, several small communities were founded on behaviorist principles. Here, a community member works at Twin Oaks Community (in Louisa, Virginia), which began as a Walden Two society in the 1960s but later evolved away from behaviorism.

© Michael Dwyer/Alamy

■ A Skinnerian approach to altering behavior is to set up environmental contingencies that reward desirable behavior. This approach has been successfully adopted in many "special" schools and treatment centers for children and adults with emotional and cognitive disabilities. In this day-treatment center for adults with intellectual disabilities, there is a "token economy" where appropriate behavior is rewarded with tokens that can be exchanged for treats and privileges—the tokens thus serve as secondary reinforcers. Here, a staff member is helping a client (on the left) select a reward to buy with his tokens in the center's store.

behaviors. As he became older, he was less and less willing to interrupt this structure. College students who seek advice about improving their grades are often advised to adopt just such a regimen—to arrange their study materials in a quiet place and go there every single day at the same time. This conditioning can produce a "productive personality." Of course, many students reject such advice, seeking to be more spontaneous, intuitive, and "free."

What about maladaptive behaviors? According to Skinner, psychopathology is learned in the same manner as all other behaviors: The adaptive or maladaptive personality (i.e., behavior) is learned by reinforcement. People have either not learned the appropriate response and have a behavioral deficit, or they have learned the wrong response. Also, some individuals may have been punished for adaptive behaviors. Thus, the treatment for "mental illness" is to set up environmental contingencies that reward desirable behavior. This approach has been operationalized to some extent in schools and group homes for children with cognitive and emotional disabilities. Interestingly, Skinner agrees with Karl Marx and Erich Fromm that an incoherent, oppressive society leads to the many problems of individuals in modern life; but for Skinner it is behavior, not consciousness or psychic stability, that is fragmented by disorganized reinforcers (Skinner, 1974). To Skinner, a neurotic is someone who has been reinforced for overly emotional behavior.

Applying Behaviorism: Personality Change and Individual Differences

Skinner agreed that Freud was an insightful observer of human behavior, but Skinner did not want to allow any vague mentalistic concepts (that could not be observed). So he continually reinterpreted the explanations of other theorists. Some examples of this reinterpretation are shown in Table 1.

If personality is merely learned behavior, as this school of thought contends, it can then presumably be unlearned using the same conditioning processes by which it was first learned. This is not a totally new idea. In fact, we present an example offered by Ben Franklin in the Self-Understanding box. What is new is that behaviorists try to do this systematically, according to scientific laws that they propose about contingencies.

Skinner did not deny that there are genetic differences among organisms. Instead, he said that the role of biological factors was to define the organism's range of responses and the organism's ability to have its behavior strengthened by environmental events. He emphasized that the environment is of primary

■ TABLE 1 Behaviorist Reinterpretation of Psychoanalytic and Neo-Analytic Concepts

Psychoanalytic or Neo-Analytic Concept	Behaviorist Reinterpretation
Freud's notion of the *id* as the instinctual energies that form the undifferentiated core of personality	Skinner asserted that this is simply humans' innate susceptibility to reinforcement, which is a product of evolution
The internal personality structure termed the *ego* or "I," which responds to the world according to the reality principle	The learned responses to the practical contingencies of everyday life; there are different behavioral repertoires for different environmental contingencies
The *superego* or "over-I" that internalizes societal rules and helps protect the ego from overwhelming id impulses	Behavior is learned from the punitive practices of society, controlling behavior not allowed by parents and society; "unconscious" simply means that people are not taught to observe it and talk about it
The ego defense mechanism of *repression*, that pushes threatening thoughts and motives back into the unconscious	We learn to avoid behavior that is punished, and by not engaging in it, we avoid conditioned aversive stimulation
Jung's notion of *archetypes* (universal emotional symbols) and the *collective unconscious* of deep, universal emotional symbols	Skinner says that this is the evolution of certain universal characteristics of the human species and the parallel cultural evolution of useful behaviors; there is thus a sameness or universality of things that are reinforcing, and a commonality of behaviors that societies need to control

importance even in hereditary characteristics because the environment selects behaviors that encourage pro-creation and survival; that is, in a relatively constant environment, the environment will "select" individuals who have the most adaptive behaviors to survive and reproduce. But ascribing any behavior to "instinct" is a mistake because it again ignores the role of environmental circumstances.

Internal Processes, External Causation, and Free Will

Skinner acknowledged that we have emotions, thoughts, and internal processes, but he dismissed these as irrelevant in the explanation and understanding of behavior. Thoughts and emotions do occur, according to Skinner, but they do not cause behavior. Thoughts, emotions, and other internal events are, as are all characteristics of the organism, *caused by* environmental events. In any case, we cannot operationalize internal processes or

Why Does It Matter?

The strong position of the behaviorist approach is that only observable behavior can provide appropriate data for a science of behavior. From this point of view, a subjective verbal report by an individual of a memory, an emotion, or an idea is only "data" to the extent that the string of words and the physical properties of the utterance constitute observable behavior. Skinner, in fact, wrote a book titled *Verbal Behavior* (1957) in which he provided a stimulus–response analysis of language behavior. As the technology to do neuropsychological measurement improves, it brings up the question of whether internal events occurring in the brain can be considered *observable*, and thus legitimate for scientific analysis if they can be measured objectively and reliably. We can do such measurement now with a variety of methods (EEG, fMRI, and so on). Does the behaviorist now need to broaden the scope of what behaviors are investigated?

Ben Franklin's Habit Chart

Although behaviorist theories of learning and reinforcement were developed in the twentieth century, key elements of the approach have been understood by some people for many centuries. One of the keenest insights into behaviorist principles was given by Benjamin Franklin (rpt. 1906) in his autobiography more than two hundred years ago. Rather than paying for a New Age course in self-improvement, you might try Franklin's method for yourself.

In an effort to improve the moral quality of his life, Franklin made a list of 13 virtues he thought desirable. For example, he wanted more temperance (not drinking to excess), frugality, industry ("be always employed in something useful"), and humility. He saw that the virtues were composed of specific behaviors, which together comprised habits. To change his habits, Ben constructed a calendar book, with rows of the virtues and columns of the days of the week (see chart). At the end of each day, he would put a black mark on his chart if he had violated the virtue that day. Aiming to create a clean slate, he had the reinforcement of seeing the number of black marks decrease. In this way, Franklin gradually minimized his bad habits.

Franklin, with great insight, went even further. At the beginning, he focused on one virtue at a time, so that he would not be distracted or discouraged by attempting too much at once. Second, he arranged or ordered the virtues in a way that each one would facilitate the learning of the next one. (For example, once he was no longer dull with too much drink, he could more easily move on to tackle the next set of habits.) Third, he gradually increased the reinforcement intervals; over time, he returned to his notebook less and less often, although he always kept it with him.

Interestingly, Franklin also recognized some of the limits of the behaviorist approach. He wrote little encouraging mottoes and sayings and poems in his notebook (a quote from Cicero here, a Bible verse from the Proverbs there), to inspire and motivate him further. Although he was not religious in the orthodox sense, he well understood and reflected on the importance of the religious underpinnings of what he was attempting. He thus integrated what today would be called a cognitive and motivational approach to behavioral change.

In the end, Ben Franklin said that although he could not achieve perfection, the endeavor made him a better and happier man than he otherwise would have been.

■ Benjamin Franklin's Habit Chart

Almost two centuries before behaviorism was formalized, Franklin had a sophisticated and insightful approach to modifying his own behavior using a form of negative reinforcement (a decrease in the black marks that signified violations of the virtues to which he aspired).

	Sunday	Monday	Tuesday	Wednesday	Thursday	Friday	Saturday
Temperance							
Silence							
Order							
Resolution							
Frugality							
Industry							
Sincerity							
Justice							
Moderation							
Cleanliness							
Tranquility							
Chastity							
Humility							

measure their magnitude. So rather than ask if someone feels tired or how tired he or she is, look to the environment—when he or she last slept, how much he or she slept, and so on. These environmental events are the factors that can be measured and studied scientifically. Thus, contrary to what many personality theorists have emphasized, personality is not something that is specially or uniquely human. Because personality is merely a group of behaviors that have been well supported by the environment, any organism could potentially have a "personality" as Skinner's theory defines it.

Like Freud, Skinner was a **radical determinist**, which means he believed that all human behavior is caused. Both believed that there is absolutely no evidence that people have "free will" in their behavior. For Freud this determinism was biological, whereas for Skinner it was environmental. According to Skinner, considering internal causes just confuses our study, diverting important attention from the real causes of behavior—the organism's reinforcement history. He was concerned that a focus on internal explanations for behavior entails the risk of eventually neglecting the key influence of the environmental events.

Radical Determinism
The belief that all human behavior is caused and that humans have no free will

Other Learning Approaches to Personality

In the 1930s and 1940s, a number of experimental psychologists became dissatisfied with the notion that behavior is totally a function of the events in the environment. They believed it was also important to take into account internal characteristics of the organism, such as how hungry or tired it was. But they still wanted to maintain a totally objective (often rat-based) approach. One of the most influential of these theorists was Clark Hull.

The Role of Internal Drives: Clark Hull

Hull was born in New York and later studied at the University of Michigan. He studied math, physics, and chemistry, intending to become an engineer, but then encountered the views of Watson and Pavlov, turned to psychology, and eventually became an influential professor at Yale. In 1943, he wrote *Principles of Behavior*. Hull's emphasis was on experimentation, an organized theory of learning, and the nature of **habits**, which were, according to Hull, simply associations between a stimulus and a response.

For Hull, the organism (usually a white rat) makes responses that lead to a goal that alleviates a drive. These responses in themselves become stimuli for further responses and *intervene* between the stimulus (e.g., hunger) and response (e.g., eating). So, for example, the rat must learn to make a variety of moves to get through the maze before it can reach the food and reduce its hunger drive. As applied to humans, this explains how a goal such as becoming rich can be learned, even though it is quite distant from an innate drive such as hunger. We learn that money and success can lead to drive reduction (such as allowing us access to good food). But it all comes back to basic innate or **primary drives**—hunger, thirst, sex, and the avoidance of pain.

Habits
In learning theory, simple associations between a stimulus and a response

Primary Drive
A fundamental innate motivator of behavior, specifically hunger, thirst, sex, or pain

SHARPEN YOUR THINKING · Current Controversy

Should Governments Encourage Gambling?

In the United States, the majority of the states sponsor state lotteries, with the proceeds going to public schools or other public purposes. More than two dozen countries run national lottery programs, also with "good causes" as the beneficiaries.

From the perspective of the principles of learning theory, playing a lottery (and most other forms of gambling) can be viewed as an example of partial reinforcement: The behavior of betting (buying a ticket) results in an outcome (winning the game and receiving money) that reinforces the behavior. In many gambling activities, small payouts occur rather frequently—for example, if you play "scratcher" games, as many as 10 percent of the tickets may provide a prize. Although these more frequent prizes tend to be very small (as little as the initial cost of the ticket in some cases), they can act as reinforcers all the same. Of course, the reinforcement is partial—the vast majority of the time, a person will not win. But partial reinforcement is very powerful in increasing the likelihood of a behavior being repeated and in making that behavior resistant to extinction. By its nature, gambling leads to more gambling.

Many governments require that their lottery officials regularly determine who is participating in the lottery. These reports, intended to address the criticism that the lottery disproportionately burdens the poor, tend to focus on the fact that lottery players are representative of the general population. While this may truly be the case, the impact of lottery gambling may still be disproportionally harmful to people who have lower incomes. For example, suppose 8 percent of those who spend $50 a month or more on lottery tickets have very low incomes, and that 8 percent of people in a state are classified as very low income. In this case, the income distribution of the group of heavy lottery players may well reflect the overall income distribution of that state as a whole. Does that mean, though, that the lottery has no greater negative impact on low-income people? A system where the poorest 8 percent of a population pay 8 percent of the taxes collected would be much less progressive than the income tax systems used by most governments, where the tax rates increase as the income level rises.

Is the promotion of gambling an activity in which governments should participate? Does running a lottery contribute to the general good of society? Is it appropriate for governments to encourage people, including those who may not have much discretionary income, to spend it on the addictive entertainment of the lottery? Should personality psychologists advise lottery boards on the most effective reinforcement schedules and lottery marketing so as to encourage more and more people to gamble?

What is important for understanding Hullian learning approaches to personality is that Hull turned attention to the internal state of the organism during learning, although he still emphasized the reinforcements provided by the environment. This allowed later development of more complex learning-based approaches than would result from a strict focus on stimulus and response.

Social Learning Theory: Dollard and Miller

A very productive and influential group of investigators from various backgrounds coalesced at Yale in the 1930s and were heavily influenced by Hull. One of these was Neal Miller, who received his Ph.D. at Yale in 1935. Interestingly, Miller did postdoctoral work at the Vienna Institute of Psychoanalysis, where he was exposed to Freud's ideas at the height of their European influence. Miller later also became an expert physiological psychologist. Putting all these background pieces together, Neal Miller worked in a research paradigm of environmental reinforcements in laboratory rats, like a good experimental behaviorist; however, he continued Hull's focus on internal drives, both in terms of physiology (such as brain mechanisms) and motivation. Furthermore, he tried to understand the deeper issues of the psyche that Freud and others had raised. He stayed at Yale until 1966, when he went to Rockefeller University and became a leader in the new field of health psychology, working on such topics as biofeedback and the voluntary control of processes like heart rate.

At Yale, Miller met John Dollard, who had received his Ph.D. in sociology at the University of Chicago. Chicago, at the time, was the center of the sociological and anthropological approach to social psychology, which emphasized the social or relative nature of the self. Dollard had also studied psychoanalysis in Berlin. So, when Dollard and Miller met and started collaborating, they together represented almost all the important traditions relevant to the study of personality—the psychoanalytic and ego aspects, the social and anthropological aspects, and the biological and cognitive aspects, all in the overall context of a learning and behaviorist framework. It is fascinating to see what emerged from this blend of fundamental ideas—an approach to personality called social learning theory.

Simply put, **social learning theory** proposes that our likelihood of responding in certain ways—termed "habits"—are built up in terms of a hierarchy of secondary, or *acquired*, drives. For example, suppose you are mugged and beaten up while walking down a dark alley. Not only would you probably learn to avoid such situations (remembering the pain), but you would feel anxiety in similar situations. This learned anxiety is now an acquired drive that can motivate new behavior. You could be reinforced (and thus learn new aspects to your personality) when this drive is reduced, such as always walking at night with a confident companion. You might even learn to enjoy sipping wine with a good-humored group of friends when the sun begins to set (if this reduced your anxiety). Note that the lighthearted companions will not protect you from being mugged in the dark alley; rather, a hierarchy of responses has been built up from the learning and reducing of new drives.

Habit Hierarchies

In other words, for Miller and Dollard (1941) there is a learned hierarchy of likelihoods that a person will produce particular responses in particular situations. They call this a **habit hierarchy**. In essence, the individual's experiences result in learning the likelihood that a specific response in a particular situation results in reward. Using this information, the individual ranks the probability of responses in the habit hierarchy. Through this implicit process, the responses most likely to result in reward become the responses most likely to occur. Social learning theories see this personal ranking as responsible for individual differences that we often term personal style or personality. Furthermore, many of the important reinforcers that determine a person's habit hierarchy are social in nature, coming from people in the social environment.

The concept of **secondary drives** attempts to describe how the (adult) human personality, in all of its complexity, can be conditioned from the infant stage, at which the child is just a bundle of undifferentiated physiological drives and responses. The concept of secondary drive explains traditional personality constructs, like the trait of extroversion, as learned secondary drives. For example, if the active orientation toward others (which characterizes an extrovert) brings milk from the mother or a clean diaper from the father, a drive toward these behaviors will be

Social Learning Theory
A theory that proposes that habits are built up in terms of a hierarchy of secondary drives

Habit Hierarchy
In social learning theory, a learned hierarchy of likelihoods that a person will produce particular responses in particular situations

Secondary Drives
In social learning theory, drives that are learned by association with the satisfaction of primary drives

Thinkstock

■ In understanding drug abuse, the behaviorist and learning approach focuses not on motives toward impulsivity, nor on neurochemical substrates, but rather on hierarchies of behaviors that have been reinforced. Addiction and abuse are seen as patterns of learned behavior. Similarly, in designing the best treatment, focus is on reinforcements (see the Classic to Current box on treatment for drug abuse).

learned—and so on, as the child develops. Such notions are useful in understanding why some cultures (like Japan, which promotes group cohesion) have more shy people than other cultures (like the United States and Israel, which reward individual activity and assertiveness). Children are socialized—they learn secondary drives and behaviors—through social rewards.

How far can this theory be extended? Does it work? An aspect of this notion of secondary drives as derived from the primary drive of feeding was applied to the concept of attachment to the mother and examined by Harry Harlow's famous studies of rhesus monkeys (Harlow, 1986; Harlow & Mears, 1979). Infant monkeys were separated from their mothers, and some of the infants were fed by feeding bottles attached to a bare wire cylinder. Harlow demonstrated that infant monkeys did not develop a secondary drive of attachment to these wire surrogate mothers; they preferred soft, terry cloth–covered surrogate mothers (even nonfeeding ones). In other words, attachment did not derive from its association with nourishment. Although this finding did not totally negate the concept of attachment as a secondary drive, it did suggest that contact comfort itself has a primary drive status in these primate infants. Not only did such studies suggest that the developing child needs more than to have primary needs like hunger satisfied, but they also showed the difficulty of simply accounting for the social needs and tendencies.

As noted, both Dollard and Miller had studied psychoanalysis, were impressed with its many insights, and were eager to combine them with experimental findings. But although Freud had (1963b) psychoanalyzed a neurotic man obsessed with images of rats (whom he called Rattenmann, or *man of the rats*), of course Freud had never psychoanalyzed a rat. Dollard and Miller (1950) agreed that Freud had identified crucial periods in the child's personality development, but they changed the explanations to ones involving learning, through rewards and punishments. For example, they named critical times during development (feeding, cleanliness training, early sex training) when the reinforcement contingencies provided by the parents are particularly relevant. If a hungry child is not fed, she may develop anxiety or passivity rather than sociability and love. If a child is punished for messes and toilet accidents, she may learn to avoid her parents to reduce anxiety. If a child is beaten for masturbation, he may learn to associate anxiety with all aspects of sexuality. Such reinterpretations and refinements to psychoanalytic notions—made by Dollard and Miller and many other psychologists during the 1930s, 1940s, and 1950s—have come to play a dominant role in current approaches to child socialization.

Drive Conflict

What about the mental illnesses and repressed conflicts that Freud wrote so much about? Extending Hull's concepts of drives, learning, and secondary drives, Dollard and Miller attempted to explain the development of internal conflicts that result in

Classic to **Current**

Treatment for Drug Abuse

From their very beginnings in the conditioning labs of Pavlov and Watson, behaviorist and learning approaches have been focused on two things: the environmental *stimulus*, and the rewards and punishments that affect the likelihood of an organism's subsequent response. Indeed, these approaches are sometimes termed "stimulus—response" (S-R) theories. Although the models have been refined, modern approaches in this perspective maintain this focus. A good example concerns therapeutic interventions for drug abuse. Or perhaps we should say, a good example concerns attempts to change societally undesirable behavior.

Whereas a psychoanalytic or neo-analytic approach to drug abusers would be focused on disrupted childhood experiences and how those experiences became manifested in a poorly functioning adult ego, and a biological perspective would be interested in the neural circuits and neurotransmitters involved in drug abuse, the behaviorist and learning perspective focuses on changing the relevant stimulus and changing the consequences. In other words, certain stimuli have become associated with taking illegal drugs, and the rewards for abstaining have not been strong enough to maintain legal behavior. In particular, what does this mean in terms of today's therapies?

In terms of dealing with the stimulus, one approach is to address the eliciting circumstances. For example, if the abuser usually meets a group of abusing friends in a seedy restaurant, the focus might be to make that setting inaccessible, such as taking a drug-abusing teenager and sending him or her to a different school in a different city or even to a residential treatment facility. Or, the focus might be to have the police monitor and harass the lawbreakers in the seedy restaurant, thus making the situation no longer associated with good times.

Another approach to changing the stimulus would be to corrupt the drug or a similar substance to make it nausea-inducing. For example, with alcohol addiction, the therapist may prescribe a medication like Antabuse (disulfiram) which, in the presence of alcohol, causes accumulation of acetaldehyde in the blood and produces highly unpleasant symptoms such as flushing, vomiting, palpitations, vertigo, and fainting. Or the therapist might attempt to pair scenes of the drug paraphernalia with unpleasant reactions (such as seeing others vomiting). If one felt awful at even the sight of the drug, the likelihood of ingestion would surely decrease (Smith, Frawley, & Polissar, 1997). But what about changing the reinforcements for not using drugs? One interesting six-month study of drug abuse treatment focused directly on reinforcement (Silverman, Svikis, Robles, Stitzer, & Bigelow, 2001). The participants (patients) were pregnant substance-abusing women who were in a drug abuse program and who had recently used opiates or cocaine. They were randomly assigned to either a special treatment group or to a usual-care control group. The treatment group women were assigned to work-training sessions and worked a three-hour shift daily for pay (vouchers). Urine samples were collected for ongoing monitoring of drug abuse. Under an escalating reinforcement schedule, the women could earn lots more if they came to training sessions and remained drug-free. (The value of the daily vouchers increased from $7 all the way up to about four times that amount if the woman remained drug-free.) The results showed that women in the treatment group were twice as likely to have urine samples that tested negative for opiates and cocaine. In other words, even in this hard-to-treat, hard-core group of drug addicts, the provision of a substantial reward (high, increasing salary, which could be used to buy various goods) for desired behavior was able to change the so-called personality patterns to a substantial degree.

This approach of rewarding addicts for remaining drug-free has come to be called contingency management. One promising recent application of it integrates the direct reinforcement system (rewarding addicts for abstinence from illicit drugs) with reward for compliance with other components of a treatment program, such as taking medication, that increase the likelihood of drug abstinence (Carroll & Rounsaville, 2007). In the behaviorist view, addiction is seen as a behavior, sensitive to modification like all behaviors.

FURTHER READING

Carroll, K. M., & Rounsaville, B. J. (2007). A perfect platform: Combining contingency management with medications for drug abuse. *American Journal of Drug and Alcohol Abuse*, *33*(3), 343–365.

Silverman, K., Svikis, D., Robles, E., Stitzer, M. L., & Bigelow, G. E. (2001). A reinforcement-based therapeutic workplace for the treatment of drug abuse: Six-month abstinence outcomes. *Experimental & Clinical Psychopharmacology*, *9*(1), 14–23.

behaviors (symptoms) of neurosis and disorders such as obsessive-compulsive behavior. For example, children have (primary) sexual drives but sometimes may be punished for acting on them. If the punishment results in the conditioning of a fear response to this drive, the primary and secondary drives may conflict in an **approach–avoidance conflict**. The individual is both drawn to and away from the sexual object, resulting in anxious, neurotic behavior. There can likewise be an **approach–approach conflict**, in which a person (or rat) is drawn to two equally attractive choices, and an **avoidance–avoidance conflict**, in which the individual is repulsed by two equally undesirable choices. This can make a rat run back and forth in a maze, not knowing which drive to reduce first—a neurotic rat!

Another important example of the work of the so-called Yale Group is their idea that aggression is always the result of blocking, or frustrating, an individual's efforts to attain a goal. This theory was propounded in the influential book *Frustration and Aggression* (Dollard, Miller, Doob, Mowrer, & Sears, 1939). Here again we have an important psychological concept—aggression—that figures prominently in both psychoanalytic and biological approaches to personality. But it is now analyzed in terms of drives, habits, and learning (including social learning), thus taking into account the complex, multidimensional nature of aggression.

For example, it is interesting that a frustration coming from the environment may lead to aggression against a different target. If your boss blocks you from achieving your promotion, you may come home and yell at your family. In some ways, this idea is similar to Freud's *displacement* defense mechanism, in which an aggressive impulse is channeled elsewhere. The **frustration–aggression hypothesis**, like the Freudian notion of a death instinct and like the evolutionary proposition of an evolved domineering aggression, allows for a biological tendency to aggress. However, Dollard and Miller's approach ties these notions more closely to the environment and the ways one has learned to satisfy basic drives (an idea derived from Hull). Aggression can be learned; it can also be unlearned or prevented. And aggression clearly varies from situation to situation, from family to family, and from culture to culture. In other words, the social learning approach endeavors to integrate key ideas from other theories, but all within a learning framework. These ideas are important because they led to modern cognitive-social learning and interactionist approaches to personality.

Patterns of Child-Rearing and Personality: Robert R. Sears

Another member of the Yale Group, Robert R. Sears, performed a series of studies designed to examine the efficacy of Dollard and Miller's theoretical explanations for personality. Specifically, Sears wanted to examine psychoanalytic constructs in terms of the real, observable behavior of parents and children. He described personality as "potentialities for action" that included motivation, expectations, habit structure, the nature of the instigators to behavior, and the environmental events produced by that behavior. For example, Sears studied the child-rearing antecedents of dependency and aggressiveness in children (Sears, Maccoby, & Levin, 1957). Childhood personality was measured by teachers' ratings, behavioral observation, and doll play. Child-rearing practices were obtained by maternal report (a major methodological limitation

Approach–Avoidance Conflict
A term used by Dollard and Miller to describe a conflict between primary and secondary drives that occurs when a punishment results in the conditioning of a fear response to a drive

Approach–Approach Conflict
A term used by Dollard and Miller to describe a conflict in which a person is drawn to two equally attractive choices

Avoidance–Avoidance Conflict
A term used by Dollard and Miller to describe a conflict in which a person is faced with two equally undesirable choices

Frustration-Aggression Hypothesis
The theory that aggression is the result of blocking, or frustrating, a person's efforts to attain a goal

because mothers' reports may be distorted). Still, Sears found that the amount that the parent reported punishing the child for dependency was highly related to both dependency and aggression in the child. Overall, the study found that although many child-rearing practices were weakly or not at all related to personality characteristics in children, Dollard and Miller's theory that many Freudian disorders and neuroses resulted from parenting practices of punishments—that punished children for undesirable behavior—was somewhat supported by the data (Sears, Rau, & Alpert, 1966). This empirical approach took the conflicts described by Freud and endeavored to test them through study of parental responses. Freud never conducted such tests, but they grow naturally out of a learning approach to personality.

Why does it matter that Dollard and Miller were working at Yale in the 1940s, where they were heavily influenced by Hull, who in turn had been influenced by the 1920s work of Watson? We are endeavoring to show that there is no simple answer to what it means to be a person. There is no single and comprehensive theory that has been established and universally adopted throughout personality psychology. Rather, there are systems of ideas and insights that derive from various intellectual traditions and historical movements of ideas. By tracing these developments and presenting them as eight fundamental perspectives on personality, we can achieve a rich, multifaceted appreciation of personality that goes well beyond the simple assumptions of a layperson.

Modern Behaviorist Personality Approaches

Most personality psychologists see a fundamental conflict in a behaviorist approach to personality: Behaviorism deals only in externally observable entities and is thus limited in its ability to address the essence of personality, which is complex, internal, and not directly observable. In recent years, one promising avenue of contact has gone back to the physiological roots of conditioning research: an interesting return to a truly Pavlovian approach. In this view (e.g., Gray & McNaughton, 2000; Pickering, 1997), characteristics of the nervous system differ systematically between individuals, producing individual differences in conditioning and corresponding individual differences in personality. This approach, sometimes termed reinforcement sensitivity theory (RST) posits that underlying biobehavioral systems influence individual responsivity to both reward and punishment. The behavioral activation or approach system and behavioral inhibition system (BAS and BIS) moderate the effects of reward and punishment and have clear correlations with reliably measured personality traits (e.g., Corr, 2002, 2008; Jackson, 2003).

Why Does It Matter?

If individuals show stable individual patterns of differential sensitivity to reward versus to punishment, then a customized approach to many types of training is appropriate—one size will not fit all. While the older behaviorist tradition generalized the superiority of reward over punishment as a training technique, there may be individuals who would learn new behaviors more quickly or more enduringly with a different mixture of reward and punishment.

Another approach connects personality psychology of traits to behaviorism. It assesses personality by looking at the frequency with which a person performs certain observable acts (Buss & Craik, 1983). This **act frequency approach** records and counts behaviors that are typical of a given trait category. For example, a conscientious person will complete work on time, persevere in a task, be prudent before spending money, and refuse an impulsive dare. This approach meets the behaviorist requirement

Act Frequency Approach
Assessing personality by examining the frequency with which a person performs certain observable actions

221

TIME LINE

The History of Behaviorist and Learning Approaches to Personality

The major developments in the behaviorist and learning approaches can be seen here in historical relation to one another and in relation to their broader societal and cultural contexts.

Behaviorist and Learning Aspects		Societal and Scientific Context
Philosophers and theologians view individual deviations as games of the gods or possession by the devil	Ancient Times and Middle Ages	Humans are seen primarily in religious terms, as created by a divine presence
Individual is increasingly understood to be shaped or set by social class and by work, following Locke's view of infant as a blank slate	1700s–1800s	Increasing emphasis on reason and rationality, philosophers search for the core of human nature; Ben Franklin develops habit chart
Pavlov studies classical conditioning; other studies of animal learning begin in earnest	1880s–1900s	Darwin's evolutionary approach leads to experimental studies in animals in search of universals applicable to people
Watson founds behaviorism	1900s–1920s	Experimental psychology develops; increased industrialization of society
Skinner dramatically expands behaviorism; Hull develops broader learning theory	1920s–1940s	Experimental psychology is increasingly dominated by behaviorism; attempts to combine behaviorism and psychoanalysis
Influence of social psychology increases; child-rearing practices are studied	1940s–1950s	In reaction to fascism and world war, studies of propaganda, attitude formation, and social structure increase
Existentialists challenge behaviorists; human freedom discussed; cognitive psychology grows; behaviorism declines	1950s–1960s	Economic boom with huge new middle class; baby boomers in public schools; new affluence removes old fears from workers
Learning approaches increasingly combined with cognitive and social approaches; personality seen as interacting with the demands of social situations	1970s–1980s	Societal problems of crime and delinquency lead to searches for more sophisticated models of teaching and learning
Ideas of conditioning and reinforcement integrated into other approaches to personality	1990s–2000s	Better understandings of the individual in specific work environments

that only events that are observable are legitimate, but connects to more conventional personality approaches by seeking stable individual trait differences in behavior. The patterns of act frequencies can be examined for evidence that the traits measured by conventional instruments manifest themselves in observable behavior, within and across cultural contexts (Church, Katigbak, Miramontes, del Prado, & Cabrera, 2007).

Evaluation

The emphasis of the behaviorist and learning approaches is on using completely controlled scientific experiments. In terms of research, this emphasis has led to a focus on laboratory pigeons and rats. In terms of concepts, this approach has led to an unwillingness to make inferences about the "mind" or the "spirit." Turning first away from introspectionism, some in this field (like Skinner) eventually refused to concede any kind of internal structures, cognitions, motives, or traits whatsoever. Further, behaviorism admits no internal motivation to self-fulfillment or self-actualization, and no true heroism; there is only history of reinforcement.

Behaviorist and learning approaches to personality have forced the field of personality to be much more experimental in its research and rigorous in its concepts than it would otherwise have been. Notions of conditioning, reward, and extinction now pervade psychology, including personality and clinical psychology. Moreover, this approach provides an empirically well-supported explanation of why behavior is not as consistent across situations as many other personality theories might imply. The situation itself must be considered an aspect of personality.

On the other hand, because radical behaviorists are unwilling to recognize any sorts of internal structures of the mind, they tend to be less able to profit from the many advances being made in cognitive psychology and the other brain sciences. Until the day he died, Skinner was relentless in his attack on cognitive psychology, even though cognitive psychologists are usually very strict in their experimental designs and scientific methods. Similarly, behaviorists are often unwilling to benefit from the many developments in trait approaches to personality.

Perhaps more important, behaviorists refuse to concern themselves with "unscientific" notions like freedom, dignity, and self-fulfillment. Such things are seen as *epiphenomena*—that is, secondary phenomena that are derived from real phenomena of experience. For example, Skinner repeatedly asserts that though people may sometimes feel free, they are in actuality always controlled by the contingencies of the environment. For Skinner, people feel free when they do not recognize that they are being controlled. Education and religion are said to be two means through which the control of behavior is disguised or concealed (Skinner, 1974). Many psychologists view this perspective as a terribly demeaning and insulting view of what it means to be a person. A person is qualitatively different from a laboratory rat. Writer Arthur Koestler (1967) charged that behaviorism "has substituted for the erstwhile anthropomorphic view of the rat, a ratomorphic view of man." Such matters are taken up in the next four chapters.

"Oh, not bad. The light comes on, I press the bar, they write me a check. How about you?"

■ Skinner liked to point out that in many social interactions, the subordinate is not only being shaped by the superior, but is also shaping the superior. For example, children quickly learn to train their parents by rewarding certain behaviors emitted by the parents. (© The New Yorker Collection 1993 Tom Cheney from cartoonbank.com. All Rights Reserved.)

Evaluating the Perspectives

Advantages and Limits of the Behaviorist and Learning Approach

■ Quick Analogy

- Humans as intelligent rats learning life mazes.

■ Advantages

- Forces attention to the environmental influences on behavioral consistencies.

- Demands rigorous empirical study (usually laboratory-based).

- Stresses the importance of applying the principles of conditioning to each organism individually.

- Looks for general laws that apply to all organisms.

■ Limits

- Extreme behaviorism may ignore insights and advances from cognitive and social psychology.

- May tend to dehumanize unique human potentials through comparisons to rats and pigeons.

- Tends to refuse any notion of enduring dispositions within individuals.

- Tends to view humans as objects to be trained.

■ View of Free Will

- Behavior is determined by environmental contingencies.

■ Common Assessment Technique

- Experimental analysis of animal learning.

■ Implications for Therapy

- Because personality is conditioned and learned, therapy is based on teaching desirable habits and behaviors, and on extinguishing undesirable ones. Disruptive or aggressive children may be rewarded when they act cooperatively or quietly. Fears of elevators or airplanes are treated through systematic desensitization, in which relaxation is slowly and progressively paired with the fear-provoking stimuli until the fear is extinguished. In aversion therapy to treat stubborn problems such as alcoholism, the therapist may prescribe a drug (e.g., Antabuse) that produces nausea when alcohol is consumed.

Summary and Conclusion

Most approaches to personality start with complex patterns of human behavior and try to break them down into simpler, understandable components; instead of breaking down, behaviorist and learning approaches start with simple stimuli and responses of lower animals and try to build up an understanding of human complexity.

Following up Ivan Pavlov's work on classical conditioning, John B. Watson, the early-twentieth-century behaviorist, rejected introspectionism and psychoanalysis, and instead demonstrated how little Albert's emotional "personality" could be trained by hitting a hammer against a steel bar to severely frighten the infant in the presence of a conditioned stimulus. Principles of learning, generalization, and extinction were also applied to children, as the learning approach explored how "personality" is located in the environment, not in the depths of the psyche.

According to B. F. Skinner, personality is a repertoire of behavior learned from an organized set of environmental contingencies. That is, personality is the group of commonly performed responses that a person has learned. Because it is environmentally determined, behavior is therefore very situation specific.

Skinner's approach emphasized the function of behavior, and it is a deterministic theory, in which there is no free will. He stressed that we must apply the principles of learning to each organism individually. In his novel *Walden Two*, Skinner describes a utopian community that is behaviorally engineered, based on principles of operant conditioning; a benevolent government rewards positive, socially appropriate behavior, and all is well.

According to Skinner, the motivations that Freud called the drives of the id are better understood as biological reinforcers of the environment; and the part of the psyche that Freud called the superego (conscience) is better understood as the contingencies that society creates and imposes to control the selfish (individualistic) nature of the individual. For Skinner, personality traits such as extroversion are just groups of behaviors that have been reinforced. Behaviorist approaches forced personality theorists to become

more empirically minded, and many untestable Freudian assumptions were discarded.

Miller and Dollard (1941) developed a complex and wide-ranging approach to understanding the relation between learning and personality based on drives, behaviors, and reinforcements. They said that in order to learn, one must "want something, notice something, do something, and get something" (p. 2). Thus, they allowed for internal motivations, both biological and cognitive, and for reinforcements, both personal and social. According to Miller and Dollard, the connection between stimulus and response is called a habit; therefore, what we call personality is primarily made up of habits, and the relations among various habits. Secondary drives are learned—acquired by association with the satisfaction of primary drives. Abstract constructs such as happiness and status are considered to be based on learned drives. Dollard and Miller and their colleagues worked to combine the insights of psychoanalysis and sociology with the laboratory experiments of the behaviorists. This in turn led to social and cognitive learning theories that are common in the study of personality and psychopathology today.

In other words, Dollard and Miller (1950; Miller & Dollard, 1941) tried to understand the development of the variety and complexity of personality in terms of conditioning and learning, broadly construed. Their theory crossed the biological and psychodynamic issues with conditioning processes. As did Skinner, they saw personality as the result of the accumulation of conditioned behaviors, but unlike Skinner, they saw value in "internal" constructs (like drives and motivations) and higher mental processes. Importantly, they recognized that human behavior was embedded in a culture.

The behaviorist and learning approaches to personality, with their emphasis on the environment, drew significant attention to the situational specificity of behavior: We should not expect that a person will behave the same way in every situation. These insights are now incorporated into the most modern conceptions of what it means to be a person.

■ Key Theorists

Ivan Pavlov	B. F. Skinner	John Dollard	Robert R. Sears
John B. Watson	Clark Hull	Neal Miller	

■ Key Concepts and Terms

partial reinforcement	operant conditioning
classical conditioning	shaping
generalization	radical determinism
discrimination	social learning theory
extinction	secondary drives
behaviorism	habit hierarchy
systematic desensitization	act frequency approach
Thorndike's Law of Effect	frustration-aggression hypothesis

Cognitive and Social-Cognitive Aspects of Personality

The ancient Chinese philosopher Meng-tsu (also called Mencius) wrote, "The superior man will not manifest either narrow-mindedness or the want of self-respect" (translated 1898). Most people today would likewise prefer to think of themselves as broadminded and as having a positive self-image. But what does it mean to have a broad mind or a narrow mind? Are there distinctive ways that individuals perceive and think about the world?

Seated Woman, 1962 (oil on canvas), Picasso, Pablo (1881–1973)/Private Collection, © DACS/The Bridgeman Art Library International © 2008 Estate of Pablo Picasso/Artists Rights Society (ARS), New York

■ The ways in which people view the world vary greatly, and from the cognitive perspective, this variability is an important source of individuality. Here, the Spanish artist Pablo Picasso (1881–1973) reveals some of his "personality" by depicting the unconventional way that he sees the face and body of his wife, Jacqueline.

Some people are dreamers and some are realists. Some are optimists and some are pessimists. Some see the glass as half empty, while others looking at the same glass see it as half full. Some people looking at a burning bush see destruction, others see the opportunity of newly cleared land, others see divine inspiration, and still others see air pollution.

How can we understand these variations in response? Why do some people face up to life's hardships while others crumble or retreat? One key approach is to understand the cognitive structures or concepts that people have and the perceptual processes they employ—what they attend to, what they comprehend, and how they conceptualize. In dealing with information both about our external environment and our internal environment (our own thoughts and sensations), we need to focus on something, interpret what we see, and place it within the framework of all the other knowledge and information we have (Norem, 1989). In this sense, we are all philosopher–scientists.

People think about and try to understand the world around them. This fact is so important that all personality theories attempt to take it into account. But cognitive approaches to personality view perception and cognition as the core of what it means to be a person. The way that people interpret their environments, especially their social milieu, is seen as central to their humanness, and the ways in which people differ from one another in how they do this is seen as central to their individuality. This chapter examines the cognitive and social-cognitive aspects of personality. We begin with basic ideas about cognition and perception, and then move on to more complex notions of cognitive styles and social expectancies.

Roots of Cognitive Approaches

Although philosophers have long been concerned with the nature of the human mind, it was not until Charles Darwin's theory of evolution expanded thinking about human nature that cognitive psychology could begin in earnest; that is, after the human mind came to be seen in biological terms, scientists could begin to explore how thinking changed as a child developed, was influenced by different circumstances, and was shaped by culture. (It is interesting to note that the explanation we have just given is a cognitive one; that is, scientists were unable to behave as psychological experimenters until they were able to *think* a certain way.)

Roots in Gestalt Psychology

Gestalt psychology was an intellectual movement that became very influential in Germany in the 1920s, and it was brought to America in the 1930s as many of its foremost thinkers fled fascism. The central tenets of Gestalt theory are: (1) human beings seek meaning in their environments, (2) we organize the sensations we receive from

Gestalt Psychology
An approach to psychology that emphasizes the integrative and active nature of perception and thought suggesting that the whole may be greater than the sum of its parts

228

■ **FIGURE I**

A Typical Gestalt Perceptual Figure

Gestalt theories claim that perception involves a search for meaning and that this meaning can be an emergent property that is not found within any single element. Here, the triangle that most people perceive "emerges" from the juxtaposition of incomplete circles; it exists in the mind of the perceiver, but not in the picture itself.

the world around us into meaningful perceptions, and (3) complex stimuli are not reducible to the sum of their parts.

The German word **gestalt** means pattern or configuration. The view from Gestalt theory is that the configuration of a complex stimulus is its essence (Kohler, 1947). From this perspective, component elements of a stimulus or experience cannot be added up to re-create the original. The essence of the original resides in its overall configuration, which is lost when subparts are analyzed separately. For example, the "triangle" in Figure 1 is not actually drawn on the page, but it is constructed by the viewer. When we are observing a triangle, it is more than three straight lines, and when we are looking at a triangular relationship among lovers, it is more than three separate relationships.

Kurt Lewin's Field Theory

Kurt Lewin came directly out of the Gestalt tradition, but unlike most Gestalt theorists, he focused his efforts in the areas of personality and social psychology rather than perception and problem solving. Lewin published his **field theory** in 1935. His notion of "field" can be seen either as a field in the mathematical sense of vector forces or as a playing field (a field of life). It focuses on the **life space**—all the internal and external forces that act on an individual—and the structural relationships between the person and the environment. For example, a person's family life might be one region of the life space and religion another. For some people, the spaces are cleanly and clearly divided, with boundaries that keep issues and emotions from each region fully independent. Other people have more openness in the boundaries, so the different regions of life exert more influence on one another.

Lewin's definition of personality focused on the momentary condition of the individual—the idea of **contemporaneous causation**. Because Lewin attended so closely to what was going on in a person's mind at any moment, his orientation can be considered a cognitive position, although its simultaneous attention to the situation also makes it an interactionist position. As we have seen, the various approaches to personality can sometimes overlap more than one of the basic aspects.

Cognitive Style Variables

All individuals have distinctive, enduring, **cognitive styles** of dealing with their everyday tasks of perception, problem solving, and decision making (Bertini, Pizzamiglio, & Wapner, 1986; Porter & Suedfeld, 1981; Scott & Bruce, 1995). People differ on

Gestalt
A German word for pattern or configuration

Field Theory
Kurt Lewin's approach to personality, suggesting that behavior is determined by complex interactions among a person's internal psychological structure, the forces of the external environment, and the structural relationships between the person and the environment

Life Space
In Kurt Lewin's theory, all the internal and external forces that act on an individual

Contemporaneous Causation
Kurt Lewin's concept that behavior is caused at the moment of its occurrence by all the influences that are present in the individual at that moment

Cognitive Style
An individual's distinctive, enduring way of dealing with everyday tasks of perception and problem solving

many dimensions, such as whether they are color reactors or form reactors (that is, when objects vary in both color and form, which dimension is seen as most important); generally attentive or inattentive; analyzers (who concentrate on separate parts of things) or synthesizers (who concentrate on patterns); evaluative or nonevaluative; people who see the world in complex, sophisticated terms or those who see it in simpler terms; and so on. These differences explain why one person shows up at a garden party wearing a Hawaiian sport shirt with polyester plaid pants and white buck shoes, while another comes dressed all in black cotton with a touch of white trim.

One such cognitive style variable is **field dependence**. People who are highly field dependent are very influenced in their problem solving by aspects of the context (or field) in which the problem occurs that are salient (highly noticeable) but not directly relevant to the solution. Other people are **field independent** and are not as influenced by contextual factors.

An important demonstration of field dependency comes from a task that requires a subject to adjust a bar so that it is fully vertical. One version of this task is shown in Figure 2. On some trials, the bar is within a rectangular frame that is slightly offset from the vertical. People who tend to align the bar with the surrounding frame (and thus do not make the bar fully vertical) are said to be field dependent on the rod-and-frame task. That is, their perception of the position of the rod is influenced by the context or field in which it occurs. This orientation is shown on the left panel of the figure. People who align the bar vertically despite the tilted frame (see the right panel of the figure) are termed field independent; that is, they escape the influence of the field in their problem solving.

In an alternative version of the task, a person sits in a special chair with controls for adjusting the tilt; the subject is then asked to position the chair so that it is fully upright, while seated in a specially constructed room that has a tilted floor. In this case, the field-independent individual is able to ignore the visual cues about which way is up—cues that are misleading in this situation—and instead is guided by internally generated cues about body positioning. The field-dependent person is so influenced by the irrelevant cues from the tilted room that he or she ends up aligned with the tilted room rather than aligned with true vertical. In these simple situations, there is a benefit to being field independent—it gets you the correct response—but over the broad range of situations people normally confront, neither extreme is universally preferable.

Field Dependence
The extent to which an individual's problem solving is influenced by salient but irrelevant aspects of the context in which the problem occurs

Field Independence
The extent to which an individual's problem solving is *not* influenced by salient but irrelevant aspects of the context in which the problem occurs

---

■ **FIGURE 2**

The Rod-and-Frame Test

The test for field independence measures how well a person ignores the irrelevant context of a problem. Given the task of rotating the central rod until it is vertical, the field-dependent individual (left panel) is led astray by focusing on the context and aligns the rod with the frame. Given the same task, the field-independent individual (right panel) can ignore the misleading frame and find the true vertical.

The field-independent style is more analytical and allows for more complex levels of restructuring in problem solving. These individuals are more influenced in their behavior by internalized aspects of the problem-solving situation. The field-dependent person, on the other hand, has a greater sensitivity to the context of a problem and tends to be more holistic and intuitive in problem solving. Field-dependent people also show greater sensitivity to their social and interpersonal contexts. Field dependence was first explored as a personality variable in the 1940s by Herman Witkin (1949) and Solomon Asch (1952) and has inspired thousands of studies. Some of the differences that have been demonstrated are listed in Table 1.

Why Does It Matter?

Field dependence is an important approach to individual differences in personality because it is reliably and objectively measurable across many different instruments; moreover it tends to be consistent in an individual over time (even from childhood to adulthood). A person's standing along this perception-based field-dependence continuum is associated with many aspects of behavior, especially interpersonal behavior.

When field dependence is examined over groups, there is a modest but consistent gender difference, with females tending more toward field dependence than males. This is certainly consistent with many aspects of gender difference in personality and cognition, such as women's greater social sensitivity and more contextually bound moral reasoning. We note that these differences have various causes, but field dependence relies on perception—a cognitive process—as the basis for the explanation.

When field dependence is examined in a cross-cultural context, interesting differences emerge. Societies can be characterized in terms of the predominant cognitive style of their members (Witkin & Berry, 1975). Witkin claimed that people in hunter-gatherer societies tended to be more field independent than people in predominantly agrarian societies. He attributed the difference to the adaptive value of each style for the differing demands on the individuals in each group; hunter-gatherers need to be more analytical in order to find game and to keep track of their locations so that they can find their way home again. Farmers tend to have more elaborate systems of social interaction, and conformity to group norms and interpersonal sensitivity would be of primary importance in that environment.

■ TABLE 1 Characteristics Associated with Field Independence

Domain	Characteristics
Children's play preferences	Field-independent children are more likely to favor solitary play over social play.
Socialization patterns	Field-independent people are more likely to have been socialized with an emphasis on autonomy over conformity.
Career choices	Field-independent people are more likely to be in technological rather than humanitarian occupations.
Preferred interpersonal distance for conversation	Field-independent people are more likely to sit farther away from a conversational partner.
Level of eye contact	Field-independent people make less frequent and less prolonged eye contact with a conversational partner.

Why Does It Matter?

Did you ever listen to a rigid fundamentalist who is stubbornly unyielding in his or her opinions and beliefs? A know-it-all? Individuals vary in their need for cognitive closure, a preference for a definite answer over ambiguity. People with a high need for cognitive closure prefer to reach a judgment quickly and to avoid changing it once it is set. This can be summarized as a tendency to seize and freeze—to seize on information allowing a quick judgment and then to freeze that choice (Kruglanski, 2004; Kruglanski, Pierro, Mannetti, and De Grada, 2006). People low on this need will avoid making choices, trying to keep their options open and not feeling bound to their choice even after it has been made.

Cognitive Complexity
The extent to which a person comprehends, utilizes, and is comfortable with a greater number of distinctions or separate elements into which an entity or event is analyzed, and the extent to which the person can integrate these elements by drawing connections or relationships among them

Learning Style
The characteristic way in which an individual approaches a task or skill to be learned

Another cognitive style variable relevant to personality is **cognitive complexity**—the extent to which a person comprehends, utilizes, and is comfortable with a greater number of distinctions or separate elements among which an entity or event is analyzed, and the extent to which the person can integrate these elements by drawing connections or relationships among them. People low in cognitive complexity see the world in more absolute and simpler terms, preferring unambiguous problems and straightforward solutions. An important component of cognitive complexity is comfort in dealing with uncertainty. People high in cognitive complexity tend to be relatively more comfortable in dealing with uncertainty, and those lower in cognitive complexity are more oriented toward certainty (Sorrentino & Roney, 2000). Individuals tend to move toward higher levels of cognitive complexity as they get older and accumulate more life experience (Pennebaker & Stone, 2003).

Individual differences in cognitive style also show up in what is termed **learning style**—the characteristic way in which an individual approaches a task or skill to be learned (Sternberg & Zhang, 2001). That is, people vary in their preferred approaches to a learning task, and these individual preferences are stable tendencies. For example, an individual student might approach his or her first course in an unfamiliar field with a holistic style, trying to build his or her own understanding of the topic and trying to see relationships between the new topic and things the student has learned in other courses. Another student might have a more analytic approach, preferring to take in information in the order presented by the course, and building his or her understanding of the topic as a separate module isolated from other knowledge. Another example involves stable individual preferences for verbal versus visual representation: some students are most comfortable and adept at thinking in words, while others prefer to use imagery. Just as in the case of field dependence/field independence, one style is not consistently superior to another, but there may be specific tasks on which one approach will be more appropriate than another. Learning style can be seen as an aspect of personality in itself, and it has also been shown to correlate with more traditional measures of personality and temperament (e.g., Busato, Prins, Elshout, & Hamaker, 1999; Harrison & Lester, 2000).

Cognitive and Perceptual Mechanisms

We can gain deeper insights into the cognitive aspects of personality by examining mechanisms of expecting, attending, and information processing.

Jean Piaget was born in Switzerland in 1896. Like Freud, Piaget was first interested in biology (he studied mollusks) and then studied for a while with Carl Jung.

However, he soon turned to a focus on intellectual development (including the development of his own children) and went on to have a major impact on cognitive conceptions of the development of personality. Piaget proposed a cognitive-structure explanation of how children develop concepts about the world around them.

Schema Theory

According to Piaget (1952), children progress through a series of cognitive stages as they mature. At each stage, the content of their knowledge and the nature of their reasoning become more sophisticated. New cognitive structures, called **schemas**, build on the structures (schemas) acquired earlier. For example, we now know that human newborns have an innate preference to listen to human speech (more than to other sounds) and to focus their eyes on human faces (more than on other visual stimuli). As babies encounter human speech and human faces, they build on this groundwork to develop complex cognitive structures—patterns of understanding the world. A nine-year-old child viewing a sexual scene on a TV soap opera actually "sees" or understands something different than does either a two-year-old or a mature adult.

The schema that is activated in a given situation is a major determinant of a person's expectations, inferences, and actions in that situation (Abelson, 1981). Such schemas exist at many levels, and schemas at different levels can simultaneously be active in influencing our behavior. Suppose, for example, a person (Pat) is going out on a first date with a new acquaintance (Chris), planning to have dinner and then see a movie. As Pat sits down at their table in the restaurant, many schemas are simultaneously relevant in guiding Pat's behavior. One of these might be a schema for the event of eating in a restaurant. (Sometimes a schema for a familiar event is called a **script** because, like the script of a play, it specifies the roles and actions of all the participants along with the props and the setting.) Pat knows, among other things, what the server is likely to say and how to respond appropriately. We usually do not think about these schemas or scripts unless they break down, as might be the case when we travel to a different country.

Another relevant schema for Pat might be the script for a first date, which influences Pat's expectations of what to do, as well as what to expect Chris will do. Pat will be using the specific conversational and linguistic schemas that govern the ways of talking to people who are in particular social categories (such as friend), or who have particular roles to play in an interaction (such as date). If Chris responds with a "business associate script," that may very well be the end of that relationship. In other words, personality can be viewed as a series of cognitive scripts.

Schema
A cognitive structure that organizes knowledge and expectations about one's environment

Script
A schema that guides behavior in social situations

Categorization
The perceptual process by which highly complex ensembles of information are filtered into a small number of identifiable and familiar objects and entities

Why Does It Matter?

Piaget's foundation, coupled with subsequent research on schemas and scripts, is so important because it suggests that our ways of understanding unfold in a fairly logical order and that new cognitions build on older cognitions (Rumelhart, 1980). According to this view, a good teacher or role model cannot directly teach, but rather must guide learners to make their own individual discoveries. This is a distinctive view of human nature.

Categorization

We all tend to organize our experiences by assigning the events, objects, and people we encounter into categories. **Categorization** is omnipresent and occurs automatically (i.e., without our effort or conscious intention). What does this mean?

© Roger Wright/Getty Images

■ In many situations, people normally begin their consideration of an object by assigning it to a category. For most of us, male or female is the first categorization we make when we encounter a new person. Many people find that their normal modes of interaction are very disrupted when one of the most salient characteristics, gender, is difficult to determine.

Stereotype
A schema or belief about the personality traits that tend to be characteristic of members of some group

The actual physical stimuli that are encountered by our sensory organs are extraordinarily complex. The visual scene in front of you right now, for example, contains millions of bits of information, even if it were to be described only in terms of the visual characteristics of each tiny sector of the visual field (such as a computer could understand). This is the information that reaches your eye, but it is not what you "see." What you experience instead are the identifiable, familiar objects that are present—things like this page, your own hand, a pen, a door. It is impossible for people *not* to categorize. We experience the world through our interpretations (Bruner, Goodnow, & Austin, 1956).

Automatic categorization of very complex scenes occurs even when the simple characteristics of the stimulus are too brief or too weak to reach our conscious awareness. One striking example involves our ability to detect information about the emotional states of other people from briefly displayed facial expressions. Without necessarily being aware that we detected a particular facial muscle twitch or a flared nostril or dilated pupil, sometimes even without our having conscious or reportable knowledge of what such a signal might mean, we recognize the emotions associated with those brief stimuli (Carney, Colvin, & Hall, 2007; DePaulo & Friedman, 1998). We perceive anger or interest or disgust without consciously analyzing the signals that conveyed that information.

Consider now what happens when you enter a classroom you have never been in before. Normally, you will perceive objects such as chairs, windows, an instructor's desk, and other classroom paraphernalia. Of course, you have never seen these particular chairs or windows before, but by an automatic and effortless process you categorize them. But there are individual differences: The set of categories a person uses depends heavily on both the expectations that are aroused by the current environment and on his or her relevant prior experience.

This same powerful, automatic process of categorization, though, can have negative effects, as it is just a tiny step from a useful category to a harmful **stereotype**. The same informational efficiency that provides us with useful expectations and interpretations can lead us to premature judgments (prejudice). The existence (and persistence) of negative social stereotypes about social, religious, ethnic, or racial groups can be explained by the confluence of several cognitive factors that play a pervasive role in our processing of information. The primary factor is the one discussed earlier—the power of categories to guide people's interpretations and expectations (Taylor & Crocker, 1981). Once a category exists for us, when we encounter something or someone who matches a few features of that category, we "fill in the blanks" with the rest of

Why Does It Matter?

From a cognitive perspective, the stereotypes associated with categories of people are no different in terms of their representation and use than, say, categories of flowers. Some people are quick to categorize other objects and other people. This is part of the reason why persons of different ethnic groups (such as White Americans versus Black Americans) often have different views of judicial proceedings in which ethnic group or color is an issue; their differing experiences have led them to different schemas and categories in processing the same information. They "see" different things.

the information that applies to the category (Srull & Wyer, 1989). Further, people are much more likely to notice information that supports their expectations than information that is contradictory to their expectations. Thus, as we look at a new person who is a member of some group or category, under most conditions we are more likely to notice those characteristics that fit the stereotype than characteristics that do not. When we believe it, we see it (Hamilton & Sherman, 1994).

People's categorization processes are not invariant over different environments; the categories and processes vary with changes in the situation (King, 2000). For example, the categorization and interpretation processes involved when a person interacts with another—called social cognition (cognition occurring in the domain of social interaction)—can vary as a function of home versus school, work versus leisure, friendship versus romance. The fact that social-cognitive processes change with changes in the situation is referred to as **situated social cognition** (Smith & Semin, 2004, 2007). How we understand the world depends in part on our goals and feelings at the time.

Situated Social Cognition
Social-cognitive processes that change with changes in the situation

Control of Attention

How do we "see" (and hear and smell and feel and taste) persons and objects and events in ways that are meaningful to us? Often it is through the control of attention. Because humans do such a remarkable job of extracting meaning from what William James (1890) called a "blooming, buzzing confusion," most of us are not aware of the sophisticated mechanisms by which we continuously control our attention and interpret our surroundings. Here, however, is an exercise you can do right now to demonstrate this capacity to yourself.

Continue to read this paragraph, and while you are reading, also listen to the background noises in your environment, feel the contact of your clothing with your skin, feel this text touching your hand, smell the scent in the air around you, taste the taste inside your mouth, and attend to the visual scene beyond the edges of this page in your peripheral vision.

Of course, paying attention to all those things at once is difficult, and also interferes with your ability to concentrate on what you are reading. What is interesting about this exercise, though, is that all the sensory information that allowed you to hear, smell, feel, taste, and see the previously unattended aspects of your internal and external environment is always present, always impinging on your sensory systems. Fortunately for our sanity, we aren't constantly noticing and attending to it all. On the other hand, we are constantly doing *some* monitoring of our environments in all modalities; for example, if there were even a faint smell of smoke, you would probably notice it (Triesman, 1964). People pick up on a few key features of their current environments and filter these in light of their current goals. But people differ in their attention to things and this is a source of stable individual differences—a cognitive approach to personality.

Individual Differences in Attention: ADHD

One striking way in which individuals differ is in the extent to which their attention is under their intentional control. People (especially school-aged children) who have atypical attentional processes are often diagnosed as having **attention-deficit/**

Attention-Deficit/Hyperactivity Disorder (ADHD)
A disorder in which a person has atypical attentional processes

hyperactivity disorder (ADHD). According to the *Diagnostic and Statistical Manual of Mental Disorders IV* (American Psychiatric Association, 1994), the term "ADHD" is used for people with or without the hyperactivity component; that distinction is made by a subcategorization into three distinct subtypes of the disorder: the Hyperactive/Impulsive type (no inattention), the Inattentive type (no hyperactivity/impulsivity), and the Combined type (both inattention and hyperactivity/impulsivity).

Many researchers argue that the relatively large population of ADHD-Inattentive individuals go undiagnosed and untreated precisely because of their lack of hyperactive and impulsive behaviors (Fisher, 1998). Attentional behavior in these individuals differs in several ways from that of most other people (Barkley & Edwards, 1998). Their symptoms appear to be associated with an inability to appropriately shift their attention from one spatial location to another (Carter, Krener, Chaderjian, Northcutt, & Wolfe, 1995; Fisher, 1998; Swanson et al., 1998). Paradoxically, attention is not uniformly worse in all respects in people with attention-deficit disorder (ADD) or ADHD; instead, it is different in ways that make it simultaneously better and worse. People with ADD are often capable of very intense concentration—"hyperattention"—on a task that engages their interest, with deeper or longer-lasting concentration than people who are otherwise comparable (in age, education, intelligence), and they sometimes have difficulty disengaging from some stimulus or activity. For example, a school-aged boy with ADHD may concentrate for long periods of time on a computer game, continuing to be engaged in the task long after his age-mates have grown bored and moved on to something else. During this period, the child may appear to be utterly oblivious to his surroundings and completely focused on his game—an ideal demonstration of paying attention to a task. Conversely, though, people with ADD often fail to shift their attention appropriately to important aspects of their environments. They might fail to notice that the other students have put away their books, not be aware that their companions have left the video arcade, not pick up on social cues from others that their behavior is inappropriate (e.g., Yuill & Lyon, 2007).

This variability across people in how their attentional processes operate is directly relevant to personality because of its significant influence on how a person interacts with social environments. It is relevant also because it influences how that person is perceived by others—as alert versus inattentive, as "with it" versus "out of it," as responsive versus standoffish. Although the specific neurological mechanisms involved in these deficits are still in question, it has become increasingly clear that the systems involved in responding to information in the periphery have developed atypically with these children (Collings, 2001). Regardless of the specific cause, these individuals' deficits frequently interfere with their ability to acquire the skills necessary to perform well academically and socially, and have lifelong consequences for children with the ADHD-Inattentive type.

The hyperactivity and impulsivity symptoms associated with the ADHD-Hyperactive/Impulsive and ADHD-Combined types may be associated with Gray's

(1987) Behavior Inhibition System (BIS), the neurological system involved in inhibiting learned responses to new stimuli (Barkley, 1997; Quay, 1997). Barkley and Quay maintain that the inability to stop (or at least regulate) immediate reactions to events in the environment results in the disruptive behaviors (i.e., hyperactivity, impulsivity, emotional outbursts) and the poor academic outcomes frequently observed among these children. Many of these children, as is the case with their ADHD-Inattentive counterparts, fail to outgrow their problematic behaviors and continue to have psychosocial problems throughout their lives (Biederman et al., 2007; Fisher, 1998). Although ADHD seems to impact males more frequently than females, both sexes are at risk for this highly heritable disorder (National Institutes of Health [NIH], 1998). Fortunately, advances in neuroscience technologies offer great hope for more effective early diagnoses and interventions for this complex disorder.

ADHD is normally diagnosed based on observed behavior, as rated by parents and teachers, but there is accumulating evidence that distinctive patterns of brain activity in specific regions also characterize the disorder. A variety of methods have shown that brain activity in children with ADHD is measurably different from that of children without the disorder. For example, the pattern of brain activity in the frontal lobe (specifically in the striatal region) differs between boys diagnosed with ADHD and same-aged boys who do not have the disorder (Mazaheri et al., 2010; Vaidya et al., 1998).

Children with ADHD are commonly treated with Ritalin or Concerta, brand names for the drug methylphenidate, which is a form of amphetamine. The intent of the medication is to improve academic performance, control classroom behavior, and improve social interactions. The treatment is controversial, however, at least in part because the nature of the disorder itself is not fully understood (Barkley & Edwards, 1998; Biederman, Spencer, Wilens, Prince, & Faraone, 2006). Some critics argue that we are merely drugging children to deal with the deficiencies of the school environment. They ask, "Whose attention disorder is being treated?" Is it the child's problem, or is it the case that the educators are not attending to the right priorities and creating appropriate learning environments in their schools?

What is clear, though, is that in those with ADHD, the drug's effect is quite different from its usual effect. In non-ADHD individuals, amphetamine (called "speed" as an illegal street drug) acts as a stimulant, increasing arousal. Paradoxically, in those with ADHD, Ritalin decreases hyperactivity, inattention, and impulsivity—it slows and inhibits their activity rather than stimulating it. This paradoxical effect is very robust (Volkow et al., 2001; Volkow, Wang, Fowler, & Ding, 2005). We are starting to see a consistent picture of both the disorder and its treatment. If current theorizing is correct in claiming that the disorder results from deficits in the ability to inhibit behavior (Barkley, 1997), then it may follow that Ritalin-type drugs produce their helpful effects in ADHD by stimulating the inhibitory system. The brain characteristics underlying the personality trait of impulsiveness typical of some forms of ADHD may soon be better understood.

Classic to Current

A Social-Cognitive Interpretation of Transference

The concept of transference is most closely associated with Freudian psychoanalysis, where the patient transfers feelings, memories, and fears from past relationships onto the therapist. But the term refers more generally to the phenomenon in which aspects of past significant interpersonal relationships influence current interactions in new relationships. In the psychoanalytic case, the analyst actually comes to represent the mother or father (or other significant figure) to the patient, and the therapist becomes the target of the patient's unresolved, unconscious, psychosexual conflicts from that earlier relationship.

Andersen and Berk (1998) developed a social-cognitive model of the transference phenomenon. This model applies to everyday social relations, and rejects the Freudian focus on psychosexual conflicts and defense mechanisms. The simplest description of this social-cognitive view of transference is that it takes fundamental processes of cognition and social cognition (such as categorization, similarity, accessibility, and schemas) and applies them to the question of how old relationships affect new social interactions. Rather than being satisfied with conjecturing that transference is an everyday phenomenon that occurs outside the psychoanalytic context, Andersen and her colleagues did clever laboratory experiments to test the hypothesis.

Because transference is a phenomenon based on significant personal relationships, the experiments had each participant come to an experimental session where the participant provided information in a standardized format about a significant other. In a session that appeared to be unrelated to the first session, and occurred weeks later, participants were presented with information about a new target person who either had been constructed to resemble the participant's significant other, or was unrelated to that person's description. After learning about the "new" person, the participants completed a recognition memory task on information about the new person and then evaluated the new person. A variety of different control conditions were used to ensure that any effects found would be due to the similarity of the new target to the significant other.

The studies showed the presence of transference in several ways. Participants falsely recognized information about the new target person that was never presented but was true of the significant other that the target resembled. Participants' evaluations of the new target person were influenced by their feelings toward the significant other that the target resembled, for both positively and negatively evaluated significant others. The

experiments also provided evidence that interpersonal roles were activated when the new target resembled a significant other (Baum & Andersen, 1999). The data showed that the motivation to approach the new target was influenced by the emotional tone of the relationship with the significant other, and that expectancies about how the new target would respond to the participant were also congruent with the relationship with the real significant other. And, when participants were asked to describe themselves after learning about the new person, these self-representations in the context of the fictional new person tended to be more similar to the self-representations in the context of the significant other when the new target resembled the significant other, showing that the self-concept was also influenced by the transference. Using a slightly different experimental approach, Brumbaugh and Fraley (2007) showed that attachment patterns toward a significant other (romantic partner versus parent) influenced feelings toward a new target person who resembled either the partner or the parent.

These experiments show that a transference-like phenomenon occurs in everyday social relations. With just the principles of cognition and social cognition, this phenomenon of transference can be created without any of the psychoanalytic baggage that it normally carries. This research shows that prior significant relationships have broad and diverse effects on new relationships, and that these effects are strong enough to show up even when the new relationship is not a deep or meaningful one (these participants were developing relationships with fictional people presented in the form of a verbal description). Without resorting to psychoanalytic constructs of the unconscious, defense mechanisms, or unresolved sexual conflicts, cognitive and social-cognitive processes alone are adequate to explain the phenomenon of transference.

FURTHER READING

Andersen, S. M., & Berk, M. S. (1998). The social-cognitive model of transference: Experiencing past relationships in the present. *Current Directions in Psychological Science, 7,* 109–115.

Baum, A., & Andersen, S. M. (1999). Interpersonal roles in transference: Transient mood effects under the condition of significant-other resemblance. *Social Cognition, 17*(2), 161–185.

Brumbaugh, C. C., & Fraley, R. C. (2007). Transference of attachment patterns: How important relationships influence feelings toward novel people. *Personal Relationships, 14,* 513–530.

Cognitive Influences on Interpersonal Relationships

How a person interacts with others is, of course, also influenced by how the individual perceives himself or herself, how the individual perceives the partner, how the individual categorizes the relationship, and the goals the individual has for the relationship. These essentially cognitive factors influence how the relationship will proceed. One influential factor is termed **rejection sensitivity.** This personality variable captures the extent to which an individual is overly sensitive to cues that he or she is being rejected by another. When a child experiences repeated and severe rejection by a parent (or other significant person), the child develops anxious expectations of rejection that are carried into other relationships (Pietrzak, Downey, & Ayduk, 2005). This hypersensitivity to cues of rejection in interpreting the behaviors of other people causes the person to behave in ways that lead, in an unfortunate spiral, to a greater likelihood of actual rejection (McDonald, Bowker, Rubin, Laursen, & Duchene, 2010; Romero-Canyas & Downey, 2005).

Rejection Sensitivity
A personality variable capturing the extent to which an individual is overly sensitive to cues that he or she is being rejected by another

Humans as Scientists: George Kelly's Personal Construct Theory

Personal Construct Theory
The approach to personality proposed by George Kelly that emphasizes the idea that people actively endeavor to construe or understand the world and construct their own theories about human behavior

Each of us tries to figure out how our worlds work. Can we therefore think of ourselves as good or poor scientists, actively trying to make sense of the world around us? This is the basic thrust of George Kelly's influential perspective on personality, that each of us tries to understand the world and that we do so in different ways. Because its focus is on people's active endeavors to construe or understand the world and construct their own versions of reality, this approach is (sensibly) called constructivism, or **personal construct theory**.

Kelly's (1955) fundamental postulate is that "a person's processes are psychologically channeled by the ways in which he anticipates events". According to this approach, people change as they reorganize their construct systems. Kelly's theorizing was especially focused on the domain of interpersonal relationships. What guides a person's behavior is his or her interpretation of the surrounding environment and the resultant expectations about it.

Individuals as Amateur Personality Theorists

Kelly explicitly used the model of the scientific method to describe general human behavior. Kelly (1995) claimed that "every man is, in his own particular way, a scientist" (p. 5). Like the scientist who specifies a hypothesis and then conducts an experiment to see if the hypothesis accurately predicts the

■ According to George Kelly, each of us is a personality theorist, developing and using our own constructs to understand people.

outcome, individuals make up their own "theories" and then use their personal experiences as the "data" that support (or invalidate) the theory.

One key feature of Kelly's theory clearly differentiates it from many other approaches to personality. Trait approaches to personality posit a specific set of traits as being central to explaining human personality, but Kelly (1963) had a radically different idea: We each have our own system of constructs that we use to understand and predict behavior (both our own and others'). Kelly argues that each person is more or less a personality theorist, with a personal system of explanations of human behavior!

The Role Construct Repertory Test

Role Construct Repertory Test
An assessment instrument designed by George Kelly to evoke a person's own personal construct system by making comparisons among triads of important people in the life of the person being assessed

Kelly devised a unique assessment instrument that was designed to evoke one's personal construct system. Rather than asking people to rate or rank a set of traits or dimensions of personality that the test creator thinks are important, the goal of this instrument is to allow the person's own understanding of personality to emerge through the process of making comparisons. This well-known instrument is called the **Role Construct Repertory Test**, or Rep test. (You can take a similar test yourself in the Self-Understanding box.) The examiner first elicits the names of 20 to 30 people who fit specific roles in the person's life (such as father, previous boyfriend/girlfriend, disliked teacher). Then, the examiner puts together triads (groups of three) of these figures and the examinee is asked to identify how two of them differ from the third. The dimension that differentiates among the group is the construct generated by the subject. For example, suppose a person is given the triad of her sister Annette, her boss Geraldine, and a disliked teacher Mr. Sorensen, and is asked to say how one of them differs from the other two. If the subject says that her sister and her boss are both nervous but her disliked teacher is calm, a construct of *nervous–calm* is generated. This procedure is repeated a few dozen times with different triads, resulting in a set of constructs that is taken to be a reflection of the hierarchy of constructs (dimensions) that the examinee believes are important in understanding and predicting behavior. Each person's constructs are a unique expression of that individual's own view of which characteristics of people are important.

Kelly's major work was published in 1955, a decade before cognitive psychology was established as a field of study within psychology. Nonetheless, Kelly's work helped pave the way for more modern social cognition approaches such as attribution approaches and social learning theories (see the following sections). These theories, like Kelly's, try to explain the ways in which the individual perceives the social world and anticipates events, and view these processes as central to understanding human behavior. But it is important to remember that each person's explanations function in an interpersonal, cultural, and historical context; that is, the explanations can change depending on the particular persons, histories, and situations involved (Hermans, Kempen, & van Loon, 1992).

Social Intelligence

People differ widely in their cognitive abilities, but does such information help us better understand their personalities? Many of the concepts we have been discussing coalesce in the idea of social intelligence (Cantor & Kihlstrom, 1987). The idea is

Cognitive Personality Assessment Using a Role Construct Approach

Based on the Work of George Kelly

From taking this brief test, you can get a sense of how a role construct approach works. If you are interested in exploring your own constructs further, you can add more roles to the list in section I, and more triads to the list in section II.

I. For each of the roles described, write the name of a specific person who has that role in your life.

_____ 1. Your mother or father

_____ 2. Your best friend

_____ 3. Your sister nearest in age (or female most like a sister)

_____ 4. Your brother nearest in age (or male most like a brother)

_____ 5. Your spouse (or boyfriend/girlfriend)

_____ 6. A teacher you liked

_____ 7. A teacher you disliked

_____ 8. Your boss

_____ 9. A successful person you know

_____ 10. An unsuccessful person you know

II. Consider each group of three listed in the first column below (the numbers refer to the people named in section I). Think of a way in which two of them are similar to each other and different from the other one. Write the numbers of the two who are similar and a term that describes how they are similar (their shared characteristic). Then, write the number of the one who is different and a term that describes how he or she differs.

Group	Which two are similar?	Shared characteristic	Who is different?	Different characteristic
1, 4, 5	_____	_____	_____	_____
2, 3, 9	_____	_____	_____	_____
4, 6, 10	_____	_____	_____	_____
2, 4, 7	_____	_____	_____	_____
6, 8, 9	_____	_____	_____	_____
1, 7, 8	_____	_____	_____	_____
4, 7, 9	_____	_____	_____	_____
5, 8, 10	_____	_____	_____	_____
1, 3, 8	_____	_____	_____	_____
3, 5, 6	_____	_____	_____	_____

III. Look over the list of contrasting pairs of terms you generated. Your list is a reflection of your personal constructs—how you think about people.

fundamentally quite simple: Just as individuals vary in their knowledge and skills relevant to many aspects of their lives (for example, in mathematical ability, in musical aptitude, in reasoning skills, and so on), they also differ in their level of mastery of the particular cluster of knowledge and skills that are relevant to interpersonal situations—their **social intelligence**.

This approach claims that people vary in their abilities to understand and influence other people. Success in interpersonal interaction is easy for some people and difficult for others. Some are diplomats while others are boors. The construct of social intelligence tries to capture the ways in which individuals differ from one another in their interpersonal skills.

This distinction can even be seen in nonhumans. Foxes from a population that had been selectively bred for friendliness and lack of aggression toward humans were able to use cues from a person's pointing and gaze to find hidden food, while the foxes not selectively bred for these traits made no use of these social cues. The genetically distinct friendly, nonaggressive foxes showed skills in interaction with humans that can be seen as a component of social intelligence, even though humans have evolved some additional specialized skills of social cognition (Hare et al., 2005; Herrmann, Hernández-Lloreda, Call, Hare, & Tomasello, 2010).

Individuals have specific emotional abilities to deal with other people, an ability termed **emotional intelligence**. For example, some people are empathic while others are clueless, and some people are charming while others are rude (Rosenthal, 1979). Psychologist Daniel Goleman (1995) claims that emotional intelligence has five components: being self-aware, controlling anger and anxieties, being persistent and optimistic in the face of setbacks, being empathic, and interacting smoothly with others. Another prominent approach conceptualizes emotional intelligence as comprising the four related abilities of perceiving, using, understanding, and managing emotions (Salovey & Grewal, 2005). Various self-report measures of emotional intelligence have been developed, but there is evidence that such self-report measures of emotional abilities are of limited applicability, because they do not reflect real-time social competence as measured by a performance test (Brackett, Rivers, Shiffman, Lerner, & Salovey, 2006; Goldenberg, Matheson, & Mantler, 2006). It is better to see what social skills individuals actually can perform (Hall, Andrzejewski, & Yopchick, 2009).

Howard Gardner, a prominent educational psychologist interested in educational implications of individual differences, devised a theory of **multiple intelligences** that has become influential in the field of education (Gardner, 1983). This theory claims that all human beings have at least seven different intelligences—seven different ways of knowing about the world—and that people differ from one another in their relative strengths in each domain. Gardner's seven intelligences include knowing the world through language, logical-mathematical analysis, spatial representation, musical thinking, bodily-kinesthetic intelligence (control of one's body as a gymnast might have), understanding of the self, and understanding of others. Under Gardner's approach, each person is characterized by a profile of intelligences rather than by a single, global measure of intelligence (such as an IQ). Gardner rejects traditional intelligence measures as too narrow. He claims that they usually reflect people's differential abilities in one or

Social Intelligence
The idea that individuals differ in their level of mastery of the particular cluster of knowledge and skills that are relevant to interpersonal situations

Emotional Intelligence
The set of emotional abilities specific to dealing with other people

Multiple Intelligences
Howard Gardner's theory that claims that all human beings have at least seven different ways of knowing about the world and that people differ from one another in the relative strengths of each of these seven ways

two of the ways of knowing, but pick up almost no information about their abilities in the other spheres. The multiple-intelligences approach is focused on the variety of domains in which people can be intelligent—the social intelligence approach is focused on the social-interpersonal domain. But both social/emotional intelligence researchers and multiple intelligence researchers argue that individual differences in people's abilities in the social-interpersonal domain should be viewed as a sort of intelligence—that these abilities form internally coherent clusters and are measurable within an individual-differences framework in the same way as any other aspect of cognitive skill. In other words, if you have the cognitive skills and attentional control to be empathic, sensitive, influential, popular, inspiring, compassionate, exciting, humorous, charming, and so on, then you are socially intelligent.

One important component of social-emotional intelligence is **emotion knowledge**—the ability to recognize and interpret emotions in the self and others. In the view of many theorists, emotion knowledge is necessary for communicating emotion and for building and maintaining interpersonal relationships (Bandura, 1986; Hobson, 1993; Izard, 1971). Emotion knowledge in children is relevant not only to the development of their social skills but to their academic success as well (Izard et al., 2001; Trentacosta & Izard, 2007). Note that the conception of social intelligence involves cognitive skills which presumably can be learned and cultivated to some degree. In this scheme, aspects of personality can be changed and improved through skill training.

Emotion Knowledge
The ability to recognize and interpret emotions in the self and others

Explanatory Style as a Personality Variable

As the cognitive approach to personality has continued to evolve, increased attention has been devoted to the cognitive styles (or characteristic perceptual modes) that people use to try to understand their environments (Sternberg & Grigorenko, 1997). **Explanatory style** refers to a set of cognitive personality variables that capture a person's habitual means of interpreting events in her or his life. There are a variety of approaches to this central idea of explanatory style.

Explanatory Style
A set of cognitive personality variables that captures a person's habitual means of interpreting events in his or her life

Optimism and Pessimism

One version of this approach sets up optimism and pessimism as the extreme poles of explanatory style. People with an optimistic explanatory style tend to interpret events in their lives with an optimistic perspective, even perceiving neutral events as positive and seeing potential or eventual positive outcomes in negative events. Those with a pessimistic style, on the other hand, tend to focus on the negative potential in a situation. For example, if a student with an optimistic explanatory style receives an uncharacteristically poor grade on an exam, she might consider that to be useful feedback, informing her that she needs to change her study or note-taking techniques. Once she makes those changes, she confidently expects a better outcome on the next exam.

If the same student's explanatory style were closer to the pessimistic pole, she might view the poor grade as a sign of her own lack of ability; this is a stable attribution to an internal cause. Or she might blame factors that are out of her control, such as an overly tough professor; this is a stable attribution to an external cause. In either case, her expectations for her future performance would be lower, and she may even become depressed (Peterson & Barrett, 1987; Peterson & Seligman, 1987).

In general, having an optimistic explanatory style is associated with better outcomes, especially in times of challenge (Carver, Scheier, & Segerstrom, 2010). In one study, students with an optimistic explanatory style (as measured by a standardized

Famous Personalities

Presidents and Achievement

Do you feel confident and able to meet your goals? Albert Bandura describes self-efficacy as an individual's belief that he or she can successfully perform a particular action. Self-efficacy beliefs are domain-specific—you have different beliefs in your self-efficacy for different tasks. You might have low self-efficacy in mathematics, but high self-efficacy in your writing ability. According to Bandura (1982), self-efficacy beliefs have important effects on—in fact are the most important motivators of—an individual's achievement. People are much more likely to engage in activities that they believe they can successfully accomplish than to undertake tasks that they do not believe they are competent to handle.

Self-efficacy decisions are based on four kinds of experiences. First, previous successful experiences with the task demonstrate the ability to perform the task competently. Second, seeing others successfully perform certain tasks increases the perception that they are "do-able." Third, the verbal persuasion of others encourages us by telling us that we are capable of succeeding at a particular activity. Finally, our levels of physiological arousal give us information as to whether or not we can cope in a particular situation. These factors together culminate in the individual's perception of ability to accomplish a task or goal—his or her self-efficacy for that situation.

Relatedly, attribution theorists like Bernard Weiner emphasize that one's achievement derives from one's manner of interpreting success and failure. There are three properties of perceived causality for events in one's life: (1) situations are perceived as being either internally caused (caused by some factor of the individual) or externally caused (due to situational issues); (2) events are seen as the result of either controllable factors or uncontrollable factors; and (3) the causes of occurrences are perceived as being either stable (lasting across time) or changing (Weiner, 1985). Weiner hypothesizes that one's usual style of explaining causes of success and failure is responsible for the expectancy of success and therefore for one's achievement-oriented behaviors. According to this theory, high achievers tend to perceive the causes of their success as internal, controllable, and stable. These ideas seem to hold true across cultures (Betancourt & Weiner, 1982; Schuster, Försterling, & Weiner, 1989).

A clear example of the importance of the response to failure in determining ultimate achievement can be seen by looking at the history of Bill Clinton's 1992 presidential campaign. When he lost the New Hampshire Democratic primary race, many political pundits considered his chance at the nomination to be doomed. But Clinton styled himself the Comeback Kid and attributed his poor showing to the scandals that had recently plagued his campaign—an external attribution. Of course, there are many factors that determined his ultimate success in that campaign, but Clinton's success expectancy and his attribution of

instrument) were more likely than their more pessimistic peers to believe that effort, improved study habits, and greater self-discipline could make a difference in their grades. And the optimists were more likely to do well (Peterson & Barrett, 1987). In another study, the work of low-achieving students was measurably improved by an intervention that was focused on overcoming their pessimistic interpretation of their performance (Noel, Forsyth, & Kelley, 1987). Students entering college who scored higher on a scale measuring their hopefulness had higher subsequent grades and were more likely to graduate than their less hopeful peers, even after controlling for the students' scores on entrance exams (Snyder et al., 2002).

Note, however, that excessive optimism may be detrimental to success in situations in which optimism leads a person to overlook or downplay potential problems. For example, it is not helpful for an optimistic dieter to think that ice cream does

failure to an external cause put him in a strong position with respect to how he ran his campaign. He had previously engineered the same remarkable reversal when he lost and later regained the governorship of Arkansas. Furthermore, he had spent almost all of his adult life either preparing for elected office, running for office, or holding elected office (previous success and lots of encouragement). His level of achievement motivation (as evaluated by David Winter through an ingenious analysis of every U.S. president's first inaugural address) was extraordinary, even when compared to earlier presidents—Clinton was more than two standard deviations above the mean for all presidents (Winter, 1987, 1994), and far above his successor George W. Bush (Winter, 2001).

Psychologist Carol Dweck and her associates take a different approach to understanding the relation between cognitions about task performance and success. She has found that children tend to show one of two behavior patterns in achievement situations: a maladaptive "helpless" response or an adaptive "mastery-oriented" response. Helpless behavior involves avoidance and poor performance in the face of challenges or obstacles. Children who show mastery behaviors, on the other hand, do well when activities are demanding and continue to strive and succeed when they encounter difficulties (Diener & Dweck, 1980; Elliott & Dweck, 1988). These individual differences in trying and persisting at difficult tasks were found even among children of similar abilities.

Children who are helpless tend to attribute their failure to internal characteristics and inadequacies such as low intelligence, poor memory, or poor problem-solving capacity. These attributions accompany low expectations for future successes. Such children also show accompanying emotional reactions such as anxiety or boredom. Helpless children's performance tends to sink into a slow decline, and interestingly, helpless children often interpret even their successful performance as deficient in some manner. Children who are mastery-oriented, however, respond very differently to difficulty. These children tend not to view the difficulty as a failure but instead, like Bill Clinton, they look at obstacles as interesting challenges to be faced and surmounted. They increase their effort and concentration, and they exhibit optimistic, positive emotions.

Some individuals have goals that permit them to see achievement situations as opportunities to learn, expand their abilities, and become more competent. Whereas Weiner thinks individual differences in attributions for success and failure cause high- and low-achievement behavior, Dweck counters that the patterns of goal-making that an individual uses are ultimately responsible for the attributions made about performance. Dweck (2006) suggests that if we don't worry about performance and evaluation but instead focus on the paths to our goals, we are much more likely to achieve them (and perhaps even become president).

not really have a lot of calories and fat. Excessive optimism may even be considered maladaptive. A person who is always upbeat and positive, even in times of sadness or crisis, is considered "abnormal." In situations where the chances for failure are high, lowered expectations may be adaptive. Julie Norem (Norem, 2008; Norem & Smith, 2006) describes the phenomenon of **defensive pessimism**, in which a person reduces anxiety and actually improves performance in a risky situation by anticipating a poorer outcome.

Learned Helplessness and Learned Optimism

What happens when an individual learns that he or she cannot control any of the things that are important? Martin Seligman (1975) uses the term **learned helplessness** to describe a situation in which repeated exposure to unavoidable punishment leads an organism to accept later punishment even when it is avoidable. In a classic series of experiments, unpleasant electric shocks were administered repeatedly to dogs who could not escape. When the restraints were removed, the dogs could easily have avoided continued shocks, but they tended to stay in place and suffer further punishment. In the initial series of shocks, they had learned that they were helpless to control the punishment, and so they gave up trying to escape or avoid it (Overmier & Seligman, 1967).

Analogous experiments with people show the same result: Once an individual learns that he or she is not in control, the motivation to seek control may be shut down, even when control later becomes possible. During the initial phase, the control truly is external. But with sufficient experience under external control, the participant no longer attempts internal, self-directed control. Depression, stress, and apathy are commonly the consequences. This line of thought is currently used in studying and treating depression, in conjunction with the idea that depressive people have a depressive schema in which they generate more and more depressive thoughts (Abramson, Metalsky, & Alloy, 1989; Beck & Freeman, 1989). (See the Famous Personalities box.)

Fortunately, there is evidence that teaching children to challenge their pessimistic thoughts can "immunize" them against depression (Seligman, Reivich, Jaycox, & Gillham, 1995); that is, a **cognitive intervention**—teaching people to change their thought processes—can affect subsequent behavior. Note again that this aspect of personality is seen here as a kind of cognitive skill. Seligman and his colleagues have gone beyond just showing that people with a pessimistic explanatory style can minimize the harm from their pessimism; they have developed methods that can help people escape their pessimistic style and become optimistic. This phenomenon of **learned optimism** is achieved by training people to think differently about themselves and the situations that arise in their lives, and to develop the healthier responses that characterize people who have an optimistic style (Seligman, 2006).

The consequences of these personality differences in explanatory style sometimes can be seen in terms of differential memory. For example, when memory is examined for information that came from an emotionally threatening source, people with a repressive coping style show reduced memory for information from that threatening source, whereas people with a more information-seeking coping style manage to remember and use the information. Other experiments show that people with dispositional pessimism may have a generalized expectancy that bad things will happen to them, and they remember bad things and even reinterpret good things as

Defensive Pessimism
The approach of anticipating a poorer outcome, thus reducing anxiety and actually improving performance in a risky situation

Learned Helplessness
The term used by Martin Seligman to describe a situation in which repeated exposure to unavoidable punishment leads an organism to accept later punishment even when it is avoidable

Cognitive Intervention
Teaching people to change their thought processes

Learned Optimism
The term used by Martin Seligman to describe an optimistic style that people can be trained to achieve

not so good (Carver & Scheier, 1981; Scheier & Carver, 1985). Certain aspects of cognitive approaches can be seen as modern realizations of directions that Sigmund Freud first proposed.

Interestingly, purely cognitive, explanatory attempts at psychotherapy sometimes run up against unconscious processes. If you try too hard to think in a certain way, you may wind up thinking in the opposite way—the antidote becomes the poison (Wegner, 1994). For example, if you are on a diet and try very hard not to think about ice cream and other delicious fatty foods, you may very well set in motion a set of unconscious thought processes focused on just those treats and be ready to spring into eating action as soon as you let down your guard.

Julian Rotter's Locus of Control Approach

The cognitive approach can be combined with social learning theories to produce a quite sophisticated view of personality. For example, it seems as if a personality theory should be able to take into account that people work to attain their goals both because of the consequences (rewards) and because of their thoughts and perceptions about the outcome and its likelihood. People plan and make choices before they act. Julian Rotter (rhymes with "voter"), a social learning theorist, considered such matters. Rotter was an important bridge between traditional social learning theories and the most modern ideas that have come to be called social-cognitive theory (Rotter, Chance, & Phares, 1972).

According to Rotter, our final choice of behavior depends both on how strongly we expect that our performance will have a positive result (**outcome expectancy**) and how much we value the expected reinforcement (**reinforcement value**). Rotter's theory focuses on why an individual performs a behavior and which behavior he or she actually performs in a specific situation.

Generalized versus Specific Expectancies

In any environment, people have a variety of possibly relevant behaviors in their repertoire. Some of these are more likely to occur in a particular situation than others. Rotter calls this likelihood that a particular behavior will occur in a specific situation its **behavior potential**. A particular behavior, like laughing loudly, may have a high behavior potential in some situations (during a hilarious movie) and a low behavior potential in other situations (during a final exam).

There are **specific expectancies** that a particular reward will follow a behavior in a particular situation and **generalized expectancies** that are related to a group of situations. For example, a person might have the generalized expectation of enjoying parties, but the additional specific expectancy of not enjoying his father's office holiday party. Using these constructs, we might think of the more stable, situationally consistent personality characteristics that we ascribe to people as being the result of their generalized expectancies (which result in similar behaviors in a variety of similar situations). Those behaviors that people engage in that are often labeled as

Outcome Expectancy
The expected consequence of a behavior that is the most significant influence on whether or not an individual will reproduce an observed behavior, in the view of Albert Bandura; also, the extent to which an individual expects his or her performance to have a positive result

Reinforcement Value
The extent to which an individual values the expected reinforcement of an action

Behavior Potential
A term used by Julian Rotter to describe the likelihood that a particular behavior will occur in a specific situation

Specific Expectancy
According to Julian Rotter, the expectancy that a reward will follow a behavior in a particular situation

Generalized Expectancy
According to Julian Rotter, expectancies that are related to a group of situations

being contrary to their personality may arise from their specific expectancies about a particular situation (resulting in a different behavior than is usual for them). Because, as outside observers, we rarely have access to the internal information that directs the actor in specific situations (which contributes to his specific expectancies and thereby affects his behavior in that situation), his behavior—in this case, avoiding the holiday party—appears to us to be inconsistent with his personality.

When do generalized expectancies influence our behavior more than specific expectancies, and vice versa? Rotter says that we tend to weigh generalized expectancies more heavily in new situations and use specific expectancies when the situation becomes more familiar (and we better know what to expect).

The Role of Reinforcements

Rotter also proposes that an individual will prefer some reinforcements more than others and this will affect the likelihood of occurrence of behaviors associated with different reinforcements. The greater the subjective value of the reinforcement, the more likely a person is to perform a behavior associated with that valued reinforcement. The value of any reinforcement is considered in relation to the values of other available reinforcers. According to Rotter, the reinforcer that will have the highest value is the reinforcement that we expect will lead to other things we value (such as money, prestige, and so on). These **secondary reinforcers** are of value because of their association with the satisfaction of important psychological needs.

Rotter describes six psychological needs that develop out of biological needs: recognition–status (need to achieve, be seen as competent, have positive social standing); dominance (need to control others, have power and influence); independence (need to make decisions for oneself); protection–dependency (need to have others give one security and help one achieve goals); love and affection (need to be liked and cared for by others); and physical comfort (need to avoid pain, seek pleasure, enjoy physical security and a sense of well-being).

The Psychological Situation

Behavior potential, outcome expectancy, and reinforcement potential all come together to form what Rotter terms the **psychological situation**. Rotter (1982) notes that the power of the situation in behavior is frequently downplayed; what is really important, he contends, is not necessarily the objective situation (as behaviorists might suggest) but the *psychological situation*. The psychological situation represents the individual's unique combination of potential behaviors and their value to him or her. It is in the psychological situation that a person's expectations and values interact with the situational constraints to exert a powerful influence on behavior.

Locus of Control

The best-known feature of Rotter's theory is the concept of external versus internal control of reinforcement, or **locus of control** (1966). There is either the generalized expectancy that the individual's own actions lead to desired outcomes—an **internal locus of control**; or, there is the belief that things outside of the individual, such as

---

Secondary Reinforcement
According to Dollard and Miller, a conditioned reinforcement; a previously neutral stimulus that becomes a reinforcer following its pairing with a primary reinforcer

Psychological Situation
According to Julian Rotter, the individual's unique combination of potential behaviors and the value of these behaviors to the individual

Locus of Control
In Julian Rotter's theory, the variable that measures the extent to which an individual habitually attributes outcomes to factors internal to the self versus external to the self

Internal Locus of Control
According to Julian Rotter, the generalized expectancy that an individual's own actions lead to desired outcomes

chance or powerful others, determine whether desired outcomes occur— an **external locus of control**. Rotter developed a scale of internal-external locus of control which measures an individual's beliefs about the determinants of his or her behavior.

Unlike the strict behaviorists, Rotter does believe that individuals have enduring dispositions, despite the important role of the situation in determining behavior. In his original conception, Rotter saw locus of control as a stable individual difference variable with two dimensions (internal and external) influencing a variety of behaviors in a number of different contexts. In later studies, locus of control (LOC) was found to have three somewhat orthogonal (independent) dimensions—internality, luck or chance, and powerful others (Levenson, 1981). That is, external people not only believe that events are beyond their control, but they do so either in terms of chance or powerful others.

Internal-LOC individuals are more likely to be achievement-oriented because they see that their own behavior can result in positive effects, and they are more likely to be high achievers as well (Findley & Cooper, 1983). External-LOC people tend to be less independent and also are more likely to be depressed and stressed, just as Rotter predicted (Benassi, Sweeney, & Dufour, 1988; Rotter, 1954).

Over the past 40 years, young Americans' locus of control has become increasingly external. They believe their lives are more controlled by external forces than their parents believed at the same age (Twenge, Zhang, & Im, 2004). Unfortunately, such feelings are consistent with increasing cynicism and depression. These people increasingly blame others for their problems and are less likely to join with others to take action to improve society.

© Thinkstock

■ Although young people today have many choices, new technologies, and inexpensive travel opportunities, there is increasing alienation. Locus of control among young people is more external for the current generation than in years past—if this tattooed young woman feels that she has little power over her life, why bother with society at large?

Albert Bandura's Social-Cognitive Learning Theory

External Locus of Control
According to Julian Rotter, the belief that things outside of the individual determine whether desired outcomes occur

Before the first time you ever drove a car, you had already learned many things about how you should and should not drive. Much of that knowledge was gained while you were a passenger, before you ever stepped into a driver's ed class. It came from observational learning processes—watching other people perform the task. This fundamental aspect of human behavior is the focus of Albert Bandura, a social-cognitive theorist whose major work addresses the nature of observational learning as well as the manner in which the inner person and the demands of a situation combine to determine a person's actions.

Unlike classical behaviorists, who insist that learning mechanisms be restricted to explaining the relationships between observable variables Bandura adopted the view of Clark Hull that there is a place in learning theory for unobservable variables (intervening or internal variables) that mediate the relationship between stimulus and response.

Self-System
According to Albert Bandura, the set of cognitive processes by which a person perceives, evaluates, and regulates his or her own behavior so that it is appropriate to the environment and effective in achieving goals

Observational Learning
Learning by an individual that occurs by watching others perform the behavior, with the individual neither performing the behavior nor being directly rewarded or punished for the behavior

The Self-System

Bandura gives an important role in personality to what he calls the **self-system**—the set of cognitive processes by which a person perceives, evaluates, and regulates his or her own behavior so that it is appropriate to the environment and effective in achieving the individual's goals (Bandura, 1978). Thus, the individual is affected not only by external processes of reinforcement provided by the environment, but also by expectations, anticipated reinforcement, thoughts, plans, and goals—that is, by the internal processes of the "self." The active, cognitive nature of the individual *during* learning is critical: Rather than just responding to direct reinforcement after the fact by altering behavior in the future, the person can think about and anticipate the effects of the environment. The individual can anticipate the possible consequences of his or her own actions and thereby choose an action based on the anticipated response of the environment and others in it. While classical behaviorist learning theory assumes that a person's behavior changes over time in reaction to the direct effects of reinforcement (and punishment) on the stimulus–response link, Bandura's theory claims that the effects of prior reinforcement are internalized and that behavior actually changes because of changes in the person's knowledge and expectations. His approach gives a central role to what he calls "human agency" (1989), the capacity of a person to exercise control not only over her actions, but also over internal thought processes and motivations. Knowing that a particular behavior (by the self or another) in a particular situation was reinforced in the past allows the individual to *anticipate* that she will be reinforced for that behavior in the same (or similar) situations in the future. This approach thus draws on the strengths of both the learning and cognitive approaches to personality.

Observational Learning

One of Bandura's (1973) key contributions was his explanation of how new behaviors can be acquired in the absence of reinforcement. Bandura noted that people learn so many complex responses that it is impossible for each learned response to result simply from the operation of reinforcement. So, he expanded the scope of learning theory beyond what was included in the traditional behaviorist approach. He theorized mechanisms by which people can learn simply by watching others perform a behavior—learning without performing the behavior themselves and without being directly rewarded or punished for the behavior. This is called **observational learning** or **vicarious learning** (vicarious because it is gained secondhand by watching the experience of another). It is also referred to as *modeling*, meaning that a person forms himself or herself in the image of another.

In Bandura's view, people do not mindlessly copy the behavior of others, but rather they decide consciously whether or not to perform a behavior that was learned by observation. Thus, there is a clear distinction between the acquisition of a behavior (adding it to the individual's repertoire of behaviors) and the later overt performance of that behavior. The individual can learn, or acquire, a vast number of behaviors through observational learning, but whether

© Edouard Berne/Getty Images

■ Many children watch many hours of television each day, seeing repeated acts of violence. Does such visual exposure to violence produce more aggression in children, or do more aggressive children have a greater preference for watching violent shows?

SHARPEN YOUR THINKING — Current Controversy

Protecting Children from Dangerous Video Games?

There is clear consensus from the research literature that there is a strong correlation between aggressive behavior by children and their prior exposure to violent video content (Anderson, 2004). The vast majority of the most popular video games include high levels of violence and antisocial behavior, along with a heavily sexist and racist slant. With an understanding of the powerful nature of observational learning, is it appropriate for society to regulate children's exposure to violent video-game content? Is that a proper role for government, or should these decisions be left to individual parents?

Consider a different risk: In many countries, it is illegal to sell cigarettes to minors. There are clearly established facts about tobacco use that are behind the legislation outlawing sale of tobacco products to minors. Smoking has serious negative effects on health and survival, and most smokers begin their habit (become addicted to nicotine) in adolescence. From the perspective of society, if children can be protected from access to tobacco until they are adults, they are saved from tobacco's harmful consequences and society is saved the costs of excessive illnesses from firsthand and secondhand smoke.

Are the same arguments applicable in the two situations? One important aspect that differs is that the specter of censorship is often invoked in the case of video games, while tobacco is a consumer product that does not have obvious first amendment implications. In the case of the video games, there are solutions available that have worked (with varying levels of success) for other media. For example, the commercial film industry has developed an industrywide "voluntary" movie-rating program run by the Motion Picture Association of America (MPAA). In fact, the video-game industry has instituted its own rating system through the Entertainment Software Rating Board (ESRB). Unlike the MPAA movie ratings, which specify only the minimum age of the appropriate audience, the ESRB ratings include both suggested age guidelines for a game and a description of the specific content that may be objectionable (e.g., "violence," "drug reference," or "crude humor"). Thousands of games have been rated.

As a society, we permit many things that have great potential for harm, but we limit or influence the social modeling. We allow adults to buy cigarettes, but we do not allow cigarette ads on TV. We allow fast-food companies to urge us to eat excessive amounts of unhealthy food, but we show fashion models and sports heroes who are lean and fit. As a society, we restrict children's rights to legally engage in behaviors such as smoking, gambling, and attending X-rated shows. Is it the job of government regulation to determine what is in the best interest of children and what children should be permitted to do, or should that be left to parents, with the government's role limited to ensuring that good information is made available to the parents as they make the choices for their families?

---

the individual actually ever performs any particular behavior depends on a variety of factors, discussed in the following sections.

Vicarious Learning
Learning achieved by watching the experiences of another person

Learning of Aggressive Behavior

Bandura and his colleagues conducted a series of studies, now quite well known, on the observational learning of aggressive behavior by children. In these studies, children watched a film that showed an adult behaving aggressively toward an inflated plastic Bobo clown—punching, hitting, kicking, and hammering it. Children who saw the aggressive behavior were more likely to behave aggressively when they were later allowed to play with the clown themselves. Further, when the children saw the adult rewarded for the aggression, the children were even more likely to behave aggressively themselves than were children in the control condition, in which the adult was neither rewarded nor punished. Conversely, the children who saw the adult punished were less likely to behave aggressively than the control children. But seeing the aggressive behavior rewarded was not necessary to induce increased aggression. Children who saw unrewarded aggression were later more aggressive than children who saw the same adult model display neutral behavior (also unrewarded). The observational learning did not require observation of the reward; just seeing the aggressive behavior itself was enough to "teach" it to the children.

A comprehensive review of research on the effects of media violence on children provided "unequivocal evidence that media violence increases the likelihood of aggressive and violent behavior in both immediate and long-term contexts" (Anderson et al., 2003). Observational learning is a very powerful force, and the level of media violence children experience (in TV, films, video games, computer games, and popular music) is staggering, given both the proportion of violence in their media sources and the vast number of hours per week that are spent experiencing those media sources.

Outcome Expectancy

Many subsequent experiments have demonstrated that people learn a variety of novel responses merely by watching others perform them. This is a concern as people watch ever larger quantities of ever more violent movies and TV shows. Bandura claimed that individuals can put together information from multiple, separate observations so that new patterns of behavior can be developed that are somewhat different from any that have actually been observed.

Note, however, that not all television viewers become homicidal maniacs. In Bandura's view, the most significant influence on whether an observer will reproduce an observed behavior is the expected consequences of the behavior—its outcome expectancy: Individuals are more likely to imitate behavior that they believe leads to positive outcomes. Outcome expectancy is based not only on observed consequences of reinforcement or punishment, but also on anticipated consequences (Bandura & Walters, 1963).

Whose Behavior Is Modeled?

In addition to outcome expectancy, other factors also influence the likelihood that another person's behavior will be modeled. These include characteristics of the model: age, gender, similarity to the observer, status, competence, and power. Characteristics of the behavior are also important in determining modeling; for instance, simple behavior is more likely to be modeled than complex behavior. Further, some categories of behaviors are more *salient*, and this salience may result in that behavior being observed and reproduced more often. In addition, a behavior that is admired or desired is more likely to be modeled.

The likelihood of modeling is also influenced by some attributes of the observer (the potential imitator): People with low self-esteem, people who are more dependent, and people who have had their imitative behavior reinforced more in the past are more likely to imitate. And, by necessity, observers' ability to imitate a model is limited by their cognitive and physical development; that is, successful modeling requires the ability to correctly perceive, encode, and reproduce the behavior. Of course, children's skills in these tasks improve with age, allowing the older child to model behavior that is beyond the modeling capability of the younger child.

Observational learning provides a mechanism for the acquisition of behavior that is so dangerous that one might not live to learn to perform it if it had to be acquired by shaping. For example, the circus tightrope walker would probably be dead (or at least maimed) long before learning to shape his behavior into an acceptable performance by successive approximation, without prior observational learning. (The same is true of driving, fencing, or crossing the street.) Relatedly, some behavior, like operating a control tower or raising a baby, is so complex that learning would take an excessive amount of time were it to be acquired solely through direct reinforcement. In domains such as these, the rudiments can and must be acquired by observational learning.

Another insight of this approach is the acceptance that complex behavior can change very rapidly—perhaps as when someone undergoes an epiphany or a conversion. As any parent can attest, children can, with very limited exposure, learn behaviors that adults consider undesirable.

■ Observational learning and modeling, according to Bandura, are likely to occur when the behavior and the model are admired.

Social-cognitive observational learning can also provide at least a partial explanation of the often-strong behavioral resemblance between parent and child. According to Bandura, observational learning allows the child not only to acquire specific behavioral sequences from the parent, but also to internalize broader patterns of behavior and emotional response—resulting in a child who seems to resemble the parent in personality. This explanation in terms of observational learning is quite different from other mechanisms that lead to parent–child similarity.

Comparison with Reinforcement-Oriented Learning Theory

In contrast to Skinner's and other conditioning theories that are completely dependent on the construct of reinforcement, Bandura's cognitive social learning theory (1977b) accounts for the learning of novel behaviors in the absence of any observable reinforcement. It allows for the learning of behavior for which neither model nor observer is rewarded—a common occurrence that behaviorist theory cannot easily explain. Observational learning also explains how a person learns to inhibit socially unacceptable behaviors without first having to produce them inappropriately. In addition, observational learning offers reasons why an individual will disinhibit a normally inhibited or suppressed behavior, and subsequently produce an unacceptable behavior, as a result of exposure to a model that performs the behavior. This explains group violence and mob behavior (like looting)—behavior in which people engage when they see others performing the behavior, but that they would never think of performing alone.

Unlike behaviorist theorists, whose research relies primarily on animals, Bandura uses the model of cognitive theorists and performs rigorous empirical study of his constructs with human subjects. In fact, observational learning can explain the acquisition of personality characteristics and behaviors that are uniquely human and not well accounted for by traditional learning theories: moral behavior, delay of gratification, self-critical behavior, and achievement orientation.

Processes Underlying Bandura's Observational Learning

According to Bandura, the observation of models and the repetition of the models' behavior are not just matters of simple imitation; observational learning also involves active cognitive processes with four components: attention, retention, motor reproduction, and motivation. *Attention* is mainly influenced by the characteristics of the model and the situation. *Retention* is influenced by the cognitive ability of the observer and his or her capacity to encode the behavior (by the use of images or verbal representation). *Motor reproduction* is influenced by characteristics of the observer, such as the ability to turn the mental representation into physical action and the ability to mentally rehearse the behavior. *Motivation* most influences the actual performance of the behavior that has been observed.

In other words, even when a person has observed and acquired a behavior, it will be performed when it leads to valued outcomes and not performed if it is expected to lead to negative outcomes. For example, TV programs model many illegal activities that we are not likely to imitate because to do so would put us at risk of punishment by law enforcement. Thus, the motivational component is highly influenced by both the expected (imagined) and the observed consequences of the behavior. Although social-cognitive learning theory has been criticized for oversimplifying the cognitive processes involved in learning, the basic structure proposed is consistent with widely accepted cognitive principles of attention and memory.

Acknowledgment of the concept of self-reinforcement—that we think about the potential consequences of our actions—leads to the construct of **self-regulation**; that is, Bandura recognizes that the individual's internal processes of goals, planning, and self-reinforcement result in the self-regulation of behavior. Self-punishment can range from feelings of self-disgust or shame to actually withholding a desired object from oneself (say, not watching a favorite sit-com). In addition, the concept of self-regulation suggests the operation of internal standards of behavior against which we measure our own success or failure. Bandura believes that these internal standards may be internalized originally through observational learning (especially from parents, teachers, and other important models) but eventually may reflect past behavior acting as a standard against which future behavior is judged.

Self-Regulation
Monitoring one's own behavior as a result of one's internal processes of goals, planning, and self-reinforcement

Self-Efficacy

If people do not believe that they can act to produce desired effects, they have little incentive to act and persevere. For example, in one study, business graduates were asked to discover and apply managerial rules to a simulated organization. Some of the participants were told that the required skills were innate—if you didn't have skills, you could not succeed. These participants lowered their goals and did not perform very well. The other participants were told that the necessary skills could be acquired with practice; these business graduates set challenging goals and developed successful organizational strategies (Wood & Bandura, 1989).

Bandura (1977a, 1997) thus adds one more important cognitive element to the formula: the personality characteristic of **self-efficacy**. Self-efficacy is an expectancy—a belief (expectation) about how competently one will be able to enact a behavior in a particular situation. Positive self-efficacy is the belief that one will be able to successfully perform the behavior. Without a feeling of self-efficacy (which is

Self-Efficacy
An expectancy or belief about how competently one will be able to enact a behavior in a particular situation

a very situationally specific belief), the person is much less likely to even try to perform a behavior. According to Bandura, self-efficacy determines whether we try to act at all, how long we persist in the face of difficulty or failure, and how success or failure at a task affects our future behavior. The concept of self-efficacy differs from the concept of locus of control in that self-efficacy is a belief about our own ability to successfully perform a certain behavior, whereas locus of control is a belief about the likelihood that performing a certain behavior affects the ultimate outcome.

Our self-efficacy beliefs are the result of four types of information: (1) our experiences trying to perform the target behavior or similar behavior (our past successes and failures); (2) watching others perform that or similar behaviors (vicarious experience); (3) verbal persuasion (people talking to us, encouraging or discouraging performance); and (4) how we feel about the behavior (emotional reactions). Of these, the most important source of information is our own performance experiences. The next most important is vicarious experience, followed by verbal persuasion and then emotion. We use these four sources of information to determine whether we think we can competently perform a behavior. This is an important personality characteristic because it is an essential cognitive determinant of our actions.

Bandura has also pursued the construct of self-efficacy in the health domain. Self-efficacy has been found to be related to physiological aspects of health: People who do not feel self-efficacious experience stress along with its concomitant health and immune system implications. Self-efficacy is also related to the individual's potential production of healthy behaviors: People who do not believe that they can effectively perform a health-promoting behavior are much less likely to try (Bandura, 1992, 1998).

Although self-efficacy is an internal characteristic that influences behavior and reactions in relatively constant and predictable ways, self-efficacy is also situationally determined. To expand the example above, an individual has specific self-efficacy beliefs about his or her ability to perform specific health behaviors. Mary may believe that she can successfully exercise on a daily basis to reduce her weight, but she may be certain that she cannot resist her craving for ice cream; Bandura would say Mary has high self-efficacy in the exercise domain but low self-efficacy about her eating habits. On the other hand, Bandura also suggests that one might have "higher order," or less specific, self-efficacy beliefs in a broader, more general domain. For example, a student may have a general belief that he can achieve academic success, even though he may simultaneously have very low

CHANGING Personality

In Albert Bandura's view, a good way to change personality is straightforward: take control of your life. That is, the social-cognitive learning approach asserts that people can exert substantial control over their own actions and their own development. His social-cognitive approach emphasizes what he calls "human agency"—the idea that individuals shape their own life circumstances (Bandura, 2006). People can create opportunities for themselves, and then make the most of those opportunities. The several key elements of human agency are: intentionality, forethought, self-reactiveness, and self-reflectiveness. First, we form intentions, including methods of achieving those intentions within the real constraints of the environment. Second, we can envision the future in ways that help guide our current action. Third, we can motivate and regulate our own behavior in executing our plans. And fourth, we can examine our goals, our actions, and our progress to refine our actions toward our goals. So, you might ask, with all these powers, why am I not achieving all my goals? Bandura might offer this explanation: Belief in your personal efficacy is critical to your success. You have to believe that you can succeed—without that belief in your efficacy, you won't have the incentive to really get started, or the perseverance to overcome obstacles. From the perspective of personality change, the good news is that there are robust techniques for increasing self-efficacy. The most effective approach is to have repeated experiences of mastery, including some easy successes, some successes that require overcoming obstacles, and some opportunities to make constructive responses to failures (Bandura, 2004). Because you are the agent in your own life, you can arrange appropriate challenges for yourself to help you build your sense of efficacy, step by step. As you overcome increasingly difficult challenges and increase belief in your efficacy, you are much more likely to achieve your goals.

TIME LINE

The History of Cognitive and Social-Cognitive Approaches to Personality

The major developments in the cognitive and social-cognitive approaches can be seen here in historical relation to one another and in relation to their broader societal and cultural contexts.

Developments in Cognitive Aspects		Societal and Scientific Context
Philosophers and theologians view individual deviations as games of the gods or possession by the devil	Ancient Times and Middle Ages	Differences in perceptions seen primarily in religious or philosophical terms
Laboratories studying perception and thinking are founded	1800s	Increasing emphasis on reason and rationality; philosophers search for the core of human nature
Gestalt psychology takes hold in Europe	1900–1930	Experimental psychology in U.S. is increasingly dominated by behaviorism; social turmoil in Europe; immigration in U.S.
Field theory ideas of Lewin and schema ideas of Piaget make their way into American psychology	1930s–1940s	In reaction to fascism and world war, increased study of propaganda, attitudes, prejudice, and child-rearing
Kelly develops personal construct theory; educators study how children learn	1940s–1950s	Cognitive psychology grows and behaviorism wanes; cybernetics, computers, and enhanced communications; new middle class becomes better educated and more mobile
Rotter, Bandura, and others adapt behaviorist approaches into the cognitive framework	1960s–1970s	Social psychology thrives; time of social and artistic change and turmoil
Research on explanatory style, optimism, and depression; learning disabilities and attention-deficit disorder receive much attention	1970s–1980s	Progress in cognitive psychology; new work roles, coupled with new family structures and fewer extended families
Studies of self-efficacy and of human–computer interactions thrive; self-regulation models develop	1990s	Better understanding of the individual in the workplace; Internet, computer, and high-tech revolutions
Greater integration of cognitive conceptions (intelligence, skill, evaluation) into personality theory	2000s–	Greater focus on the role of motivation, expectations, social factors in achievement

self-efficacy about his ability to perform well in a particular history class. Self-efficacy can also be viewed as arising from the interaction of knowledge structures (what one knows about the self and the world) and appraisal processes by which a person continuously evaluates the situation (Cervone, 2004). Bandura extends the concept of self-efficacy to apply to groups as well, which he terms collective efficacy (Bandura, 2000). To take action as a member of a group (whether a team, a religious congregation, a club, an army, or any other human group), a person needs a belief in the efficacy of the group to accomplish its goals.

Self-Regulation Processes

Self-regulation is the process by which people can control their own achievements and actions: Setting goals for themselves, evaluating their success at reaching those goals, and rewarding themselves for accomplishing those goals. The concept of self-efficacy is an important component of this process, influencing the choice of goals and the expected levels of achievement for those goals. Also important are the individual's own schemas, by which the person understands and operates on the environment. The construct of self-regulation focuses on the internal (intrapersonal) control of our behavior. (Notice how different this is from a behaviorist view of control of behavior.) This specific cognitive approach to behavior is at least two decades old, but is becoming very prominent on the interface between social psychology and personality psychology (Boekaerts, Pintrich, & Zeidner, 2000; Carver & Scheier, 1990). It has very broad relevance to many applied areas as well—especially education and health, which are domains where a better understanding of how people exercise control over their own behavior could have implications for improving our society's success in teaching and in promoting health.

If an individual's cognitive schemas and styles of information processing normally produce consistencies in behavior, what will happen if these processes break down? Consider, as an example, the following processes sometimes affecting a first-year college student. First, the student moves away from family, community, and high school friends to a new set of surroundings with new expectations and belief systems. New college friends may have social or religious beliefs that are unfamiliar and different from those in the student's childhood community. Further, new ideas learned in college courses and new philosophies espoused by professors could help alter the student's worldview. At the least, old schemas may be thrown into temporary turmoil.

Second, cognition and perception may be changed or impaired more directly by biological factors. For example, a student who often stays up late to study for exams may become sleep deprived. Commonly, alcohol enters the picture. Alcohol is well known to disrupt one's usual ways of thinking (Knight & Longmore, 1994; Parker & Noble, 1977).

Third, the students may encounter environments where deindividuation processes are active. Deindividuation is a process by which one loses one's usual sense of identity (Reicher, Spears, & Postmes, 1995). It is most likely to occur in situations of anonymity or lack of emphasis upon one's personal identity. This might mean losing one's self in a crowd, being less self-conscious in conditions of low light, or being in a group that is transient or quick-changing.

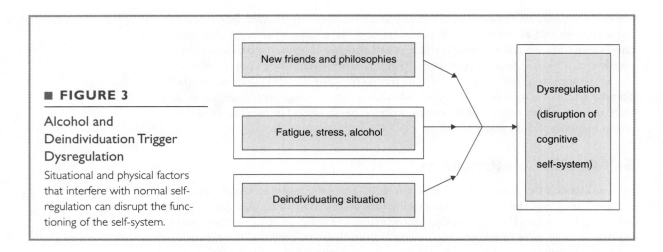

■ FIGURE 3

Alcohol and Deindividuation Trigger Dysregulation

Situational and physical factors that interfere with normal self-regulation can disrupt the functioning of the self-system.

For example, all of these conditions might hold for a first-year college student who attends a large party on a Saturday night after midterm exams. The student's old ideas have been challenged by new friends and professors, there is stress and fatigue from the exams, and a keg of beer is available. Further, the student feels anonymous at the party, the situation is a novel one, and previously unknown activities are going on. In this circumstance, the student may do things that are "out of character," and possibly even dangerous or illegal. If there are negative consequences, family, friends, and even the student may be very surprised that a person with a "good" personality could have done such "bad" things. The self-system, the cognitive processes that influence a person's usual way of perceiving and self-regulating, has broken down (as illustrated in Figure 3).

Humans as Computers

Is human personality analogous to a sophisticated computer program that processes information from the environment? Computers manipulate information as their central function—all they are is information processors. Perhaps that is all that people are as well?

Is it reasonable to think we can build a computer that has a "personality"? Could we simulate a generic person, or even a specific person—a Martin Luther King Jr.? Can the linking of on–off switches be made to represent consistencies and motives in human behavior? If we were successful in creating a humanlike program using the capabilities of a computer, that would support the idea that humans can be understood (to a significant degree) as information-processing devices.

There have been interesting attempts to apply computer simulation methodology more broadly to personality. In such an approach, theoretical constructs are translated into a computer model, and the "behavior" of the model is examined under a variety of conditions. For example, a neural network simulation model (where a very large number of simple program elements combine to produce outcomes) has been used to create "Virtual Personalities" (Read et al., 2010; Read &

Evaluating the Perspectives

Advantages and Limits of the Cognitive Approach to Personality

■ **Quick Analogy**

- Humans as scientists and information processors.

■ **Advantages**

- Seeks to explain personality through study of the uniquely human processes of cognition.
- Captures active nature of human thought.
- Differences in cognitive skills are viewed as central to individuality.
- Studies perception, cognition, and attribution through empirical experimentation.

■ **Limits**

- Often ignores the unconscious and emotional aspects of personality.
- Some theories (social learning theory) can tend to oversimplify complex thought processes.
- May underemphasize situational influences on behavior.

■ **View of Free Will**

- Free will through active human thought processes.

■ **Common Assessment Techniques**

- Decision tasks, biographical analysis, attributional analysis, study of cognitive development, observation.

■ **Implications for Therapy**

- Uses understanding of perception, cognition, and attribution to change thought processes. For example, to treat marital problems, each partner might be shown the workloads and viewpoints of the other, might role-play the other's role, might receive training in listening carefully to his or her partner, and also might be shown examples of couples engaging in cooperative interactions. Cognitive-behavioral therapy promotes self-efficacy by giving the client successful experiences with the task, showing that similar others can successfully perform the task, using verbal encouragement, and conditioning control of excess physiological arousal. Self-help support groups (such as for coping with serious illness) often use this approach.

Miller, 2002). Such models can learn relationships between different situations and the behaviors that are appropriate in those situations.

Even when a computer is not programmed by psychologists to have a personality, human characteristics are commonly ascribed to computers. We tend to anthropomorphize complex machines: "The computer thinks I wanted to reformat the whole document," or "The program is trying to print the letter," or "The statistics package is mixing up my dependent and independent variables." We attribute goals, beliefs, and mental states to machines because of how *we* process information. As we have seen, when we observe ourselves or others in action, we make such attributions, and we tend to carry that process over to our understanding of other complex entities—often inappropriately.

Research on what are termed sociable robots (e.g., Breazeal, 2003) has looked at what characteristics tend to lead people to perceive robots as appealing partners for social interaction. One study (Lee, Peng, Jin, & Yan, 2006) varied the programming of a robotic dog to give it more extroverted versus more introverted patterns of speech and nonverbal behavior, and found that the "personality" of the robotic dog had different effects on humans who were selected on the basis of their introverted versus extroverted personality. The human participants had different impressions of the dog when the dog's "personality" was similar versus complementary to their own, just as is the case when people interact with other humans.

Turing Test
A standard test by which to judge whether a computer can adequately simulate a human; in this test, first proposed by Alan Turing, a human judge interacts with two hidden others and tries to decide which is the human and which is the computer

Shortly after World War II, when primitive computers were first under development, the British mathematician Alan Turing proposed a standard test by which to judge whether a computer could adequately simulate a human. The **Turing Test** sets up a situation in which a human judge interacts (via computer keyboard or teletype) with two hidden others. One of the hidden others is a person; the other is a computer program. The judge asks questions of each party and, on the basis of the answers typed back by each one, attempts to determine which is the person and which is the machine (Crockett, 1994). If the judge cannot accurately distinguish between the person and the machine, the computer "passes" the Turing Test. So far, no computer has robustly passed the test; that is, no computer program can fully simulate a human well enough to fool a human judge, but that day may be coming soon. For example, the IBM supercomputer named Watson can not only find facts (like a Google search can) but can go through its huge database and find correct answers to the types of subtle or toying questions asked on the game show *Jeopardy* (Thompson, 2010). And, in chess, expert computer programs can beat chess grand masters—even the highest-ranked human chess player in the world. If a machine can be programmed to play world-class chess, why can't it appear convincingly human in conversation? One answer is that you don't need a human personality to play excellent chess, but you surely need one to seem human.

Summary and Conclusion

All the cognitive approaches to personality described in this chapter have in common the view that the essence of personality is to be found in the way people think—that is, in how we understand the events in our world, how we understand the nature and actions of other people, how we learn from our social environments, and how we control and understand our own behaviors.

In many cases, the cognitively oriented theories of personality were outgrowths of prior theories that were more directly cognitive. Kurt Lewin took the Gestalt approach, which had previously been applied chiefly to perception and problem solving, and developed it into his field theory of personality. Another outgrowth of Gestalt psychology was the development of the concept of field dependence as a personality variable.

People who are more field dependent are more influenced by the surrounding context in their perception and problem solving; that is, the "field" in which the object or problem appears is viewed as an integral part of it. This sensitivity to context leads a field-dependent person to respond more holistically and intuitively, in contrast to the more analytical and abstract responses of the field-independent person. Field dependence is reliably measurable across many different instruments, tends to be consistent in an individual over time, and predicts many aspects of behavior, especially interpersonal behavior.

Cognitive and perceptual mechanisms of expecting, attending, and information processing are a central part of our understanding of human behavior, and they have been applied to the study of personality by many of the more cognitive approaches. Schemas are the cognitive structures that organize our knowledge and expectations about our environments. Schemas exist on many levels of complexity, and many can simultaneously be part of our understanding and expectations of a single event or entity. Complex schemas (also called scripts) guide our behavior in social situations. Our personality, according to this view, is seen as the series of scripts that direct and circumscribe our behavior.

Categorization processes are central to human cognition (and underlie our ability to evoke appropriate schemas). Our perceptual processes take in highly complex ensembles of information consisting of millions of bits of information, but what we experience is filtered through our categorization processes into a small number of identifiable and familiar objects and entities (words, individual people, household objects, and so on). It is impossible for people *not* to categorize—we experience the world through our interpretations. Our categorization processes pick up on a few features of some entity and automatically invoke a category. This is informationally efficient, allowing us to assign categories without in-depth analysis, but it leads us to miss details that may not match the usual ones for the category. To the extent that individuals have had different experiences, they may have developed somewhat different categories, and thus the same event or object may be interpreted quite differently by different people.

George Kelly developed the personal construct theory, whose fundamental postulate is that "a person's processes are psychologically channeled by the ways in which he anticipates events." Kelly's theorizing was especially focused on the domain of interpersonal relationships. Kelly proposed that we each have a unique system of constructs that we use to understand and predict behavior (both our own and that of others). Kelly's Role Construct Repertory Test results in a set of constructs that reflects the hierarchy of dimensions that the examinee believes are important in understanding and predicting behavior.

Social intelligence theory proposes that people vary in the abilities pertinent to understanding and influencing other people. Success in interpersonal interaction is easy for some people and difficult for others. The level of mastery of the particular cluster of knowledge and skills relevant to interpersonal situations is called social intelligence.

Explanatory style refers to a set of cognitive personality variables that captures a person's habitual means of interpreting events in her or his life. There are a number of different approaches to this central idea of explanatory style. One version has poles of optimism and pessimism as the extremes of explanatory style. People with an optimistic explanatory style generally interpret events in their lives with an optimistic perspective, whereas those with a pessimistic style tend to focus on the negative potential in a situation. People whose explanatory style is closer to the pessimistic pole may be more prone to depression. Conversely, having an optimistic explanatory style is associated with better outcomes. People can learn to have a more optimistic style—learned optimism. Another approach to explanatory style is the attributional model of learned helplessness. The term "learned helplessness" describes what happens when an individual learns that he or she cannot control any of the things that are important: Repeated exposure to unavoidable punishment leads an organism to accept later punishment even when it *is* avoidable. Depression, stress, and apathy are commonly the consequences. There is evidence, though, that cognitive intervention—teaching people to change their thought processes—can affect subsequent behavior. Overcoming learned helplessness assumes that personality is seen as a kind of cognitive skill.

Rotter's social-cognitive theory claims that people choose their behaviors on the basis of the likelihood of the behavior in that specific situation (its behavior potential), an expected result (its outcome expectancy), and how much we value that outcome (its reinforcement value). These factors constitute the "psychological situation," which ultimately determines behavior. The best-known feature of Rotter's theory is the concept of external versus internal control of reinforcement, or locus of control. Either individuals hold the generalized expectancy that their own actions lead to desired outcomes—an internal locus of control; or they believe that things outside the individual, such as chance or powerful others, determine whether desired outcomes occur—an external locus of control. Internal-LOC individuals are more likely to be achievement-oriented and high achievers, whereas external-LOC people tend to be less independent and also are more likely to be depressed and stressed.

Bandura's social-cognitive learning theory can be seen as an application and refinement of the classical learning theory that dominated psychology for much of the twentieth century. Bandura drew attention to observational learning (vicarious learning), which was poorly explained in classical behaviorism. He showed that learning by observation did not require any overt reinforcement. In Bandura's theory, the individual's internal processes of goals planning, and self-reinforcement result in the self-regulation of behavior. Bandura adds one more important cognitive element to the formula: the personality characteristic of self-efficacy, a belief (expectation) about how competently one will be able to enact a behavior in a particular situation.

All of these cognitive approaches to personality share the view that human perception and human cognition are at the core of what it means to be a person. The way that people interpret their environments is seen as central to their humanness, and the ways in which people differ from one another in how they do this are seen as central to their individuality.

■ Key Theorists

Kurt Lewin	George Kelly	Julian Rotter
Jean Piaget	Martin Seligman	Albert Bandura

■ Key Concepts and Terms

Gestalt psychology	emotional intelligence
field theory	multiple intelligences
life space	explanatory style
contemporaneous causation	learned helplessness
cognitive style	behavior potential
learning style	internal versus external locus of control
schemas and scripts	self-system
categorization	observational learning
personal construct theory	self-regulation
Role Construct Repertory Test	self-efficacy
social intelligence	Turing Test

Trait Aspects of Personality

After the terrorist airplane attacks on the United States of September 11, 2001, an unknown person suddenly started attacking with a biological weapon: anthrax. Spores of the deadly bacteria were sent through the mail and a number of people died. Who was to blame? Months later, the Federal Bureau of Investigation (FBI) was still stumped. But it put its behavioral scientists to work and released a profile of the person behind the anthrax attacks. The perpetrator was said to be most likely an adult male who has difficulty with social relationships. If he has a relationship at all, it is probably of a selfish, self-serving nature. He may hold grudges for a long time, vowing that he will get even one day. How can the FBI say such things about the personality of an unknown suspect?

This FBI profile was strangely reminiscent of another deadly case. Starting in 1978, an unknown person began sending letter bombs to scientists around the country. More than a dozen such bombs over 17 years led to the critical injury of 23 innocent

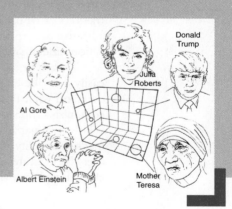

people and three deaths. The FBI, analyzing construction of the explosive devices, determined that they were made by the same person, years before the media started receiving letters from the "Unabomber." And the FBI had used the pattern of the bombings to construct a psychological profile of the bomber. The FBI profiled the bomber as an obsessive-compulsive male in his late 30s or early 40s, educated, who likes to make lists, dresses neatly, is a quiet neighbor, and probably has poor relations with women. The FBI did not know this person—rather, it assembled a psychological profile that the person would likely fit.

Such criminal profiles are often uncannily accurate. In many cases, it seems as if details of an individual's personality can be inferred from certain distinctive patterns of behavior. (In the case of the Unabomber, the FBI was only partly correct. In the case of the anthrax mailer, the prime suspect died before being charged, but the FBI personality profile was apparently accurate.) What is interesting about such cases is that they rely quite heavily on a trait approach to personality; that is, they assume that much about an individual's consistent reaction patterns can be predicted from knowing his or her core personality traits. A **trait approach** to personality uses a basic, limited set of adjectives or adjective dimensions to describe and scale individuals.

Trait Approach
Use of a limited set of adjectives or adjective dimensions to describe and scale individuals

How many traits are there? This question turns out to be the pivotal one in the **trait approach** to personality. Francis Galton (1884) explored Roget's thesaurus and found over a thousand core words expressive of character. In fact, broadly speaking, the English language contains thousands of words that can be used to describe personal qualities (Allport & Odbert, 1936): *aberrant, abeyant, abhorrent, able, abominable, . . . zany, zingy, zombied, zoned-out*. Gordon Allport counted about 18,000 adjectives. Does this mean that there are thousands of personality traits? If so, it would be very difficult to study personality.

For a trait approach to succeed, it should use a relatively small number of traits to account well for a person's consistencies. The approach would be even easier if the same traits could be applied differentially to all people—that is, if everyone could be rated on every such trait. But this is not absolutely necessary; perhaps a subset of traits could be used for each person. Furthermore, we need not be limited to simple adjective descriptions of personal qualities; people also differ in terms of their motivations and abilities.

Trait approaches to personality are certainly common in popular culture. We easily describe an acquaintance as extroverted or conscientious or selfish. We understand what it means to say that a bomber is quiet and reserved yet obsessive-compulsive and shy around women. Can such traits be reliably measured, and do they validly summarize and predict reactions? Can the FBI accurately anticipate a criminal's personality? It turns out that the successful trait psychologist must be a detective every bit as astute and observant as the famous fictional detective Sherlock Holmes. This chapter explains the trait aspects of personality.

The History of Trait Approaches

Ancient Conceptions

For thousands of years, narrators have characterized individuals using traits. The biblical book of Genesis, for example, tells us that Noah was a "just" man who walked with God. Descriptions of such righteous men were often illustrated with narratives of their righteous deeds, but the trait itself was assumed to be a stable characteristic.

The first systematic approach to analyzing traits arose in ancient Greece. Hippocrates described human temperament in terms of the so-called bodily humors—sanguine (blood), melancholic (black bile), choleric (yellow bile), and phlegmatic (phlegm). The dominance of a humor—the prevalence of one of the four fluids—supposedly determined typical reaction patterns. The sanguine was hopeful and cheerful, the melancholic was sad and depressive, the choleric was angry and irascible, and the phlegmatic was slow and apathetic. Intriguingly, although the idea turned out to be biologically groundless, the humoral approach did an excellent job of describing basic reaction patterns. It was not until the seventeenth-century renaissance in biology that humoral notions began to be discarded.

In addition to temperaments, character descriptions also began in classic Greece. Theophrastus, a pupil of Aristotle, is one of the earliest known creators of character sketches. The sketches are brief descriptions of a type of person that can be recognized across time and place—such as the buffoon, the temptress, the miser, or the boor (Allport, 1961). Theophrastus's famous "Penurious Man," described over 2,000 years ago, divides up the dinner check at a restaurant according to what each person ate; he searches out bargains and is stingy

■ This seventeenth-century Dutch painting titled *The Miser*, reflects the long-standing notion that there are people whose essence can be captured by describing them in terms of a single notable trait. This "miser" has a great deal in common with the "penurious man" profiled by Theophrastus 2,000 years earlier, and with comedian Jack Benny's persona 300 years later.

with his guests; he would move all the furniture in the house to find a penny; and so on. Such a person is still easy to recognize. In the twentieth century, two millennia later, the vaudeville and TV comedian Jack Benny made a very successful career out of portraying just such a "cheapskate." (On one of his shows, Jack was accosted by a mugger who said, "This is a stickup. Your money or your life." Jack paused, and the audience laughed. The mugger repeated, "I said your money or your life!" Jack Benny: "I'm thinking it over!") Trait approaches to personality attempt to capture such notions of personality reliably and validly, through systematic, scientific means (Asendorpf, 2006).

In the nineteenth century, after Charles Darwin liberated conceptions about the sources of human variation, replacing demons and spirits with mutation and natural selection, individual differences became a prime topic for scientific study. Consistencies could be sought in psychobiological characteristics of the person. Francis Galton's (1907) extensive attempts to measure human abilities spurred intelligence testing and the assessment of other aptitudes. The final necessary ingredient was the development of modern statistical techniques, which provided the quantitative foundation for the study of traits to begin in earnest.

Jung's Extroversion and Introversion

Carl Jung (who worked on neo-analytic aspects of personality) helped launch trait approaches. Jung set in motion an influential stream of work on traits when he employed the terms extroversion and introversion in a theory of personality (Jung, 1921/1967). For Jung, extroversion refers to an orientation toward things outside oneself, whereas introversion refers to a tendency to turn inward and explore one's feelings and experiences. Thus, for Jung, a person could have tendencies toward both introversion and extroversion, but one would be dominant. It was not until Hans Eysenck's work in the early 1950s that the terms took on their current meaning, discussed below. (Some theorists prefer the spelling "*extra*version," but we will stick with the more common "*extro*version.")

The **Myers-Briggs Type Indicator** is a widely used instrument that attempts to measure introversion and extroversion as Jung defined them. In addition to global introversion–extroversion, there are subclassifications. The **Sensation–Intuition scale** indicates whether a person is more prone to realism or imagination. The **Thinking–Feeling scale** indicates whether a person is more logical and objective or more personal and subjective. There is also a **Judgment–Perception scale**, which indicates one's orientation toward evaluating or perceiving things. Some people are more structured and judgmental, while others are more flexible and perceptive.

This Myers-Briggs scheme has often been successfully used by vocational counselors (Bayne, 1995). Thus, for example, some people direct their attention inward (i.e., are introverted) and rely on feelings and intuition in evaluating new situations. Such people might make good clinical psychologists or artists (Gridley, 2006). How about an extrovert who is realistic, thinking, and judging? Such a person might make a good military officer. What is interesting about this pioneering approach is that it systematically classifies individuals according to a psychologically rich yet understandable set of categories.

In general, subsequent research has validated the importance of the introversion–extroversion division, but the usefulness of further dividing people into subtypes along

Myers-Briggs Type Indicator
A widely used instrument that attempts to measure introversion and extroversion and several other subclassifications as defined by Carl Jung

Sensation–Intuition Scale
Subclassification of the Myers-Briggs Type Indicator that reflects whether a person is more prone to realism or imagination

Thinking–Feeling Scale
Subclassification of the Myers-Briggs Type Indicator that reflects whether a person is logical and objective or personal and subjective

Judgment–Perception Scale
Subclassification of the Myers-Briggs Type Indicator that reflects whether a person is oriented toward evaluating or perceiving things

the lines of Jung's theory has shown mixed results as a general approach to personality. Empirically speaking, Jung's divisions are not the best ones. Rather, schemes such as the Big Five dimensions of personality (see section later in this chapter) are clearer and more helpful (Carlson, 1980; Costa & McCrae, 2006; McCrae & Costa, 1989; Myers & McCaulley, 1985). Jung set the stage by drawing attention to the observation that some people are oriented to look inward, others outward, and that this dichotomy is a stable individual difference. Subsequent empirical research refined and developed these ideas.

The Use of Statistics: R. B. Cattell

As the psychoanalytically based theorists like Jung were proposing theories of the basic tendencies motivating personality, more quantitatively oriented psychologists began using statistical approaches to try to simplify and objectify the structure of personality. Some of the major steps along this path were taken by R. B. Cattell (1905–1998), starting in the 1940s.

Remember that Allport had found thousands of personality adjectives in the English language, but he concluded that his list must be reduced by eliminating terms that were clearly synonymous. Cattell went much further with this lexical (language-based) approach. The traits listed by Allport were further grouped, rated, and then "factor analyzed" by Cattell.

Factor analysis is a statistical technique. Like other statistics, it helps us rework or reduce information we already have in order to make it more understandable. For example, a list of numbers (scores) can be summarized in terms of two statistics—a mean (average) and a measure of variation (such as the standard deviation). Similarly, the relation of two variables—that is, pairs of scores—can be summarized in terms of correlation coefficients (such as r). Factor analysis goes one step further: It is a way of summarizing correlation coefficients. For instance, if we know the correlations (associations) among a number of variables, factor analysis can help us summarize these relations in terms of a small number of dimensions. By taking into account the overlap (that is, the shared variance), factor analysis mathematically consolidates information. Variables that are correlated with each other but not with other variables form a dimension, or "factor." Factor analysis thus can help us reduce or even eliminate the redundant information in a list of personality descriptors.

Cattell, like Allport, assumed that language has evolved to capture the important aspects of personality. So, he started with a list, derived from Allport's, that seemed to contain all the nonsynonymous adjectives that refer to personality. People were then rated on these characteristics, and the ratings were combined through factor analysis. Cattell repeated this basic process in many ways and on various data sets throughout the years.

Cattell did his graduate work with Charles Spearman, the English psychologist and statistician who is famous for his pioneering work on assessing intelligence, including the development of the idea of a general factor of intelligence termed g. Cattell, like most psychologists of his day, also received training and experience in clinical psychology. He moved from England to the United States in 1937 to work with E. L. Thorndike. Thorndike, like Spearman, was very interested in the measurement details of assessing intelligence, so it is not surprising that Cattell's approach to personality is reminiscent of factor analytic approaches to intelligence.

© Stockbyte/Getty Images

■ Activities of everyday life provide a window into personality. It turns out that music preferences can be reliably categorized and are somewhat associated with personality (Rentfrow & Gosling, 2003, 2006). Some people like classical, jazz, blues, and folk music; these people tend to be politically liberal and high on Openness. Others like rock, alternative, and heavy-metal music; these people tend also to be high on Openness but also high on athleticism. Some people prefer pop, country, religious, and soundtrack music; these people tend to be high on Extroversion and Conscientiousness, and also on conservatism. Finally, others prefer rap, soul, funk, and dance music; these people tend to be higher on Extroversion, Agreeableness, and also on liberalism. Further, individuals use music to communicate something about their personalities to others.

Q-data, T-data, L-data, and the 16PF

Q-data

The term used by R. B. Cattell to describe data gathered from self-reports and questionnaires

Q-data is the name that Cattell gave to data that are gathered from self-reports and questionnaires (questionnaire data). But recognizing that people often do not have a good understanding of their own personalities, Cattell argued that two other kinds of information should also be collected. **T-data** are data collected by placing a person into some controlled test situation and noting or rating responses; these data are observational (test data). **L-data** consist of information gathered about a person's life, such as from school records (life data). Obviously, a valid personality trait should show up in the course of life; for instance, we would expect more club presidents to be extroverts than introverts. In other words, Cattell endeavored to see if the same trait could be captured in different ways. This approach to construct validation has been used frequently since then in assessing the validity of personality traits.

Cattell was well versed in personality theory and relied on theory to select the variables to consider in his analyses. He well knew that in factor analysis, as in many other spheres of life, "garbage in" yields "garbage out." In other words, if we have poor information to start with, then even the most sophisticated attempt to summarize or analyze the data will yield useless results. He was theoretically sophisticated in generating the raw data, yet his approach to personality from that point on was unequivocally statistical.

Based on his factor analytic findings, Cattell (1966) proposed that there are 16 basic personality traits.

Why Does It Matter?

Cattell argued that there are strata, or layers, of traits; certain tendencies are more fundamental and serve as the source for other traits. Traits are uncovered and distilled through statistical analysis of self-report, observational, and demographic data from questionnaires (Q), testing situations (T), and life paths (L). Cattell also showed the necessity of testing trait schemes in applied settings—in clinical work, in business organizations, in schools, and so on—and then using the findings to understand the traits better. His process—going from theory to assessment to applied work, and then back to theory and more assessment—has become the standard process for all modern trait approaches to personality.

■ **TABLE 1** Cattell's Sixteen Personality Factors (16PF)	
outgoing—reserved	suspicious—trusting
more—less intelligent	imaginative—practical
stable—emotional	shrewd—forthright
assertive—humble	apprehensive—placid
happy-go-lucky—sober	experimenting—conservative
conscientious—expedient	self-sufficient—group-tied
venturesome—shy	controlled—casual
tender-minded—tough-minded	tense—relaxed

Cattell labeled the factors that emerged with letters of the alphabet rather than trait names to emphasize that they were an objective result of the statistical method, not biased by preconceived notions. These 16 factors are shown in Table 1, with each represented by the labels of the opposite ends of the continuum for that factor. These factors are typically assessed in an individual using the Sixteen Personality Factors Questionnaire (16PF).

In the late 1930s, and continuing through the '40s and '50s, Cattell's quantitative approaches, as well as the then-popular behaviorist and psychoanalytic approaches, exerted a significant influence on Gordon Allport. Allport saw serious problems with all three approaches! Yet it was Allport who had a tremendous influence (probably the greatest influence) on trait psychology.

Gordon Allport's Trait Psychology

Variability and Consistency

Anyone who has observed people knows that the same person may behave differently in different situations. The same person may also behave differently at different times, with different people, and at different ages. Thus, a simplistic notion of stable traits is obviously inadequate—even the most cheerful and friendly person will at times be angry and aggressive. This variability was well recognized by Gordon Allport, who argued that although behavior is variable, there is also a constant, core portion for each person. It is this constant portion that is captured by the modern conception of **traits**.

The notion of traits assumes that personality is rooted very much within the person. Allport (1961) defined personality as the "dynamic organization within the individual of those psychophysical systems that determine his characteristic behavior and thought" (p. 28). According to this view, each person has unique, key qualities. In recent years, some influential approaches to personality have expanded the focus on the individual to incorporate aspects of

T-data
The term used by R. B. Cattell to describe data gathered from placing a person in a controlled test situation and noting or rating responses

L-data
The term used by R. B. Cattell to describe data gathered about a person's life from school records or similar sources

Trait
According to Gordon Allport, a generalized neuro-psychic structure or core tendency that underlies behavior across time and situations

■ If you had been a student of personality at Harvard in the 1950s, you probably would have rated this man as conscientious. A cardinal disposition of Gordon Allport was his meticulous and wide-ranging approach to the study of personality.

the situation as well. These so-called *interactionist* approaches simultaneously study the person-by-situation interactions.

Gordon Allport was born in Indiana in 1897. He spent a long career at Harvard University and died in 1967. His father was a doctor, his mother a teacher, and his older brother Floyd also became a distinguished psychologist. An excellent and well-educated student throughout his life, Allport was renowned for his scholarly knowledge. He was one of those scholars who picked interesting topics to study and then brought to bear a wide assortment of relevant evidence and original thinking.

At the age of 22, Allport visited Europe and wrote to Sigmund Freud asking for a meeting. Allport reports that Freud opened their meeting with an expectant stare. After all, Freud was a master clinician, and people generally came to him seeking advice. Not knowing what to say, Allport reported an incident he had seen on the tram: A clean little boy seemed to have a severe phobia about dirt or getting dirty. Allport himself was rather fastidious and well starched. Freud looked at him and asked, "And was that little boy you?" (Allport, 1968).

Allport was appalled that Freud would seek to see a deeper meaning in such a simple remark. Recalling this meeting later, Allport reported that it taught him to look more at surface-level, manifest aspects of personality before probing deeply into the unconscious. Freud emphasized instinctual drives but Allport emphasized traits. Of course, a Freudian might speculate that Freud was right on the mark in his question to Allport and that is why Allport was so shocked and bothered. A psychoanalyst would see Allport's later explanation ("rationalization") as merely a defense mechanism. To the contrary, Allport saw himself as a man of great common sense and rationality. It is interesting to note how a down-to-earth, scholarly boy from the American Midwest would develop a meticulous but commonsense-based theory of personality.

How meticulous and rational was Allport? We have seen that he pored over the entire English language to gather a database of adjectives for thinking about traits. Allport's fascination with words evidently began at a young age. He reports that when he was 10 years old, one of his jealous schoolmates pointed at him and said, "Aw, that guy swallowed a dictionary" (Allport, 1968). His personality remained stable—as a professor he reported reading summaries of *everything* published in psychology each year (in a huge compendium called *Psychological Abstracts*) (Allport, 1968). Similarly, he examined dozens of definitions of personality before constructing his own. His definition is so carefully worded that it has been quoted in many books. The idea of personality as "the dynamic organization within the individual of those psychophysical systems that determine his characteristic behavior and thought" (Allport, 1937) is the essential trait perspective. It sees personality as an organization within the individual.

The Importance of Culture

Allport held a lifelong concern with studying prejudice. Like Kurt Lewin, Allport believed that theories would be helpful in practice, and that theories in turn should be informed (and enriched) by practice. Allport studied American prejudice against Negroes (as they were then called) and Jews at a time when it was not fashionable to do so. He was one of the first American intellectuals to recognize the truth about the Nazi genocide, and his book *The Nature of Prejudice* (1954) remains remarkably up to date on the practical uses of personality theories.

Well aware of cultural influences on personality, Allport helped found Harvard's Department of Social Relations, which grouped the areas of personality and social psychology with sociology and anthropology. (This department was dissolved in 1972, as many psychologists began to shun such a broad perspective on human behavior.) Allport emphasized that no one would confuse a Viennese with a Vietnamese or a Venetian, as their culture provides each with ready-made ways of approaching their lives. The interesting questions arise when people immigrate to different cultures—say from Vienna, Vietnam, and Venice to Los Angeles—and try to raise their children. To what extent and in what ways do these new Americans become more alike in their traits? These are important questions of culture.

In all of these matters—doing applied work in sensitive areas, examining cultural variations, questioning approaches that were too deep or too shallow—Allport was ahead of most of his contemporaries and indeed ahead of many modern personality researchers. Allport integrated the ideas of hundreds of philosophers and scholars, from classical times onward, into his writings. One perspective that particularly bothered him, however, was the behaviorist work of B. F. Skinner. Allport could not stomach any attempts to reduce the complexity and nobility of each human being. Allport thus heartily encouraged the development of humanistic psychology, fearing humans would be degraded if their behavior were explained in terms of the conditioning of rats and pigeons.

Functional Equivalence

Allport also thought that factor analysis could not possibly depict in full the life of an individual (Allport, 1961). Thus, he was no fan of Cattell. Because a factor is no more than a statistical composite, it could not possibly do justice to an individual. Taking bits of information from studying many people could not disclose what is revealed by intensive study of a single individual. Furthermore, Allport pointed out that factor analysis produces a cluster (a factor) but does not name the factor; naming the factor falls to the factor analyst, and there is often reason to doubt whether the name truly captures the essence of the factor. In this way, the factor analyst may be misled by his or her own statistics.

Yet Allport obviously could not deal with thousands of personality traits. How did he reduce and structure the mass of individual thoughts, feelings, and actions? He believed that regularities arise (1) because the individual views many situations and stimuli in the same way, and (2) because many of the individual's behaviors are similar in their meaning—that is, they are **functionally equivalent**. In his words, a trait is an internal structure that "renders many stimuli functionally equivalent" and can "guide equivalent forms of adaptive and expressive behavior" (1961). Functional equivalence is the essence of Allport's approach to traits.

For example, a so-called superpatriot (Allport made up the name "McCarley") might view socialists, college professors, peace organizations, Jews, the United Nations, civil rights activists, and so on as objects to be despised and scorned; they

Functionally Equivalent Gordon Allport's concept that many behaviors of individuals are similar in their meaning because the individuals tend to view many situations and stimuli in the same way; for Allport, the trait is the internal structure that causes this regularity

are *seen as equivalent* by this extremist. Such a person might in turn give hate-filled speeches or join a lynch mob; these are equivalent behaviors. These consistencies are what form the basis for Allport's conception of personality. He analyzed these consistencies in terms of common traits and personal dispositions.

Common Traits

Common Traits

The term used by Gordon Allport to describe organizing structures that people in a population share

Because people have a common biological heritage, and because people within a culture have a common cultural heritage, it makes sense to assume that people have in common many organizing structures (traits). Allport termed these **common traits**. Common traits are traits that people in a population share; they are basic dimensions.

For example, in American society, some people constantly push to get ahead of others and to dominate their environment. Other people develop a comfortable style of going along with the flow of things (including yielding to or ignoring the pushy people). Allport thought people could usefully be compared on such dimensions, but he did not believe that such an analysis provides a full understanding of personality.

Functionally Autonomous

A term used by Gordon Allport to describe the idea that in adulthood many motives and tendencies become independent of their origins in childhood and that finding out where such tendencies originated is, therefore, not important

What about the motivation driving a person to keep everything clean and well ordered (sort of like Allport himself)? Allport accepts the Freudian idea that such motivation could have its origins in the childhood socialization of instinctual tendencies. However, in adulthood these motives or strivings take on a life of their own. Allport said that this means that many motives are **functionally autonomous**—they have become independent of their origins in childhood. Thus, it would not make sense to try to trace them back to early childhood (except perhaps in cases of serious psychopathology). The childhood experiences may be the root or origin of the adult tendencies, but they do not continue to influence these tendencies. It would be useful to understand that a desire for neatness and order dominates a person's approach to life, but it is not necessary to unearth where these tendencies originated.

Proprium

Gordon Allport's term for the core of personality that defines who one is; Allport believed that the proprium has a biological counterpart

Allport sometimes used the term **proprium** to refer to the core of personality. (Proprium simply means "one's own" or "one's self.") By this he meant that there are layers within the human psyche, including an irreducible core that defines who we are. In this narrow sense, Allport's view was close to Freud's. Both theorists felt that there are central forces underlying our everyday diverse behaviors. Presumably this core has a biological counterpart (as both Freud and Allport explicitly expected); but such biological structures have not been fully identified, at least not yet. In any case, Allport thought these core motivations were much more rational and positive than the Freudian approach described them to be.

Personal Dispositions

We learn to recognize thousands of different people by their faces. No two people look exactly alike (except for some cases of identical twins), so it should not be surprising that no two personalities are exactly alike. To fully understand individuals, we need to use methods that take into account each person's uniqueness. Such methods are termed "idiographic." Useful idiographic methods include document analyses (such as of diaries), interviews, behavioral observations, and flexible self-reports such as Q-sorts. Using these methods, different people can be described differently, rather than in terms of the same few dimensions.

Allport conceived personal dispositions in terms of a person's goals, motives, or styles; he called it a **nuclear quality**. A Justin Bieber or a Bono (Paul Hewson) has a style that is quite distinctive. Or, consider the complex personality of an artist like Picasso, whose unique personality is revealed through his expressive style. This is a complex personality that can be and has been studied in depth, but not in terms of common traits. Thus, for Allport (1961), a **personal disposition** is a trait—a generalized neuropsychic structure—that is peculiar to the individual.

Personal dispositions that exert an overwhelming influence on behavior are termed **cardinal dispositions** (or ruling passions of a life). Allport gives examples such as Albert Schweitzer's reverence for life, realized in his total devotion to missionary doctoring, or the Marquis de Sade's sexual cruelty, realized in his consuming sexual passions. For the bomber described at the beginning of this chapter, the cardinal disposition might be a compulsion toward control over a certain self-appearance or worldview, coupled with an immense frustration and insecurity that led to the painstakingly planned violence. Usually, however, personality is organized around several **central dispositions**, fundamental qualities that can succinctly portray an individual. For example, central dispositions are qualities that a professor would mention in writing a letter of recommendation for a student.

The idea that each individual has some organization of personality that is unique is troubling to some quantitatively oriented psychologists. If each person is unique, we cannot validly assess each person on the same dimensions, and, so the argument goes, we cannot uncover basic laws of personality. Plus, what a headache the study of personality will be if we cannot administer the same personality tests to everyone, but must tailor them to the individual!

Allport's response to such criticisms was not to dismiss nomothetic searches for common traits (seeking general laws for all persons) as futile. He said only that such efforts are incomplete. From a biological perspective, Allport has a good point: Modern biology recognizes the unique variations of each individual. The artistic vision of Picasso cannot be placed in the same framework as the vision of most people. And from a psychological perspective, no two people share the same upbringing and experiences. Allport thus sees great value in the in-depth psychological study of the individual.

It is an empirical question as to whether Allport is correct about the need for an idiographic approach—the need to assume personal dispositions. If Allport is wrong, then evidence will eventually demonstrate that everyone can be fully described in terms of a set of common traits. But don't underestimate the dangers of *assuming* that personal dispositions can be ignored. Researchers who rely only on common traits may assume that a single test can be used in all cultures or subcultures. This assumption has, in the past, repeatedly been proven wrong, as exemplars of the dominant culture (European White males) have been used as the standard by which to evaluate others. Interestingly, an early personality text by Ross Stagner (1937) that gave significant emphasis to the social and cultural aspects of personality has been

Nuclear Quality
Gordon Allport's term for describing personal dispositions in terms of a person's unique goals, motives, or styles

Personal Disposition
A term used by Gordon Allport to describe a trait that is peculiar to an individual

Cardinal Dispositions
A term used by Gordon Allport to describe personal dispositions that exert an overwhelming influence on behavior

Central Dispositions
A term used by Gordon Allport to describe the several personal dispositions around which personality is organized

Why Does It Matter?

Gordon Allport emphasized the complex uniqueness of each individual and acknowledged that behavior varies across situations; but he still believed that an individual has a stable personality that can be understood and scientifically studied. His approach helped point researchers to today's understanding that personality can be distinctive and somewhat variable but still very useful for studying and understanding people.

Big Five
The trait approach to personality that is supported by a great deal of research and suggests personality can be captured in five dimensions: Extroversion, Agreeableness, Conscientiousness, Neuroticism, and Openness

Extroversion (Big Five)
The personality dimension that includes enthusiasm, dominance, and sociability; people low on this dimension are considered introverted

Agreeableness (Big Five)
The personality dimension that includes friendliness, cooperation, and warmth; people low in this dimension are cold, quarrelsome, and unkind

Conscientiousness (Big Five)
The personality dimension that includes dependability, cautiousness, organization, and responsibility; people low in this dimension are impulsive, careless, disorderly, and undependable

Neuroticism (Big Five)
The personality dimension that includes nervousness, tension, and anxiety; people low in this dimension are emotionally stable, calm, and contented

Openness (Big Five)
The personality dimension that includes imagination, wit, originality, and creativity; people low on this dimension are shallow, plain, and simple

mostly ignored until recently. Allport did not make such ethnocentric mistakes. An approach to personality that is too ready to discard idiographic approaches may also be an approach that misses important unique information about women, about elderly people, and about people from different religions, cultures, and ethnic groups.

With these caveats from Allport in mind, we now turn our attention to the most successful modern efforts to establish a useful nomothetic scheme—the factor analytic search for common traits.

A Contemporary Trait Approach: The Big Five

One of the most remarkable but controversial developments in the trait approach to personality has been the emergence of a high degree of agreement about an adequate dimension scheme—one based on five dimensions. Starting in the 1960s but accelerating since then, a vast body of research has converged on the idea that most common trait approaches to personality can be captured by five dimensions. Listed below, they have come to be called the **Big Five**:

Extroversion (also called surgency): Extroverted people tend to be energetic, enthusiastic, dominant, sociable, and talkative. Introverted people tend to be shy, retiring, submissive, and quiet.

Agreeableness: Agreeable people are friendly, cooperative, trusting, and warm. People low on this dimension are cold, quarrelsome, and unkind.

Conscientiousness (also called lack of impulsivity): Conscientious people are generally cautious, dependable, persevering, organized, and responsible. Impulsive people tend to be careless, disorderly, and undependable. Early research in personality called this dimension Will.

Neuroticism (also called emotional instability): Neurotic people tend to be nervous, high-strung, tense, moody, and worrying. Emotionally stable people are calm and contented.

Openness (also called Openness to experience, culture, or intellect): Open people generally appear imaginative, witty, original, and artistic. People low on this dimension are shallow, plain, or simple.

How Was the Big Five Model Developed?

This model emerged from extensive factor analyses of the adjectives used to describe personality and from equally extensive factor analyses of various personality tests and scales (Goldberg, 1990; John, 1990; McCrae & Costa, 1985; Norman, 1963). Note that the Big Five approach to personality is mostly research-driven, rather than theory-based. It is an inductive approach to personality, which means that the theory emerges from the data.

■ Self-Understanding

Assessing Yourself on the Big Five

Ten-Item Personality Inventory (TIPI)

Here are a number of personality traits that may or may not apply to you. Please write a number next to each statement to indicate the extent to which you agree or disagree with that statement. You should rate the extent to which the pair of traits applies to you, even if one characteristic applies more strongly than the other.

1 = Disagree strongly 2 = Disagree moderately 3 = Disagree a little
4 = Neither agree nor disagree 5 = Agree a little
6 = Agree moderately 7 = Agree strongly

I see myself as:

_____ 1. Extroverted, enthusiastic.

_____ 2. Critical, quarrelsome.

_____ 3. Dependable, self-disciplined.

_____ 4. Anxious, easily upset.

_____ 5. Open to new experiences, complex.

_____ 6. Reserved, quiet.

_____ 7. Sympathetic, warm.

_____ 8. Disorganized, careless.

_____ 9. Calm, emotionally stable.

_____ 10. Conventional, uncreative.

After completing the inventory about yourself, do it again about a classmate, and have the classmate rate himself/herself and rate you. Then calculate the scores for each test.

TIPI scale scoring ("R" denotes reverse-scored items—invert ratings of these items before adding to the other rating for that characteristic):

Extraversion: 1, 6R

Agreeableness: 2R, 7

Conscientiousness; 3, 8R

Emotional Stability: 4R, 9

Openness to Experiences: 5, 10R

See how your classmate rated himself or herself and how she or he rated you. Average scores for college students are Extroversion 4.40, Agreeableness 5.23, Conscientiousness 5.40, Emotional Stability 4.83, and Openness 5.38.

As noted, factor analysis is possible because certain characteristics are associated (correlated) with each other. For example, people who are outgoing also tend to talk more than average, and they also tend to be more sociable. The statistical analysis, therefore, takes apart the scores on each characteristic and places the commonality into an underlying (shared) dimensional score. In this way, it reduces the observed characteristics into a smaller number of dimensions (the *factors*). So, if someone scores high on the statistical dimension we label Extroversion, we know that this person probably tends to be outgoing, talkative, and sociable. Of course, in this example, in reducing these three characteristics to one dimension, we usually lose some information, and some people do not fit the pattern as well as others; but, overall, we gain simplicity and parsimony (economy).

Are the Big Five traits really there? Can these traits be confirmed in some way other than through analyses of language-based ratings? Dimensions that emerge from a factor analysis or other clustering techniques do not necessarily represent real entities. If we mathematically cluster a number of masculine and feminine characteristics (such as dominant, aggressive, tough, tender, nurturing, feminine), we find evidence for two dimensions—male–like and female–like. These are, of course, "real" categories; that is, we can find biological counterparts to the clusters—men and women. If we cluster personality characteristics, can analogous biological characteristics be found? Allport points out that at one time, the atom—the smallest component of an element—was merely a hypothetical construct. But the development of new theories and new measuring instruments then proved the atom's existence, its "reality." There can be hypothetical constructs that represent something that is really there, even if we are not yet sure exactly what that "something" is. Many researchers believe that the biologically based origins of the Big Five will eventually be found.

On the other hand, the Big Five dimensions derive mostly from lexical approaches to traits. In other words, people (either naïve raters or professional psychologists) have described and tested and categorized others, and these ratings have been reduced to five dimensions. The problem with this is that the raters may be wrong. Raters can be wrong in two ways. First, they can see things that are not really there. It may be that people are prone to see other people in terms of five dimensions. This type of biasing tendency is sometimes called **implicit personality theory**. It means that there are consistencies (and biases) in how we see things, particularly other people's personalities. We may erroneously tend to see certain traits as going together. Just as stereotypes bias our perceptions of an out-group, implicit personality theories may bias our perceptions of others. If this is the case, then factor analyses may be capturing the implicit personality theories rather than the basic dimensions of personality.

Second, raters can be wrong by missing (not seeing) things that are really there. Even the best scientists viewed our world as three-dimensional until Einstein showed mathematically that time is a fourth dimension, continuous with the other three. Everyone thought we lived in a three-dimensional world, but everyone was wrong. Analogously, perhaps observers of personality are wrong, missing a key aspect of others' patterns of responding.

How can these issues be resolved? There is now good reason to believe that at least some basic trait dimensions really do exist; perhaps 3, perhaps 16, but most probably 5 or so dimensions. Research using behavioral genetic and other biological

Implicit Personality Theory

A type of biasing tendency for people, perhaps erroneously, to see certain traits as going together and to perceive consistencies when viewing the personalities of others

approaches confirms that it makes sense to say there is biological evidence for a small number of dimensions, although somewhat greater or lesser numbers of basic dimensions are not precluded by these analyses (Borkenau, Riemann, Angleitner, & Spinath, et al., 2001; Carver & Connor-Smith, 2010; Loehlin, 1992). For example, regardless of whether extroversion will eventually be understood in terms of a responsivity of the nervous system, a genetically programmed orientation, a developed pattern of behavior, or even as a compound product of several other elements, there seems little doubt that there is great value in seeing the construct as representing something that is probably real in a biological sense. Certainly, we can point to real individuals who seem to exemplify an end point of each of the dimensions (see Figure 1).

Cross-cultural research confirms the utility of five or so dimensions, as does research in populations of young and old, educated and uneducated (McCrae & John, 1992). If the Big Five dimensions were the result of some sort of biasing stereotypes, then they would not replicate in other cultures. So far at least, the scheme seems to work quite well throughout the world (Allik & McCrae, 2004; McCrae & Costa, 1997b; McCrae et al., 2004). Some studies in non-English-speaking cultures find evidence for a spirituality dimension or an honesty-humility dimension that includes sincerity, fairness, modesty, and greed avoidance (Ashton & Lee, 2007). This approach is not merely adding a sixth factor, but rather is attending more to issues of a person's tendency toward antagonism and psychopathology, also a concern of Hans Eysenck's third factor called psychoticism (see the following discussion of Eysenck).

Cross-cultural research also yields warnings about uncritical usage of the Big Five dimensions of personality. Although many cultures recognize that people vary along such dimensions, cultures differ markedly in how much they value each trait. A good example concerns pressures toward competition versus cooperation— striving independently for success versus helping others. Comparisons between Mexicans and Americans, and between Mexican Americans and European Americans, have shown fascinating differences. Americans (and Euro-Americans) are expected to compete, to dominate, to win. Mexican (and Mexican American) culture, on the other hand, prizes trust, cooperation, and helping one's peers. These preferential differences can have important implications, such as in the classroom. Should we continue the traditional American practice of encouraging competition in the classroom, in which students compete for the highest grades? Or, should we strive to develop more cooperative learning environments, in which children must help one another to learn? Such issues remind us that individual differences in traits do not develop or have their effects outside a specific cultural context; culture is always relevant (Aronson, 1978; Kagan & Madsen, 1972).

Would subcultural influences also be observable? For example, does personality vary in different states or regions of the United States? One study used the Internet to collect personality information on over half a million Americans (Rentfrow, Gosling, & Potter, 2008). North Dakotans were very sociable and friendly but less anxious and imaginative than people in other states. New Yorkers were much less agreeable than average but much more neurotic and creative. In general, the Great Plains, Midwest, and Southeast are high in Extroversion but the East Coast and Northwest are low in Extroversion. Openness is high in the Northeast and the West Coast, but low in the Midwest. The Eastern third of the country is much more

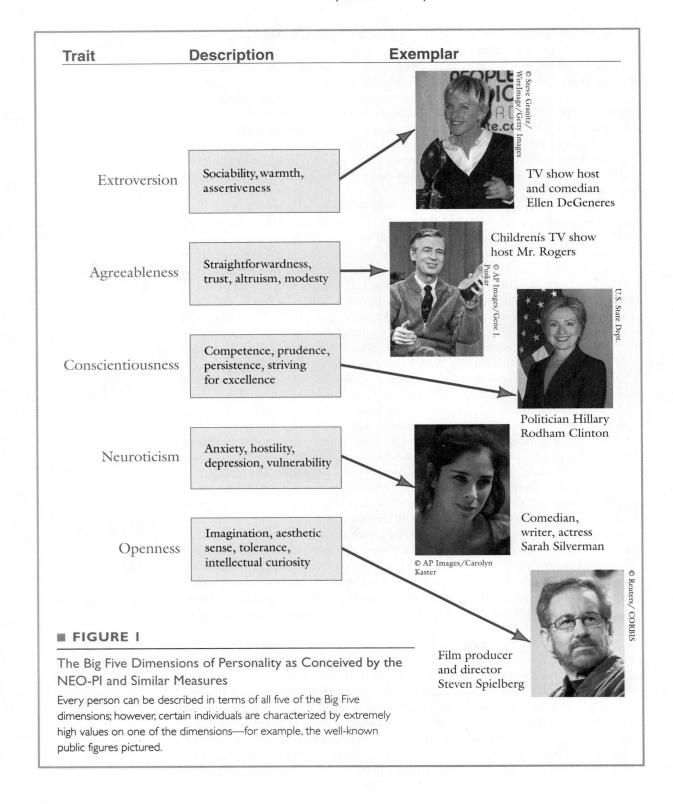

Trait	Description	Exemplar

Extroversion — Sociability, warmth, assertiveness → TV show host and comedian Ellen DeGeneres *© Steve Granitz/ WireImage/Getty Images*

Agreeableness — Straightforwardness, trust, altruism, modesty → Children's TV show host Mr. Rogers *© AP Images/Gene J. Puskar*

Conscientiousness — Competence, prudence, persistence, striving for excellence → Politician Hillary Rodham Clinton *U.S. State Dept.*

Neuroticism — Anxiety, hostility, depression, vulnerability → Comedian, writer, actress Sarah Silverman *© AP Images/Carolyn Kaster*

Openness — Imagination, aesthetic sense, tolerance, intellectual curiosity → Film producer and director Steven Spielberg *© Reuters/ CORBIS*

■ **FIGURE 1**

The Big Five Dimensions of Personality as Conceived by the NEO-PI and Similar Measures

Every person can be described in terms of all five of the Big Five dimensions; however, certain individuals are characterized by extremely high values on one of the dimensions—for example, the well-known public figures pictured.

neurotic than the West. Knowing these differences can spur an analysis of geographic differences in artistic accomplishment, crime, religiosity, health, and so on. The states highest and lowest on each Big Five trait are shown in Table 2.

Career Pathways and Other Important Outcomes

Do the Big Five factors have useful applications in understanding people's career paths? Extroverts, with their enjoyment of others, boldness, energy, ambition, and, yes, big mouths, tend to be successful as politicians or other high-visibility leaders.

■ **TABLE 2** Geographic Variation in Personality among States in the U.S.

HIGHEST	LOWEST
Extroversion	
North Dakota	Maryland
Wisconsin	New Hampshire
Nebraska	Alaska
Agreeableness	
North Dakota	Alaska
Minnesota	Nevada
Mississippi	Wyoming
Conscientiousness	
New Mexico	Alaska
North Carolina	Maine
Georgia	Hawaii
Neuroticism	
West Virginia	Utah
Rhode Island	Colorado
New York	South Dakota
Openness	
New York	North Dakota
Oregon	Wyoming
Massachusetts	Alaska

Note: Data from Rentfrow, Gosling, & Potter, 2008

People scoring high on Conscientiousness seem to do well at work, especially in corporate settings. Their persistence, responsibility, and strong sense of purpose help them accomplish goals and secure their bosses' admiration. They also do well in college (Barrick & Mount, 1991; Martin, Montgomery & Saphian, 2006; O'Connor & Paunonen, 2007; Wagerman & Funder, 2007).

Comparisons of entrepreneurs and managers suggest that entrepreneurs tend to be higher on Conscientiousness and Openness, and lower on Neuroticism; that is, entrepreneurs have an especially high achievement motivation, an innovative orientation, and are more resilient to stress (Zhao & Seibert, 2006). People high on Agreeableness are likely to be altruistic, involved in helping others (Graziano & Eisenberg, 1997; Roccas, Sagiv, Schwartz, & Knafo, 2002). They may be fine leaders of nonprofit organizations, members of the clergy, or perhaps good moms and dads.

Neurotics, who may be anxious, tense, and fretful, can move in one of two main directions—either channeling their worrying into a kind of compulsive success or else letting their anxiety lead them into recklessness. You probably know both kinds

Famous Personalities

Madonna

Sensuous, eccentric, frank, proud, creative. Men find her erotic, yet many women have admired her unique style as a strong female figure. "Who's that girl?" It's Madonna.

With her records, videos, concert tours, movies, flames (both male and female), marriages, motherhood, and children's books, she has been on the cover of almost every magazine, from *Time* to *Penthouse*. As a feminist, she emphasizes the importance of being attractive, sensual, energetic, ambitious, aggressive, and humorous. Although known for controversial videos that explicitly display messages about sex, race, and religion, her concerts are just as controversial; her choreography has included rubbing her female endowments and masturbating. Taking an active role in political issues such as the rights of gay people and support for AIDS research, this opinionated woman openly criticized Catholicism as disgusting and hypocritical. Is there one dimension or a few traits that could accurately capture her personality?

Jung might have seen aspects of introversion because of the importance to Madonna of dealing with feelings, intuitions, and experiences. On the other hand, she is also realistic and thinking, aggressively standing up for her own discontents and unashamed to speak her mind in a variety of controversial arenas. So, Jung might have seen her as having strong extroverted tendencies as well.

Modern trait psychologists, using the Big Five personality dimensions, would describe Madonna as highly extroverted because of her frequent displays of energy and the active enthusiasm that fuels her dominant, social, and talkative characteristics. Indeed, it takes stamina to tour the world performing theatrical concerts, staging dance routines, releasing hit albums, starting a record label, and on and on. Her imagination, aesthetic sense, and curiosity would also qualify her as very high on Openness. Yet Extroversion and Openness do not fully capture her personality. Although she strives for excellence, her vanity and her willingness to throw caution to the wind show her as initially low on Conscientiousness, but gradually increasing on this trait, as most adults do.

Perhaps we should look to Eysenck's work. He also would label Madonna as an extrovert, based on the insensitivity of her nervous system. Because Madonna surrounds herself with people and engages in activities that constantly promote stimulation and draw attention, she reveals that her nervous system inherently is not very sensitive and is seeking arousal from the outside.

Could we say her personal dispositions are centered about exploration and expression of sexuality? Featured in *Penthouse*, Madonna harbors no inhibitions or insecurities about who she is as a female. When dressed, she's been noted for wearing conical shaped brassieres, pink

of people. Note also that although extroverts may perform risky behaviors, it is to increase positive rewards and experiences; neurotics, however, engage in risky, reckless behavior such as alcohol abuse in an attempt to cope with their negative moods (Cooper, Agocha, & Sheldon, 2000).

People high on Openness tend to be creative and to value aesthetic and intellectual pursuits, and because they seek a wide range of experience, they may be artists or writers (McCrae & Costa, 1997a). (Of course, because people are thought to vary on all five dimensions, such an illustration is only a useful example.) Overall, personality traits can predict a variety of important outcomes, including spiritual health, physical health, longevity, empathy, altruism and even relationship quality (Ozer & Benet-Martínez, 2006; Roberts, Kuncel, Shiner, Caspi, & Goldberg, 2007). Importantly, the magnitude of the associations of personality with these life incomes is comparable to the well-known effects of intelligence and socioeconomic status.

© Vadim Ghirda/AP Wide World

girdles, men's pin-striped suits, and boxers. Her videos also usually feature a masculine figure whom she lusts for, or who lusts for her. Because this nuclear quality influences much of her behavior, it can be seen as a cardinal disposition. But that simple summary does not seem to do her justice. It appears that a richer analysis of motives is in order.

Perhaps she fears being left alone and therefore situates herself so that she is always surrounded by people—motivated by strong needs for sex, for power, for affiliation. She comments, "Power is a great aphrodisiac." In every situation she is the center of attention and her word is treated as law. She is off the scale on Murray's notion of exhibition—a need to perform and be the center of attention. Madonna's expressive style is a key to her personality. Yet she continually reinvents her public persona, intriguing her multitudes of fans and remaining the best-selling female rock star ever.

■ Singer/actress Madonna. Whether theorizing in terms of traits, dimensions, motives, needs, types, personal strivings, or expressive style, personality psychologists seek a systematic description of what makes each person unique. Individuals who represent extreme points on the aspects being measured can illustrate a theory—or challenge it.

As noted for entrepreneurs, many times it is helpful to understand *combinations* of personality traits to best predict outcomes. For example, people low on conscientiousness and high on neuroticism are especially likely to smoke and be unhealthy (Kern, Martin, & Friedman, 2010; Terracciano & Costa, 2004). Similarly, individuals low on conscientiousness and high on extroversion are especially likely to drink alcohol, especially if they have access to drinking peer groups (Friedman & Martin, 2011; Hong & Paunonen, 2009).

More Than Five? Fewer Than Five?

In the view of Allport and others, certainly more than five trait dimensions are needed to characterize each individual—that is, when an idiographic approach is taken. The Big Five are meant to be used in nomothetic analyses—that is, when the same dimensions are applied across individuals. But are five dimensions enough for summarizing common traits? This question cannot yet be answered. The reason, again, is that there is no compelling and comprehensive theory that explains why five dimensions are sufficient to capture what we need to know when comparing and contrasting individuals.

What might such a theory look like? It might be derived from new knowledge of brain biology; for example, perhaps five distinct kinds of biological responding might be identified. Or it might be derived from a functional analysis of evolutionary pressures on survival; for example, perhaps five sorts of skills—such as bonding with others, or finding resources—may be key to what it means to be a human being. Relatedly, however, it may have been most useful (in an evolutionary sense) for people to be able to ascertain these five dimensions in others. It can be argued that we need to know who will cooperate with us (i.e., be agreeable), who is going to be a successful leader (i.e., be extroverted), and who is going to be dependable (i.e., be conscientious) (Buss, 1995a). Therefore, people may have evolved an ability to detect and understand these individual differences in others.

Despite progress in understanding the Big Five, Cattell continued to assert that 16 general personality factors are essential. Cattell was impatient with psychologists who did not accept his scheme, frustrated that psychologists do not, he says, want to remember 16 things at the same time (Cattell, 1990). Cattell himself also turned his attention to motives and interests. He believed that a psychometric approach should be used to analyze instinctive drives—sex, fear, assertion, self-protection—and attachments such as love of home, or spouse, or job. Importantly, Cattell also urges analysis of changes over time. For example, does getting

CHANGING Personality

Many people wonder how they can change their personality to be more extroverted and less neurotic. Even more, they wonder how they can change their partner (significant other) to be more honest, caring, and agreeable. The trait approach views personality as an emotional temperament (Allport's "psychophysical system") organized by socialization into stable, characteristic thoughts and action patterns—that is, traits (Rothbart, 2007). So the trait approach will not look to introspection, dream analysis, medication, cognitive therapy, nor programmed reinforcement to change personality. Instead, traits can best be changed, slowly over time, through experiences that develop our old predispositions into new directions. What are some good ways to do this? How can a person be re-socialized? One powerful example is readily available to college students, even if they don't realize it—namely, going to college. College students often change quite a bit as compared to their high school friends who didn't go to college or who went to a very different kind of college. The same is true later in life. The jobs you choose, the organizations you join, and the friends you have will develop your inclinations in new directions. If you are studious but too shy and timid, do you think your personality will improve if you become a physician or a computer engineer? If you join a meditation group or a singing chorale? What if your partner is extroverted but much too assertive and self-centered—do you think he or she would become more humble by moving to Salt Lake City and becoming a minister or by moving to Hollywood and working in television? By working in education or by entering elective politics?

married tend to change the conscientiousness factor of personality in systematic ways, making one more conscientious? How is this transformation best represented mathematically? By turning attention beyond fixed traits located within the individual, and toward everyday motives, interests, and behaviors, personality researchers are now pointing to the complexity of human personality and to the necessity of considering the broader context of personality.

Interestingly, even proponents of the Big Five approach to personality generally find it expedient to turn to additional trait descriptions to describe personality fully. (They do this even when talking about common traits.) Sometimes these are called subfactors or **facets**, but they all involve a further elaboration of the Big Five model (Block, 2001). For example, anxiety and depression are closely related aspects of Neuroticism, but clinicians treating anxiety disorders and depressive disorders find the distinction to be a very significant one. In fact, different psychotropic drugs may be prescribed to treat the two conditions— for example, Valium for anxiety and Prozac for depression. The fact that these drugs act in different ways in the brain suggests that Neuroticism may prove to be too broad a factor. But if anxiety and depression turn out to be two variants of what can go wrong with the same underlying neurological system, then the superordinate category Neuroticism may prove correct after all.

■ Your credit card company may know almost everything about what you purchase. Can this be used to measure your traits and predict your future behavior, including your risk of defaulting on your payments? Can you tell something about the personality of someone who buys birdseed to help out starving birds in the winter? Many businesses seem to think that you can (Duhigg, 2009; Zhao, Zhao, & Song, 2009).

Facet
Within the Big Five trait approach, the component characteristics (also sometimes called subfactors) that underlie each of the Big Five factors

Eysenck's Big Three and Related Alternatives

Could there be fewer than five basic dimensions of personality? It might be that two or three of the Big Five trait dimensions are a core part of the organism, with the other two or three merely derivatives; that is, perhaps biological factors predispose a person to behave in one of three basic types of ways, but that these can be clearly subdivided. For example, the basic extroverted individual could then be further categorized in terms of activity level, sociability, and excitability. This is the position of Hans Eysenck.

Eysenck was born in Germany in 1916 and fled to England in 1934, where he was long an important voice in psychology. He died in 1997. Relying on his biological approach, Eysenck believed that fewer than five basic dimensions are the basis of personality. Rather, he proposed that all other traits derive from three biological systems.

Whereas Cattell believed that personality theory should be the criterion for selecting the variables—that is, the data—to be used in factor analyses, and whereas many Big Five researchers take a fully inductive approach, Eysenck goes further and believes that various other sorts of evidence should also guide the selection of the factors (Eysenck, 1994; Eysenck & Eysenck, 1985), that factor analyses alone

SHARPEN YOUR THINKING | Current Controversy

Should Political Candidates Reveal Their Big Five Profiles?

When candidates run for public office, it is common for them to release information about their recent income tax returns and wealth profiles, along with information about their physical health profiles. The information provided allows the voting public to form some idea about how the candidate conducts her or his financial life, and to have confidence that there is no hidden medical problem that might interfere with the candidate carrying out the duties of office, if elected. Is there an equally compelling need for the public to have information from a candidate's personality test? Traditionally, psychological testing has not been part of the normal public disclosure process, but might that be helpful?

There are many reasons why a candidate's results on a Big Five test (or other personality inventory) might be deemed unhelpful. First of all, knowing that the test results would become public, the candidate could respond in a manner that would misrepresent his or her real beliefs and preferences—this would certainly be a situation in which there would be a strong incentive for positive self-presentation. The candidate could be presenting a false persona to the public through manipulated test results. On the other hand, this same criticism seems applicable to the medical and financial reports as well—the desire for positive self-presentation could well influence those measures just as much as it would influence the personality test results. Yet the public still has an expectation that the financial and medical disclosures will be made. Are personality test results really more subject to manipulation?

Another possible criticism of the disclosure of personality test results is that most members of the electorate are not in a good position to interpret or evaluate this information. Again, is it really any different for financial or medical disclosures?

Including personality tests among the expected disclosures would be useful only to the extent that a candidate's Big Five profile gives the voters information about the candidate that would be useful in deciding how to vote. In evaluating a candidate, the voter often wants to know whether the candidate can be trusted to act in the public interest rather than for private gain. Could that be captured at all by the Conscientiousness and Agreeableness factors? The voter wants a candidate who will find new ways to solve persistent problems. Would high Openness be a desirable characteristic, or would we prefer inflexible commitment to a cause? The voter wants a candidate who will be able to work productively with others who hold differing views on an issue. Do low neuroticism and high extroversion make for a better leader?

Currently, we do not expect candidates to reveal personality test results. But might the public be administering its own version of a personality test? Candidates are expected to state their positions on current public issues, to justify their past actions, to predict (or promise) their future actions, to interact with one another in debates, to respond to tough interviewing by the media, and to have their spouses and children put on view. Could this kind of intensive examination provide much of the same information that would be provided by a personality test?

Extroversion (Eysenck) In Hans Eysenck's biologically based theory, the term is used to describe the characteristic of being generally sociable, active, and outgoing; extroverts are thought to have a relatively lower level of brain arousal and thus tend to seek stimulation

should not guide our structuring of the basic dimensions. For example, there is evidence that people's tendencies on at least several characteristics—anxiety level, friendliness, self-esteem, and openness to new experiences—generally remain fairly stable throughout adult life (Costa & McCrae, 1987a; Trzesniewski, Donnellan, & Robins, 2003). If you are calm and outgoing at age 25, you will probably not be crotchety and nervous and dogmatic at age 60. However, people do tend to become more conscientious and somewhat more agreeable as they age (Helson, Kwan, John, & Jones, 2002; Srivastava, John, Gosling, & Potter, 2003).

The first dimension of personality, according to Eysenck, is **extroversion**. It includes Cattell's factors of outgoingness and assertiveness. The second is **neuroticism**; this dimension includes Cattell's factors of emotional instability and apprehensiveness. The third factor is **psychoticism**—a tendency toward psychopathology, involving impulsivity and cruelty. Psychoticism includes Cattell's factors of tough-mindedness and shrewdness. In terms of the Big Five, Eysenck's psychoticism involves low Agreeableness and low Conscientiousness; his extroversion and neuroticism dimensions are similar to those of the Big Five. Eysenck does not directly account for the Openness factor, and indeed, Openness is the least defined and most murky Big Five factor, both theoretically and statistically.

Eysenck's approach (along with the related work of Jeffrey Gray) is one of the few to endeavor to take into account the biological bases of personality (what Allport termed its "psychophysical" aspects), personality theory, and evidence arising from rigorous empirical and statistical analyses of traits. Interestingly, Eysenck's parents were actors and he himself became an extremely passionate and outspoken psychologist and intellectual, often at the center of intellectual controversy. Thus, it is not surprising for Eysenck to ask such intriguing questions as whether extroversion runs in families.

© Thinkstock

■ Recent evidence on the biological aspects of traits suggests that extroverts are attracted to parties primarily because of the potential for good times and positive rewards, but not because they like other people more than introverts do.

Evidence for Eysenck's Approach

Are there three core trait dimensions? One study examined self-reported traits as well as related emotions and motivations (Zuckerman, Joireman, Kraft, & Kuhlman, 1999). People who were sensitive to signals of punishment were high on neuroticism. People who were sensitive to signals of reward were high on the extroversion factor. People who were basically hostile, cynical, and unhappy scored high on psychoticism. Such high psychoticism individuals are not well integrated into social norms of work, family, and helping others (Lodi-Smith & Roberts, 2007).

Other research along these lines tries to determine whether the essential characteristic of extroversion is the tendency to enjoy social situations (sociability) or a sensitivity to reward seeking and the experience of pleasant emotion (consistent with the postulated biological activation system) (Wilt & Revelle, 2009). One study had introverts and extroverts rate situations that varied as to how social they were and how pleasant they were (Lucas & Diener, 2001). It turned out that extroverts rated social situations more positively than introverts did only when the situations were pleasant. Extroverts also rated nonsocial situations more positively than introverts if the situations were pleasant, again suggesting that the reward (pleasantness) rather than the sociability is more important to extroverts.

Another study (of women only) used functional magnetic resonance imaging (fMRI) to study brain reactivity to positive, pleasant images. This study found that extroverts (but not introverts) showed greater brain activity to these positive stimuli than to negative

Neuroticism (Eysenck) One of Hans Eysenck's three biologically-oriented personality dimensions; it includes emotional instability and apprehensiveness

Psychoticism (Eysenck) This dimension includes a tendency toward psychopathology, involving impulsivity and cruelty, tough-mindedness, and shrewdness

Why Does It Matter?

Why does it matter how many basic trait dimensions there are? First, because knowledge of core dimensions is very helpful in assessing individuals and understanding their likely future paths. Second, because the core dimensions may lead us to better understand the core biosocial nature of who we are and why we vary.

stimuli (Canli et al., 2001; Canli, 2006). Thus, extroversion may indeed be related to biological differences in the brain's reward system. Neuroticism, on the other hand, may be related to brain activity relevant to the detection of perceived unusual situations such as threats (Eisenberger, Gable, & Lieberman, 2007; Eisenberger, Lieberman, & Satpute 2005).

Interestingly, the scores of American college students on extroversion (scales of the Eysenck Personality Inventory and the Eysenck Personality Questionnaire) have been increasing in recent years (Twenge, 2001). This finding is remarkable because extroversion is postulated to be heavily biologically based. Because it is unlikely that the biology of the population is changing in any dramatic, systematic, and relevant way, this finding points to the likelihood that extroversion is a complex combination of biological predispositions, socialization experiences, and societal expectations.

Personality Judgments

Is "love at first sight" merely a lustful attraction, or can we really tell something instantly? What happens when we first see a stranger? Can we make reliable and valid initial judgments about personality or are we usually misled by stereotypes? These questions bear directly on the validity of a trait approach to personality.

Consensus in Personality Judgments

Can observers make accurate judgments about others' personalities—that is, judgments that are confirmed by other testing? Most basically, observers can usually tell whether a stranger is male or female; this gives us a lot of important information about how that person will behave on many dimensions. We can also sometimes judge age, ethnic group, and perhaps ill health; here again we are gathering important information. But what about judging aspects of personality like extroversion or neuroticism?

Suppose we have strangers rate a group of people on a number of trait dimensions. We then factor analyze the ratings, and the factor analysis shows five basic dimensions (the Big Five). How can we be sure that the consistency does not result from cognitive representations in the minds of the raters? Perhaps raters "see" certain traits as naturally occurring together (Passini and Norman, 1966). Perhaps factor analysis detects something about the minds of the raters rather than something about the personalities of those being rated.

Analogously, if the ratings that are used in factor analyses of traits are self-ratings, then a similar problem of inference arises; that is, let us say that a group of people rate themselves on a number of traits, and factor analysis of their self-ratings shows that they can be summarized in terms of five dimensions. The question that arises is whether we have uncovered people's ideas about how their traits can be grouped—that is, their self-images—rather than objective dimensions of their personalities.

Suppose, however, that we have the subjects' peers—friends of the people—rate them on a number of trait dimensions, and this factor analysis also shows five dimensions (the Big Five). Suppose further that the friends' ratings agree with the self-ratings and are more accurate than the strangers' ratings. This would start to indicate valid judgment of personality rather than stereotyped judgments. Just these sorts of studies have been conducted (Funder & Colvin, 1988, 1991; Norman & Goldberg, 1966; Watson, 1989).

When we observe someone with whom we have never interacted—such as a new classmate—we are in a state that has been termed the **zero acquaintance** state (Kenny et al., 1992). As the trait approach predicts, observers do indeed tend to agree in their judgments—there is consensus at zero acquaintance. In other words, consensus among observers is one additional piece of evidence for the reliability of personality. But are observers depending on some stereotype, thus making invalid, inaccurate (though similar) judgments? And which traits are most reliably judged?

Zero Acquaintance
Observation and judgment of someone with whom one has never interacted

Another clever solution to this matter is to use self-ratings, peer ratings, and even add spouse ratings. People's spouses presumably know a lot about their personalities. When this is done, the same Big Five dimensions emerge (McCrae & Costa, 1987). These corroborations are good evidence that the Big Five scheme is valid and is not some kind of artifact. Furthermore, the Big Five factors can be recovered from (found in) Q-sort assessments of personality, as well as in assessments using other traditional self-report measures such as the Myers-Briggs scale and the MMPI (McCrae & Costa, 1989).

A remarkable illustration of the importance of the "visibility" of familial personality (even beyond what personality scientists usually imagine) is the case of Luz Cuevas and her lost daughter, Delimar, who disappeared as an infant after a house fire. Philadelphia authorities thought that the infant had burned to ashes, but her mother never believed it. Six years later, Cuevas was at a children's birthday party and met a young girl. She somehow surmised this girl to be her daughter and pretending the six-year-old girl had gum in her hair, removed several strands. Sure enough, DNA tests confirmed her hunch, and the daughter (who had been kidnapped) was eventually returned to her.

As hinted at above, a final confirmation of validity comes from the fact that trait ratings can be used successfully to predict future behavior and outcomes, especially when coupled with self-report personality measures (Friedman, Kern, & Reynolds, 2010; Friedman & Martin, 2011; Ozer & Benet-Martínez, 2006). For example, conscientious people have better marriages, do better at and are more productive on the job, and stay healthier and live longer. Open individuals are more artistic and more likely to succeed at creative activities. Agreeable persons tend to have good friends, be admired at work, and stay healthy if they follow their inclinations to be altruistic and help others. Neurotic people tend to become worriers and complainers, and may self-medicate with alcohol, but may sometimes be more realistic in the face of challenges. Extroverted people rise to leadership positions, attract romantic interest, and generally feel happy and healthy. All in all, studies keep finding encouraging evidence for the idea of several stable and valid dimensions of personality—although not necessarily five factors precisely. (See the Classic to Current box for further discussion.)

Classic to Current

Human Nature, Five Factors, and the Personality of Personality Psychologists

The historian of science Thomas Kuhn (1962) popularized the idea of paradigms and paradigm shifts in understanding how scientific theories develop and change. The basic idea is that scientific thinking grows and changes, not by a slow, incremental accumulation of knowledge, but by sudden shifts in the way we view the world. For example, the view of physics proposed by Newton was instantly outmoded by the relativity theories of Einstein. The view of health as determined by bodily humors proposed by the ancients, Aristotle and Galen, was replaced by the modern conceptions of anatomy and physiology discovered during the Renaissance. Interestingly, it is often not the case that existing theories are discarded by their proponents in light of new evidence. Rather, a new generation of scientists comes along and enthusiastically adopts the new perspective. It seems to take a fresh mind to reject the conventional wisdom and embrace the new paradigms that discoveries bring. Unfortunately, sometimes new paradigms are wrong, and it is foolish to adopt them.

Similar but smaller paradigm shifts seem to occur in psychology. We emphasize that personality psychology can be used to examine the basis of human nature—what does it mean to be a person? Different psychologists are comfortable with different assumptions and perspectives. These disagreements occur even among personality psychologists who generally accept the value of a trait approach. Currently, major controversies continue to swirl around the validity and utility of a five-factor approach.

Paul Costa Jr., R. R. McCrae, and Lewis Goldberg, for example, are vociferous proponents of the five-factor model. Jack Block doubts the wisdom of this approach. And Hans Eysenck insisted that a three-factor model is much superior (Block, 1995a, 1995b, 2001; Costa & McCrae, 1995a, 1995b; Eysenck, 1992; Goldberg, 2001; Goldberg & Saucier, 1995). How can we decide?

One of Block's (and Eysenck's) major objections to the five-factor approach is that it is grounded in the statistical technique of factor analysis. Simply put, factor analysis reduces or restates the data (usually correlations) that are fed into it. If the data points fed in are not adequate to capture fully the nature of personality, then no amount of analysis or reduction will come up with the "basics." Relatedly, the five-factor approach is usually heavily dependent on language, which may have its own artificial structures, although the five-factor model has been replicated in other languages and some claim it represents a "human universal" (McCrae & Costa, 1997b). Also relevant is the point that there is no strong a priori theoretical reason why there should be 5 (not 3, 4, 16, or whatever) basic factors. (It's not as if someone has discovered the corresponding five basic parts of the brain.)

The other main area of disagreement about the five-factor model involves how well it explains existing data. Does it capture and simplify what we already know about personality? Part of the answer is statistical—in the jargon, this comes out as "unexplained variance." Part of it is conceptual—does it help us in a subtle yet comprehensive manner to be more insightful? In short, can we describe personality well with five factors, or is there a lot of "stuff" left unexplained? Here, much of the argument has the flavor of a discussion about whether the glass is half empty or half full. Is the five-factor model an elegant edifice or an ugly obstruction?

For this paradigm shift to general acceptance of the five-factor approach to personality to occur, the bottom line is really fairly simple: The approach must be able to fully (sufficiently) account for personality in an economical and efficient (parsimonious) way, and it must lead to new research that provides a broader and deeper understanding of personality. Many researchers argue that the five-factor approach is doing just this, but doubters remain unconvinced. We will have to wait and see whether future generations of personality psychologists will feel most comfortable with this approach, believing that it accounts for the most data, fits best with other knowledge, and does so in the most parsimonious and elegant fashion. In the meantime, you might want to explore the advantages and limits of the Big Five in your own studies of the personalities of yourself and others.

FURTHER READING

Block, J. (2001). Millennial contrarianism: The five-factor approach to personality description 5 years later. *Journal of Research in Personality, 35*(1), 98–107.

Goldberg, L. R. (2001). Analyses of Digman's child-personality data: Derivation of Big-Five factor scores from each of six samples. *Journal of Personality, 69*(5), 709–743.

Limits of Trait Conceptions

There is always some danger that we will not be careful in how we use the idea of traits. We might underestimate the role of other aspects of personality and the role of the social situation. We might overlook the individual's personal dispositions or the fact that basic dimensions do a better job in describing some persons than others. Trait conceptions generally lie in direct contradiction to behaviorist and social learning approaches, which emphasize the environmental causes of patterns of behavior (Costa & McCrae, 1994). Still, when we follow the lead of Gordon Allport (1968) and apply the empirical approach to understanding the person as a whole (as a Gestalt), we can indeed succeed in achieving a significantly greater understanding of what it means to be a person.

Do professional profilers of criminals at the FBI do even better? One study compared professional profilers to other detectives, psychologists, and college students (Pinizzotto & Finkel, 1990). When presented with actual materials from a sex crime case, the professional profilers were indeed more accurate and comprehensive, but the experienced police detectives and the psychologists also did quite well. Only the college students did poorly. At the least, this and related studies suggest that experience in studying personality and motivation can lead to some documentable improvements and successes, but the optimal way to proceed is as yet unknown.

Types

Should we divide people into certain categories or classes, rather than rate them along trait dimensions? For example, it is easy to distinguish men from women, or preadolescents from sexually mature adults. In discussions of personality, these categories or classes are termed **types**. When discussing psychoanalysis, we mention the Freudian idea of an anal character type, who is stingy. In our discussions of the biological aspects of personality, Sheldon's theory of body types (somatotypes) is considered.

The idea of types is that there are discrete classes of people. Boundaries between classes are usually not so clear-cut, however, when we are dealing with psychological characteristics (Costa, Herbst, McCrae, Samuels, & Ozer, 2002; McCrae, Terracciano, Costa, & Ozer, 2006). Categories such as extroversion and introversion are broad, but no one is completely introverted or completely extroverted. Rather, it is a matter of degree. Theories of personality that include distinct types are usually just the first step on the way to a more complete understanding of traits. Nevertheless, type theories may be useful in providing ideals or models of personality to which real people can be compared (Allport, 1961; Asendorpf, 2006; Asendorpf & Denissen, 2006).

Might there indeed be certain ways in which people are categorically different and do not fall along a continuum? That is, are some personality differences not just a matter of degree—with qualitative (not just quantitative) differences? Rather than make blanket assertions about type theories at this time, it is prudent to examine each such theory as it is proposed (Vollrath & Torgersen, 2008).

Types
A theoretical approach to personality in which people are divided into discrete categories or classes as opposed to being placed along a continuum

Motives

Motives
Internal psychobiological forces that induce behavior towards a goal or push for expression

Closely related to traits, but distinct from them, are motives. **Motives** are internal psychobiological forces that help induce particular behavior patterns toward a goal. The concept of motives captures the idea that there are forces within the human organism pushing for expression—needs for food, for play, for pleasure, and so on. In some sense motives are more basic than traits because motives can be seen as underlying traits.

Consider the case of explaining why Linda goes to lots of parties with her friends. A trait explanation might find she is very high on agreeableness and extroversion—she is friendly, cooperative, and warm. This might be a good summary, useful in predicting other aspects of Linda's life. But what if we explain Linda's party-going in terms of a fear of being left alone, or a high sex drive, or a desire for happiness, or a need to be around people? These latter explanations are motivational—they involve a goal. Needs, drives, and emotions are all related to motives. The concept of a motive has the advantage of taking into account the emotional dynamism of a person (Schultheiss, Kordik, Kullmann, Rawolle, & Rösch, 2009). At the same time, it has the significant danger of being imprecise.

Need
Term used by Henry Murray to describe a readiness to respond in a certain way under given conditions

Henry Murray, a founder of the motive-based study of personality, used the term **need** to refer to a readiness to respond in a certain way under given conditions (Murray, 1962). Basic needs include needs for achievement, affiliation, dominance, and exhibition. Murray's sophisticated approach is heavily dependent on the social situation and so we consider it, in our focus on person-by-situation interactionist approaches to personality.

Some of the most modern approaches to personality use the concept of "motives" to understand personality but are more modest in their scope. For example, we might analyze a specific set of goals or "life tasks" such as doing well in school (Cantor, Norem, Niedenthal, Langston, & Brower, 1987). Many college students see this as a key motivation in their lives. But note that this life task is not a vast and complex trait like extroversion. Rather, it helps us understand specific behaviors and consistencies in college-related situations.

Need for Achievement (n Ach), Need for Affiliation (n Aff), and Need for Power (n Power)

Need for Achievement (n Ach)
According to Henry Murray, the need to succeed on tasks that are set out by society

In America, where people's identities are closely tied to their success, it is not surprising that there has been tremendous interest in the **need for achievement (n Ach)**.

People with a high need for achievement are persistent and even driven to succeed on tasks that society sets out for them. They enjoy individual challenges and may obtain a string of college degrees or a shelf of awards. They tend to rise to the top in business, especially if quantity is more important than quality, or if shrewdness or persistence can lead to triumph. For example, they may be first-rate stockbrokers or salespeople or entrepreneurs (Brunstein & Heckhausen, 2008; McClelland, 1961; Rauch & Frese, 2007). However, they may be less successful once skills of diplomacy or cooperation become more important to the job.

In the motivational approach to traits, this achievement motivation is usefully contrasted with two other basic needs that have also attracted significant research attention—the need for affiliation and the need for power.

Early in the twentieth century, one of the founders of modern psychology, William McDougall (1908), wrote about a "gregarious" instinct, which causes people to want to come together in groups. McDougall then developed the notion of a "sentiment," which is an instinct that is socialized to be attached to an object. The instinct to seek out other people might become the motivation to have lots of friends. This idea of a motivation to affiliate set in motion a century of research. For example, Henry Murray proposed both a need for affiliation and a need to reject. But it has been the **need for affiliation (n Aff)**—the need to draw near to and win the affection of others—that has attracted the most attention.

People with a high need for affiliation want to come together and spend time with other people. It is an intriguing motive because it prompts people both to have friends and to please their friends (to maintain the friendship). Such people may be extroverted, agreeable, and conscientious: They are extroverted because they seek the stimulation of other people; they are agreeable because they want to act friendly; and they are conscientious because they are dependable. Such a motivational approach thus cuts across a five-factor trait approach (Winter, 1993). With a need, the goal determines the behavior. For example, in this case the goal is to have friends, and the goal can be realized through certain traits, such as agreeableness. Such affiliation may be part of a biologically based means of coping with stress (Taylor & Gonzaga, 2007). On the other hand, a lone bomber with a very low need for affiliation might be unwilling or unable to reach out and have friends and a lover; conflict over a desire to express one's ideas but having no intimate listeners might lead to a violent striking out.

Murray also identified a need for dominance (n Dominance), which has come to be termed **a need for power (n Power)**. People with a high power motivation naturally seek positions and offices that allow or invite them to assert control over others. We all know some people like this: They like to usurp the leadership of small groups, accumulate possessions, and control territory, although they may be quarrelsome and somewhat insecure (Hermann, 2005). Of course, many politicians are high on power motivation, although some are more motivated by achievement; that is, some want to gain credit and status and success (achievement) rather than money and influence (power) (Winter, 1992). An interesting study of the inaugural speeches of American presidents indicated that those scoring high on the need for power were more likely to make important decisions that led to their being viewed as great presidents (Winter, 1987).

■ Could the popular television show *Survivor* be viewed as based on the tension between the needs for affiliation—the need to belong—and the need for power—the need to achieve one's own goals over others? It has been argued that *Survivor* serves a therapeutic function for TV viewers working to reconcile these two needs in their own psyches (Schapiro, 2007).

■ By understanding his colossal need for power (n Power), one can capture the essence of the personality of emperor Napoleon Bonaparte.

Need for Affiliation (n Aff)
According to Henry Murray, the need to draw near to and win the affection of others

Need for Power (n Power)
According to Henry Murray, the need to seek positions and offices in which one can exert control over others

Measuring Motivation

Individual differences in motivations can be assessed by observing behavior across time and situations. This is, however, a difficult and time-consuming process. Is there an easier way to measure motivations? Standardized self-report tests like the Personality Research Form (Jackson & Messick, 1967), which was based in part on Henry Murray's theories of needs, can sometimes do a good job at assessing motives by forced response to short standardized items. In a different sort of self-report approach, personal goals can be assessed by asking people to write about those things that are the focus of their daily efforts.

However, if people are mostly unaware of the needs that are motivating their behaviors, then a subtler approach may sometimes be necessary. Motivational psychologists like John Atkinson (1958), David McClelland (1984), and David Winter (1973) have therefore attempted to use more projective measures—such as Murray's Thematic Apperception Test, or TAT—to measure motivation. For example, a person might be presented with an ambiguous scene in which an attractive man is seen to be pushing ahead of an attractive woman while entering a hotel lobby doorway. If the person explains the scene as an attempt by the man to meet his client and complete a sale he has been pursuing, then this would be classified as indicating high achievement motivation. How we perceive the world around us is influenced by our internal state (see Figure 2).

Need for Exhibition (n Exh)
According to Henry Murray, the need to show one's self before others and to entertain, amuse, shock, and excite others

Need for Exhibition (n Exh)

Another key motive involves the need for emotional communication, which Henry Murray called **need for exhibition**, n Exh. People high on this need want to show themselves before others and amuse, entertain, excite, or even shock others. They are colorful, spellbinding, noticeable, dramatic, and showy. This is usually studied through a focus on their expressive style (Friedman, Prince, et al., 1980).

■ FIGURE 2

Motivation Can Influence Perception

When people are standing on a very high hill that they will have to climb down, the perceived distance to the bottom is influenced by the perceived effort involved (Proffitt, 2006). That is, a deep-seated motivation can affect perceptions and behaviors. Similarly, people tend to see desirable objects (such as a cold bottle of water on a hot day) as physically closer than less desirable objects (Balcetis & Dunning, 2010). That is, we do not see the surrounding world exactly as it really is; instead our perceptions and efforts are distorted. Such findings confirm the importance of dynamic needs and motives to the understanding of traits.

Expressive Style

Mickey Mouse and Donald Duck are not only known but also liked around the world. What makes a cartoon character successful? Walt Disney should know. Disney said that showing individual personality in a cartoon is the key to success.

How can a cartoon character have a personality? Of course it cannot have a real, biologically based personality. But a successful cartoonist, or a successful novelist for that matter, can use intuition to capture distinctive styles of behaving. What is especially interesting about a cartoon character is that much of this information is communicated through expressive style—elements such as vocal characteristics, facial expressions, and body gestures and movements. After just a few minutes of watching Donald Duck in action (and listening to his quackish speech), we know what kind of character he is. A personality test like the 16PF is not necessary.

As Gordon Allport and other personality psychologists have long known, we can similarly gather important information about an individual's personality by observing expressive style. In 1933, Allport and Vernon published a book called *Studies in Expressive Movement*, which was one of the first major works on personality and expressive style. A consummate observer, Allport was not blind to the limits of simple approaches to expressive movement. He did not expect that an individual would always show the same expressive movements. Rather, he felt that there was some underlying consistency in a person's style, and that this would reveal itself in characteristic ways in certain situations. For example, an extrovert would not necessarily gesture expansively when she was feeling nervous. Even so, subsequent research suggests that a noteworthy degree of consistency characterizes an individual's gesturing, body incline, and voice cues, even across interactions with different people (Levesque & Kenny, 1993).

> ## Why Does It Matter?
>
> Given that much of the trait approach to personality uses statistical techniques originally developed for the study of intelligence, it is odd that an ability approach has rarely been taken in the study of personality. Intelligence is the ability to *do* certain things but personality traits have generally been conceived as *being* rather than *doing* something. We believe that it is important to include a focus on styles, motives, and nonverbal social skills when we employ a trait approach to personality.

Emotional Expressiveness

How or why is expressive style related to personality? There is evidence that it is the emotional aspect of expressive behavior (which Allport usually called temperament) that is the key to understanding its ties to certain personality traits (Buck, 1979, 1984; DePaulo & Friedman, 1998; Friedman, 2001; Friedman, DiMatteo, & Taranta, 1980; Friedman, Riggio, & Segall, 1980); that is, an individual likely has typical ways of expressing or inhibiting feelings like anger or joy. Some of this seems to be innate; there are consistencies in inhibited and uninhibited expressive styles that have been first seen in babies and then documented in longitudinal research spanning many years (Kagan, Reznick, Snidman, Gibbons, & Johnson, 1988). Note, however, that personality traits in adulthood are more stable than temperament-based trait development (Roberts & DelVecchio, 2000). This is probably because relatively stable situational and other factors (such as interacting with the same spouse) generally help us maintain a consistency of reactions in adulthood.

Perhaps the most significant individual dimension of style is overall expressiveness. People vary in the intensity, expansiveness, animation, and dynamism of their nonverbal (and verbal) behaviors (e.g., Friedman, Prince, et al., 1980; Gallaher, 1992; Halberstadt, 1991; Manstead, 1991). This expressiveness can be measured and defined as the ease with which people's emotions can be read from their expressive behaviors, even when they are not trying deliberately to communicate their feelings to others. Such people are often uninhibited and charismatic (Friedman, Riggio, et al., 1980; Friedman, Riggio, & Casella, 1988).

Expressive people are often perceived as more attractive than unexpressive people (DePaulo, Blank, Swain, & Hairfield, 1992; Friedman et al., 1988; Larrance & Zuckerman, 1981; Riggio, 1986; Sabatelli & Rubin, 1986); that is, expressiveness makes one seem more attractive. In fact, studies of personal charisma that look at both fixed attractiveness (in photographs) and expressiveness suggest that expressiveness is at least as important as physical attractiveness—and perhaps even more so—in accounting for favorable first impressions (Friedman et al., 1988). Many charismatic and captivating actors would be judged plain and unappealing from photographs; conversely, a positive perception of a striking beauty can be obliterated by the first few minutes of a conversation.

Extroversion is the trait that is most readily seen in expressive style. In other words, extroversion is somehow "behaviorally visible." People who score as extroverted on personality tests look animated when they are observed by others, both friends and strangers (Albright, Kenny, & Malloy, 1988; Borkenau & Liebler, 1993; Cunningham, 1977; Funder & Sneed, 1993; Kenny et al., 1992; Riggio & Friedman, 1986; Scherer, 1978, 1982; Watson, 1989). In fact, not much information is needed by observers in order to make accurate judgments of extroversion (see Figure 3). The judgments are not perfect, but they are reasonable, given the limited information that is available. Other traits of social importance such as affiliation, exhibition, dominance, nurturance, and playfulness also seem to be closely tied to nonverbal expressive cues. Expressive people are more extroverted, dominant, impulsive, playful, and popular. In contrast, more individually oriented characteristics, such as motivations toward achievement, autonomy, order, understanding, and so forth, may be less evident nonverbally (Gifford, 1994).

Sometimes disease intervenes. People with Parkinson's disease often become less expressive as their muscles move less, especially in their facial expressions. A result is that they may be misjudged as less extroverted and more neurotic than they really are, and so their social interactions may be distorted (Tickle-Degnen & Lyons, 2004).

Dominance, Leadership, Influence

Dominant people (like kings on thrones or judges on benches) sit higher, stand taller, talk louder. They are likely to invade the space of others, as when they put their feet up on their desk or your desk. Dominant people also have more expansive gestures, walk at the front of the line or parade, and sit in the first row or at the head table. During interactions, they can interrupt more, control time (as you wait in their waiting room), and can stare at you more if they want, but can also look less if they so

■ **FIGURE 3**

Expressive Style

Some personality traits are associated with characteristics that can be picked up by casual observation. Posture and gestures are visible cues as to whether a person is more extroverted (like the person on the left) or more introverted (like the person on the right).

choose (Ardrey, 1966; Exline, 1972; Exline, Ellyson, & Long, 1975; Goffman, 1967; Henley, 1977; Mehrabian, 1969; Sommer, 1969, 1971). Even among children, those who lower their brows and thrust their chins forward are more likely to win competitions and keep disputed toys than those whose faces appear less dominant (Camras, 1982; Zivin, 1982).

Expressive people grab attention (Sullins, 1989), and they may inspire or activate the expressive behavior of other people, whose own feelings then become clearer. In addition, nonverbally expressive people are more likely to individuate themselves and become leaders; that is, you know who they are and they are likely to differentiate themselves in ways that lead to a relatively strong impact on others (Riggio & Reichard, 2008; Whitney, Sagrestano, & Maslach, 1994).

The most successful communicators are able to read the cues of others and, in return, are spontaneously able to express the appropriate emotions; that is, they are nonverbally sensitive, nonverbally expressive, nonverbally self-controlled, and motivated to perform for their "audiences." Former president Ronald Reagan was an outstanding example of such a communicator. His personality was such that most people liked him as a person, even if they strongly opposed his politics. Not surprisingly, Reagan had been a successful movie actor before entering politics.

Expressiveness and Health

Researchers of the so-called Type A, coronary-prone personality (Rosenman, 1978) study and attend to many of the same nonverbal characteristics (such as emphatic movements and fluency of vocal cues) that are relevant to extroversion

TIME LINE

The History of Trait Approaches to Personality

The major developments in the trait approaches can be seen here in historical relation to one another and in relation to their broader societal and cultural contexts.

Developments in Trait Aspects		Societal and Scientific Context
In ancient Greece, the ideas of character and temperament develop, as caused by the so-called bodily humors	Ancient Times	Nature is thought to be composed of air, earth, fire, and water
Religious interpretations view persons as divine creations possessed by good or evil	Middle Ages	Humans are seen as agents in a struggle between good and evil
Search for basic traits of individual differences begins, unsuccessfully	1800s	Following the Enlightenment, emphasizing reason and rationality, philosophers search for the core of human nature
Carl Jung and colleagues search for deep-rooted individual differences in orientation toward the world	1920s–1940s	Experimental psychology is dominated by behaviorism, and clinical psychology is dominated by psychoanalysis
Gordon Allport defines traits as neuropsychic structures that make certain stimuli functionally equivalent and guide consistent behavior	1930s	Rise of fascism stimulates interest in propaganda and individuals with authoritarian traits
Statistics (especially factor analysis) are developed and applied by Cattell and others to assess intelligence and other individual differences; Henry Murray develops a motive-based approach termed "personology"	1930s–1950s	Testing, based on statistics, becomes the norm for college admission, psychological screening, and other applications; clinical psychology attempts to become more science-based; and experimental psychology considers clinical applications
"Crisis" in personality as traits fail to fully predict behavior across situations	1960s–1970s	Time of social change, as Americans open new roles in civil rights and women's rights
The Big Five approach to traits takes hold	1990s	Increased use of longitudinal approaches reveals long-term stability of certain individual differences
Traits, motives, goals, and expressive styles are studied in more sophisticated ways; more attention paid to the behavioral manifestations of traits	2000s–	Personality psychology is reestablished as major subfield; more societal interest in predicting outcomes such as work success, health, and longevity

and expressiveness. A charismatic expressiveness, involving fluid, outward-focused gestures, is a sign of health, whereas nonverbal cues of an impatient hostility (for example, explosive, accelerating speech and clenched fists) are signs of an unhealthy personality. Unexpressiveness is not necessarily an indicator of an unhealthy personality if the lack of expressiveness results from a calm, content, yet reserved orientation. But unexpressiveness is unhealthy when it is a sign of alienation, depression, or repressed anxiety (Friedman, 2000b; Friedman & Booth-Kewley, 1987a, 1987b; Friedman, Hall, & Harris, 1985; Hall, Friedman, & Harris, 1986; Pennebaker, 1990).

Characteristic modes of emotional responding are likely biologically determined by birth or soon thereafter, but expressive responses are heavily socialized during childhood, both in general and for specific social situations, with implications for health. As a simple example, take an inherently unexpressive child and place him in a family who expects the child to become an aggressive salesperson. Or take an inherently expressive child and place her in a setting where the expectations are that she will be a "good girl"—reserved and obedient. For both children, the effects on adjustment, coping, and health are likely to be striking.

Further evidence that expressive style is tapping some basic element of personality, just as Allport suspected, is supplied by studies in which people try to control or to increase their expressiveness. Although expressive people generally are talented at enacting emotions, they are less successful than unexpressive people at deliberately appearing neutral—they still appear emotional (Friedman, Riggio, et al., 1980). Even when it is important to hold back their expressions so as not to embarrass others, expressive people may have trouble squelching their emotional expressions (Friedman & Miller-Herringer, 1991). Interestingly, expressive people who are deliberately trying to act unexpressive do not seem as unexpressive as unexpressive people who are acting naturally (DePaulo et al., 1992). On the other hand, culture subtly affects or "accents" nonverbal emotional expression; a study that compared Japanese and Japanese Americans expressing the same emotions found that observers could detect nationality (Marsh, Elfenbein, & Ambady, 2003).

Trait research that focuses on expressive style is often termed the study of "nonverbal social skill," or more simply, "social skill" (Riggio, 1986, 1992; Rosenthal, 1979). The study of nonverbal skills in personality is different from the usual focus on traits in at least three ways (Friedman, 1979). First, the concept of nonverbal skills shifts attention toward emotion; that is, aspects of personality like empathy, sympathy, and anger communication come to the fore. Second, there is a shift away from the usual focus on internal traits and motives and toward observable abilities. For example, instead of studying extroversion per se, the focus might be on facial, bodily, and vocal expressiveness. This is important because these expressions can be learned to some extent. Third, there is a shift toward the ongoing process of social interaction. That is, with a focus on expressiveness there is more concern with personality in the context of communication with others, consistent with the most modern understandings of personality.

Evaluating the Perspectives

Advantages and Limits of the Trait Approach

■ Quick Analogy
- Humans as clusters of temperaments and traits.

■ Advantages
- Simplifies personality to a small number of basic dimensions.
- Looks for a deeper consistency underlying surface variations in behavior.
- Good individual assessment techniques.
- Allows for comparisons to be made between individuals.
- Uses both lab and field studies, theoretical and applied.

■ Limits
- May reach too far in trying to capture the individual in a few ways.
- May label people on the basis of test scores.
- Sometimes underestimates variability across situations.
- May be biased by implicit personality theories.
- Difficult to determine the number of reliable personality dimensions.
- May underestimate the influence of unconscious motives and early experience.

■ View of Free Will
- Allows for free will at the margins, after predispositions and motives exert their influence.

■ Common Assessment Techniques
- Factor analysis, self-reports, testing of styles, document analysis, behavioral observation, interviews.

■ Implications for Therapy
- If much of personality is structured around a small number of key dispositions, motives, or traits, then we can change our goals, skills, and orientations but probably not our basic dispositional "natures." So, for example, if you are introverted, conscientious, and hard-working but lonely, it is not sensible to try to become a glad-handing class president or the life of the party; but you might set a series of limited goals aimed at making a few close friends who share your intensity and conscientiousness. You might also pay attention to improving your conversational skills.

Summary and Conclusion

The trait approach to personality searches for a small number of core dimensions that can usefully summarize a person's consistent patterns of responding. The number of such dimensions is still in dispute. Cattell's factor approach to personality sees the necessity of 16 traits. Eysenck believes that theory should guide the selection of the factors, and he sees all traits as deriving from three biological systems, producing the three factors of extroversion, neuroticism, and psychoticism. But many, if not most, researchers now agree that five dimensions do a satisfactory job in most circumstances—the so-called Big Five of Extroversion, Agreeableness, Conscientiousness, Neuroticism, and Openness.

From roots in ancient Greek notions of temperaments and characters, the trait approach bloomed in the 1930s, fed by Jung's notions of inward and outward orientations, the statistical analyses of quantitative psychologists, and Gordon Allport's extensive theorizing about capturing the fullness of each individual's life. Modern approaches have adopted Allport's notion that traits are the invariant aspects of a person that accompany the changing parts. In other words, there are core tendencies that give a life its uniqueness and consistency, even though personalities undergo variations across time and situation.

Common traits are traits that people in a population share, and personal dispositions are traits (generalized neuropsychic structures) that are peculiar to the individual. Motives are internal psychobiological forces that induce behavior or push for expression; motives always involve a goal, such as food, friends, or power. For Allport (as opposed to Freud), motives are functionally autonomous—they have become independent of their origins in childhood. Recent research on expressive style suggests that there is a noteworthy degree of consistency in an individual's gesturing, body incline, and voice cues, even across interactions with different people, and that the emotional facet of expressive behavior is a key aspect of personality. For example, people vary systematically in the intensity, expansiveness, animation, and dynamism of their nonverbal and verbal styles. Such expressive style approaches may view personality in terms of social skills.

Most trait psychologists assume that there are biological bases to these consistencies, and so they are quite interested in the proliferation of knowledge about the biological bases of personality. Most trait psychologists are also willing to accept that there are cognitive and psychodynamic influences on traits. Yet a trait approach, like any other single approach to personality, has proved inadequate to capture fully what it means to be a person. In particular, trait approaches need to be complemented by approaches that recognize the noble, spiritual aspects of human beings and that consider the situational demands on behavior.

■ Key Theorists

Carl Jung	Gordon Allport	Paul Costa Jr. and Robert McCrae
B. Cattell	Hans Eysenck	Henry Murray

■ Key Concepts and Terms

Myers-Briggs Type Indicator	central dispositions
factor analysis	Big Five approach
functionally equivalent	implicit personality theory
common traits	types
functionally autonomous	motives
proprium	needs
cardinal dispositions	expressive style
personal dispositions	

Humanistic, Existential, and Positive Aspects of Personality

Humanistic, Existential, and Positive Aspects of Personality

© AP Images/Alessandro Trovati

Confirming one of the greatest sports comebacks ever, cyclist Lance Armstrong returned to win and dominate the Tour de France bicycle competition. But Lance had previously faced an even greater crisis and challenge. At the age of 24, he was diagnosed with testicular cancer, which had spread to his lungs and brain. With less than a 40 percent chance of survival, Lance had a testicle removed and underwent aggressive chemotherapy. His physical strength, a core of his self, was suddenly challenged and devastated. Yet Lance not only returned to cycling triumph, he returned to create his own cancer foundation. He then

Lance Armstrong. What does personality psychology have to say about spirit, courage, and peak experiences?

added record Tour de France titles, was awarded virtually every sports honor possible, and became an international symbol of motivation and inspiration.

Mohandas Gandhi, called the "Mahatma," or "Great Soul," led a life defined by commitment to principle. He had the personal strength to become one of the most influential leaders ever, pioneering nonviolent political resistance and winning political freedom for India. Anatoly (now Natan) Sharansky was falsely convicted of treason in the former Soviet Union; his only "crime" was being a civil rights activist trying to emigrate to Israel. Facing more and more pressure and long-term imprisonment, he became more and more resolute, eventually winning his freedom and freedom for thouands of others. Martin Luther King Jr. faced down police dogs, fire hoses, and a long-entrenched racist U.S. society to win dramatic civil rights reforms. Aung San Suu Kyi spent over 14 years under house arrest in her home in Myanmar (Burma), refusing to leave her country as she continued to advocate its return to democracy and human rights.

How are we to understand such personalities, such modern-day heroes, who represent what is spiritual and noble about human beings? What is the nature of the human spirit? Why are we here? Why are we born and why must we die? How do we measure human success? What is the path to happiness? At certain times these questions become burning issues in the lives of many ordinary people. Most adolescents agonize over their true identity, their purpose, and their future. Many middle-aged adults face an existential midlife crisis. Many elderly people contemplate the value and meaning of their lives. Issues of love, responsibility, anxiety, and self-fulfillment permeate these thoughts at each stage of life.

These questions and quandaries are uniquely human. Dogs do not ponder the meaning of their existence. Yet even young children ask about death, and why people suffer, and what is right and wrong. Any full psychological understanding of what it means to be a person should provide a psychological perspective for addressing individual differences in approaching these age-old questions. These questions are the focus of the work of humanistic and existential approaches to personality.

During the past 40 years, only about one-third of the American public has been reporting they are very happy (Pew Research Center, 2006). This percentage of happy people has been remarkably steady. During this same time period, the average per capita income (adjusted for inflation) has more than doubled. So, rising incomes have not raised happiness levels. On the other hand, the data also show that individuals with higher incomes are more likely to report being very happy than their poorer associates. How can we understand this seeming contradiction? The answer is that psychological issues are paramount. It is not how much money you have that directly influences whether you are happy or miserable, but rather how you think about your existence, including comparing yourself to other people.

The filmmaker Woody Allen captures the existential crises that can dominate a person's life in his Academy Award–winning movie *Annie Hall*. When—in a crisis of love—the Woody Allen character breaks up with his girlfriend, Annie Hall, they must divide up all the belongings from their shared apartment. Annie reminds him that all the books on death and dying are his. He is obsessed with death. But he is also obsessed with the meaning of life. He bombards Annie with discussions of philosophy, Nazi death camps, illness, aging, the meaning of love, and other central issues of human existence, all in a chronic search for life's meaning. He is appalled by people who continue on their merry way in life, wallowing in self-deception and oblivious to real human suffering, as symbolized by his visit to "tinsel-town" Hollywood at Christmastime, portrayed as the height of superficiality, where even the snow is fake. Analogously, comic Stephen Colbert satirizes the contradictions among what we think, what we say, and what we do, as he plays the character of an uninformed but high-status and self-important fool.

Not only in films and TV but in real life, people who are struggling for a sense of value and direction in their lives are often overwhelmed with anxiety; they become neurotic and otherwise psychologically impaired. On the other hand, people who are totally self-absorbed and lead egocentric or hedonistic lives often wind up even more unhappy than the neurotics. This chapter explains how existential and humanistic perspectives on personality point the way toward resolution of basic human conflicts about value, meaning and happiness, issues that are often ignored by other approaches to personality.

■ Existentialism

Existentialism

An area of philosophy concerned with the meaning of human existence

Being-in-the-World

The existential idea that the self cannot exist without a world and the world cannot exist without a person or being to perceive it

Positivism

The philosophical view of the world that focuses on the laws that govern the behavior of objects in the world

In the most simple terms, **existentialism** is an area of philosophy concerned with the meaning of human existence. Existentialists sometimes speak of **being-in-the-world**. This idea comes from Martin Heidegger (1962), an early-twentieth-century German philosopher. It addresses a thorny philosophical problem that challenges psychological science. A traditional **positivist** view of the world focuses on the laws that govern the behavior of objects in the world. For example, rats who are reinforced with food pellets for turning left in a maze soon become left-turning rats. This is regular, lawful behavior. But would this law exist if there were no people to think about it? To answer this question, other, nonpositivist philosophers have focused on the subjective nature of existence, arguing that nothing would exist if people were not here to see it.

In the extreme subjective view, the world changes as people's ideas about it change. In other words, the idea of a world is a distinctly human construction. The problem with this subjective approach is that positivist science often works—it makes valid predictions; that is, taking a positivist approach, scientists have established that there are indeed laws or regularities that do an excellent job of describing the world. Both the positivist, objective viewpoint and the nonpositivist, subjective viewpoint each makes an important point. Existentialists, therefore, address these matters by referring to "beings-in-the-world." Simply put, the self cannot exist without a world and the world cannot exist without a person (a being) to perceive it.

This existential philosophical orientation is especially important for personality psychology. A physical scientist, such as an astronomer, can usually safely ignore these issues, at least up to a point. When tracking comets or analyzing radio waves, the scientist's conception of human existence is irrelevant. (However, when issues of cosmology arise, such as the origin of the universe, even an astronomer must consider philosophy.) But for a personality psychologist, existential puzzles have direct and constant implications. People are active, conscious beings, always thinking. Is true love a product of the mind of the lover, or is it an ephemeral and unimportant product of some neurophysical state? Probably it is simply neither. Existential theories suggest that attempts to focus exclusively on self-concepts and cognitive structures, or exclusively on environmental contingencies, must ultimately fail. Instead, we also must examine people striving to make sense of their worlds by examining human beings in their worlds (Hoeller, 1990).

The existential examination is not tuned to uncovering logical inconsistencies or rationalizations. For example, take the cases of religion, belief in the afterlife, and anxiety about death. The existential approach does not consider *why* we think this way, but *that* we think this way. Similarly, questions about choosing to be ethical and moral, and guilt about being immoral, are seen as essential aspects of being human, rather than as incidental by-products of the biological nature of human beings (Vandenberg, 1991). Ethical and spiritual matters are neither to be ignored nor explained away.

The Phenomenological View

The existential perspective received a strong push in the years following World War II from French writers Albert Camus and Jean-Paul Sartre. Camus, concerned with the fundamental absurdity of existence, nevertheless saw value in the individual's having the courage to attempt to correct injustice as he or she perceived it. Relatedly, Sartre emphasized the responsibility of all individuals for their own decisions, and he believed we need to see ourselves as free actors in order to achieve authentic human existence. For example, in his powerful play *No Exit* (*Huis Clos*), Sartre shows us that hell is being trapped in a room with people we hate. It is our own perceptions (not fire and brimstone) that can torture us. Interestingly, both Camus and Sartre were active in the French resistance to the Nazis, at a time when courage, responsibility, and individual freedom were issues of the utmost importance.

Phenomenological
The concept that people's perceptions or subjective realities are considered valid data for investigation

Aspects of existential approaches are sometimes termed **phenomenological**. This means that people's perceptions or subjective realities are considered to be valid data for investigation. Two people can perceive the same situation very differently, and this difference—this phenomenological discrepancy—is often a focus of attention in existential approaches to personality. In a dispute between a husband and wife, for example, a phenomenological approach would attend to the needs and perceptions of the participants rather than to their psychological history or the rewards and contingencies of the situation. However, because the situation influences the perceptions, it would by no means be ignored.

Why Does It Matter?

Because existentialism argues that it is an oversimplification to view people as controlled by fixed physical laws, the approach is nondeterministic; that is, people cannot be correctly viewed as cogs in some vast machine. This approach, therefore, encourages theories that consider issues of individual initiative, creativity, and self-fulfillment. These are especially matters of concern for humanistic psychologists. Humanistic approaches to personality psychology focus on the active, positive aspects of human growth and achievement.

Humanism

Humanism
A philosophical movement that emphasizes the personal worth of the individual and the importance of human values

Humanism is a philosophical movement that emphasizes the personal worth of the individual and the centrality of human values. A humanistic approach to personality likewise attends to matters of ethics and personal worth. Many approaches to personality, being deterministic, emphasize the degree to which our behavior is controlled by unconscious forces or prior experiences. For example, we have seen that the psychoanalyst sees humans as driven by the primitive instincts of the id, and we have seen that the behaviorist sees people as conditioned by the contingencies of the environment.

Giving a Role to the Human Spirit

Humanistic approaches, however, resting on the more complex philosophical foundation of existentialism, are freer to give credit to the human spirit. Abraham Maslow thus called humanistic psychology the "third force" (the first two forces being behaviorism and psychoanalysis).

Humanistic approaches emphasize the creative, spontaneous, and active nature of human beings. These approaches are usually optimistic, as when they focus on the noble human capacity to overcome hardship and despair. Sometimes, however, these approaches turn pessimistic, as when they contemplate the futility of one person's actions. Nevertheless, these approaches are willing to take on the spiritual and philosophic aspects of human nature (Rychlak, 1997). (See the Self-Understanding box on creativity.)

Relations with Other People Define Our Humanness

I-Thou Dialogue
A phrase used by philosopher Martin Buber to describe a direct, mutual relationship in which each individual confirms the other person as being of unique value

I-It Monologue
A phrase used by philosopher Martin Buber to describe a utilitarian relationship in which a person uses others but does not value them for themselves

Building on existentialism, the humanistic approach stresses the "being" in human beings. In other words, it emphasizes the special active and aware quality of human beings. Life develops as people create worlds for themselves. This view also often moves from humans "being" to humans "becoming"; that is, the healthy personality exhibits an active movement toward self-fulfillment. In addition, the humanistic approach adopts the existential idea that our existence comes especially from our relations with other human beings (Buber, 1937). An important focus is on direct, mutual relations, which philosopher Martin Buber called the **I-Thou dialogue**. In this dialogue, each human confirms the other person as being of unique value. This is distinguished from a utilitarian relationship (called the **I-It monologue**), in which a person uses others but does not value them for themselves. Although Buber proffered this argument in a religious context, many humanistic psychologists focus on spiritual matters without religious content.

Why Does It Matter?

The impact of the human potential movement can now be seen in mainstream society. For example, protecting humans' relations with an unsullied, unpolluted natural eco-sphere is now a major political force worldwide. In the area of business, promoting the individual worker's self-development and concern with the feelings and ideas of small groups of workers are now major issues in industrial psychology and corporate culture. And in psychotherapy, concern with unconscious conflicts has often been replaced with techniques to facilitate personal growth. The implications of humanistic approaches for healthy personality development are being felt throughout society.

The Human Potential Movement

The so-called **human potential movement**, which began in the 1960s, is one example of the existential–humanistic approach to personality. Through small-group meetings, self-disclosure, and introspection, people are encouraged to realize their inner potentials. In the 1960s and '70s, the "human potential" milieu was more often than not a hippie commune in the woods, where encounter groups, body massage, meditation, consciousness-raising, organic health foods, and communing with nature were heavily employed. Today it echoes in movements of environmentalism, grassroots democracy, civil liberties, worker dignity, and unselfish self-fulfillment.

Human Potential Movement
An existential–humanistic movement in which people are encouraged to realize their inner potentials through small group meetings, self-disclosure, and introspection

Self-Understanding

Are You Creative?

One modern researcher working in the humanistic tradition is positive psychologist Mihaly Csikszentmihalyi, known for his work on self-actualized people. Csikszentmihalyi (1996, 2000) outlines some of the characteristics of highly creative people. Of interest is his finding that creative people often have traits that are seemingly contradictory. These antithetical traits seem to produce a **dialectical tension** that may play a role in creativity. (Dialectic refers to the process by which two contradictory forces or tendencies lead to a resolution or synthesis, in this case creative production.) What exactly does this mean?

Creative individuals are usually very smart, but they may be naïve at the same time. For example, Albert Einstein needed his wife's help to manage his financial affairs. Or they may be wise but childish, as Wolfgang Amadeus Mozart was reported to be. Furthermore, they may value playfulness; yet creative accomplishment, such as in the arts, usually requires incredible discipline. They take risks when necessary for creative achievement.

Creative people usually have very high levels of energy. As Freud suggested, this is often sexual energy, and they may have huge sexual appetites. On the other hand, they can usually focus this energy and so may, in fact, avoid sexual involvements. Similarly, creative people can seem quite extroverted and be the life of the party, but they often consider themselves introverted and even shy. They can be simultaneously humble and deeply proud of their significant accomplishments.

According to Csikszentmihalyi, creative people tend to have both masculine and feminine characteristics. Creative men are often sensitive and nurturing, and creative women are often assertive and dominant. They can suffer because of their extreme sensitivity, but they can also achieve the peak experiences of self-actualization.

Note that this sort of analysis is uniquely humanistic and existential in flavor. It is not an explanation in terms of hormones and brain structures, conditioning and reinforcement schedules, or instincts and socialization. Rather, it often involves a phenomenological examination of matters that are uniquely human, and it is comfortable with notions of creativity, freedom, and self-fulfillment.

Dialectical Tension
Concept used by Mihaly Csikszentmihalyi for the idea that creative people tend to have traits that are seemingly contradictory but that play a role in their creativity

Love as a Central Focus of Life: Erich Fromm

Most parents say that love is the most important thing that they can give to their children. Most adults say that love is the most fulfilling aspect of their lives. Yet many approaches to personality pay little heed to love, or else they dismiss it as an unimportant by-product of the true determinants of personality. On the contrary, existential and humanistic approaches often focus directly on love.

Loving as an Art

The humanistic psychoanalyst Erich Fromm (1900–1980) maintained that love is an art (Fromm, 1956). Love is not a state that people stumble into, nor is love some nebulous epiphenomenon that has no real meaning. Love requires knowledge, effort, and experience. The capacity to love must be developed with humility and discipline. According to Fromm, love is the answer to the unavoidable question—the problem of human existence. Love alone enables us to overcome our isolation from others but still maintain our individual integrity. But Fromm maintains that love cannot exist apart from a mature, productive personality; therefore, Fromm's approach to a healthy and fully human person is idealized in the "productive character," who endeavors to transcend biology and society and who uses the large human brain to love and create in uniquely human ways (Fromm & Maccoby, 1970).

Fromm is concerned that in modern society, we are alienated from ourselves, from others, and from nature. We are often unaware of our longing for transcendence and unity. We try to cover this inner alienation by "having fun." When we are immature, the world is seen as one big breast, and we are the sucklers. To overcome this existential alienation of modern society, Fromm suggests that we must master the discipline to be patient, to concentrate, and to live actively in the present, overcoming our narcissism. Paradoxically, as humans have gained more and more freedom through the ages, we have felt more and more anxious and alone. If we do not fight this loneliness and isolation by working in a loving way to help others, then we may choose the opposite extreme: We may escape from the burden of freedom by giving it up, such as to a dictator or other authoritarian force.

Fromm and his followers are willing to tackle some of the basic philosophical and religious issues in Western and Eastern thought; and to do so in terms of the psychological idea of a fully realized and fully developed personality. The mystical aspects of Judaism, Islam, and Christianity have long emphasized the importance of deep prayer and spirituality, and Eastern philosophies have long pointed out the psychological advantages of meditation, sensation, and playful thought. For example, Zen Buddhism emphasizes that life's mysteries can be successfully

■ New forms of positive, growth-focused social interaction were developed as part of the human potential movement. Although the heyday of such groups is past, many of the ideas and approaches they espoused have become integrated into the mainstream.

addressed through intuition and active consciousness of one's life. Fromm and his colleagues reinterpret philosophical, meditative, and religious musings with systematic accounts based on understanding of human personality psychology.

Fromm would undoubtedly be distressed with a society that has replaced communal activities with solitary TV viewing; with a society that has relinquished cultural traditions to standardized Big Mac hamburgers; and with a society that has traded charitable concerns about helping others for self-indulgent trips to visit Mickey Mouse. He would predict that individuals in such a society would be alienated, unloving, and unfulfilled, and further, that they would be susceptible to the appeals of a totalitarian government. But he would be pleased with the increasing equality for women, the embracing of ethnic diversity, and society's openness to social innovation.

■ Humanistic theorist Erich Fromm believed that the essential isolation of each human being could be overcome by love, but that love requires maturity and effort. He feared that the alienation characteristic of modern society would erode the quality of our lives.

Dialectical Humanism: Transcending Conflict

Like many twentieth-century intellectuals, Fromm was influenced by the Marxist preoccupation with the exploitation of workers, as well as by Freud's theories of unconscious motivation. Born into an Orthodox Jewish family, Fromm was heavily shaped by the Talmud, the collection of ancient Jewish commentaries on, and interpretations of, the Hebrew Bible. Although Fromm was trained in psychoanalysis in Berlin, he soon discarded many of its tenets and began to emphasize the effects of social and societal factors on personality. Fromm's approach, sometimes called **dialectical humanism**, tries to reconcile both the biologically driven and the societally pressured sides of human beings with the belief that people can rise above, or transcend, these forces and become spontaneous, creative, and loving.

Dialectical Humanism Erich Fromm's approach to personality, which tries to reconcile the biological, driven side of human beings and the pressures of societal structure by focusing on the belief that people can rise above or transcend these forces and become spontaneous, creative, and loving

As Fromm well knew, the struggle between concepts of free will and determinism is a long-standing one. In the twelfth century, the influential religious philosopher Maimonides wrote, "Do not think that character is determined at birth. . . . Any person can become as righteous as Moses or as wicked as Jereboam. We ourselves decide whether to make ourselves learned or ignorant, compassionate or cruel, generous or miserly" (Mishnah Torah, Hilchot Teshuva, 5.1). People were not to blame their failings on others or on evil spirits. Although God was considered all-knowing, it would not make sense to ask people to live righteous lives if they had no free will. This dilemma was sharpened when Freud gave a scientific explanation for evil spirits—namely, the inner drives of the id. A Freudian view of personality is a pessimistic, deterministic one.

Consistent with the existential assumptions of beings-in-the-world and free will, Erich Fromm traces human behavior to neither inner drives nor societal pressures but rather to a conscious person with certain needs existing within a network of societal demands. Mature people achieve a productive orientation as they enrich the world through their own creative endeavors and humanitarian ethics.

Evidence Supporting Fromm's Approach? The Age of Anxiety?

Evidence for Fromm's ideas necessarily comes from analysis of cultures or subcultures rather than from a context-free analysis of an individual. What are the personalities of people raised to love, help, and have faith in others, as opposed to people raised to disregard ethics and exploit others?

Many trends support Fromm's ideas: For example, as society has become more individualistic and consumerist, the rate of major psychological depression and other serious mental health problems in Western countries has risen steadily (Cross-National Collaborative Group, 1992; Twenge et al., 2010). In addition, as Fromm predicted, an alienated, noncommunal American society is increasingly afflicted with violence, divorce, and unrest (as shown in Table 1). Observation of the alienation and destruction present in many modern cultures suggests that existential ideas about the importance of an active love deserve serious attention.

Further evidence emerges from studies of anxiety. How did college students at the end of the twentieth century compare with college students of a half-century earlier? Despite the huge increase in big business and societal wealth, anxiety levels have risen dramatically (Twenge, 2000). (This rise occurred even before the terrorist attacks of 2001.) The same increase occurred for children, with the average American child now reporting more anxiety than child psychiatric patients from the 1950s. Many of today's students tend to be narcissistic and over-confident (Twenge and Campbell, 2009). As we will see, although there are undoubtedly many causes of this increase, the results are precisely those predicted by Fromm and the other existential–humanistic psychologists, who viewed twentieth-century social trends with alarm.

■ TABLE I   Existential Alienation? Social Indicator Changes, 1950–2000

Social Indicator	Change from 1950 to 2000
Divorce rate	doubled
Out-of-wedlock birthrate	up 7 times
Percentage of population in prison	up 5 times
Reported anxiety and depression	up 5–10 times

Note: Numbers and time periods are approximate.

Source: Data from the *Statistical Abstract of the United States*, www.census.gov/compendia/statab/. See also www.lib.umich.edu/govdocs/stcomp.html.

Responsibility: Carl Rogers

A key postulate of existential–humanistic approaches is that each person is responsible for his or her own life and maturity. This idea is best exemplified in the work of the influential humanistic psychologist Carl Rogers. Rogers believed that people have an inherent tendency toward growth and maturation. But this maturation is not inevitable. Although people are potentially free to exercise control over their own selves, they must strive to take on this responsibility for themselves, with a supportive psychosocial environment. Responsibility, like love, is a term often heard in humanistic analyses of personality but rarely heard elsewhere.

CHANGING **Personality**

Erich Fromm advised that the best way to improve one's personality is to fight loneliness and isolation by working in a loving way to help others. Rather than looking to hormones or resolving inner conflicts, a productive character will work to transcend biology and societal demands by becoming loving and creative. What are some good ways to do this? The humanistic–existential approach to personality change relies on honest relationships with others and on productive community involvement. This is illustrated by simple acts of kindness, and by larger campaigns to "pay it forward" by working with others to make things better in our communities. Particular actions include expressing thanks and gratitude to others, and remembering and celebrating joyful and helpful activities. In other words, personality change comes from exercising one's free choice to self-actualize and to love.

Rogers's Background

Carl Rogers, born in 1902, was raised in a strict Christian religious atmosphere with close family ties. His upbringing was so sternly ruled by ethical demands that he reports feeling slightly wicked when he had his first bottle of soda pop. He spent his teenage years on his family's farm learning principles of scientific agriculture. Rogers attributed his later success in part to the independence, scientific approach, and observational skills he developed during this period.

After graduating from the University of Wisconsin, Rogers attended the Union Theological Seminary in New York to prepare for the ministry but gradually moved into child and clinical psychology. It is interesting to note that many humanistic ideas (from Rogers, Fromm, and others) are derived from religious or quasi-religious sources. In contrast to those psychologists who learned about personality from the perspective of evolutionary biology or neurological impairment or animal behavior or information processing, humanistic psychologists often have had a lifelong concern with matters of the human spirit. Rogers died in San Diego in 1987, after surgery for a broken hip; to the end he was active at his Center for the Study of the Person.

Growth, Inner Control, and the Experiencing Person

A linchpin of Rogers's perspective is that people tend to develop in a positive direction; that is, unless thwarted, they will fulfill their potential. This idea can be traced back to the eighteenth-century French political philosopher Jean Jacques Rousseau, who believed in the natural goodness of human beings. Rousseau argued that schools should encourage self-expression rather than disciplining "improper" behavior. According to Rogers, a psychologically healthy person is one who has a broad self-concept capable of

■ From Carl Rogers's perspective, the role of the therapist is to be empathic and supportive, and to reflect back the client's own tensions and conflicts.

understanding and accepting many feelings and experiences. Inner self-control is healthier than forced, external control.

In addition, Rogers takes a phenomenological approach: Important issues must be defined by the individual. The focus of humanistic psychology is on what he called the **experiencing person**. Of special concern are discrepancies between what a person thinks of herself and the total range of things she experiences. Inabilities to accept aspects of oneself are stumbling blocks on the path to personal growth.

Rogerian Therapy

Rogers had a tremendous influence on the practice of psychotherapy. In **Rogerian therapy**, the therapist is empathic, supportive, and nondirective. During his years in child guidance and clinical psychology, Rogers came to understand that it is the client and not the therapist who best understands where the problems are and in what directions therapy should proceed. Consistent with the existential viewpoint, Rogers viewed a person as a process—a changing constellation of potentialities, not a fixed quantity of traits. In the supportive psychological atmosphere of client-oriented Rogerian therapy, a person learns to drop his or her masks and become more open and self-trusting. The client is the one who, with the support of the therapist, accomplishes growth and change (see Figure 1).

For constructive personality change to occur during psychotherapy, Rogers includes the following two necessary conditions: First, the therapist demonstrates unconditional positive regard for the client; and second, the therapist experiences an empathic understanding of the client's internal frame of reference and communicates this experience to the client (Rogers, 1951). In other words, a genuine integrated therapist can sense the client's tensions and incongruent feelings, reflect them back to the client, and thereby assist the client to become more mature and self-integrated. These ideas have guided the training of countless therapists. Note, however, that Rogers is willing to be rigorous in his approach; for example, he suggests that the empathy of each therapist might be evaluated by independent judges. He welcomed systematic testing of his ideas. In fact, Rogers was among the first to conduct demanding evaluations of psychotherapy.

Becoming One's Self

From a Rogerian perspective, it is of the utmost importance that we come to terms with our own nature. Although we all have ideas of what we *should be like*, Rogers says that

Experiencing Person
In Carl Rogers's phenomenological view, important issues are defined by each person for himself or herself in the context of the total range of things the person experiences

Rogerian Therapy
The client-oriented psychotherapy developed by Carl Rogers in which the therapist tends to be supportive, nondirective, and empathetic, and gives unconditional positive regard

---

■ FIGURE I

"How many psychologists does it take to change a light bulb?

Just one, but the light bulb has to want to change!" This joke reflects the view of humanistic psychologists: People have free will and can will themselves to grow and change for the better, but all such change must be driven from within.

a person should "become one's self." A healthy personality can trust his or her own experience and accept the fact that other people are different. Existential anxiety and inner conflict often arise, according to Rogers, when we put up a façade and try to conform to the expectations of others. For example, toward the end of successful therapy, one of Rogers's clients writes, "I've always felt I had to do things because they were expected of me or, more important, to make people like me. The hell with it! I think from now on I'm going to just be me" (Rogers, 1961 p. 170).

Take the case of a feisty schoolyard bully or a pushy, disgruntled coworker. How do we react to such a person? Should we reciprocate aggression toward such a person? Should we place blame on hidden dysfunctional aspects of this annoying person's personality? Rogers tells us that such behavior would be inherently destructive to ourselves. Instead, a healthy person should be optimistic and understanding toward obnoxious colleagues, searching for their humanity. Sometimes this orientation will result in a dramatic shift in the bully's behavior; but even if it does not, the important thing (for Rogers) is that we have maintained our own humanity.

What about our own feelings? Should we try to deny our feelings of anger toward an obnoxious coworker? On the contrary, Rogers urged experiencing or getting in touch with our feelings, but then using our ethical standards to take responsibility and not to let our angry feelings lead to aggressive behaviors. A fully functioning person leads a spiritually enriching, exciting, and courageous life.

One assessment technique that is well suited to a Rogerian perspective is the Q-sort. For example, a person might sort self-descriptions of a real self and an ideal self before psychotherapy and then again after psychotherapy; the therapist could evaluate whether the therapy has led to a greater integration of personality (Rogers & Dymond, 1954).

Rogers, a humanistic psychologist, viewed responsibility in a positive, self-liberating, and self-enhancing light. But some of his existential counterparts were not so sanguine and optimistic. For example, French writer Jean Paul Sartre (1956) agreed that the individual should find meaning for her or his own life—meaning would not be provided by some external world. But although Sartre, like Rogers, stressed responsibility, it was as a counterweight to existential anxiety and despair, not as a launching pad for maturity.

Why Does It Matter?

The Rogerian approach has implications for international relations, and indeed humanistic psychologists are quite concerned not only with personal peace but with world peace. For example, late in life Rogers began to tackle religious strife in Northern Ireland. In simple terms, the basic issue is whether acquiring the toughest war machine is the best path to world peace or whether the use of military force ultimately backfires by sowing the seeds of further destructiveness, despair, and aggression. In real-world situations, the considerations and the policy details are, of course, much more complex. Yet arguments about international relations and policy often depend on assumptions about human personality!

Anxiety and Dread

Computers do not become anxious, and information-processing approaches to understanding people mostly ignore matters like anxiety. Ironically, when placed in a high-tech environment, surrounded by computers, many people feel anxious. Think about how you feel on a day when every phone call you make is answered by a computer-generated electronic voice, you use the automatic teller machine, the gasoline station has a credit-card-controlled self-service pump, and your professor grades your multiple-choice exam by machine. Does anyone know you're alive? Many people under

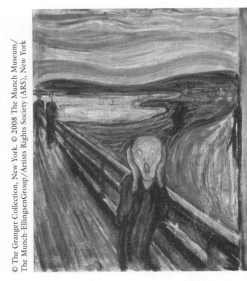

■ *The Scream,* by Edvard Munch. A Norwegian artist and a founder of modern expressionism, Munch revealed a tormented sensibility in his art, suggesting a modern alienation and despair.

this electronic onslaught feel depersonalized, anxious, and even a sense of dread, as their spiritual lives—their spirits—are ignored. This sense of alienation from modern society was foreseen by nineteenth-century Danish philosopher Søren Kierkegaard, who emphasized the importance of human faith, and nineteenth-century German philosopher Friedrich Nietzsche, who showed the importance of passion and creativity.

Anxiety, Threat, and Powerlessness: Rollo May

Existential psychologists are willing to consider anxiety, dread, and even despair as core elements of human existence—of what it means to be a human being. Anxiety was a particular focus of the existential psychologist Rollo May (1909–1994), who saw anxiety as triggered by a threat to one's core values of existence. A sense of powerlessness is often key. For example, a young woman's anxiety could be engendered by her being ignored by her parents, or alienated from her religion, or treated as an object by her peers. Or, perhaps, she is a victim of abuse or rape. To combat the alienation, she may turn to drugs or sexual promiscuity or to a violent cult. In Western societies, psychotropic drugs like Valium are among the most

Famous
Personalities

Aung San Suu Kyi

Sometimes the best examples of strength of spirit arise from unlikely sources. Aung San Suu Kyi was born into a prominent and affluent family, and could readily have taken the easy road to a comfortable life. But, despite the many opportunities she has had to choose that path, she has instead devoted her life to the cause of freedom and democracy, at tremendous personal sacrifice.

She was born in Burma (Myanmar) shortly after the end of the Second World War. Her father, Aung San, had played a critical role in establishing Burma's independence from the British Empire, but was the victim of a political assassination during the transitional period to a new government. His daughter, Aung San Suu Kyi, was only two years old when he was killed, but he became a model for her of dedication and sacrifice for

one's people. She was so young when he died that she has no direct memory of him, but his legacy inspired her to a life of service to her people. Her other role model was Mahatma Gandhi, who preached non-violent resistance—she became very familiar with Gandhi's philosophy during the years she lived in India as a teenager, accompanying her mother who had been appointed Burmese ambassador to India. Aung San Suu Kyi is motivated not only by the models of her father and of Gandhi, but also by her Buddhist beliefs in the importance of truth, righteousness, non-violence, and loving kindness, as she states in her essay "In Quest of Democracy."

For her very public leadership of the movement against the brutal military dictatorship that rules her country, she has been placed under house arrest multiple times, each time for many years, punctuated by multiple outright imprisonments. She went on a hunger strike at one point, to force better treatment of the student demonstrators who were imprisoned with her. She

widely prescribed medications, with hundreds of millions of pills swallowed every year. And alcohol is even more widely used and abused, often to ward off anxiety.

Rollo May's sense of deep inner reflection intensified when, as a young tuberculosis sufferer, he was forced to spend several years in a sanitarium. In institutions, feelings of depersonalization and isolation can be especially intense. Later, as a therapist, May saw many patients searching for meaning in their lives, an observation that refined his interest in isolation and anxiety. It is also interesting to note that May, like the other founders of existential–humanistic approaches to personality, received both divinity training and psychoanalytic training (including study with Fromm).

Rollo May (1969, 1977) bridges the gap between existential and humanistic approaches to personality. Although he focuses on the anxiety that must accompany any attempt to live life to its fullest, May sees the human journey as a noble and dignifying one. The only way to have no anxiety would be to have no freedom. In this sense, his view is consistent with much religious philosophy about the inherent worth of humankind: There must be struggle for there to be dignity. The current world, though full of threats, provides opportunities for the deepest accomplishments.

Personal Choice: Victor Frankl

Existential–humanistic theorists like Victor Frankl (1962, 1984) emphasize the benefits of personal choice. If people choose to grow and develop, the challenge of the

has spent more than a dozen years confined to her home, much of the time without access to the media or to international visitors. She has been given many opportunities for freedom, but only if she will leave her country—which she is not willing to do. When her husband was dying of cancer in England, the government refused to grant him a visa to visit her in Burma, but they offered to release her from her house arrest so that she could visit him in England. Understanding that this offer on the part of the government was an attempt to get her out of the country permanently, she believed she would not be permitted to return if she left. So, she refused the offer and thus did not see her husband at all in the last three years of his life.

The strength of her dedication to her people and her willingness to sacrifice for them has been shown repeatedly. She has spoken out against the government, led marches and campaigns for democracy, and has made Burmese government repression a prominent international human-rights issue. In 1988, she faced down the rifles of government forces trying to disperse a march she was leading; when the armed soldiers ordered her to halt, she kept walking, directing her followers to stay back. She must have been convinced that she would win the encounter one way or another—either she would be shot to death and the struggle for democracy would be strengthened by her martyrdom, or the government troops would allow her to pass unharmed and her supporters would be heartened by their success in defying the government order to disband.

She has gained international recognition for her cause, and has been personally honored with many prestigious awards, including the Nobel Peace Prize. But the prize that she truly values, democracy and human rights for the Burmese people, motivates her continued work. The theorists in the existential, humanistic, and positive psychology traditions help us understand the personality of someone like Aung San Suu Kyi, who spends her life in pursuit of goals far beyond the personal.

■ Existential-humanistic approaches have fostered the proliferation of support groups for people facing serious illness. There is some evidence that participation in such groups eases adaptation and promotes recovery.

unknown produces anxiety; but this anxiety can lead to triumph and self-fulfillment. Frankl was imprisoned in a Nazi concentration camp. He survived psychologically by choosing to find meaning in the suffering, and by adopting the responsibility to control the little bit of his life that was left to him. He did not passively accept and comply with the horrors that surrounded him.

Although Frankl's parents and pregnant wife were killed in the camps, he went on to become one of the most influential existential psychologists, reaching out to those weighed down with despair or emptiness. He called his approach *logotherapy*—the search for the meaning of existence. True to his theory of personal mastery, Frankl died in Vienna in 1997 at the ripe old age of 92. An existential struggle can lead to a triumph of the human spirit. Our modern-day heroes are those who can resist the pressures of an authoritarian society run wild.

One area in which such existential–humanistic approaches have had a tremendous effect is among people facing life-threatening illnesses. Small groups of similarly affected people now commonly come together for weekly intimate discussions. Such groups initially sprang up among people with cancer but today have spread to almost every serious medical problem (Gottlieb & Wachala, 2007; Kelly, 1979; Taylor, 2006). In these groups, people typically disclose their fears and anxieties about bearing pain and facing death, consistent with the existential emphasis on actively facing such challenges. Participants also assist one another in both tangible (e.g., informational) and spiritual ways. Typically, the results of such experiences are the affirming of human feelings of trust and companionship, and a sense of inner triumph. These positive outcomes are right in line with existential–humanistic predictions. Yet rarely is the existential–humanistic source of this orientation explicitly acknowledged. This is an example of how our assumptions about personality subtly pervade many areas of our daily lives, whether we are aware of them or not.

Many years ago, we saw a debate between B. F. Skinner and Rollo May. The arguments focused around whether people have free will or whether their actions are predetermined, but the discussion ranged freely to other fundamental life questions as well. After about 90 minutes, it became clearer and clearer to many in the audience that both May and Skinner were correct. Each had highly developed ideas and deep insight into what it means to be a person. But because of their different perspectives and different interests, they never dealt with precisely the same matters. It was impossible to prove one or the other wrong through any simple psychological arguments or studies. That is why this text repeatedly argues that a full understanding of personality requires a willingness to study and understand eight basic but differing approaches. The question of free will is still one of active debate in psychology (Dennett, 2003; Wegner, 2003).

Self-Actualization: Abraham Maslow

Do people value wisdom, creativity, insight, and communion, or do they prefer food, drink, and sex? Humanistic psychologists cannot deny the importance of basic urges; after all, humans are also animals. But people are also more. Many theorists in this area, therefore, speak of three aspects of human nature—the biological, the social, and the self-fulfilling or personal (Frankl, 1962; Maddi, 1970). Being deprived of companionship or being deprived of meaning for one's life can be just as terrifying, and deadly, as being deprived of food.

Early Ideas about Self-Actualization in Jung's Work

Self-actualization is the innate process by which a person tends to grow spiritually and realize his or her potential. Few people become highly self-actualized but many go far along this path. Interestingly, the idea of self-actualization was first propounded by Carl Jung. Unlike humanistic psychologists, Jung (like Freud) strongly believed that unconscious forces were important, but he counterbalanced this orientation with the belief in a human tendency to integrate the various psychic forces and thereby become a "whole" person. For Jung, unconscious, selfish drives were undeniable, but they could be explored and integrated with the more spiritual aspects of human beings. In this way, through self-exploration and dealing with one's shadows (the dark forces within us), a person could live in harmony with nature and with all of humanity, the community with which each person shares deep biological ties.

> **Self-Actualization**
> The innate process by which one tends to grow spiritually and realize one's potential

Is it surprising that Jung, trained in psychoanalysis, propounds many humanistic notions? Not if we recall that Jung was well read and extremely knowledgeable about Eastern religions and about psychological anthropology. These literatures exalt the universal importance of nature, spiritual matters, symbols, and spiritual integration. Jung took these disparate conceptualizations and developed an optimistic, even mystical, approach. He was well aware of the dangers of alienation. Although Jung believed in unconscious motivation, he also believed in **teleology**—the idea that there is a grand design or purpose to one's life (Jung, 1933). Thus, Jung's ideas about what it means to be a person cannot be neatly categorized. For Jung, quasi-religious, spiritual integrations are a key part of human nature, but Jung well appreciated the instinctual inner demons that can torment us.

> **Teleology**
> The idea that there is a grand design or purpose to one's life

Peak Experiences

Consider now the other extreme, a self-actualization approach that is so positive that it sees people's spirits as not only without demons but in fact almost godly. Consider how at certain times in our lives, everything seems to fall into place. This special moment might occur while listening to a moving piece of music, creating an ingenious solution to a nagging problem, experiencing a tremendously sensual or artistic moment, or the like. At such times, people seem to transcend the self and be at one with the world. They are completely self-fulfilled. Are not such positive, meaningful experiences a significant aspect of personality? Abraham Maslow thought so and investigated these so-called **peak experiences**.

> **Peak Experiences**
> According to Abraham Maslow, powerful, meaningful experiences in which people seem to transcend the self, be at one with the world, and feel completely self-fulfilled; Mihaly Csikszentmihalyi describes them as the "flow" that comes with total involvement in an activity

The idea originated in the late-nineteenth-century work of philosopher–psychologist William James, who wrote of "mystical experiences"—indescribable, fleeting, and truth-illuminating spiritual happenings. It was expanded by the phenomenological therapist Fritz Perls, who urged increases in self-awareness by integrating the fringe parts of one's nature into a healthy whole (or "gestalt") (Perls, Hefferline, & Goodman, 1951). In more recent years, such phenomena have been studied by researchers like Mihaly Csikszentmihalyi (2000; Nakamura & Csikszentmihalyi, 2009), who writes about the "flow" (complete absorption) that comes with total involvement in a meaningful activity.

Abraham Maslow, best known for his work on self-actualization, was born in New York in 1908. He died in California in 1970. A very bright child, Maslow endured a terrible relationship with a strict mother who often engaged in bizarre behaviors. He described himself in his early years as shy, bookish, and neurotic. Yet Maslow did not remain neurotic or become self-hating. Rather, he fully realized his potential, becoming a leading humanistic psychologist who inspired much positive societal change.

Interestingly, Maslow was initially trained in behaviorism. He did his graduate work with Harry Harlow, the behaviorist-oriented primatologist. But as a professor at Brooklyn College in the 1930s and '40s, Maslow was exposed to the flood of brilliant intellectuals fleeing to New York from the Nazis, including Erich Fromm, Alfred Adler, and Karen Horney. His intimate knowledge of behaviorism facilitated Maslow's serious and repeated attacks on behaviorism and its ignoring of creativity, play, wonder, and love.

Peak experiences are common to people who are fully self-actualized. The insights these epiphanies provide help to maintain the mature personality. Such people are spiritually fulfilled—comfortable with themselves and others, loving and creative, realistic and productive. Examples include Albert Einstein, Thomas Jefferson, Eleanor Roosevelt, and of course Maslow himself. (See Table 2 for examples of individuals Maslow pointed to as models of self-actualization.)

■ **TABLE 2** Examples of Self-Actualized Historical Figures Identified by Maslow

Self-Actualized Person	Self-Actualizing Accomplishment
Albert Einstein	Applied his creative genius to rethink fundamental assumptions of time and space.
Eleanor Roosevelt	Showed concern for all humankind and worked to help improve human lives.
William James	As a founder of psychology, he brought a creative new perspective.
Baruch Spinoza	Defied the religious orthodoxy of his time to propound ideas considered heretical.
Abraham Lincoln	He fought for a moral idea of freedom, at great personal cost.
Thomas Jefferson	He was an architect and philosopher of a new form of government built on democratic principles.
Pablo Casals	Became what many considered to be the greatest cellist of the twentieth century.
George Washington Carver	Showed great creativity and achievement in the face of hardship and discrimination.

Interestingly, although many theories of personality are derived from studies of hysterics or neurotics or other unhealthy people, Maslow examined ideal, healthy lives. The orientation is thus optimistic and spiritual, and, like Rogers, Maslow stresses the positive potentialities inherent in all human beings. Many personality theories were built on the study of patients who were psychologically disturbed; Maslow turned the tables to study those people with the greatest mental health.

Self-actualized people have a realistic knowledge of themselves and accept themselves. (Unactualized people may occasionally have a peak experience but are more likely to be frightened than enlightened by it.) They are independent, spontaneous, and playful. They tend to have a philosophical sense of humor; you will not find them cracking ethnic jokes or engaging in crass sexual innuendos. They can establish deep, intimate relationships with other people, and they generally have a love of humankind. They are nonconformist but highly ethical. And they have had peak experiences.

A sexual orgasm is not a peak experience, but it may lead to a peak experience if it opens the way to a deep spiritual love for another. In this regard, humanistic psychology is again quite close to many religious teachings, which see sexuality as a divine gift to be used for positive ends. During a peak experience, time may seem to stop and the immediate environment may recede.

Peak experiences are not necessarily other-worldly or sacred. Rather they may be found in friendship, in family, in work—in the pattern of ordinary life. In this and other aspects of his theorizing, Maslow reflects the influence of the Eastern philosophies and religions, in which he was well read. Spiritual growth and awareness are grounded in the full appreciation of the everyday world.

■ Abraham Maslow put self-actualization at the top of the hierarchy of human needs. He focused on understanding the self-actualized person as a way to better understand what it means to be human.

The Internal Push for Self-Actualization

For Maslow, as well as for Rogers and Jung, there is a natural tendency or pressure toward self-actualization; that is, the push for development comes from inside the growing organism rather than from outside, in the external environment. Such theories are sometimes termed **organismic** because they assume a natural unfolding or life course of each organism (Goldstein, 1963). For example, the influential neuropsychiatrist Kurt Goldstein emphasized the natural unity and coherence of the lives of most individuals. (Maslow met Goldstein when both were at Brandeis University.)

Note, however, that the motivation to grow and self-actualize is different from the drives to satisfy hunger, thirst, or libido and thus relieve tension, in that it is not strictly necessary for survival. Rogers emphasized a mature harmony of the self-concept, whereas Maslow focused on growth toward a higher plane. Whether this organismic unfolding is genetically determined or is more complexly influenced is not clearly specified. Rather, an evolved tendency for growth is simply assumed. Here we see the influence of Charles Darwin on humanistic approaches that are quite distant from modern biological thinking, where we might take his impact for granted.

Organismic
A term sometimes used to describe theories that focus on the development that comes from inside the growing organism and that assume a natural unfolding, or life course, for each organism

There is another way that Darwin's influence is felt in existential–humanistic psychology. In the nineteenth century, most scientists focused on each species as a whole collective. It took the genius of Darwin to note the uniqueness of each individual and the importance of each individual's characteristics (Mayr, 1991). Individual variation forms the basis for natural selection. Humanistic psychologists are similarly focused on the uniqueness of each individual, appreciating the natural—inherent—value of each variation.

Maslow's Hierarchy of Needs

Deficiency Needs
According to Abraham Maslow, needs that are essential for survival including physiological, safety, belonging, love, and esteem needs

Maslow divided organismic needs into two categories. First, he identified several categories of **deficiency needs**—"D-needs" (or "D-motives")—which are necessary for survival. The *physiological needs* are the basic biological necessities such as food, water, sex, and shelter. The so-called *safety needs* involve the necessity of a generally predictable world, one that makes some sense. *Belongingness* and *love needs* involve psychologically intimate relations with other people. And *esteem needs* involve respect for oneself and for others. All of these D-needs motivate us through deficits—we need something to fill a drive or void, and thereby reestablish homeostasis (bodily balance).

Maslow argued that the correct social conditions are needed to encourage the highest level self-actualization; that is, people cannot reach the "being" level ("B-level," with "B-values" or "B-motives") if they are preoccupied with satisfying their more basic needs. We cannot usually fulfill our complete human potential and search for truth and beauty if we lack food, safety, love, and esteem.

Maslow (1987) arranged all of these needs into a hierarchy, as shown in Figure 2. As in psychoanalytic theory, the lower, biologically based drives are shared with most animals. But in a departure from psychoanalytic theory, the higher, uniquely human needs are seen as also biologically based but transcendent. Like Jung, Maslow said that the highest evolved state is to be at peace with oneself, a peculiarly and preciously human quality. Ironically, this assumption is contradicted by modern evolutionary thought. Although most modern biologists admit that humans are more intelligent on most dimensions than other animals, biologists do not believe

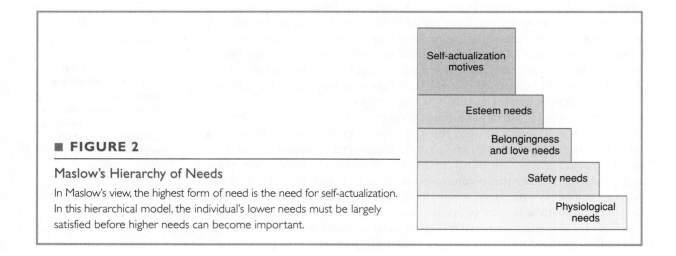

■ FIGURE 2

Maslow's Hierarchy of Needs

In Maslow's view, the highest form of need is the need for self-actualization. In this hierarchical model, the individual's lower needs must be largely satisfied before higher needs can become important.

that humans are "superior" in an evolutionary sense. In other words, humans are not thought to be at the top of the evolutionary tree, merely on one of its branches. (Humans are not the fastest animals nor the strongest, not the best of hearing nor the most monogamous, not the most peaceful, and on and on.)

Although research does suggest that people who generally reach a mature state of personality—people like Mahatma Gandhi—are more likely to act in self-actualized ways, there are also some cases in which people coming from very difficult circumstances and struggling with extraordinary challenges do become self-actualized. It thus seems that Maslow was incorrect in assuming a hierarchy of needs in a literal sense. For example, consider a poor, single mother concerned with issues of beauty and with an artistic bent—she loves to visit art museums and to sketch. Such a person may achieve many elements of self-actualization despite facing many unfilled survival needs. Note also, however, that it is Maslow and the humanistic psychologists who are most willing to emphasize the importance of issues like beauty in the first place.

Measuring Self-Actualization

What evidence is there for Maslow's humanistic conceptualization of self-fulfillment? Are self-actualized people physically and mentally healthier? Maslow himself used any assessment techniques he could—interviews, observations, self-report questionnaires, projective tests, biographical study, and others. This broad approach is necessitated in part by the subjects themselves. Self-actualized people tend to be independent, resist social pressures, love freedom, and have a high need for privacy. Further, their personalities are complex. Thus, they may be difficult to find, assess, and evaluate.

The problem with this loose assessment approach is also a problem with the whole theoretical approach—namely, that it provides insight and perspective but few scientifically verifiable conclusions. One scale that attempts to be more rigorous in its assessment of self-actualization is called the **Personal Orientation Inventory**, or **POI** (Shostrom, 1974). A self-report questionnaire, this inventory asks people to classify themselves on a number of dimensions such as whether they can develop intimate relations with other people, whether they are spontaneous and uninhibited, and so on for the various characteristics of self-actualization. It also assesses whether the person lives optimistically and realistically in the present, as opposed to worrying excessively about the past or the future.

Research using this inventory does seem able to identify people whose life orientations and behaviors are in line with what Maslow would expect. This is not surprising, however, as these matters are what the questionnaire asks about in the first place. More sophisticated, comprehensive research on such topics tends not to be done; personality theorists who adhere to Maslow's ideas generally feel uncomfortable translating lofty humanistic notions into cut-and-dried questionnaires. The research that has been done using the POI finds that the scale has various validity and reliability weaknesses but does capture at least some aspects of a healthy personality

Personal Orientation Inventory (POI)
A self-report questionnaire that asks people to classify themselves on a number of dimensions for the various characteristics of self-actualization or mental health

Mohandas Gandhi
(India)

The Reverend Martin Luther King Jr.
(United States)

Aung San Suu Kyi
(Burma [Myanmar])

 How are we to understand the spirituality, nobility, and courage exemplified by these leaders?

(Burwick & Knapp, 1991; Campbell, Amerikaner, Swank, & Vincent, 1989; Weiss, 1991; Whitson & Olczak, 1991). In other words, self-actualization does seem to be a component of mental health, but we do not yet know exactly what it is or how best to measure it. Research on gratitude finds that people who score high on dimensions of spiritual transcendence—fulfilling prayer, universality, and connectedness—tend to report higher levels of gratitude in their feelings from day to day (Herringer, Miller-Herringer, & Lewis, 2006; McCullough, Tsang, & Emmons, 2004; Sheldon, Elliot, Kim, & Kasser, 2001).

In the best existentialist tradition, Maslow pointed out that science does not exist outside the humans who create it. Thus, science is never value-free. This viewpoint is increasingly recognized throughout the fields of science, as scientists question whether they should build nuclear bombs or chemical weapons or genetically altered embryos. In personality psychology, the issue is especially important because personality psychologists claim to have scientific evidence about human nature—about what it means to be human. Maslow was rightly concerned that a pessimistic view of humans as a collection of base biological drives or as environmentally controlled robots would soon become a self-fulfilling prophecy, as the spiritual and noble aspects of people were increasingly discounted.

In the last years of his life, Maslow became more philosophical in his thinking and more realistic in his insights; he recognized the weaknesses inherent in each person and the conflicts inherent in society. For example, Maslow (1982) wrote in his journal about his self-actualized friends, "all at the top & yet all limited. . . . the top are far from perfect". Lamenting that so many intellectuals are self-centered and unable to work together—he called them prima donnas—Maslow devised a scheme by which each "king of the hill" would control his own empire. (Most universities in fact function just this way.) In other words, Maslow strived to

SHARPEN YOUR THINKING Current Controversy

Is Self-Actualization a Helpful Life Goal?

In Maslow's hierarchy of needs, self-actualization sits at the pinnacle, separated from the more mundane needs beneath it. There is a paradox that may arise when a person has transcended the D-needs and is on the path to the "being" level of self-actualization. The lower needs can be addressed by strongly focusing on them—if your survival is on the line, and you will starve unless you eat, it is helpful to give a great deal of your attention and effort to finding suitable food. Focusing on the goal of finding food makes it more likely that you will reach that goal. Moving up the hierarchy, though, and especially as a person has met all the D-needs, it may be counterproductive to focus directly on self-actualization as a goal. Are the characteristics and criteria for self-actualization consistent with a focus on seeking self-actualization?

Reaching spiritual fulfillment and making creative, constructive, even courageous contributions to humanity may have something in common with looking at stars in the night sky—in both cases, a direct focus on the goal may make the goal harder to reach. In the case of looking at a star, focusing slightly to the left or right of it gives a brighter, clearer image than a direct focus. In the case of self-actualization, reaching the heights of creativity, spiritual harmony, maturity, and sensitivity may be impeded rather than helped by excessive focus on these dimensions as the goal. Self-actualization seems to require a deep immersion in important and fulfilling activities, with the self-actualization coming as a side effect.

If you yourself wished to become more self-actualized, how could you go about achieving that? From a Rogerian perspective, if you wanted to "become yourself," how would you proceed? Would this be the same path that would lead you toward self-actualization?

believe the best about the potentialities of human beings, but, like Jung and many others, ultimately had to admit that the darker, weaker side of people could never be eliminated.

Happiness and Positive Psychology

In the 1776 Declaration of Independence, Thomas Jefferson and his colleagues went somewhat beyond then-current philosophical notions about sanctity of life and individual liberty, and asserted "unalienable Rights, that among these are Life, Liberty and the pursuit of Happiness." Many now pursue happiness, but who is happy?

From the point of view of an outside observer, we might hypothesize that someone with good food to eat, a safe place to live, good friends, good health, and a family filled with love has a high quality of life. Such factors do indeed emerge in comparisons across large groups of people. But, more commonly, we want to know what the individuals themselves think. This approach to happiness is termed **subjective well-being** (Diener, 2000). People want to feel self-fulfilled, but many do not achieve this goal.

Research confirms that happy people, who feel mildly or moderately happy most of the time, are not enthralled by acquiring big houses, fast cars, fashionable furnishings, luxury travel, and glittering jewelry. Conversely, injury and adverse circumstances do not necessarily make one unhappy! In fact, research suggests that

Subjective Well-Being
What individuals think of their own level of happiness or their quality of life

most people soon adapt somewhat to changes in their situations (Diener, 2000; Myers, 2000; Wortman & Silver, 1991). Winning the lottery (or losing one's job) will not necessarily produce more than temporary elation (or distress). This hedonic adaptation means that most people stably approach life changes, without chronic and severe mood swings. Yet, full adaptation is not inevitable, and significant changes like permanent disability that remove one from one's meaningful social activities can cause a significant drop in one's sense of well-being (Lucas, 2007).

Notions of the ultimate emptiness of materialism date back thousands of years to the very beginnings of Western religions: "Happy is the person who finds wisdom, And the person who gains understanding; For its proceeds are better than the profit of silver, and the gain better than fine gold" (Proverbs 3:13). Yet few college students plan to forego future wealth and instead spend their lives studying subjects like personality psychology.

One echo of the existential dilemma that thus occurs in modern affluent countries is the conflict between the pull (and support) of the community versus the individual freedom that wealth allows. Instead of sharing a bedroom, children (and sometimes even each parent) now sleep alone in a private bedroom. Instead of crowding together in one family room, there is plenty of room ("space") in many of today's large houses. Rather than living close to many neighbors in cities, many well-off people spread out to the suburbs and vacation in remote retreats. Loneliness or anomie is often a result.

What then characterizes happy individuals, if not wealth, space, and unlimited freedom? It is not age, gender, or income, nor traditional traits. There are only minor to moderate associations with extroversion (presumably because extroverts are more sensitive to rewards), and agreeableness (presumably because agreeable people are trusting and altruistic). There is an inverse association with neuroticism, as neurotics tend to be anxious, cynical, and pessimistic (DeNeve & Cooper, 1998; Mroczek & Spiro, 2005; Watson, 2000). But these traits often do not capture what we mean by "happy" people. Further, the matter is complicated by the situations people seek out for themselves. For general well-being and life satisfaction, personality

■ Recent research confirms the ancient wisdom that wealth does not buy happiness. Even people who are unimaginably rich seek meaningful activities and social values, just as humanistic psychology predicts. Warren Buffett, one of the wealthiest people in the world, donated over $30 billion (the bulk of his net worth and the largest charitable donation ever recorded) to the Bill and Melinda Gates Foundation. Buffett (on the right) is shown here with Bill and Melinda Gates, announcing his gift. The foundation focuses its efforts on fighting global poverty and disease, and promoting education and access to technology.

■ Three popular paths to seeking happiness are pursuit of material possessions, seeking pleasure in love and learning, and immersion in spirituality and community. Ironically, none of the three by themselves is a direct road to happiness, just as the existentialists warned many years ago.

is a predictor of relevant life achievements like job and marital satisfaction, which in turn are often relevant to overall satisfaction (Heller, Watson, & Ilies, 2004). Both personality factors and situational factors are important.

Interestingly, psychologists studying subjective well-being have often found that the best rationalizers are the most content. People who see things as always working out for the best are happiest. Furthermore, perceived financial situation and perceived control over life affect happiness, and these are not directly related to one's objective circumstances. And some people simply seem chronically more happy, again probably due to internal psychological processes (Diener, 2000; Johnson & Krueger, 2006; Lyubomirsky, 2001; Myers, 2000).

Happy individuals are less bothered when their peers do better than they do, whereas unhappy individuals are disappointed in their peers' accomplishments, and are relieved by their acquaintances' failures. Happy individuals look for information that is "good news," but otherwise don't worry much about how they compare to others. Happy people tend to think about and remember positive events in their lives. Happy people create meaning in their lives by interpreting events in terms of humanistic values of personal growth, meaningful social ties, and giving back to society. Unhappy people tend to dwell on negative happenings, and ruminate about their problems and distress (Bauer, McAdams, & Sakaeda, 2005; Lyubomirsky, 2001; Lyubomirsky & Ross, 1999; Lyubomirsky, Sousa, & Dickerhoof, 2006).

Happy people do have good relations with an intimate other, a sense of purpose and hope, and work or hobbies they enjoy. They often help others and have a sense of faith or trust. Yet it is not clear to what extent one can *make* oneself happy by getting married, becoming a volunteer, or going to church (Diener, Lucas, & Scollon, 2006; McCullough, Bono, & Root, 2005) (see also the Classic to Current box).

Positive Psychology

Positive Psychology
The movement in modern psychology to focus on positive attributes rather than on pathology

As Abraham Maslow and Carl Rogers urged a half-century ago, a significant segment of modern personality is now turning toward exploring the positive forces of life, a movement that has been named **positive psychology**. Positive psychology is more concerned with creativity, hope, wisdom, and spirituality and less troubled with aggression, weakness, and pathology (Seligman & Csikszentmihalyi, 2000).

In the health arena, this focus means attention to positive illusions (which help us cope with misfortune) and to self-healing processes (which promote an emotional stability or balance) (Friedman, 2000b; Friedman et al., 1995; Taylor, Kemeny, Reed, Bower, & Grunewald, 2000). In other words, people who are enthusiastic, trusting, feel in control, and have coping resources to meet challenges and personalities that match situations tend to stay healthier and live longer.

Yet the existential psychologist Rollo May believed that although many superficial things (like happy hours) can make us temporarily happy, true joy is something much deeper. True joy and fulfillment come from using your talents—indeed the totality of your being—to strive for important accomplishments. Rollo May thus foreshadowed the most recent emphases of positive psychology on studies of wisdom, thriving, and excellence in performance. There is increasing attention to patterns that prevent an unhealthy personality from developing, and promote healthy psychological growth, as well as attention to how and why some people remain resilient in response to crises and stress (Peterson & Park, 2009). Yet stubborn dilemmas remain, including one that has come to be called the American paradox.

The American Paradox

American Paradox
The contemporary situation where we have material abundance co-occurring with social recession and psychological depression

People in Western, developed countries have entered the twenty-first century with a societal wealth unimaginable in other times or places. House sizes are large, computers and cell phones are everywhere, and cruise ships are plentiful. Are we better off than we were? Psychologist David Myers (2000) answers: materially yes, morally no. He terms this phenomenon the **American paradox**. On the one hand we have material abundance, but on the other hand, we have social recession and psychological depression.

There are high rates of divorce, suicide, depression, and conflict, with significant numbers of nonmarital births, abusive families, teenage criminals, and poverty of the spirit. Community ties have decreased and happiness has not increased. We have more sexual partners and more sexual disease, more freedom and more disillusionment, more gadgets and more therapists. Are we happy yet?

To address this paradox, Myers and others recommend altruism, fidelity, family, community, and spirituality, which they believe will lead to fulfillment. They see hope in neighborhood organizing, in youth volunteering, and in communitarian faiths. Although there is some evidence to support this view, it is hardly a new one. More than 2,500 years ago, the prophet Jeremiah denounced false worship and social injustice, and urged a turning away from selfishness and materialism.

Classic to **Current**

Thinking, Doing, Self-Actualization, and Happiness

Classic existentialist–humanistic personality theorists wrestle with the tension between a focus on internal self-concepts versus external environmental contingencies. One does not live in a world wholly of one's own creation, but one is not merely a cog in a mechanical world either. People must struggle to make sense of their worlds, combating anxiety and dread to transcend struggle and strive for self-actualization in challenging circumstances.

A similar tension emerges in modern research on happiness. Although researchers agree that material possessions do not, in themselves, bring happiness, there is disagreement on the importance of internal-based rationalizations and environment-based interactions. Some researchers focus outwardly and point happiness seekers toward such environment-based social behaviors as altruism, fidelity, forgiveness, and community. But other researchers point toward such internal-based rationalizations as remembering positive events, being unbothered by others' triumphs, and adapting to one's own situation. For example, in one study about college applications, self-reported happy and unhappy high school seniors evaluated colleges after applying for admission, and then later after making their college choices. Happy students turned out to be more satisfied with all the college choices they had, and they more sharply devalued the desirable colleges that rejected them, thus maintaining their happiness (Lyubomirsky & Ross, 1999). Happiness, in this study, was more a function of internal rationalizations than external encounters. Many other studies, however, show the benefits of altruistic acts, such as behaving kindly toward strangers. Even more, sometimes external acts help shape one's own positive self-image.

Based on the work of David G. Myers (2000), one of the wisest interpreters of research on what makes people happy, and the work of leading researchers like Ed Diener (2000; Diener, Lucas, & Scollon, 2006) and Sonja Lyubomirsky (2001), we can derive the following suggestions for pursuing happiness.

1. Help others. As one pays less attention to one's own problems and builds positive, intimate relations with others, one's sense of well-being increases.

2. Monitor one's wealth-seeking. Because people soon adapt to newfound wealth, material possessions themselves do not guarantee happiness. Resources that help one to engage in productive or absorbing activities may, however, promote happiness.

3. Avoid television. Being inactive, being unengaged with others, being passive, and limiting one's physical activity all can promote unhappiness.

4. Keep lists or journals of your accomplishments and other things to be grateful for, to remind yourself of the good things in your life. Do this weekly and monthly.

5. Seek spiritual or awe-inspiring experiences in life, especially experiences that fit with your temperament. These could be religious, nature-based, artistic, scientific, or creative.

6. Set long-term goals and move on quickly after any short-term failures. Recognize and relish the fact that life has many difficult challenges.

7. Recognize that many people have tendencies to be relatively unhappy, due to a combination of biology, early experiences, past learning, thoughts and abilities, and current situations. If you are such a person, don't dwell on it. Like personality, happiness levels can improve, but usually change only very slowly over long periods of time.

FURTHER READING

Diener, E. (2000). Subjective well-being: The science of happiness and a proposal for a national index. *American Psychologist*, *55*(1), 34–43.

Diener, E., Lucas, R., & Scollon, C. N. (2006). Beyond the hedonic treadmill: Revising the adaptation theory of well-being. *American Psychologist*, *61*(4), 305–314.

Lyubomirsky, S. (2001). Why are some people happier than others? The role of cognitive and motivational processes in well-being. *American Psychologist*, *56*, 239–249.

Lyubomirsky, S., & Ross, L. (1999). Changes in attractiveness of elected, rejected, and precluded alternatives: A comparison of happy and unhappy individuals. *Journal of Personality and Social Psychology*, *76*(6), 988–1007.

Myers, D. G. (2000). *The American paradox: Spiritual hunger in an age of plenty*. New Haven, CT: Yale University Press.

TIME LINE

The History of Humanistic and Existential Approaches to Personality

The major developments in the humanistic and existential approaches can be seen here in historical relation to one another and in relation to their broader societal and cultural contexts.

Developments in Humanistic–Existential Aspects		Societal and Scientific Context
Philosophers and theologians discuss the good and evil natures of individuals	Ancient Times and Middle Ages	Humans are seen primarily in religious terms, as created by a divine presence
Individual is increasingly understood to have a unique nature, entitled to pursue happiness	1700s–1800s	Increasing emphasis on reason and rationality; philosophers search for the core of human nature
Radical alternative worldviews discussed, in reaction against positivism and the dominance of empirical science	1920s–1940s	Experimental psychology is dominated by behaviorism, while clinical psychology is dominated by psychoanalysis; rise of fascism
Influence of existentialism grows as philosophers and writers emphasize individual choice, commitment, and responsibility	1940s–1950s	Intellectual reactions against fascism; world war followed by emergence of United States as leading power
Humanistic psychology flourishes as Carl Rogers and Abraham Maslow emphasize self-trust and self-actualization	1960s	Clinical psychology attempts to become more science-based, and experimental psychology considers clinical applications
Encounter groups, support groups, and other manifestations of the human potential movement emerge	1960s–1970s	New roles for women and new family structures; cultural revolutions (sexual, gender, social) and experimentation with new ways to live
Studies of happiness, flow, and religiosity increase; positive psychology founded	1990s–2000s	Concern with the dignity of the individual in an increasingly technological and threatening world; ethical considerations accompany medical breakthroughs

Similarly, as we have seen, Erich Fromm (1956) argued that capitalist societies create the culture of consumption to maintain themselves; and he predicted that alienation, without love and without individual freedom to "be" rather than merely to "have," would lead to high rates of depression and discontent. There is indeed evidence that money leads to a self-sufficient orientation in which individuals prefer to be more independent of others and have others less dependent on them; further, people experimentally encouraged to be thinking about money were less helpful to other people (Vohs, Mead, & Goode, 2006).

Happiness levels rise in countries that move from having widespread poverty to having adequate levels of food, shelter, and security—just as Maslow predicted. Once basic needs are met, however, materialism becomes less important and more abstract matters like freedom can play a role in feelings of happiness (Ingelhart, Foa, Peterson, & Welzel, 2008). But within a given society, happiness is often influenced by one's position relative to others (Boyce, Brown, & Moore, 2010). As the humanistic psychologists warned, the more you compare yourself to those who seem to have more than you, the worse you feel.

Capitalism, education, and investment in science have produced a true information and communication revolution, in which we have record numbers of college graduates and instant access to a fantastic array of information. Paradoxically, much of this material "progress," when not tuned to pornography or sports scores, is often used to search for wisdom in ancient texts and prophecies, written with quills onto parchment. These are ongoing dilemmas raised by humanistic and existential approaches to personality. Perhaps national leaders should have a "council of well-being advisors" in addition to a council of economic advisors (Diener & Seligman, 2004).

A different emphasis is well articulated by the imaginative astronomer Carl Sagan (1996). In one of his last works, Sagan instead offers science as a "candle in the dark," as a beacon against superstition. Like the humanists, Sagan bemoans our society of murder, rape, cruelty, and consumerism. Sagan, however, sees rigorous science as the golden road to protection against world-altering and community-destroying technologies. Science, which demands the free exchange of ideas, logical values, and critical evaluation, is seen as the path toward a real understanding of human nature. He fears the demon-haunted world of superstitious religion.

Further Evaluation of Existential–Humanistic Approaches

Existential and humanistic approaches to personality are in some ways reminiscent of psychoanalytic approaches: They derive from complex and dynamic inner motivations. This is in contrast to theories that look for structures within the individual or for structures in the environmental reinforcers. However, existential and humanistic theories allow for free will and for true creativity, heroism, and self-fulfillment. Existential approaches are necessarily idiographic approaches; they consider each individual experience unique.

Why Does It Matter?

Why does it matter that humanistic approaches, based on existentialism but rejecting pessimism, are such optimistic approaches to personality, viewing humans and their spiritual matters in a positive light? The humanistic orientation, with its emphasis on studying self-fulfilled, fully mature individuals, brought much-needed attention in personality psychology to these positive and spiritual aspects of what it means to be a person.

Evaluating the Perspectives

Advantages and Limits of the Humanistic–Existential Approach

■ Quick Analogy

- Humans as free, sentient beings seeking spiritual fulfillment.

■ Advantages

- Emphasizes courageous struggle for self-fulfillment and dignity.
- Appreciates the spiritual nature of a person.
- Often based on the study of healthy, well-adjusted individuals.
- Considers each individual's experience unique.

■ Limits

- May avoid quantification and scientific method needed for science of personality.
- Sometimes insufficiently concerned with reason or logic.
- Theories are sometimes ambiguous or inconsistent.

■ View of Free Will

- Free will is essential to being human.

■ Common Assessment Techniques

- Interview, self-exploration, art, literature, biographical analysis of creativity and special achievement, self-report tests, observation.

■ Implications for Therapy

- Encourages self-knowledge through experiences (including spiritual experiences) appropriate to the individual. Values retreats (get-aways), self-disclosure, communal trust. May encourage creativity and self-expression through art, writing, dance, or travel. Rogers's client-centered therapy offers a genuine, empathic therapist who offers unconditional positive regard. Encourages realization of your own goals through supportive reflections (by friends or therapist) of your own advances. Encourages devotion and service to combat anxiety and alienation.

Existential philosophers place responsibility for personality squarely on the shoulders of the individual. How will I deal with love, ethics, anxiety, freedom, death? Will I allow alienation to sink me into the deepest despair, or will I use my free will to triumph and self-actualize? Inherent in existential dilemmas are the possibilities for the triumph of the human spirit.

The humanistic approach to personality is conducive to cross-cultural study and the study of ethnic groups. Many existential and humanistic psychologists were terribly shocked—both personally and intellectually—by the fascism of the 1930s and '40s. For example, Fromm repeatedly warns of the dire consequences of trying to run from the existential anxiety produced by modern freedoms. Humanistic theorists are willing to explore alternative views—such as Eastern views or religious views—of what it means to be human.

One area in which humanistic approaches to personality have had a large practical and continuing impact on general society is in the area of personal retreats. Today we do not think it odd if a hard-working adult (or even a small group of coworkers) goes away for a retreat. This "get-away" differs markedly from a traditional vacation of sports or sightseeing. During a personal retreat, we might hide away in a scenic location, try to get in touch with our feelings, renew our love for our partner, work on our music or creativity, exercise, and perhaps meditate or pray. Such activities derive from the humanistic assumption that each individual has a unique inner potential that will unfold if properly nurtured.

Humanistic personality psychology differs from other approaches not only in its subject matter and its philosophy, but also in its ideology. Humanistic theories explicitly condemn reductionistic psychology that strives to "reduce" human beings to drives or neurons or conditioned reflexes. Although this orientation has implications for the conduct of science (such as strict protection of the rights of human subjects), it is also in part a set of personal preferences about the nature of humanity. Rogers, Maslow, and other humanistic psychologists were particularly irked by B. F. Skinner's views of personality. It was not just that Skinner claimed to be studying human psychology by observing pigeons and laboratory rats. What was particularly irksome was that Skinner boldly spelled out the parameters of a utopian society (*Walden Two*). Skinner, purporting to move beyond freedom and dignity, proposed setting up the contingencies of the environment so that humans would learn to behave responsibly. This was anathema to Rogers and Maslow, whose approaches are forged on just such notions of freedom, dignity, and individual responsibility.

Nondeterministic
The idea that it is an oversimplification to view people as controlled by fixed physical laws

Summary and Conclusion

What is the nature of the human spirit? What is love? How do we measure human success? Any full psychological understanding of what it means to be a person should provide a relevant psychological perspective for addressing these age-old questions. Existential–humanistic approaches to personality tackle these issues head on.

Existentialism is an area of philosophy concerned with the meaning of human existence. Existentialists speak of beings-in-the-world; simply put, the self cannot exist without a world, and the world cannot exist without a person (a being) to perceive it. People are active, conscious beings, always thinking. Similarly,

questions about choosing to be ethical and moral, and about feeling guilt and anxiety, are seen as essential aspects of being human, rather than as incidental by-products of the biological nature of human beings.

Aspects of existential approaches are sometimes termed "phenomenological," in that people's perceptions or subjective realities are considered to be valid data for investigation. The existential approach is also **nondeterministic** because it argues against viewing people as controlled by fixed physical laws.

Humanism is a philosophical movement that emphasizes values and the personal worth of the individual; a humanistic approach to personality likewise attends to matters of ethics and personal worth. Abraham Maslow called humanistic psychology the "third force" in psychology, with only humanistic approaches emphasizing the creative, spontaneous, and active nature of human beings. Life develops as people create worlds for themselves. This view moves from humans "being" to humans "becoming"; that is, there is an active movement toward self-fulfillment in the healthy personality. The human potential movement, which began in the 1960s, is one example of the existential–humanistic approach to personality, but the implications of humanistic approaches for healthy personality development are being felt throughout society.

The humanistic psychoanalyst Erich Fromm maintained that love is an art—not something that one stumbles into, and not some nebulous epiphenomenon that has no real meaning. Love requires knowledge, effort, and experience. Fromm's concern was that in modern society, we are alienated from ourselves, from others, and from nature. We try to cover this inner alienation by "having fun." If we do not fight loneliness by working in a loving way to help others, then we may escape from the burden of freedom by giving up our freedom, such as to a dictator. For Fromm, the most mature personality is one that transcends the ordinary demands of life and creates an active positive identity involving productive, respectful love of others. As Fromm predicted, an alienated, noncommunal society is increasingly afflicted with violence, divorce, and civil strife.

The influential humanistic psychologist Carl Rogers likewise believed that people have an inherent tendency toward growth and maturation. But the maturation is not inevitable. Rather, people can gain self-understanding in a supportive psychosocial environment if they take responsibility. According to Rogers, a psychologically healthy person is one who has a broad self-concept that can understand and accept many feelings and experiences. Inner control is healthier than imposed control. Of special concern are discrepancies between what a person thinks of himself and the total range of his experiences. Inabilities to accept aspects of oneself are impediments on the path to personal growth. Rogers says that a person should "become one's self."

Some existential perspectives are not so sanguine and optimistic, focusing instead on the anxiety and dread that the freedom to create one's own meaning brings. This sense of alienation from modern society was foreseen by two nineteenth-century philosophers: Søren Kierkegaard, who emphasized the importance of human faith, and Friedrich Nietzsche, who showed the importance of passion and creativity. In this tradition, Rollo May bridges the gap between existential and humanistic approaches to personality with a focus on the anxiety that must accompany any attempt to live life to its fullest. Such existential–humanistic approaches have had a tremendous impact among people facing life-threatening illness.

Self-actualization is the innate process by which one grows spiritually and realizes one's potential. Although few people become completely self-fulfilled, Abraham Maslow thought positive and peak experiences to be a significant aspect of personality. During a peak experience, time may seem to stop and the immediate environment may recede. According to Maslow, self-actualized people have a realistic knowledge of themselves and accept themselves, and are independent and spontaneous. Such aspects of humanistic psychology are close to many Western and Eastern religious teachings. Maslow helped divert the study of personality away from psychopathology and toward the study of the most well-adjusted, self-actualized people. And in the best existentialist tradition, Maslow pointed out that science does not exist outside of the humans who create it. Thus, science is never value-free. Existential–humanistic theories allow for true creativity and heroism.

Happiness is not a simple function of being in favorable circumstances. Rather, happy individuals are less bothered when their peers do better than they do, and happy people look for information that is "good news." These people see things as always working out for the best. They think about and remember positive events in their lives, whereas unhappy people tend to dwell on negative happenings, and ruminate about their problems and distress. As the humanists proposed, happy people do have good relations with an intimate other, a sense of purpose and hope, often help others, and may have a sense of faith or trust. Further, some people simply are chronically more happy, probably due in part to internal psychological processes.

Existential–humanistic approaches, which are necessarily idiographic approaches, consider individual experience unique. Proponents vehemently denounce reductionistic psychology that strives to "reduce" human beings to drives, neurons, or conditioned reflexes. On the other hand, critics have accused humanistic approaches to personality of being insuffi-ciently concerned with logic and reason; indeed, the intellectual forefather of humanistic psychology Jean-Jacques Rousseau was similarly condemned for pro-claiming the value of feelings over reason.

■ Key Theorists

Erich Fromm	Victor Frankl	Carl Rogers
Rollo May	Abraham Maslow	Ed Diener

■ Key Concepts and Terms

existentialism

being-in-the-world

phenomenological

nondeterministic

the experiencing person

Rogerian therapy

self-actualization

teleology

peak experiences

organismic

humanism

I-Thou dialogue versus I-It monologue

human potential movement

dialectical humanism

hierarchy of needs

deficiency needs

Personal Orientation Inventory (POI)

dialectical tension

subjective well-being

American paradox

Person–Situation Interactionist Aspects of Personality

From Chapter 10 of *Personality: Classic Theories and Modern Research*, Fifth Edition. Howard S. Friedman, Miriam W. Schustack. Copyright © 2012 by Pearson Education, Inc. Published by Pearson Allyn & Bacon. All rights reserved.

Person–Situation Interactionist Aspects of Personality

Fraudulent investment advisor Bernie Madoff, with a sterling reputation, stole billions of dollars from charities and pension funds in a massive Ponzi scheme, enriching himself and forcing others to later face deprivation and struggle.

In recent years, many other well-known, wealthy, and highly successful corporate executives including Jeffrey Skilling of Enron, Bernard Ebbers of World-Com, John Rigas of Adelphia Corporation, Dennis Kozlowski of Tyco, Samuel Waksal of ImClone, and Martha Stewart of Martha Stewart Living were likewise convicted of felonies including conspiracy, fraud, obstruction of justice, making false statements to authorities, and the like. Many did the *perp walk* in which the police intentionally parade the perpetrator in

© AP Images/Bebeto Matthews

336

front of the public, as a lesson that even highly educated, thoughtful, responsible, trusted, and tested individuals can sometimes behave in ways that are very wrong and even criminal. Because of these crimes, many innocent employees, investors, and associates lost their jobs, pensions, marriages, family security, and more. How can we understand this?

In 1927, a number of schoolchildren were placed (by researchers) into a situation in which they had the opportunity to copy correct answers to an examination from an answer key. The researchers wanted to measure the students' degrees of honesty—to see if they would cheat! As we might expect, some of the students cheated, but others did not. They were then given the opportunity to "find" money that had been planted in a puzzle box by researchers. Some students kept (stole) the money, but others did not. What was the personality of the cheaters and thieves? One interesting result of this research was that students who appeared honest on some tasks appeared dishonest on others (Hartshorne & May, 1928). A "cheating personality" could not be found.

Is this result so surprising? On the one hand, most people consider themselves quite different from "crooks," whom they believe should be locked away. (And when caught, they might insist, "I am not a crook!") On the other hand, many people consider themselves to be basically honest but know that they may not do the perfectly honest thing in all situations. They may unfairly get help with their homework, or claim extra dependents on their tax returns. There are few people who are always honest or always dishonest.

S tudies like the 1927 cheaters study, which observe behavior in order to measure personality, have the advantage of relying on tangible, meaningful data. But a problem arises from the fact that people are inconsistent. Such inconsistencies led researchers in the 1930s to wonder about the general importance of personality, and these concerns were picked up again by researchers in the 1960s (Mischel, 1968). How can we talk about personality if people change their behavior from situation to situation?

The founders of modern personality psychology grappled with these same problems. For Kurt Lewin (1935), behavior was clearly a function of both personal characteristics and the immediate social situation. In fact, he summed it up in the equation $B = f(P, E)$—behavior is a function of the person *and* the environment. Gordon Allport (1961) addressed the dilemma and concluded that part of each behavior pattern represents an unvarying, underlying predisposition, but that the propensity to act is realized in different ways in different situations. And for Henry Murray (1938), needs motivated the individual from the inside *and* an environmental "press" (such as family conflict) affected the individual from the outside.

Thus, the idea that personality and the situation interact to affect behavior is an old one. People express their personality in different ways in different situations. What is new about person–situation interactionist approaches to personality is that they attempt explicitly to consider the social situation. This chapter traces the roots of the interactionist approach to personality and explains some of its most modern realizations. It helps us understand who is a crook.

Interpersonal Psychiatry: Harry Stack Sullivan

Imagine a baby boy whose needs for love and tenderness are not being met by his mother. His mother behaves erratically, is unhappy, and is often absent. His father, frustrated and unemotional, withdraws into himself. Further imagine that the boy is a Catholic growing up in a prejudiced Protestant farming community. Finally, add in the pressures of homosexual feelings stirring within a boy growing up in an aggressively heterosexual world. This describes the early life of the influential psychiatrist Harry Stack Sullivan (Chapman, 1976; Pearce, 1985; Perry, 1982). Although Sullivan proposed his theories in the 1940s, his ideas are very relevant to the personality theories of today.

Perhaps the easiest way to understand a key contribution of Sullivan to personality theory is to consider his idea of **chumship**, the important role played by peers in the formation of identity. Think about the influences—the social situations—of a 10-year-old boy like Harry. (Sullivan focused on boys but analogous issues occur for girls.) The preadolescent is putting some distance between himself and his parents, but earnestly seeking acceptance by his peers. Significant psychosocial threats to well-being are loneliness, isolation, and rejection. Note that all of these threats are inherently *social*: It makes no sense to speak about rejection unless some group is doing the rejecting. For Sullivan, it is of the utmost importance to understand the feelings of anxiety that arise when interpersonal rejection occurs (Berndt, 2007). He thus locates healthy or unhealthy psychological development in the reactions of one's peers. The most modern research confirms that social acceptance or rejection is a core element influencing individual behavior (Baumeister, Brewer, Tice, & Twenge, 2007).

Chumship

Harry Stack Sullivan's idea, derived from the sociological concept of the social self, that a preadolescent's chums serve as a social mirror for forming his or her identity

Interpersonal Psychiatry Contrasted with Psychoanalytic Theory

Others trained in psychoanalysis, such as Karen Horney and Erich Fromm, had begun turning away from Freud's focus on internal drives and struggles and had begun emphasizing the social environment. But the major shift came from Harry Stack Sullivan. For Sullivan (1953), personality is inextricably tied to social situations; personality is "the relatively enduring pattern of recurrent interpersonal situations" that characterizes a person's life (p. 111). Sullivan's approach is thus sometimes known as the **interpersonal theory of psychiatry**. It focuses on the recurring social situations that we face. It constituted a major break from psychoanalytic and ego traditions.

Sullivan's approach, like that of Kurt Lewin, is closely tied to social psychology. Sullivan (who, like Lewin, developed his main ideas in the 1930s) was heavily influenced by the so-called Chicago School of sociology and philosophy, particularly by George Herbert Mead (1968) and Edward Sapir.

Mead is best known for his intriguing writings about the **social self**. The social self is the idea that who we are and how we think of ourselves arises from our interactions with those around us. While Freudians were focusing on the child's struggle with internal Oedipal conflicts, Mead was looking at the child's ongoing social interactions with significant others. If a four-year-old says, "I'm a very smart and handsome little boy," where does this self-concept come from? For Mead, the source was clearly the child's understanding of his interactions and discussions with his parents.

■ According to Sullivan's idea of chumship, a preadolescent's pals serve as a social mirror for forming his or her identity. Just as we look in a real mirror to adjust our clothing, we look in a mirror of friends for feedback about our values and our personal strengths and weaknesses. This notion is derived from the sociological idea of a social self.

Personality as a Pattern of Interpersonal Interactions

Edward Sapir, the other key influence on Sullivan, was an anthropologist. By studying diverse societies, Sapir (1956) saw that behavior was heavily influenced by culture. Harry Stack Sullivan integrated the work of Mead and of Sapir and concluded that enduring patterns of human relationships—shaped by family and society—form the essence of personality. Sullivan believed that to understand personality, we must look to recurring patterns of social relations in a real societal context. A 10-year-old farm boy who cannot develop interaction patterns of mutuality and reciprocity with a chum may be at high risk for a life of loneliness and possibly despair.

Sullivan was born in upstate New York in 1892. His first professional work was in a series of mental hospitals, and there is some indication that Sullivan himself struggled mightily to maintain his emotional equilibrium. (It often seems that "it takes one to know one." Theorists rely heavily on their own personal insights in their theorizing.) But his career blossomed as his intriguing personality and his unorthodox ideas gained greater and greater acceptance. Although he had much in

Interpersonal Theory of Psychiatry
Harry Stack Sullivan's approach to personality that focuses on the recurring social situations faced by an individual

Social Self
George Herbert Mead's idea that who we are and how we think of ourselves arise from our interactions with those around us; also, having an identity in a social world

© Thinkstock

■ This student is very serious and conscientious in this situation, where she is attending a course lecture. To what extent can we use this information about her to predict her behavior in other situations? What other information would be helpful?

Illusion of Individuality
According to Harry Stack Sullivan, the idea that a person has a single, fixed personality is just an illusion

common with Karen Horney, Sullivan's approach is not neo-Freudian (Pearce, 1985). For Sullivan, personality is not built around the unconscious impulses of the id, nor is it fixed in early childhood. Rather, it constantly changes as a function of relations with others. Ironically but perhaps not surprisingly, Sullivan died alone after attending a meeting in Paris in 1949.

To a personality psychologist like Sullivan who believes in the idea of a social self, we actually become "different" people in different social situations! In each social situation, we imagine how others think of us and respond accordingly. Sometimes people move to a new town to make a "fresh start"—they try to present a new image to new friends, new neighbors, new coworkers. This can be successful if they are careful not to fall back into re-creating old patterns. Or a college student may behave very differently when she or he returns home on vacation and interacts with old high school friends; the high school friends have different expectations than the new college friends, and the student responds appropriately. The situation affects (elicits) the personality. Personality emerges as a combination of individual inclinations and the social situation. In fact, Sullivan termed the idea that a person has a single, fixed personality the **illusion of individuality**. In a sense, we may have as many personalities as we have interpersonal situations.

Since personality is primarily a function of social expectations, Sullivan blames society (not internal neuroses) for most of the individual's problems. Society is seen as stifling the creative growth needs of the individual. Anxiety comes from without, not from within. So, for example, Sullivan promoted the idea that it is more often harmful than helpful to lock away people who are mentally "ill" in mental "sanitariums." And indeed, social policy gradually changed and many mental hospitals closed, an example of how personality theory can sometimes have dramatic effects on social policy. Sullivan was often successful as a psychiatrist by having himself and his staff become like "chums" to his patients. He overcame many of his own problems and he believed that healthy, positive interpersonal relations could help other people overcome their problems.

With this emphasis on the social situation—that the focus of personality study should be on the interpersonal situation, not solely on the individual—Sullivan and others who well understood social psychology helped lay the groundwork for modern interactionist approaches. But perhaps the most influential precursor of the modern movement was Henry A. Murray.

Motivation and Goals: Henry A. Murray

In 1933, Henry Murray read a scary story to children at his daughter's birthday party, and he found that they projected their fear onto others—they saw images of men as more insidious and threatening. During World War II, Murray had to give up his lectern and put his theories and methods to patriotic work: The U.S. Army had him screen men who would be trained as spies and sent on dangerous missions. Murray's (1948) team used interviews and projective tests but also created challenging, stressful situations for the select recruits to react to. For example, who would climb to a dangerous height and why? Murray thus combined his deep knowledge of human motivation with his sensitivity to social and situational demands to create a view of personality that has stimulated much work. By the way, spy and counterspy agencies like the CIA and FBI now routinely conduct such psychological screening on their potential employees.

Henry Murray (1938) defined personality as the "branch of psychology which principally concerns itself with the study of human lives and the factors which influence their course, [and] which investigates individual differences" (p. 4). Because Murray viewed personality as the study of human lives across time, he necessarily watched and analyzed the interactions of individuals and the situations they encountered throughout their lives. Murray took the unconscious motivations from Freud, Jung, and Adler, the environmental pressures from Lewin, and the sophisticated trait concept from Allport and synthesized them into a comprehensive approach to personality. Murray thus can be considered a primary founder of the interactionist approach to personality.

Henry Murray was born in New York and became a physician doing biochemical research (with a Ph.D. from Cambridge University) before turning to psychology after a visit to Carl Jung in Zurich. Murray was psychoanalyzed first by Jung and then by Franz Alexander, a leader in psychosomatic medicine. He reports that these giants led him to experience the great power of unconscious motivation. Murray became director of the Harvard Psychological Clinic (treating people with psychological problems) but decided that he could learn more by studying healthy people. He blended psychoanalytic and neo-analytic ideas into a basis for empirical research.

The Personological System

Due to his emphasis on studying the richness of the life of each person, Murray preferred the term *personology* to the term *personality*; even today, psychologists working in the Murray tradition often call themselves *personologists*. Furthermore, Murray was influenced by twentieth-century philosopher Alfred North Whitehead to focus on the process of personality rather than to rely on static concepts such as enduring structures in the mind. **Systems**—dynamic influences with feedback—are key. Thus, he referred to his theory as a **personological system**.

Murray emphasized the integrated, dynamic nature of the individual as a complex organism responding to a specific environment. Therefore, on the one hand, Murray stressed the importance of needs and motivations, an emphasis that has proved quite influential. (See Table 1 for some of the needs identified by Murray.) On the other hand, Murray also emphasized the **environmental press**—the push of the situation. These are directional forces on a person that arise from other people or events in the environment. For example, seeing one's friends getting good grades in school might be a press spurring one's own efforts to excel. Take the case of whether a student will cheat: We might find that a high need to achieve in school might combine with a situation in which a lot can be gained by cheating, at low risk or cost; in this situation, cheating would more likely be the result.

Systems
According to Henry Murray, sets of dynamic influences with feedback

Personological System
Henry Murray's term for his theory of personality that emphasizes the richness of the life of each person and the dynamic nature of the individual as a complex organism responding to a specific environment

Environmental Press
The push of the situation emphasized in Henry Murray's approach to personality; it is a directional force on a person that arises from other people and events in the environment

■ TABLE I   Examples of Murray's Needs

Need	Description
Affiliation	Need to be near and enjoyably reciprocate with another.
Autonomy	Need to be free and independent of others.
Dominance	Need to control or influence others.
Exhibition	Need to be seen and heard, to entertain and entice.
Harm-avoidance	Need to avoid injury, take precautions.
Nurturance	Need to help, console, comfort, nurse the weak.
Order	Need for organization and neatness.
Play	Need for enjoyment and fun.
Sex	Need to form an erotic relationship.
Succorance	Need to be nursed, loved, controlled.
Understanding	Need to speculate, analyze, generalize.

Note: Needs are internal (but can be provoked by the environmental press), and they necessitate taking action in the social environment. The approach is thus interactionist. Examples of environmental press range from simple exigencies of life, such as getting out of the rain and getting enough to eat, to more complex sociopsychological demands, such as dealing with rejection or competition.

Source: Based on Murray, 1938.

Unlike behaviorists such as Skinner, Murray accepted (and studied) unconscious fantasies and instinctual drives. Unlike trait theorists like Allport, who stressed internal structure and self-consistency, Murray emphasized social roles and situational determinants. He was a humanist who assumed and applauded creativity, but he allowed that some of this energy arose in unconscious urges. But most important, he looked at the *combination* of internal motivations and external demands.

Thema

Thema
According to Henry Murray, a combination of needs and presses typical for the individual

For Murray, a typical combination of needs and presses was termed a **thema**. He measured them with his Thematic Apperception Test, or TAT. Remember that the TAT is a projective test, in which a person is presented with a series of ambiguous pictures (for example, two women who could be mother and daughter) and composes a story. It is an "apperception" test because the person reports not what he or she sees ("perception") but rather a narrative or imaginary interpretation. One's own needs are found in (projected upon) the ambiguous stimulus, just as Murray's daughter's friends projected their own fears onto pictures of "threatening" men. Themes of identity are thus then derived. For example, if the TAT-taker says that one of the two women in the cue picture is probably a loving, giving, saintly person who has been jilted by two insensitive boyfriends, then we may have a clue that such conflict is an

© Stockbyte/Getty Images

■ What do you think might be happening in this picture? In Murray's Thematic Apperception Test (TAT), a person is asked to provide a narrative or imaginary interpretation of an ambiguous photograph. The response is interpreted as a reflection of an important thema for that person.

organizing theme or pattern in her own life. The thema is an interaction between her need to be spiritually close to others and the environmental press of the men she dates, who want her to have sex without love.

Although there is still ongoing controversy about the validity of the TAT as a measure of personality, it seems to be the case that it is a valuable tool when it is not used alone but in conjunction with other means of discovering themes that govern an individual's identity. Murray's explicit statement of this interaction between needs and presses provided the cornerstone for interactionist approaches to personality.

The Narrative Approach: Murray's Influence

A modern example of Murray's emphases in thinking about personality is the work of psychologist Dan P. McAdams and his colleagues, who endeavor to study the full life context of the whole person (McAdams & Olson, 2010). They do this (as Murray urged) by studying motivations through biographies—that is, life stories. The idea is that the story of one's life becomes one's identity. This approach is sometimes termed the **narrative approach** to personality. For example, McAdams (1991, 2009) studies morality and the **intimacy motive**—the need to share oneself with others in intimate ways. How can we do this in a broad context? Let us consider the hypothetical case of Susan.

Narrative Approach
Dan P. McAdams's approach to personality that involves studying motivations through biographies in order to understand the full life context of the whole person

Intimacy Motive
The need to share oneself with others in intimate ways as studied by Dan P. McAdams

First of all, Susan developed a trusting nature thanks to positive, stable interactions during infancy and childhood (she was very close to her loving mother). In later childhood and adolescence, Susan was drawn to reading stories and joining groups associated with love, cooperation, and communion (Girl Scouts, her youth group, and the church choir). As a college student, Susan was idealistic, very concerned with issues of justice. Now, later in life, Susan creates a self-identity of altruistic helper (teacher, doctor, child psychologist)—she is a pediatrician. Her patients and their parents love her as a sincere and dedicated physician, and Susan loves sharing what is innermost in others. In later years, Susan may become a "generative" senior (as Erik Erikson put it), making a positive contribution to future generations by offering mentoring guidance and acting as an intimate confidante.

At each stage of life, internal inclinations lead us to seek out and respond to certain situations, which in turn help to further shape our inclinations and identity (Duncan & Stewart, 2007). In one study of these issues, generative, award-winning school teachers were interviewed for several hours about their lives—their important memories—and these accounts were then later coded by trained scorers. As predicted by McAdams, themes of love, caring, and community were especially likely to appear in the self-reported identities of these generative teachers (Mansfield & McAdams, 1996). On the other hand, while oil poured into the Gulf of Mexico from a faulty and ruinous deep-sea oil well, BP chief executive Tony Hayward enjoyed himself at a yachting race off the coast of England. While New York investment banks collapsed, plunging the economy into deep recession with millions of job losses, many bank executives continued to receive millions of dollars of salary and bonuses annually from the banks, enjoying their lavish lifestyles. They lived their lives according to a different narrative, not feeling at all sorry or responsible for the plight of their fellow citizens.

Murray was influenced significantly by the field theories of social psychologist Kurt Lewin. Lewin, well known for his proposition that behavior is a function of the person and the environment, believed this, however, in the sense of contemporaneous causation; that is, behavior is caused *at that moment* as a function of a variety of influences. Some of these influences may be residues of past behavior or previous events, but Lewin (1947) and the other field theorists did not see earlier events such as a childhood conflict or repressed drives as directly causing adult behavior. Murray's concept of needs, however, also left him closely tied to the dynamic motivational ideas of the neo-analysts like Jung, who saw unconscious motivation as a prime element of personality; to this, Murray added the weight of the environmental press and the organic quality of behavior across time.

Further, influencing Murray and the move to a more interactionist approach were behaviorists such as B. F. Skinner. For Skinner, personality exists in the environment, not in the individual—in a sense, we are whatever is reinforced. According to Skinner, similar situations evoke similar responses. These concepts helped pave the way for interactionists, making it natural to pay more attention

Why Does It Matter?

From the 1930s to the '50s, personality theorists grappled with ways to move beyond the internal, person-based notions of personality, by integrating the influence of the situation and the interaction between the person and the situation. Harry Stack Sullivan turned to the recurring social situation; for Sullivan, personality does not exist outside of social relations. For Henry Murray, the individual brings needs and motivations to recurring social situations. Together, the ideas of these insightful theorists and their colleagues laid the basis for key modern interactionist approaches to what it means to be a person.

to the effects of the situation. Murray's view was, of course, very, very different from Skinner's, but Murray (who knew Skinner at Harvard) did incorporate situational influences into his theory. Finally, Murray and his students were influenced by the humanistic notions of internal motivations toward creativity and self-fulfillment.

Modern Interactionist Approaches Begin: Walter Mischel

In 1968, echoing the conceptual breakthroughs of the 1930s, psychologist Walter Mischel again stirred up significant interest in interactionist approaches by arguing that a person's behavior varies so much from situation to situation that it simply did not make sense to think in terms of broad personality traits.

Mischel's Critique

Although it was by then well accepted that situations influence behavior, Mischel (1968) looked at the *size* of the relations between a person's behavior across situations and their variability. He claimed that you could not validly predict what an individual was going to do based on a previous measure of that person's traits. For example, one person might be fearful and anxious when speaking in front of a group, another person has that same reaction when on top of a mountain, and a third person feels that way when going out on an intimate date; no general trait of fear and anxiety could account for these variations. So, should we give up trying to understand or assess personality and instead look at the situations that affect behavior?

Many of Mischel's arguments rested on the size of the relations between personality and behavior, and between behaviors across situations. In other words, how well could we predict people's behavior knowing something about their traits, and just how consistent is personality-based behavior across differing situations?

Mischel relied on the correlation coefficient r. As we have seen, this statistic tells us how well one variable predicts, or is correlated with, another variable. With perfect positive correlation, the coefficient equals 1.0. (This would mean, for example, that knowing a woman was extroverted, we could always correctly predict extroverted behavior from her.) But Mischel claimed that most such correlations involving traits were around 0.30 or slightly higher. Therefore, it did not make much sense to talk about personality traits.

Mischel's critique stirred up a lot of soul-searching among personality psychologists about the nature of personality (Roberts et al., 2007), but two problems weaken this analysis. First, it assumes a fixed, simple model of personality in which traits lead directly to behavior. Second, what does it mean to say that most correlations of personality with behavior are "only" 0.30?

There is no reason to expect that traits or other aspects of personality will be straightforward predictors of behavior. Personality is complicated, and behavior is partly dependent on the situation. We have seen that personality (say, as viewed by the neo-analysts) sometimes involves opposites; for instance, feelings of inferiority may cause an individual to act superior.

If a man with an Adlerian inferiority complex tries to compensate (cope) by acting superior, or if a man defending his psyche against strong libidinal urges instead behaves in a puritanical, straitlaced manner, his behavior might seem unpredictable, but only until we better understand the underlying personality dynamics. (See the Self-Understanding box.)

Furthermore, we have seen that variability was well recognized by trait psychologist Gordon Allport, who argued that although behavior is variable, there is also a constant portion for each person (Allport, 1966). In other words, some invariant aspect of behavior always accompanies the changing parts. Allport believed that regularities arise because (1) the individual views many situations and stimuli in the same way and (2) many of the individual's behaviors are similar in their deeper

Self-Understanding

Some of the People Some of the Time

Although there is ample evidence that people behave differently in different situations and at different times, and although people may change as they grow and age, perhaps we should not be too rigid and demanding in our search for personality. Perhaps we should try to build these variations into our personality theories—trying to take them into account.

One way to do this is to classify people as to how consistent they are on a given trait (Bem & Allen, 1974). For example, we can ask people if they are consistently friendly or consistently honest. Some honest people, like clergy, might indeed be more consistently honest across situations, for a variety of reasons. In fact, there is evidence that consistency varies across people; traits do a lot better at predicting behavior for people who are consistent on that trait.

We might also examine the stability of one's identity. Someone whose identity is still evolving, such as a teenager or a person from an unstable home, might behave inconsistently compared to someone whose identity is much more solidified. Similarly, someone facing significant challenges to self-identity, such as those brought on by a divorce or a major move or a job loss, might behave inconsistently during the period of flux but might later behave much more consistently.

Finally, we might analyze people in terms of their life paths or life courses. A variation in behavior that might seem puzzling in isolation might make sense when the person's whole life history is understood. A rebel leader might seem warm and nurturant to his allies but amazingly hostile and devious to his oppressors, but only during the time of the conflict.

See for yourself, either by talking to a close friend or by studying the biography of a famous person. You could examine the extent to which your target person intends to be consistent on a set of behaviors (as someone devoted to a heartfelt cause might), or, on the other hand, feels the necessity to be expedient (as a politician might). You could then examine the extent to which his or her behavior is more variable at times of flux and identity change, as during career changes. Finally, you could examine the extent to which inconsistencies are more understandable in light of the person's long-term mission or ideology.

meaning—that is, they are *functionally equivalent*. A racist may do different things in different situations, but the behaviors may all derive from his racist personality structure. Even the biological perspective on personality does not assume an invariant link between dispositions and behaviors; rather, each biological inclination develops and is realized in a particular environment.

The second limitation on Mischel's analysis is the assumption that a correlation between personality and behavior (that arises in personality studies) of "only" $r = 0.30$ or 0.40 is small. In a statistical sense, such a correlation is small *if* we expect to be able to predict perfectly. But in real life, an effect this large is often considered very important and meaningful (Ozer & Benet-Martínez, 2006). For example, the effects of dietary intake of cholesterol on mortality risk, or the effects of airbags on the automobile death rate, or the effects of greenhouse gases on global warming are all smaller than this, yet no one would dismiss them as irrelevant. From this perspective, personality traits actually do quite well in predicting behavior. Furthermore, if we take into account that some traits are useful for understanding only some people or some situations, we can do even better.

The argument that personality is not a valuable concept because it is not highly correlated with behavior across situations has the implicit assumption that it is more important to understand situations than people. If traits do not predict behavior well, then focus on situations. However, if we examine the influence of the situation on behavior, we find that situations are no better predictors. Most studies in social psychology (which manipulate situations) also have an effect size in the range of $r = 0.30$ or so (Funder & Ozer, 1983). It is true that a shy person may sometimes be quite sociable, even rowdy, at a party, but it is also true that a person's behavior at one party is not a perfect predictor of that person's behavior at other parties! Still Mischel's work served a highly useful purpose in drawing further attention to the interaction of the person and the situation, which was one of his primary goals all along.

Mischel's Theory

Mischel was born in Vienna in 1930 and immigrated to the United States when young. He was an undergraduate at City College of New York, went to graduate school in clinical psychology at Ohio State University, and worked with psychologists who took both a cognitive and learning approach to personality. While a professor at Stanford University he was also influenced by the social learning theories of Albert Bandura.

If you are offered a piece of chocolate cake at a birthday party, do you gobble it down and hope for seconds, or do you push it aside so that you will later be able to fit into your sexy clothes? Mischel's early work dealt primarily with cognitive and situational (i.e., social learning) factors that influence behaviors like the delay of gratification in children. **Delay of gratification** is a specific aspect of self-control that occurs when an individual chooses to forgo an immediate reinforcer to wait for a later, better reinforcer. Mischel has studied the variables that influence the individual's ability to delay gratification: modeling (i.e., seeing another person delay), the visibility of the desired object (out of sight helps keep it out of mind), and cognitive strategies like thinking about other things (distraction).

Mischel moved on to examine individual differences in the meanings people give to stimuli and reinforcements—he calls these personal meanings **strategies**, or styles. Mischel suggests that these "cognitive personality characteristics" are

Delay of Gratification
A specific aspect of self-control that occurs when an individual chooses to forgo an immediate reinforcer in order to wait for a later, better reinforcer

Strategies
According to Walter Mischel, individual differences in the meanings people give to stimuli and reinforcement that are learned during experiences with situations and their rewards

Competencies
According to Walter Mischel, a person's abilities and knowledge

Encoding Strategies
According to Walter Mischel, the schemas and mechanisms one uses to process and encode information

Expectancies
According to Mischel, a personality variable encompassing a person's outcome expectancies and self-efficacy expectancies

Plans
According to Mischel, a personality variable encompassing our intentions for our actions

Behavioral Signature
According to Walter Mischel, the set of situation-behavior relationships that are typical of an individual and that contribute to the apparent consistency of an individual's personality

learned during experiences with situations and their rewards. Thus, despite Mischel's apparent emphasis on the situation (which grows out of cognitive psychology and learning theories), he also lends some credence to internal person characteristics that look suspiciously like personality. Traits are reconceived to be cognitive strategies. In particular, Mischel has discussed four personality variables: **competencies**—the person's abilities and knowledge; **encoding strategies**—the schemas and mechanisms one uses to process and encode information; **expectancies**, including outcome expectancies for our own behavior and self-efficacy expectancies (that is, whether we think we can do something and how likely it is that we will succeed); and **plans**. His studies demonstrate that personality is not merely an internal condition that pushes the individual toward behavior regardless of the situation, nor is the individual simply at the mercy of environmental events. Instead, an individual's actions, like delay of gratification, are the result of both environmental constraints (such as the visibility of and experience with the desired object) and internal, cognitive characteristics of the individual (such as self-regulatory strategies). All in all, this work supports the basic tenet that the person and his or her behavior and the environment are continuously interacting with and influencing one another. We have personality, but it is in flux.

In short, in much research using this social-cognitive personality approach, Mischel and colleagues (e.g., Mischel, 1973, 1977, 1990; Mischel & Shoda, 1995) find that part of the "consistency" of personality seems to be due to similarity of the perceived features of situations—that is, people identify situation–behavior relationships that become **behavioral signatures** of their personalities (Holmes & Cavallo, 2010; Lord, 1982; Mischel, 2007; Shoda, Mischel, & Wright, 1994). In a sense, one might say that personality is in fact the interaction, or intersection, of the cognitive "person" characteristics and the environment (Krahe, 1990). Similarly, personality is sometimes viewed as a "transaction" that occurs when a

Famous

Personalities

What Is His True Identity—or Is There One? Borat, Brüno or Cohen?

Consider a prominent British man who comes from a religiously observant family, and who follows many of the traditional practices of his Jewish faith. He was educated through secondary school at an expensive private academy for boys and then went on to study at the University of Cambridge. He graduated with a degree in history, writing his thesis about the civil rights movement in the United States, and showing a deep concern for justice. He routinely refuses to comment publicly on his personal or family life. Based on this description, a characterization of his personality would probably focus on traits such as seriousness, conscientiousness, introversion, respect, and dignity.

Compare that man to a well-known comedian, who has several well-developed comic personae in his repertoire, each an outrageous, uninhibited, vulgar figure. In the guise of these characters, he interacts with unsuspecting members of the public, exposing them as gullible, racist, prejudiced, narrow-minded people. He goes head-to-head on camera against people who are prominent and of good standing in their communities or in the larger public arena, and he shows them to be foolish and bigoted. He speaks crudely and explicitly about sexuality, including topics of incest, rape, and bestiality. There is a great deal of bathroom humor and nudity. A personality

person's unique personal strategies and styles interact with the particular styles of others (Thorne, 1987). These are more modern conceptions of the social nature of personality that Harry Stack Sullivan so cleverly argued. They are now common in modern approaches to personality (Ozer, 1986).

Validity of Traits

Are traits merely in the observer's mind? **Attribution theories** in the field of social psychology examine the ways we draw inferences about other people's behavior. They often find that we have biases and make errors when judging others (Jones & Nisbett, 1987). For example, we are likely to explain some observed behavior of our friend as a quirk of his personality, while the friend may see the same behavior as situationally determined. We may see our friend Sam as selfish or fearful because he refuses to donate blood during a blood drive, but Sam may know that he was exposed to hepatitis and so is not an acceptable donor. In other words, we as observers are often focused on Sam's particular behavior and draw an inference about his personality, but Sam sees different forces pressuring him to behave as he does. Because we do not see those forces, we sometimes overexplain—incorrectly—in terms of personality.

For example, you may always see your professor in formal settings—the lecture hall or the office—and therefore you might assume that your professor is rather rigid and serious. However, if you could see your professor on a vacation in Hawaii,

Why Does It Matter?

Modern advice about the combined individual and situational synergies that are necessary to lose weight, or become a successful professional athlete, or develop a rewarding marriage depend heavily on an interactionist approach to personality. We shouldn't just target the person and we shouldn't just focus on the optimal training or strategy. Instead, it is best to take account of how particular individuals (with particular predispositions) will respond in specific situations (e.g. Kober, Kross, Mischel, Hart, & Ochsner, 2010; Morf & Horvath, 2010).

Attribution Theories
Theories that examine the ways in which individuals draw inferences about other people's behavior

description of such a man might include terms like *outgoing, exhibitionist, boorish, extroverted, spontaneous, daring, creative, sensation-seeking,* and *rude.*

Those two men have little in common, it would seem—except that they are both the same person, the actor-writer-comedian Sacha Baron Cohen. He has been much more successful than most celebrities at keeping the spotlight on his public life, and keeping his personal life out of view. The apparent contradictions between who he is in public versus in private illustrate the interaction of the person with the situation.

He was quoted in an interview—one of the few he has done out of the role of one of his characters—saying, "I think that essentially I'm a private person, and to reconcile that with being famous is a hard thing" (Strauss, 2006). That sentiment is not unusual, with many celebri-

ties feeling stalked and exposed. Baron Cohen's method of dealing with that conflict, though, is creative: He normally appears for publicity interviews from within one of his characters. When the film *Borat* came out, the promotional interviews were done by Borat, not by Baron Cohen, continuing a pattern set earlier, with interviews about *Da Ali G Show* done by Ali G (a politically incorrect hip-hopper). When Baron Cohen was invited to give a speech at Harvard University as part of its commencement festivities, it was Ali G who showed up and gave the speech. The elegance of this solution, for Baron Cohen, is that he can keep his nonpublic persona out of the media without losing the benefits of media exposure.

So who is this man? Is he really Baron Cohen, or is he really Ali G, or Borat, or Brüno, or some other character waiting for the limelight? From the perspective of a person–situation interactionist, the answer is yes.

or flirting at a party, or dancing at a nightclub, you might make a very different inference. Does this mean that personality traits do not exist? Not really. We often overgeneralize about someone's personality, but this does not mean that we could not come to a better inference if we undertook a more comprehensive assessment. (Funder, 2001; Funder & Fast, 2010; Funder, Kolar, & Blackman, 1995). Although we sometimes make biased or distorted inferences, in general there is good evidence for validity. For example, different judges of a personality (such as if your parents, your friends, and your classmates judge your personality) tend to agree, and knowing the target in the same context enhanced but was not necessary for interjudge agreement; so cross-situational consistency is common. Furthermore, personality judgments by your acquaintances show better interjudge agreement (and agreement with your own judgments of your personality) than do judgments by strangers. In short, observers agree in their judgments of personality, and this interjudge agreement seems to arise, at least in part, from mutual accuracy. But as we will see, understanding and prediction are much enhanced when the situation is simultaneously considered.

The Power of Situations

One reason that personality is sometimes a weak predictor of behavior is that the power of the situation is sometimes so strong that it overrides our inclinations. To take an extreme example, if a fire breaks out in a theater and the crowd panics and rushes toward the exits, it is not surprising that a calm, rational person caught in the crowd will act excitedly and irrationally.

Or consider college students of the late 1960s, caught up in antiwar protests and the hippie revolution against the establishment. Even some of the most conscientious and law-abiding young people used illegal drugs, burned draft cards, engaged in illegal demonstrations, and so on. On a more massive scale, millions of otherwise decent and devout Germans cooperated with the Nazi regime, even with their murderous extermination camps and their brutal invasions. It would be foolish to try to explain such behaviors solely in terms of internal personality constructs. Sometimes the power of the situation is all but overwhelming. Yet it is also an oversimplification to explain Germans' obedience to Hitler only in terms of the situation (Blass, 1991). Some people are eager to be swept up in an authoritarian movement, while others are more hesitant, and still others actively resist (see Figure 1). Often, the power of the situation over our actions depends on the source of our identity in that situation (Milgram, 1974). For example, many individual clergy, deriving their identity from a higher morality, actively opposed the Nazis, even though most organized churches in Germany and Italy did not.

Trait Relevance and the "Personality" of Situations

Modern personality work sometimes tries to attend directly to trait relevance. Just as Allport argued, it seems likely that all traits are not equally relevant to all people. Furthermore, certain situations provide an opportunity for certain traits to be expressed (Britt & Shepperd, 1999; Tett & Guterman, 2000). For example, if you

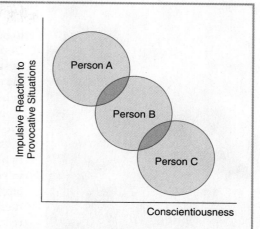

■ **FIGURE I**

Individual Behavior at a Given Point in Time Is Difficult to Predict Because of the Power of Situations

However, traits predict behavior fairly well over longer periods of time (Fleeson, 2004). This is illustrated in this figure, in which the behavior of Person A, who is low on conscientiousness, will vary a lot (behaving anywhere inside her circle) but remain pretty impulsive; but Person C, who is higher on conscientiousness, will react less impulsively on average, even though his behavior varies a lot as well.

score high on risk-taking, and that trait is central to your personality, this may show up as relevant in situations involving travel to exotic destinations or moving to new jobs, but it might not be so relevant to situations involving going out of your way to help a friend or to repair a flat tire. For other people, risk-taking would not be a very useful trait in predicting their behavior in any situation.

With the emphasis of the interactionist approach on situations, a key problem is deciding how to classify situations (Funder, 2006). For example, take the case of Michael, who reports himself as being quite shy. Forced to speak in front of a group of fellow students, Michael shakes and sweats with fear, yet at home or at family gatherings, he is an active loudmouth. How will Michael behave at dinner parties? how about in his school play? how about on a date with his dream girl? Are any of these situations comparable and relevant to his shyness trait?

How can we systematically classify situations? One way is to place people into a carefully controlled situation and see who behaves as expected. For example, we could create a situation that provokes aggression or one that rewards delaying gratification and then note who behaves "appropriately" (Bem & Funder, 1978). Once we identify the characteristics of people who aggress in a situation that we think is "aggressive," we can then see if these same people also behave aggressively in another situation that we also believe to be "aggressive." If the second situation does indeed elicit aggressive behavior from the same individuals, then we can deduce that it is similar to the first aggressive situation. But if the people who aggress in the second situation have different characteristics, then we conclude that the two situations are dissimilar.

Although this idea is a clever one, imagine how difficult it would be to measure all the situations we encounter. This could take forever. A simpler way would be to ask psychologists to rate or evaluate various situations, classify the situations, and then see if they elicit similar behaviors in people who score similarly in relevant personality tests. Perhaps we could someday create a comprehensive atlas of situations (Kelley et al., 2003).

Some psychologists try to focus directly on how each individual evaluates, interprets, and reacts to the different situations he or she encounters (Magnusson, 1990;

In evaluating other people's intentions and emotions toward us, we often rely on the size of the pupils in their eyes. (We do this both consciously and unconsciously.) In an important study of so-called pupillary contagion, it was shown that the observed pupil size of another was mirrored by the observer's own pupil size. Because we have no conscious control of our pupil size (it is autonomically controlled), this finding means that our judgments of and subsequent reactions to other people are partially determined by direct sociobiological processes, a startling example of the interaction between person and situation (Harrison, Singer, Rotshtein, Dolan, & Critchley, 2006).

Aggregation
According to Seymour Epstein, the averaging of behaviors across situations (or over time), to improve the reliability of behavior assessments

Magnusson & Endler, 1997; Torestad, Magnusson, & Olah, 1990). For example, we might measure people on self-reported or physiologically assessed anxiety and then place them in different situations. In this way, we could try to tease apart the contributions to behavior of stable anxiety (personality), the situation (seen as anxiety provoking), and the interaction (only some people become anxious in certain anxiety-provoking situations).

An additional complication is the fact that no two situations are ever exactly alike; the world changes over time (Elder & Caspi, 1988). Consider a suburban American family of two parents and two children in 1957 versus 55 years later, in 2012. Certainly many important factors are likely to be extremely different—among others, the education and employment of the mother, the entertainment choices, the proximity of extended family, and the family's relations with other ethnic groups. Although personality theorists generally look to the influences of genes and family environment, one's birth cohort—the generation born at the same time—can also play a significant role (Twenge, 2002). It matters whether one is a baby boomer, in Generation X (born in the 1970s), in Generation Y (also called the Millennial Generation—born in the 1980s to 1990s, a baby boomer "echo"), and so on.

Does this make it impossible to generalize about personality and situations? The two families—from 1957 versus 2012—undoubtedly share many common elements: rivalries between the children; love and attachment to the parents coupled with strivings for independence; the need for cooperative efforts for food, cleaning, transportation; and so on. Successful approaches to personality can capture recognizable patterns and regularities while also taking into account changes that occur across time. This is why ancient stories about people from Greek mythology or from the Bible can still be understood and appreciated by us today.

Consistency Averaged across Situations

Consider a situation in which Sue, a highly extroverted woman, attends a lively party but sits by herself and hardly talks to anyone. How can this be? When personality tests fail to predict behavior in a specific situation, two issues may be relevant. First, there is the issue of reliability. Perhaps chance factors affected the behavior in that particular situation; one sample of her behavior was not a reliable indicator of her personality. Second, there is the question of the appropriateness of that situation as being associated with the personality trait in question (Murtha, Kanfer, & Ackerman, 1996). Perhaps this party was not the right sort of occasion to elicit extroverted behavior. A way to deal with both of these issues is to gather information (observe behavior) across many situations. We could observe Sue at other parties and at other sorts of social gatherings. Her behavior could then be seen as her "average" behavior—the average across situations. This averaging is termed **aggregation** (Epstein, 1983).

Approaches to the Big Five dimensions of personality generally take this sort of path. They assume that there are relatively few dimensions of personality and relatively few basic sorts of situations. They are not at all disturbed when an extroverted person does not talk at a party; they assume that the extrovert will appear sociable when her various behaviors are considered together (aggregated). And in fact such approaches do provide a fairly accurate account of behavior. They might be fine, for example, in judging someone's temperamental suitability to be a salesperson. However, such "average" approaches would not be at all satisfying to Lewin, or Allport, or Murray, or Mischel. These theorists would want to try to understand why Sue is sitting alone at *this* party even though internal forces are pushing her to be an extrovert.

Mirror Neurons

Striking evidence that individual behavior can best be understood in a social context comes from the discovery of mirror neurons. **Mirror neurons** are brain cells that react (fire) in the same way both when the person (or animal) acts and when the person (or animal) sees another person act in the same way (Iacoboni, 2009; Rizzolatti & Craighero, 2004). In other words, there is a built-in brain system that links our actions to the actions and emotions of others. If we see another person reaching back to throw a punch, we understand it at a deep level because our own brain cells fire as if we were going to throw the punch (Borroni & Baldissera, 2008; Keysers & Fadiga, 2008). Because of individual differences in the brain, some persons are more sensitive to the social milieu and situation while other persons are more independent: Individual differences in empathy, for example, have been linked to differential mirror neuron activity (Kaplan & Iacoboni, 2006). At the extreme, the deficiencies in understanding social cues and the intentions of others that are characteristic of autism may be related to abnormal mirror neuron systems (Dapretto, Davies, & Pfeifer, 2006; Oberman & Ramachandran, 2008).

Mirror Neurons
Brain cells that react (fire) in the same way both when a person (or animal) acts and when that person (or animal) sees another person act in the same way

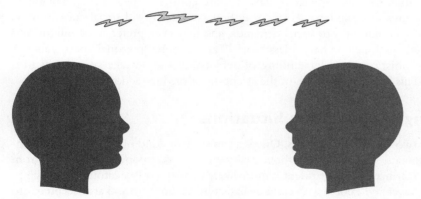

■ *Mental Telepathy?* Sometimes two very close, long-term friends or two identical twins seem to be able to read each other's thoughts. One starts thinking "Let's go play tennis" and the other blurts out, "Let's go play tennis!" Are the personalities "in sync"? Mirror neurons might provide an explanation for this sort of phenomenon.

If the first person starts thinking about tennis and makes very subtle body or hand movements indicating a preparation for the game, the partner may unconsciously sense and copy (imitate) these slight movements, whereby the partner's brain would think "tennis." This is not really mental telepathy, which would, by definition, involve some paranormal force that goes beyond the five senses. But it may capture what people often mean by mental telepathy. People with certain common inclinations and experiences who are placed in the same situation can profoundly influence each other, even when they don't realize it (Manusov & Patterson, 2006).

Personal versus Social Situations

As we have seen, one of the first things a child learns is to separate the self from others. That is, one of the tasks of infancy is to learn that one's mouth is one's own, but the breast belongs to someone else (mother). By the age of two or three, the child is further learning the no-no's of public behavior (initially, these range from masturbation to picking one's nose) as well as learning the niceties of social interaction (saying please and thank you, taking turns, helping others). Some children also learn to be charming or manipulative or charismatic.

In other words, although we develop a social self, the social self is more prominent in certain people, or at certain times, or in certain situations. One of the first theories of this psychosocial differentiation involved "field dependence versus field independence" (Witkin & Goodenough, 1977). Field-dependent people have a harder time separating the figure from the background in a perceptual task but field-independent people can disregard compelling background influences. Thus, in the social realm, they tend to act more independently. Field-dependent people are more reliant on others and respond in line with the demands of the social situation.

Shyness, self-consciousness, performance anxiety, and self-monitoring become very relevant to these matters (Scheier & Carver, 1988; Snyder, 1987). Some people are so tied to social roles that, almost chameleon-like, they take on the colors—the demands—of the social situation. For example, some actors seem to have almost no identity of their own—they become their current roles. On the other hand, other people are so unable to play social roles that they find social situations very uncomfortable. They may be called nerds. This could produce a consistency in personality; for example, they act conscientiously in private and continue to act conscientiously even when at a riotous party.

We all probably knew a schoolmate who didn't seem to understand that he shouldn't keep his finger up his nose and, to the extent that he *did* understand, did not seem to care what others thought of him. Some people who are little influenced by social situations may appear to have a more consistent personality. They may perceive things more independently, may be less able to read social cues, may be unmotivated to conform to social demands, and may even prefer to be unique and uninhibited. Such people have a less "social" and a more "personal" personality. A full and sophisticated understanding of personality should take such issues into account. This broad view is one of the strengths of the interactionist perspective.

Seeking and Creating Situations

Consider two high school seniors. One is a top student, kind of preppy, from a family of diplomats. The other plays three varsity sports, is very popular and earthy, from a family of farmers. Which student is more likely to apply to Princeton, and which to Indiana University? People with certain characteristics apply to and are accepted into certain colleges. People with certain characteristics are then selected and self-selected into corresponding sororities and fraternities. These houses in turn further reinforce these tendencies. We seek out situations that reinforce our self-conceptions.

In one interesting study of personality and life events, researchers followed 130 University of Illinois students for four years (Magnus, Diener, Fujita, & Payot,

SHARPEN YOUR THINKING   Current Controversy

Is Juvenile Delinquency Situational?

Parents of teens and preteens are often very concerned about preventing their children from hanging out with the wrong crowd. The parents worry that the influence of some unsavory peers will lead their child down a bad path. Are these concerns realistic, in light of interactionist views of personality? If you believe that a person's behavior changes with the situation, as an interactionist might claim, are teens at risk when they spend time with peers whose lifestyle and values are different from those at home?

Acceptance by the peer group tends to be very important during adolescence. Teens are influenced in their tastes, behaviors, activities, and preferences. Within one clique or "crowd" in a high school, teens will be listening to the same music, wearing similar clothing and hairstyles, watching the same set of TV shows, using the same slang. But how deep does that conformity go? Does it extend to the students' values, to their beliefs and life aspirations? to their personalities?

Are teens fully adopting the views of the peer group, or are they joining a group because the views of its members are similar to the views they already hold? Is it accurate to view these young people as being formed or molded by their situation, or is it more accurate to see them as selecting situations for themselves that support the identities they are trying to create? Would a gang member change if he spent many hours a week with the chess club? with a church group? All of these aspects matter at certain times, which helps explain why there is no simple, general "cure" for such troubling problems (Hagell & Jeyarajah-Dent, 2006).

1993). First, the students were administered the NEO Personality Inventory, a general measure of the Big Five factors of personality. They were then sent follow-up measures four years later, including assessments of life events (like marriage) that the students had experienced. It turned out that extroversion predisposed the students to experience positive life events, but neuroticism (tendency toward anxiety and depression) tended to predict negative life events. Anxious people went on to experience more anxiety-provoking events; that is, personality leads us to experience certain kinds of events, which then, in turn, can affect personality. Of course anxious, depressed people do not always encounter bad life events, but they are more likely to.

Consider also what happens when a child who is an aggressive bully enters the schoolyard. With the bully's arrival, the playground may soon turn into a war zone as that child's personality elicits and provokes certain behavior in others (Rausch, 1977). Bullies wind up tormenting themselves by setting in motion a long-term pattern of self-defeating aggression, which creates problems for them in school and at work, in addition to their problems with peers (Huesmann, Eron, & Yarmel, 1987).

All in all, we deliberately choose to enter some situations and to avoid others that do not match our inclinations, our self-conceptions, or our moods. The selection of situations is a key principle of the interactionist aspect of personality (Ickes, Snyder, & Garcia, 1997; Kendler & Baker, 2006).

Finally, there is evidence that consistency results in part from our own active, conscious efforts. One interesting series of studies assessed the influence of self-conceptions on the type of feedback solicited during social interactions (Swann & Read, 1981). In one experiment, undergraduates displayed a clear preference for feedback that would confirm their self-perceived level of emotionality. Another

CHANGING Personality

How can you change personality in a way that is long-lasting and very significant? The person–situation interactionist perspective suggests that individuals who get on a path and develop a trajectory toward the relevant situations are most likely to succeed. Step-by-step, the traits will lead into situations and the situations will help deepen the traits. The only detailed lifelong study of such matters (of the personality-situation interaction) followed over 1,500 California children for over eight decades—that is, for their whole lives. The traits and lifestyles nurtured by individuals on trajectories that led to thriving, a sense of well-being, and a long life were: those involving a conscientious and persistent pursuit of important goals; stable and deepening relationships; worthwhile careers with a strong sense of accomplishment; and a growing maturity and satisfaction with life. These individuals did not have a giddy sense of happiness or self-indulgence. In fact, a general cheerfulness was often not relevant to their later health and happiness. Instead it was those prudent people who developed a large social network, stayed physically active, were involved with and gave back to their communities, thrived in their careers, and nurtured a healthy marriage or close friendships who became the kinds of self-actualized personalities that many of us desire to become. You can read about this lifelong study of personality, situations, and subsequent health, happiness, and longevity in Friedman & Martin's (2011) book, *The Longevity Project: Surprising Discoveries for Health and Long Life from the Landmark Eight-Decade Study*.

study in this series found that the participants regarded self-confirmatory feedback (consistent with their self-images) as especially informative. In other words, people tend to regard confirming information as more compelling than disconfirming information about themselves—an instance of a more general cognitive preference for seeking out and attending to confirmatory over disconfirmatory feedback (Wason & Johnson-Laird, 1972). For example, optimists gaze less at unpleasant pictures than do pessimists (Isaacowitz, 2006). We also often seek out friends and listen to discourse that tells us what we want to hear about ourselves. For example, people tend to become less distressed and more content as they age, and this is, at least in part, due to an increasing willingness to disengage from offending situations and ignore those who want to bother us (Charles & Carstensen, 2008)! By seeking and eliciting confirming feedback from others, we may make our social environments and self-conceptions seem more stable than they really are.

Time: The Importance of Longitudinal Study

Human beings are not mannequins with fixed collections of attributes, but rather we are always in the process of becoming something new. As we grow and develop, how do we change? Changes over time have often been left out of modern scientific personality theories because they are so difficult to study. The only good way to study personality over time is to follow people as they react, grow, and change in the real world. Psychologist Jack Block (1993) defines **longitudinal study** as "the close, comprehensive, systematic, objective, sustained study of individuals over significant portions of the life span". Simply put, this means following people over time.

Longitudinal Study
According to Jack Block, the close, comprehensive, systematic, objective, sustained study of individuals over significant portions of the life span

Of course we all do this to some extent as amateurs; we watch our siblings, parents, children, spouses, and perhaps close friends over periods of many years. But doing this scientifically is much more difficult. Who can do a study that lasts many years? What about securing research funding and publishing (or face perishing)? How can we keep track of people as they move around? What if someone loses interest in participating in our study? How do we deal with changing times and changing measures? The obstacles seem insurmountable. Yet, as Block (1993) points out, "There is no alternative scientific approach that can begin to discern and disentangle the specific influential factors conjoining, interweaving, reciprocating with each other as the individual reaches out to life, is enveloped by circumstance, and forges character" (p. 7).

Classic to **Current**

Personality across Time

One of the oldest and most important sets of questions about personality concerns personality stability across time. When does personality form and how much does it change as we age? Who changes most, and why? How much future behavior can be predicted? Through the past 100 years, such questions have been addressed by many personality theorists, but they have often had to rely on casual observations of children or on retrospective reports of adults (who think back on their lives). Such evidence is notoriously weak.

The best evidence about personality stability and change necessarily comes from long-term longitudinal studies, which follow children into adulthood and then into old age. Longitudinal personality psychology is now the focus of a great deal of attention. For example, longitudinal studies have been the focus of the important work of the personality psychologist Avshalom Caspi (Caspi, 2000; Caspi & Roberts, 2001; Roberts & Caspi, 2001, 2003; Caspi, Roberts, & Shiner, 2005).

One key question is the age at which personality takes on a stable shape. Freud and the psychoanalysts thought that this occurred around age five, but the neo-analysts like Erikson thought development continued throughout life. Biologically oriented psychologists tend to think that personality is launched during conception and prenatal development, and fully formed when adulthood (sexual maturity) is reached (in the teenage years). Allport seemed to agree that basic personality traits have emerged by late adolescence, although some individuals remain childish (immature) at this age. One key study followed 1,000 children from age 3 to 18 (Caspi & Silva, 1995). Some associations and continuities did indeed emerge, but they were not conclusive. For example, young children who were impulsive and restless tended to grow up into adults who were reckless and sensation seeking. Note, however, that we say "tended to"; the associations were far from perfect.

One source of uncertainty is in defining and measuring stability or continuity of personality. For example, if one person changes situations often during childhood (say, the parent is in a military career) while another person stays in the same childhood family community, how should this difference in situations be taken into account? Second, because there is always unreliability in the measurement of personality, how much variation might be due to inadequate measurement? Third, what if a person retains her high-ranking position relative to her peers on conscientiousness, but average conscientiousness of the whole group increases from young adulthood into midlife; is that stability or change?

As we have noted, people may seek out situations that fit their personality. For example, extroverts may find themselves in stimulating situations and jobs. In turn, these situations teach and bring out different aspects of personality. Further, even when facing similar environments, different people view the same situation in different ways. Despite all these complicating factors, at least some consistencies can be observed in many people, especially in midlife and later years. Different theorists disagree as to whether these modest consistencies, dependent on multiple factors, mean the glass is half full (i.e., that there is meaningful stability) or half empty (i.e., that we should speak in terms more complex than "personality").

Our own opinion is that it makes sense to think about a moderate degree of personality stability across time, if the situations of corresponding life pathways are simultaneously taken into account. For example, consider a young boy, prudent and conscientious, who seeks out prudent and conscientious friends who help him avoid drinking and smoking, works for an education and toils hard in college, achieves a career in science, marries a fellow scientist, and lives a long life. It can be argued that it would be an oversimplification to conclude that his childhood conscientiousness led to his longevity. But we believe that it is valuable to examine such life pathways using personality as a guiding concept.

FURTHER READING

Caspi, A. (2000). The child is father of the man: Personality continuities from childhood to adulthood. *Journal of Personality and Social Psychology, 78*(1), 158–172.

Caspi, A., & Silva, P. A. (1995). Temperamental qualities at age three predict personality traits in young adulthood: Longitudinal evidence from a birth cohort. *Child Development, 66,* 486–498.

Caspi, A., Roberts, B. W., & Shiner, R. L. (2005). Personality development: Stability and change. *Annual Review of Psychology, 56,* 453–484.

Why Does It Matter?

We can help children grow up along a healthier path through a better understanding of these matters. For example, children who have highly reactive autonomic nervous systems and live in high-risk families (such as with insufficient income) are especially likely to develop an undercontrolled personality and have later problems in social behavior (Hart, Eisenberg, & Valiente, 2007). They might be good targets for early interventions such as early school programs.

Ego-Resilient
A term used to describe people who are calm, socially at ease, insightful, and not anxious

Life-Course Approach
Approach to personality by Avshalom Caspi that emphasizes that patterns of behavior change as a function of age, culture, social groups, life events, and so forth, as well as because of internal drives, motives, and traits

Following their own advice, Berkeley professors Jack and Jeanne Block began a long-term longitudinal study of children back in 1968. They collected various types of data—life data (like school information), observational data (like parents' ratings), test data (formal testing procedures), and self-report data. What did they find across three decades? One interesting finding has been that girls who became depressed by college age tended to have been shy, reserved, oversocialized, and overcontrolled at age seven. But boys who became depressed had been aggressive, unsocialized, and self-aggrandizing in their early years (Block, Gjerde, & Block, 1991). Further, children who were indecisive, overcontrolled, and vulnerable were also more likely to become politically conservative when they grew up, possibly attracted to more stability in their lives (Block & Block, 2006). Such childhood bases of later political views has generally been confirmed in studies of adults (Jost, 2009). It is not fully rational who becomes more conservative and who becomes more liberal.

Boys who were **ego-resilient**—calm, socially at ease, resourceful, insightful, not anxious—at a young age were still relatively ego-resilient two decades later. But girls' scores on this dimension in childhood were not related to their scores in adolescence. You might anticipate that boys who were aggressive and unsocialized as children later faced a lot of strict disciplining or school failure, which would make them tend toward depression. Girls who were resilient at a young age might weaken as they reach the severe pressures of American adolescence, just as girls are subtly pressured to give up their interests in math and science. The beauty of a comprehensive longitudinal design is that such hypotheses can be tested; for example, we could compare the school records of these boys and girls.

The Life-Course Approach

In studying personality across the life span or life path, psychologist Avshalom Caspi prefers the term **life-course approach**. Such terms emphasize that patterns of behavior change as a function of age, culture, social groups, life events, and so on, as well as because of internal drives, motives, abilities, and traits. In fact, these internal aspects unfold or develop in certain ways in certain contexts. Thus, they are very much interactionist. A girl with a weak ego, low self-control, and high drives toward intimacy, sexuality, and expressiveness might develop and behave very differently if she lived in a Muslim family in Saudi Arabia and went to the local girls' school than if she lived in an agnostic family in California and went to Beverly Hills High.

Caspi and his colleagues, among others, take the idea of a life course even further, arguing that individuals to some extent *create* their own person–situation interactions, even over many years, by varying how they interpret situations, by eliciting reactions from others, and by seeking out certain situations (e.g., Caspi & Bem, 1990). For example, think of all that may have happened over the years to a very aggressive young boy who grew up in your community. The aggression brings on certain events in certain situations, but it is impossible to know what behaviors will result without understanding the interactions between the person and the situation.

We knew a boy who was very smart and likable in elementary school but had an attention-deficit disorder and was something of a class clown. As his teachers increasingly punished him for being disruptive, even somewhat deviant, he began looking for ways to make trouble, and he began to seek out more deviant situations and behaviors. Eventually, he dropped out of college and was arrested for pushing heroin.

A model termed **cumulative continuity** (Roberts & Caspi, 2003) sums up these various ways in which personality tends to remain stable even though it is possible to change. By interpreting situations as similar, by eliciting similar reactions from others, and by seeking out certain similar situations, as well as by responding to stable genetic influences and stable environments (social and economic), the average adult maintains a fairly consistent personality. Note, however, that unusual circumstances can produce dramatic personality change, such as in the case of a war, depression, or natural disaster that interrupts one's family structure, friends, career, and self-view of one's usual responses.

There is one study of personality and its effects across the full life span (Friedman & Martin, 2011). In 1921, Stanford psychologist Lewis Terman began one of the most comprehensive and best-known studies in psychology. To investigate his theories of intelligence, Terman recruited 1,528 bright California boys and girls, intensively studied their psychosocial and intellectual development, and tracked them into adulthood. Most of these participants are now dead, and we (your text author and colleagues) have gathered their death certificates and coded their dates and causes of death (Friedman et al., 1995; Friedman & Martin, 2007, 2011). These life-span data provide a unique opportunity to address intriguing questions about the role of personality in physical health and longevity, using a **prospective design**—that is, using early measures to predict later outcomes.

Some of the most interesting findings from this project concern the role played by childhood personality. We all imagine that we can look at children and envision at least a little about their later life, but could childhood personality possibly predict premature mortality decades later? Can we validly speak of a "good little boy"? The most striking discovery in this study is that childhood conscientiousness (or "social dependability") is predictive of longevity. Children, especially boys, who were rated as prudent, conscientious, truthful, and free from vanity (four separate ratings by their parents and teachers, which we averaged) live significantly longer. They are about 30 percent less likely to die in any given year (Friedman et al., 1993; Martin, Friedman, & Schwartz, 2007).

This finding that childhood personality predicts survival across the life span raises many fascinating questions concerning causal mechanisms. Why are conscientious, dependable children who live to adulthood more likely to reach old age than their less conscientious peers? Statistical analyses called *survival analyses* showed that the protective effect of conscientiousness is partly but not primarily linked to a reduction in the risk of injury: Although there is some tendency for the unconscientious boys to grow up to die a violent death, conscientiousness is also protective against early death

Why Does It Matter?

Why does a life-course approach matter? One example is the complexity of depression: Depression is made more likely by a genetic predisposition and a difficult childhood, which can lead to poor social skills and stressful situations in adulthood. This, in turn, can alienate others and further decrease social support, which can further impair self-esteem, thereby increasing the severity of the depression (Caspi et al., 2003; Coyne & Whiffen, 1995).

Cumulative Continuity
The tendency of personality to remain stable over time through consistency of interpretations, environments, and reactions

Prospective Design
Using early measures to predict later outcomes

from cardiovascular disease and cancer. An examination of unhealthy behaviors shows them also to be somewhat relevant as explanatory mechanisms. The unconscientious have less healthy habits, but a significant effect of conscientiousness still remains after controlling for such factors as drinking and smoking. What seems to be the case is that this aspect of childhood personality (unconscientiousness) sets in motion a whole string of adult actions that all lead to shortened life span. For now it is important to understand that early personality can sometimes have very long-term and far-reaching effects, even on how long we will live.

A review of various studies of personality consistency across time indicates good but not perfect personality stability across adulthood (Roberts & DelVecchio, 2000; Terracciano, Costa, & McCrae, 2006). Interestingly, as shown in Figure 2, trait consistency (test–retest correlations of traits) generally increases in a linear fashion until around age 50. That is, personality generally seems most stable for people in their 50s. However, longitudinal studies of personality change often reveal individual and trait differences. Many people do change. For example, one study found that neuroticism tended to change at a more rapid rate (a quadratic decline) than did extroversion in later years, and that individual trajectories were influenced by social factors like marriage (Mroczek & Spiro, 2003).

People generally tend to become more conscientious, less neurotic, and somewhat more extroverted (dominant) as they move from youth into midlife, although their relative position on conscientiousness is fairly stable across many years (Friedman & Martin, 2007; Hampson & Goldberg, 2006; Roberts, Walton, & Viechtbauer, 2006). Later in life, as they mature, most people continue to become less impulsive, more reliable, and more content, although here too there can be significant individual variation depending on one's friends and life paths (Charles & Piazza, 2009; Jackson et al., 2009; Lüdtke, Trautwein, & Husemann, 2009; Roberts & Mroczek, 2008).

■ **FIGURE 2**

Trait Consistency at Different Ages

Personality generally seems most stable for people in their 50s. However, because this information comes from a compilation of various smaller studies rather than a major study of the same people across their lives (Roberts & DelVecchio, 2000), we must be careful in interpreting such findings. Longitudinal studies show that some traits, such as conscientiousness, are fairly stable and important throughout life (Friedman & Martin, 2007; Hampson & Goldberg, 2006; Roberts, Walton, & Viechtbauer, 2006; Shiner, Masten, & Roberts, 2003)

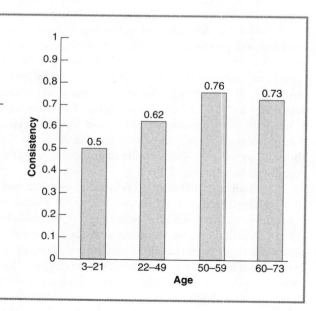

Readiness

The old saying tells us "You can't teach an old dog new tricks." This is not precisely correct, of course, as people (and dogs) can learn at any age. The adage does, however, capture two important elements of the time dimension of interactionist approaches. First, each experience has its effects in the context of previous experiences. For example, a shy young person may be intimidated enough by a pushy salesperson to buy an unwanted item (or go on an unwanted date) the first time she is so pressured. However, the fiftieth time, she is much less likely to succumb ("Get lost, Bud!"), although she may still find the encounter unpleasant. Note that this is a characterization of the environment—it is the "fiftieth time of encountering pressure"—but the characterization only has meaning as it relates to the person experiencing the events. Thus, we should not expect personality always to lead to the same behavior in the same situation. After all, people learn from and react to their experiences!

The second key point about time is that we are more affected by certain environments at certain times in our lives (Hampson & Friedman, 2008). Who is more affected by a very sexy peer—an 8-year-old, an 18-year-old, or an 80-year-old? Who can learn a new language more quickly—an immigrant couple in their early 40s or their 9- and 10-year-old children? Somewhere around puberty, children lose some of their abilities to learn language. Ironically, this is often precisely the age when our junior high and middle schools begin foreign language instruction.

This leads us into the topic sometimes termed **readiness**. Konrad Lorenz, the famous ethologist (scholar of animal behavior), knew ducks and geese so well that he could induce them to trail him around, thinking he was their mother (Lorenz, 1937). During a certain **critical period**, shortly after hatching, ducklings will **imprint** on their mother, or a clever substitute. If Lorenz walked past the nestlings at just the right time (and if their duck mother had been removed), guess who the young ducks readily adopted as their mother? Similarly, it is well established that our brains and perceptual systems need to interact with the environment to develop properly. For example, if a young animal is kept in total darkness from birth through a young age, its visual system will never develop properly, even if later experiences are normal.

People who face severe stress as children (such as molestation or a contentious parental divorce) are at higher risk for disorders such as depression later in life. There are many reasons why this dysfunction may occur. For example, if they grow up fearing other people, they may have less social contact and fewer sources of social support. But there is also evidence that an early biological predisposition may be created (Shonkoff, Boyce, & McEwen, 2009). For example, one study stressed baby rats when they were young and nursing but otherwise let them grow up normally. These rats had much higher levels of stress hormones in their blood when they were later subjected to a stressor (mild foot shock) as adults (Heim et al., 2000; Ladd, Owens, & Nemeroff, 1996). People with major depression as adults may be reacting so severely to stress because their nervous systems were impaired by their early experiences.

We can also imagine a more transient readiness, one that may not be biologically based. For example, after a death or divorce, there may be a period during which a person is not psychologically ready to begin a mature new relationship. Although the phenomenon is not well documented, it does seem that relationships

Readiness
The extent to which individuals are likely to respond appropriately in a given situation, as a function of their prior experiences with that situation

Critical Period
The point during development when an organism is optimally ready to learn a particular response pattern

Imprinting
A term used by ethologists to describe a type of learning that occurs at a particular early point in an organism's life and cannot be changed later on

that begin "on the rebound" are more often problematic. The effects of our personality may not be understandable unless this time-based situational variable is taken into account.

We can go even further and posit hour-to-hour fluctuations. It is known, for example, that most people are alert in late morning but have a drowsy period after lunch. But these circadian fluctuations vary somewhat from person to person. At which time would a flirtatious gesture, or an aggressive gesture, have its greatest impact on a given person? We would need to know something about both the person and the time. In short, full understanding of person–situation interaction effects should take into account the various changes that occur over both long and short periods of time (Robins, Fraley, Roberts, & Trzesniewski, 2001).

Interactionist approaches accept the idea that personality has a biological basis, but they do not concede that personality unfolds in an automatic, preprogrammed sequence. Rather, just as personality cannot be understood without a focus on the individual organism, it likewise cannot be understood without a focus on the social environment.

Interactions and Development

Social interactions can be categorized along two basic, independent dimensions: (1) an *affiliation dimension* of warmth and harmony versus rejection and hostility; and (2) an *assertiveness dimension* of dominance and task-orientation versus submission and deference. Personality researchers have found it useful to arrange these dimensions into a circle, or **circumplex model** (Bales, 1958; Freedman, Ossorio, & Coffey, 1951; Plutchik & Conte, 1997). An illustration of a circumplex approach to personality is shown in Figure 3.

For example, in your group of friends, one person may naturally become the task leader and dominate discussion, while another might strive to promote harmony

Circumplex Model
An arrangement of two basic dimensions of social interaction that shows the circular pattern of the combined characteristics

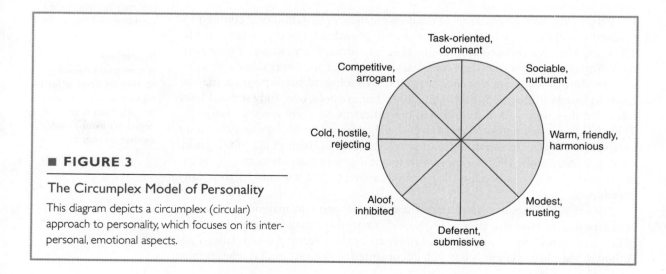

■ FIGURE 3

The Circumplex Model of Personality

This diagram depicts a circumplex (circular) approach to personality, which focuses on its interpersonal, emotional aspects.

among members of the group, counteracting the bad feelings instigated by a troublemaker (Helgeson, 1994). Someone who is nurturant might be both assertive and harmony-seeking, and so might fall in between. In other words, seeing where a person falls in terms of being cooperative and assertive in ongoing interactions, and why he or she behaves this way, is a useful and simple approach.

A more general such interpersonal and longitudinal approach to personality focuses on psychosocial maturity in terms of what is called **ego development** (Loevinger, 1966, 1997). Undeveloped egos are impulsive, self-protective, or conformist; they tend to be focused on the self and are either manipulative or blindly loyal. But highly developed egos are individualistic (broad-minded), autonomous (self-fulfilled and respectful of others), or "integrated" (Loevinger et al., 1985).

This integrated stage corresponds to Maslow's portrait of the self-actualized person. Thus, ego development involves a notion of maturing to higher levels. The Washington University Sentence Completion test is a projective measure of level of ego development that endeavors to reach deeper motivations than is possible with an objective, multiple-choice questionnaire. In a sentence-completion test, the subject is prompted with an emotionally loaded phrase like "Regarding my family, . . . " and completes the sentence. A self-protective, conformist answer completion like "I think my family's the best in the neighborhood" is a sign of immaturity; but a complex, nuanced response like "I know that my parents had their weaknesses but I have come to resolve our conflicts by recognizing my own fears of sharing those weaknesses" is an indication of a mature ego.

Just as Henry Murray and Harry Stack Sullivan assumed, researchers are now documenting that, in the right circumstances, a deep personal wisdom and a psychological maturity in relating to others may develop as one ages (Staudinger, 2008; Vaillant, 2007). This maturity is characterized by an adaptive coping style and an ability to be a positive leader for others—whether as a nurturant parent, a productive citizen, or a wise political or religious leader (Friedman & Martin, 2011; Vaillant, 2002).

Understanding Surprising Criminality

In the late 1940s, an impulsive man named Millard Wright was desperate to stay out of jail. A dishonest person, he had been a thief all his life. In an attempt to curb his urge to steal, Wright had a prefrontal lobotomy—a surgical operation on his brain. Alas, five years later he was arrested with a house full of stolen goods. It was reported that neither the detectives nor the neurosurgeons were any nearer to knowing what makes an incurable thief ("It Didn't Work," 1952). Perhaps today they would instead make use of the sophisticated person–situation interactionist approach to personality to help poor Wright and others who want to understand and alter their behavior. Like Diogenes, the ancient Greek philosopher who wandered through the streets of Athens searching for an honest man, we are still searching, but we know better where to shine our lantern.

Why Does It Matter?

Looking at combinations of personality traits and situations lets us understand phenomena that otherwise appear puzzling. For example, some children become very hostile and aggressive after repeatedly playing with violent video games, but most children and most game players seem unaffected. How can this be? It appears that children who are high on neuroticism, low on agreeableness, and low on conscientiousness and who then play violent video games are especially likely to be negatively affected (Markey & Markey, 2010).

Ego Development
An individual's level of psychological maturity

TIME LINE

The History of Person–Situation Interactionist Aspects of Personality

The major developments in the person–situation interactionist approach can be seen here in historical relation to one another and in relation to their broader societal and cultural contexts.

Developments in Person–Situation Interactionist Aspects		Societal and Scientific Context
Philosophers and theologians view individual deviations as games of the gods or possession by the devil	**Ancient Times and Middle Ages**	Humans are seen primarily in religious terms, as created by a divine presence
Individual is increasingly understood to have a unique nature, but shaped or set by social class, work, or core motivations	**1700s–1800s**	Increasing emphasis on reason and rationality; philosophers search for the core of human nature
Studies of values and moral behaviors show individual inconsistencies	**1927–1945**	Experimental psychology is dominated by behaviorism, while clinical psychology is dominated by psychoanalysis; economic depression and rise of fascism
Influence of social psychology increases, as Fromm, Sullivan, Murray, and others try to shift the focus of personality to the interpersonal situation	**1940s–1950s**	In reaction to fascism and world war, studies of propaganda, attitudes, prejudice, and social structure increase; many families move to suburbs and discard old ways
As influence of existentialism grows, writers emphasize complexity of individual choices and behaviors	**1950s–1960s**	Intellectual reactions against fascism; economic boom with huge new middle class; new affluence frees workers from old fears
Mischel's critique argues that traits are not predictive of behavior, because of the influence of situations	**1960s**	Social psychology thrives; dramatic social changes with sexual revolution and focus on civil rights
Research in personality declines, as psychologists attempt to come to grips with personality as interacting with the demands of social situations	**1970s–1980s**	New roles for women, changes in employment structures and social relations, new family structures, emphasize the importance of social and societal influences on behavior
Studies of personality rebound strongly as more sophisticated views of person-by-situation interactions are developed	**1990s**	Better understandings of the individual in the workplace, as well as new views of culture's role in individual behavior
Increased focus on change and stability over time, and on the neuropsychological mechanisms relevant to social interaction	**2000s–**	Concern about how to understand social interaction in a more globalized and more technologically mediated world

Evaluating the Perspectives

Advantages and Limits of the Interactionist Approach

■ Quick Analogy
- Humans as an ongoing dialogue between self and environment.

■ Advantages
- Emphasizes interpersonal influences.
- Can draw on best aspects of other approaches.
- Understands that we are different selves in different situations.
- Often studies personality across time.

■ Limits
- Difficult to define situations and to study the many complexities of interactions.
- Extreme positions can fail to take into account the complexity of the relationship between personality, behavior, and the situation.
- May overlook biological influences.

■ View of Free Will
- Free will exists but only to a limited degree.

■ Common Assessment Techniques
- Observation and empirical testing of cross-situational consistency, classifying situations, self-report tests, projective tests, biographical study, longitudinal study.

■ Implications for Therapy
- Personality can change slowly over time, as you seek out and influence situations and as the situations in turn interact with you. So, for example, if you have a strong orientation toward others and greatly like helping people, you might choose medicine if you want to further develop a biological healing orientation to life; or you might choose the clergy if you want to further develop a theological and philosophical orientation to life; or you might choose personality psychology if you like the scientific orientation and want to become more like your personality professor.

Person–situation interactionist approaches endeavor to take into account the many ways personality "is realized in," or "unfolds in," or "interacts with" the situational context. Intelligent, successful executives from Enron, BP, WorldCom, or Martha Stewart Living can make shocking blunders and even find themselves in jail when they head down pathways and wind up in situations where their moral compass is lost as the patterns that served them well in the past now lead them into mistakes. The most modern notions about personality help us understand this, but it is important to recognize that they derive from and are closely tied to the other seven basic aspects of personality.

Of course, to some extent, human behavior is unpredictable. In the J. D. Salinger (1951) novel *Catcher in the Rye*, the narrator scorns this "psychoanalyst guy they have in there who keeps asking me if I'm going to apply myself when I go back to school in September. It's such a stupid question. I mean, how do you know what you're going to do till you do it?" (p. 213).

Taken together, the eight basic aspects of personality provide a sophisticated understanding of what it means to be a person.

Summary and Conclusion

How can we talk about personality if people change their behavior from situation to situation? Interactionist approaches to personality explicitly attempt to consider the social situations in which people find themselves or create for themselves. Person–situation interactionist approaches to personality draw on various other perspectives and insights to create a more sensitive yet complex view of patterns of human behavior.

From the late 1930s to the mid-1950s, converging influences forever changed our notions of personality to be more situational and interactionist. Although coming out of a psychoanalytic tradition, the work of Erik Erikson and Harry Stack Sullivan transformed personality psychology. For Sullivan (1953), personality is "the relatively enduring pattern of recurrent interpersonal situations" that characterize a person's life (p. 111). To a personality psychologist like Sullivan, who believes in the idea of a social self, we actually become different people in different social situations. In a sense, we may have as many "personalities" as we have "interpersonal situations."

Henry Murray viewed personality as the study of human lives across time, and so he observed and analyzed the interactions of individuals and the situations they encountered during their lives. For Murray, typical combinations of needs and presses are termed "thema" and might be measured with his Thematic Apperception Test.

Echoing the 1930s, the psychologist Walter Mischel in the 1960s again stirred up significant interest in interactionist approaches by arguing that a person's behavior varies so much from situation to situation that it simply did not make sense to think in terms of broad personality traits. However, there is no reason to expect that traits or other aspects of personality will be perfect, straightforward predictors of behavior. Personality is complicated, and Mischel's criticisms helped personality theorists become more sophisticated in their thinking about personality. Mischel also criticized the size of the simple relations between personality and behavior, but it turns out that situations do no better job than traits in predicting behavior. Plus, a correlation of 0.30 in this domain is actually quite important and meaningful.

Research suggests that although biases do sometimes cause us to overattribute to personality and overemphasize its importance, there is good reason, converging from multiple sources, to believe that many aspects of our inferences about personality are quite valid. Sometimes the situation is so strong that it overrides our inclinations. Sometimes we can classify situations or focus directly on how each individual evaluates, interprets, and reacts to the different situations she or he encounters. Or, the social self can be found to be more prominent in certain people, or at certain times, or in certain situations.

Some people may be less motivated to conform to social demands and may even prefer to be unique and uninhibited. Such people have a less "social" and a more "personal" personality. A full and sophisticated understanding of personality should take such motivation and preferences into account.

Sometimes personality elicits and provokes certain behavior in others, and in some cases that consistency of response results in part from our own active, conscious efforts. We may seek and elicit confirming feedback from others. And we are more affected by certain environments at certain times in our lives. But, alas, to some extent, human behavior is unpredictable.

Although an "honest" personality who is always honest or a "cheating" personality who is always dishonest has not been found, psychologists today have a much clearer understanding of the consistencies (and inconsistencies) in people's lives and the forces that maintain them. When all the relevant knowledge is taken into account, there is no reason to be disappointed or even surprised that a highly extroverted person may be sitting silently, avoiding a party; or that a highly neurotic person is sitting in a composed, poised manner, calmly comforting a child; or that there are few if any people who will always be perfectly honest. Personality psychology has provided and continues to provide important insights about the complexities of what it means to be a person.

■ Key Theorists

Harry Stack Sullivan   Walter Mischel   Jack and Jeanne Block   Konrad Lorenz
Henry Murray   Mark Snyder   Avshalom Caspi

■ Key Concepts and Terms

chumship
interpersonal theory of psychiatry
social self
illusion of individuality
personological system
needs
environmental press
thema
Thematic Apperception Test (TAT)
contemporaneous causation
delay of gratification

behavioral signatures
personal strategies
attribution theories
"personality" of situations
mirror neurons
self-monitoring
longitudinal study
life-course approach
cumulative continuity
readiness
circumplex model

Male–Female Differences

From Chapter 11 of *Personality: Classic Theories and Modern Research*, Fifth Edition. Howard S. Friedman, Miriam W. Schustack. Copyright © 2012 by Pearson Education, Inc. Published by Pearson Allyn & Bacon. All rights reserved.

Male–Female Differences

Ayaan Hirsi Ali was raised in a traditional culture (in Africa) but lives as a feminist in the West. She was raised as a Muslim but has strongly criticized the unequal treatment of women in many Islamic societies and speaks out with unusual courage despite constant death threats. *Time* magazine called her one of the 100 most influential people in the world and she has bravely taken on political leadership roles traditionally dominated by men.

What does it mean to be masculine, and what does it mean to be feminine? Gender has played a key role in all personality theories, from Freud onward. Why is gender such an important aspect of personality?

Common beliefs and stereotypes about males and females are that "boys are adventurous," "girls are dependent," "men are aggressive," and "women are nurturant." Are they reasonable and accurate descriptions of personality? Is personality circumscribed by gender-linked personality traits? In other words, does being male or female alter the likelihood of certain traits or even strictly limit an individual's personality?

© AP Images/Bas Czerwinski

n this chapter, we use the eight basic aspects of personality to examine in more depth a particular applied topic of individual differences. Are there gender-based psychological differences? What is the etiology (causal origin) of these differences? How do different personality theories explain how these differences emerge and how they are maintained? What research evidence does or does not support the reality of gender-based personality characteristics? Not only do we aim to achieve a more sophisticated understanding of these issues, but we also strive to deepen our understanding of the basics of personality psychology.

Biological differences in male and female genitalia (and the underlying chromosomal difference) determine one's "sex"—male or female. So traditionally, differences between men and women were studied under the rubric "sex differences." However, psychologists now more clearly recognize that the complex ways in which people determine what is "male" and what is "female" are heavily socially based, and therefore many prefer to use the term "gender differences."

Masculinity—the qualities generally associated with being a man—and **femininity**—the qualities generally associated with being a woman—are usually of more interest than "maleness" and "femaleness" per se because they subsume the psychological characteristics of interest (such as boldness, nurturance, and so on). As we will see, men and women can have both masculine and feminine characteristics, in various ways and for various reasons.

Masculinity
The qualities associated with being a man

Femininity
The qualities associated with being a woman

Do Males and Females Differ?

In terms of physical development, there are obvious differences between men and women in average height, external genitalia, breasts, facial hair, and hair growth/baldness patterns. Moreover, there are substantial internal, physiological differences between men and women. For example, men and women have different levels of the hormones that are responsible for a variety of biological features such as fertility.

Although men tend to be physically stronger than women, baby girls and women appear to be constitutionally stronger than boys and men. Male children are more susceptible to a variety of diseases and disabilities than are females, and girls are more neurologically mature than boys at birth and through puberty (Nicholson, 1993; Parsons, 1980). Women tend to outlive men, but no one fully knows why (see Figure 1).

Sigmund Freud declared, "Anatomy is destiny." Are the physical differences between males and females causes of psychological gender differences? This is an important question because the fact that men and women differ physically and physiologically often leads to a simple biological justification for all personality differences between men and women. After all, males and females look so different, and have such different sex organs and hormones, that (it is assumed) they must think, act, and feel differently, and for primarily biological reasons. Remember that for Freud, a boy acquires his superego as he resolves the Oedipus complex and recasts the idea of marrying his mother. Girls, already lacking a penis, develop a much weaker conscience. This explanation conveniently fit in with the dominant (male) prejudices of

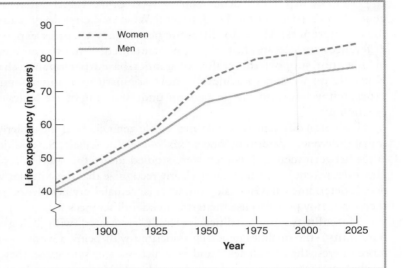

■ FIGURE I

Projected Life Expectancy at Birth in the United States

As overall life expectancies in the United States and Canada (and the rest of the world) have increased, women's life expectancies have remained greater than men's. The reasons for this difference are still being researched, but in addition to biology, differences in masculinity–femininity seem highly relevant. (Data are projections from U.S. Census Bureau.)

the time, in which Freud and everyone else "knew" that women had a lesser sense of justice and reason than did men. Yet we have seen the dangers of such simple biological explanations. Biological differences exist in the context of and are shaped by a complex social world. It is thus challenging and interesting to explore the multiple influences on gender differences in personality.

In a casual, unscientific sense, females are often described (and describe themselves) as emotional, nurturant, submissive, communicative, sociable, poor at math and science, subjective, passive, and suggestible, with a lower sex drive than men. Men are described (and describe themselves) as more rational, independent, aggressive, dominant, objective, achievement-oriented, active, and highly sexed. In a classic large-scale study from the 1970s, males and females of a variety of ages were asked to list characteristics and behaviors on which men and women differed (Broverman, Vogel, Broverman, Clarkson, & Rosekrantz, 1972). Two interesting results stood out: First, most subjects agreed that men and women differed on over 40 personality characteristics; and second, both men and women found most "masculine" characteristics to be more desirable than "feminine" characteristics. This phenomenon of higher desirability of masculine over feminine characteristics has not disappeared in the intervening decades, although the difference appears somewhat diminished (Seem & Clark, 2006). Regardless of whether substantial gender discrepancies in personality actually exist, many people perceive significant differences between men's and women's personalities, and these perceptions influence their attitudes about and behaviors toward others, thereby influencing personality. However, studies evaluating the reality (validity), and extent (size) of these perceived gender-based personality differences often have not supported the existence of many gender-specific traits. Starting with a comprehensive review of the literature on sex differences conducted in 1974 (Maccoby & Jacklin, 1974), researchers have found that, in many ways, men's and women's traits and behaviors are very similar (Halpern, 2006; Haworth, Dale & Plomin, 2009b; Hyde,

■ The women's movement of the 1970s signaled a major shift in women's roles in society. We have come a long way since the days when the jobs offered in the help wanted ads were separated into Male and Female sections. Interestingly, personality research on gender and on women's abilities also started changing in the 1970s.

1991, 2007); that is, there is substantial overlap between the distributions of male and female traits and behaviors.

It is interesting to note that this changing perspective on gender differences began at the same time that women gained more rights in society, during the 1970s. That decade saw women being admitted for the first time to many prestigious colleges, gaining equal rights regarding property and marriage, and moving in large numbers into higher-status careers such as medicine, law, and business. As people became less likely to assume that women were inferior, they began finding less evidence of inferiority; and, at the same time, changes in beliefs helped bring about these social changes. This is another illustration of the way in which our understanding of personality is partially influenced by our culture and our times, and likewise, how new insights into the nature of personality can also change our culture and our times.

There are a few areas in which reliable gender differences in psychological abilities have been found, especially in those related to thinking, perception, and memory. Boys and men have better spatial abilities, on average, whereas girls and women are more verbally advanced. Girls usually start to talk at a slightly earlier age, tend to have larger vocabularies, generally earn higher grades in school, and do better in reading and writing (at least through elementary school) than boys. They attend college in significantly higher numbers than boys (see Figure 2). Boys do better in tasks and measures of spatial ability from grade school on, know more about geography and politics, and beginning in high school, boys do better in mathematics, although these differences are small and do not explain different career patterns in the sciences (Else-Quest, Hyde, & Linn, 2010; Halpern, 1992, 2004; Halpern et al., 2007). And the math advantage for boys may no longer be present (Hyde et al., 2008).

■ Following puberty, there may be a slight superiority of boys over girls in math. How do we separate out the effects of differences in brain organization, differences in hormones, and differences in expectations about performance?

373

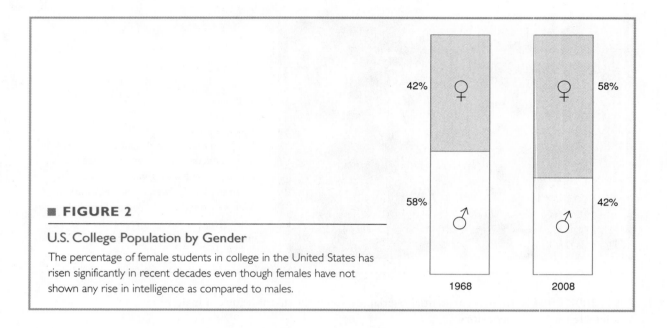

■ FIGURE 2

U.S. College Population by Gender

The percentage of female students in college in the United States has risen significantly in recent decades even though females have not shown any rise in intelligence as compared to males.

There is also some evidence for gender differences in the expression of two social characteristics: aggression and communication. Boys and men are more verbally and physically aggressive than females (Eagly, 1987; Hyde, 1986a). Males commit more violent crimes. Females are better at nonverbal communication, more sensitive to nonverbal cues, and more nonverbally expressive than are males (Hall, 1990). Other commonly proclaimed gender differences in personality and behavior, such as dependency, suggestibility, and nurturance, are more difficult to confirm (Eagly, 1995; Wood & Eagly, 2010). Men are more likely to take charge in small groups, and women are more likely to be concerned about and involved with child-rearing, but there is considerable overlap, with many men being nurturant and many women being independent.

One study went beyond the traditional self-report measures of masculinity–femininity and instead used people's preferences and interests in various types of occupations. For example, mechanical engineers and chemists were male-type occupations, preferred by the men in the study. Interior decorator, florist, and librarian were female-type occupations, generally preferred by the study's women. Occupational interests were then used to assess masculinity–femininity. There were some more masculine men and some more feminine men, as well as more masculine women and more feminine women. Following these individuals for many decades (for the rest of their lives) yielded a striking result: Although the women on average outlived the men, masculine men and masculine women were more likely to die at a younger age, while the more feminine women *and* the more feminine men were relatively less likely to succumb (Friedman & Martin, 2011; Lippa, Martin, & Friedman, 2000) Why might this be? Biology, socialization, learned behavior, activities, and thoughts and feelings are all likely relevant.

A Brief History of Gender Difference in Personality

Evidence from Ancient Civilizations

Archeological excavations of hunting societies that existed 4,000 to 6,000 years ago have unearthed early portrayals of women—in petroglyphs, hieroglyphs, and burial statuettes—representing essentially "female" characteristics of fertility and nurturance. On the other hand, men were most often represented in prehistoric art either hunting or warring. Some of the earliest Asian religious beliefs dichotomized humanity into a female and male component, *yin* and *yang*. The yin represents the female—passive, shaded, and cold—whereas the yang portrays the male element—active, light, and hot. Leaders and priests were more likely to be male although status differences were not necessarily rigid.

As time went on, ideas about the differences between men and women were formalized into the identification of women as not only different but lesser. For example, Plato described women as weaker and inferior. Aristotle more specifically depicted women as incomplete and incompetent because of their inability to produce semen. Together with the conception of women as being deficient men was the view of women as possessing frail personalities—emotional, unprincipled, suggestible, and indecisive. In the Hebrew, and later the Christian, Bible, men not only wielded the power but also held the higher moral authority, although women occasionally played important roles. The view of females as incomplete or imperfect males persisted for centuries, and the influential theologian Thomas Aquinas (1225–1274) perpetuated this idea, providing a religious rationale for the inferiority of women.

Maternal Instinct
According to the functional school of psychology, an inborn emotional tendency toward nurturance that is triggered by contact with a helpless infant

Nineteenth-Century Views

Under Darwin's influence, the functional school of psychology (in the late 1800s to the early 1900s) declared that behavior and thought evolve as a result of their functionality for survival. For example, proponents emphasized the issue of **maternal instinct**, which was defined as "an inborn emotional tendency toward nurturance that was triggered by contact with a helpless infant" (Lips & Colwill, 1978, p. 29). According to the (male) functionalists, most of a woman's energy was to be expended on pregnancy, childbirth, and lactation; as a result women had no remaining resources for developing other abilities. These theorists also explained that the maternal instinct revealed itself in other domains where women nurtured others, such as in their relationships with their spouses and close friends. These concepts were used to both explain and justify the

photovat.com

■ Many religions explicitly exclude women from the formal role of spiritual leader of the community (including Roman Catholicism, Islam, and Orthodox Judaism). Is this because women are seen as inherently unsuited to the demands of providing moral and practical leadership to groups that include men?

dominant position of men and the submissive position of women in the contemporary society.

Biological Influences on Gender Differences

Sex Hormones in Normal Prenatal Development

Genetic Sex
Whether an individual has XX chromosomes (female) or XY chromosomes (male)

Estrogen
The class of sex hormones typically considered the "female" sex hormone

Androgen
The class of sex hormones typically considered the "male" hormone

Genetic sex is determined at the moment of conception when the female's egg with its X chromosome joins with the male sperm with its X or Y chromosome, resulting in a girl (XX) or a boy (XY). Interestingly, although each embryo has the physiological structures from which both male and female genitalia can develop, at around 6 weeks' gestation, testes begin to develop only in embryos with XY chromosomes. The testes begin to produce sex hormones: some progesterone and **estrogen** (typically considered the "female" hormone) and a larger amount of **androgen** (typically considered the "male" hormone). The genetically male fetus then develops the internal and external male sex organs. When the embryo has XX sex chromosomes, the gonad buds begin to develop into ovaries at about 12 weeks' gestational age. It appears that in the absence of testes producing large amounts of androgen, female external and internal genitalia develop.

Thus, for the male embryo, androgen initiates the development of male genitalia and influences, to some extent, the organization of the brain. In addition there is some evidence that hormones secreted by the mother, the placenta, and the female fetus's ovaries additionally may influence female development. Thus, during this prenatal stage, physiological sex differences that will appear later in life are established by the influence of the hormones (Knickmeyer & Baron-Cohen, 2006). Effects on the brain are incompletely understood, but, for example, the prenatal hormones may affect the brain by influencing the manner in which the hypothalamus will regulate the pituitary gland as it controls the secretion of gonadal hormones after puberty (such as in the regulation of menstruation).

The Effects of Prenatal Sex Hormones on Gender Behavior

The fact that androgen affects the physical development of the fetus suggests that prenatal androgen exposure might also affect personality in some gender-specific manner. Two kinds of evidence support the possibility of an effect of prenatal hormones on gender behavior: (1) experimental data from animal studies, and (2) studies of humans who have experienced prenatal genetic or hormonal anomalies.

When researchers expose developing animal fetuses to androgens during early prenatal development, a typical finding is that greater amounts of androgens affect later behavior: Such animals have higher levels of rough and tumble play, more aggressive behavior, and higher activity levels. This is true for both genetic males (XY) and genetic females (XX) who are so exposed (Parsons, 1980; Ramirez, 2003).

An analogous kind of natural experiment occurs in humans who experience abnormal prenatal sexual development. Genetic anomalies include mutations in the number of sex chromosomes contained within the embryo's cells. In other cases, the embryo or fetus may fail to be exposed to the appropriate hormones or may be overexposed to inappropriate hormones. For example, now and then individuals are born with too many sex chromosomes, most often of the configurations XXX, XXY, or XYY. XXX people are anatomically female and fertile, whereas XXY and XYY are anatomically male (Stockard & Johnson, 1992). Despite early assumptions to the contrary, there is little evidence that the extra Y sex chromosome (in XYY) has much influence on behavior. Some researchers suggested that individuals with an extra Y chromosome experienced greater quantities of testosterone in their system and that, as a result, they were more aggressive. These individuals were identified in a prison population, however, and it was not determined properly whether or not there was an equivalent (and also unusually aggressive) proportion of XYY males in the non-incarcerated population. This lack of appropriate controls and the fact that XY males in these populations were actually responsible for a larger portion of the more violent crimes such as murder and physical and sexual assault has resulted in the conclusion that there is no greater tendency toward aggression in these XYY males (Hargreaves & Colley, 1987; Lips & Colwill, 1978).

On occasion, a child is born with a single X chromosome, an X0. This anomaly is known as **Turner's syndrome**. Individuals with Turner's syndrome have female external genitals but no ovaries. Because they are not exposed to androgen they remain female, but they are sterile. At puberty, with no ovaries to excrete estrogen, the young women must receive hormone supplements if they are to develop secondary sexual characteristics (Nicholson, 1993; Parsons, 1980). There is some evidence that these girls engage in timid and feminine behavior and may display weaker mathematical and spatial skills (Saenger, 1996). Such findings have been used to argue that at least certain aspects of feminine behavior have a direct genetic basis (Boman, Hanson, Hjelmquist, & Möller, 2006; Gatewood et al., 2006).

The development of genetically female or male fetuses may be influenced by irregularities in prenatal hormonal exposure. For example, genetically female embryos may be prenatally exposed to an excess of androgen, possibly the result of defects in the adrenal gland, or because the pregnant mother takes external sources of male hormones. If the influence is more than minor, then these androgenized genetic females are born with either masculine genitals or ambiguous genitalia. In most cases, children with ambiguous genitalia undergo surgery to reconstruct normal female structures. These **androgenized females** show more tomboy behavior and are more active than other girls (Auyeung et al., 2009). It is unclear whether these so-called masculine personality traits and behaviors (1) result from the exposure to androgen, (2) are induced by parental expectations for the behavior of daughters who were exposed to male hormones and who were born with ambiguous (or malelike) external genitalia or other male-typical appearances, or (3) result from the girls' own awareness of their hormonal and physical masculinity.

In some rare cases of androgenized genetic females, the external genitalia look male, and the child's "femaleness" is not detected early. These children are raised as boys and the condition is not noticed until puberty when secondary sexual

Turner's Syndrome
An anomaly in which an individual is born with only a single X chromosome; such a person has female external genitals but no ovaries

Androgenized Females
Genetically female individuals who were prenatally exposed to excessive levels of androgens and are born with either masculine or ambiguous external genitalia

■ Some young girls prefer the activities of their male peers rather than their female peers. Are their hormone levels and brain structures more "masculine" than those of the typical girl, or have they had different socialization experiences?

characteristics do not develop. At that time, because these children have experienced an extended period of sexual identification as males, they may be given extra male hormones to encourage the development of male secondary sexual characteristics, and sometimes may live successful (although sterile, being genetically XX) lives as adult "males."

One sad case of the reverse situation involved David (Bruce) Reimer, who was born as a boy but had a botched circumcision that maimed him. A famous doctor, John Money, convinced David's mother to have the boy's testicles removed, give him hormones, and rename him Brenda. Dr. Money used "Brenda" as an example to claim that children are not born masculine or feminine but are socialized those ways. But when the boy reached his teenaged years (after an unhappy childhood), he assumed his male identity and took the name David. He lived a troubled life and killed himself at age 38. The point is that underpinnings of gender are often not as clear-cut as some would like to think.

Overall, although prenatal exposure to sex hormones does seem to influence the development of masculine/feminine behaviors to some extent, gender is also affected by the strong influence of both parental expectations and gender socialization. For example, in the 1950s and '60s, many pregnant women took the hormone diethylstilbestrol (DES) in an attempt to prevent miscarriage. DES, like testosterone, can have a masculinizing influence, and indeed, many of the daughters of these women later developed reproductive problems. However, any behavioral effects that have been found (such as a tendency toward bisexuality) have tended to be weak (Hines & Sandberg, 1996; Jacklin, Wilcox, & Maccoby, 1988; Meyer-Bahlburg, Ehrhardt, Rosen, & Gruen, 1995). It is an oversimplification to assume a simple genetic basis for *any* aspect of personality. Rather, biology sets the stage for the various other key influences on personality.

The Influence of Hormones during and after Puberty

The influence of biological and hormonal factors is, of course, not limited to the prenatal period. Starting in puberty, there are major differences in the proportions of and variations in hormones produced by men versus women. For example, increases in male testosterone and aggression are commonly linked (Archer, 2006). Testosterone levels may be related to dominance and achievement (Dabbs, Karpas, Dyomina, Juechter, & Roberts, 2002).

Puberty and menstruation bring a cyclical process of hormonal release in women that has been related to changes in women's feelings and behavior at various times during the monthly cycle. At the start of the cycle, the pituitary gland instructs the ovaries to release a large amount of estrogen, which causes growth in the lining of the uterus. Halfway through the cycle, the pituitary releases a hormone that causes ovulation, the amount of estrogen drops, increases on the 20th day, and decreases again to the end of the cycle (see Figure 3).

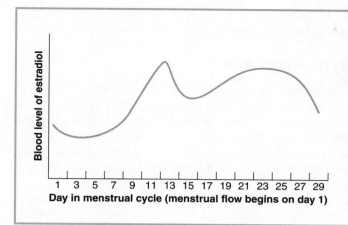

■ FIGURE 3

Cyclical Variation in Blood Levels of Estradiol in Females

Estradiol, a form of estrogen, shows a distinctive pattern of variation over the course of the menstrual cycle in premenopausal women, which is often related to mood and behavior. It has been argued that these and related hormone swings help account for emotionality, as well as females' varying interest in sexual activity and varying appeal to men at different times of the month.

Cyclical oscillations in women's hormones are said to be related to female personality characteristics including mood swings, violence, inability to make decisions, mental illness, and decreases in coordination (e.g., Lips & Colwill, 1978; Moir & Jessel, 1991; Nicholson, 1993). The most persistent personality characteristic associated with female hormone cycles is emotionality, or mood swings. In fact, the concept that menstruation results in emotional instability in women is quite old, reported by the early Greek philosophers, among others. The word *hysteria* (uncontrolled outbursts of emotion) derives from the Greek word for "uterus." It was thought that women's emotionality was caused by a wandering womb, and hysterectomies were performed as a cure for mental illness, even into modern times. This is a painful example of how ancient prejudices against women sometimes can make their way into modern pseudoscientific theories. A kernel of truth—hormonal fluctuations affecting mood—can be exaggerated by society into a stereotyped myth: feminine weakness and mental instability.

The actual influence of hormonal cycles on personality appears to be quite small in most women, although there are real variations as a function of the menstrual cycle (Dreher et al., 2007). Nevertheless such reasoning has played a role in keeping women out of politics and limiting their advancement in military careers and space exploration.

Gender Differences in Personality from the Eight Perspectives

The assumptions we make about differences (or lack of differences) between men and women, and their causes, may lead to various important consequences. As noted, if gender differences are seen to be primarily physiologically and biologically determined, then they will tend to be considered permanent, unchangeable, and even morally correct or divinely ordained. If these differences are seen as learned through reinforcement, they can probably be more readily changed; if they are seen as basic and large rather than as changing and overlapping, then different social roles will be assigned men and women;

and so on. That is why we focus on understanding eight basic aspects of personality and how each affects the ways we think about what it means to be a person.

The Psychoanalytic Approach

In a sense, the psychoanalytic theory of psychological gender differences is a biological theory. It assumes that differences in a variety of traits including aggression, jealousy, passivity, rationality, and dependency arise from emotional responses to differences in the physical structure of boys and girls. If the basic mechanism by which gender-specific personality traits are attained is that of identification with the same-sex parent (which takes place at the completion of the third psychosexual stage of development at about five years of age), it is clear why Freud equated anatomy with destiny.

Remember that during the phallic stage, the boy is presumed to develop a strong desire for his mother, and as a result, aspires to replace his father. However, because the father is much larger and more powerful, the boy fears retribution—that is, that Dad will castrate him for desiring Mom. This castration anxiety, according to Freud, has been enhanced by (1) the importance of his penis for pleasure, (2) threats from his parents about masturbation, and (3) the fact that he has noted that girls do not have this valued appendage and therefore must have been castrated already for some devastating misdeed. To deal with this overwhelming anxiety, the boy identifies with his father, thereby taking on his father's personality traits, while additionally being able to possess his mother vicariously through his father's experience. This resolution of the Oedipus crisis results in boys incorporating "male" characteristics into their own personalities, including paternal ethics and values, resulting in the development of the superego, or conscience.

Famous Personalities

The Personalities of Professor Jonathan Joan

There are few individuals in a unique position to see the role of gender in personality through their own personal experience: those who have lived on both sides of the male–female boundary. Dr. Joan Roughgarden, professor of biological sciences and of geophysics at Stanford University, spent the first 52 years of life as Jonathan Roughgarden. Joan claims that she has always seen herself as female, despite all external evidence to the contrary: she was born with male genitals and raised as a male; had the outward appearance of a male; and dressed, acted, and took on social roles that were male. She, like other male-to-female transsexuals, describes herself as a woman who was born into the body of a man.

One summer, Jonathan Roughgarden left campus to begin his sabbatical leave. Colleagues with whom Roughgarden had worked for many years were shocked when, at the end of the leave, Joan Roughgarden arrived to resume teaching and research in the Roughgarden laboratory. The full transition—bodily changes, a new wardrobe, a new hairstyle, a new legal name, and a new social identity—was not all completed over just that year, but it was during that time that Joan became the public face of this distinguished scientist.

What happened to the personality of this individual, formerly Jonathan and now Joan? The personality of Jonathan, as reported by the *New York Times*, was that of "the quintessential macho academic: aggressive, abrasive, and competitive" (Yoon, 2000). But, according to Joan, that was not her true personality—it was just a persona that Jonathan had adopted to succeed, and it never felt natural. As Joan says, "It became clear to me that I wasn't ever going to figure out how to do the guy thing." The

Females, according to Freud, also begin the phallic period with mother as the strongest love object. Girls discover at this age that they do not have a penis, resulting in penis envy (which is similar to the historical notion of women as incomplete men); and girls are overwhelmed with envy, inferiority, and jealousy. To resolve this crisis, the little girl withdraws her affection from her equally inferior mother, takes on her father as a love object, and unconsciously replaces her desire for a penis with the desire for a child. Thus, the female incorporates the feminine personality characteristics of jealousy, envy, inferiority, nurturance, and dependence. The lack of the extreme anxiety and fear that drive the male's resolution of the Oedipal stage means that women experience a weaker repression of the crisis and, consequently, develop a weaker superego.

The Neo-Analytic Approaches

Erik Erikson provided an alternative explanation, rooted in psychoanalytic notions but shaped by society, for the development of masculine and feminine traits. It was, however, still based on the physical construction of the genitalia. Erikson's conceptualization described male traits such as being active, exploring, warring, and pragmatic, in a sense corresponding to their external, outwardly extended genitals. Little boys build phallic towers out of toy blocks. He portrayed female characteristics such as nurturance, gentleness, and peacefulness coinciding with the internal nature of female genitals. Little girls create refuges and enclosed, secure spaces. Although Erikson also saw the importance of ego factors, here too the relationship between male and female biology and personality is strong. Certainly our society is very concerned with covering up genitalia. Although erections are natural and common, when was the last time you saw an erect penis on network TV or in a magazine ad?

male style didn't come naturally to her, because she was, in her own view, not really a male. Joan claims that she realized one day that the competitive, often hostile, status-oriented struggle to be the alpha male didn't match her view of herself and was not comfortable, even though that style had brought great success. Joan's personality, in contrast to Jonathan's, reflected a more feminine style. Presiding at a conference after her transition to Joan, Roughgarden surprised colleagues who were accustomed to Jonathan's hard-charging style—Joan encouraged others to participate in dialogue, gave them positive feedback, and worked to bring the group to consensus. She has been described as now being warmer, more nurturant, and friendlier; a reflection of her female self.

Underscoring the importance of gender roles in guiding how people interact, Joan found that she is now often treated less respectfully, although of course the body of her work has not changed—as a woman, she is more likely to be "interrupted, ignored and condescended to by men." And because gender roles are so central to identity, when she reappeared at Stanford as Joan, she felt the need to be reintroduced to her own department, since her colleagues had never met Joan (although they had known Jonathan for years).

A professional biologist, she has focused on changing the way biologists think about sex. As her own thinking about the complexity of sex and gender has evolved with her personal experience, she has pointed out how evolutionary biology has evaluated sexual life in the animal kingdom too narrowly, underemphasizing the diversity of gender and sexuality, and the important implications of that variety for evolution. Her views have aroused a great deal of scientific controversy (Jolly, 2004; "Letters," 2006). Roughgarden's biological sex was male but her socially construed gender became female. Finding a deeper understanding of sex and gender is not only a personal matter but a scientific one as well.

Karen Horney, in her rejection of strict Freudian notions, suggested that penis envy was often a minor influence on personality, and in fact males envied the female ability to bear children. She turned the tables and postulated that men's efforts to control and achieve more and more in life result from feelings of inferiority due to this envy. Horney also noted the effect of a society that defines women as inferior and severely limits their opportunities, suggesting an interaction of social forces with biological factors. Although Horney brought a new, female perspective to the psychoanalytic view, she still emphasized a strong influence of biological factors (such as the woman's ability to bear children) on personality.

Carl Jung blended the psychoanalytic theory of gender differences with the earlier Asian conceptions of yin and yang, male and female, as each being a part of the complete individual. Jung described two archetypes that represented the maleness and femaleness of humans. The anima is the female component, the feminine inner personality, as present in the unconscious of the male—the "relationship" part of the personality. The animus is the male archetype, the abstract, analytic, logical component. Jung (in contrast to Freud) generally did not attach values to male and female characteristics. Instead, Jung posited the existence of both the anima and the animus in every person and emphasized the importance of recognizing and integrating these and all other aspects of the unconscious when developing a healthy personality. This represented the first discussion of **androgyny**, the consolidation of both female and male traits, as the most adaptive and healthiest orientation.

Androgyny
The consolidation of both female and male traits

Feminist neo-analyst Nancy Chodorow brought an object-relations perspective to the question of gender differences and the self. In her view (Chodorow, 1999b), the self is not fully autonomous, but fundamentally influenced by relations with others. (This is a central principle in object-relations approaches.) That is, children develop their gender identity in the context of their relationship with the mother, who is the key influence on the process for both boys and girls. Chodorow accepts the traditional psychoanalytic position that both boys and girls have their primary identification with the mother. The gender identity that develops in the daughter will match that of her mother, even though her individual self-identity will be distinct from her mother's. The same process cannot hold true for her son, though, who must develop a male gender identity in the context of his relationship with his mother, as well as developing his individual self-identity. Over time, the boy's developing gender identity must break from that of his primary relation in order for him to develop a healthy male identity. Because the object-relations view claims that the self is socially constructed in the context of the interaction with the mother, boys and girls must diverge in the nature of those interactions in order for their appropriately gender-identified selves to develop. This distinction between boys and girls in their processes of developing gender identity is universal, but Chodorow suggests that the way it occurs in any particular environment (such as our contemporary Western culture) is also influenced by the specific parenting practices in that cultural environment. Such ruminations by neo-analysts clearly strike a chord with the general public, as seen in the popularity of books like *Men Are from Mars, Women Are from Venus* (Gray, 1992), which focus on the ways men and women unknowingly (unconsciously) fail to communicate with each other.

Biological/Evolutionary Approaches

The evolutionary explanation for gender differences is based primarily on the argument that successful reproduction requires different sexual behaviors of women and men (Archer, 2009). Because the adaptive challenges in this evolutionarily critical domain differ between the sexes, the sex differences that exist are explained as resulting from natural selection. According to this theory, it is evolutionarily imperative for men to have as many sexual contacts as possible in order to perpetuate their genes. Men have almost inexhaustible supplies of sperm with which to impregnate and need squander little energy or thought on propagation. Men, however, cannot be 100 percent sure that a given child is theirs. These considerations (or lack of consideration, as the case may be) result in men trying to make as many women pregnant as possible; that is, they have an inherited tendency to engage in numerous sexual contacts with multiple partners (Ehrlichman & Eichenstein, 1992).

Females, on the other hand, having limited child-bearing years, must be more selective in their mating practices to avoid wasting their very limited reproductive opportunities on pregnancies involving unfit sperm. Furthermore, females must invest nine months of their time and substantial bodily resources (especially stored energy and minerals) in each pregnancy, followed by many years in child-raising. It is helpful to choose a mate who will assist with the child-rearing (Kenrick, Neuberg, Zierk, & Krones, 1994). Thus, an evolutionary interpretation provides a rationale for men being more sexually promiscuous and active than women, and for women being more nurturant and more sensitive to men's character (so they don't waste precious eggs on haphazard sexual contacts), although women presumably have been selected to want to become pregnant.

Most studies and surveys of American males and females have demonstrated that the average man has more sexual partners than the average woman, although of course the evolutionary psychologists knew this before they constructed their theories! Men do engage in most indicators of sexual activity—including masturbation, heterosexual and homosexual contacts, and casual sex—more often than do women at just about every age (Buss, 2007; Nicholson, 1993). However, these differences in sexual activity do not only imply a biological or evolutionary explanation; many other factors such as cultural norms and expectations, social learning, and peer influences are known to have an extensive influence on sexual behavior. Because we are unsure of the precise selection pressures on our ancestors, it is very difficult to be sure that certain behaviors proved biologically adaptive (Shibley-Hyde & Durik, 2000).

■ Would it bother you more if your partner (or future spouse) was feeling sexually attracted to someone else, or if your partner started falling in love with someone else? Are there male-female differences here?

■ The functionalists viewed women's so-called maternal instinct as central to their lives, precluding their development of other pursuits. But pregnancy, childbirth, and lactation are central pursuits for only part of a woman's life.

Classic to **Current**

Sex Differences in Jealousy

Charles Darwin's astonishing work on evolution directly influenced many pioneers of personality psychology, including Pavlov, Freud, Watson, and Eysenck. From the start, evolutionary theory had obvious and dramatic implications for understanding male–female differences and male–female relations, because successful mating is obviously central to reproductive success (passing on one's genes). Although evolutionary concepts moved into the background as personality psychology developed during the twentieth century, recent years have seen a great resurgence of interest in these topics.

David Buss and his colleagues have focused directly on male–female differences in jealousy (Buss, Larsen, Westen, & Semmelroth, 1992). Men (and other mammalian males) face the evolutionary problem of uncertain paternity; that is, males are not 100 percent certain that a mate's child is their own. A cuckolded male has spent effort and resources (time, money, protection) but gotten no genetic return from his unfaithful spouse. So, the argument goes, men evolved high levels of sexual jealousy, going ballistic at the hint that their mate might become sexually involved with another man. Females, on the other hand, are sure of their maternity, but face a different risk. Females face the risk and threats to their offspring if their mates abandon them and take off with an alternative mate or mates. So, the argument goes, women evolved high levels of emotional jealousy, worrying most about emotional attachment.

Buss and colleagues have collected an impressive amount of data supporting the prediction that men are more distressed at the thought that their partners might be enjoying passionate sexual relations with another man, whereas women are more distressed imagining that their partners are falling deeply in love with another woman. There are, however, many relevant arguments and studies that fail to confirm this point of view.

One of the problems is that most of us believe, even before any data are collected, that men and women differ markedly in their orientations toward love and sex. It is not news that relatively more 20-year-old men are thinking about sex while relatively more 20-year-old women are thinking about marriage. The question is, why is this the case? Some studies fail to confirm the hypothesized explanation, finding only, for example, that men react more to sexual imagery than to emotional imagery, even when infidelity is not involved (Harris, 2000). Others point out that men and women may have different understandings and interpretations of flirting by their partners, rather than an evolved, biological difference in jealousy (DeSteno & Salovey, 1996; Penke & Asendorpf, 2008). A third line of counterargument comes from the finding that masculinity and femininity (which measure gender roles) mediate the effect of biological sex on differences in jealousy (Bohner & Wänke, 2004).

In other words, many psychologists assert that sociocultural theories provide an alternative to the evolutionary psychology explanation of male–female differences in jealousy (and in many other domains) (Wood & Eagly, 2000, 2010). So are some personality differences between men and women directly evolved from issues of cuckoldry versus loss of a mate's resources? Most human behavior, especially concerning a matter like sexual jealousy, is complex and so needs to be approached from multiple perspectives to be thoughtfully examined. Even when there is an evolved biological basis, behavior patterns are shaped by culture, socialization, and learning.

FURTHER READING

Bohner, G., & Wänke, M. (2004). Psychological gender mediates sex differences in jealousy. *Journal of Cultural and Evolutionary Psychology, 2*, 213–229.

Buss, D. M., Larsen, R. J., Westen, D., & Semmelroth, J. (1992). Sex differences in jealousy: Evolution, physiology, and psychology. *Psychological Science, 3*, 251–255.

DeSteno, D., & Salovey, P. (1996). Evolutionary origins of sex differences in jealousy? Questioning the "fitness" of the model. *Psychological Science, 7*, 367–372.

Harris, C. R. (2000). Psychophysiological responses to imagined infidelity: The specific innate modular view of jealousy reconsidered. *Journal of Personality and Social Psychology, 78*, 1082–1091.

Penke, L., & Asendorpf, J. B. (2008). Evidence for conditional sex differences in emotional but not in sexual jealousy at the automatic level of cognitive processing. *European Journal of Personality, 22*, 3–30.

Wood, W., & Eagly, A. H. (2000). A call to recognize the breadth of evolutionary perspectives: Sociocultural theories and evolutionary psychology. *Psychological Inquiry, 11*, 52–55.

Animal research provides strong evidence for a biological basis of maternal instincts and other prosocial behaviors in subhuman species (MacDonald & MacDonald, 2010; Nicholson, 1993). For example, when injected with the blood from rats who have recently given birth, female rats exhibit a variety of maternal behaviors such as nest-building and retrieving young. Male rats that are injected with testosterone, on the other hand, also exhibit some maternal behavior toward pups. After birth, nursing causes female primates (including humans) to produce large quantities of **prolactin**, the hormone that causes lactation, or milk production. However, despite the apparent influence of this hormone and others—especially oxytocin—on mothering, female monkeys are often unable to successfully care for their offspring if they have been deprived of normal opportunities to model and practice maternal behavior. In humans, the biology provides only the core of a more complex cognitive-motivational system—motherhood "instincts" have a strong learned component. Furthermore, such hormonal influences apply primarily to the nursing of, and bonding with, newborns and other intimates, and they do not necessarily generalize to a feminine desire to chauffeur children to their piano lessons and soccer games.

Prolactin
The hormone that causes lactation

In line with an evolutionary perspective on maternal instinct, it also has been argued that humans evolved in environments where the survival of any infant was far from guaranteed, and mothers needed to avoid investing their resources in an infant who (due to its own characteristics or to the circumstances into which it was born) was unlikely to survive. Selfless devotion to an unhealthy or unwelcome infant would interfere with the mother's overall reproductive success. In the view of anthropologist and primatologist Sarah Blaffer Hrdy (1999), it is common for females of many species—including our own—to abandon, starve, or outright murder their own infants under certain circumstances. A woman's lifetime reproductive success might be enhanced by choosing *not* to nurture under certain circumstances. In Hrdy's view, the harsh reality of our evolutionary heritage is that sentimentally appealing notions of instant maternal–infant bonding at birth would not lead to adaptive fitness. Thus, the maternal instinct, as Hrdy understands it, is not the instinct to protect and nurture an individual infant who needs that care to survive, but rather the instinct for a female to cut her losses when she is dealt a losing hand.

The Behaviorist Approach: Social Learning

According to social learning approaches, gender-typed personality characteristics are attained through the same processes by which other behaviors are learned: reinforcement (operant learning), modeling, conditioning, generalization, vicarious learning, and other such learning processes (Bandura & Bussey, 2004). According to this perspective, parents, as the primary sources of modeling and reinforcement, serve as primary socializers of sex-typed traits. For example, Jenny's mom chastises her for dirtying her party dress, and compliments her for playing quietly in the corner with her dolls, encouraging passivity and compliance. Even Jenny's dress limits her activity as she must be careful to keep her legs together and not flip cartwheels (Henley, 1977). Alternatively, Peter's father wrestles with him during their playtime, rides bikes and go-carts, and Peter and his dad watch the weekend football game, cheering the tackles that immobilize members of the opposing team, promoting more active, aggressive forms of interaction.

■ Observational learning is more likely to occur when the model is similar to the learner. A child is more likely to model the same-sex parent than the opposite-sex parent, so the behaviors of children in a family will likely echo and thus perpetuate any gender-typed behaviors of the parents.

In addition, other powerful models, such as peers, teachers, and the mass media, demonstrate vicariously reinforced gender-typed behavior. Arnold Schwarzenegger provides a commanding model of the supermasculine hero, whose positive behaviors bring him extremely attractive rewards; meanwhile, the cute, feminine girls of TV sitcoms employ their winsome ways and feminine wiles to accomplish their goals. Among the characteristics of models that most clearly influence children's imitation is similarity of the model to the child (Bandura, 1969). Because gender is such a salient characteristic, boys imitate the traits and behaviors they see in men, whereas girls are more likely to learn to perform like the women they see.

Learning approaches thus tend to see gender differences as both deriving from the society and changeable by society. Many modern Western notions—such as the importance of providing proper role models for girls in our society—grow directly out of this social learning perspective. This is an example of why a thorough understanding of personality psychology can help us become more sophisticated in our approaches to many areas of social life and society.

The Cognitive Approach: Gender Schema Theory

Gender Schema Theory
The theory that argues that our culture and gender-role socialization provide us with gender schemas

Gender Schemas
Organized mental structures that delineate our understanding of the abilities of, appropriate behavior of, and appropriate situations for males and females

Gender schema theory argues that our culture and gender-role socialization provide us with **gender schemas**—organized mental structures that delineate our understanding of the abilities of, appropriate behaviors of, and appropriate situations for men and women, boys and girls (Bem, 1981; Martin et al., 2002; Ostrov & Godleski, 2010).

Gender schemas operate as cognitive filters or lenses through which we process gender-relevant information. For example, the schemas determine which characteristics of a situation will capture our attention, and they restrict which features of a situation we will process. That is, these schemas affect our perceptions of others (and ourselves) and assist us in making decisions about our resulting behavior. For example, when in a new doctor's office, the men are presumed to be doctors whereas the women working in the doctor's office are often assumed to be nurses or office staff. In a mixed-gender group, medical questions are more likely

■ When a baby is born, the parents announce either "It's a boy!" or "It's a girl!" and most parents try to dress their baby so that its sex is obvious. From the moment of birth, boys and girls are treated differently. It looks like this girl is being set up for a life where sweetness and prettiness are valued, while the boy is being readied for competition and sports as important activities.

to be addressed to the males. When we first meet someone (or hear someone calling on the telephone), we immediately want to know if this is a male or female. This category and our corresponding assumptions about masculinity and femininity are a key influence on our resulting perceptions and interactions.

Highly **gender-typed** (very masculine or feminine) individuals are more likely to organize their conceptions of themselves and others around the gender schema (Bem, 1974; Hargreaves, 1987) than are individuals who are not as gender-typed. Thus, feminine females (who see themselves as nurturant and dependent) are more likely to support political candidates whose policies promote traditional gender roles.

Gender stereotypes are more likely to be activated in certain situations such as beauty shops and automobile repair shops (Deaux & Major, 1987). Furthermore, a male car salesperson will interact differently with a 19-year-old female college cheerleader wearing a halter top than he will with a 30-year-old male football player. The cognitive approach to personality thus draws attention to the many aspects of thinking and perceiving and interpreting that are strongly influenced by gender.

Gender Typed
Describes an individual whose conception of self and of others is unusually strongly organized around gender schemas

Trait Approaches to Masculinity and Femininity

Masculinity and femininity have often been considered lasting, internal personality characteristics, or traits. Although many psychologists agree that masculinity and femininity are important traits, few have actually attempted to define these characteristics. Much of the pertinent literature becomes tied up in a tautology that suggests that the traits of masculinity and femininity are composed of the characteristics exhibited by males and females respectively. The issue is further confused by the fact that culturally prescribed social roles sometimes identify different characteristics as masculine or feminine in different cultures.

Self-Understanding

Measuring Your Masculinity/Femininity

Have you ever wondered how your own personality might be evaluated in terms of masculinity and femininity? There are many elaborate and psychometrically sophisticated scales that have been developed, but you can get a pretty good reading from this quick and simple scale.

For each characteristic, choose the number between zero (not at all true of me) to 4 (very true of me) that represents your standing on that characteristic.

	Not at All True of Me				Very True of Me	M	F
1. Able to devote myself completely to others	0	1	2	3	4	_____	_____
2. Able to make decisions easily	0	1	2	3	4	_____	_____
3. Active	0	1	2	3	4	_____	_____
4. Aware of the feelings of others	0	1	2	3	4	_____	_____
5. Competitive	0	1	2	3	4	_____	_____
6. Emotional	0	1	2	3	4	_____	_____
7. Feel superior to others	0	1	2	3	4	_____	_____
8. Gentle	0	1	2	3	4	_____	_____
9. Give up easily	0	1	2	3	4	_____	_____
10. Helpful to others	0	1	2	3	4	_____	_____
11. Independent	0	1	2	3	4	_____	_____
12. Kind	0	1	2	3	4	_____	_____
13. Self-confident	0	1	2	3	4	_____	_____
14. Stand up well under pressure	0	1	2	3	4	_____	_____
15. Understanding of others	0	1	2	3	4	_____	_____
16. Warm in relations with others	0	1	2	3	4	_____	_____
					Total	_____	_____

Scoring: Copy your chosen self-rating into column M for items 2, 3, 5, 7, 11, 13, and 14. Then, reverse your score on item 9 (a 0 becomes a 4, a 1 becomes a 3, a 2 is unchanged, a 3 becomes a 1, and a 4 becomes a 0), and put that number in column M as well. Copy your chosen number into column F for items 1, 4, 6, 8, 10, 12, 15, and 16. Sum up each column. The sum of the M column is your masculinity score, the sum of the F column is your femininity score. Each score will be between 0 and 32. Median scores for a large sample of college students, combining the scores of males and females, are about 23.5 for femininity and 21.5 for masculinity. This measure reflects a modern understanding of masculinity and femininity as orthogonal (independent) dimensions—your score on one does not predict your score on the other.

Based on Helmreich, Spence, and Wilhelm, 1981.

Masculinity and femininity have historically been considered two opposite poles of a single trait, but there are problems with this conceptualization. The concept of masculinity and femininity as a bipolar continuum fails to explain those individuals who exhibit many masculine *and* many feminine traits or, alternatively, individuals who display few of either. Indeed, statistical analyses of bipolar measures of the masculinity/femininity (M-F) trait have often demonstrated that the traits are multidimensional (Stockard & Johnson, 1992)—a person can be both masculine and feminine. The most frequently used instruments thus now measure masculinity and femininity as separate traits.

Using the **Bem Sex Role Inventory**, Sandra Bem classified individuals as (1) feminine—that is, high in endorsement of feminine characteristics; (2) masculine—endorsing masculine characteristics more; (3) androgynous—high in both masculine and feminine traits; or (4) undifferentiated—low in both categories. Because individuals encounter many circumstances in life requiring a variety of appropriate responses and behaviors, Bem suggested that the androgynous person would be most functional in a number of situations, being able to nurture, to be assertive, to express appropriate emotionality, while being rational and independent when appropriate (Bem, 1974). However, the findings of empirical studies of the correlation between gender-typing and behavioral flexibility have been inconsistent. In many cases, having the "masculine" traits of independence, agency, self-esteem, and so on is healthier and more adaptive than being more balanced on masculine and feminine characteristics.

Bem Sex Role Inventory
A measure designed by Sandra Bem to classify individuals as masculine, feminine, androgynous, or undifferentiated (low in both masculinity and femininity)

Aggression and Dominance

An assortment of experimental and observational studies suggest that when differences in aggression are found, they tend to be in the direction of male aggressiveness, including greater verbal aggression in males than in females. Indeed, when Hyde (1986b) meta-analyzed 143 studies of gender variation in aggression, she found males more aggressive than females, with the largest effect in studies of physical aggression. In addition, Hyde found that the method of the study had an impact on the result, with naturalistic observations resulting in larger gender differences than did experimental studies. The impact of higher levels of the personality trait of aggression in young males has powerful consequences for their survival—young men between 18 and 24 are overwhelmingly more likely to die than their female peers, with the vast majority of deaths among young people due to automobile accidents, homicide, and suicide (see Figure 4).

Do men have a more dominant personality than women? If aggressive behaviors are defined as dominance, then the answer is yes. If, however, leadership qualities, or controlling behaviors, or behaviors that resist control are included in the description, gender differences in dominance pale (Stockard & Johnson, 1992; Wood & Eagly, 2010). Because children tend to interact with members of their own gender, dominance in children has primarily been studied in these single-gender groups. In these interactions it is found that boys engage in more behaviors that are commonly thought to establish dominance, including interrupting,

■ Although women have been integrated into all U.S. military forces, their presence is far from universally accepted. Some personality theories claim that women tend to lack the aggressive instincts it may take to make a good soldier.

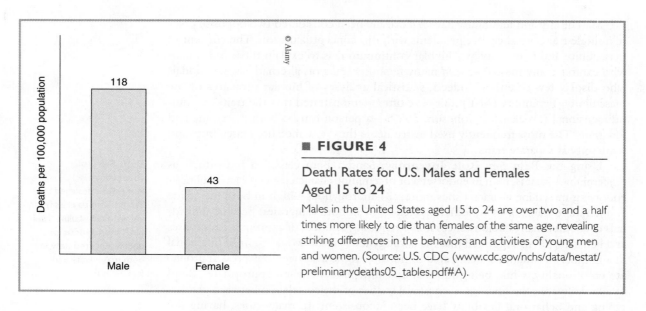

© Alamy

■ **FIGURE 4**

Death Rates for U.S. Males and Females Aged 15 to 24

Males in the United States aged 15 to 24 are over two and a half times more likely to die than females of the same age, revealing striking differences in the behaviors and activities of young men and women. (Source: U.S. CDC (www.cdc.gov/nchs/data/hestat/preliminarydeaths05_tables.pdf#A).

commanding and threatening, resisting the requests of others, and so on. Alternatively, girls take turns in conversation, make requests more politely, and agree with one another more often. These findings have also been documented in cross-cultural studies (Whiting & Edwards, 1988). A simple trait focus on gender and aggression may be misguided (Richardson & Hammock, 2007).

Emotionality

Popular belief, expressed in song and story, often defines women as creatures of emotion, swayed by their excitable and emotional natures. These beliefs are further represented in descriptions (and expectations) of women as subjective, sentimental, and illogical. Men, on the other hand, are expected to be under control—rational, logical, and unemotional. How accurate are these representations? A corollary question is this: Does the actual amount of emotion experienced by males and females differ? Or do men just demonstrate or openly express emotion less often or easily than women? Or, are differences in male and female emotionality simply cultural myths that act as gender schemas, affecting our perceptions of male and female behavior?

Do girls and women cry more than men and boys? Observational studies of babies and preschool children have found that *boys* cry more often as infants, toddlers, and preschoolers. On the other hand, both self-report and observation demonstrate that older girls and women in our society probably do cry more often than older boys and men (Nicholson, 1993). During children's socialization (at least in modern, middle-class culture), crying is discouraged in little boys, whereas tears remain an acceptable means of expressing negative emotion for little girls. Although women are generally more moody and emotional than men (Schmitt, Realo, Voracek, & Allik, 2008), it is a matter of dispute whether observable sex differences in emotionality reflect differences in the external expression of emotion rather than important differences in the level of emotion experienced—that is, it is often argued that there is not a sex difference in emotionality, but rather a sex difference in the display of emotion (Fischer, 1993).

Girls are just as adventurous and brave as boys. In fact, among children, girls tend to be more persistent and less distractible than boys, but not more fearful

■ Do women cry more in public than men do because of their hormones or because of their socialization? The observed differences between cultural groups in the relative levels of male and female crying imply that hormonal differences alone provide an inadequate account. Men are less likely to cry in public than women, but this does not imply that their distress or grief is any less—only that the display of their emotions is controlled by different rules. This man and woman lost a family member in a suicide bombing in Bali, Indonesia.

(Else-Quest, Hyde, Goldsmith, & Van Hulle, 2006). However, children are socialized to believe that females are more fearful, whereas boys learn early that it is not "manly" to admit to fear. Similarly, as adults, men are less likely to admit to anxiety than are women (and receive fewer prescriptions for tranquilizers, but drink more).

In terms of emotional sensitivity, girls and women are generally more influenced by the emotions of others. For example, baby girls are more likely to start crying when other infants cry. Women do better at interpreting the emotion displayed in photos and are better at expressing emotions so that they are interpretable by others. These findings suggest that women may be more attuned to both their own and others' emotional states (Hall & Matsumoto, 2004).

Achievement Motivation

Are there sex differences in ambition and ability, in the desire and capability for success? A common means of measuring achievement has been by utilizing the construct of **achievement motivation** (McClelland, Atkinson, Clark, & Lowell, 1953)—the drive to strive for success. According to performance measured by the projective Thematic Apperception Test (TAT), McClelland and colleagues concluded that women were not as motivated to achieve as men. After all, women do not run the major institutions of society—government, military, corporate, or academic—to the same extent that men do. In addition, some explanations suggest that women's higher need to be accepted and liked disrupts achievement. However, by now it should be clear to you that trait theorists can overgeneralize and overinterpret their data just as much as adherents of the other perspectives can.

It has also been suggested that females get their rewards from other persons whereas males are rewarded by task performance. However, Maccoby and Jacklin's (1974) study of sex differences demonstrated that there were no gender differences in person versus task orientation; in fact, in some studies boys were more sensitive to peer presence than were girls. Another characteristic of women sometimes said to be responsible for their lack of professional success (compared with men) is their "fear of success," but empirical evidence of any such phobia has not appeared. In short, gender differences in occupational and professional success seem to derive from something other than gender differences in personality. Or, as novelist George Eliot

Achievement Motivation
According to David McClelland, the drive to strive for success

(1859), who was a woman writing under a male pseudonym, put it: "I'm not denyin' the women are foolish: God Almighty made 'em to match the men" (p. 569).

Humanistic Approaches

Abraham Maslow's personality theory minimized the importance of masculine and feminine personality traits, highlighting instead the importance of self-actualization. He noted that both men and women who had successfully become the best they could be had a variety of traits in common including empathy and openness (often considered female qualities) and creativity and autonomy (classically male characteristics). Thus, according to Maslow, the self-actualized person has transcended the traditional conceptions of male or female personality.

Maslow noted that people vary on their feelings of dominance, which are related to self-evaluation, and he associated feelings of low dominance with feelings of inferiority, introversion, and suggestibility—characteristics our culture often identifies as feminine. In contrast to psychoanalytic and biological approaches, Maslow hypothesized that it was cultural influences such as norms, education, status, and expectations that connected women to low dominance. In a 1942 study, Maslow found that women who had strong feelings of self-worth were independent, successful, assertive, and healthy, with healthy sexual orientations.

SHARPEN YOUR THINKING   Current Controversy

Is a Single-Sex Classroom Discrimination or Sensitivity?

Over half a century ago, the Supreme Court of the United States decided a case that had a tremendous impact on public education. By the decision in *Brown v. Board of Education*, segregated public schools were ruled to be a violation of the U.S. Constitution. The Fourteenth Amendment to the Constitution assures equal protection of the laws to all citizens, and the Supreme Court determined that schools segregated by race denied such equal protection. The previously accepted doctrine was that "separate but equal" was adequate to ensure equal protection (as established in *Plessy v. Ferguson*), but the *Brown* decision declared that separation carried with it the implication of inferiority and resultant psychological harm. For the second half of the twentieth century, then, public schools were forbidden to use race as an official criterion in assigning children to schools. De jure segregation (segregation by law) was no longer legal, although the lack of residential integration meant that many schools remained de facto segregated.

Can we draw any parallels between racial segregation in public schools and sex segregation? For generations, single-sex public schools (especially high schools)

had been very common. By the 1960s, almost all of these had become coeducational (although some courses like home economics and auto shop were open only to one sex). More recently, there has been a resurgence of interest in creating single-sex classrooms and schools for girls. The goal of such sex segregation is to allow the female students to excel in academic domains such as science and math, where the academic performance of girls tends to be poorer than that of boys. The relevant federal laws and court rulings permit sex segregation, but only in situations with "an exceedingly persuasive justification." While the results of educating girls in single-sex classrooms appear to be mixed, the fact that they are permitted under the law raises interesting issues.

Oppression and discrimination, limited educational opportunities, and inferior status characterized the treatment both of racial minorities and of women for many centuries. In what way, if any, is sex segregation in public schools different from racial segregation? Are there differences in the nature of the categories of gender versus race that make one type of segregation less objectionable than the other?

Humanistic approaches to personality are usually the most willing to assume psychological equality of men and women, as each individual seeks fulfillment. They tend to expect that personality differences between men and women will become smaller as societies give more equal rights and opportunities to women.

Interactionist Approaches: Social and Interpersonal Characteristics

Many gender-relevant activities are not based solely on individual traits but rather are also heavily tied to the demands of social situations. Thus, the interactionist approach to personality is often very useful in understanding these phenomena.

Nurturance, Caring, Sociability, Nonverbal Sensitivity

Both anecdotal reports and many empirical studies suggest that our societal stereotype that girls and women are more nurturant and caring than boys and men (Deaux & Lewis, 1984) is grounded in differences that can be empirically measured with good reliability (Feingold, 1994; Taylor et al., 2002). Cross-cultural studies (Whiting and Edwards, 1988) likewise indicate that in most societies young girls nurture more than their male counterparts. There is also substantial literature suggesting that older girls and adult women nurture more than do males of corresponding ages (Stockard & Johnson, 1992). Suggestions that females are more sociable than males, however, seem to have little or no solid empirical basis. Although female children are often described as more likely to "attach" themselves to their parents, there is little empirical evidence of significant differences in attachment behaviors of boys and girls (Lewis, 1987). When women are raised to be nurturing and are placed into social roles that expect nurturing, they tend to act in a nurturant and caring manner.

Women have a distinct advantage in both expressing and decoding nonverbal messages. Women are better at understanding (decoding) others' nonverbal behaviors, including facial and body cues, and at recognizing faces. Women are also better at expressing accurate, decipherable nonverbal messages, especially facial cues (Eagly, 1987; Hall, 1990; Hall, Bernieri, & Carney, 2005).

In terms of specific social nonverbal behaviors like smiling and gazing, women smile and gaze more than men (Hall, 2006; Hall & Halberstadt, 1986). However, the reasons (i.e., the psychological processes) responsible for these differences depend on a host of socialization pressures, different experiences, and situational demands, which compound any biological predispositions that may exist. Here, as elsewhere, both the personality and the immediate social situation need to be considered.

Sometimes male–female differences in empathic accuracy are a function of differential motivation, rather than differential ability. An examination of more than a dozen studies of empathic accuracy found reliable gender differences in situations in which the perceivers are aware that they are being evaluated on an empathy-relevant dimension, or when the relevance of gender to the empathy perception is clear (Ickes, Gesn, & Graham, 2000). Thus, Maslow's humanistic argument is consistent with the interactionist approach, as the self-actualized person can transcend the common situational expectations of others.

Influenceability

What about the popular belief that women are more susceptible to influence? Is there a gender difference in suggestibility such that females are more easily influenced, conform more readily, and are more easily persuaded to change their beliefs than are males? When Maccoby and Jacklin (1974) reviewed the literature, they found that whereas there were no gender differences in situations in which there was no face-to-face contact with the persuader, in personal encounters women were a little more likely to conform than were men. Others examined differences in influenceability and find small to moderate gender differences in studies of persuasion and conformity, with women conforming slightly more than men (Becker, 1986; Eagly, 1978; Eagly & Carli, 1981; Hyde & Frost, 1993). How can we understand these differences?

Instrumentality versus Expressiveness

Instrumental Behavior

Behavior that is oriented to objectives that are task-focused and beyond our interpersonal system; contrasts with expressive behavior

Expressive Behavior

Behavior that involves the emotional well-being of one's social or family group; contrasts with instrumental behavior

Social Roles Theory

Alice Eagly's theory that the social behaviors that differ between the sexes are embedded in social roles; that is, the different roles in which men and women find themselves specify their behaviors

Social Roles

Gender roles and many other roles pertaining to work and family life that involve expectations applied to a category of people

Instrumental behavior involves being oriented to objectives that are task-focused and separate from the interpersonal system, whereas **expressive behavior** involves the emotional well-being of one's social or family group. Women are often identified as engaging in more expressive actions, whereas men are more instrumental, although both qualities exist in all individuals to some degree (Hyde & Linn, 1986; Wood & Eagly, 2010). Both instrumentality and expressiveness require skills and both are useful and beneficial. Being expressive does not imply being emotion-driven and incompetent, nor does instrumentality intimate an utter lack of interpersonal skills.

The social psychologist Alice Eagly has not been satisfied with traditional socialization theories and trait theories. First, she notes that the study of gender differences has focused on biology and on childhood development and socialization rather than examining what actually maintains the differences in adulthood. In addition, Eagly notes that much of the adult research has involved short-term interactions with strangers, a limited situational context that constrains the types of behaviors men and women display (Eagly, 1987, p. 9). Rather than simply generalizing from these narrow instances, Eagly offers, instead, her theory describing the function of social roles as the determinants of gender differences. According to this **social roles theory**, "the social behaviors that differ between the sexes are embedded in **social roles**—in gender roles as well as in many other roles pertaining to work and family life" (Eagly, 1987). This is a structural and interactionist explanation of gender differences that emphasizes the fact that members of different groups, such as males and females, often also occupy different social roles that fulfill social needs. This means that men and women tend to occupy social roles (structures), including gender, occupational, and family roles, that elicit different social behaviors from the men and women who enter these roles with caring inclinations.

Eagly thus suggests that the different roles in which men and women find themselves specify behaviors. Roles more often occupied by women, such as family roles of wife and mother, and occupational roles, such as nurse, teacher, and secretary, tend to evoke communal behaviors of relationship-maintenance and caring for others. Roles in which men find themselves more often, such as the family roles of breadwinner and father, and occupational roles of surgeon or manager, tend to require agentic qualities of independence and self-reliance (Eagly, 1987).

Gender roles (i.e., social roles based on gender) constrain general, broad categories of behavior as individuals respond to their own and others' behavioral expectations. For example, there are strong expectations that men (in our society) will not cry in public; just about everyone agrees that this is expected, and we are aware that everyone agrees. These expectations result in men's conforming to these gender role constraints (by not crying in public), thereby producing the characteristics of the controlled, unemotional "nature" of males. These social behaviors look superficially like the result of stable, internal gender traits. All in all, Eagly provides an explanation for gender differences that is based on neither biology and evolution nor learning and modeling. Instead differences arise from the different social roles men and women fulfill, and to particular gender roles in particular situations (Eagly & Carli, 2007).

The strong influence of social expectations and social comparison on gender-relevant behavior has been confirmed by social psychologist Brenda Major and her colleagues whose work has emphasized that individuals tend to make in-group (same sex) comparisons when evaluating their behavior. These in-group comparisons are in part responsible for an individual's satisfaction with her or his social roles, even when the roles involve inferior status or compensation. For example, Bylsma and Major (1994) found that because women base their judgments of "entitlement, performance and pay satisfaction" on same-sex, rather than opposite-sex, comparisons, women are more likely to express satisfaction with their status. This is true even when they have a clearly disadvantaged position; that is, women tend to compare themselves to other women, and as a result cross-gender inequities in status and pay are more likely to be ignored.

■ Billy Tipton (center in photo) was a well-known jazz pianist. Born a woman, Billy wanted to be a jazz player and pretended to be a man; even "his" trio companions did not know for many years that Billy was a woman. Billy married (saying he had been genitally injured in a car accident), and he and his wife adopted three children. It is not clear how Billy is best understood: as a cross-dresser, a lesbian, a transsexual, or simply a woman passing as a man to escape gender discrimination.

Gender Roles
Social roles based on gender

Cross-Cultural Studies of Gender Differences

Studies of the roles of men and women across cultures have found a wide variety of evidence that many gender characteristics are culturally determined through socialization and social expectations.

When Margaret Mead studied two New Guinea peoples, the Arapesh and the Mundugamor, she reported that whereas male and female Arapesh both displayed what we think of as feminine characteristics such as nurturance, among the Mundugamor both sexes seemed to be characterized by what we think of as masculine traits such as aggressiveness (Mead, 1935). Ann Oakley (1972) described the Bamenda group in Cameroon, among whom women are considered the stronger individuals and are expected to do most of the heavy agricultural labor.

Beach volleyball player Misty May-Treanor won gold medals in the Olympics twice (first in Athens and then again in Beijing) with her teammate Kerri Lee Walsh-Jennings. One hundred years ago, "ladies" played the genteel sports of tennis and golf wearing their long skirts and big hats. In recent years, female players have become more prominent in many sports that involve rough contact between players, perhaps as a reflection of a shift in social roles and social expectations.

Egoistic Dominance
According to Whiting and Edwards, trying to control the behavior of others in order to meet one's own needs

On the other hand, some gender differences are dependably demonstrated in a number of different cultures. For example, Whiting and Edwards (1988) studied children from 13 different cultures, finding consistent gender differences in nurturant behavior (with girls more nurturant than boys) and **egoistic dominance**, defined as trying to control the behavior of others in order to meet their own needs (with boys more egoistically dominant). Of course, socialization of certain behaviors could be consistent throughout a variety of cultures. Nevertheless, these investigators also found no dependable gender differences in several other areas, including dependency, prosocial dominance, and sociability. By now it should be clear that gender effects are not simply biological nor learned nor cultural. A sophisticated understanding requires an integration of various sorts of evidence using various relevant perspectives.

Love and Sexual Behavior

In American society, stereotypes of gender differences in love and in sexual approach and behavior abound. Men are described as dominating women in sexual relationships and as enjoying sex more than women, whereas women are said to give sex to men in exchange for getting what they (women) want in other domains. Women are stereotyped as interested in love, men as interested in sex. But these views have not always been the case. History and literature provide a multitude of opposing stereotypes of female sexuality, with women described as excessively sexual, insatiable, and therefore more likely to be vulnerable to possession by demons or the devil. In many parts of Africa, girls were (and sometimes still are) given clitoridectomies (genital mutilations) in order to interfere with sexual drives viewed as shameful. In fact, the concept of women's lack of sexuality is quite recent, stemming from the Victorian era. The fact that, despite these historical inconsistencies, the conception of men as innately more sexual than women has prevailed (with biological and evolutionary explanations routinely invoked) suggests that we should be especially wary of pseudoscience and distortion when considering these matters.

Culture provides the context in which our sexual behaviors are learned. Thus, gender differences in sexual behavior result from differential socialization for boys and girls, different models to whom they are exposed and to which they attend, and systems that reward boys and girls, women and men, differently for certain sexual behaviors. Gender differences in sexual behavior can also be classically conditioned, and likewise, socially "inappropriate" sexual behaviors may be extinguished. For example, a double standard has long existed in American society whereby married men can dally (cheat with impunity), but women who are promiscuous are seen as whores. Through these processes, boys and men learn to emphasize the physical and superficial aspects of sex, and girls and women learn to focus on the relational, love aspects of sex (Lips & Colwill, 1978). Further, cognitive processes (such as expectations and fantasies derived from mass media like movies) intercede in much sexual response and probably play an important part in gender differences in this behavior.

Although sexual behavior is very similar for males and females before puberty, adolescence can change everything. Whereas some of the physical changes accompanying female puberty (such as menstruation) are not attended by sexual pleasure, the boy's pubertal manifestations of erections and sexual dreams do draw his attention to the gratification that his genitals can provide. Teenage boys find themselves more focused on their genitals as a source of pleasure. In our culture and many others, boys discuss their genitals and masturbation with their peers more often than girls do (Nicholson, 1993). Girls focus their growing interest in the opposite sex more on romance and love, and they engage in less masturbation than boys. However, female interest in sexual relations may keep increasing into their 20s and 30s.

Changes in cultural understanding of female sexuality are resulting in a closing of the gap in sexual activity between the sexes. In some subcultures, women are approaching men in the age of first sexual experience and in the number of sexual encounters, both premaritally and extramaritally. Two other aspects of sexuality for which women are now considered to be much more similar to men than previously thought are women's interest in, and arousal by, erotica, and women's fantasies and erotic thoughts. Here again, our simplistic assumptions about the nature of men and women can turn out to be wrong when they are rigorously evaluated from multiple points of view.

A longitudinal study of Boston-area college students provided some interesting findings on courtship. In opposition to the stereotype, the researchers found that men had more romantic notions than women and more often initiated a relationship with the hope of falling in love. Men were also more likely to "love" more than women in the relationship. When relationships ended, the demise was more likely to have resulted from the woman's misgivings than from the man's, and the men were more devastated (Rubin, 1973).

Summary and Conclusion

One of the oldest philosophical questions concerns the nature of man versus the nature of woman. Personality psychology provides its own answers to this question using psychological theories, observations, and studies. A century of research on this topic has overturned many old stereotypes and prejudices, and has refined many of the relevant issues. One of the refinements has been to understand the multiple influences on masculinity and femininity, and to therefore be less concerned with sweeping generalities about categorical differences. Although there are some striking differences between being a man and being a woman, it is also the case that there is more variation among women and among men than between men and women; the distributions significantly overlap. That is, the personalities of men and women are more similar than they are different.

Because of a combination of biological predispositions and physical differences that are then acted upon by the expectations of others and the strong socialization pressures of society, men tend to develop psychologically masculine traits, behaviors, and abilities, whereas women tend to develop feminine ones. These may then be maintained by adult social roles. In the area of cognitive abilities, men tend to do better on visual and spatial tasks; in contrast, women generally have more advanced verbal abilities. Women are more expressive and more nonverbally sensitive, and they are also more nurturant, while men are more violent and aggressive. Men are more casual in their approach to sexual relations, but women (like men) have strong sexual drives. In addition to these fairly sizable differences, men and women may develop a host of other more masculine and feminine tendencies, depending on their environments and immediate surroundings. For example, in many times and places, men have been more athletic than women, but this difference decreases rapidly when women are allowed to participate in sports and have access to the proper facilities and training. Gender is a key influence on our perceptions of another's personality; we are frustrated when we cannot tell if someone is male or female, masculine or feminine. However, our perceptions and expectations are often incorrect.

Overall, gender differences in personality are generally not innate and unchangeable, but are influenced by a combination of biological tendencies, motives and abilities, social expectations, learning and conditioning, strivings, and situational pressures; that is, gender differences are, in this regard, like other aspects of personality. By understanding the various forces that make one a person, we can understand the forces that make one masculine or feminine. With this knowledge, we become less burdened and deceived by stereotypes or false assumptions.

■ Key Theorists

Sandra Bem   Alice Eagly   Brenda Major   Margaret Mead

■ Key Concepts and Terms

functionalism
maternal instinct
genetic sex
Turner's syndrome
androgenized females
Oedipus conflict
castration anxiety

penis envy
gender schema theory
Bem Sex Role Inventory
androgyny
social roles theory
in-group comparisons

Stress, Adjustment, and Health Differences

Disease-Prone Personalities
Health Behaviors and Healthy Environments ■ The Sick Role ■ Disease-Caused Personality Changes ■ Diathesis–Stress: The Interactionist Approach ■ Personality Disorders

Personality and Coronary-Proneness
The Type A Behavior Pattern and Choleric Struggle ■ Giving Up ■ Other Diseases

The Human Termites
Conscientiousness ■ Sociability ■ Cheerfulness ■ Stressed Termites ■ Mental Health

Blaming the Victim

The Self-Healing Personality
Control, Commitment, and Challenge ■ Trust and Devotion

The Influence of Humanistic and Existential Aspects on Understanding Self-Healing
Growth Orientation ■ Identity, Morality, and Purpose ■ Sense of Coherence

Photo by Russ Warner, Courtesy of Jack LaLanne

Jack LaLanne was one of the first fitness gurus, opening the original health and exercise club back in 1936. He promoted strength-building (including for women) while doctors said it would make you "muscle-bound"; he promoted vegetables and vitamins while doctors were promoting protein-rich meats, milk, and cheese; and he promoted enthusiasm and a positive psychological orientation while doctors focused on blood tests. When we last checked, Jack was 96 years old and all the doctors were long dead.

Jack LaLanne was widely ridiculed for promoting exercise, vegetables, and vitamin supplements decades before those practices became part of mainstream health advice. His approach was revolutionary for the times, claiming that health, happiness, and longevity would be improved by diet, exercise, and the right psychological orientation.

From Chapter 12 of *Personality: Classic Theories and Modern Research*, Fifth Edition. Howard S. Friedman, Miriam W. Schustack. Copyright © 2012 by Pearson Education, Inc. Published by Pearson Allyn & Bacon. All rights reserved.

Jack's motto always was to "inspire people to help themselves to a better life, physically, mentally, and morally" (www.jacklalanne.com). Is there a strong relationship between physical health, mental health, and moral health?

Is it true that worriers get headaches, and repressed women get breast cancer, and Type A men get heart attacks? Are there cancer-prone personalities and coronary-prone personalities? Are there self-healing personalities who manage to live a long and healthy life? These are some of the most fascinating yet complex questions in personality psychology.

Some people seem susceptible to all types of health problems but others rarely get sick. People differ. Even when there is a life-threatening disease, people with similar medical conditions can respond in dramatically different ways to their medical treatment. For example, some diabetics show a dangerous increase in blood sugar when stressed, but other diabetics do not (Stabler et al., 1987). How is personality relevant?

In the 1940s, Franz Alexander, a leading proponent of psychosomatic medicine, described the cases of two middle-aged women with breast cancer. Two years after their mastectomies, Ginny was dying but Celia was back at her job with new responsibilities. Dr. Alexander could not find a biological explanation for the different outcomes—the case histories and tumors had been similar. So he looked for personality differences. He found that Ginny was ostentatiously brave and asserted that she was going to get well, but she seemed unable to face her disease or her feelings about losing her breast. Celia, on the other hand, was neither excessively optimistic nor full of despair. She admitted that losing a breast was hard and tried to find out how she could adjust (Alexander, 1950).

We have all heard about hard-working executives who drop dead while relatively young—in their 40s or 50s. On the other hand, many people of prominence have led very demanding and productive lives well beyond age 70. For example, Eleanor Roosevelt and Benjamin Franklin made major contributions to world affairs late in life. Could it be that this commitment to a better world was relevant to their health? Katharine Hepburn, Vladimir Horowitz, Pablo Picasso, and many other artists have acted, played, and painted well into very old age. Not only could such performers continue working late in life, but they retained that joyful enthusiasm that audiences find so appealing. The longevity of extraordinary individuals like Katharine Hepburn and Benjamin Franklin is not in itself scientific proof. However, such personalities provide insights into the findings that emerge from scientific research.

T his chapter examines the relations among personality, stress, adjustment, and health. We do so with a critical eye, but also with a fascination about the many intriguing findings. By considering personality in an applied sphere such as health, we are following the advice of Kurt Lewin, Gordon Allport, Sigmund Freud, Carl Rogers, and other great theorists that the individual is best understood when studied in a real-world social context. It turns out that not only do we better understand health by studying personality, but we also come to a better understanding of personality by studying health.

Disease-Prone Personalities

Psychosomatic medicine is based on the idea that the *psyche* (mind) affects the *soma* (body). In the 1920s and '30s, many interesting ideas about psychosomatic medicine grew out of the psychodynamic theorizing of Sigmund Freud. For example, a classic work described a patient named Agnes, an unhappy and unattractive woman of 50 plagued with a serious heart condition that her doctors labeled "cause unknown" (Dunbar, 1947). Agnes went in and out of hospitals until, finally, she died in the hospital on her birthday. Why did she die on her birthday? Agnes had always wanted to show her resentment at being born.

Agnes had grown up in a hateful environment, with her mother constantly reminding her that Agnes was a mistake—the mother had never wanted a child. Of course, Dunbar's explanation of Agnes is a classic psychoanalytic interpretation: deep conflict with a parent leading to the symbolism of death on one's birthday. Is this understandable in terms of modern knowledge of personality and health? Can we influence *when* we will die? In fact, there is epidemiological evidence that people can sometimes prolong life briefly until they have reached a symbolically meaningful occasion (Phillips, Van Voorhees, & Ruth, 1992; Shimizu & Pelham, 2008); that is, dates of deaths are not randomly distributed.

More difficult than observing such phenomena is *explaining* them using modern scientific understanding. Why and how is personality related to illness and health? There are a number of ways in which personality has been shown to be relevant. These are illustrated in Figure 1.

Health Behaviors and Healthy Environments

The first major link between personality and health involves health behaviors—what people do. For instance, people with certain personalities take greater risks with their health and thus die sooner. However, this connection is not as simple as it sounds.

Psychosomatic Medicine Treatment based on the idea that the mind affects the body—that mental health affects physical health

© Thinkstock

■ Personality can influence the likelihood of engaging in behaviors such as smoking and drinking that have negative consequences for health. Personality thus can be considered a risk factor for disease.

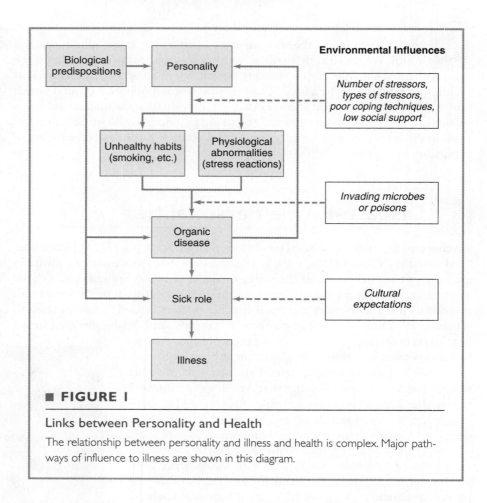

■ **FIGURE 1**

Links between Personality and Health

The relationship between personality and illness and health is complex. Major pathways of influence to illness are shown in this diagram.

Anyone could be hit by a car or run off the road by a truck. Sometimes such a tragedy is just bad luck. But who is more likely to wander aimlessly across a busy street—a happy, fulfilled person or a lonely, depressed, preoccupied person? Who is more likely to go out for a late-night drive alone and without wearing a seat belt? Who is more likely to inject illegal drugs into his or her veins? People who are impulsive, depressed, isolated, angry, or otherwise psychologically impaired are more likely to put themselves into unhealthy situations. In other words, one very important way that personality affects health is through behaviors that lead to more or less healthy habits and environments.

It is well established that smoking cigarettes and drinking alcohol are related to a number of personality characteristics such as rebelliousness, aggressiveness, alienation, low self-esteem, and impulsivity (Conrad, Flay, & Hill, 1992; Friedman, 2007; Hawkins, Catalano, & Miller, 1992; Tucker et al., 1995). Often, it is personality and social problems in childhood that lead to drinking in adolescence, smoking, and other drug abuse (Chassin, Presson, Sherman, & Edwards, 1991; Chassin, Rogosch, & Barrera, 1991; Friedman & Kern, 2010; Maddahian, Newcomb, & Bentler, 1986; Webb, Baer, McLaughlin, McKelvey, & Caid, 1991). These unhealthy behaviors in turn significantly increase the risk of health problems and premature death.

Why are these particular personality characteristics associated with these unhealthy behaviors? There are two sets of reasons. First, people with problems in emotional regulation may seek the stimulating or tranquilizing effects of cigarettes, alcohol, illicit drugs, and even junk food in an attempt to change their physiologically based moods (Wood, Cochran, Pfefferbaum, & Arneklev, 1995). For example, if your innate temperament or your early experiences lead your body often to feel sluggish, you may seek out substances such as cigarettes, or situations such as parachuting, that are stimulating. On the other hand, if you are often nervous and fidgety, you may seek out drugs that are tranquilizing.

Second, certain social factors tend to encourage unhealthy behaviors. For example, an alienated, rebellious teenager might seek out a peer group or gang that uses drugs or rides fast motorcycles (Clapper, Martin, & Clifford, 1994). If such an alienated teenager, in contrast, found meaning in a religious peer group or a green political movement, he or she might behave more like a divine angel than a Hell's Angel. In short, the personality trait of conscientiousness is a strong and reliable predictor of health and longevity, in part because it predicts healthier behaviors and in part because it predicts to healthier situations (Friedman & Kern, 2010; Kern & Friedman, 2008).

Furthermore, many unhealthy behaviors that place people at high risk for medical problems are instigated by stress, which is likely to be a special problem for impulsive and emotionally unstable people. For example, stressed individuals tend to eat more and gain excessive weight, an effect mediated by chronic stimulation of the hypothalamic-pituitary-adrenal (HPA) axis (that is, stress hormones) (Adam & Epel, 2007). Obesity, chronic stress, and chronic inflammation are involved in a variety of diseases.

Risk taking, thrill seeking, and sensation seeking are known to be relatively stable personality characteristics. Zuckerman's (1979, 1983a, 1983b) sensation-seeking scale (which is related, for example, to a love of travel and active sports) has subscales of Thrill and Adventure Seeking, Experience Seeking, Disinhibition, and Boredom Susceptibility. Is this propensity related to health? One study examined the personality correlates of drivers convicted and not convicted for offenses such as speeding or reckless driving (Furnham & Saipe, 1993). Compared with good drivers, the convicted drivers did indeed score high on sensation seeking and high on Eysenck's psychoticism scale.

A related approach is Frank H. Farley's **Type T theory** of psychobiological motives. Type T stands for "Thrill Seeking" (Morehouse, Farley, & Youngquist, 1990). This theory, too, derives from Eysenck's ideas about the physiological basis for introversion and extroversion. It suggests a psychobiological need for stimulation

© Thinkstock

■ Thrill-seeking Type T personalities may be able to get the stimulation they seek from activities that do not pose serious threats to their safety. Riding a roller coaster, for example, may be a good substitute for truly dangerous pursuits that are also attractive to a Type T.

Type T Theory
Frank H. Farley's theory that suggests a psychobiological need for stimulation due to an internal arousal deficit; Type T stands for "Thrill Seeking"

Should We Promote the Self-Healing Personality?

There are personality predictors of disease-proneness, and people with those characteristics are more likely to engage in unhealthy behaviors (such as smoking, drinking to excess, and unsafe driving) and to enter unhealthy environments. There are likewise self-healing personalities, who tend to engage in healthy behaviors, achieve emotional balance, and become well-integrated into their social communities. To what extent should society as a whole bear the medical costs for illness or injury that is caused by reckless behavior and lifestyles? As the costs of health care rise rapidly, would it be appropriate or beneficial to distinguish between costs that can be closely tied to an individual's behavior or personality and those that are random or due to uncontrollable circumstances? If a teenaged motorcyclist riding without a helmet is permanently paralyzed in an accident caused by his own reckless, drunken driving, should all of the costs of maintaining him for the rest of his life be covered by his health insurance plan? Is it up to society to promote self-healing personalities? If a chronic alcoholic who is serving a life sentence for murders committed under the influence needs a liver transplant due to his cirrhosis (associated with alcohol abuse), should his position on the transplant list reflect any of these factors? If we assign blame for illness, are we in danger of blaming the victim, that is, unfairly accusing sick people as being responsible for their condition? Is this reminiscent of saying that sick people have been possessed by the devil? As you examine your own thinking on these issues, consider both the ethical and practical consequences of ignoring these variables, and the complexity of evaluating them.

due to an internal arousal deficit. But if Type T people's needs for stimulation and risk taking can be satisfied by appropriate experiences in appropriate environments, they will be less likely to get into trouble. So it may be a mistake to forbid thrill seekers from their heart-pounding activities. Rather, it may be better to channel these motives into activities that are safe as well as exciting.

The Sick Role

Sick Role
A set of societal expectations about how a person should behave when ill

A second key reason for an association between personality and illness comes from society's idea of the **sick role**. Certain people respond to stressful life events by entering the sick role (Mechanic, 1968)—the set of societal expectations about how you should behave when you are not healthy: you should go see a doctor, stay home from work, be uncomfortable, act grumpy or moody, avoid strenuous activity, and so on.

Sometimes, people take on the sick role even though there is no organic (medical) condition that can account for their activities. For example, people under extreme stress or people who are not well adjusted may respond to the pressure of moving to a new job by avoiding this responsibility, losing their appetite, oversleeping, being lethargic, and calling in "sick." These actions, or "illness behaviors," may lead to the person being defined as ill. It is not only the classic hypochondriac who is "ill" because of personality more than disease. Rather, many neurotic people retreat to the safety of the sick role when they encounter challenges in their lives. Also, note that in our society it is considerably easier and more socially acceptable for a person to seek medical care from a doctor and to adopt the sick role than it is to seek psychological help for an emotional problem.

As behaviorists like B. F. Skinner would predict, escaping from stressful situations by becoming "sick" is rewarding. You may receive sick pay, days off, sympathy from friends, care from relatives, and so on. The sick role thus exemplifies the behaviorist view that personality can be "located" in the environment.

Cognitive factors are also quite relevant. When are we more likely to feel pain or decide that our body is not functioning correctly? Symptom perceptions are affected by factors such as a person's attention to bodily sensations and what he or she thinks about the sensations (Pennebaker, 1982; Pennebaker, Burnam, Schaeffer, & Harper, 1997). For example, if people think prolonged fatigue is a symptom of illness, they are much more likely to define themselves as ill when they experience fatigue; others might see fatigue as a normal part of everyday life. In addition, the interpretation of a bodily sensation as a symptom of illness is affected by the person's mood and chronic emotional state. Negative moods such as depression increase the likelihood of defining symptoms as indicative of illness. In fact, it has been suggested that in many cases symptom reporting is better regarded as an indication of neuroticism (anxiety, hostility, and depression) than as a sign of organic disease (Costa & McCrae, 1987b). Many people undergo tests for organic disease (such as cardiac tests for heart disease) when their pain is, in reality, a psychophysiological reaction to stress. The pain is real but there is no underlying organic disease that any physician can find.

Disease-Caused Personality Changes

A third set of reasons for associations between personality and health arises from the fact that disease can affect personality. This is sometimes termed a **somatopsychic effect** because the body affects the mind. For example, the physical weakness or oxygen deprivation resulting from a serious illness can induce chronic depression. Alzheimer's disease slowly but surely affects both personality and health as the brain deteriorates.

Somatopsychic Effect
Disease or genetic predispositions to illness that affect personality

Sometimes, genetic conditions can lead both to organic diseases and personality effects. For example, Down syndrome affects both personality and health. Or, there may be a physiological predisposition to both impulsivity and heart disease. In such cases the links between personality and health are real, not imagined, but health cannot be improved through psychological intervention or personality change because both are caused by the underlying third variable (such as genetic makeup or infection). Personality differences in health and well-being may begin before birth (due to genetics or *in utero* hormonal influences), and be influenced by genetic-environmental interactions throughout life (Hampson & Friedman, 2008).

Photostogo

■ Each society in each historical period has its own well-developed set of behaviors that are associated with illness—the sick role. There are expectations we share about how a person should behave when ill, and how the ill person should be treated by others, and these may encourage certain neurotic or stressed individuals to see themselves as ill.

Diathesis–Stress: The Interactionist Approach

Different things are stressful for different people. Some people hate having to stand up in front of an audience, others go crazy sitting at a desk all day, and still others dread dogs, exams, or even sex. Interestingly, most people know these things about themselves. Sir Francis Bacon, in the year 1625, put it this way: "A man's own observation, what he finds good of and what he finds hurt of, is the best physic to preserve health."

In the late 1940s, a number of medical students at Johns Hopkins University were studied in terms of their biological and psychological characteristics. The students were categorized as either slow and solid (wary, self-reliant), rapid and facile (cool, clever), or irregular and uneven (moody, demanding). They were then followed for 30 years. During this time, about half of them developed some serious health problem. Most (77 percent) of the previously labeled "irregular and uneven" types developed a serious disorder during these 30 years, but only about a quarter of the rest suffered a major health setback. In a follow-up study on later classes of medical students at Hopkins, the "irregular and uneven" temperament types were again much more likely to have disease or to have died (Betz & Thomas, 1979). They seemed constitutionally predisposed to poor health. But the environments in which they grew up were also highly relevant.

Personality has different implications in different places and different cultures. In Japan, there are well-defined social expectations concerning cooperation with the group and polite deference toward others' feelings. A Japanese individual who is loud-mouthed, aggressive, and brusque will face sanctions by the society and will likely feel distressed as a result. He may be labeled "sick" or "crazy" and may indeed become sick. In America or Italy or Israel, the opposite is common. It is the very shy, reserved, and deferential individual who is likely to feel unsuccessful and isolated. Such a mismatch between a person and his or her social group can be a source of stress and an important factor in illness.

Health psychologists refer to a **diathesis–stress model** of disease. **Diathesis** is the predisposition of the body to a disease or disorder. The predisposition or weakness might come from genetics or upbringing—for example, having weak back muscles. However, the illness (such as chronic back pain) would not materialize unless and until it is elicited from the environment: for example, by engaging in an occupation such as farming or construction that strains the back. Or someone who might be prone to mental illness may in fact have had a previous episode but may not have another bout of mental illness until the environmental conditions are ripe (see Figure 2). This model of illness has much in common with the idea of personality interacting with the situation

© AP Images/Lefteris Pitarakis

■ Redhead Pain. People with red hair may be physiologically more sensitive to pain and more resistant to the effects of anesthesia. One study confirmed that redheads are more anxious about receiving dental treatment, presumably because they feel more pain, even under anesthesia (Liem, Joiner, Tsueda, & Sessler, 2005; Binkley et al., 2009). This is a good example of the subtle interaction of a genetic predisposition and situations in producing consistent patterns of behavior. Such unusual effects may be hard to detect.

Diathesis-Stress Model
Model of disease that suggests that although a predisposition to illness exists because of genetics or upbringing, the illness itself will not appear unless or until it is elicited by the environment

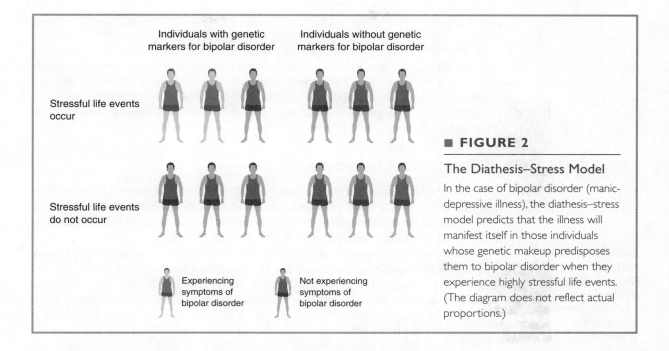

Individuals with genetic markers for bipolar disorder

Individuals without genetic markers for bipolar disorder

Stressful life events occur

Stressful life events do not occur

Experiencing symptoms of bipolar disorder

Not experiencing symptoms of bipolar disorder

■ FIGURE 2

The Diathesis–Stress Model

In the case of bipolar disorder (manic-depressive illness), the diathesis–stress model predicts that the illness will manifest itself in those individuals whose genetic makeup predisposes them to bipolar disorder when they experience highly stressful life events. (The diagram does not reflect actual proportions.)

(Caspi, Roberts, & Shiner, 2005). Thus, studying personality and health also helps us understand better the person–situation interactionist approach to personality.

Some of the greatest insights of the influential cardiologist Bernard Lown involved psychology—his focus on the emotional reactions of the individual. Lown found that the most potent stress relates to the recall of emotionally charged experiences. Such psychological stress is uniquely individual. For example, one woman did not display a heart arrhythmia (technically called a ventricular premature beat, or VPB) when told that she had advanced malignancy (cancer), but she did show a cardiac arrhythmia when she was asked to discuss her gay son (Lown, 1987, 1988).

It is known that stress can bring on a heart attack (Kamarck & Jennings, 1991). But why do only some people drop dead from emotional shock? Lown proposes a three-part model to account for the variability in sudden cardiac death after encountering stress. First, some electrical instability must already be present in the heart muscle; this is often the result of partially blocked arteries. (This is the medical diathesis, or predisposition.) Second, the person must be feeling a pervasive emotional state such as depression. (This is the psychological diathesis.) Third, there must be a triggering event, such as the loss of a job or the death of a loved one, with which the person cannot cope. In other words, as Gordon Allport often argued, we should not expect straightforward and direct links between personality and health. Personality is complicated and does not exist in a vacuum.

Research findings do not allow a simple inference that personality causes disease. In the first place, the associations are variable. Many people with personality problems or emotional disturbances do not become sick, and many ill people do not have unusual or differing personalities. Second, personality is associated with a multitude

Diathesis
The often hereditary predisposition of the body to disease or disorder

of behavior patterns, bodily reaction patterns, and social circumstances, any of which may be routes by which disease is more likely to take hold and progress. For many life-threatening diseases, risk factors are neither necessary nor sufficient causes. This unsettling state of affairs makes exact prediction from personality to disease impossible, but it does not make associations wrong or not worth knowing. As we will see, quite a bit is understood about personality and health (Friedman, 2007). And there are things to be done to change one's personality that can improve one's health (Friedman & Martin, 2011).

Personality Disorders

In modern American society, the most common form of severe stress faced by children is sexual or physical abuse. Such stress and abuse clearly places the individual at much higher risk for later problems with mental and physical health. In particular, the risk of experiencing borderline personality disorder clearly rises.

Borderline personality disorder is the term applied to people with serious problems of impulsive, self-destructive behavior; fragile self-identity; and moody, stormy relationships (Herman, 1992; Kroll, 2001; Linehan, 2000). These unstable individuals may suddenly shift moods, blow up, or even make suicide threats or attempts, while feeling empty and struggling to avoid abandonment. Not surprisingly, such people are often encountered by clinical psychologists and psychiatrists, but they are difficult to understand and treat. Why? Such disorders may be the result of various sorts of risks and so cannot be understood or treated from a single perspective.

From the psychoanalytic viewpoint, a child who faces severe, abusive disruptions in psychosexual development cannot develop a normal personality; sexual feelings have been misdirected and unresolved. The neo-analytic focus on identity seems especially relevant to abused children; such children cannot develop the basic trust and attachment that forms the basis for later close relationships. It is also the case that people suffering from borderline disorder are likely to come from extended families in which affective (emotional) disorders are common, suggesting a biological, temperamental basis for increased risk. (Not all abused children later develop this syndrome.) In addition, such children are often raised by parents who give them a distorted view of the world, and they cannot understand their parents. For example, they may have an abusive father and a mother who seems not to see the abuse. There is thus a *combination* of harmful influences.

More generally, borderline personality is one example of a type of deep-rooted, ongoing pattern of behavior that impairs the person's functioning and well-being. These patterns are termed **personality disorders**. Personality disorders are usually stable by early adulthood and last for many years. People suffering from personality disorders just cannot seem to fit well into their families and jobs—there are regular *significant* disruptions—and these individuals may be excessively suspicious, exceptionally emotional, or markedly anxious. A description of 10 common personality disorders is presented in the Classic to Current box.

But just as we now know that personality often can gradually change throughout adulthood, so too can personality disorders (Clark, 2009; Crowell, Beauchaine, & Linehan, 2009). Individuals with these problems of identity, emotional instability, and severe lack of trust can sometimes slowly become more stable, secure, and

Borderline Personality Disorder
Combination of impulsive, self-destructive behavior, fragile self-identity, and moody, stormy relationships

Personality Disorder
Deep-rooted, ongoing pattern of behavior that impairs the person's functioning and well-being

Classic to **Current**

Personality Disorders

Some people have ongoing significant maladaptive styles of behaving, which impair the person's functioning and well-being; these are termed "personality disorders." Such disorders are usually stable by early adulthood and may last for many years. Such people may be excessively suspicious, exceptionally emotional, or markedly anxious. They tend to be the troubled people we encounter in daily life, but they are not delusional or depressed. Listed below are 10 personality disorders. They are sometimes grouped into three clusters, based on whether suspiciousness, emotionality, or anxiety is the main problem. You can probably recognize some of these characteristics in a mild form in yourself, but that does not mean that you have a personality disorder. Rather, all of these patterns are extremes, which create ongoing problems. You can think in depth about the various, interrelated causes of these conditions.

1. *Paranoid*. Paranoid people are very suspicious and assume that others are against them. They take offense very easily and often have difficulties in the workplace. They are suspicious of and bear grudges against their spouses and coworkers.
2. *Schizoid*. Schizoid people choose to be alone and generally do not express their feelings. Praise or criticism from others does not matter much to them. (Note that these people are not especially prone to schizophrenia, which is a disease of delusions.) They have few close friends and few sexual encounters.
3. *Schizotypal*. Schizotypal people are also extreme loners, but they often act or dress in odd or eccentric ways. For example, they may laugh at unusual times or wear unseasonable clothing. They may tend to believe in magic—noticeably peculiar.
4. *Antisocial*. People with Antisocial personality disorder are very irresponsible, cold-hearted, and often criminal. For example, in adolescence they may be truant, lying, and thieving. Such people have patterns of fighting, and often are attracted to illegal drug use. They may be cruel to animals.

5. *Borderline*. Borderline people are so emotional and unstable that they often make suicide threats or attempts. They may have faced physical or sexual abuse earlier in life and have significant problems with their identity and self-esteem. They may engage in binge eating, reckless driving, or promiscuous sex.
6. *Histrionic*. People with Histrionic personality disorder are extremely emotional and attention seeking. They need to be assured about their attractiveness and so they dress in striking or seductive clothing (and may be taken advantage of).
7. *Narcissistic*. Narcissistic people are self-important and try to take advantage of others. Yet they constantly need the approval and attention of other people, even though they misunderstand others.
8. *Avoidant*. People with Avoidance personality disorder are very timid and easily embarrassed. They avoid close friends, as they are self-critical and fear any slights from others. They feel inferior.
9. *Dependent*. Dependent people will do almost anything to gain the approval of others. They may have very submissive relationships and are very fearful of being abandoned. They volunteer for unpleasant tasks simply to gain approval from others.
10. *Obsessive-Compulsive*. Obsessive-compulsive people are rigid perfectionists. They may work too hard, be preoccupied with details, and worry whether things will be done exactly their way.

It is important to remember that many of us have some of these traits to some degree. The labels can, however, sometimes be helpful in understanding and helping someone who behaves in extreme patterns that create ongoing problems and misery. Because these characteristics are based in biology and in early childhood disruptions that lead to chronic cognitive and behavioral patterns and social disruptions, they can be best approached with a thorough understanding of the eight basic aspects of personality.

adaptable with enough good interpersonal support. Although the Antisocial young hoodlum on your block or the Histrionic drama queen in your dorm can be unbelievably disruptive, there is hope that a multi-pronged effort to repair the internal and external sources of stress can eventually be effective. Of course the immediate threatening or criminal behavior patterns need to be addressed first.

Personality disorders are especially relevant to the perspective taken in this text in that they cannot be understood by considering only one or two aspects of personality. Rather, there seems to be a biological predisposition, a disturbed childhood, impaired social learning, and ongoing maladaptive social interactions, all leading to an individual with chronic life difficulties. The various categories of personality disorders therefore also have some overlap.

Recent Developments on Stress, Adjustment, and Health

Personality and health has become a major field of research (Friedman, 2007; Hampson & Friedman, 2008). There is now little doubt that individuals who are well adjusted and are well integrated into their communities are at significantly lower risk for disease and premature mortality than those who are regularly more unstable, impulsive, isolated, alienated and distressed (Friedman, 2000a; Smith & Gallo, 2001). When dealing with illness, medical investigators often think they are asking the question, "*Why* do people become sick?" but they are really often studying "*Who* becomes sick?" Yet research in this area is full of single-variable models and potentially misleading or erroneous assumptions of causality, when the reality is that the causal ties are usually complex.

Some of the best recent evidence for the idea of disease-proneness comes from studies of coronary heart disease (Suls & Bunde, 2005), and it is this topic that we consider next.

Personality and Coronary-Proneness

A century ago, the medical educator Sir William Osler argued that there was a link between personalities always engaged in stressful activity and the development of coronary heart disease. In the 1930s, the well-known psychiatrists Karl and William Menninger (1936) maintained that heart disease is characteristic of those with repressed aggressive tendencies. But such vague propositions could not be systematically and rigorously tested until the 1950s, when two cardiologists, Meyer Friedman and Ray Rosenman (1974), proposed the idea of the **Type A behavior pattern**. As one source of their insight, these cardiologists noted that when their upholsterer arrived to repair the chairs in their office waiting room, he noticed that only the front edges of the cushions were worn out. Their heart patients literally sat on the edges of their seats.

Type A Behavior Pattern/Type A Personality
A tense, competitive style that is especially likely to be associated with coronary heart disease

The Type A Behavior Pattern and Choleric Struggle

They proposed that Type A people, who are in a constant struggle to do more and more work in less and less time, would unleash their nervous systems in ways that would damage their hearts through excessive arousal of the sympathetic nervous system. Type As were said to be hasty, impatient, impulsive, hyperalert, potentially hostile, and very tense—a volatile package sometimes summarized as a "workaholic" personality. This idea inspired several decades of intensive research on the idea of a coronary-prone personality.

The struggle of a Type A person is most likely to be the one of a "choleric," angry against the arbitrary controls of his or her job or life. Such a person will also have generally poor interpersonal relations. There is now good evidence that people who lead confrontational, bitterly competitive, and driven lives are more likely to suffer heart disease. *But it is not hard work, activity, or a challenging job that is the key problem.* Rather it is the hostile struggle that is the problem. Many people are told to slow down, take it easy, take vacations, and even to retire from their jobs. In fact, though, there is not a shred of evidence that regular hard work increases the likelihood of heart disease in healthy people. (A different situation, of course, is a patient with an impaired heart whose doctor has advised strict limits on activity.)

Everyone likes to achieve a sense of mastery or competence. Such feelings of control are generally healthy. But people prone to cardiovascular problems (and other diseases) are especially driven to *excessive* achievement and to total mastery of their worlds. This argument was developed by David Glass, one of the first researchers to study seriously the psychological elements of coronary-proneness. In various studies, Glass showed that Type A people refused to feel tired and were especially likely to react with hostility when frustrated. In other words, their excessive contentiousness and competitiveness can be traced to a desire to maintain control (Glass et al., 1980). These feelings of desire for control are not necessarily bad; they are a key aspect of good health for most people. It is only when they are excessive (Figure 3) that there is a problem. With constant struggle, high levels of neuroticism and low levels of agreeableness—being chronically depressed, anxious, and angry—predicts heightened risk of coronary disease (Denollet, 2000; Smith & Gallo, 2001; Suls & Bunde, 2005).

■ FIGURE 3

Type A Man

(© Howard S. Friedman; drawing by Robin Jensen)

Giving Up

What happens when a person loses all control and "gives up"? This was the lot of many U.S. soldiers who were captured during the Korean War and imprisoned under hopeless circumstances. Soldiers called the phenomenon "give-up-itis." Such POWs were especially likely to die soon in captivity. But give-up-itis sounds amateurish: If you want to achieve scientific respectability for this condition and inspire others to conduct research, you have to develop the idea, cast it into a more conceptual framework, and give it a fancier title. Martin Seligman (1975) did this in his influential "Theory of Learned Helplessness".

The basic idea is a simple one. Imagine a situation in which a person cannot control the outcome, no matter what he or she does. This person might be a child who is totally ignored by her parents, an adult in an unbending job, or a person in a scientific laboratory facing uncontrollable noise. Very often, that individual learns to be helpless. In other words, he or she will not make any efforts at controlling his or her surroundings, even when subsequently placed in a controllable environment.

In the early 1940s, a number of healthy young Harvard undergraduates entered a study in which they underwent a physical examination and completed a battery of personality tests. Many of these men were then followed for the next 40 years. In light of recent developments in the area of psychology and health, researchers dug the old questionnaires out of a closet and analyzed responses given by the men in 1946. The responses were categorized as indicating either a negative and pessimistic explanatory style or a positive, optimistic outlook. For example, one pessimistic man wrote, "I have symptoms of fear and nervousness . . . similar to those my mother has had." What were the relations to subsequent health? Starting at about age 45, a clear difference in the health and longevity of these men emerged. The men with the pessimistic explanatory style were less likely to be alive and healthy (Peterson, Seligman, & Vaillant, 1988). This was replicated in a study of the Terman participants (see Human Termites section of this chapter) which found that pessimistic catastrophizers, who over-generalize the extent and meaning of bad events, were more likely to face premature mortality (Peterson et al., 1998); but this was mostly because they died from accidents or violence (homicide, suicide, car crashes, etc.).

When comedian George Burns (1976) was 80 years old, he said he would never retire: "I think the only reason you should retire is if you can find something you enjoy doing more than what you're doing now. I don't see what age has to do with retirement" (p. 11). Burns was right (and kept working all his life). Sociologists have shown that retirement is healthy for some but not all. If retirement means giving up an interesting daily routine, losing economic status, and moving away from friends, then retirement is likely to be unhealthy (Antonovsky, 1979). In other words, it is an unfortunate oversimplification to think that health will improve when people retire and take it easy. George Burns died at the ripe old age of 100. Renowned cellist Pablo Casals put his view this way: "To stop, to retire even for a short time, is to begin to die" (Kirk, 1974. In short, hard work is not unhealthy, but excessive hostility or depression can be very bad for physical as well as mental health.

Other Diseases

What about personality and proneness to other diseases? To organize this field and place these various studies into a single conceptual framework, a meta-analysis was conducted (Friedman & Booth-Kewley, 1987a). **Meta-analysis** is a statistical technique of combining the results of various studies to see what they say when taken together.

Some of the most widespread speculation about health concerns the effects of emotional states on arthritis and asthma. Other attention focuses on headaches and ulcers. So the meta-analysis examined these and heart disease. In total, over 100 studies were included in the statistical meta-analyses. These studies in turn had included many thousands of people. They contained almost all the relevant published scientific work on the question, "Why are some people more likely to become ill?"

The results revealed associations between various psychological disturbances (like chronic anger, or anxiety, or depression) and several diseases. In other words, it was not the case that anxiety was related only to ulcers and repression exclusively to asthma. Rather, there was evidence for what Friedman termed a generic **disease-prone personality** (Friedman & Booth-Kewley, 1987a; Friedman & VandenBos, 1992).

Meta-Analysis
A statistical technique for combining the results of multiple research studies

Disease-Prone Personality
Personality characteristics associated with an increased likelihood of becoming ill

Remember again that disease is not necessarily or solely caused by unhealthy emotional patterns. Some emotionally imbalanced people live long and healthy lives, and some balanced people become very ill. In order to clarify matters further and ascertain how personality interacts with time and circumstances to affect health, it is necessary to follow large numbers of people throughout their lives. This was done in the study of the so-called human Termites.

The Human Termites

The psychologist Lewis Terman was one of the leading intelligence researchers of the twentieth century. Among other contributions, he developed the well-known Stanford-Binet IQ test. In 1921, Terman began one of the most comprehensive studies in psychology. He recruited bright California schoolchildren—856 boys and 672 girls—intensively studied their psychosocial and intellectual development, and followed them into adulthood. These clever participants nicknamed themselves Terman's "Termites."

In what ways are aspects of personality related to longevity in general and to specific diseases in particular, across the life span? To address this question directly, we need to follow people for a lifetime. Obviously, this assignment is impossible for any single researcher, but we have been able to approximate just such a lifetime study, based on the Terman archives. By 2010, almost all of Terman's participants had died, and your text coauthor and colleagues gathered their death certificates and coded the dates and causes of death (Friedman et al., 1995; Friedman & Martin, 2011). By the way, Friedman's graduate students decided that if the Terman participants could be "Termites," then the researchers could be "Termanators," and they named Professor Friedman "Chief Termanator." As the research was being done at the University of California in Riverside, only about fifty miles east of Hollywood, the name seemed to fit.

Back in 1921, Terman's aim was to secure a reasonably random sample of bright California children, and so most public schools in the San Francisco and Los Angeles areas were searched for bright kids, nominated by their teachers and tested by Terman to have an IQ of at least 135 (Terman & Oden, 1947). They have been followed at 5- to 10-year intervals ever since. In this remarkable study, only small percentages (less than 10 percent) of participants are unaccounted for. Analyses by Terman's researchers as well as our own comparisons indicate that those lost from the study do not differ systematically from those who remained, so there is not a bias due to dropouts. The Termites were a bright, well-educated group, integrated into American society, similar in many health-relevant ways to most bright, educated middle-class Americans of the twentieth century.

When the average Termite was about 11 years old, Terman collected trait ratings about the participants from their parents and teachers. The scales he used are remarkably modern in their appearance and provide a better assessment than the primitive personality tests that were available at the time. It is reasonable to expect that parents and teachers have a good idea of whether an 11-year-old child is a sociable, popular child, is conscientious, is self-confident, and so on. Friedman and his

■ The "Termites" were first studied as children in California by Lewis Terman in 1921, and they are still being intensively studied by Howard Friedman and his colleagues (see *The Longevity Project*, Friedman & Martin, 2011). Some of the Termites have allowed themselves to be publicly identified. Pictured here are Shelley Smith Mydans (left), who was a journalist for *Life* magazine, and Jess Oppenheimer, the creator of the *I Love Lucy* show (right with Lucille Ball). Most of the Terman children grew up to be successful contributors to society (as Terman had hoped), but a good number headed for rough times and were at high risk for premature mortality. Certain key aspects of their personalities seem most relevant. (Right photo courtesy of www.lucynet.com.)

collaborators constructed six personality dimensions from Terman's scales and used them to predict longevity and cause of death throughout their lives using a statistical technique called *survival analysis* (which computes the fraction of a population that will survive past a certain time) (Friedman et al., 1993; Friedman et al., 1995; Martin et al., 2007). We will now examine the intriguing findings in some detail.

Conscientiousness

Does childhood personality predict premature mortality decades later? The most striking finding is that childhood social dependability or conscientiousness is predictive of longevity. Children, especially boys, who were rated as prudent, conscientious, truthful, and free from vanity (four separate ratings, which were averaged) live significantly longer throughout the life span. They are about 30 percent less likely to die in any given year. Personality did indeed predict longevity.

This finding that personality predicts survival across the life span raises many fascinating questions concerning causal mechanisms. Why are conscientious, dependable children who live to adulthood more likely to reach old age than their less conscientious peers? Further survival analyses suggest that the protective effect of conscientiousness is partly but not primarily due to a reduction in the risk of injury. How does it operate? Although there is some tendency for the unconscientious to be more likely to die a violent death, conscientiousness is also protective against early death from cardiovascular disease and cancer. Furthermore, a focus on unhealthy behaviors such as smoking and drinking shows them to be somewhat relevant as explanatory mechanisms, but a significant effect of conscientiousness remains after controlling for drinking and for smoking and other aspects of personality. In other words, a person who was conscientious as a child is less likely to suffer an early death from injury, and less likely to engage in unhealthy habits, but stays healthier and lives longer for other reasons as well. Further, conscientiousness, measured independently in childhood *and* adulthood, predicts mortality risk across the full life span, and the link from childhood remains robust when adult conscientiousness is statistically controlled (Friedman & Martin, 2007; Martin et al., 2007).

Follow-up studies indeed confirm that conscientiousness is important to health and longevity, for a variety of reasons (Bogg & Roberts, 2004; Kern & Friedman, 2008; Weiss & Costa, 2005; Wilson, Mendes de Leon, Bienias, Evans, & Bennett, 2004). Conscientious individuals not only engage in better health habits and fewer risky activities, it is also the case that they are physiologically predisposed to health and their conscientious personality leads them into much healthier situations and relationships (Carver, Johnson, & Joormann, 2009; Friedman & Martin, 2011).

■ In the Terman sample, children who were rated by their parents and teachers as high in conscientiousness lived longer than their less conscientious peers.

Sociability

The Terman research found no evidence that the personality trait of sociability is strongly related to health and longevity. Having good social relations is healthy, but those people high on the trait of sociability are not necessarily those who develop the best social ties. Rather, the locus of health-relevant effects seems to be centered in such traits as impulsivity, egocentrism, and undependability. For example, childhood ratings on such variables as popularity and preference for playing with other people did not predict longevity.

To further explore the lifelong effects of sociability, Friedman followed up on Terman's (1954) study of scientists. Terman had found that the Termites who grew up to be scientists had been much less sociable early in life than the nonscientists. (Only male scientists were studied by Terman.) In fact, Terman considered the differences in sociability to be quite remarkable. Re-creating Terman's groups and comparing their longevity, survival analyses found that the scientists did not die sooner. In fact, the scientists tended to live longer (Friedman et al., 1994). So having a very sociable personality did not by itself forecast a long life. This is in part because highly sociable extroverts in American society are generally at greater risk for smoking and alcohol abuse; health associations with extroversion are best understood in particular contexts.

Cheerfulness

A very interesting and paradoxical finding concerned childhood cheerfulness—that is, rated optimism and a sense of humor. Contrary to expectation, childhood cheerfulness was inversely related to longevity. The cheerful kids grew up to be adults who died somewhat sooner.

Why might this be? The cheerful children, like extroverted people, grew up to be more likely to smoke, drink, and take risks, although these habits did not fully explain their increased risk of premature mortality (Martin et al., 2002). It might also be the case that cheerfulness is helpful when facing a stress such as surgery, but harmful if it leads one to be careless or carefree throughout one's life (Tennen & Affleck, 1987; Weinstein, 1984). For example, they might say to themselves, "It doesn't matter if I smoke; it won't affect me." In other words, people who behave in an amusing way are not necessarily those whose attitudes and behaviors are most healthy, but an optimistic person facing health challenges may be more willing to cooperate fully with treatment prescriptions and regimens; such effects are *interactions* of the person and the situation. It is probably also the case that happier people are generally healthier people (Pressman & Cohen, 2005), but not necessarily because the happiness is producing the health; rather, other factors are simultaneously influencing both one's mental and physical well-being.

Stressed Termites

In terms of relevant social factors, the longevity project also looked at those children who faced the divorce of their parents. It is well known that divorce of one's parents during childhood can have ill effects on one's future mental health. For example, children of divorce, especially boys, are at greater risk for observable behavior and adjustment problems (Amato & Keith, 1991; Block, Block, & Gjerde, 1986, 1988; Hetherington, 1991; Jellinek & Slovik, 1981; Shaw, Emery, & Tuer, 1993; Zill, Morrison, & Coiro, 1993). Here, too, the explanations often concern a lack of social dependability or ego control—that is, impulsivity and nonconformity—although neuroticism (low emotional stability) is also often implicated. But there had never before been a lifelong prospective study of family stress predictors of mortality and cause of death, although family stress (particularly parental divorce) has been found to predict unhealthy behaviors such as smoking and drug use in adolescence as well as poor psychological adjustment (Amato & Keith, 1991; Block, Block, & Keyes, 1988; Chassin, Presson, Sherman, Corty, & Olshavsky, 1984; Conrad et al., 1992; Hawkins et al., 1992). Would these detrimental effects of parental divorce reach across the life span and affect longevity and cause of death?

Friedman and his colleagues looked at the children whose parents either did or did not divorce before the child reached age 21. Children of divorced parents faced a one-third greater mortality risk than people whose parents remained married at least until the children reached age 21. Among males, for those whose parents divorced while they were children, the predicted median age of death is 76; for those whose parents remained married, the predicted median age of death is 80. For females, the corresponding predicted ages of death are 82 and 86 (Schwartz et al., 1995).

Although fewer people in the Terman sample had faced divorce of their parents during childhood compared to children today, this finding does provoke serious concern in light of the overwhelming evidence from other studies indicating damaging psychological impacts of parental divorce. Death of a parent had very little effect, consistent with other research indicating that parental strife and divorce has a greater influence on subsequent psychopathology than parental death (Tennant, 1988).

Using the information gathered and coded from the death certificates, the study then examined whether divorce of one's parents relates differentially to cause of death. Parental divorce was not associated with whether one is more likely to die of cancer, or heart disease, or other disease; it was a general risk factor. Also, the overall higher mortality risk could not be explained away by a higher injury rate, although the possibility of an especially increased risk of injury death cannot be ruled out. In addition, personality and parental divorce were shown to be independent predictors of longevity. Figure 4 shows the effects of conscientiousness and parental divorce on longevity in males; the effects are analogous for females. It is interesting to note that the size of the combined effect of conscientiousness and parental divorce is equal to the effect of gender on longevity, which is one of the largest known effects on that variable.

Is the increased mortality risk of children of divorce due in part to these people's own subsequent divorce? People whose parents divorced were indeed more likely to divorce their own partners. Further, individuals who were divorced or remarried reported that their childhoods were significantly more stressful than did those who got and stayed married. In other words, Terman participants who experienced a marital breakup were more likely to have seen the divorce of their own parents, and they were more likely to report having experienced a stressful home environment as children (such as "marked friction among family members"). Given that parental divorce is associated with one's own future divorce, and that one's divorce is predictive of increased mortality risk, it is indeed the case that one's unstable adult relations "explain" some of the detrimental effects of parental divorce. However, after controlling for one's (adult) divorce, parental divorce during childhood remains a significant predictor of premature mortality, suggesting that it has some additional adverse consequences in adulthood.

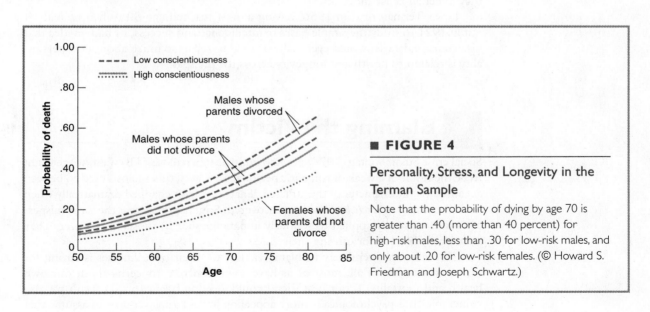

■ FIGURE 4

Personality, Stress, and Longevity in the Terman Sample

Note that the probability of dying by age 70 is greater than .40 (more than 40 percent) for high-risk males, less than .30 for low-risk males, and only about .20 for low-risk females. (© Howard S. Friedman and Joseph Schwartz.)

Mental Health

What about personality and mental state in adulthood? In 1950 (when they were about 40 years old), the Termites were asked about tendencies toward nervousness, anxiety, or nervous breakdown. Based on their responses, on personal conferences with participants and with family members, and on previous related information in the files dating back a decade, Terman's team then categorized each participant on a three-point scale of mental difficulty: satisfactory adjustment, some maladjustment, or serious maladjustment. Almost one-third experienced at least some mental difficulty by this stage. For males, mental difficulty as of 1950 significantly predicted mortality risk through 1991, with unstable males at high risk of premature mortality (Martin et al., 1995).

All in all, undependability, impulsivity, and family instability (parental and one's own divorce) are predictive of premature mortality. It may be the case that such psychosocial factors affect a whole host of health behaviors—drinking and smoking, exercise patterns, diet, use of prophylactics, adherence to medication regimens, avoidance of environmental toxins, and more—which, when put together, may explain a lot of the associations between psychology and longevity. Taken together with the increasingly well-documented associations of stress with both cardiovascular disease mechanisms and effects on the immune system ("psychoneuroimmunology," Friedman, 2008; Kemeny, 2007; Temoshok, 1998), it is probable that there are multiple pathways linking personality to longevity.

Overall, there is reliable confirmation in the physical health arena of the importance of what psychologists have typically called mental stability or ego strength—dependability, trust, and lack of impulsivity. How large are these effects? These effects are smaller than the influences of gender or smoking on longevity, but they are comparable to common biological risk factors such as systolic blood pressure and serum cholesterol, and to common behavioral risks such as exercise and diet, as they affect all-cause mortality.

Lewis Terman died in 1956, having almost reached age 80. When he had set out in 1921 to study the simple bases of intelligence and success, he had no idea that his extensive data set would eventually be used to tell us so much about how personality is related to health and longevity across the life span.

Blaming the Victim

Social critic Susan Sontag (1978) pointed out that tuberculosis (TB) was once thought to be the result of a weak or romantic personality; that is, tuberculosis used to be seen as caused by the character of the afflicted. That viewpoint changed dramatically when the TB-causing *tubercle bacillus* was discovered. Sontag argues that the same misperception is currently applied to seriously ill patients such as those with cancer: They are unfairly blamed for causing their illness.

This (illogical) tendency to blame victims for their own illnesses is strong for two reasons. First of all, most of us have some concrete concerns about our own health and mortality. If our best friend could develop breast cancer, aren't we also vulnerable? It is psychologically more appealing for us to answer no—to assume that we are different from her and that our friend was somehow responsible for her own illness. That way, we distance and protect ourselves from feeling personally threatened. The second reason we tend to blame people for their own disease has to do with our desire for a predictable world. We like to believe that if we work hard and take care of ourselves, things will work out reasonably well. But illness sometimes arises suddenly and progresses unpredictably. Blaming the victim reestablishes cause-and-effect predictability, and our own worldview is safe again.

There is a danger that an undiscerning student will conclude that people with disease have brought it on themselves. Aside from the inhumanity and lack of compassion for suffering people that this view entails, it may lead to further problems and suffering for the victim, as others withdraw financial or emotional support. On the other hand, it is a disservice to both healthy and ill people to pretend that they can have no effect on their prognosis. It is a big problem that about half of Americans agree with the statement "There is not much a person can do to prevent cancer." Quite the contrary, there are indeed things that make disease and early death more likely. We must walk this fine line between blaming patients on the one hand and absolving them of any role in their health on the other hand. There are healthy and unhealthy personalities.

The Self-Healing Personality

Mohandas K. Gandhi was one of the greatest workaholics of all time. He was not sickly even though he spent over 2,300 days in prison and endured numerous self-imposed fasts. On the contrary, he had the personal strength and commitment to be one of the most influential leaders of the twentieth century, perhaps of all time. He pioneered nonviolent political resistance (*satyagrapha*), instituted numerous social reforms, and won political freedom for India. He was assassinated at age 78. What defined Gandhi's life was a commitment to principle. As he aged, he grew more and more content with his life, but he remained humble. He certainly was not blindly optimistic. People who are constructively challenged find it easier to remain healthy.

Although thousands of pages are published each year debating the question "Why did Ms. X become ill, and how can she be treated?" little is asked about "Why did Ms. Y remain healthy?" Fortunately, personality researchers studying health have drawn much inspiration from the humanistic and existential approaches, which do indeed consider positive aspects (Friedman, 2000b).

Control, Commitment, and Challenge

An analysis by Salvatore Maddi and Suzanne C. Ouellette Kobasa (1984) of business executives under stress in a large midwestern firm examined the psychological differences between those who became ill and those who did not. Over a period of eight years, several key factors emerged. First, the executives' feeling of control was a significant factor in terms of health. Those who remained healthier did not

■ Victor Frankl, once an inmate in a Nazi concentration camp, showed that a person's sense of dignity has more than ethical importance—it is also an aspect of health.

© AP Images/Ronald Zak

feel powerless in the face of external challenges but instead had a sense of power. They tended to believe that challenging situations could be influenced by their personal efforts. For example, an executive named Andy clearly lacked this sense of control. He appeared polite and eager to please despite feeling increasing pressures of job responsibilities. He carefully transmitted job orders from his superiors to his subordinates but exerted little authority himself. He worried that his workload was getting out of control. At home, trouble was developing with his wife and children. Andy developed an ulcer and was on a restricted diet. He experienced sleeplessness, appetite loss, and heart palpitations. Although only in his 40s, he had a tendency toward high blood pressure. He lacked the strength of personality to cope with his job stress.

The second characteristic of executives who remained healthy was their commitment to something they felt was important and meaningful. Those individuals who felt committed to their work, their communities, and their families were less likely to become ill. One executive, Bill, was seen as especially successful and healthy, even though his wife had been killed in an accident seven years earlier. He had a twinkle in his eye and a zest for his work. He enjoyed learning from his work, felt its social importance, and welcomed changes in the company as interesting and worthwhile.

Third, executives who remained healthy were those who responded to life with excitement and energy. They welcomed change and innovation while remaining true to the fundamental life goals that they had already established. One of the successful, healthy executives, Chuck, was involved in difficult customer relations work. As his company began reorganizing, Chuck reported feeling more challenge but said that it made his work that much more interesting and exciting. He was not threatened. Chuck is the kind of executive who views every problem as an opportunity to improve on the status quo. Contrary to some pop psychology theories, happy-go-lucky, lackadaisical people are not especially healthy.

Trust and Devotion

These ideas about self-healing have been confirmed by many other sorts of studies, though often indirectly. For example, the personality psychologist Julian Rotter is well known for work on the idea and measurement of *locus of control*. Some people feel pushed around by external forces, whereas other people feel the *locus* (the location) of control over their lives is within themselves. We have seen that this is relevant to health and coping. In an incisive analysis, Rotter (1980) asserts and presents evidence that people who trust others are less likely to be unhappy, conflicted, or maladjusted. They are more dependable and have more friends. They are not necessarily more gullible; they are just less cynical. In brief, they are healthier. This is not a moral judgment; it is merely a summary of the empirical evidence. Trust is a motivation directly relevant to the healing personality.

In 1978, Anatoly (now Natan) Sharansky was convicted of treason in communist Moscow and was sentenced to many years of hard labor. His real crime was that he was a Jewish activist who was trying to emigrate to Israel. At the end of his trial, the outcome of which had been predetermined, Sharansky stood up in court and expressed his faith and determination to be free. Sharansky survived many years in Soviet prison and was eventually permitted to emigrate, in good health. Although few Westerners face the challenges Sharansky faced, almost everyone is subject to environmental pressures. Yet many hard workers thrive anyway, even in arduous or hectic circumstances. In precise opposition to what writers about workaholism and the Type A personality often claim, living life to the fullest seems to provide protection from disease. A key element of this healthy style, however, is a commitment to an ideal greater than oneself.

It is useful to think about two major types of self-healing personalities. The first is the more active, zealous type. This includes the busy but confident lawyer, and the hard-working, productive executive. These people seek out stimulation, are highly extroverted, and tend to be spontaneous and fun-loving. The second type of self-healing personality is the calmer, more relaxed type—active, alert, involved, and responsive, but calm, philosophical, and bemused. Although these people also enjoy the presence of others, they tend to prefer the company of a few close friends.

These two types of healthy people have different optimal levels of stress. For the second, more reserved and content, type of person, it is better to have conflicts resolved and stimulation under control. For the first, more excitement-seeking, type of personality, a higher level of challenge is healthier; unsolved dilemmas are not a bother for this person. In line with this thinking, research suggests that in similar situations these two types of people have different tendencies toward negative emotions and stress hormones. The low-key, goal-oriented individuals show more distress and greater release of stress hormones when challenges remain unresolved. The more spontaneous and arousal-seeking individuals, on the other hand, are especially likely to be distressed by a lack of stimulation and are threatened only when challenges become overwhelming. Thus, here again we see that blanket health recommendations for the whole population can lead to serious problems. The individual must also be considered.

Famous Personalities

Self-Healing or Doomed?

As an exercise to encourage thinking about self-healing and disease-prone personalities, sort the following public figures into the personality–health categories of self-healing or doomed, and try to defend your choices based on information from this chapter.

Prince Charles	Tom Hanks	Willie Nelson	Martha Stewart
Hillary Clinton	Paris Hilton	Barack Obama	Donald Trump
Tom Cruise	Jesse Jackson	Rosie O'Donnell	Mike Tyson
Leonardo DiCaprio	Beyoncé Knowles	Sean Penn	Denzel Washington
Snoop Dogg	David Letterman	Julia Roberts	Shaun White
Jodi Foster	Bill Maher	Chris Rock	Oprah Winfrey
Bill Gates	Nelson Mandela	Jerry Seinfeld	Tiger Woods
Whoopi Goldberg	Dennis Miller	Britney Spears	

The Influence of Humanistic and Existential Aspects on Understanding Self-Healing

The influential humanistic psychologist Carl Rogers was one of the first to call scientific attention to personal growth and fulfillment—the joy of being alive. Rogers saw each person as having an inherent tendency to grow and enhance her or his being (discovering a true self that may be hidden) in order to produce more positive inner feelings. The fully functioning person lives up to her or his potential and completely develops and uses any talents.

Rogers was primarily concerned with psychological health, but we now see that it turns out that his description applies to general, overall health. This is not so surprising because the many patients Rogers saw in therapy were facing major emotional imbalances, which are associated with psychological disruptions. Rogerian therapy involves helping patients clarify their feelings so that they can integrate their unique life experiences into their self-concept.

An example from our own research is a male heart attack victim who worked very hard at his job but did little more than lie on the couch at home. He was not satisfied with his occupational level, and he would have preferred to live and work in a more relaxed environment. For him, the beginning of the road to recovery came in his recognizing that he was in the wrong line of work and should really be pursuing his love of the outdoors. Once this insight was achieved, his other problems began to resolve. This line of thinking supports the idea that a healing personality is necessarily somewhat different for each individual.

Growth Orientation

Like Rogers, the humanistic psychologist Abraham Maslow also spent a good part of his influential career focused on the positive, growth-oriented aspects of human beings. We saw that Maslow recognized that healthy people first need to achieve balance in their basic biological needs, and then they need to obtain affection and self-respect; finally, he emphasized self-actualization. People with this growth orientation are spontaneous and creative, are good problem solvers, have close relationships to others, and have a playful sense of humor.

As people become more self-actualized, they become more concerned with abstract issues of beauty, justice, and understanding. They develop a sense of humor that is philosophical rather than hostile. They become more independent and may march to the beat of a different drummer. They become more ethical and more concerned with the harmony among members of the human race. These characteristics of the self-healing personality are not merely the opposite of such disease-prone characteristics as suspiciousness, bitter cynicism, despair and depression, or repressed conflicts. Rather, they are positive, meaningful motives, behaviors, and goals in their own right.

Even positive emotions may be self-enhancing. One approach called the **broaden-and-build model** of positive emotions proposes that experiences of positive emotions, like joy, interest, pride, contentment, and love, can broaden people's modes

Broaden-and-Build Model
Proposes that experiences of positive emotions, such as joy, interest, pride, contentment, and love can broaden people's modes of thinking and responding, bringing more possible actions to mind

Self-Understanding

Assessing the Self-Healing Personality through Nonverbal Expressive Style

One way to assess personality aspects of health-proneness is to observe a friend and then have a friend observe you for an hour a day for two weeks. Simply count up the number of expressive behaviors that indicate a healthy psychoemotional state, and compare them to those indicating a possible problem. Of course, the following checklist is only a rough guide, but it illustrates the kinds of cues used by experienced clinicians (Chesney, Eagleston, & Rosenman, 1980; Friedman, 2000b; Hall, Friedman, & Harris, 1986).

Nonverbal Cues Usually Associated with a Self-Healing Personality
- Calm, well-modulated, even speech
- Symmetrical hand gestures directed away from one's body
- Natural smiles; natural enthusiasm
- Open, relaxed body position (when sitting)
- Good mutual gaze with others
- Smooth body movements
- Seems charismatic and optimistic

Nonverbal Cues Usually Associated with a Disease-Prone Personality
- Uneven or accelerating speech; interruptions
- Loud voice with explosive words; too quick to answer
- Sighs, stutters, "ums"
- Clenched fists; clenched teeth
- Touching, scratching, picking one's body
- "Closed" body position of arms and legs (when sitting)
- Fidgeting and shifting; tapping or drumming with fingers
- Shifty-eyed; downcast gaze
- Facial grimaces of anxiety or anger
- Vocal or body gestures of impatience or intolerance
- Overcontrolled unexpressiveness; looks repressed or too calm

of thinking and responding; that is, they bring more possible actions to mind (Cohn, Fredrickson, Brown, Mikels, & Conway, 2009). In turn, this helps build social resources, as one's positive emotions and creativity can reverberate in those around us. According to this line of thinking, it is helpful to cultivate positive emotions to build psychological resiliency (Fredrickson, 2001; Lyubomirsky, King, & Diener, 2005).

Identity, Morality, and Purpose

Talking to victims of serious illness, it is intriguing to note the ways many of them have changed their philosophies of life after their brushes with death (Taylor, 2010). A reasonable expectation is that recognition of the fragility of life might lead to a callous and hedonistic rampage—"I might as well maximize my fun because I won't live forever." In fact, such reactions are rare. For people who make changes (many do not), the direction is almost always toward greater self-fulfillment. For example: "I try to spend more time with my family"; "I stop to smell the roses"; "I try to see the other person's side of things"; "I do volunteer work at the hospital." Note that these changes are hard to understand without an appreciation of existential personality psychology.

Remember that Viktor Frankl, the existential philosopher and therapist, developed his theories of a healing personality as a prisoner in a Nazi concentration camp. Although most inmates died, the quickest to go were those who were stripped of their sense of identity and purpose. On the other hand, survival was more likely for those who tried living in a meaningful way, even in dire straits. A person's sense of dignity has more than psychological and ethical importance. It is also an aspect of health. Lack of attention to this crucial factor during medical treatment seems to be what angers cancer patients the most. Much more distressing than the cancer itself is the sense of *being* a "cancer," a "tumor," a "disease." Thousands of writers with cancer, representing millions and millions of cancer sufferers, have pleaded, "Don't talk to my spouse about me as if I'm not here"; "Don't pretend that everything is OK"; "Don't be afraid to look at me and touch me"; "Treat me as a person, not as a disease." Once a sense of dignity and meaning is gone, the will to live disappears as well.

Sense of Coherence

Sense of Coherence
A person's confidence that the world is understandable, manageable, and meaningful

Salutogenesis
Aaron Antonovsky's theory of how people stay healthy; according to this approach, the world must not necessarily be controlled or ordered for the healthy individual, but the individual must have a sense of coherence

Central to health, says medical sociologist Aaron Antonovsky (1979, 1987), is a **sense of coherence**—a person's confidence that the world is understandable, manageable, and meaningful. Antonovsky proposed a general theory of how people stay healthy called **salutogenesis**. According to this approach, the world must not necessarily be controllable but controlled or ordered, in the grand scheme of things. For example, someone with a strong perception that she was carrying out God's purpose might have a high sense of coherence. Antonovsky describes the case of a male survivor of the Nazi holocaust (Antonovsky, 1987). As a Jewish teenager in Nazi Europe, this individual was quite pessimistic, doubting that he would survive. Yet he had no sense of personal affront or distress. He saw all the Jews in the same sinking ship and carried on with his life as best he could, including participating in resistance efforts. After the war, it seemed natural to him that he would go to Israel and start a new life. This healthy man was hardly an optimist; rather he had a remarkable ability to take extraordinary challenges in stride.

This understanding of meaning and dignity, more common among anthropologists and European thinkers than among American psychologists (who tend to be more ethnocentric), adds an important new twist to our comprehension of health maintenance. For self-healing personalities, life matters. In their own ways, individuals come to a view of life as ordered and clear, rather than as chaotic and inexplicable. In their own ways, they are intact, thriving protagonists, not isolated, alienated drifters. One large-scale study that followed over 20,000 European adults for up to six years found that those with a strong sense of coherence were 30 percent less likely to die, even after adjusting for risk factors such as smoking, blood pressure, cholesterol, and neuroticism (Surtees, Wainwright, Luben, Khaw, & Day, 2003).

Each perspective has implications for our understanding of health (see Table 1). As we have said throughout this text, each of the basic approaches to understanding personality provides insight that can prove useful in coming to a full understanding of human personality.

■ **TABLE 1** Health and the Eight Aspects of Personality

Perspective	Implications for Health
Psychoanalytic	Repressed conflicts in the unconscious can show themselves in medical symptoms; this idea was the basis for the development of psychosomatic medicine. Today, this process is usually termed *somatization*.
Neo-Analytic/ Ego	Child-rearing practices and resulting degrees of attachment and security (or insecurity) direct children toward healthy patterns (conscientious, self-efficacious, trusting, with social integration) or unhealthy patterns (substance use, promiscuity, violence).
Biological	A person with stress or with unhealthy habits like alcoholism is seen as having a disease; treatment, therefore, usually involves administration of pharmaceuticals that affect hormones or neurotransmitters.
Behaviorist	Healthy and unhealthy habits are learned through conditioning reinforcement; health promotion involves changing the reward contingencies.
Cognitive	As a function of how people process information, they come to understand how their behavior affects their health and how to best maintain health. A sense of control allows people to respond to the challenges in their lives.
Trait	Certain traits such as conscientiousness are seen as healthy, whereas other traits such as impulsivity, cynicism, and sensation seeking can prove unhealthy.
Humanistic-Existential	Self-actualization, personal growth, and sense of coherence are related to self-healing. Good, altruistic social relations are integral to health.
Interactionist	Health is optimized when the individual achieves a good match between self and environment, thus maximizing homeostasis.

Summary and Conclusion

Much insight into the complexities of personality can be gained by studying an applied area such as stress, disorder, illness, and health. By considering personality in an applied sphere such as health, we are following the advice of Kurt Lewin, Gordon Allport, and other great theorists that the individual is best understood when studied in a real-world social context. Not only do we better understand health by studying personality, but we also better understand personality by studying health.

There are a number of ways in which personality has been shown to be linked to health. One key link between personality and health involves health behaviors. Certain types of people, because of their biology and/or socialization, are more likely to engage in risky behaviors, ranging from cigarette smoking to sky diving. A second key association between personality and illness comes from society's idea of the sick role and the rewards that it conveys. Individuals enter into more or less healthy situations. A third set of associations between personality and health involves disease affecting personality—a somatopsychic effect in which the body affects the mind. The fourth and most fascinating connection between personality and health involves the diathesis–stress link.

Diathesis is the predisposition (often hereditary) of the body to a disease or disorder. However, the illness does not surface unless and until it is elicited by the environment. For example, someone might be prone to mental illness, and may have had a previous episode, but may not have another episode of mental illness until the environmental conditions are ripe. This model of illness has much in common with the idea of personality interacting with the situation.

There is now strong evidence that people who lead hostile, depressed, competitive, and driven lives are more likely to suffer heart disease than are more easygoing people. But it is not hard work, activity, or a challenging job per se that is the key problem. Rather it is the bitter struggle that is the problem. On the other hand, if you are in a situation in which you cannot control the outcome, no matter what you do, you may learn to be helpless, a condition that can lead to depression and ill health. There are associations between various psychological disturbances (like chronic anger, or anxiety, or depression) and several diseases. In other words, it is not the case that anxiety is related specifically to ulcers and repression solely to asthma. Rather, there is evidence for a generic "disease-prone personality."

The Terman Life-Cycle study, which began in 1921–1922, provides a means of seeing the effects of personality on health across the life span. Childhood social dependability, or conscientiousness, is a good predictor of longevity, as is conscientiousness in adulthood. A person who was conscientious as a child is less likely to suffer an early death from injury, and less likely to engage in unhealthy habits, but also stays healthier and lives longer for other biopsychosocial reasons as well.

In studying self-healing, personality researchers have drawn much inspiration from the humanistic and existential approaches, which consider positive aspects of human functioning. There are two major types of self-healing personalities. The first is the more active, "gung-ho" type. This category includes the busy lawyer and the hard-working, but committed, executive. These people actively seek out stimulation, are highly extroverted, and tend to be spontaneous and fun-loving. The second main type of self-healing personality is the calmer, more relaxed type. Both types achieve a balance that is appropriate for themselves. There is increasing evidence that fulfillment and playfulness are key aspects of the self-healing personality.

■ Key Theorists

Franz Alexander
Flanders Dunbar
Marvin Zuckerman

Frank H. Farley
Bernard Lown
David Glass

Ray Rosenman and
  Meyer Friedman
Lewis Terman

Howard Friedman
Aaron Antonovsky

■ Key Concepts and Terms

psychosomatic medicine
sensation-seeking scale
Type T theory
sick role
somatopsychic effect
borderline personality disorder
personality disorder

diathesis–stress model
Type A behavior pattern
Terman Life-Cycle study
self-healing personalities
broaden-and-build model
salutogenesis
sense of coherence

Culture, Religion, and Ethnicity: Processes and Differences

It is sometimes said that American psychology is the study of White college sophomores and white laboratory rats. More than three-quarters of psychology study participants come from Western, educated, industrialized, rich, and democratic societies (Henrich, Heine, & Norenzayan, 2010, who use the clever acronym WEIRD). This indictment of the failures of some psychologists to reach out to study other cultures and subcultures does not apply directly to personality psychology. Many

From Chapter 13 of *Personality: Classic Theories and Modern Research*, Fifth Edition. Howard S. Friedman, Miriam W. Schustack. Copyright © 2012 by Pearson Education, Inc. Published by Pearson Allyn & Bacon. All rights reserved.

influential personality theorists were born in Europe and were heavily affected by European events. Europeans, with their close contact with many different nations and cultures (and their many ethnic wars), have tended to be quite sensitive to cultural influences on personality. For example, Freud thought deeply about the psychological bases of culture, religion, and literature; Jung studied Far Eastern philosophy and mysticism; Lewin did experiments on intergroup relations; Erikson studied Native Americans; and Fromm compared the structures of societies worldwide. Personality psychology has a rich tradition of cultural awareness, even though such matters are sometimes overlooked in modern personality research.

Personality psychologists have been less attentive, however, to religious influences and to cultural and ethnic influences on personality in groups that have been the object of social and economic discrimination, such as Asians, Africans, Hispanics, and Native Americans. One important exception was Gordon Allport, who wrote extensively about anti-Semitism and about American racial prejudice and discrimination toward African Americans. Allport believed that the behavior of Americans could not be understood without knowledge of Black–White relations in America. But Allport's insightful work in this area from the 1950s has been followed up only infrequently by other personality psychologists, even those who pursue other of Allport's ideas. Such omissions have hindered the development of personality psychology.

Why the gap in knowledge about ethnic and cultural aspects of personality? One reason for the narrowness of certain areas of American psychology is simply experience and tradition; that is, most young researchers study what their professors (advisors) have studied, and it can take a long time for nonmainstream orientations such as a cross-cultural emphasis to enter forcefully into the arena of ideas. Further, because many individuals are multicultural—that is, experience a mixture of cultures (Hong, Benet-Martínez, Chiu, & Morris, 2003)—some researchers have shied away from doing cultural work due to the perception that it is too complicated for theory testing. But culture is a key determinant of what it means to be a person, and so the systematic study of these cultural influences should be, as Allport noted, an essential part of personality psychology. Modern personality psychology should draw on its rich traditions of cultural awareness. These influences are the subject of this chapter.

Group Influence

The poet John Donne told us that "No man is an island." He meant that the course of everyone's life is related to that of everyone else. Each person is embedded in a complex social system—families, friends, neighbors, communities, and societies.

The most direct and immediate influence on personality development is, of course, the family, which is why personality theorists give so much attention to the effects of our parents. But we are also heavily influenced by our peers. Harry Stack Sullivan's emphasis on the importance of "chums," especially during adolescence, has been confirmed, as the teen years are very important to forming an ethnic identity (Phinney, 1993, 2003). Yet even as adults, the ways we think about ourselves depend on our friends and associates. For example, imagine that we have a cocktail party to which we invite 10 lawyers, 10 surgeons, and 10 psychology professors. Very likely, it would be relatively easy to pick out who is who (perhaps even before they congregate together) on the basis of mannerisms or politics or even shoe styles or other articles of apparel and aspects of appearance! In other words, each social (in this case occupational) grouping influences its members.

■ An ancient Olmec figure from Mexico. Culture influences what we regard as acceptable for public display. In American culture, many men buy pornography, and that behavior is seen as normal in many segments of society—but it would generally be seen as deviant to display it on the coffee table or work desk.

Cultural Effects

Beyond these direct social influences, but tied to them, are the pressures of societal institutions. For most people, who they are is influenced by religious upbringing, the educational system, government, and nationality. A person raised in private Catholic schools in Boston is likely to have quite different patterns of responses than a person raised in communist schools in Beijing. These influences go beyond genetic differences and differences in family relations. They are **cultural effects**—the shared behaviors and customs we learn from the institutions in our society.

There are also dramatic differences within each culture that result from the effects of ethnicity and class. Even within the same city, within the same high school, individuals may develop strikingly different reaction patterns as a function of the history of their ethnic group (family customs and subcultural traditions) and class (economic and educational status). For example, in the same Boston classroom, a middle-class African American will often have different experiences than an immigrant Latin American or a wealthy German American. This is not to minimize the fact that all are human beings and all are Americans. Rather, it is important to understand that cultural as well as biological and social influences profoundly shape personality.

Cultural Effects
The shared behaviors and customs learned from the institutions in society

History of Research on Personality and Culture

To a fish, the whole world is aquatic because that is the only world a fish can know. A similar problem challenges our knowledge of culture: It is difficult to see the peculiarities of our culture without an outside perspective. Things that seem natural and normal to us can often only be identified as culture-specific through comparison with other cultures. To many Americans, it is unusual and repulsive to eat insects; but to many Africans, insects are tasty but it is unusual and repulsive to eat pigs (ham, bacon). Even complex behaviors are culture-specific. For example, Europeans traditionally recorded their history in books, whereas Africans relied heavily on oral traditions; each method seems odd (and inadequate) to the other culture.

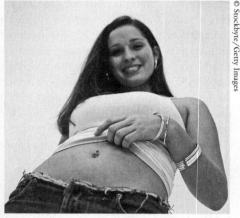

■ Sexual modesty or flamboyance in dress is heavily influenced by culture but is not necessarily indicative of personality. It is interesting that controversy over dress often centers around young women, again revealing sexuality and sexual power as key human concerns.

All people have a biological sex drive. Yet culture and religion can influence people to refrain from premarital sex, to avoid adulterous relations during marriage, and even to refrain from sexual activity completely, as in the cases of monks, priests, and nuns. Preferred sexual positions vary cross-culturally, as do masturbation objects, homosexual practices, display of nudity, and bestiality (sexual relations with animals) (Kluckhohn, 1953). The habits—including prescriptions and proscriptions—of other cultures may often appear quite strange to an unsophisticated observer. During the colonial era, Europeans often described other peoples as heathen, uncivilized, and perverse (and prescribed the "missionary position" for sex). Evaluating others from one's own cultural point of view is termed **ethnocentrism**.

Ethnocentrism

Evaluating others from one's own cultural point of view

Contributions from Cultural Anthropology

In the early 1900s, as the field of cultural anthropology began to develop, insightful researchers such as Margaret Mead traveled to exotic locales and observed the native customs, families, and societies. In the 1920s, Mead violated expectations for educated young women in American society and took off to observe children and adolescents in Samoa (an island chain in the South Pacific). One particular focus of Mead's study was child-rearing. For example, Mead found that the difficulties of adolescence are not the same in all cultures. Although adolescence in the United States is a time of rebellion, in some cultures adolescents experience a smoother transition into adulthood. Of course, all teenagers everywhere undergo the hormonal changes of puberty. But the *effects* of the biological (hormonal) changes can vary dramatically as a function of society's response.

Modern-day researchers are still concerned with the potential "problems" of adolescence—substance abuse, promiscuity, violence. Are these the result of innate processes of development? Not necessarily. It is important to remember Mead's pioneering point that the full story cannot be simply located inside each individual; rather, the dramatic effects of society are equally relevant (Mead, 1929, 1939).

Like Gordon Allport, Margaret Mead did feel, however, that the individual's inclination to respond in certain ways (i.e., their personality) was relatively stable when the cultural context was understood. For example, she studied the Manus tribe of the Admiralty Islands in Polynesia in 1928. She returned 25 years later, after the community had undergone a profound social revolution influenced by modern life. Mead found that she could recognize stable individual patterns, even though the actual behaviors had changed as a function of culture (Mead, 1954). Similarly, when one travels to a new culture, it may be hard at first to separate behavior that is clearly culturally normed (e.g., running in front of bulls in Pamplona, Spain) from an individual's own idiosyncratic behaviors (e.g., jumping into a park's fountain). But once you understand the cultural context (e.g., Pamplona's San Fermin festival), individual patterns of behavior become clear.

In some cultures, such as Mexican and Filipino societies, children must help care for their younger siblings and also cooperate with many family chores (Whiting & Whiting, 1975). These children tend to grow up to be prosocial—in other words, they are helpful to others. In contrast, in the dominant American culture (and now in the Asian American subculture), most children grow up learning to achieve success, to "fulfill their potential" by participating in sports, artistic performances, academic endeavors; in sum, to become number one. Such children are often less altruistic and more competitive. These ideas, derived from cross-cultural research, are important as researchers endeavor to understand how children thrive or fail in public schools (Cook-Gumperz & Szymanski, 2001). For example, a student of Latino background might not thrive academically in a classroom in which cutthroat competition is the norm, but be otherwise described as mature, given his or her family's emphasis on learning *respeto* (respect) and *simpatía* (warmth), two important values in Latin cultures (Greenfield et al., 2006; Marín & Marín, 1991).

Other anthropological studies, in attempts to prove or disprove Freudian psychoanalytic notions, examined exposure of children to sexual behavior. For example, one analysis concluded that some societies do not hide sexual matters as Americans do. Children may have opportunities to see adults copulate (for example, where the whole family sleeps together in one room), or they may receive explicit instruction at a young age (Ford & Beach, 1951). On the other hand, in the Victorian Europe of Freud's time (and in much of American society today), children may hear about sexual behavior as a dirty little secret, and they may be severely punished or humiliated for sexual curiosity. Because it is these negative encounters that may lead to repression, anthropological study suggested that key aspects of Freudian theory needed substantial modification or outright rejection. In other words, the Freudian idea of sexual repression probably cannot be directly applied to a society that encourages open sexual expression.

In an influential book called *The Cultural Background of Personality*, anthropologist Ralph Linton (1945) pointed out that any boy from a hunting tribe who finds himself alone in the woods after dark will know how to build a shelter and survive the night, even if he has never been alone and done this before. Linton's point was

■ The same behavior or attribute can be seen very differently from differing cultural perspectives. Business negotiations in Japan involve communication that is more indirect (in both verbal content and nonverbal style) than most Americans are accustomed to. Conversational statements that Americans view as appropriately bold, frank, and direct may be viewed by their Japanese hosts as pushy, tactless, and rude.

that a person comes to situations armed with much knowledge derived from culture. We share many of our reactions with those who live in our culture (such as current American culture) or subculture (such as American teenagers of Hispanic background). For example, the daily behaviors of many college students have much in common—awakening to pop music, washing, brushing teeth, putting on jeans, eating bagels, or cereal, or Egg McMuffins, greeting friends, going to classes, visiting campus clubs or houses, and so on. It would be a mistake to try to show how the individual's personality explains all these behaviors. Rather, people are shaped by their cultures and subcultures and so, in many ways, are like those in the same culture or subculture but different from those in other cultures.

In short, when we meet people from a different cultural environment, the culturally consistent aspects of their behavior are so salient that we tend to overlook the individual differences in personality. Anthropologist Bradd Shore (1996) found in his fieldwork in Samoa that it was only after becoming familiar with the culture of the community he studied that he was able to recognize personality differences among the Samoans he encountered. He was initially so overwhelmed by the striking *shared* (culturally determined) aspects of the Samoans' personalities that he was not initially able to detect that the individuals within that culture differed from one another just as much as did individuals within his own culture (Shore, 1996).

Emic versus Etic Approaches

Emic Approach

An approach that is culture-specific, focusing on a single culture on its own terms

Etic Approach

An approach that is cross-cultural, searching for generalities across cultures

F-scale

A scale developed at the University of California, Berkeley, to measure a person's proneness to being rigid and authoritarian

Cross-cultural personality psychologists often distinguish between emic and etic approaches. An **emic approach** is culture-specific; it focuses on a single culture, understood on its own terms—for example, the ways that Americans toilet train their children, or the way anxiety is expressed in some Latin cultures (known as *ataque de nervios*). An **etic approach** is cross-cultural; it searches for generalities across cultures—for example, all cultures have ways of saying hello and good-bye. By the way, the terms "emic" and "etic" derive from a distinction made in the field of linguistics between language-specific versus universal ways of describing speech sounds.

Why is this relevant to personality? Problems arise when concepts, measures, and methods developed in one culture are carelessly transferred to another culture in an attempt to make cross-cultural generalizations about personality. For example, consider the **F-scale**, developed in Berkeley, California, to measure a person's proneness to being rigid and authoritarian. It works fairly well in detecting Americans prone to be prejudiced. But this scale cannot be validly and directly used in other cultures. In a study in South Africa, scores did not predict antiBlack prejudiced behavior among White South Africans (Pettigrew, 1958). Does this mean that an analogous authoritarian personality cannot be isolated in other cultures? Not at

© K. Kai / Fujiphotos / The Image Works

all. Rather, various culture-specific variables must also be considered. Emic approaches call for indigenous, locally derived methods (e.g., interviews with locals, focus groups) that are sensitive to the culture-specific elements of the topic under study. These are then complemented by etic approaches, which rely on translated, imported methodology (e.g., translated personality tests) that facilitate quantitative comparisons across cultures (e.g., Benet-Martínez, 2007).

Carl Jung, the Swiss psychoanalyst, searched mythology, religion, ancient rituals, and dreams for the roots of personality. Jung described a collective unconscious, which is the depository of memories of human evolution. In other words, people evolved to share certain guiding thoughts and motivations. For example, take the case of the mother. All people through all generations had mothers. Jung (1959) suggests that just as it is clear that the infant has evolved to suck milk from the breast, it is also the case that all children have inborn tendencies to react in certain ways to their mothers. It is thus not surprising that all societies have myths and images that involve mothers. Archetypes are the universal structures of the collective unconscious—all people are born expecting (psychologically) to have a mother. But the role of the mother varies from culture to culture in many respects. Jung thus pointed to ways that personality psychology must be universal while at the same time allow for important cultural variations.

Collectivist and Individualistic

A key dimension of cultural effects on personality involves the centrality of the autonomous individual versus the centrality of the collective. More individualistic themes tend to be found in Western cultures, but more collectivist themes in Eastern cultures (Church, 2009; Kitayama & Markus, 1999; Markus & Kitayama, 1991; Triandis & Trafimow, 2001). Individualists emphasize autonomy and independence, whereas collectivists are more interdependent and group-focused. Americans admire the lone cowboy or the all-star athlete, whereas Asians may prefer a group leader or a winning team. Many Asian cultures insist on the fundamental relatedness of individuals; Americans, on the contrary, prize doing one's own thing. Euro-Americans and Japanese thus hold correspondingly different predictions for future life events. In one study, Japanese subjects expected that positive life events would happen more often to others than to themselves, but Americans did not show this pessimistic bias (Chang, Asakawa, & Sanna, 2001). This American, individualistic tendency to perceive oneself as unique and worthy is confirmed by studies showing that people in individualistic cultures report themselves to be more competent, intelligent, and attractive than their average peers (Heine, Lehman, Markus, & Kitayama, 1999). Paradoxically, the vast majority of Americans want to be "above average" and think that they are (Ariely, 2008), a phenomenon mocked by radio host Garrison Keillor's fictional Lake Wobegon, where all the children are above average.

Visiting a teeming city such as collectivist Calcutta, India, you might find great hospitality, but visiting New York City might leave you very conscious of the meaning of rugged individualism. It is no accident that New York is a world center of capitalism. Thus, differences in behavior might be badly misjudged if the surrounding cultural milieu were not considered.

These collectivist versus individualist cultural differences also impact people's cognitive approaches and general worldviews (Nisbett, 2003). Systems of perception and thought vary systematically between East and West, in ways that are both broad and deep: The relational, interconnected, and context-sensitive Eastern approaches contrast with the decontextualized, logic-driven Western approaches. For example, when viewing a conflict or competition, those from a collectivist culture might be more interested in the circumstances and more tolerant of ambiguity, while persons from an individualistic culture would want to know who is right and who is the winner. From a cognitive perspective on personality, these cultural distinctions in how people perceive, understand, remember, and think about themselves and their environments are important parts of personality. There is also some evidence that Asians and Asian Americans benefit relatively less from seeking and using advice and emotional comfort from others, and instead benefit more from attending to the deeper cooperative values of their social groups; western Europeans and European Americans, in contrast, seek and benefit from the demonstrative social support of others when they are stressed (Kim, Sherman, & Taylor, 2008).

One interesting cross-cultural study compared decision-making strategies among 1,123 adolescents who grew up in Finland experiencing Western, individualistic educational practices to 428 adolescents who grew up in Estonia during the period of Soviet collectivist culture. The teenagers were asked to solve problems about such matters as teasing and stealing. The researchers found that the (collectivist) Estonian adolescents were more aggressive and showed lower levels of social responsibility than their Finnish peers; they also tended to withdraw more from the problem. The researchers argue that personal responsibility is not likely to develop if a focus on collective identity interferes with the initial development of personal identity and responsibility (Keltikangas-Jarvinen & Terav, 1996). Thus, it is understandable that many Americans, who grow up in close-knit families that emphasize individual accomplishment but also justice and decency, mature into charitable, religious, and peace-minded adults, despite the strongly individualistic society.

Errors of Scientific Inference: The Case of Race

A chapter on ethnic, religious, and cultural influences on personality is important as a means of helping us to be accurate and scientifically rigorous. We have seen that an ignorance of social and cultural influences leads even the most brilliant scientists to errors of judgment. For example, Galton and other ability and intelligence researchers convinced themselves that White males had the highest intelligence and thus it was only fitting that they occupied the leading positions in universities, businesses, and governments. Freud viewed a healthy woman as one who would be a good wife and mother, and who would be most satisfied sexually by sexual intercourse with her husband. Indeed, for many years, psychologists, like other leaders, rarely questioned the idea that a president, a senator, a surgeon, a corporate executive, a judge, or a professor should be a wealthy White male.

These were not the views of ignorant or malicious bigots. They were the views of many thoughtful, educated people. In an interesting book called *Joining the Club: A*

SHARPEN YOUR THINKING | Current Controversy

The Bell Curve

In 1994, Richard Herrnstein and Charles Murray published a controversial treatise called *The Bell Curve*. They claimed that they had compiled evidence for an inherited general factor of intelligence that is responsible for most categories of success and failure. This factor, they contend, is quite accurately and fairly measured by currently available IQ tests. The authors assert that IQ ("native intelligence") is highly correlated with success in our culture, including income level (poverty versus financial success), amount of schooling, employment (versus unemployment), job success (and one's position within one's company), laziness, receiving public assistance (welfare), out-of-wedlock births, divorce, quality of parenting, involvement in criminal activities, political and civil participation, and voting behavior (Herrnstein & Murray, 1994).

Although such a broad and sweeping attribution of personality to genetics should make us suspicious in the first place (given all we know about the complexity of personality), our suspicions are confirmed by the next claim: These authors additionally contend that genetically transmitted intelligence is the primary factor causing differences in success between ethnic groups. Rather than looking to social and cultural advantages and traditions as possible causes of differential levels of success between ethnic groups, Herrnstein and Murray claim that these differences are primarily due to group differences in IQ.

This argument has also been adopted uncritically by less-informed others. We saw an editorial in a major newspaper arguing that society should not worry so much about providing educational enrichment to students because "scientists have proven" that abilities and success are genetically determined. As a student of personality psychology, would you accept such a vague assertion?

Most basically, we should be suspicious and even alarmed when someone tries to make policy conclusions based on ethnic group. Even if it were the case that group differences in outcomes had some biological basis, so

what? There is tremendous variation within each group. When considering an *individual* applicant to a school or for a job, of what relevance is this person's ethnicity or gender if he or she may be the next Picasso or Einstein or Marie Curie (the first person to win two Nobel prizes)?

Are achievement and failure due primarily to allegedly "race-based" innate (in)ability? Many psychologists have countered these arguments by pointing out inaccuracies in the evidence and inconsistencies in the reasoning that nullify any conclusions about an inherited component of achievement. For example, it is known that high heritability values do not eliminate, or even often limit, the strong effects of environmental change on outcome (Wahlsten, 1995). This means that even to the extent that intelligence is highly inherited, a relatively minor environmental change (such as strong, well-educated parents) can still significantly change the achievement level of an individual with a particular IQ. Errors in *The Bell Curve* authors' use of statistics have also been criticized (Bateson, 1995; Fancher, 1995; Fraser, 1995; Krishnan, 1995). It has also become clear, with the mapping of the human genome, that the racial groupings commonly used in the United States are more social categories than genetic ones (e.g., Bonham, Warshauer-Baker, & Collins, 2005; Smedley & Smedley, 2005). The lack of unambiguous and consistent genetic markers for race undermines a basic assumption of a genetically based race–IQ correlation.

Because of cultural influences, IQ tests have frequently been demonstrated to be inaccurate if misused (Nisbett, 2009). Although they are accurate about certain skills for many people of similar backgrounds, they have routinely been found to lead to the mistaken placement of intelligent students in special (remedial) education classes (Barrow, 1995; Siegel, 1995). Personality theories bring with them assumptions about human nature, assumptions that can have the most dramatic implications.

History of Jews and Yale, the author documents the reactions of Yale College's leaders in the 1920s, as the numbers of Jewish immigrant students began increasing at top colleges (Oren, 1985). For example, consider the comment of a psychologist—and dean of freshman—who advised that, though the Jewish students were doing very well academically, they should be excluded from Yale because of personal flaws: "I feel they are in the nature of a foreign body in the class organism. They contribute very little to class life" (Oren, 1985. In other words, they came from a different culture.

Such prejudiced feelings led to exclusionary quotas that allowed only small numbers of nonmainstream students (and no women) to attend Yale College (and most other elite colleges) until the late 1960s. Subtle cultural prejudices and influences were distorting the judgments of even the most educated men in America.

Race as a Flawed Approach to Grouping People

Humans form groups based on many different sorts of criteria. Many groups are based on professed beliefs, such as political or religious beliefs. Political parties are examples. It is usually possible for a person to change between such groups (i.e., convert) by adopting new beliefs.

Other groups are based primarily on cultural habits or extended family customs, such as eating spaghetti or tacos, or dressing in kilts, or beads, or *kaffiyehs* (Arab headdresses), perhaps in addition to religious beliefs. These groupings are generally termed **ethnic groups**. Irish Catholics are an example.

Some large groupings are based on physical characteristics tied to geographical origin, such as skin color, or eye shape, or height. Such groupings are often called **races**. But racial groupings are the source of much confusion and scientific misunderstanding because they confound culture and tradition with physical appearance, erroneously assuming that the physical characteristics are inherently tied to the customs. People can change religion or eating habits but cannot easily change skin color. Further, we can readily see if someone is "black," "white," or "yellow," but not if she is Catholic or Buddhist.

Ethnic Group
A group whose membership is based primarily on shared cultural habits or customs

Race
Large groupings based upon physical characteristics, such as skin color, eye shape, or height, tied to geographical origin

■ Former actor and governor Arnold Schwarzenegger wound up in hot water himself when he referred to a Latina California assembly woman as "very hot." Referring to Caribbean islanders, he said, "I mean, they are all very hot ....They have the, you know, part of the Black blood in them and part of the Latino blood in them that together makes it." Such an overgeneralization illustrates two mistakes that even well-educated people often make. First, they confuse culture with "blood" (i.e., biology), even though there is clear evidence that their culture, not anything in their blood, strongly influences the common responses of a group of people. Second, by stereotyping a group, one makes the error of over-generalizing and thus ignoring the fact that among Latinos and any other group, there are still huge variations in how passionate, emotional, and "hot" an individual may be.

Because physical characteristics are so obvious, we often overgeneralize and overattribute personality characteristics based on them. An Arab man living in Saudi Arabia might have a large nose, dark hair, speak Arabic, wear a *kaffiyeh*, have conservative politics, follow traditional Arab customs, and, if a Muslim, not eat pork. But how about a grandson of such an Arab, who was born and grew up in Los Angeles and worked as an actor? He also might have a large nose and dark hair but otherwise might not be at all like his grandfather. It would not be logical to generalize on the basis of a few physical characteristics and assume that these two men would have similar behavior patterns. Yet this sort of confusion and overgeneralization is common, especially on the basis of skin color.

The American Dilemma

In America, Black–White differences are the most significant such grouping, largely because of American history. The United States was founded on the principle that "All men are created equal," yet the U.S. Constitution allowed slavery (and counted slaves as three-fifths of a man for purposes of taxation and representation). Gunnar Myrdal (1944) called this problem the **American dilemma**. How could there be a country in which all men are created equal but many were slaves?

In 1933, racial stereotyping was studied among male undergraduates at Princeton University (Katz & Braly, 1933). The students were asked to select those traits that they believed most characterized 10 so-called racial groups (such as Americans, Chinese, Irish, and so on). "Americans" (like the students themselves) were seen as industrious, intelligent, and progressive, but prejudiced judgments of other groups were pervasive. For example, "Negroes" were viewed as superstitious, lazy, happy-go-lucky, and musical. It is remarkable how illogical these distorted perceptions can be. For example, California imported Asian workers as manual laborers, forced them to live in segregated areas, and then often stereotyped them as ignorant and clannish. Interestingly, modern research using valid measures of personality in different cultures has shown no support for simple notions of national "character"; ideas that the English are especially reserved or Canadians are unemotional are unfounded stereotypes (McCrae & Terracciano, 2006).

It is clear that genetic makeup can have an important influence on personality, but it does so in complicated ways. Skin color is just one particular observable manifestation of genes, as are eye color, height, build, eye shape, nose shape, and on and on. As we have seen, such physical attributes are poor substitutes for a more sophisticated biological, social, cognitive, existential, and cultural analysis of individuals. And a focus on skin color leads to needless controversial political conflict, which produces more heat than light (Klineberg, 1935; Rushton, 1995; Spearman, 1925; Yee, Fairchild, Weizmann, & Wyatt, 1993). In the case of Nazi Germany, a focus

American Dilemma
Gunnar Myrdal's term for the paradoxical idea that slavery was allowed and endorsed despite the claim that the United States was founded on the principle that all men are created equal

Official White House Photo by Pete Souza

■ The case of Barack Obama illustrates many of the complexities in thinking about "race and culture." Born to a Black man from Kenya (Africa) and a White woman from Kansas, Obama lived part of his childhood in Hawaii (at times with his mother and at times with his White grandparents), part in Indonesia, and part at Ivy League schools in the northeastern U. S. He then married an African-American woman and worked as a community organizer in the African-American sections of Chicago. To understand him as an individual, one needs to consider the cultural, social, and ethnic forces that helped shape his development, in addition to his individual cognitive, biological, and experiential traits, drives, and abilities. To understand his success in reaching the highest elective office, one needs to consider how he learned to draw from and be comfortable with diverse and sometimes-clashing ethnic influences.

on physical differences and so-called race differences led to mass murder of groups ranging from children in wheelchairs to Jews and Gypsies, all in the name of "scientific improvement" of society. (See the Self-Understanding box)

Should personality psychologists study "race"? On the one hand, it certainly makes sense to take into account that personality is influenced by the reactions of others, and that others often react to us based on perceived physical characteristics. (In the United States, this is often skin color.) Relatedly, it sometimes makes sense to study narrow biological similarities (such as genetic proneness to certain diseases) among subgroups of people. On the other hand, there is no known scientific advantage in trying to categorize heterogeneous groups like Americans into one of several races (Dole, 1995; Graves, 2001; Phinney, 1996). Rather, it is more fruitful to study the effects of ethnic identification, history, family, subculture, religion, and social class as they interact with temperament and affect personality. These classifications are more readily definable and less susceptible to scientific and social distortion.

Religion

If a devoutly Christian member of the college football team is the butt of a classmate's derogatory comment, will he respond by "turning the other cheek" as instructed by his religion, or will he respond in kind with a put-down of the offender (or even a physical retaliation) to maintain his macho image and not be seen as a wimp? Cultural and religious expectations can be contradictory, and people can find themselves in situations where there are two or more sets of rules to follow. If you are a member of a minority religion, you encounter these conflicts more often, as cultural practices tend to be aligned with the majority religion. Although religion sometimes can be seen as an aspect of culture, each domain reflects its own understanding of human nature and how people should behave. In pluralistic societies, with multiple religions existing within a shared cultural framework, religious beliefs and practices can clearly differentiate the reaction patterns of many individuals; religion can be a key aspect of individual identity.

Yet religion has often stayed at the periphery of personality investigations, as researchers endeavored to develop personality on a firm empirical basis. In fact, Sigmund Freud and many other psychoanalysts were vocally antireligion, as they tried to differentiate their new science from the unscientific beliefs of the religious milieu of the time. On the other hand, Carl Jung was very interested in religious symbolism, mythology, and mysticism (Browning, 1987). Now, with increases in interests in religion among college students, and with global strife involving fundamentalist extremists, religion is beginning to assume a more important place in the study of personality (Cohen, 2009; McCullough, Friedman, Enders, & Martin, 2009; McCullough & Willoughby, 2009). Religion is very relevant to self-regulation, health, and social integration. For example, religious women tend to stay healthier and live longer; not only because of healthier behaviors, but also because of better social ties (Friedman & Martin, 2011). On the other hand, religious Christians seem more likely to attribute rare events to fate ("it was meant to be") instead of chance ("it was a coincidence") than are nonreligious individuals (Norenzayan & Lee, 2010). This remained true whether they were of Asian or European ancestry.

■ Christianity, Judaism, and Islam are all monotheistic religions, share certain ancient Semitic traditions, and place fundamental historical events in Jerusalem. Yet each also sees itself as the true or most valid religion and transmits this sense of special identity to its children and converts. For many individuals, religious identity and associated customs and traditions are a key aspect of personality. Gordon Allport distinguished the religious beliefs predominantly influenced by culture and experience from the more fundamental beliefs deeply rooted in the character structure of the individual. However, each orientation could lead either to positive values or to prejudice.

In the Protestant religion, which rebelled against the more hierarchical nature of Catholicism, there is an emphasis on the individual's direct relationship with God. This observation, coupled with the fact that the American colonies and government were founded mostly by Protestants, is often offered as an explanation of the individualistic nature of Americans. Indeed, the so-called Protestant work ethic—the idea that the individual should work hard to benefit himself and (thereby) society—is sometimes invoked to explain the economic prosperity of the United States and (Protestant) northern Europe (Bellah, Sullivan, Tipton, Madsen, & Swidle, 1985; Weber, 1930/2001). Is it therefore true that American Protestants are more individualistic than members of other religions that are more community-focused or focused on social religious ritual? Indeed there is evidence that American Protestants tend to be more personal with their religious philosophy and beliefs (including a personal experience with God), whereas American Jews and Catholics are relatively more concerned with social, ritual, and community matters (Cohen & Hill, 2007). Still, there is much individual variation within groups.

The humanistic–existential approach to personality, of course, is very willing to consider spirituality as a core element of being human. In fact, a focus on spirituality is one of the key differences between the Christianity-influenced humanists like Carl Rogers and the behaviorists like B. F. Skinner. (Skinner saw religion as a set of contingencies—a government—that uses its own jargon like "pious" and "sinful.") Today, the Judeo-Christian religious view of humans as stewards of God's earth is often manifest in individuals who feel they must devote their lives to saving the planet (ecologically), protecting human and animal life, and nurturing families. A nonreligious person might be equally committed to such causes, but the underlying motivations and associated behaviors (such as whether the activities are accompanied by prayer) could be quite different. Sometimes a non-religious person will strive (unknowingly) to act according to religious directives, as the religious ideas have become embedded in the secular culture in a non-religious formulation (Cohen & Rankin, 2004).

Although Carl Jung was encouraging of religious exploration but wary of Westerners running to adopt Eastern religions, recent years have seen an upsurge of Western interest in Buddhism, sometimes inspired by the Dalai Lama, the exiled Buddhist leader of Tibet. The simple, peaceful, calm aura of such trained Buddhist monks evinces healthy spiritual growth, somewhat analogous to the transcendental higher states of fulfillment urged by Abraham Maslow and Victor Frankl. Meditation is employed to train the mind to combat neurotic tendencies, and some people so trained do indeed appear to show high levels of left prefrontal brain activation and less emotionality (Davidson, 2004; Goleman, 2004). In contrast to the Judeo-Christian tradition, Buddhism emphasizes core elements of a cognitive approach to personality, because the focus is on the individual's consciousness and its development, rather than on the socialization practices of the environment or relations with other people. There is a focus on individual mindfulness (awareness of the moment) to counter anxiety, which may involve a distancing from the chronic troubles of the world; it is quite different from a psychoanalytic search for repressed conflict from childhood or a humanistic search for awe-inspiring experiences.

SES Gradient
A phenomenon in public health in which the higher the person's socioeconomic status, the lower is that person's risk of getting sick and dying prematurely

Socioeconomic Status [SES]
A measurement of one's level of education and income

Socioeconomic Influences on Personality

There is a fascinating phenomenon in public health called the **SES gradient**. This term refers to the fact that the higher a person's socioeconomic status, the lower that person's risk of getting sick and of dying prematurely. (**Socioeconomic status [SES]** is a measure of one's level of education and income.) This relation has been found in various times and places and income levels (Adler, Boyce, Chesney, & Cohen, 1994). For example, older women who are rich live longer than older women who

Famous Personalities

Comedians and Their Ethnicity

Korean American comedian Margaret Cho uses her outrageous stand-up routines to address issues of racism, gender equality, and gay rights. Many people find her brand of comedy uproariously funny, but others see her humor as crude and (paradoxically) promoting ethnic stereotypes by telling jokes about her own ethnic group. It may be that Cho generates additional outrage because of expectations that Asians (especially Asian women) won't "rock the boat."

African American comedian Chris Rock relies heavily on issues of race in his performances, highlighting characters and situations that are uniquely identified with the African American experience. Is it humor or bad taste if he says, "I ain't scared of Al-Qaeda! I'm from Bedford-Stuyvesant, Brooklyn!"

Hispanic comic Carlos Mencia jokes about the Latino experience, bringing issues of race and social class to his stand-up act. He uses terms that many consider politically incorrect (in fact, one of his DVDs is subtitled "Not for the Easily Offended").

All of these comedians, along with the many others who use their often-painful experiences as members

are merely affluent. There are many sorts of explanations for this gradient, but none of them has yet to be found to be fully adequate (Saegert et al., 2007).

What is interesting about this phenomenon for personality psychologists is that social class can have such sweeping effects on individuals. If social class can affect one's likelihood of getting sick and how long one is likely to live, it probably also has significant effects on one's usual patterns of psychological reactions (e.g., Pearson, Lankshear, & Francis, 1989). Even among the middle class, there are differences among the well-off middle class, the average middle class, and the working class (blue collar or lower middle class). Such issues are obvious to investigators in countries like India, which has a clear history of social classes or castes (e.g., Dubey, 1987). But in American academic settings, studies of social structure and personality appear primarily in the field of sociology (House, 1990). Personality psychologists have had little to say.

Karl Marx and Alienation

Relatedly, some scholars emphasize the effects of the economic system on individual behavior. This type of approach took formal shape with the work of the German social philosopher Karl Marx (1818–1883). Marx, a student of history and economic oppression, concluded that many societal institutions (including religion) served mainly to maintain the economic power of the elite (1872). His ideas led to modern socialism and communism. Socialists believe in a society structured so that people work directly for the benefit of the society rather than for themselves. Communists believe in the use of revolutions by the working class to eliminate private property because property is thought to encourage a selfish and dehumanized society.

How is Marxist thought relevant to personality? Marx contended that psychosocial attributes such as alienation and selfishness could be traced directly to the economic structure of a capitalist society. He

■ Karl Marx thought that individual attributes such as alienation could be traced directly to the economic structure of a capitalistic society rather than to biology or the unique history of the individual.

of ethnic minority groups as a major source of their comedic material, are walking the fine line that separates the celebration of their cultures through comedy from the exploitation and stereotyping of their communities. The complaints are not that the comedians are not funny, but that it is disrespectful and inappropriate to take serious social problems of minority communities (such as drug abuse, welfare dependency, illegal immigration, gangs) and turn them into fodder for entertainment.

The alternative perspective (which many of the comedians would endorse) is that comedy can serve to highlight the positive aspects of a culture, showing its unique and rich customs and worldview. Giving outsiders the opportunity to see the cultural group portrayed through humor increases appreciation of the diverse communities that make up our world. And many of the fans, of course, are themselves members of these communities—highlighting the group's problems and challenges can strengthen an audience member's identification with the group. There are painful truths that can be told about any cultural group, but our shared sense of in-groups and out-groups makes it more acceptable for such truths to be brought to light from the inside.

thus saw strong socioeconomic influences on what it means to be a person. The socialist and communist revolutions of the twentieth century did not confirm Marxist predictions: The abolition of private property and the enforcement of economic equality did not lead to a workers' paradise of psychological fulfillment. However, the basic orientation of Marx and his followers—that socioeconomic class and related factors of social structure are key concepts in understanding human behavior—has indeed been adopted in many modern analyses in sociology, social psychology, and political science (Kohn, 1999). For example, much modern distress and disaffection can be traced to the fact that Americans participate in fewer social organizations, are less likely to know their neighbors, and even socialize less frequently with friends (Putnam, 2000). It is not that each person has decided independently to socialize via computers, put up fences, and quit his or her bowling league; rather, there is a collapse of social structure.

In personality psychology, Marx's greatest influence was on Erich Fromm and his associates, as they thought deeply about existential alienation in modern society. Like Marx, Fromm struggled to determine what is the basic nature of a human being and what kind of culture best promotes human fulfillment. Fromm accepted and extended the idea that the socioeconomic basis of society will shape its culture, but he was not deterministic or pessimistic. Fromm believed that capitalist societies must create, by their nature, a culture of consumption. If people are not shaped to crave and constantly consume newer and fancier products, then the capitalist society cannot function. (For example, think of the businesses that would collapse if most people most valued meditation, neighborhood sports, and good conversation, and were satisfied with simple clothes, simple foods, and simple means of transportation.) On the other hand, Fromm believed that societies could be created that promoted self-fulfillment through an emphasis on community, love, and mutuality.

Language as a Cultural Influence

Language is one of the most central and influential features of any culture. In Canada, the French speakers of Quebec have had many cultural clashes with the English speakers of the rest of the country in their push toward political independence. In the United States, people from Spanish-speaking cultures, such as Mexican Americans, Cuban Americans, and Puerto Ricans, have been remarkably successful in maintaining key aspects of their subculture by maintaining their culture's language. Many other American subcultures also strive to treasure and preserve the original language of their culture. Speaking and listening—that is, language in its oral form—are a pervasive mode of interpersonal interaction in all human societies, and a central part of who we are. Particular characteristics of a particular language help shape us toward being a particular type of human.

Language and Identity: Idiolects and Dialects

To some extent, you are what you speak. In the words of Martiniquan psychiatrist Frantz Fanon (1952/1967), "To speak means to be in a position to use a certain syntax, to grasp the morphology of this or that language, but it means above all to assume a culture, to support the weight of a civilization". This role of language is a double-edged sword in its effects on social identity, keeping out those who do not proficiently speak a group's defining language, and reinforcing the ties among those who do.

Because we each have different experiences, each individual speaks a unique version of his or her native language, called an **idiolect**. The idiolect is a form of self-expression and thus a part of personality (Johnstone & Bean, 1997). This peculiarity has allowed historians and literary critics to attempt to determine whether all the Shakespearean plays were written by the same person and which books of the Bible come from one voice. Of course, the greater the similarities between any two people in terms of factors such as where they have lived, where they were educated, their social class, religion, and interests, the greater the similarity is likely to be between their idiolects. Variations between groups of people who share regional characteristics or cultural characteristics create distinct **dialects**. When two groups speak related but distinguishable dialects, dialect can be an important aspect of group identity. Within some African American communities, for example, group identity is supported by speaking Black English—and members who "talk White" are viewed as abandoning their roots.

The everyday concept of "accent" focuses on pronunciation, but the concept of dialect is much more comprehensive, encompassing variations in vocabulary and unique syntactic forms as well. For example, there are many subcultural differences in slang terms. Certain dialecticians are as skilled as the fictitious Professor Henry Higgins (from *My Fair Lady/Pygmalion*) who could listen to someone speak and pinpoint that person's neighborhood or tiny village, and thus know something important about personal identity.

Language allows people to maintain a strong identification with their group; the dialect of a subcultural group like a street gang serves many of the same social functions as the technical jargon used within a narrow scientific specialty. In both cases, members of the group use words and expressions that are unique to the group or have special meanings within the group. Language can, therefore, be used both to assert the speaker's membership in the group and to prevent outsiders from understanding communications among members.

Creating a Culture through Shared Language: The Deaf Community

An interesting example of the importance of shared language in creating a culture comes from the Deaf community. There is a "culture of the Deaf" to a much greater extent than there is a culture of the blind, at least partially because deafness seriously interferes with the ability of most deaf individuals to communicate with the larger society (that is, with those who cannot communicate in sign). People who are blind also face many extra difficulties in everyday life, but they are not especially impaired in using the common language of the community at large. Although the Deaf community shares a language within the group but not outside it, it differs from the more common ethnic and regional and linguistic communities because often the hearing families of the Deaf community's members are not fully part of the same community. The Deaf community is clearly part of the larger culture, and deaf children readily learn

Idiolect
Each individual's own unique version of his or her native language

Dialect
Regional variations in phonology, vocabulary, and syntactic forms

the larger culture (Van Deusen-Phillips, Goldin-Meadow, & Miller, 2001). Yet the differences that do exist help us step outside our usual perspective and become like fish who can learn that the world is not entirely aquatic.

Language as Politics: The "English Only" Movement

The "English Only" movement in the United States provides striking evidence of the psychological importance that most people attach to the idea of their mother tongue as part of who they are. Consider first those people who favor limiting all governmental communication to English (including government documents, election materials, etc.). One interpretation of their position is that they believe that immigrants and their children cannot become full participants and contributors to the society at large unless they are forced to become proficient in the language of the majority. An alternative interpretation of their position is that the United States was established by speakers of English and that the English language embodies the essence of public life. Out of respect for that heritage, they believe English must remain the only "official" language.

People on the other side of the dispute want the government to continue to offer services in the languages preferred by the recipients of the services. Many of them view the "English Only" movement as a racist, exclusivist, bigoted attempt to undermine the cultures of minority-language groups—a movement intended to take away the rights of non-English-speaking people to live their lives and conduct their public business in their own native languages. What is clear from looking at both positions is how deeply people care about what language is used in the public sphere, and how important they think this issue is in defining the nature of individual and national identity.

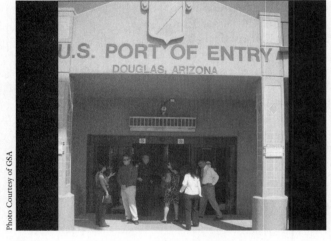

Photo Courtesy of GSA

■ Although all law-abiding citizens oppose illegal immigration, some Americans oppose substantial legal immigration as well, worrying that American values will be undermined by foreigners. Ironically, studies on the personality of immigrants suggest that they are likely to desire challenges, be work-oriented, have a high standard of excellence, seek freedom, be willing to engage in risk-taking entrepreneurship, and have a desire to effect change. In other words, as American history well demonstrates, immigrants typically help sustain American values, especially if the immigrants are welcomed and appreciated (Berry et al., 2006; Boneva & Frieze, 2001; Deaux, 2006).

Language and Thought

Why should it matter what language people speak, as long as all the parties to a conversation can understand and express themselves? As noted, the issue of identity is central, with language functioning as an expression of cultural solidarity. But language also functions as an influence on how people communicate and, to some extent, as an expression of the worldview of their culture. What can be easily expressed, and what must be included in an utterance, varies among languages. For example, the Swedish language has a limited vocabulary for emotion words (relative to English). Hebrew, the oldest language revived for modern use, makes relatively less use of abstract terms, pressing its speakers to use concrete ones. In some Native American languages, the form (shape) of an object being acted on changes the form of the verb used. In all of these cases, the requirements of the language become part of how the speaker casts an intended communication into words, as well as how those words are interpreted by the listener. Anyone who has ever tried to translate a prose passage (or, worse yet, a poem) from one language to another soon becomes aware of how enormously difficult it is to preserve the meaning while shifting the language.

An even stronger role can be afforded to specific features of individual languages in shaping communication: Our language influences not only how we say things, but even how we think about and understand and perceive the world. In other words, the specifics of your language not only determine how your thought is transformed into words, but also shape the very nature of the thoughts you can think. One well-known statement of this idea is often referred to as the Whorfian hypothesis or the Sapir-Whorf hypothesis (after anthropologists Benjamin Lee Whorf, who promoted it in the 1950s, and Edward Sapir, who had promulgated it 10 years earlier). Their idea, often termed **linguistic relativity**, claims that our interpretation of the world is, to a large extent, dependent on the linguistic system by which we classify it. Imagine, for example, that your language has many familiar words for different types of clouds (terms like "nimbus" and "cumulus") but lacks a generic word for "cloud." The linguistic relativity hypothesis claims that you would then think about clouds very differently from the way a native speaker of English (who has the generic term "cloud") does.

The empirical data on this question are mixed because of the methodological complexity of operationalizing the linguistic relativity hypothesis. Still, there is scattered evidence about the relevance of language-influenced thought processes to personality. For example, one study found that people who tend to use active verbs also tend to have field-independent personalities (Doob, 1958); their perceptions are less passive. Other evidence can be found in literature: As Roger Brown pointed out (1970), one of the most powerful features in George Orwell's fictional totalitarian civilization in *1984* is that Newspeak—the language invented by the dictatorship—makes it impossible to express or even to think rebellious thoughts (Orwell, 1949). There is little doubt that some aspects of who we are derive from the words and phrases we use to understand and communicate about things and ideas. Or as the Czech proverb puts it, "Learn a new language and get a new soul."

Kofi Annan of Ghana, who served as the seventh secretary-general of the United Nations, is widely recognized for his commitment to human rights, human development, human dignity, tolerance, and peace. He was educated in Ghana, the United States, and Switzerland, is fluent in English, French, and several African languages, and is married to a Swede (Nane). With his uncanny ability both to appreciate different cultures and yet move effortlessly among cultures, Kofi Annan won the Nobel Prize for Peace.

Linguistic Relativity
The idea of Benjamin Lee Whorf and Edward Sapir that claims that our interpretation of the world is, to a large extent, dependent on the linguistic system by which we classify it

Bilingualism: Two Personalities?

If language is a key aspect of personality, do people who speak two languages have two "personalities"? Research has begun to support this idea, suggesting that people behave in line with the language they are speaking at the time, especially if they see their two cultural identities as compatible (Benet-Martínez, Leu, Lee, & Morris,

2002; Benet-Martínez & Oishi, 2008; Hong et al., 2003; see also Fivush & Nelson, 2004). For example, Chinese American biculturals, comfortable with their bicultural identities, behaved more in line with the Chinese side of their personalities when that aspect of their identities was made salient—and vice versa. In other words, if one grows up speaking two languages (as many people do), then certain thoughts and behavior patterns are learned in, and triggered by, a certain linguistic–cultural context.

A series of studies on bilinguals in English and Spanish showed that they can respond differently to personality assessments when questioned in English versus in Spanish (Ramírez-Esparza, Gosling, Benet-Martínez, Potter, & Pennebaker, 2006). So it is not surprising that Hispanic American college students in the United States often speak Spanish when attending social-focused holiday gatherings of the extended family but speak English when discussing a more formal or scientific topic with their bicultural peers. From a scientific point of view, such findings confirm the importance of culture to personality, as well as the importance of language to the influence of culture.

Language and Social Interaction

Imagine a world in which, before you can speak to another person, you first have to determine where that person stands relative to you in the social hierarchy. If you determine that you are lower in the "pecking order," you will speak differently than if you are higher, and differently again if you are equals. For such a system to work smoothly, of course, the social ranking has to be unambiguous—you have to be able to tell where each of you stands. What makes for high rank varies somewhat among societies but frequently includes factors of wealth, age, sex, occupation, family or clan, ethnicity, and education. In many traditional societies, social rank is obvious from visible signs (such as tattoos, hairstyles, or clothing). One very clear example of this phenomenon is in the use of personal pronouns (Brown, 1970). In languages originally derived from Latin (e.g., French, Italian, Spanish) as well as in German, there is no generic "you." Instead, one form is used toward intimates and subordinates, and a different form for those to whom respect is due. In French, one says *tu* or *vous*; in Spanish, *tu* or *usted*; in German, *du* or *Sie*. While there is some variation among languages in exactly who receives the familiar versus the polite form (and under what circumstances), making the distinction correctly is always extremely important. English uses a generic "you," and without even the option of different forms. So, for many monolingual English speakers, incorporating this distinction when learning another language requires substantial effort. But look out if you address a superior with the wrong pronoun, such as addressing your Spanish father-in-law with the subordinate *tu*. Further, you had better not address your Japanese boss by his or her first name. Each language community enforces norms of politeness that are reflective of its view on proper conversational interaction (Brown & Levinson, 1987).

Gender and Language

Gender is a very important domain where many of these issues of status, power, and identity are tied up with language. Many languages include distinctions between word forms that are used by females versus males (and *about* females versus males). English makes very few such distinctions that are purely linguistic. English has male and female pronouns for the third-person singular (*he* and *she*), with their associated forms (*his/hers* and *him/her*). Other than that, I am just "I" whether I am male or female, you are just "you" of either sex, or status, or even number, and so on. Many other languages have different pronouns for each sex for first, second, and third person (e.g., *we, you, they*) and also put distinctive endings on many words that denote gender. A cousin in French is either *un cousin* (male) or *une cousine* (female); your professor in Spanish is either *un profesor* (male) or *una profesora* (female). If I say "I am an American," my statement is the same whether I am male or female, and perhaps what it means (to speaker and listener) refers to a truly gender-neutral concept. Compare that to a French person, who must say either *Je suis Français* or *Je suis Française;* these are two different terms that sound quite distinct, and they may denote rather different underlying concepts—different types of personalities.

■ Given what is known about the psychology of language, it is clear that terms such as "freshman," which is often used to refer to a first-year college student of either sex, are not truly gender-neutral.

Most of the formal guidelines about English usage (for example, the *New York Times* style book, the American Psychological Association manual) now require gender-neutral reference unless only one group is included in the reference; that is, we shouldn't say "Each senator should vote according to his own conscience" or "Scientists and their wives" For centuries though, the formal guidelines promoted the use of *he/him/his* for both all-male and mixed groups. This notion of the male pronoun as the default or generic has sometimes led to almost comical phrasing, such as the biology text statement "Like all mammals, the human bears his young alive."

From a psychological perspective, the masculine pronoun is (not surprisingly) closely linked to males. Experiments have demonstrated (in a variety of ways) that when people hear "he" and "his," they are not likely to think of female examples (e.g., Gastil, 1990; McConnell & Fazio, 1996). But most of the people who have had significant influence in the codification of language rules (especially rules for written language) over the centuries have been male and have reflected the male experience. Going back to the linguistic relativity hypothesis, it is informative to note that even for writers and speakers committed to egalitarian language, it can be a challenge to phrase certain ideas in ways that are gender-neutral but not awkward. The absence of a gender-neutral third-person singular pronoun (for *he* or *she*) in English makes some things hard to say gracefully. Feminist critic Andrea Dworkin (1981) put it this way: "Male supremacy is fused into the language, so that every sentence both heralds and affirms it" (p. 17). While this statement is more extreme than most would endorse, it does capture the resistance of the English language to comfortable gender-neutrality. The language we use reflects and influences how we think and behave.

Culture and Testing

Like any intellectual endeavor, psychological testing rests on a number of assumptions. If the assumptions are met, the test may yield valuable information. However, when the assumptions are not met and the tester does not recognize the problem, then the testing can prove not only unhelpful but harmful.

■ An additional factor when considering cultural issues in testing goes beyond the content of the test to the context of the testing: The relationship between the test administrator and the test-taker can also play a role in test performance.

One problem arises when the assumptions underlying the test are culturally biased. Most obviously, the item content of a test may not adequately capture some cultural experiences. For example, someone growing up on a farm will have different experiences than someone growing up in an inner city, and so certain general knowledge questions or psychological reaction questions could be appropriate for one group but totally inappropriate for the other group. Similarly, "hearing the voices of angels" may be seen as a valuable religious experience in some cultures but as a sign of psychopathology (schizophrenia) in another culture. Test scores are also known to be affected by such things as motivation, previous test-taking experience, the qualities of the examiner (test administrator), and socioeconomic status.

Culture-Free and Culture-Fair Tests

One attempt to deal with such problems was the development of what were called culture-free tests. For example, in an intelligence test called the Raven Progressive Matrices test (Raven, 1938), people analyze geometric figures. The test-taker has to identify recurring patterns in drawings. Because all children develop perceptual abilities—learn to see the world—it is hoped that such tests are not dependent on culture. However, more sophisticated analysis of this issue makes it clear that some cultural assumptions creep into every such test. For example, children in some cultures have more experience in taking tests (and certain kinds of tests). So researchers turned to trying to develop tests that are culture-fair.

Culture-fair tests attempt to control for or rule out effects that result from culture rather than from individual differences. So, for example, an intelligence test might see how quickly individuals respond to presentation of a stimulus such as a sound or a picture. The idea is that response time is more biological than influenced by learning and one's environment. However, we have seen that all biological processes unfold in some environment. Some cultures value quick responses and others encourage slower, more deliberate responses. And, frankly, some cultures are more motivated regarding test-taking.

Another way to approach the issue is to include some subscales that are known to be culturally biased and other subscales that are thought to be more culture-fair (Cattell's Culture Fair Intelligence Test takes this approach). Then, if an individual scores differently on the two types of subscales, we have an indication that standard testing may be inappropriate for this individual. This is, of course, what teachers do naturally when they observe that a student from an unfamiliar background performs well on most tasks but has trouble on others.

Some tests now try explicitly to take culture into account. For example, the **System of Multicultural Pluralistic Assessment (SOMPA)** (Mercer, 1979) assumes that test results cannot be divorced from the culture. Therefore, the focus of comparisons is among individuals *within* a cultural group rather than between cultural groups. Such ideas have been mostly applied to ability and intelligence testing because of a concern about misclassification of disadvantaged minority students

System of Multicultural Pluralistic Assessment (SOMPA)

A system developed by Jane Mercer that assumes that test results cannot be divorced from the culture and focuses on comparisons among individuals within a cultural group rather than between cultural groups

as having less intellectual potential. There has been much less attention to such matters in the assessment of personality constructs like conscientiousness and extroversion, but the same sorts of errors will be made if cultural matters are not deliberately considered.

When tests are constructed, the thorny issue arises as to which items are culturally biased and which indicate valid cultural differences. For example, let us say that Group A scores higher than Group B on an item thought to indicate tendency toward depression. Should this item be included in the scale? If Group A is truly more prone to depression, then it should be. If the groups are not truly different in this way, then the item reflects a cultural bias and should be excluded. Note that the only way to resolve such an issue is to look at the validating criterion—that is, to look at other sources of information about the two groups. This is almost always true: Tests have no value outside the contexts in which they are created, but they may be quite useful when the context is well understood.

Consider now this more practical issue: Suppose a paper-and-pencil problem-solving test is used as an employment test to choose firefighters. Such a test is certainly not predictive of courage, or stamina, or of ability to carry a 150-pound person down a rescue ladder. However, this test might be relevant to the directing of a firefighting team's strategy or to making the correct split-second decision. In short, there are no simple rules that can be developed to ensure the complete validity of all tests.

One of the main problems with testing is not that the tests are culturally biased but rather that they are used inappropriately. For example, it does not much matter if a Japanese psychologist develops a test that shows that Americans are "too extroverted." What matters is what is done with this conclusion. Is an attempt made by the Japanese psychologist to change Americans because of their "deficiency"? Is an attempt made to exclude Americans from visiting Japan or from buying Japanese products or from reading Japanese scientific journals?

Stereotype Threat

Even the testing situation, with its accompanying social expectations, can be relevant. Psychologist Claude Steele (1997) has shown that people faced with a difficult evaluative challenge such as an SAT test may react poorly if they see themselves as identified with a group that is expected to do poorly. For example, a woman taking an advanced math test and an African American taking a GRE test before graduate school may become anxious and do poorly if they believe that "women don't do as well as men on advanced math" or "Blacks don't do as well as Whites in graduate school." This is termed **stereotype threat**—the threat that others' judgments or their own actions will negatively stereotype them (and will lead to inadvertent confirmation of the stereotype). If, however, they come to believe that the test or evaluation is not relevant to these characteristics (that the test is not gender-relevant or race-relevant), then their performance improves. In other words, this theory combines ego approaches, cognitive approaches, and interactionist approaches, in which the individual's identity in a specific situation depends on how she or he construes that challenge and affects behavior in predictable ways.

Stereotype Threat
The threat that others' judgments or one's own actions will negatively stereotype an individual

Physiological reactions can also result from stereotype threat. For example, one study examined changes in blood pressure in African Americans and Euro-Americans

■ Masako Owada was educated at Harvard and Oxford and had a very active career as a diplomat for the Japanese government. That all changed when, at age 29, she married Crown Prince Naruhito. Owada immediately "changed" her personality, stayed at home, became traditional, and deferred to her husband, the prince. Although reports suggest that the change was sometimes very difficult for her, do you think it was any easier because she lived in a collectivist, interdependent society? Would it be more difficult for an American female executive to "change" in a similar manner if she married a senator or the president? (Left photo was taken prior to marriage, right photo after her marriage.)

when faced with stereotype threat. These college students were randomly assigned to one of two conditions. In the high stereotype threat condition, the participants saw a Euro-American male professor who explained that they would take a new intelligence test, being studied at Princeton and Stanford, which would help see if tests are biased. In the low stereotype threat condition, participants saw an African American professor, who explained that researchers at Tulane and Howard University were trying to develop a fair, culturally unbiased test, in which Black and White students generally performed equally well. They were then all given the same standardized test. The results showed that African Americans taking a challenging test under the condition of high stereotype threat performed worse and had higher blood pressure reactions than did African Americans in the low stereotype threat condition, or the Euro-Americans in either condition (Blascovich, Spencer, Quinn, & Steele, 2001). Here we see again how individual differences cannot be explained solely in terms of traits, biology, situation, or culture; rather, all these elements together play a role. Furthermore, there are individual differences in susceptibility to stereotype threat; persons who are especially conscious of their group stigma are especially at risk (Brown & Pinel, 2003). Recent work suggests that stereotype threat is a multi-dimensional concept and extends beyond school to work and other settings; combating the effects of a given threat thus requires a refined understanding of its nature (Roberson & Kulik, 2007; Shapiro & Neuberg, 2007).

What about more general implications? **Cultural imperialism** is extending one's own cultural approaches over those of another culture or subculture. For example, in many American history books, the cultures of Native Americans (American Indians) have often been disparaged or ignored. More recently, there have been countercharges that so-called multiculturalism (which, for example, might insist on non-Western books in literature and philosophy courses) has gone too far in attacking traditional Western forms of scholarship.

Cultural Imperialism
The extending of one's own cultural approaches over those of another culture or subculture

As a social science, psychology has an interesting role in this debate. In physical sciences such as chemistry, there can be no sincere debate: The laws of molecular structure are the same in all cultures. Conversely, in the humanities, no scientific standards can be applied: Literature and philosophy operate in a different sphere of discourse. But a social science such as personality psychology is subject to cultural influences and distortions while at the same time it is held to the standard of scientific methods. A fully valid personality psychology must take into account cultural variations, but must simultaneously construct theories that are verifiable through the collection of data. This is a significant challenge for the future of personality psychology.

A More General Model of Personality and Culture

Imagine a case in which the police in San Francisco picked up a five-year-old boy wandering in the park. When the officers questioned him, he refused to respond. When they served him food, he refused utensils and ate with his fingers. When they went out for a walk, he stopped and urinated behind a tree. For a child raised in San Francisco, this would indicate a very unusual personality. But suppose you discovered that the child had just immigrated with his refugee mother from a poverty-stricken, war-torn region of the world? Our judgments about his personality would change—and soften—dramatically. The point is that ideas of personality and predictable behavior are meaningless outside of a framework—a cultural context—in which they are to be understood (Betancourt & Lopez, 1993).

Some of the saddest examples of the results of failures to understand the role of culture in personality arose from relations between representatives of the U.S. government and Native Americans. In addition to the unsavory history of wars, betrayals, and misunderstandings, even relations within the last 100 years have often been characterized by misinformation because Indian cultural assumptions are often so radically different. Interest was spurred in such matters when Erik Erikson (1950) undertook a study of the Sioux in South Dakota. He found that White teachers viewed the Native American students as having a fundamental personality "flaw." In other words, the Indians didn't cooperate with or do well in traditional American classrooms.

Erikson traced the problem to a long history of contradictory government policies: Independent Indian reservations were established, but the inhabitants were

Self-Understanding

Culture and Acceptable Behavior

To understand and provoke discussion of cultural differences, consider doing the following exercise. First, gather together a diverse group, such as students taking a popular class (like introductory biology) or students from a heterogeneous dorm. Second, ask each person to rate whether they *agree* or *disagree* with the following statements about appropriate behavior. Third, discuss where these individual differences arise: from temperament, family, religious affiliation, sex hormones, gender roles, unique personal experience, evolutionary selection, early socialization experiences, existential thought, rational deduction, and so on.

It is appropriate for either party in a relationship to formally propose marriage.

A daughter should not marry against her father's wishes.

Barrier birth control is important to help prevent overpopulation and the spread of AIDS; it should be made freely available.

It is fine to eat pork.

It is fine to eat dog meat, since there is a surplus of dogs.

It is fine to eat beef hamburgers on occasion.

College women who show off their navel piercings are attractive.

Mink and fox coats are beautiful, and mink and fox farms are a reasonable source of clothing material.

A gay or lesbian couple with a deep love and commitment should be allowed to marry.

It is fine for college-age couples, very much in love, to engage in passionate kissing in public.

It is fine for elderly couples (in their 70s), very much in love, to engage in passionate kissing in public.

It is fine for college-age gay couples, very much in love, to engage in passionate kissing in public.

If one does not follow the teachings of Mohammed, one cannot be admitted to heaven.

If one does not follow the teachings of Jesus, one cannot be admitted to heaven.

It is OK for a man to divorce his wife if she cannot bear children.

If you win a significant prize in sports or academics, it is fine to display it in your room.

Rap music should be permitted to use profanities, because it is part of the art and the norm.

If a woman is widowed while still in her 20s, before having children, it is fine for her to quickly get back into the dating scene.

It is fine for a father to beat (on the buttocks) his misbehaving young daughter, to punish her for improper behavior, so long as the beating is mild and is part of a regimen of moral upbringing.

made dependent on the government for their livelihood. Trust and cooperation were preached, but agreements were often broken. Indian culture was conceded to be distinct, yet government policies often tried to force the norms of the dominant culture onto the reservations. Not surprisingly, the children did not behave like White Americans. However, only in recent years have such matters of cultural clashes and personality begun to be explicitly studied. To fully understand personality stability and change as people age, it seems wise to consider their early predispositions, their developmental stage, *and* the culture in which this unfolds (Whitbourne, Zuschlag, Elliot, & Waterman, 1992).

Incorporating Culture into Personality Theory

One solution to the problems of cultural ignorance in approaches to personality is not to try to eliminate culture (or "control for" culture) but rather to bring culture into key consideration as a basic element of personality. Everyone grows up in some culture. And culture is certainly part of what it means to be a person—there are no people without cultures. So it makes sense to incorporate culture into personality theories and personality research.

When Gordon Allport (1954) studied prejudice, he saw that it was a mistake to locate prejudice totally inside an individual's personality. Which sociocultural conditions foster prejudice? Allport proposed a mix of societal, economic, historical, and communication factors as complementary to internal personality dynamics. For example, prejudice was more likely during times of social change, when economic rivalries exist (such as for jobs), when government authorities sanction scapegoating, when societal traditions support hostility, and when the society has unfavorable attitudes toward assimilation and pluralism. In the last century, such conditions occurred when World War I swept away many of the socioeconomic and geographic divisions of the late nineteenth century, and again when the Great Depression (beginning in 1929) produced worldwide economic hardship and chaos. Indeed, fascism grew in power and popularity in the 1930s, especially in countries that did not have a long history of democracy and freedom.

Culture and Humanity

Culture provides the individual with basic information about what it means to be a human being, even though the specific content may vary (Shweder, 1990). Indeed, it seems as if humans are uniquely suited for (adapted for) culture (Tomasello, 2000). Things that no child is born knowing but all cultures teach include answers to these fundamental questions: What does society value and expect of me? Who is like me, on my side, in my family? What should a man do versus what should a woman do? What is mature, rational behavior, and what is childish, impulsive behavior? It is interesting to recall that these are the same questions that Sigmund Freud asked a century ago. Personality psychology has come full circle in the understanding of the importance of culture. A listing of how the eight aspects of personality approach culture is presented in Table 1.

Some of the most modern approaches to personality and culture focus on roles and cognitive sets. Culture, by influencing what roles we are likely to assume, likewise influences our behavior. For example, in modern American culture, success in

Classic to Current

Culture and Personality from a Gay and Lesbian Perspective

Most college students now understand that certain behavior patterns among gay men and lesbian women are reflective of a certain subculture, rather than an inherent part of a homosexual "personality." Many students would be surprised to learn, however, that the nature of these homosexual subcultures can vary dramatically from place to place.

Contemporary cultures have developed stereotypes about people with sexual interest in someone of the same sex. Often gay individuals are seen as having the stereotypical qualities of the "opposite sex"; this provides an easy but oversimplified means of understanding their homosexual attraction. For example, men who are attracted to men typically may be seen as having so-called feminine attributes—being flighty, overly emotional, perhaps even cowardly or deceptive. Women attracted to other women are assumed to have exaggerated masculine attributes—being confrontational, aggressive, interested in sports, loud, and even brutish or threatening (Halberstam, 1998; Rottnek, 1999).

However, there is cultural variation. Ethnographic studies indicate that various contemporary gay male subcultures forcefully reject the alleged link between male homosexuality and stereotypically feminine attributes. In fact, gay men within some subcultures sometimes even link same-sex desire primarily with an exaggerated masculinity (Connell, 1992; Murray, 1996). A comparative study of personal advertisements demonstrated that while gay men across several Western cultures show common concern about their masculinity, definitions of masculinity as a personality trait vary considerably from one gay culture to another (Allison, 2000). In the United States, for example, men tend to claim a gay identity that they define as inherently masculine, but in France, gay men predominantly reject Anglo-American gay identity, equating membership in a gay subculture with effeminacy. Gay men in the Netherlands frequently link their masculinity with the rejection of the bars and discos of the big cities, instead linking masculinity to the adoption of domestic partnerships similar to heterosexual marriages.

Other issues of gay or lesbian personality have nothing to do with masculinity and femininity, but still have something to do with the dominant society's reluctance to accept same-sex desire. For example, when gay men first began appearing regularly on major TV networks in the United States, they were often cast in the role of the funny gay neighbor. Although a fairly successful strategy to ease social discomfort about the existence of same-sex desire, such a repeated formula gave some viewers the impression that gay men are inherently humorous or all share the personality trait of wit. Although gay sarcasm and wit have been recognized as a means of nonconfrontational resistance to social rejection, such coping through humor emerges only in specific times and places. Social and even family rejection has led many gay men and lesbian women to develop a range of unhealthy coping behaviors, including alcoholism.

Strikingly, studies that began in the 1950s by research pioneer Evelyn Hooker (1956, 1993) have revealed no consistent differences when comparing the personalities of those with same-sex desire and those with different-sex desire; that is, clinicians and researchers typically have not been able to detect personality differences between homosexuals and heterosexuals. Although casual observers think that they see personality differences, they are most often viewing subcultural differences.

Social perceptions in different cultures each create a portrait of the "typical" personality of a gay man or lesbian woman, but gays or lesbians within each of these cultures may embrace or reject aspects of the stereotypical personality. Gays and lesbians share the full range of personality attributes of people in the societies in which they live. As with other cultural influences, their personalities must be understood through the interaction of self, dominant culture, and sexual subculture.

FURTHER READING

Allison, T. L. (2000). *The good gay citizen: A cross-cultural analysis of the rhetoric of good gay citizenship.* (Doctoral dissertation, University of California, San Diego, Literature, 2000.) UMI No. AAT 9989256.

Connell, R. W. (1992). A very straight gay: Masculinity, homosexual experience, and the dynamics of gender. *American Sociological Review, 57,* 735–751.

Halberstam, J. (1998). *Female masculinity.* Durham, NC: Duke University Press.

Hooker, E. (1956). A preliminary analysis of group behavior of homosexuals. *Journal of Psychology, 42,* 217–225.

Hooker, E. (1993). Reflections of a 40-year exploration: A scientific view on homosexuality. *American Psychologist, 48,* 450–453.

Murray, S. O. (1996). *American gay.* Chicago: University of Chicago Press.

Rottnek, M. (Ed.). (1999). *Sissies and tomboys: Gender nonconformity and homosexual childhood.* New York: New York University Press.

■ **TABLE 1**   Culture and the Eight Aspects of Personality

Perspective	Primary View of Cultural Aspects of Personality
Psychoanalytic	Long-ago evolutionary forces have shaped the primitive impulses of the id, and each society develops ways to try to control the id.
Neo-Analytic/Ego	Differing child-rearing practices and attachments in different cultures shape children to have certain tendencies, such as to be calmer and more trusting, or more anxious and aggressive.
Biological	Culture emerges after evolution shapes genetic tendencies.
Behaviorist	Culture is the set of reinforcement contingencies in place at a certain geographic location or shared environment.
Cognitive	As a function of how people process information, they come to certain shared or unique understandings about how the world is constructed and how to best behave in it.
Trait	Culture transmits shared knowledge within a group or civilization, but personality is more than the subjective side of culture; individual traits or tendencies show themselves in a way particular to each culture, but are individual nonetheless.
Humanistic–Existential	Culture is the realization of human beings' strivings to create enduring meaning and value in their lives.
Interactionist	Culture is a collection of common situations; but behavior cannot be understood without a simultaneous focus on the particular individual in the particular situation; thus, culturally influenced behavior can undergo rapid change.

competitive sports is highly valued for boys, and so the attributes of a successful competitive athlete are adopted by many. Furthermore, culture helps the growing child determine the ways or dimensions in which to think about the world. For example, if an adolescent girl is socialized to think primarily in terms of families and children and domestic chores, she may be more likely to leave school and start a family at a young age (Caspi, Bem, & Elder, 1989). Culture thus helps us set our goals. With a knowledge of cultural influences on personality, we are more hesitant to accept universal proclamations about, and more willing to look for socioenvironmental influences on, the nature of human beings (Shweder & Sullivan, 1990).

Modern approaches also understand that historical and socioeconomic influences on personality make it unwise to overgeneralize the concepts that emerge from the dominant or mainstream culture (DuBois, 1969; Gaines & Reed, 1995). As noted, a White Italian American child growing up in a Catholic suburban school may have dramatically different experiences from a Black child attending an inner-city school that emphasizes African-American culture. It may be difficult to compare the personalities of these students without taking culture directly into account. This does not mean that there cannot be universal theories of personality; it only means that the theories must not ignore these cultural, historical, and socioeconomic factors.

What about conceptions of personality that arise from cultures outside those of Europe and America? In Japan, the term *amae* is sometimes used for a kind of dependent love that arises in childhood as the child comes to understand that he or she will always have the parents' love. But it is seen as a common feature of Japanese adult behavior, with adults assuming that others in a collectivist society will treat them with benevolence and good will. Such a concept would be missing in the West, as Americans assume that each child will want to develop as much independence and self-fulfillment as possible (Berry et al., 2002; Doi, 1981). Likewise, in Africa, personality is often understood in relation to the good of the community (Nsamenang, 2004).

Culture is also important for understanding personality's effects on applied fields such as physical health. The Seventh-day Adventist (SDA) church is a group of individuals whose doctrines center around their beliefs in the seventh-day sabbath (Saturday, not Sunday) and the physical return (advent) of Jesus. Interestingly, they are one of the healthiest groups of Americans. Since the earliest days of the SDA church, their "health message" has been of paramount importance. This message directs church members to abstain from smoking, drinking, and the eating of flesh (although in recent years, more SDAs have begun to eat meat). Because Seventh-day Adventists believe their bodies to be sacred and dedicated to God, church members also are encouraged to pursue good health in other ways, such as through regular exercise and a wholesome diet. Their supportive social structure may also be health promoting. Furthermore, Adventists believe in abstaining from premarital sex, although the reasons for this are primarily moral rather than health-related. In total, these strong cultural beliefs help shape the personalities of most of the church's members, and the striking result is that Adventists are among the healthiest and longest-living groups in the United States (Fraser, Beeson, & Phillips, 1991). An explanation of the personality and health behavior of an Adventist that disregards this religious and cultural milieu would be superficial, if not totally inadequate.

Culture and Theory

An understanding of cultures also affects how we develop theories. When Kurt Lewin was a student and then a researcher and teacher in Berlin in the 1920s, he naturally adopted ideas from the Gestalt psychologists with whom he worked. Rather than focusing on specific stimuli and responses as the behaviorists did, Lewin tried to understand complex applied situations such as behavior in restaurants, leadership in groups, and people's motivations and aspirations (Ash, 1992). He knew that personality was not located solely inside a person but also depended on the social and cultural environment. When the Nazis came to power in Germany in 1933, Lewin fled to the United States.

As a psychologist who moved from the autocratic and obedient culture of Germany to the relatively democratic and free culture of America, Lewin began thinking about cultural differences in child-rearing, education, leadership, and societal expectations. Rather than being oblivious to the environment in which he was immersed, Lewin was forced to focus even more on the environment itself and was able to exert a tremendous influence on American social and personality psychology. In other words, this type of analysis suggests that the kinds of personality theories that are developed by a researcher will depend in part on the researcher's culture. Culture influences theory (Bond & Smith, 1996; Gergen, 2001).

Does this mean that the theories cannot be scientifically valid? Not necessarily. Human behavior is so complex that it is natural that different but overlapping theories will emerge to try to explain it. As we have advocated, each theory and explanation of what it means to be a person should be rigorously evaluated on logical and empirical grounds; some theories are better than others. However, we also believe that it is helpful to understand each theory in its context and to be open-minded about differing points of view.

Current Research Directions ·

One interesting focus of current research on cultural aspects of personality involves differences between Western and Eastern (Asian) cultural views of the self. In America, the underlying assumptions about people grow out of the idea of the unlimited potential of the divinely inspired free man or woman. In America, it is assumed that each person should strive to be independent and self-reliant. Because the focus is on the individual, not on the social context, this view can lead to an underemphasis on cultural factors. In contrast, in a society such as Japan, the success of the society (rather than the success of the individual) is seen as of utmost importance. Selflessness and even self-sacrifice of one's life is admired in Japanese culture but often scorned in American society. For Americans, heroes are often those people who rebel against and overcome social expectations, such as suffragist Susan B. Anthony, civil rights leader Martin Luther King Jr., or Apple computer coinventor Steven Jobs.

Consider then people's emotional reactions across cultures (Benet-Martínez & Oishi, 2008; Kitayama, Markus, & Matsumoto, 1995). For example, when does a person feel embarrassment or shame? In Japanese society, making a faux pas (false step) at work, say by violating or overlooking an expected ritual of greeting or honor, could be a source of extreme embarrassment. In contrast, in certain aspects of American business (or American football), triumphing brazenly over an opponent might be cause for celebration of individual accomplishment. Note that attributing these different reactions to the individual's personality would be a mistake if culture is not also taken into account.

The Situation May Elicit Cultural Differences

There are times when ethnic identity must be elicited from the social situation. In an experimental demonstration of this phenomenon, Anglo (European American) students and Hispanic undergraduates were exposed to either cooperative or competitive feedback while working together in small (six-person) same-sex groups. When the experimental situation was a competitive one, the response patterns of the two ethnic groups were quite similar. However, the ethnic composition of the group had a dramatic impact on the behavior of Hispanics when the situation was cooperative. Hispanics were intensely competitive when they were in a minority in the small group; but they cooperated when they were in the majority. In contrast, the behavior of Anglos exposed to the cooperative feedback was not affected by changes in the ethnic balance of the group.

In other words, the Hispanic students functioned like the Anglos, except when the cooperative norms of their culture were salient; in that case, the ethnically influenced aspect of their personality emerged (Garza & Santos, 1991). Such situationally influenced aspects of cultural identity may be especially likely to occur in collectivist cultures or subcultures (Kanagawa, Cross, & Markus, 2001). Now with increased globalization and migration, college classrooms are filled with a diverse student body, and there are often stimulating and delightful situational elicitations of culturally based patterns of behavior. However, more research is needed into naturally occurring situations facing cultural minorities, such as the experiences of working-class Mexican American women with more ethnically oriented acculturation who may often face sexual harassment (Cortina, 2001).

Just as the study of traits is turning more towards understanding behavioral outcomes (like success and achievement), cultural personality psychology is becoming more focused on cultural products. One research review (Morling & Lamoreaux, 2008) examined a number of products across cultures—magazine ads, books, news coverage, Internet content, TV ads, song lyrics, and even art. For example, does the art focus on an individual person (individualistic) or more on the surrounding context (collectivist)? Sure enough, cultural products from the West are more individualistic and less collectivist than cultural products from East Asia and Mexico.

Ethnic Socialization

In diverse societies, parents face the dilemmas of instilling pride in their children without encouraging feelings of superiority, and preparing their children for prejudice without instilling anxiety. For example, African American parents must socialize their children to understand that they may face discrimination (Allen & Boykin, 1992; Bowman & Howard, 1985; DuBois, 1969). Should parents explicitly talk about racial issues? Should they emphasize the unique aspects of African American culture or should they minimize differences in the hope that their children will then have an easier time dealing with—or merging into—the mainstream society? Of course, such matters face parents of many ethnic groups, trying to maintain pride and tradition while being full participants in society.

How will majority people react when their stereotypic information is disconfirmed—that is, when they see someone acting less "ethnic"? Some research suggests that attention to information that is inconsistent with stereotypes depends on one's implicit theories about traits—that is, people who believe that traits are fixed show greater attention to stereotype-consistent information, rather than inconsistent information (Plaks, Stroessner, Dweck, & Sherman, 2001). They thus maintain their stereotypes. People who better understand the complex nature of personality may be more flexible in changing their views. These varying perceptions in turn affect minority group members as they move between associating with and identifying with various groups throughout the general culture. For example, theory and research by psychologist William Cross has analyzed racial identity and racial socialization of African Americans as they shift their reference comparison groups among Blacks, Whites, biculturalism, and multiculturalism (Cross & Vandiver, 2001; Vandiver, Cross, Worrell, & Fhagen-Smith, 2002). Various outcomes are possible, with some individuals coming to feel more comfortable only in minority or majority groups while other individuals develop a more bicultural or multicultural identity (cf Benet-Martínez & Haritatos, 2005). People comfortable with multiculturalism tend to be politically tolerant (van der Noll, Poppe, & Verkuyten, 2010).

What about people's tendencies to confirm the negative expectations of others? Is it good for children to know that sometimes they will fail through no fault of their own but rather due to prejudice and discrimination? Is it better to minimize such potential obstacles but at the risk that the child will not have a firm ethnic identity? Such complex matters have no simple answers but are starting to attract significant research interest as the United States and many other countries increasingly try to face up to the conflicts that exist in their multiethnic societies. A broad and deep understanding of personality, which includes cultural aspects of personality, will be necessary for significant progress to occur on these issues. (See the Famous Personalities box.)

Summary and Conclusion

Understanding cultural influences is important to understanding all eight of the basic aspects of personality. Cultural differences involve the shared behaviors and customs we learn from the institutions in our society, and they are an essential component of who we are.

Many influential personality theorists were born in Europe and were heavily affected by European culture, and so personality psychology has a rich tradition of cultural awareness even though such matters are sometimes ignored in modern personality research. Because culture is one key determinant of what it means to be a person, the systematic study of these cultural influences should be, as Gordon Allport noted, an essential part of personality psychology. A person raised in private Catholic schools in Boston is likely to have patterns of responses quite different from those of a person raised in communist schools in Beijing.

It would be a mistake to try to show how the individual's personality explains all these behavioral variations. Rather, people are shaped by their cultures. More individualistic themes tend to be found in Western cultures, more collectivist themes in Eastern cultures (Triandis, 1994). In America, Black–White differences are the most significant cultural grouping, because of American history. The United States embraced principles of both equality and racial stratification, a problem

Gunnar Myrdal called the American dilemma. Rather than studying the vague notion of "race," it is more fruitful to study the effects of ethnic identification, history, minority status, family, subculture, religion, and social class as they interact with temperament and affect personality. These classifications are more readily definable and less susceptible to scientific and social distortion.

The effects of social class—social and economic status—on personality can be dramatic. Such issues are obvious to investigators in countries like India, which have a clear history of social classes or castes, but in America, personality psychologists typically have had little to say about social structure and personality. Karl Marx argued that psychosocial attributes such as alienation could be traced directly to the economic structure of a capitalist society, and his writings greatly influenced Erich Fromm and his associates as they thought deeply about existential alienation in modern society.

Language is one of the defining features of a person's identity. Because we each have different experiences, each individual speaks a unique version of his or her native language, called an idiolect. The "English Only" movement in the United States provides striking evidence of the psychological importance that most people attach to the idea of their mother tongue as part of who they are. Not only does our language influence how we say things, it also impacts how we think about and understand and perceive the world. Gender is one important domain where many issues of status, power, and identity profoundly influence how we use language.

A major problem with psychological testing is not simply that the tests are culturally biased but rather that the test results are used inappropriately. A fully valid personality psychology must take into account cultural variations and must simultaneously construct theories that are verifiable through the scientific collection of data. One solution to the problems of cultural ignorance in approaches to personality is not to try to eliminate culture (or "control for" culture) but rather to bring culture into key consideration as a basic element of personality.

■ Key Theorists

Margaret Mead
Beatrice and John Whiting
Ralph Linton

Harry Triandis
Hazel Markus
Shinobu Kitayama

Karl Marx
Claude Steele

■ Key Concepts and Terms

culture
ethnocentrism
emic approach versus etic approach
archetypes
individualistic and collectivist cultures
American dilemma
SES gradient

idiolect and dialect
linguistic relativity
pronouns and status
"English Only" movement
System of Multicultural Pluralistic Assessment (SOMPA)
stereotype threat

Love and Hate

Legend tells us of beautiful Helen of Troy, the daughter of Zeus, whose abduction by Paris caused the terrible Trojan War. Love and beauty led to death and destruction. The young lovers Romeo and Juliet (of Shakespeare's play) face the hatred and opposition of their feuding parents. When Juliet's father insists that she marry someone else, she takes a potion that makes her appear dead, so that Romeo will come and rescue her. When Romeo returns, he thinks she is really dead and, in despair, kills himself with poison. Juliet awakens, sees her lover dead, and kills herself. Here, however, the love tragedy has a positive aspect: When the families see what has happened, they put an end to their bitter fighting.

It certainly seems that many of the most central aspects of what it means to be a person revolve around issues of love and attraction. It is difficult to find better insights than those in Homer's epics or Shakespeare's plays, but personality

Romeo and Juliet, Leonardo DiCaprio, Claire Danes, 1996, TM & © 20th Century Fox Film Corp. All Rights Reserved.

From Chapter 14 of *Personality: Classic Theories and Modern Research*, Fifth Edition. Howard S. Friedman, Miriam W. Schustack. Copyright © 2012 by Pearson Education, Inc. Published by Pearson Allyn & Bacon. All rights reserved.

psychology endeavors to be scientific. As we have seen, modern personality psychology takes ancient insights and intuitions and tries to evaluate them in systematic, testable ways. Is love really the most potent motivator of people's behavior, both negative and positive?

Or is hate the greatest force underlying human endeavor? Why would an Adolf Hitler or a Joseph Stalin order the murders of millions of innocent people? Why would so many people cooperate in the annihilation of their fellow citizens? Why would a terrorist like Mohammed Atta fly a passenger plane into the World Trade Center, killing thousands of innocent civilians at work in their offices?

Adolf Hitler was born in April 1889, and killed himself in the same month in the year 1945, as his Third Reich collapsed around him. During his lifetime, he exuded a hatred so potent that he was able to mobilize an amazing enmity in the German populace. It resulted in the implementation of a policy culminating in the death of over 11,000,000 of those he hated. Millions of children were butchered, starved, shot, and burned. Hitler said, "It is not by the principles of humanity that man lives or is able to preserve himself above the animal world, but solely by means of the most brutal struggle" (Bullock, 1962).

How can someone come to hate so much? Hitler's father died when Hitler was still a young boy, and his mother was said to be overindulgent. Hitler was a poor student and a failed artist. Even in his youth, he had a temperament that led him to be passionate, intolerant, and unable to form the usual types of social ties. (These events are not that uncommon, and so of course do not fully explain his later behavior; they are *part* of the picture.) Hitler welcomed his participation in World War I, in which he repeatedly risked his life (Davidson, 1977). Yet Hitler was one of the world's shrewdest politicians, outmaneuvering the leaders of other countries. Despite his own unusual nature, he often well understood the nature of others.

We are also fascinated by so-called serial killers such as David Berkowitz, the "Son of Sam," who crept up on young men and women sitting in parked cars and shot them. And consider this: Why would a serial killer like Jeffrey Dahmer, a seemingly handsome and intelligent young man, strangle a series of male lovers, have sexual relations with their dead bodies (necrophilia), keep their heads in his freezer, mummify a penis, and eat his victims' dead flesh (using a meat tenderizer when it was too tough)? Can personality psychology explain this kind of apparently unprovoked hostility?

his chapter examines specific applications of personality psychology to individual differences. We believe that although personality psychology should be scientifically rigorous, it also must confront head-on the basic issues of human nature.

The Personality of Hate

Throughout history, love and hate were viewed as divinely inspired. For example, the ancient Roman god Cupid appeared as a winged infant carrying a bow and a quiver of arrows; if he shot you, the wound inspired love. Hate was often seen as the result of possession by the devil. For example, parts of the Christian church persecuted witches for several centuries, and in 1692, twenty so-called witches were cruelly executed after the famous witch trials in Salem, Massachusetts. The goal was to drive away the devil. However, when Charles Darwin turned attention to the "animal" nature of humans, the centuries-old stories of angels and devils were reinterpreted into psychological and psychobiological theories. Personality theory and theorists provide varying explanations for these motivations—for why we hate.

Why did Hitler, on a massive scale, and Dahmer, with his own hands, hurt others? What about serial killer Ted Bundy, an outwardly attractive, normal man who physically and sexually tortured young women? Women liked him and he gained their trust by faking injuries (such as wearing a cast). He viciously killed at least 20.

How did these killers come to have such aggressive, hateful personalities? What makes a person hateful? Is it innate, inborn, part of the person? Is hate the by-product of a biological defect of some kind? Does it emerge from what the individual has learned or witnessed? Is hate the result of one's cognitive interpretation? Or does some aspect of the situation in which the person finds himself or herself trigger his or her hateful behavior?

Biological Explanations of Hate

Several personality perspectives see aggression, and its internal manifestation in hatred, as a natural, biologically based aspect of humanity; that is, we are biologically predisposed to hate by our genetic heritage. The psychoanalytic and neo-analytic views are part of this tradition, but they have been surpassed by more modern biological theorizing. Perhaps most influential of these today is the ethological perspective, based on evolution, and we will begin there.

Ethological Explanations

Ethology is the study of animal behavior patterns in natural environments. Ethologists draw inferences about the function of the behavior for survival. The ethologists Konrad Lorenz (1967) and Irenäus Eibl-Eibesfeldt (1971, 1979) characterized aggression as the product of adaptive evolutionary

Bureau of Land Management

■ Ethologists view aggression in animals (and by extension, in humans) as innate and adaptive. These wild horses are ferocious in their struggle for dominance. Does the innateness perspective shed any light on why cultural differences (across time and locale) and individual differences (within a cultural group) are so strikingly great?

Ethology
The study of animal behavior patterns in natural environments

processes. According to this argument, hatred is innate because aggression was adaptive in the evolution of our species. Just as brightly colored male fish attack and kill their fellow fish in tropical waters to protect territorial and mating rights, so too humans defend their beachfront property to the death. A "Son of Sam" may kill young dating couples in part because he himself does not have access to a date. Consistent with evolutionary theory, mass murderers are usually men rather than women, and they are usually men of prime mating age rather than old men. Further, despots like Hitler and Stalin and their lackeys are always expansionist—seeking new territories for their empire.

These ethological theories also state that natural aggressive tendencies may be distorted and sometimes expressed inappropriately. For example, because our modern society restrains aggressive actions, this frustrating of natural aggression may result in modern individuals' experiencing a buildup of aggressiveness, which requires some kind of expression or outlet. Consistent with this view, there is some evidence that serial killers often have unusually strict parents, who may foster a buildup of aggressive feelings.

Or, on a larger scale, Hitler may have been expressing his territorial aggressions, accumulated through years of societal repression and intensified when Germany was forced to give up territory after losing World War I. So he ordered the extinction of all individuals who, he believed, should not remain in his territory, especially Gypsies and Jews. According to the evolutionary view, those who were disabled, disfigured, and gay were "naturally" repellent to Hitler because of a biologically based aversion to deviancy; it follows that they too had to be eliminated. Ethologists point out that mutant members of a species are often destroyed. (Ethologists acknowledge that such notions are repugnant to our sensibilities but reply that nature is cruel.)

SHARPEN YOUR THINKING Current Controversy

Who Becomes a Suicide Bomber?

Who would become a suicide bomber, going against the drive for self-preservation, and blowing oneself up to strike terror into the innocent civilian population? One popular stereotype posits that suicide bombers are poor, uneducated pawns, and that the solution to this threat involves spreading money and education throughout the world. However, the evidence suggests that the issue is more complicated than that, and so multiple factors influencing personality should be considered.

Let us consider some of the misconceptions. First, it is often assumed that suicide bombers or attackers are not too intelligent or are psychologically unstable fanatics. In fact, they often leave behind messages or videos that explain their mission in intelligent detail. Second, it is often suggested that suicide bombers have very low self-esteem and feel they have nothing to lose.

In fact, such terrorists often have high self-esteem, perhaps even having an exaggerated sense of self. Third, suicide bombing is often analyzed as a rational act, with attention to arguments that might dissuade a potential bomber (such as giving them "something to live for"). In fact, suicide bombers are often young and concerned with issues of identity, and have been living in an isolated social group, where social influence of an extreme ideology defines their reality. Further, they may be motivated by revenge (for some previous attack on their family or country) and are highly emotional in their responses. Finally, the importance of the immediate social situation is often overlooked. Most attacks need careful planning, indoctrination, preparation of dangerous materials, and transportation by and cooperation with significant others. Suicide bombers are not empty pawns.

There are, however, serious problems with these explanations when we try to utilize them in a scaled-down way to explain the hateful actions of an individual. This theoretical orientation helps us understand why people have a deep-rooted capacity for aggression, but why do we find so many individual and cross-cultural differences in aggressiveness? Many people who grow up with strict parents do not have an explosion of hostile aggression. They do not murder their neighbors or wage war against children. Many cultures and subcultures have a very low incidence of individual aggression (like Japan, or Madison, Wisconsin, or western Pennsylvania), while in others it is sky-high (as in the United States overall, or in Miami and New Orleans). Similarly, although evolutionary psychologists would not be surprised that invaders would want to rape and impregnate the local women, why would some soldiers relish this but others refuse?

Ethological solutions to aggression have often proved ineffective. For example, Lorenz suggests organized sports as a safe means for people to release inner aggressive tendencies. Yet sports matches (such as soccer matches and hockey games) regularly inspire fistfights among players and spectators, and sometimes even lead to stadium riots. And the armed forces engage in war games to *encourage* toughness and aggression in their troops. If anything, competition often seems to bring out aggressive tendencies rather than dissipate them. Finally, ethological explanations generally bring with them a sense of inevitability about aggression: If it is in our genes, then it cannot be halted (Silverberg & Gray, 1992; Stoff & Cairns, 1996).

Brain Disorders

Another biological explanation for individuals with particularly aggressive, hateful personalities involves structural and drug-induced brain disorders. For example, many homicides are committed under the influence of alcohol or amphetamines (Brain, 1986). It is well known from experiments on laboratory animals that stimulation of certain brain centers can produce intense, unremitting rage (Adams, Boudreau, Cowan, & Kokonowski, 1993). Indeed, some people who have evidenced fits of rage or intense hatred have been found to have abnormalities of brain structures involving lesions on and near the hypothalamus and amygdala (temporal lobe). Might Hitler have been the victim of such a brain abnormality? There is some anecdotal evidence that Hitler did indeed blow up in violent outbursts at times. Obviously without postmortem access to his central nervous system, we will never know for sure, but note that Hitler and his associates often functioned quite rationally in a sophisticated German society. Brain disorder is usually associated with sudden, uncontrollable rages rather than with the cold, calculated planning of the deaths of millions.

Biochemical, brain-imaging, and genetic studies all point to disorders of serotonin and dopamine, key neurotransmitters (chemical messengers), in excess impulsivity and aggression (Seo, Patrick, & Kennealy, 2008). Such neurotransmitter deficiencies or gluts are at least partly genetically controlled

■ Sniper Charles Whitman, shown here (back row, right) with his family in earlier days, was found to have had a malignant brain tumor. Does this explain (or excuse) the murderous behavior?

(Hendricks et al., 2003). Indeed, psychopathic behavior and drug abuse are often correlated, but both genetic and environmental factors play established roles in these syndromes of antisocial behavior (Tsuang, Bar, Harley, & Lyons, 2001).

In the mid-1960s, one mass murderer, Charles Whitman, took possession of the campus tower at the University of Texas and shot (killing or injuring) dozens of people. A postmortem examination determined that Whitman had a malignant brain tumor near the amygdala. Was that lesion responsible for his sudden rage? Or did it merely contribute to other influences? If so, should a killer like Whitman be excused from his actions because of his "illness"? Such questions illustrate ways in which the study of personality psychology is relevant to many matters of societal concern.

Gene–Environment Interactions

Hateful behavior often tends to run in families, but this phenomenon could be due to genetic influences, family or subcultural influences, or some combination of the two. It is known that problematic parenting, including various forms of neglect or abuse, is associated with hateful, aggressive behavior in the children (Lahey, Moffitt, & Caspi, 2003). But will changing the poor parenting practices lead to a reduction in the likelihood of violence in their offspring? First of all, it turns out that twin studies, adoption studies, and sibling studies reveal that both genetic and environmental factors contribute to aggressive, antisocial behavior (Moffitt, 2005; Odgers et al., 2008). Second, there is evidence that some children are born with very difficult temperaments and can evoke "negative" behaviors from their frustrated parents. Yet overall there is indeed evidence that genes and environment often interact in affecting aggression in children (Jaffee et al., 2005; Jaffee, Caspi, Moffitt, Polo-Tomás, & Taylor, 2007; Moffitt, 2005). That is, some children are especially vulnerable in a biological sense, and it is these children who are most affected by certain troubling or unusual family or environmental circumstances.

Psychoanalytic Approaches to Hate

After viewing the destruction caused by World War I, Sigmund Freud more fully developed his ideas of the aggressive, destructive side of the id as a counterforce to lustful urges. Freud postulated the existence of an aggressive instinct or drive—that all people have a death instinct: **Thanatos** is the drive toward death and self-destructive behavior, named after the Greek god of death. Self-destructive behavior is, however, a sign of psychopathology in modern society (Weininger, 1996; Yates, 2004). As with socially unacceptable sexual impulses, this energy must either be released or be dealt with in another, more socially appropriate, manner. Consistent with a Freudian analysis of defense mechanisms (especially reaction formation), serial killer Dennis Rader, who hanged young girls and then masturbated over their dead bodies, also was president of his church congregation and was a Boy Scout leader.

Another commonly used defense mechanism involves projecting the unacceptable death impulse onto the hated object(s)—that is, attributing the hatred to others. One might see others as aggressive, hateful, and dangerous, which results in hatred and paranoia toward the object of the projection. Alternatively, if an individual feels hatred toward a dangerous, unsuitable object such as his father, he might displace that hostility to a more suitable and less threatening object—perhaps

Thanatos
According to Freud, the drive toward self-destructive behavior or death

toward a disadvantaged social group. Thus, Freudian theory can lead to the prediction that a dictator's scapegoating of out-group members (blaming them for all the ills of his society) results from his own problems and the consequent use of defense mechanisms. In fact, a study that examined the defense mechanisms of violent individuals found that they were more likely to use projection as a defense mechanism and that the use of displacement differentiated violent from nonviolent individuals (Apter et al., 1989).

In modern psychiatric terminology, many of these hateful people, including many serial killers, would be diagnosed as having an **antisocial personality disorder** (Meyer, Wolverton, & Deitsch, 1998). Such people are also called *psychopaths* or sometimes *sociopaths*. They violate rules even as children; for example, a 13-year-old boy who pulls the wings off insects, carries a knife to bully his classmates, likes to destroy property, and generally lies to and cons others would be so diagnosed. As adults, such people are remorseless, exploitive, and irresponsible. Not surprisingly, serial killer Ted Bundy tortured animals as a teenager.

Antisocial Personality Disorder
A personality disorder in which an individual is excessively impulsive, violates the rules of society, and lacks anxiety or guilt for his or her behavior

Neo-Analytic Views of Hate

Neo-analytic theorists go beyond Freud's description of an innate death instinct when explaining aggression. Jung hypothesized that of the personality elements that are common to all human personality—the archetypes—one particular archetype, the shadow, is where the primitive, animal instincts reside. Thus, according to Jung, inappropriate or uncontrolled expression of one's shadow could result in the type of primal hatred and aggression evidenced by Hitler. Additionally, remember that Jung described psychological types based on the individual's placement on personality trait typologies: introversion/extroversion and thinking/feeling/sensing/intuiting. The thinking-extroverted type is described as stubborn, intolerant, and opinionated, aspiring to tough, unyielding principles—a type not incompatible with dictators.

Alfred Adler and Karen Horney also believed (along with Freud and Jung) that hostile, hateful personalities developed during childhood, but these neo-analysts did not claim that they arose directly from a biological instinct or drive. (This is in line with the neo-analytic emphasis on the role of society.) When explaining the etiology of hostility in the individual, Adler focused on early social experiences, especially coping with rejection. Children who are rejected by their parents may come to view the world as inhospitable and hostile. These children are more likely to grow up to be criminals. Remember that Adler emphasized that although it is a natural part of childhood to experience feelings of inferiority, most of us learn to compensate for these inferior feelings by succeeding in a variety of endeavors. However, individuals who develop an inferiority complex (including feelings of helplessness and incompetence) may sometimes overcompensate (developing a superiority complex), which leads them to attack and denigrate others in an attempt to increase their own feelings of importance. Hitler and Stalin seem to fit the type that Adler called dominant or **ruling type**—the kind of person who proceeds for his or her own gain without consideration of others. (See the Famous Personalities box.)

Ruling Type
According to Alfred Adler, a type of person who proceeds for his or her own gain without consideration of others

Why did 28-year-old Timothy McVeigh blow up the federal building in Oklahoma City, sending body parts of 19 small children flying? Was he the popular class president in high school? No, he was small, thin, the son of divorced parents, did not date, and had a strong, early fascination with guns. Was he a family man with

Classic to **Current**

Terrorism: The Interactionist View

On the morning of September 11, 2001, a small group of terrorists flew hijacked commercial airliners into the massive World Trade Center in New York, totally demolishing it. They also damaged part of the Pentagon in Washington, DC, again killing many workers sitting in their offices. What types of people would commit such acts? A single explanation will not suffice, but a combination of personality and environment yields some important clues.

President George W. Bush called the terrorists "evil." In the sense that a young man would give his life to indiscriminately murder thousands of civilians without warning and simply for horror and terror, such an attack fits any definition of evil. Evil, however, implies a moral or even religious explanation. Indeed, each side claimed "God is on our side and will help us destroy the devils on the other side." We have seen that such explanations for human behavior were common throughout the ages, but are not at all scientific.

At the most basic, biological level, this capacity for "evil" arises out of our evolutionary history, which gives people the capability for terrible violence and aggression. It is also not a coincidence that the attackers were young men rather than middle-aged women. As we have seen, there is a greater potential for aggression in young men. Importantly, however, most young men are not violent. We need to understand more about these men and their situations.

The attacks were not really "mindless" or "insane." The terrorists' leaders were educated, intelligent, and had specific goals in mind. However, they were probably not popular, agreeable, hard-working extroverts. Rather they were dissatisfied in some way, perhaps alienated, cynical, and somewhat depressed. Yet even this is not nearly enough to explain their behavior. We need to understand the situations that take such people and turn them into ruthless killers.

First, there is a supporting emotional ideology. Just as Hitler had grand theories about race superiority, the September 11 terrorists were devoted to a complex religious and cultural ideology that saw Americans as the enemy. Second, this ideology helped the terrorists to dehumanize their victims, thus believing not that they were killing innocent workers and tourists, but devils, enemies, and worthless vermin. Third, this ideology, and a strong sense of solidarity built up in terrorist training camps, helped the terrorists feel a sense of comradeship with and duty to one another. They "lost" their individual identity or ego, submerged in a common cause.

To some extent, the terrorists also were well trained to be obedient to authority (Milgram, 1974). It is not as if they suddenly awoke one day and decided to leave college and murder thousands of civilians. Rather, they saw themselves as foot soldiers who were only following the orders of their supreme leader; they themselves did not make the decision to attack. The worst evils often occur when individuals give up their own sense of self, their own goals for the future, their own self-actualization, and instead see themselves as part of a vast system or army that must follow its commanders.

Some commentators try to blame poverty for terrorism. But most people in poverty throughout history and throughout the world do not turn to evil acts. Other commentators try to blame lack of education. Yet the attacks were carefully and intelligently planned and executed. Education itself does not prevent evil. Rather, the likelihood of evil is minimized when society produces fewer people prone to evil and more social institutions and circumstances that counter evil.

© Eric J. Tilford/U.S. Navy/Getty Images

■ Although certain individuals are more likely to become terrorists, it is the interaction of such personalities with the appropriate eliciting circumstances that actually creates a terrorist.

Think about a boy in these circumstances: He is raised in a stable home, with good attachments to his parents; develops a sense of accomplishment and future goals; has good relations with friends and associates; is rewarded for helping others in need; learns to take responsibility for his actions and question authority when necessary; lives in a society that values human life, respects others, allows free discussion without threats, and models heroes who peacefully do good deeds for others. Compare this child to a second child: a boy who is raised with unpredictable parents who beat him when they are unhappy; is ridiculed in school and ignored by his overworked teachers; is out of the mainstream and so seeks a small group of oddball friends; lives in a closed society that represses free discussion; sees people who are accused of crimes swiftly arrested, beaten, and executed; learns to view others, especially women, as mere property and servants; is taught to blindly believe all religious teachings as the road to salvation; lives in a culture where autocratic, powerful men rule by intimidation; and can find a sense of identity by adopting the ideology of a dictator and joining with other powerful forces. Which child is more likely to commit evil acts?

In short, although it is true that certain individuals are more likely to become terrorists, it is the interaction of such personalities with the appropriate eliciting circumstances that actually creates a terrorist. Hate will never disappear from the human race, but the right combinations of people and situations can make evil acts increasingly rare.

FURTHER READING

Post, J. M. (2007). *The mind of the terrorist: The psychology of terrorism from the IRA to al-Qaeda.* New York: Palgrave Macmillan.

Sanford, N., & Comstock, C. (Eds.). (1971). *Sanctions for evil.* San Francisco: Jossey-Bass.

Staub, E. (2003). *The psychology of good and evil: Why children, adults, and groups help and harm others.* New York: Cambridge University Press.

a loving wife and four kids? No, he wanted to join the army's Special Forces (Green Berets) but didn't make it. He read racist, anti-Semitic literature and admired terrorists for their individualism.

Karen Horney also looked to childhood as the time of life when an individual may become hateful, arguing that children must feel safe during childhood to develop properly. When children experience an extended time when they do not feel safe (for example, when they repeatedly experience undue punishment or when parents embarrass or shame them), their security is undermined. Repressed anxiety becomes basic anxiety, and neurosis.

Horney proposed self-protective measures to which the abused child might turn. One of these mechanisms is to achieve power and superiority over others, which counteracts the feeling that one is impotent or being mistreated. A person with an **aggressive personality** sees most others as being hostile and believes that only the most competent and cunning survive; so he behaves accordingly—is hateful and hostile, denigrating and abusing others—and in this manner maintains his feelings of control and power. Someone with this aggressive personality uses the neurotic coping strategy Horney calls "Moving Against" people. As a child, Joseph Stalin (who became the ruthless Soviet dictator) was savagely beaten by his drunken father. He was physically strong but short, and his face was severely scarred by a childhood bout with smallpox. Like Hitler, he became strong-willed and revenge-minded. Stalin even scorned his own son as a "weakling." Millions of peasants died under his policies of forced collectivization of farming and production and his political purges. Modern research confirms that people who have inflated views of themselves, and encounter social rejection, are especially prone to become aggressive

Aggressive Personality According to Karen Horney, a neurotic trend to see most others as being hostile, to believe that only the most competent and cunning survive, and to behave hatefully and hostilely toward others in order to maintain a feeling of control and power

(DeWall, Twenge, Gitter, & Baumeister, 2009). For example, one study found that narcissistic college students—who were told that no one wanted them on their team in a laboratory experiment—were especially likely to become angry (Twenge & Campbell, 2003).

Erik Erikson, in his theory that people are presented with conflicts to overcome during each stage of life, viewed individual aggression as emerging during the social interactions of early childhood. According to Erikson, three unsuccessfully resolved psychosocial stages may result in an individual who is angry, hostile, and hateful: (1) The child who does not develop an adequate trust during infancy will likely

■ Under Stalin's rule over the Soviet Union (beginning with his rise to power during the revolution of 1917 and continuing to his death in 1953), many millions of citizens—peasants, military leaders, political figures, the intelligentsia, and industrialists—disappeared during the "Great Terror," killed by starvation, execution, or forced labor. Here, a woman and her child, suffering from the famine and carrying all their possessions, look desperately for food. Stalin (which translates as "man of steel," and is the name he adopted as a *nom de guerre*) is viewed as a brutal, totalitarian tyrant. Was Karen Horney right that aggressive personalities arise from abuse in childhood?

© London Express/Hulton Archive/Getty Images

Famous Personalities

The Murder of Cara Knott

Cara Knott was a bright, attractive, energetic 20-year-old college student in San Diego whose battered and strangled body was found beneath a well-traveled freeway overpass. What was so surprising about her murder was that Cara was an extremely careful and conscientious person who always took the utmost precautions. She would never have associated with dangerous characters.

What was even more surprising, however, was the identity of her murderer. Craig Peyer was a distinguished officer of the California Highway Patrol (CHP) with a spotless record. Married with three children, Peyer was known as a friendly man and a "straight arrow."

When Cara's body was discovered near a little-used freeway off-ramp, the police were at first stumped. But then an increasing number of young women—dozens of them—alerted by the publicity, called in to say that they previously had been pulled over on the same off-ramp at night and detained by a CHP officer. These women likewise were pretty and had been driving alone. Evidently, Officer Peyer liked to use his authority to force

develop a pattern of continuing to be distrustful later in life; (2) the child who is treated in a hostile manner when pursuing autonomy may become destructive and angry; (3) finally, if the child's initiative is punished and thwarted rather than realistically channeled, the child may fail to develop an adequate superego. This individual, whose parents are so woefully lacking during these three important stages of psychosocial development, may become a hateful, aggressive adult.

In sum, the neo-analytic perspective spans both biological and nonbiological explanations for hate. Neo-analysts see hate as arising from improper channeling of drives and from failures to resolve the conflicts of childhood. Although powerful instincts exist, aggression is not inevitable but rather is the result of poor parenting and an unstable social environment. This view is commonly seen today in explanations of inner-city violence committed by children of immature single mothers.

Hate and Authoritarianism: Erich Fromm

Like many social scientists, Erich Fromm struggled to understand why many Germans willingly accepted Nazi totalitarianism. Fromm emphasized the cultural milieu as well as the individual's personal history as sources of hostility and hatred. Fromm theorized that individuals feel more and more alone and isolated as civilization advances and as people attain more and more individual freedom. In order to counteract these feelings of loneliness and alienation, he theorized, some people renounce their freedom, surrendering their individuality and principles in order to belong to the group, at any cost.

However, Fromm accepted psychic mechanisms within the individual similar to the neurotic trends defined by Horney. People with an **authoritarian personality** type often have a cruel penchant for exerting power over others, abusing them, and taking their possessions. This personality characteristic, according to Fromm, is generated by a particularly negative relationship with one's parents but is not inevitable. Thus, Fromm straddles the line between biological and nonbiological determinants of hate. He accepts that we have a biological heritage that yields the capacity for

Authoritarian Personality Type
According to Erich Fromm, a person who has a cruel penchant for exerting power over others, abusing them, and taking their possessions; such a personality characteristic may result from a particularly negative relationship with one's parents

personal conversations with women, until something went very wrong when he tried to do this with Cara Knott.

Although this case is certainly unusual, many people thought it to be impossible. How could such a man, sworn to law enforcement and with a perfect record, be a murderer? (Although Peyer claimed he was innocent, he was convicted. He later refused an opportunity to provide his DNA for testing. He remains in prison.)

Surface consistencies in personality may spring from a deeper set of forces. Should we be suspicious when someone is too "perfect"? It was reported that Craig Peyer was a super-

responsible officer; the district attorneys loved to work with him on cases. The CHP sometimes used him as their TV spokesperson because of his confident and friendly manner. Other officers even liked to use his patrol car on the next shift because he kept it so clean! Yet remember that this super-straight officer was also attracted to and professionally trained in the use of authority and, when necessary, deadly force.

Such unusual cases remind us of the complexity of evil. No simple explanations will suffice. But some level of understanding is possible.

If you travel I-15 in San Diego today, you drive over the Cara Knott Memorial Bridge.

Self-Understanding

The Authoritarian Personality

At various times and places in history, the world is troubled by extremely militaristic and repressive leaders who act against what most of us consider to be ethical and moral. The fascist leaders of the 1930s and 1940s are notorious examples. Does personality psychology have anything to say about this? How can we assess a tendency toward fascism?

After World War II, a number of social scientists tried to make sense of the brutal deaths of millions of people. One research group, based at the University of California, Berkeley, conducted a large study of what they came to term the "authoritarian personality" (Adorno, Frenkel-Brunswik, Levinson, & Sanford, 1950). Drawing heavily on Freud's theories (but also considering ego notions and social learning), these social scientists profiled a typical person with antidemocratic tendencies.

The authoritarian personality has a strong id but a weak ego, and so sexual and aggressive urges are not dealt with in a rational manner. Rather, there is a very strong superego, evidenced in the person's holding very conventional values and an uncritical acceptance of and admiration for authority. The authoritarian personality typically deals with sexual urges by projecting them onto the external world. To deal with anxieties and inadequacies about power and sexuality, the authoritarian blames and scapegoats others. In the case of a psychologically weak, threatened White man, this may result in stereotyping such as that Blacks are uncontrollably oversexed, that Jews are plotting to grab world power, that people with disabilities are immoral polluters, that Asians are untrustworthy scavengers, and so on. The out-groups, who in reality lack much power, are portrayed as immoral, dangerous, power-hungry, and worthless, so that the authoritarian personality can feel good.

Authoritarians usually grow up in very strict homes, in which there is typically physical punishment from a domineering father intolerant of ambiguity and change. Or the father may be absent altogether. Authoritarians cope with their own uncertainties and problems in relationships by believing that wild happenings and orgies are going on somewhere out there in the world around them, especially among members of the stereotyped out-group. They have a high respect for authority and believe in severe punishment for lawbreakers, such as castration for rapists. They desire to look tough and avoid dealing with inner feelings. These characteristics are measured with the F-scale (F for fascist).

Although the concept of authoritarianism is not problem-free, the main idea has survived the test of time. It may not be the source of most prejudice, but there is little doubt that this syndrome can be useful in understanding the behaviors of certain repressed individuals. Prejudice does form patterns. For example, such individuals are attracted to symbols of adolescent masculinity, such as wearing imposing uniforms or carrying weapons.

The prejudice, narrow-mindedness, and defensiveness of many people can be better addressed by understanding the personality dynamics that often underlie such patterns. It should be remembered, however, that the actions taken by authoritarians will be heavily influenced by the society and the precise social situations in which they find themselves.

violence, and he accepts that improper channeling of drives during childhood can create lifelong problems; but he places the bulk of the blame on our failure to find meaning in an empty society. He thereby incorporates elements of an existential and humanistic view of hate.

Interestingly, the British actor Anthony Hopkins was able to overcome a lonely childhood and alcohol problems as an adult to star as the psychopath Hannibal Lecter in the chilling film *The Silence of the Lambs* (1991). Lecter (the character) was a seemingly charming and intelligent gentleman, but one who would bite off the nose of someone who got too close. Hopkins (the actor) was able to relate to the dark forces of personality that might motivate such vile behavior, yet Hopkins himself was able to overcome the forces that had afflicted him.

The Humanistic Perspective on Hate

Humanistic psychologists take a viewpoint nearly opposite to the biological approaches to hatred. In contrast to the ethologists, humanistic theorists emphasize the many ways in which people are different from animals. They underscore the importance of morality, justice, and commitment, which involve complex thought and self-awareness. In contrast to the psychoanalysts and neo-analysts, humanistic psychologists focus more on the mature self-actualizer than on the inordinately hateful individual. They look at what can go right rather than what can go wrong during upbringing. However, humanistic explanations for individual hatred can be derived from the theories.

The humanistic psychologist Carl Rogers believed that negative emotion stems from a lack of positive regard in the individual's life, particularly from parents during childhood. Rogers emphasized the individual's need for unconditional positive regard, acceptance, and love from others, especially from one's mother. Parents who place conditions on their positive regard for their child (such as a mother who coldly withdraws her love each time her child misbehaves) will likely have an anxious child. Such children grow up afraid to realize their full potential; they are threatened by experiences that challenge their self-concept. As the amount of discrepancy (incongruence) between one's perceptions of oneself and one's real experiences increases, the greater is the tendency to distort reality and possibly even become psychotic. For example, someone who hoped to be a friendly, well-liked, and well-respected leader but had to deny or distort negative reactions from peers because of inner fears and insecurities cannot become a self-confident, fully functioning, and growing individual. Instead, such a person might be stagnating, cruel, and antisocial. However, Rogers (1961) was so optimistic that he believed *all* persons—regardless of their circumstances—could unleash their internal tendencies toward positive growth.

Abraham Maslow (1968) also pointed out that our fears and doubts about ourselves are at the root of immaturity and hate. He focused on unmet safety needs as afflicting the neurotic adult. Like Rogers, Maslow insisted that evil and hatred are not a basic part of people's personalities but instead result from experiencing a deficient environment. In a world without child abuse, poverty, divorce, and discrimination, the incidence of children growing into hating adults presumably would plummet. Yet Maslow, unlike Rogers, did not urge unconditional acceptance of others. Rather, he argued that children (and adults) need structure and regulation as well as love and feelings of safety. Further, Maslow, reflecting on Hitler's atrocities, did not share Rogers's optimistic view that every person could be redeemed.

Hatred as a Trait

After a number of women were ambushed and murdered while hiking in the San Francisco Bay area, David Carpenter was arrested. He had suffered under an emotionally abusive father, a physically abusive mother, and childhood peers who made fun of his stuttering. He was cruel to animals and had a violent temper and a strong sex drive (Douglas, 1995). Remember that trait theorist Gordon Allport (1961) described cardinal traits as personality characteristics that are ubiquitous and highly influential in an individual's personality and that dominate the individual's day-to-day actions. When we consider Carpenter and similar others filled with hatred and aggression (like Ted Bundy), it seems clear that these are cardinal traits, defining characteristics of their personalities.

For trait theorists, traits like aggression are part of the dynamic organization of personality, parts of personality that incline an individual to behave in certain ways. Raymond Cattell (1966), using factor analysis to extract the common human traits, isolated those source traits that, if manifest to an extreme degree, seem to characterize a killer. Individuals low on factor A are aloof and critical, people low on factor C are emotionally unstable, people high on factor E are dominant and aggressive, those low on Factor I are tough-minded, and those high on factor L are suspicious. Extreme scores on these factors could conceivably combine to describe a cold-blooded killer. Because these traits are descriptive (derived from factor analysis), they are not incompatible with other theoretical formulations. They are merely a different view of the same phenomenon.

For Hans Eysenck, the personality dimension most relevant to hate is psychoticism. As we have seen, a person high on this dimension is impulsive, cruel, tough-minded, and antisocial. (In terms of the Big Five scheme, the counterpart would be low Agreeableness and low Conscientiousness.) For Eysenck, these dispositional differences are assumed to be based on differences in neurophysiology.

In applied research on aggression, psychologist Seymour Feshbach (1971) viewed anger as an *emotional reaction* that culminates in hateful behavior. Feshbach found that other emotional responses such as empathy and altruism could counter aggression. That is, Feshbach says that empathy inhibits one's response to the social contexts that elicit aggressive feelings and behaviors. Children who are more empathic are less aggressive, and low-empathy children are more aggressive (Feshbach & Feshbach, 1969). Interestingly, participation in an empathy training program reduced aggression in both aggressive and relatively nonaggressive children (Feshbach & Feshbach, 1982). Indeed, people who ruminate less about their anger, and who get along well with and understand others, are less likely to become aggressive (Miller, Pedersen, Earleywine, & Pollock, 2003).

In an analysis of Hitler's personality, Henry Murray thought that Hitler's aggression involved an intense effort to overcome early weaknesses and humiliations, and a counteractive need for revenge (Murray, 1943). Would it be helpful to try to understand a trait like vengefulness from a more modern perspective? One study examined vengefulness, defined as the disposition to seek revenge following interpersonal offenses. It was measured using self-report on a forgiveness scale. Vengeful people were found to be less forgiving, having greater negative feelings, and less satisfied with life. They also tended to ruminate more about offense. In terms of the Big Five, they were less Agreeable and more Neurotic (McCullough,

Bellah, Kilpatrick, & Johnson, 2001; see also Lecci & Johnson, 2008; Sibley & Duckitt, 2008).

Cognitive Approaches to Hate

Remember that cognitive approaches to personality pay little direct attention to biology and the actual events of childhood. Rather, they emphasize that it is not an individual's real experiences, but the manner in which a person interprets (construes) his or her relationships and experiences that determines his or her actions. According to this view, hatred and aggression depend on the ways we learn to explain the world.

George Kelly, for example, looked at personal constructs toward others. He found that some people do not make many distinctions among others—they are more likely to perceive other people as similar to one another. People who are more authoritarian are like this, exhibiting what Kelly (1963) called **cognitive simplicity**. This permits one to dismiss whole groups of people as "enemies."

Kelly additionally explained that hostility may result when an individual's construal of others is not supported by experience. Well-adjusted people evaluate others realistically and alter their concepts if evidence indicates they are incorrect; maladjusted people do not. Instead, hostile people try to constrain others to fit their construal, rather than changing their interpretation of reality. Hitler attempted to alter the composition of an entire nation to fit his construal of it. Did Berkowitz perhaps "eliminate" those who did not meet his view of reality? Indeed, differences have been found in the manner in which violent people perceive threat compared to people who are not hostile. For example, violent criminals are more likely to perceive events as threatening and to see other people as having hostile intentions. It is believed that psychopaths have deficits in the processing of both social and cognitive tasks (Kirsch & Becker, 2007; Serin & Kuriychuk, 1994).

These distortions of the meaning of social interactions begin at an early age. Preadolescent and young adolescent boys who are aggressive are more likely to misperceive hostility in a variety of aspects of their social engagements (Lochman & Dodge, 1994). Therefore, according to these cognitive models, extreme hostility and hatred result from the individual's misconstrual of situations, frequently attributing malevolent intentions to events and people that are actually benign (Harmon-Jones & Harmon-Jones, 2007).

Cognitive Simplicity
According to George Kelly, the tendency for some people to fail to make distinctions among other people and to perceive other people as similar to one another

Learning Theory: Hate as Learned Behavior

B. F. Skinner held that we gain little except confusion by arguing that someone has hatred, or aggressive tendencies, or a motivation to aggress. Instead, we should simply note if and when someone (or some pigeon) actually does aggress. By focusing directly on the behavior, we can begin to see which environmental contingencies make the aggressive act more likely to occur. Learning theories state that aggression is acquired through the same mechanisms as all behavior.

Classic learning theory says that hateful emotions are conditioned responses, whereas operant learning theory emphasizes the role of reinforcements and punishments in shaping learned aggressiveness. Social learning theory incorporates the point that the hateful behavior of others is modeled, observed, imitated, and vicariously reinforced (Morgan, 2006).

What about the serial killer who murders only women? A series of events, such as violent abuse by one's mother during childhood, would, according to the theory of conditioned learning, result in the eventual pairing of the conditioned response of hatred and aggression to women, even when the abuse was not occurring. This hatred might be quite specific to women who look like, or have some specific characteristics similar to, the original unconditioned stimulus—Mom. Or the hateful emotions might generalize to a larger group of individuals, for example, all middle-aged women; that is, the sight of the conditioned stimulus (any woman) would elicit hateful feelings and would provoke the behaviors that accompany them. Examination of the childhoods and life histories of several mass murderers indicates that many of them indeed did suffer at the hands of individuals similar to their victims, lending some credence to the premise that, in at least some cases, hatred is a conditioned response.

It is certainly true that if hateful behavior (toward a group) is reinforcing, either because it attracts attention to an otherwise ignored individual, or because it evokes the adulation of others, or because it brings material possessions (loot), then the person will continue to behave in a hostile manner. In fact, the aggression may actually escalate.

When Dollard and Miller further expanded the conditioned response paradigm, they demonstrated that defense mechanisms such as projection, and one's thoughts (including angry and hostile ones), can be conditioned. Some of these may become secondary drives that motivate much of the individual's actions. Hatred can thus be learned and become a drive that impels one to behave in an aggressive, hostile manner.

Children who live in homes filled with hate (fighting parents) often grow up to be hateful themselves, learning hostility from their parents' example. Further, a person who was abused as a child is more likely to become an abusive parent. These social learning processes—vicarious learning and modeling—can be quite powerful, especially for children who have antisocial tendencies (Biederman, Mick, Faraone, & Burback, 2001; Kazdin, 2005).

Cultural Differences in Hatred

Anthropologists have provided a significant amount of evidence that there are huge societal differences in the average (and the culturally acceptable) level of hostility in a society (Goldstein & Segall, 1983). Whereas some societies have been characterized as extremely aggressive, others demonstrate little interpersonal hatred or hostility. Something in the social structure must be relevant.

Even within the boundaries of the United States, cultural differences have been found to predict differential levels of hostility. Nisbett and Cohen (1996) compared the northern part of the United States to the southern states and found that the higher rate of homicide in the South seems to be due to a culture of honor that advocates violent responses to perceived insults.

© Erich Lessing/Art Resource, NY

■ The boys depicted in this Bronze Age frieze (discovered in excavations on the Aegean island of Santorini) did their fighting over 3,000 years ago. Each boy wears a boxing glove on his right hand—they were participating in an activity that was organized and approved by their social group. Maybe the biggest change over the thousands of years from their time until ours is that now we have thicker padding in boxing gloves.

■ Within the United States, the states of the deep South have a higher rate of homicide among Whites than in the northern states. Specific cultural beliefs or practices in the region may produce this effect.

Interestingly, there is little regional difference in the North–South homicide rates for African Americans, suggesting that it is something about White southern culture that causes the violence, instead of just living below the Mason-Dixon line (Nisbett & Cohen, 1996). Also, a widespread presence of guns contributes to a cycle of violence in which arguments lead to deadly retribution. With dramatic cultural and subcultural differences in aggression, personality theories that focus solely on characteristics of the individual are clearly inadequate. Thus, some sort of person-by-situation interactionist approach is needed.

Evaluating Hate

In sum, there is usually no simple explanation of hatred and aggression. The different personality perspectives make different assumptions and collect differing evidence about what it means to be a person—in this case, what it means to be an evil, hateful person.

Occasionally, a brain tumor or other severe provocation is the simple explanation for hate, but those cases are extremely rare. Rather, hate and aggression often seem to arise from a combination of forces. Most basically, there does seem to be an innate capacity for hate and aggression. Many animals defend their offspring, their territories, and their mates through vicious aggression. And specific parts of the brain are central to rage. The evidence supports the idea that we have a capacity but not an inevitability for hate and aggression in our natures.

Several perspectives agree that hate and aggression are especially likely if one faces an abusive and unstable childhood environment. These orientations take the emphasis away from biology and place it in the identities and patterns that are set in motion through parent–child relations. Children who are treated with abuse and contempt by their parents or their society are likely to become abusive and contemptuous adults. Further, the ways we learn to interpret events, and the rewards we see and receive, can have dramatic effects on our likelihood of aggression. Even whole societies differ markedly in the amount of hate and aggression they contain and display. The specific situation also matters, as certain people in certain situations are more likely to aggress.

It is interesting to consider the supposed simple "cures" for hate and aggression that our complex analysis tells us will generally *not* work as a comprehensive solution: medications or brain surgery for violent offenders; school education programs; threats of whipping or death; organized intensive sports competitions; or hoping the inherent good inside each person will eventually surface or prevail. Such simple solutions are often proposed by politicians, but they are too narrow to be generally effective. Rather, tendencies toward hatred and aggression can be minimized by serious efforts to create a society with physically healthy individuals (who also avoid substance abuse) who develop good relations with their parents; a society that models and rewards only cooperative behavior; a society that fosters justice and guides its citizens along a disciplined and productive life path. However, even in such a stable, well-balanced society, certain individuals will still need more intensive interventions.

The Personality of Love

Is love the counterpart of hatred? Are they opposite sides of the same coin? Or is love, in its own right, the most potent motivator of behavior? How do the personality theorists explain love? .

Evolutionary/Ethological Explanations of Love

British journalist Woodrow Wyatt (1981) said, "A man falls in love through his eyes, a woman through her ears". He meant that a man is attracted by a woman's beauty but a woman is attracted by what she hears about a man's status. Evolutionary psychology explains that love through the millennia developed because of its adaptive consequences. Attraction to members of the opposite sex is obviously necessary if we are to reproduce. In addition, for our genes to produce offspring that will themselves grow to reproduce, two basic elements must immediately come into play: (1) characteristics that ensure that a healthy offspring is born and (2) characteristics that ensure that the helpless child will survive (to reproductive age).

Such arguments underlie the research of evolutionary psychologists like David Buss, who draws on the work of biologist Robert Trivers (1996) and psychologists Martin Daly and Margo Wilson (Daly & Wilson, 2005b; Daly, Wilson, & Weghorst, 1982). Buss hypothesizes that there are different characteristics for which males and females look when selecting a mate because of their different biological roles during reproduction. The male, according to this argument, is attracted to females who have physical characteristics indicating their suitability to conceive and carry a healthy offspring through a successful pregnancy. Thus, the male should be attracted to females who are young, fit, and healthy—characteristics represented, in part, by the degree of physical attractiveness. Another possible ramification of this theory is that older men would be attracted to younger women. Buunk, Dijkstra, Kenrick, and Warntjes (2001) found this to be true; men, regardless of their age, desired to have relationships with women who were in their reproductive years.

■ The evolutionary perspective claims that the optimal mate has different characteristics for males than for females. A male should prefer females who appear young and fertile, whereas a female should prefer males who appear able to provide resources for her offspring.

Females are also somewhat attracted to males based on their physical attractiveness because of the ability of physical attractiveness to indicate potential fertility and genetic health (Kenrick, 2006). (Males with disease and infirmity are less likely to be suitable gene carriers.) Females, however, must invest nine months during gestation, and a long period of time during the child's helpless infancy and childhood, taking care of the child. Because the female's energies are concentrated on child care, she requires a male who can provide her with the necessities of life, such as food and shelter, while her offspring are children. Thus, females prefer men who are able to provide for these needs. According to Buss, this means that females are attracted to men who have skills required to successfully acquire resources (Buss, 2009; Buss, Haselton, Shackelford, Bleske, & Wakefield, 1998). Evolutionary considerations are seen to be as salient today as they were in earlier times. In one study of this theory, German and American men and women demonstrated the predictable sex differences in attraction: Men routinely emphasized physical attractiveness as important for mate selection, whereas women consistently highlighted earning ability as important when choosing a partner (Buss, 1989).

Are these differences just due to gender role expectations? Cross-cultural evidence yields some support to the contention that these preferences reflect inherent, genetic characteristics. Irrespective of culture, women are more likely to prefer mates who have an ability to acquire resources. Ambitious, hard-working men are consistently valued by women across cultures (Buss, 1989, 2009). Moreover, men in all cultures were more likely to value youth and physical attractiveness in females.

Where does love come into this picture? From the male perspective, it is necessary for males (but not females) to ensure the paternity of their offspring. (Females know that their infant is theirs, but males cannot be certain.) Emotional commitment between sexual partners has adaptive value because it bolsters monogamy, helping ensure that the female will not mate with others. From the female perspective, love, and the commitment that accompanies it, helps ensure that the male will stick around, providing resources, until the child is grown (Buss & Schmitt, 1993).

One of the problems with confirming these ideas is that we do not know for sure what specific evolutionary pressures were faced by our ancestors. Furthermore, most of us know that men are attracted to healthy and sexy young women and that women prefer men who are stable and have talents and resources. So the evolutionary "prediction" was not a difficult or intriguing one to make or confirm. Women are also attracted to men with a sense of humor or certain tastes in music. What evolutionary pressures could be relevant to that? In other words, this line of reasoning holds great promise but is far from proven.

Psychoanalytic Explanations for Love

Freud viewed love as arising from sexual instincts. During the oral stage of development, mothers provide one's first erotic pleasure—oral gratification. As a result, mother becomes the child's first object of love. Much later, during the genital stage, the individual learns that sexual satisfaction can be provided by a sexual partner. The strong feeling accompanying mature sexual attraction, according to Freud, is love; that is, love is a result of the fact that one's sexual partner is responsible for sexual satisfaction. Love for a partner arises out of adult sex, just as love for the mother first arose out of oral gratification. This perspective suggests that what a person does for love is really done for sex, a somewhat limited and pessimistic outlook (Miller & Siegel, 1972).

■ Psychoanalytic and neo-analytic theories stress the lasting influence of the mother as the first love object. Is it just a coincidence that when the little boy on the left grew up to become the young man on the right, he chose to marry a woman who resembles what his mother looked like as a young woman?

Further, there is some biological evidence that the motivation to sex and the motivation to romantic love involve different neurological systems (Fisher, 2006).

Melanie Klein and the object relations theorists noted that for almost all children the mother is the nurturer, and therefore the mother is the first and most salient love object. Object relations theory diverges from Freudian theory at this point, avoiding Freud's use of the Oedipal stage to explain the transfer of affection to the parent of the same sex. Instead, object relations theorists emphasize the importance of this first mother–child relationship, stating that the child internalizes the nature of this relationship, which becomes, in a sense, the prototype or template for future loves. Our adult love is based on our mother love, perhaps being imitative, perhaps opposite. If mother teases with her breast, we may seek a teasing lover in adulthood (or may avoid teases). Some theorists highlight the feeding and drive-reduction elements of the early relationship, while others emphasize the attachment aspects—the tactile comfort and feelings of safety and security offered by one's mother.

Neo-Analytic Explanations for Love

Erik Erikson (1963) focused on the sixth stage of psychosocial development, when the individual is in his or her early 20s (and has established an adult identity) as the time at which mature love develops. Erikson noted that during this stage, Intimacy versus Isolation, the young adult is ready to commit to another, forming an intimate relationship and experiencing love. According to Erikson, only those who have found their identity will be able to experience true intimacy—and love—whereas those whose ego identity is not complete will either remain isolated or will engage in false relationships by being sexually promiscuous or by having shallow relationships. Thus, Erikson saw love as the result of healthy, normal development.

A modern approach by psychologist Phillip Shaver and his associates also relies on understanding a child's development, but Shaver uses models of attachment learned during childhood to account for differences in the quality of adult relationships. The idea is that the nature of one's childhood attachment relationship is reflected to some extent in later romantic relationships (Brennan & Shaver, 1995; Hazan & Shaver, 1987; Shaver & Mikulincer, 2005). Note that this way of thinking derives directly from the neo-analytic theory of Karen Horney (1945), involving unresolved basic anxiety, and from related studies of the biological bases of infant attachment (Ainsworth, 1979; Ainsworth & Bowlby, 1991; Bowlby, 1969).

There are three **romantic attachment styles**, according to Shaver and colleagues: (1) **secure lovers**, who easily form close relationships with others and let others become close to them; (2) **avoidant lovers**, who feel uncomfortable when they are close to another or when others are close to them, and who have trouble trusting and being trusted by others (adult children of alcoholics may often fall into this group); (3) **anxious-ambivalent lovers**, who want to get close but are insecure with the relationship and may scare away partners by being desperate about the relationship. About half of people studied were found to be secure, but unfortunately the rest were found to be avoidant and anxious-ambivalent. Individuals' adult attachment styles were found to be predicted by the quality of their relationships with their parents, further supporting the theory that people form models of these early relationships that influence later attachments. But there is also some evidence that these various attachments arise in part from individual

Romantic Attachment Styles
According to Phillip Shaver, one's style of adult romantic relationships, which is modeled on and reflects the nature of one's childhood attachment relationships to the parents or caregivers

Secure Lovers
According to Phillip Shaver, people who have a romantic attachment style in which they easily form close relationships with others and let others be close to them

Avoidant Lovers
According to Phillip Shaver, people who have a romantic attachment style in which they feel uncomfortable being close to others or having others close to them and have trouble trusting and being trusted by others

Anxious-Ambivalent Lovers
According to Phillip Shaver, people who have a romantic attachment style in which they want to get close but are insecure with the relationship

differences in the serotonin and dopamine systems (Gillath, Shaver, Baek, & Chun, 2008; Stein & Vythilingum, 2009).

Cognitive Approaches to Love

Can we count the ways we are able to love? The cognitive approach to love tries to classify the different types of loving and, further, to distinguish our passions from our thoughts. It seems clear that there are some good friends whom we like a lot but would not want to be intimate with; some to whom we are very self-disclosing but not physically attracted; some we are madly passionate about but don't really like that much; and so on.

Unfortunately, love has eluded any simple classification scheme. Most approaches distinguish liking and respect from love and passion. Some distinguish a respectful, companionate love from an emotional devotion. Still others try to use several such dimensions simultaneously, comparing infatuation to sexual exploitation to true love, and so on. What is clear from these analyses is that our thoughts are very much involved with our feelings. There are so many kinds of love because there are so many ways that we reflect on and interpret our drives, motivations, and interpersonal relations (Beall & Sternberg, 1995; Berscheid, 1994; Fehr & Russell, 1991; Rubin, 1973; Sternberg & Barnes, 1988).

Humanistic–Existential Perspectives on Love

The humanistic personality psychologists have devoted a considerable amount of energy to explaining the etiology of love. They disdain the simple behaviorist view that we love someone who provides us with reinforcements. Their theories emphasize that people who realize their potential, becoming the best that they can be, are the people who can have the truest love. They also focus on the idea that a person must accept (and love) himself or herself before he or she can give real love to others. For example, Carl Rogers argued that children who learn to accept themselves can grow up to be fully functioning individuals, able truly to love others.

Maslow's View on the Need for Love

Abraham Maslow placed the need for love on the third rung of his need pyramid. He meant that only after one's physiological needs (as for food) and one's safety needs (as for order) are met can one work on satisfying needs for love and affiliation (belongingness). As the individual moves successfully up the need pyramid, satisfying belongingness and esteem needs, she or he can become more able to fully love and self-actualize.

Maslow (1968) described two types of love, **being love** (referred to as "B-love") and **deficiency love** (referred to as "D-love"). D-love is selfish and needy, whereas B-love is unselfish and cares for the needs of the other. B-lovers are more self-actualized and help their partners toward self-actualization. This perspective implies that people bring different personality orientations to loving—self-actualizing people love unselfishly (B-love), but needy, immature people experience D-love. We all know some immature people seeking selfish D-love. In fact, research on successful marriage suggests that partners in long-term happy marriages see each other as having a caring, responsive personality, and acting as true friends (Huston, Niehuis, & Smith, 2001).

Being Love
According to Abraham Maslow, love that is unselfish and cares for the needs of others; a person who is involved in being love is more self-actualized and helps his or her partner toward self-actualization

Deficiency Love
According to Abraham Maslow, love that is selfish and needy

Erich Fromm's Theory of Love

Erich Fromm combines the humanistic–existential and psychoanalytic perspectives in his theory of love. Remember that Fromm believes that modern humankind suffers from a societally induced sense of alienation and loneliness. Unlike Freud, who saw love and sex as expressions of the instinctual, animalistic nature of humans, Fromm sees love as a special characteristic that actually humanizes men and women. In order to alleviate feelings of loneliness, people seek contact with the world around them and, in particular, with other individuals. Love is the positive result of individuals striving to join with others.

Fromm goes on to describe characteristics that discriminate between different qualities and types of love. For Fromm, **motherly love** is completely one-sided and unequal—the mother gives unconditional love, asking for nothing. From this love the child acquires a sense of stability and security. **Brotherly love** involves loving all others—all of humankind. This kind of love reunites the isolated individual with others. **Erotic love** is, however, directed toward a single individual; erotic love is a momentary, short-lived intimacy. In such cases (when this dominates), the individual may move from one lover to the next fairly rapidly. People who engage solely in erotic love do not experience true mature love but rather satisfy sexual needs, alleviate anxiety, or control or are controlled. It is **immature love** when the taking of love overwhelms the giving of love, which may occur in (immature) adult–adult, as well as adult–child, unions. But when an individual's personality is mature, the person is capable of true giving and therefore of genuine, mature love.

Real **mature love**, according to Fromm, incorporates elements of brotherly love and self-love. In mature love, each partner is caring for the other. In addition, mature lovers feel a sense of responsibility toward each other, not out of obligation, but freely given (Miller & Siegel, 1972). Mature love also encompasses respect for the development of the partner. Finally, in order to love maturely, each person must have knowledge of the partner. One must be able to love oneself and one must have the sense of devotion that accompanies brotherly love before one can successfully and maturely love another.

Thus, Fromm sees love as much more complex than simply a means of reducing sexual tension. Fromm's view of mature love has been adopted by most modern marriage counselors. Interestingly, in contrast to Freud, Fromm believed that immediate sexual satisfaction did not facilitate love but rather that sexual satisfaction would follow true love. This is the idea that the best sex comes in the most loving relationships. If a woman is seeking the relationship she never had with her father, or if the man is seeking childish motherly love, neither will ever be fully satisfied. These are examples of neurotic love. Similarly, if an individual gives up her or his own identity and worships the partner, the result is a form of pseudo-love.

Rollo May: Types of Love

Because Fromm saw love as crucial to addressing questions of meaning and existence, his can be thought of as an existentialist point of view. Rollo May, the existentialist psychotherapist and author, followed Fromm and published influential books that described modern humans as depersonalized by modern culture and technology. He believed that this resulted in the numbing of the individual's ability to love. Violence and dehumanization may be the result (May, 1972).

Motherly Love
According to Fromm, the type of love that is completely one-sided and unequal, in which the mother gives love and asks for nothing, and from which a child acquires a sense of security and stability

Brotherly Love
According to Fromm, the type of love that involves loving all of humankind and that reunites isolated individuals with one another

Erotic Love
According to Fromm, the type of love that is directed toward a single individual; it is a short-lived intimacy that satisfies sexual needs and alleviates anxiety

Immature Love
According to Fromm, the type of love in which the taking of love overwhelms the giving of love

Mature Love
According to Fromm, the type of love in which each partner cares for the other, feels responsibility to the other, and gives love freely

■ According to Rollo May, "free love" as practiced by the hippies was not an ideal form of love—it lacked the discipline and will that characterize meaningful and lasting love.

Sex
According to Rollo May, a form of love consisting of lust and tension release

Eros
According to Rollo May, a type of procreative love that is experiential and savoring

Philia
According to Rollo May, a type of brotherly love or liking

Agape
According to Rollo May, a type of unselfish love characterized by devotion to the welfare of others

Authentic Love
According to Rollo May, a type of love that incorporates all other types of love

In particular, Rollo May described various types of love. These are **sex** (lust, tension release); **eros** (procreative love—savoring, experiential); **philia** (brotherly love); **agape** (devotion to the welfare of others; unselfish love); and **authentic love**, which incorporates the other types of love. May argued that modern society unfortunately promotes the dividing up of the different types of love, but he believed that love is usefully understood from the different perspectives.

May developed these ideas during and after the sexual revolution of the 1970s, at the height of the hippie subculture. He suggested that our technological age has had important negative consequences for love, resulting in people who are obsessed with sex, independent of other aspects of love. As a result, tenderness and closeness are missing from many sexual unions. (It was also not surprising that the divorce rate rose dramatically in the 1970s.)

In addition, as an existentialist, May emphasized the importance of will. He noted that love and will are intertwined: that love needs will (or effort, volition) to be lasting and meaningful. He noted that the difficulty with the hippies was that although love was given freely, it lacked will. It was too unrestrained and irresponsible (May, 1969). The hippie culture overthrew the sexual hang-ups that resulted from sexual repression, but it sometimes went too far by eliminating all discipline and commitment. It is apparent that Rollo May's perception of the impact of will is similar to Fromm's inclusion of knowledge, accomplishment, and development in mature love.

Cultural Differences in Love

Just as cultural context influences aggressive tendencies, there are cultural differences in the experience and expectations for love. This again suggests that love cannot simply be a biological phenomenon or an instinctual (id-dominated) phenomenon, nor even simply a family-based concept.

In many cultures and in many times throughout history, marriages were arranged by the bride's and groom's parents. Economic, religious, and social factors played a key role. Matchmakers were important forces in society. Yet few modern-day college students would want their parents to find their mates for them. We often assume that there is an ideal partner out there for us, and all we have to do is find this person and fall deeply in love. However, to the extent that the neo-analysts and the humanists–existentialists are correct, it might make more sense to allow some forms of matchmaking to return. Rather than choosing on the basis of immediate sexual attraction or fulfillment of immature needs, an experienced matchmaker might choose pairings on the basis of respect, maturity, similar values, and the potential for a deep, integrative love, as well as physical compatibility. The result might be better marriages and deeper love.

In fact, one undergraduate studying personality, a recent immigrant from Afghanistan, confirmed to us that in her family, her parents and aunts and uncles all have healthy arranged marriages, whereas the only divorce in her whole extended family was the relative "who married for love." This is another example of how understanding the assumptions about human nature that accompany the different approaches to personality can help us become more sophisticated in understanding many key issues in our lives.

A study of 80 married Mexican American and Euro-American volunteers found that practical attitudes about love, and less idealism about sex, were related to level of acculturation in the Mexican American group—with more Hispanically oriented individuals being more pragmatic. However, passionate love was correlated with marital satisfaction for all groups (Contreras, Hendrick, & Hendrick, 1996). In other words, we certainly would not want to carry the argument too far and assert that passionate love and attraction are unimportant. A balance of the two approaches is needed. Other studies have found that members of individualistic cultures tend to place more emphasis on romance and personal fulfillment than people from collectivistic societies, but they are not necessarily more loving (Dion & Dion, 1993; Levine, Sato, Hashimoto, & Verma, 1995). Furthermore, Wan, Luk, and Lai (2000) found that personality correlates of loving style differed between subjects from the East and subjects from the West.

■ Most American college students would not want their parents (or a matchmaker, shown here to the right of the mother of the prospective bride in a scene from *Fiddler on the Roof*) to select their mates for them, as happens in many traditional cultures. Young adults selecting their own partners may use different criteria from those used by parents and matchmakers.

Fromm was distressed by the modern capitalist structure in which the highest goals of life often seem to be consumption and "having fun." The result of this lifestyle is often loneliness.

The Trait and Interactionist Approaches: Loneliness

Consider the case of Joe, a 20-year-old college student who is somewhat of a loner. He keeps to himself, has difficulty relating to others, and does not much share his thoughts or feelings with others. Although Joe is uncomfortable about his lack of social interactions, he rarely talks about being lonely.

A significant number of people have difficulty finding love and forging meaningful relationships. They feel lonely and isolated. Is there a relationship between personality and loneliness? The study of loneliness has provided an informative picture of the typical personality of the lonely individual.

Lonely people have trouble forming relationships, trusting others, and getting close. They have difficulty talking about themselves, disclosing their feelings to others, forming social relationships, and feeling comfortable in social interactions (Berg & Peplau, 1982; Peplau & Caldwell, 1978; Peplau & Perlman, 1982). They may be generally less sociable (Perlman & Joshi, 1987). In trait terms, they may be very low on extroversion and somewhat low on agreeableness and emotional stability. In other words, loneliness is a common and stable condition (Hawkley & Cacioppo, 2007). Cognitive personality theorists point out that lonely people often have a negative explanatory style—they see things as beyond their control and tend to view others in a negative light (Snodgrass, 1987).

Other personality characteristics that are not as intuitively obvious have also been shown to be related to loneliness. People who are high in both masculine and feminine traits (androgynous people) seem to be the least lonely, possibly because they feel comfortable in a variety of social situations and are able to make friends with an assortment of people with different interests and outlooks (Berg & Peplau, 1982). They may have better social skills and higher self-esteem.

Loneliness is associated both with psychosocial problems like social inadequacy, and also with instrumental problems like health ailments and lower incomes (Cacioppo & Patrick, 2008; Perlman, Gerson, & Spinner, 1978). As Erik Erikson would expect, different issues affect loneliness as we age. This information suggests that environmental characteristics might take a significant toll as well. In fact, for a behaviorist like Skinner, the loneliness of college results from having to move to an environment in which one cannot emit one's usual responses to obtain rewards.

This line of thinking suggests that loneliness can be overcome by developing skills and changing environments. That is why many counselors (treating lonely people) suggest their getting involved with social groups and clubs related to their interests, knowledge, and skills, even if they feel awkward at first. Loneliness cannot be considered only a personality trait; rather, an interactionist view that takes the situation fully into account is needed (Rook, 1988, 1991). Loneliness occurs when there is a mismatch between a person's actual relationships and needed relationships (Perlman & Peplau, 1998).

Love Gone Wrong: Risky or Violent Sexual Behavior

As poets have long surmised, in some paradoxical ways, love and hate are closely related. Intimate relations are most often tied to deep love, but they are also linked to risky behavior and aggression. What personality traits may encourage one to participate in risky sexual practices? This question is receiving increasing attention as a result of the spread of AIDS (acquired immunodeficiency syndrome).

Many investigators have been interested in determining the relations between personality and sexual behavior—in particular, between personality and unsafe sex. Most basically, extroverts are more sexually adventurous because they seek extra stimulation. Extroverts have even been found to be more apt to engage in "French kissing" and to engage in a wider variety of sexual activities (Barnes, Malamuth, & Check, 1984; Fontaine, 1994). People who are dispositionally impulsive and less controlled also tend to act impulsively in their sexual encounters. For example, a study of college students found that those who were likely to make impulsive decisions and take risks in their daily lives were also more likely to take more risks in their sexual behaviors. This was true regardless of their understanding of safe sex, so risk-taking is not primarily a cognitive factor (Seal & Agostinelli, 1994). These students were also more sensitive to situational cues, suggesting that they might be more likely to be carried away by the moment, a response that is associated with not using condoms. Overall, impulsivity, emotionality, and sensation seeking are strongly related to sexual risk-taking, but the person, the situation, and the relationship context all matter (Cooper, 2010; Donohew et al., 2000).

Such people are also generally more extroverted, less restrained, and more likely to have sex earlier in relationships, to have more than one sexual partner at a time, and to be in relationships that are less committed (Simpson & Gangestad, 1991). According to an ethological explanation, such people prefer physical attractiveness and are more sexually active, compared to people who care more about partner *investment* and so are more sexually selective (and inhibited). The people who are more sexually active and indiscriminate do not necessarily have a greater sex drive or greater sexual satisfaction, however.

Psychoticism is also related to sexual risk. Indeed, as Eysenck conceived the dimension, this is one of the core components of psychoticism. Fontaine (1994) used the Eysenck Personality Questionnaire to examine the personalities and sexual activities of men aged 18 to 35 and found that high scores on psychoticism were related to risky sexual practices such as having unprotected sex and having sex with bisexual, intravenous drug-using, or multiple partners.

One study examined the relationship, across the life span, between teenage sexual activity and subsequent mortality risk, using data derived from the archival prospective study begun in the 1920s by Lewis Terman. Teenagers who were more sexually active were at increased mortality risk years later. It turned out that, again consistent with Eysenck's concept of psychoticism, such sexually active teenagers were also lower on conscientiousness, greater abusers of alcohol in adulthood, and less willing to get a good education (Seldin, Friedman, & Martin, 2002).

How is it that sex, which we most often identify with love (or at the very least, with caring), can become a venue of anger, force, and violence? Neil Malamuth and his associates have investigated the types of personality characteristics that are associated with sexual aggression toward women and with sexual violence such as rape. They have found that men's level of dominance, hostility toward women, favorable attitudes toward violence against women, and higher levels of psychoticism predict sexual aggression (Barnes et al., 1984; Hunter, Figueredo, & Malamuth, 2010; Malamuth, 1986). In other words, sexual aggressors tend to be cold, impulsive, tough, and cruel. They may be odd but charming like Ted Bundy. Serial killers are often found to have collections of pornography: Of course, most people with pornography are not predators or killers, but pornography consumption is a significant predictor of sexual aggression (Vega & Malamuth, 2007).

A scale such as the Attraction to Sexual Aggression is somewhat capable of identifying men who are apt to engage in sexual violence toward women (Malamuth, 1989; Malamuth, Huppin, & Paul, 2005). Such men tend to believe in rape myths (e.g., that women enjoy rape), and they have a strong need for dominance. For Freud, it was clear that such men had not resolved their Oedipal complex nor developed an adequate superego; and for the neo-analysts, it was clear that such men faced deficient parenting. From a cognitive viewpoint, such men may lack an understanding of the humanness of others. From a trait point of view, they lack empathic abilities and are oblivious to many of the rules that govern society. To a humanist, they are simply immoral. In all these cases, there is agreement that it is difficult to change a sexual predator. Increasingly, when they are convicted of felonies, these men are being sentenced to life in prison. Society's views are coming into line with psychology's views.

In sum, most perspectives on love agree that it has a strong biological basis, presumably one that is related to the benefits for reproductive success of being sexually

attracted to and supportive of a mate. This explanation, however, is a long way from saying that love is predominantly biology. The precise influences of biology on love are still poorly understood.

In Western industrialized society, the romantic ideal tells us that we should marry someone with whom we fall passionately in love. Yet there is also much evidence that love can grow out of a meaningful friendship. Many of the wisest personality psychologists have emphasized that true love, long-lasting love, thrives best when it is part of an unselfish, mature concern for another.

Summary and Conclusion

This chapter attempts to bring to life the eight basic aspects of personality by considering some of their implications for understanding love and hate. We are shocked but fascinated by serial killers, who kill victims one by one, and by brutal dictators, who kill by the thousands. They show us the truly evil side of humanity. Yet we are also inspired by the devotion and true love of which people are capable. We have seen that a simple explanation of these complex motivations and behaviors is not possible.

Evolutionary (ethological) approaches characterize aggression as the product of adaptive processes; that is, hatred is innate because aggression was adaptive in the evolution of our species. These natural aggressive tendencies may be distorted and sometimes expressed inappropriately and grotesquely due to biological aberrations, drug abuse, or unusual environmental circumstances. However, why are there so many individual and cross-cultural differences in aggressiveness? All people have a capacity for hatred but the capacity is usually not realized to any significant degree.

For Freud, aggression is ultimately traced to defense mechanisms against the death instinct—thanatos. It may be displaced onto others, projected onto others, or repressed, only to emerge in drastic or dramatic ways. But for the neo-analysts, hatred arises from the insecurities, anxieties, and traumas of childhood, especially in parent–child relations. In a world of stable parenting and emotional health, aggression would be rare. For trait theorists, aggressive or domineering patterns become defining styles of how the individual interacts with his or her world.

In the humanistic–existential view, aggression results from the thwarting of the natural tendencies toward fulfillment, as a result of the combination of fail-

ures in family life, societal life, and individual choices. Also nonbiological are the learning approaches, which examine the reward structures and models of aggression that show and sustain violence.

In the cognitive approach, hateful people are often characterized by cognitive simplicity. This leads them to dismiss whole groups of people as "enemies." Violent criminals are more likely to perceive events as threatening and to see other people as having hostile intentions; psychopaths have deficits in the processing of both social and cognitive tasks. These views imply that aggression can be lessened as people are taught to take a more accurate and benign view of their worlds. Given the dramatic cultural differences in aggression, nonbiological influences must play an important role. The interaction of personality and situation provides a good approach to addressing the sources of terrorism.

Is love, not hate, the most potent motivator of behavior? Evolutionary psychologists propose that there are different characteristics for which males and females look when selecting a mate because of their different biological roles during reproduction. The male is attracted to females who have physical characteristics indicating their suitability to conceive and carry a healthy offspring through a successful pregnancy. But because the female's energies are concentrated on child care, she requires a male who can and will provide her with the necessities of life, such as food and shelter, while her offspring are children. Love derives from its adaptive value in promoting survival.

For Freud, what we do for love is really a fulfillment of the sexual drives of the id. Freud's successors, such as the object relations theorists, emphasize the importance of the first mother–child relationship, stating that the child internalizes the nature of this relationship, which becomes in a sense the prototype or template for future loves. But according to Erikson and other ego psychologists, only those who have found their identity will be able to experience true intimacy—and love. Those whose ego identity is not complete will either remain isolated or will engage in false relationships—promiscuous or shallow.

The humanistic personality psychologists devote considerable energy to explaining love, and they disdain the simple behaviorist view that we love someone who provides us with reinforcements. In mature love, each partner is caring for the other. Mature lovers feel a sense of responsibility toward each other, but love is freely given, without selfish conditions. For Maslow, "being" lovers (but not "deficiency" lovers) help their partners toward self-actualization. The existentialists like Rollo May emphasize the importance of will: Love needs will (or effort, volition) to be lasting and meaningful.

Customs and feelings about love and marriage vary significantly across time and culture, warning us against simple acceptance of our own common views about love. Loneliness, sexual promiscuity, and sexual violence are complex issues at the intersection of love and hate, and they are fruitfully viewed from multiple perspectives to be fully comprehended.

We have endeavored to apply the eight basic perspectives on personality to important topics of individual differences: male–female differences, health differences, cultural differences, and love–hate differences. We have seen that personality is by no means a dry academic exercise or a historical curiosity. Rather the study of personality goes to the heart of what it means to be a person.

■ Key Theorists

Seymour Feshbach   Melanie Klein   Neil Malamuth
David Buss   Phillip Shaver

■ Key Concepts and Terms

ethological theories   evolutionary psychology
thanatos   romantic attachment styles
antisocial personality disorder   "being" love versus "deficiency" love
ruling type   Erich Fromm's types of love
authoritarian personality type   Rollo May's types of love
cognitive simplicity   Attraction to Sexual Aggression scale

Where Will We Find Personality?

Where Will We Find Personality?

The Brave New World of Personality
Designer Personalities ■ A Utopian World versus Abuse of Reward and Punishment ■ Genetic Superhumans ■ Can I Change My Personality?

The Eight Perspectives Revisited
Is There One Correct Perspective? ■ Are There Exactly Eight Perspectives? ■ Can the Perspectives Be Merged?

What is the future of personality psychology? Will new combinations of gene therapies, psychotropic drugs, computer-augmented brains, refined conditioning techniques, and strict control over the situational environment mean that the future human being is a well-behaving cyborg or android that now seems so far, far away? Will we eliminate hatred and war, creating loving families realizing their human potential? Will humanity fade into robotics?

Why would anyone want to study personality psychology anyway? Why would students take a course about personality when they could spend time learning useful computer or accounting or engineering skills, or becoming culturally enriched through the study of literature, music, or art? Who is interested in what makes people tick? Although there is not much research directly on this topic, some related findings have emerged from the California Psychological Inventory (CPI), a well-constructed personality test (Gough, 1987). One of the CPI scales is termed "psychological-mindedness"; it identifies individuals interested in the needs, motives, and experiences of others. Such people also may be good judges of what others feel. There is some evidence that this tendency toward psychological-mindedness can be improved through study (perhaps through taking courses in personality!) and that it is predictive of a more mature and wise adulthood (Donohue, 1995; Gough, Fox, & Hall, 1972; Helson & Roberts, 1994; Staudinger, Lopez, & Baltes, 1997).

Personality psychology has implications for a wider philosophical view of what it means to be a person. We have considered age-old issues of human nature, but we have done so in terms of the conceptual and empirical advances of psychology through the beginning of the twenty-first century. In this vein, it is not at all surprising that many of the leading contributors to the field of personality were not content to limit their writings to probing individual differences, processes of change, or enlightening psychotherapies; but rather, they went on to articulate visions for creating restructured societies, utopias, and new worlds. The process continues.

The Brave New World of Personality

Three dramatic scientific developments are changing the way psychologists think about what it means to be a person. First, better understanding of brain biochemistry may raise the possibility of chemically controlled designer personalities. Second, more accurate control of environmental contingencies will improve society's ability to control individual behavior through **social engineering**. Third, better understanding of the human genetic code may lead to a dramatic change in our understanding of and control over the genetic bases of personality, so-called behavioral genomics (Plomin, & McGuffin, 2003).

Social Engineering
Control of environmental contingencies to influence individual behavior

Designer Personalities

Since the beginnings of humankind, people have used psychoactive substances such as alcohol and opium to influence the brain and thereby influence behavior. For example, the Aztecs and other early and Native Americans used peyote, a small, spineless, psychedelic cactus native to Texas and Mexico. How and why such substances affected personality were not of much concern; they were consumed either as part of a religious experience or for recreation. Now, however, breakthroughs in understanding brain chemistry—the neurotransmitters through which brain cells communicate—are making possible drugs that, in a targeted fashion, scientifically change the nature of who we are.

Research in this new field—termed *social neuroscience*—began as an attempt to help people suffering from mental illnesses such as depression, chronic anxiety, and schizophrenia. A century ago, Freud highly recommended the use of cocaine and used it himself (it was even one of Coca-Cola's original ingredients), until its addictive qualities became recognized. Amphetamines to treat depression, and tranquilizers like Valium to treat anxiety, have been available for half a century. They are heavily prescribed legally, and heavily abused illegally. But now, designer drugs are being synthesized to create designer personalities. Perhaps the best example of this new type of drug is Prozac (fluoxetine).

Prozac blocks the reabsorption of the neurotransmitter serotonin in the brain and thus enhances the user's mood and alters emotional reaction patterns. Prozac was created to treat severe depression. It is now being used, however, by people who want to overcome a wide range of perceived problems ranging from shyness

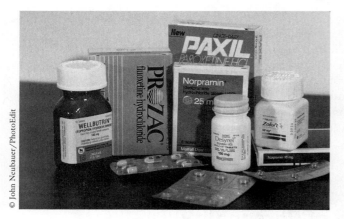

■ Pharmaceuticals used to alter behavior.

Lysergic Acid Diethylamide (LSD)
Hallucinogenic drug derived from a fungus that evokes dreamlike changes in perception and thought

and moodiness to a tendency to be obsessive. Because Prozac seems to interfere with obsessive-compulsive tendencies, it is even being tried as a treatment for compulsive gambling and for lack of concentration. Although the number of people taking Prozac in an attempt to "improve" their usual personality is not well documented, the number seems substantial—millions of prescriptions are written for Prozac every year. A popular book, *Listening to Prozac*, describes how Prozac works wonders as a mood enhancer for grumpy people (Kramer, 1993).

Around 1960, Timothy Leary was a well-established psychology professor at Harvard University, making important contributions to our understanding of the interpersonal nature of personality. Turned on by an anthropologist to "magic mushrooms," Leary and others then began studying and advocating the use of the psychedelic drug **lysergic acid diethylamide (LSD)** for its potential to expand the mind and promote creativity and well-being. A fungus derivative, LSD is a hallucinogenic drug that evokes dreamlike changes in perception and thought. Hollywood psychiatrists jumped on the bandwagon; one of the more famous patients to use LSD during therapy was actor Cary Grant ("Psyche in 3-D," 1960). Unfortunately, many users jumped out windows. As LSD's effects—among them, delusions and bizarre behaviors—became better understood, Harvard fired Leary and LSD was outlawed.

Most people agree that mind-altering drugs should indeed be used to treat patients with long-term clinical depression, who sit in their rooms crying miserably, incapacitated, unable to work or to lead anything approaching a normal life. But what about treating unhappiness, or poor concentration, or shyness? There is evidence that 10 to 30 percent of the population have a biological tendency toward shyness. Should we boost their sociability with pills?

With the sophisticated understanding of personality developed in the preceding chapters, we can see that such a simple approach to the person is naïve and uninformed—such treatments by themselves will not prove effective over the long term. Personality is much more than the release of chemicals in the brain, although such elements of biology are surely very important. Personality is a function of many brain systems and has a cognitive aspect and a trait aspect. Personality depends heavily on learning, socialization, and the social situation. And who we are has an important spiritual element of freedom, consciousness, and nobility, which is overlooked at our peril.

What kind of world would it be if we all had our brain chemistries continually adjusted so that no one would yell at you, no one would rush to get ahead of you, no one would cry, and no one would worry whether she had turned the oven off? For every psychosocial problem, a pill would be there. Further, all artists could take creativity pills for enhanced performance, and academics could take intelligence pills for clear thinking. (Currently available, Aricept or donepezil is a prescription drug that inhibits the breakdown of acetylcholine and is used to treat mild to moderate dementia. And many students use amphetamines such as Adderall to concentrate

© John Neubauer/PhotoEdit

better, despite the risk of side effects.) Even if such a world of drug-shaped people does not sound so appealing, the issues will not simply go away. Drugs that alter our thinking and feeling are now being created at a rapid pace, and society will have to decide if, when, and how to use them.

A Utopian World versus Abuse of Reward and Punishment

Henry David Thoreau (1854) emphasized the freedom and dignity of the individual, arguing that each person should march in step with the music that he or she hears, seeking simplicity, integrity, and individuality. In B. F. Skinner's version of utopia, the perfect community is one in which convention and coercive societal restrictions are likewise eliminated, but are replaced by a reward system that shapes people's desires to fit the community's needs. Because freedom and dignity are seen to be only illusions, Skinner can move beyond them to a place where society pleasantly manipulates the work force through positive reinforcement. All tasks are willingly done because cleaning sewers is more highly rewarded than tending community flower gardens.

Skinner's ideas have sometimes made their way into the modern work force, where the threat of being fired for low-quality work has been superseded by enticing incentives for high-quality work—bonus resort meetings for high sales output, special health-club or bathroom privileges, or even written notes of praise from the boss. Inner-city schoolchildren at high risk of academic failure may be paid for reading books. Preschoolers may be given candies or trinkets when their behavior conforms to teacher desires. Advertising campaigns are designed on the basis of extensive studies of social learning. (Ironically, even Thoreau's Walden Pond is often used in tacky advertising campaigns.) Especially effective rewards can be offered as more and more is known about the individual's earlier inclinations and past experiences. Corporate computer banks are rapidly filling with such information about each person in the country. Computer cookies on your laptop track the Internet sites you have visited. All sorts of websites influence you to reveal your valuable personal information.

© Spencer Grant/PhotoEdit

■ Experts at interrogation generally oppose torture, feeling that better information can be gathered by using a deep knowledge of personality and motivation to elicit desired disclosures. As personality-based interrogation techniques become more and more effective, should limits or oversights be placed on these procedures? Should they be available to advertisers and salespeople?

Less effective means of control—coercion, fear, and punishment—are still a popular force to contend with, as there is strong public support for high-security prisons with hard labor, long prison terms, corporal (physical) punishment of unruly students, fines and taxes, and spread of sophisticated guns and other weapons of self-defense. Although much is known about shaping personality through learning and rewards, it remains to be seen which approach will come to dominate society. The smart money is on the social engineering—understanding each individual and then targeting what you will want to do, who you will vote for, and what you will buy.

In our discussion of designer personalities, we posed some questions about what a world ruled by drugs would look like. Now we ask, what if everyone's behavior were continually shaped by environmental contingencies? For every psychosocial problem, a new conditioning regimen would be there. Even if such a world does not seem appealing, the issues that arise must still be confronted. We must become and remain educated about personality.

Cartesian Dualism
The concept proposed by René Descartes that there is a separation of the mind and body

■ Are parents willing to select desired characteristics of their offspring? In a survey (Clifford, 2001), almost 60 percent of those who responded would select for kindness, almost 30 percent for intelligence. Good looks and athletic ability were under 15 percent. Would you genetically alter a fetus? If the next generation were kinder and smarter, would our world be a better place?

Genetic Superhumans

At least some manic-depressive personalities clearly have a strong genetic basis. Further, some of the genetic bases for thousands of diseases are being documented (Online Mendelian Inheritance in Man [www.ncbi.nlm.nih.gov/omim]; McBride et al., 2010). As more and more is discovered about the human genome, there will inevitably be implications for our understanding of the genetic bases of personality. How genes affect behavior—behavioral genomics—(Plomin & Crabbe, 2000; Plomin, Haworth & Davis, 2009) is perhaps the greatest challenge in the brave new world of personality. For some researchers, the ultimate goal of the research is human genetic therapy—manipulation of the genes—just as is now commonplace with certain crop plants.

The biological approach to personality is often misunderstood. Much of this confusion can be traced back to the perceived separation between the mind and the body, forcefully analyzed in the early seventeenth century by René Descartes (1961). The separation, known as **Cartesian dualism**, grew out of a worldview in which the life of the spirit, derived from God, was distinct from the goings-on of the earthly world. However, since the time of Darwin, we have known that the "mind" must have a physical basis. As we have seen, this does not mean that personality can be "reduced" to biology. Take, for example, the case of people who have gene-based mood swings. There must be physiological correlates of these mood swings in the person's brain. This does not in any way mean that the person's moods are not affected by her perceptions, her interactions with her friends and family, her early childhood experiences, her religious beliefs, her learning experiences in specific situations.

The genetic code affects the development of our brains, the rest of our nerves, and our hormones and neurotransmitters. In other words, the genetic code affects the biological bases of our consistencies in behavior. The activity levels of our nervous systems, in turn, likely account for much of the temperamental differences seen in infants and young children. This does not mean that all of personality is inherited. With the "unraveling" of the human genome in the year 2000, it does seem likely, however, that the biological tendencies that underlie some of our traits will increasingly be documented as more and more of the human genome is explored. Presumably, some of these tendencies will soon be changeable through genetic engineering; but who will decide which, and whose?

What kind of world would it be if all fetuses had their future behavior programmed by genetic engineering? For every psychosocial problem, a new genetic intervention would be designed, just as we now engineer corn seeds to be healthier and more productive. Even if a genetically engineered world sounds no more appealing than a world of designer personalities or a world of conditioning-shaped utopias, the issues will not just disappear. We must be educated about what it means to be a person.

In our rapidly changing world, other dramatic new conceptions of personality will also undoubtedly arise. For example, there is increasing computer modeling of brain function and behavior, and there are, of course, many computer-based technologies that change our daily behaviors. However, all these changes can be thoughtfully evaluated and understood if one has a good understanding of the basic aspects of personality.

Can I Change My Personality?

When students first enroll in a course on personality, they are often very interested in personality change. They want to become a more extroverted or charismatic person; or they want their boyfriend or girlfriend to become more devoted; or they want to avoid becoming like their parents. By now it should be clear that there are no simple roads to personality change in adulthood, but some some tips are available and some change is possible, indeed is often inevitable.

As we have just seen, although some dramatic personality change is possible through drugs, extreme conditioning, and genomics, such drastic interventions are usually not what people have in mind for personality change for themselves. It turns out that more gradual and fulfilling change is indeed possible, but it is not easy. People can learn to change how they think about things, what they do in their daily habits, their deeper beliefs, and the people and situations they associate with. For example, a student who felt lonely, unappreciated, and unattractive in high school might indeed begin to remake his or her personality in college. Such a person might start interpreting the world in a new light; might improve nutrition and physical activity; might join clubs or volunteer groups composed of friendly, decent people; might learn and practice new skills like public speaking; might join a suitable religious or ethical community; and, if necessary, might talk to a counselor about problems with parents, peers, and so on. Because personality is multifaceted, effective personality change takes a multipronged effort.

The Eight Perspectives Revisited

We have studied personality in terms of eight basic perspectives. We believe that to fully appreciate modern understandings of personality, it is important to be well grounded in the rich intellectual history of the field. We have looked at the psychoanalytic aspects of personality, which focus on the complex inner workings of the mind; the ego aspects, which focus on the self; the biological perspective, which is currently witnessing great advances in the understanding of evolution and neuroscience; the behaviorist approach, which brings to bear the insights of learning theories; the cognitive perspective, which relies on the insights of modern experimental psychology into human thought processes; the trait approach, which looks for underlying consistencies in the individual; the humanistic and existential approach, which draws on the rich traditions of the humanities in understanding human existence and thriving; and the interactionist perspective, which looks at the person in the environment. Table 1 reviews these perspectives.

Is There One Correct Perspective?

Which perspective is most correct? There is no simple answer to this question. Theories that lead to testable hypotheses can be evaluated by collecting data, but the eight basic perspectives are not scientific theories. It is very important to note, however, that the theories that grow out of these perspectives can indeed be tested, and as we have seen, some theories about particular aspects of personality are preferable to others. We have used empirical data to show that some predictions and hypotheses about personality are false, some are true, and many need further evaluation.

Do we need to choose our favorite perspective the way we might choose a religious affiliation or political philosophy? Not necessarily. Being open to different assumptions about human nature can expand theoretical potentials as well as facilitate discovery of problems with entrenched assumptions (Gergen, 2001). It is important to understand the dangers and weaknesses of each perspective, so that when we hear about a "new" idea regarding personality, we can thoughtfully evaluate (in an informed way) its potential for good or bad, success or failure. For example, we might be suspicious of a new "miracle" drug that claims to cure school-behavior problems in children, and we might be equally suspicious of a "miracle" behavior therapy for curing marital conflict. We should be skeptical of a questionnaire that claims to assess our "money personality" and advises us how to invest, and we should wonder about a "dream and consciousness" seminar that promises to erase our neuroses and heal our diseases. To be sure, we should not dismiss all such approaches as inherently valueless. Rather, we should be able to evaluate such ideas and techniques from the perspective of a highly educated and sophisticated person who has achieved an advanced and complex understanding of what it means to be a person.

Are There Exactly Eight Perspectives?

Are eight basic perspectives too few or too many? This is a matter of personal preference. Rather than arguing about the correct number of perspectives and about which theorists should be grouped together into a given perspective, it is more important to understand what each perspective has to offer and its strengths and weaknesses.

Because all the perspectives are trying to explain patterns in people's lives, they necessarily will have some overlap with one another. It is interesting to note that some early reviewers wrote comments like, "I knew they (the authors) were really Freudians at heart"; or "The text is sympathetic to the humanistic approaches"; or "Great knowledge of and influence by the biological perspective"; and so on. In other words, readers could detect that we find something very valuable in each perspective. But it should be clear that we do not believe that any single perspective provides the royal road to understanding personality.

Can the Perspectives Be Merged?

Should we try to merge these eight perspectives into one grand approach? There are certainly ways in which this could be attempted. For example, we could search for the evolutionary and biological bases of psychoanalytic defense mechanisms like repression (Nesse, 1990). Indeed, Freud was trained as a biologist and would probably feel quite at home today in a modern biological or evolutionary perspective. Notions of the unconscious have much in common with modern cognitive approaches.

Or we might search for the cognitive or biological bases for the Big Five or Big Three trait approaches to personality. Traits are presumably based in inherent perceptual or temperamental differences. Or the social learning approaches might be integrated with the cognitive approaches. Both emphasize experimental study of thinking and learning.

Work from the learning and behaviorist perspective fits nicely into current notions that personality manifests itself differently in different situations. Similarly, work from the ego perspective overlaps with modern interactionist approaches that propose we have different selves in different situations. Humanistic and existential notions of freedom and self-fulfillment echo notions of motives and skills, not only elevating human dignity and free will but also in forcefully attacking the behaviorist ideas of Skinner. The existential perspective is also, of course, concerned with concepts of the self. In short, there is plenty of overlap among perspectives.

However, often these various perspectives cannot and perhaps should not be merged; it may be that personality is too complex to be understood from any single perspective. Just as biology needs different levels of scientific analysis—the biochemical level, the cellular level, the organ level, the organism level, and the population level—so, too, personality psychology needs different sorts of analyses to

■ **TABLE I**   The Eight Basic Aspects of Personality

Perspective	Free will?	Structures	Key Concepts	Key Methods
Psychoanalytic	No	Id, ego, superego	Psychosexual stages, Oedipus complex, defense mechanisms	Free association, dream analysis
Neo-Analytic/Ego	Usually no	Unconscious, conscious self, social self, archetype	Identity; sociocultural influences on self-esteem; life goals	Varies from free association to situational and autobiographical, with an emphasis on self-concept
Biological	No	Genes, instincts, brain structure	Evolution, hormones, neurotransmitters	Neuroscience, heritability studies
Behaviorist	No	External regularities in rewards	Reinforcement, conditioning, learning, extinction	Experimental analysis of animal learning
Cognitive	Sometimes yes	Constructs, expectancies, cognitions, schemas	Perception, observation, human as scientist/decision maker	Decision tasks, attribution experiments, computer simulation of personality
Trait	Sometimes yes	Traits, motives, skills	Basic dimensions of personality; unique personal styles and dispositions	Factor analysis, self-reports, testing of styles and skills
Humanistic	Yes	Spirit, being-in-the-world	Self-actualization, alienation, well being	Interviews, self-exploration, art, biographical analysis of creativity
Interactionist	Usually yes	Predispositions, situations	Person-in-situation	Observation and testing of cross-situational consistency; classifying situations

Vision of Utopia	Some Leading Theorists	Key Strength	Key Weakness
Unconflicted psychosexual development, mature socialization of id instincts	S. Freud	Attention to unconscious influences; importance of sexual drives even in non-sexual spheres	Many ideas superseded by more modern research on the brain; speculations often unverified or unverifiable; influenced by sexist assumptions of the times
Mature self, adapted to the many situations to be faced	C. Jung, A. Adler, K. Horney, E. Erikson	Emphasis on the self as it struggles to cope with emotions and drives on the inside and the demands of others on the outside	Sometimes a hodgepodge of ideas from different traditions; difficult to test in rigorous manner
Improvement through medication of the brain and gene manipulation or selection, understanding how our biological inheritance affects society	I. Pavlov, R. Plomin, H. Eysenck, D. Buss, M. Daly	Focuses on tendencies and limits imposed by biological inheritance, can be combined with other approaches	Tends to minimize human potential for growth and change, serious danger of misuse by politicians who oversimplify its findings
Conditioning and reinforcing of individual behaviors so the person wants to do what benefits society	B. F. Skinner, J. Dollard, N. Miller	Can force a more scientific analysis of the learning experiences that shape personality	May dehumanize unique human potentials through comparisons to rats and pigeons, may ignore advances from cognitive and social psychology
Rational decision making through understanding thought processes, computer simulation of personality	G. Kelly, A. Bandura	Captures active nature of human thought and uses modern knowledge from cognitive psychology	Often ignores unconscious and emotional aspects of personality
Understanding unity of each individual, accurate assessment of abilities	G. Allport, R. B. Cattell, H. Eysenck, P.T. Costa Jr., R. R. McCrae	Good individual assessment techniques; captures personality in 5 or so basic dimensions	May reach too far in trying to capture individual in a few ways, may label people on the basis of test scores
Self-actualization; overcoming existential crises; love and dignity	A. Maslow, C. Rogers, E. Fromm, E. Diener	Appreciates the spiritual nature of a person, emphasizes struggles for self-fulfillment and dignity	May avoid quantification and scientific method needed for science of personality
Understanding how the individual creates and maintains appropriate or inappropriate roles and identities	H. Murray, H. S. Sullivan, W. Mischel, A. Caspi	Understands that we are different selves in different situations	No good ways to define situations or to study the many complexities of interactions

understand different sorts of issues. Early concepts can be refined, not totally discarded, as new insights emerge from research.

In studying personality, we have seen that there is no simple understanding of the self (ego). There are aspects of ourselves that are hidden from our view, but yet our conscious self-concept is an important element of who we are. Furthermore, although extroverts can act in an introverted fashion and vice versa, people do maintain a certain consistency over time. Although there are striking differences across cultures and culture must be considered when studying personality, the nature of an individual can be understood across great reaches of time and place. It is also now clear that, to some extent, we are different people in different situations; that is, our social self continually redefines and re-creates itself as we take on new roles and negotiate new social identities throughout life.

There is a constant tension between notions of self-fulfillment and notions of deterministic control. We have seen that there are many ways in which who we are and what we do is affected by forces beyond our control and often beyond our knowledge—by our genes, and by our early socialization and rewards, and by our thoughts and inclinations, and by the demands of the situation. On the other hand, there is good reason to assume that people have a creative and spiritual nature, and sometimes make conscious choices toward spiritual self-fulfillment or acts of nobility. Perhaps the actress Mae West expressed this unresolved tension best in the film *My Little Chickadee* (1940): "I generally avoid temptation unless I can't resist it."

In studying personality, we have seen that it is necessary to study both the individual and the group. For example, women share some qualities with other women, but each woman is different from all other women. As Gordon Allport (1955) noted, most of psychology searches for general processes and laws of behaviors, but personality psychology places major emphasis on individual differences—the individual is central. As Allport repeatedly asked, "How shall a life history be written?"

Summary and Conclusion

Why would anyone take a course about personality? As we have seen, our knowledge of "human nature" affects many of the most important decisions we make as individuals and as a society. Further, the questions of personality derive from fascinating, age-old intellectual puzzles. But where philosophers relied on theology, observation, and logical analysis, personality psychologists turn to systematic empirical investigations of the correlates and causes of individual differences.

Many people interested in personality will think about ways to improve society, or even to create a utopia. The goal may be designer personalities or brave new worlds. We've speculated about what the world would look like if everyone had his or her brain chemistries continually adjusted by medications, if

behavior was continually shaped by government or corporate-run environmental contingencies, and if all fetuses had their future behaviors programmed by genetic engineering. Such notions are not so far-fetched. Politicians and business leaders around the world are toying with these concepts even now. Other dramatic new conceptions of personality will also undoubtedly arise, such as using computer modeling of brain function and behavior to "improve" society. These changes can be thoughtfully evaluated and understood if and only if one has a good understanding of the basic aspects of personality.

We have studied personality in terms of eight basic perspectives. We have seen that there is no simple answer as to which perspective is correct—each has its strengths and weaknesses. To some extent, the eight perspectives overlap. This is not surprising because all are attempting to explain the same thing—personality.

Some readers might be more comfortable integrating various ideas and findings into your own theory of what it means to be human and why each person is unique. In our view, the most important caution is that the shortcomings and dangers of each approach not be overlooked; there is a significant chance of harmful, or even evil, results when the college-educated among us do not fully appreciate the implications of each view of humankind.

Personality has not yet yielded all its secrets. They will be unearthed only as the best personality students demand the integration of complex theory and solid empirical data. For these reasons, personality psychology can be one of the most challenging yet rewarding areas of academic study.

References

References

Abelson, R. P. (1981). Psychological status of the script concept. *American Psychologist, 36*, 715–729.

Abramson, L. Y., Metalsky, G. I., & Alloy, L. B. (1989). Hopelessness depression: A theory-based subtype of depression. *Psychological Review, 96*(2), 358–372.

Adam, T. C., & Epel, E. S. (2007). Stress, eating and the reward system. *Physiology and Behavior, 91*, 449–458.

Adams, D. B., Boudreau, W., Cowan, C. W., & Kokonowski, C. (1993). Offense produced by chemical stimulation of the anterior hypothalamus of the rat. *Physiology & Behavior, 53*, 1127–1132.

Adams, H. E., Wright, L. W., & Lohr, B. A. (1996). Is homophobia associated with homosexual arousal? *Journal of Abnormal Psychology, 105*, 440–445.

Adler, A. (1930). *The neurotic constitution; outlines of a comparative individualistic psychology and psychotherapy* (B. Glueck & J. E. Lind, Trans.). New York: Dodd, Mead.

Adler, A. (1959). *The practice and theory of individual psychology.* Totowa, NJ: Littlefield Adams.

Adler, N. E., Boyce, T., Chesney, M. A., & Cohen, S. (1994). Socioeconomic status and health: The challenge of the gradient. *American Psychologist, 49*, 15–24.

Adorno, T. W., Frenkel-Brunswik, E., Levinson, D., & Sanford, N. (1950). *The authoritarian personality.* New York: Harper.

Aiken, L. R. (1999). *Personality assessment: Methods and practices* (3rd ed.). Seattle, WA: Hogrefe & Huber.

Ainsworth, M. S. (1979). Infant-mother attachment. *American Psychologist, 34*, 932–937.

Ainsworth, M. S., & Bowlby, J. (1991). An ethological approach to personality development. *American Psychologist, 46*, 333–341.

Albright, L., Kenny, D. A., & Malloy, T. E. (1988). Consensus in personality judgments at zero acquaintance. *Journal of Personality and Social Psychology, 55*, 387–395.

Alessandri, S. M., Sullivan, M. W., Bendersky, M., & Lewis, M. (1995). Temperament in cocaine-exposed infants. In M. Lewis & M. Bendersky (Eds.), *Mothers, babies, and cocaine: The role of toxins in development* (pp. 273–286). Hillsdale, NJ: Erlbaum.

Alexander, F. (1950). *Psychosomatic medicine.* New York: Norton.

Alexander, K. W., Quas, J. A., Goodman, G. S., Ghetti, S., Edelstein, R. S., Redlich, A. D., et al. (2005). Traumatic impact predicts long-term memory for documented child sexual abuse. *Psychological Science, 16*, 33–40.

Allen, B. A., & Boykin, A. W. (1992). African-American children and the educational process: Alleviating cultural discontinuity through prescriptive pedagogy. *School Psychology Review, 21*, 586–596.

Allik, J., & McCrae, R. R. (2004). Escapable conclusions: Toomela (2003) and the universality of trait structure. *Journal of Personality and Social Psychology, 87*, 261–265.

Allison, T. L. (2000). *The good gay citizen: A cross-cultural analysis of the rhetoric of good gay citizenship* (Doctoral dissertation, University of California, San Diego, Literature, 2000). UMI No. AAT 9989256.

Allport, G. W. (1937). *Personality: A psychological interpretation.* New York: Holt, Rinehart & Winston.

Allport, G. W. (1954). *The nature of prejudice.* Cambridge, MA: Addison-Wesley.

Allport, G. W. (1955). *Becoming: Basic considerations for a psychology of personality.* New Haven, CT: Yale University Press.

Allport, G. W. (1961). *Pattern and growth in personality.* New York: Holt, Rinehart & Winston.

Allport, G. W. (1965). *Letters from Jenny.* New York: Harcourt Brace.

Allport, G. W. (1966). Traits revisited. *American Psychologist, 21*, 1–10.

Allport, G. W. (1968). *The person in psychology.* Boston: Beacon Press.

Allport, G. W., & Odbert, H. S. (1936). Trait names: A psycho-lexical study. *Psychological Monographs, 47*(211), 171.

Allport, G. W., & Vernon, P. E. (1933). *Studies in expressive movement.* New York: Macmillan.

Amato, P. R., & Keith, B. (1991). Parental divorce and the well-being of children: A meta-analysis. *Psychological Bulletin, 110*, 26–46.

Ambady, N., & Rosenthal, R. (1993). Half a minute: Predicting teacher evaluations from thin slices of nonverbal behavior and physical attractiveness. *Journal of Personality and Social Psychology, 64*, 431–441.

American Psychiatric Association. (1994). *Diagnostic and statistical manual of mental disorders* (4th ed.). Washington, DC: Author.

Andersen, S. M., & Berk, M. S. (1998). The social-cognitive model of transference: Experiencing past relationships in the present. *Current Directions in Psychological Science, 7*, 109–115.

Andersen, S. M., Reznik, I., & Glassman, N. S. (2005). The unconscious relational self. In R. Hassin, J. S. Uleman, & J. A. Bargh (Eds.), *The new unconscious* (pp. 421–481). New York: Oxford University Press.

Anderson, C. A. (2004). An update on the effects of violent video games. *Journal of Adolescence, 27*, 113–122.

Anderson, C. A., Berkowitz, L., Donnerstein, E., Huesmann, L. R., Johnson, J. D., Linz, D., et al. (2003). The influence of media violence on youth. *Psychological Science in the public interest, 4*, 81–110.

Anderson, M. C., Ochsner, K. N., Kuhl, B., Cooper, J., Robertson, E., Gabrieli, S. W., et al. (2004). Neural systems underlying the suppression of unwanted memories. *Science, 303*(5655), 232–235.

Antonovsky, A. (1979). *Health, stress, and coping.* San Francisco: Jossey-Bass.

Antonovsky, A. (1987). *Unraveling the mystery of health: How people manage stress and stay well.* San Francisco: Jossey-Bass.

Appelbaum, P. S., Uyehara, L. A., & Elin, M. R. (Eds.). (1997). *Trauma and memory: Clinical and legal controversies.* New York: Oxford University Press.

Apter, A., Plutchik, R., Sevy, S., Korn, M. L., Brown, S., & van Praag, H. (1989). Defense mechanisms in risk of suicide and risk of violence. *American Journal of Psychiatry, 146*(8), 1027–1031.

Archer, J. (2006). Testosterone and human aggression: An evaluation of the challenge hypothesis. *Neuroscience & Biobehavioral Reviews, 30*(3), 319–345.

Archer, J. (2009). Does sexual selection explain human sex differences? *Behavioral and Brain Sciences, 32,* 249–311.

Ardrey, R. (1966). *The territorial imperative: A personal inquiry into the animal origins of property and nations.* New York: Atheneum.

Arenberg, I. K. (1990). Van Gogh had Ménière's disease and not epilepsy. *Journal of American Medical Association, 264,* 491–493.

Ariely, D. (2008). *Predictably irrational: The hidden forces that shape our decisions.* New York: HarperCollins.

Aronson, E. (1978). *The jigsaw classroom.* Beverly Hills, CA: Sage.

Asch, S. E. (1952). *Social psychology.* New York: Prentice Hall.

Asendorpf, J. B. (2006). Typeness of personality profiles: A continuous person-centred approach to personality data. *European Journal of Personality, 20,* 83–106.

Asendorpf, J. B., & Denissen, J. J. A. (2006). Predictive validity of personality types versus personality dimensions from early childhood to adulthood: Implications for the distinction between core and surface traits. *Merrill-Palmer Quarterly, 52,* 486–513.

Ash, M. G. (1992). Cultural contexts and scientific change in psychology: Kurt Lewin in Iowa. *American Psychologist, 47,* 198–207.

Ashton, M. C., & Lee, K. (2007). Empirical, theoretical, and practical advantages of the HEXACO model of personality structure. *Personality and Social Psychology Review, 11*(2), 150–166.

Atkinson, J. W. (Ed.) (1958). *Motives in fantasy, action, and society.* Princeton, NJ: Van Nostrand.

Auden, W. H. (1970). *Behaviorism. A certain world.* New York: Viking Press.

Auyeung, B., Baron-Cohen, S., Ashwin, E., Knickmeyer, R., Taylor, K., Hackett, G., & Hines, M. (2009). Fetal testosterone predicts sexually differentiated childhood behavior in girls and in boys. *Psychological Science, 20,* 144–148.

Bacon, F. (1625). *The essayes or counsels, civill and morall of Francis Lo. Verulam, Viscount St. Alban.* Newly enlarged. London: Printed by John Haviland for Hanna Barret & Richard Whitaker.

Baddeley, A. (1990). *Human memory: Theory and practice.* Boston: Allyn & Bacon.

Bailey, J. M., & Pillard R. C. (1991). A genetic study of male sexual orientation. *Archives of General Psychiatry, 48,* 1089–1096.

Bailey, J. M., & Pillard, R. C. (1995). Genetics of human sexual orientation. *Annual Review of Sex Research, VI,* 126–150.

Bailey, J. M., Dunne, M. P., & Martin, N. G. (2000). Genetic and environmental influences on sexual orientation and its correlates in an Australian twin sample. *Journal of Personality and Social Psychology, 78*(3), 524–525.

Baker, L. A., & Daniels, D. (1990). Nonshared environmental influences and personality differences in adult twins. *Journal of Personality and Social Psychology, 58,* 103–110.

Balcetis, E., & Dunning, D. (2010). Wishful seeing: More desired objects are seen as closer. *Psychological Science, 21,* 147–152.

Bales, R. F. (1958). Task roles and social roles in problem-solving groups. In E. E. Maccoby, T. M. Newcomb, & E. L. Hartley (Eds.), *Readings in social psychology* (3rd ed.). New York: Holt.

Bandura, A. (1969). *Principles of behavior modification.* New York: Holt, Rinehart & Winston.

Bandura, A. (1973). *Aggression: A social learning analysis.* Englewood Cliffs, NJ: Prentice-Hall.

Bandura, A. (1977a). Self-efficacy: Toward a unifying theory of behavioral change. *Psychological Review, 84*(2), 191–215.

Bandura, A. (1977b). *Social learning theory.* Englewood Cliffs, NJ: Prentice-Hall.

Bandura, A. (1978). The self system in reciprocal determinism. *American Psychologist, 33,* 344–358.

Bandura, A. (1982). Self-efficacy mechanism in human agency. *American Psychologist, 37*(2), 122–147.

Bandura, A. (1986). *Social foundations of thought and action.* Englewood Cliffs, NJ: Prentice-Hall.

Bandura, A. (1989). Human agency in social-cognitive theory. *American Psychologist, 44,* 1175–1184.

Bandura, A. (1992). Exercise of personal agency through the self-efficacy mechanism. In R. Schwarzer (Ed.), *Self-efficacy: Thought control of action* (pp. 3–38). Washington, DC: Hemisphere.

Bandura, A. (1997). *Self-efficacy: The exercise of control.* New York: W. H. Freeman.

Bandura, A. (1998). Health promotion from the perspective of social cognitive theory. *Psychology & Health, 13*(4), 623–649.

Bandura, A. (2000). Exercise of human agency through collective efficacy. *Current Directions in Psychological Science, 9,* 75–78.

Bandura, A. (2004). Swimming against the mainstream: The early years from chilly tributary to transformative mainstream. *Behaviour Research and Therapy, 42,* 613–630.

Bandura, A. (2006). Toward a psychology of human agency. *Perspectives on Psychological Science, 1,* 164–180.

Bandura, A., & Bussey, K. (2004). On broadening the cognitive, motivational, and sociostructural scope of theorizing about gender development and functioning: Comment on Martin, Ruble, and Szkrybalo. *Psychological Bulletin, 130*(5), 691–701.

Bandura, A., & Walters, R. H. (1963). *Social learning and personality development.* New York: Ronald Press.

Bargh, J. A., & Williams, E. L. (2006). The automaticity of social life. *Current Directions in Psychological Science, 15,* 1–4.

Barkley, R. A. (1997). Attention-deficit/hyperactivity disorder, self-regulation, and time: Toward a more comprehensive theory. *Journal of Developmental & Behavioral Pediatrics, 18*(4), 271–279.

Barkley, R. A., & Edwards, G. H. (1998). Attention Deficit/Hyperactivity Disorder (ADHD). In H. S. Friedman (Ed.), *Encyclopedia of mental health* (Vol. 1, pp. 169–182). San Diego, CA: Academic Press.

Barnes, G. E., Malamuth, N. M., & Check, J. V. (1984). Personality and sexuality. *Personality and Individual Differences, 5*(2), 159–172.

Barrick, M. R., & Mount, M. K. (1991). The Big Five personality dimensions and job performance: A meta-analysis. *Personnel Psychology, 44*(1), 1–26.

Barrow, R. (1995). Keep them bells a-tolling [Special issue: Canadian perspectives on *The Bell Curve*]. *Alberta Journal of Educational Research, 41*(3), 289–296.

Bartlett, F. C. (1932). *Remembering: A study in experimental and social psychology.* Cambridge, UK: Cambridge University Press.

Bartoshuk, L. M., Duffy, V. B., Fast, K., Kveton, J. F., Lucchina, L. A., Phillips, M. N., et al. (2001). What makes a supertaster? *Chemical Senses, 26,* 1074.

Bateson, D. J. (1995). How can *The Bell Curve* be taken seriously? [Special issue]. *Alberta Journal of Educational Research, 41*(3), 271–273.

Bauer, J. J., McAdams, D. P., & Sakaeda, A. R. (2005). Interpreting the good life: Growth memories in the lives of mature, happy people. *Journal of Personality and Social Psychology, 88*(1), 203–217.

Bauer, P. J. (2007). *Remembering the times of our lives: Memory in infancy and beyond.* Mahwah, NJ: Erlbaum.

Baum, A., & Andersen, S. M. (1999). Interpersonal roles in transference: Transient mood effects under the condition of significant-other resemblance. *Social Cognition, 17*(2), 161–185.

Baum, A., & Dougall, A. L. (1998). Stress. In H. S. Friedman (Ed.), *Encyclopedia of mental health* (Vol. 3, pp. 599–606). San Diego, CA: Academic Press.

Baumeister, R. F., & Leary, M. R. (1995). The need to belong: Desire for interpersonal attachments as a fundamental human motivation. *Psychological Bulletin, 117*(3), 497–529.

Baumeister, R. F., Dale, K., & Sommer, K. L. (1998). Freudian defense mechanisms and empirical findings in modern social psychology: Reaction formation, projection, displacement, undoing, isolation, sublimation, and denial. *Journal of Personality, 66*(6), 1081–1124.

Baumeister, R. F., Brewer, L. E., Tice, D. M., & Twenge, J. M. (2007). Thwarting the need to belong: Understanding the interpersonal and inner effects of social exclusion. *Social and Personality Psychology Compass, 1,* 506–520.

Baumeister, R. F., Campbell, J. D., Krueger, J. I., & Vohs, K. D. (2003). Does high self-esteem cause better performance, interpersonal success, happiness, or healthier lifestyles? *Psychological Science in the Public Interest, 4,* 1–44.

Bayne, R. (1995). *The Myers-Briggs Type Indicator: A critical review and practical guide.* New York: Chapman and Hall.

Beall, A. E., & Sternberg, R. J. (1995). The social construction of love. *Journal of Social and Personal Relationships, 12*(3), 417–438.

Beck, A. T., & Freeman, A. (1989). *Cognitive therapy of personality disorders.* New York: Guilford Press.

Becker, B. J. (1986). Influence again: An examination of reviews and studies of gender differences in social influence. In J. S. Hyde & M. C. Linn (Eds.), *The psychology of gender: Advances through meta-analysis.* Baltimore: Johns Hopkins University Press.

Beer, J. M., & Horn, J. M. (2000). The influence of rearing order on personality development within two adoption cohorts. *Journal of Personality, 68,* 789–819.

Begley, S. (2007, June 4). Reading the book of Jim. *Newsweek,* 48.

Bellah, R. N., Sullivan, W. M., Tipton, S. M., Madsen, R., & Swidler, A. (1985). *Habits of the heart: Individualism and commitment in American life.* Berkeley: University of California Press.

Bellak, L. (1993). *The Thematic Apperception Test, the Children's Apperception Test, and the Senior Apperception Technique in clinical use* (5th ed.). Boston: Allyn & Bacon.

Bellugi, U., & St. George, M. (Eds.). (2001). *Journey from cognition to brain to gene: Perspectives from Williams syndrome.* Cambridge, MA: MIT Press.

Bellugi, U., Järvinen-Pasley, A., & Doyle, T. F. (2007). Affect, social behavior, and the brain in Williams syndrome. *Current Directions in Psychological Science, 16*(2), 99–104.

Bem, D. J. (1996). Exotic becomes erotic: A developmental theory of sexual orientation. *Psychological Review, 103,* 320–335.

Bem, D. J., & Allen, A. (1974). On predicting some of the people some of the time: The search for cross-situational consistencies in behavior. *Psychological Review, 81,* 506–520.

Bem, D. J., & Funder, D. C. (1978). Predicting more of the people more of the time: Assessing the personality of situations. *Psychological Review, 85*(6), 485–501.

Bem, S. L. (1974). The measurement of psychological androgyny. *Journal of Consulting and Clinical Psychology, 42*(1), 155–162.

Bem, S. L. (1981). Gender schema theory: A cognitive account of sex typing. *Psychological Review, 88*(4), 354–364.

Benassi, V. A., Sweeney, P. D., & Dufour, C. L. (1988). Is there a relation between locus of control orientation and depression? *Journal of Abnormal Psychology, 97,* 357–367.

Benet-Martínez, V. (2007). Cross-cultural personality research: Conceptual and methodological issues. In R. W. Robins, C. Fraley, & R. F. Krueger (Eds.), *Handbook of Research Methods in Personality Psychology,* New York: Gilford Press.

Benet-Martínez, V., & Haritatos, J. (2005). Bicultural Identity Integration (BII): Components and psychosocial antecedents. *Journal of Personality, 73*(4), 1015–1050.

Benet-Martínez, V. & Oishi, S. (2008). Culture and personality. In O. P. John, R. W. Robins, & L. A. Pervin (Eds.), *Handbook of personality psychology: Theory and research* (3rd ed.), (pp. 542–567). New York: Guilford Press.

Benet-Martínez, V., Leu, J., Lee, F., & Morris, M. (2002). Negotiating biculturalism: Cultural frame-switching in biculturals with "oppositional" vs. "compatible" cultural identities. *Journal of Cross-Cultural Psychology, 33,* 492–516.

Benjamin, L. S. (1996). A clinician-friendly version of the Interpersonal Circumplex: Structural Analysis of Social Behavior (SASB). *Journal of Personality Assessment, 66*(2), 248–266.

Benjamin, L. T., Jr. (Ed.). (1988). *A history of psychology: Original sources and contemporary research.* New York: McGraw-Hill.

Berg, J. H., & Peplau, L. A. (1982). Loneliness: The relationship of self-disclosure and androgyny. *Personality and Social Psychology Bulletin, 8*(4), 624–630.

Bergen, S. E., Gardner, C. O., & Kendler, K. S. (2007). Age-related changes in heritability of behavioral phenotypes over adolescence and young adulthood: A meta-analysis. *Twin Research and Human Genetics, 10,* 423-433.

Berglund, H., Lindström, P., & Savic, I. (2006). Brain response to putative pheromones in lesbian women. *Proceedings of the National Academy of Sciences of the United States of America, 103*(21), 8269–8274.

Berndt, T. J. (2007). Children's friendships: Shifts over a half-century in perspectives on their development and their effects. In G. W. Ladd (Ed.), *Appraising the human developmental sciences: Essays in honor of Merrill-Palmer Quarterly* (pp. 138–155). Detroit: Wayne State University Press.

Berns, G. S., McClure, S. M., Pagnoni, G., & Montague, P. R. (2001). Predictability modulates human brain response to reward. *Journal of Neuroscience, 21*, 2793–2798.

Bernstein, A. (1976). Freud and Oedipus: A new look at the Oedipus complex in the light of Freud's life. *Psychoanalytic Review, 63*, 393–407.

Berry, J. W., Phinney, J. S., Sam, D. L., & Vedder, P. (Eds.). (2006). *Immigrant youth in cultural transition: Acculturation, identity, and adaptation across national contexts.* Mahwah, NJ: Lawrence Erlbaum Associates.

Berry, J. W., Poortinga, Y. H., Segall, M. H., & Dasen, P. R. (2002). *Cross-cultural psychology: Research and applications.* Cambridge: Cambridge University Press.

Berscheid, E. (1994). Interpersonal relationships. *Annual Review of Psychology, 45*, 79–129.

Bertini, M., Pizzamiglio, L., & Wapner, S. (Eds.). (1986). *Field dependence in psychological theory, research, and application: Two symposia in memory of Herman A. Witkin.* Hillsdale, NJ: Erlbaum.

Betancourt, H., & Lopez, S. R. (1993). The study of culture, ethnicity, and race in American psychology. *American Psychologist, 48*, 629–637.

Betancourt, H., & Weiner, B. (1982). Attributions for achievement-related events, expectancy, and sentiments: A study of success and failure in Chile and the United States. *Journal of Cross-Cultural Psychology, 13*(3), 362–374.

Betz, B., & Thomas, C. (1979). Individual temperament as a predictor of health or premature disease. *Johns Hopkins Medical Journal, 144*, 81–89.

Biederman, J., Mick, E., Faraone, S. V., & Burback, M. (2001). Patterns of remission and symptom decline in conduct disorder: A four-year prospective study of an ADHD sample. *Journal of the American Academy of Child & Adolescent Psychiatry, 40*, 290–298.

Biederman, J., Spencer, T. J., Wilens, T. E., Prince, J. B., & Faraone, S. V. (2006). Treatment of ADHD with stimulant medications: Response to Nissen Perspective in the New England Journal of Medicine. *Journal of the American Academy of Child & Adolescent Psychiatry, 45*(10), 1147–1150.

Biederman, J., Petty, C. R., Fried, R., Doyle, A. E., Spencer, T., Seidman, L. J., et al. (2007). Stability of executive function deficits into young adult years: A prospective longitudinal follow-up study of grown up males with ADHD. *Acta Psychiatrica Scandinavica, 116*(2), 129–136.

Bierce, A. (1911). *The devil's dictionary.* Washington, DC: Neale Publishing.

Binet, A., & Simon, T. (1916). The development of intelligence in children (E. S. Kite, Trans.). Baltimore: Williams and Wilkins.

Binkley, C. J., Beacham, A., Neace, W., Gregg, R. G., Liem, E. B., & Sessler, D. I. (2009). Genetic variations associated with red hair color and fear of dental pain, anxiety regarding dental care and avoidance of dental care. *Journal of the American Dental Association, 140*, 896–905.

Biondi, M., Parise, P., Venturi, P., Riccio, L., Brunetti, G., & Pancheri, P. (1993). Frontal hemisphere lateralization and depressive personality traits. *Perceptual and Motor Skills, 77*(3), 1035–1042.

Blascovich, J. (2000). Using physiological indexes of psychological processes in social psychological research. In H. T. Reiss & C. M. Judd (Eds.), *Handbook of research methods in social and personality psychology* (pp. 117–137). New York: Cambridge University Press.

Blascovich, J., Spencer, S. J., Quinn, D., & Steele, C. (2001). African Americans and high blood pressure: The role of stereotype threat. *Psychological Science, 12*(3), 225–229.

Blass, T. (1991). Understanding behavior in the Milgram obedience experiment: The role of personality, situations, and their interactions. *Journal of Personality and Social Psychology, 60*(3), 398–413.

Blatt, S. J., Cornell, C. E., & Eshkol, E. (1993). Personality style, differential vulnerability, and clinical course in immunological and cardiovascular disease. *Clinical Psychology Review, 13*, 421–450.

Block, J. (1993). Studying personality the long way. In D. C. Funder, R. D. Parke, C. Tomlinson-Keasey, & K. Widaman (Eds.), *Studying lives through time: Personality and development* (pp. 9–41). Washington, DC: American Psychological Association.

Block, J. (1995a). A contrarian view of the five-factor approach to personality description. *Psychological Bulletin, 117*(2), 187–215.

Block, J. (1995b). Going beyond the five factors given: Rejoinder to Costa and McCrae (1995) and Goldberg and Saucier (1995). *Psychological Bulletin, 117*(2), 226–229.

Block, J. (2001). Millennial contrarianism: The five-factor approach to personality description 5 years later. *Journal of Research in Personality, 35*(1), 98–107.

Block, J., & Block, J. H. (2006). Nursery school personality and political orientation two decades later. *Journal of Research in Personality, 40*, 734–749.

Block, J., Block, J. H., & Gjerde, P. F. (1988). Parental functioning and the home environment in families of divorce: Prospective and concurrent analyses. *Journal of the American Academy of Child & Adolescent Psychiatry, 27*, 207–213.

Block, J., Block, J. H., & Keyes, S. (1988). Longitudinally foretelling drug usage in adolescence: Early childhood personality & environmental precursors. *Child Development, 59*, 336–355.

Block, J. H. (1984). *Sex role identity and ego development.* San Francisco: Jossey-Bass.

Block, J. H., Block, J., & Gjerde, P. F. (1986). The personality of children prior to divorce: A prospective study. *Child Development, 57*, 827–840.

Block, J. H., Gjerde, P. F., & Block, J. (1991). Personality antecedents of depressive tendencies in 18-year-olds: A prospective study. *Journal of Personality and Social Psychology, 60*, 726–738.

Bloom, F. E., & Kupfer, D. J. (Eds.). (1995). *Psychopharmacology: The fourth generation of progress.* New York: Raven Press.

Bloom, H. (1998). *Shakespeare: The Invention of the Human.* New York: Riverhead Books.

Bobrow, D., & Bailey, J. M. (2001). Is male homosexuality maintained via kin selection? *Evolution and Human Behavior, 22,* 361–368.

Boekaerts, M., Pintrich, P. R., & Zeidner, M. (Eds.). (2000). *Handbook of self-regulation.* San Diego, CA: Academic Press.

Bogg, T., & Roberts, B. W. (2004). Conscientiousness and health behaviors: A meta-analysis of the leading behavioral contributors to mortality. *Psychological Bulletin, 130,* 887–919.

Bohan, J. S. (Ed.). (1992). *Seldom seen, rarely heard: Women's place in psychology.* Boulder, CO: Westview Press.

Bohner, G., & Wänke, M. (2004). Psychological gender mediates sex differences in jealousy. *Journal of Cultural and Evolutionary Psychology, 2,* 213–229.

Bolger, N., & Zuckerman, A. (1995). A framework for studying personality in the stress process. *Journal of Personality and Social Psychology, 69,* 890–902.

Boman, U. W., Hanson, C., Hjelmquist, E., & Möller, A. (2006). Personality traits in women with Turner syndrome. *Scandinavian Journal of Psychology, 47*(3), 219–223.

Bond, A. J. (2001). Neurotransmitters, temperament and social functioning. *European Neuropsychopharmacology, 11,* 261–274.

Bond, M. H., & Smith, P. B. (1996). Cross-cultural social and organizational psychology. *Annual Review of Psychology, 47,* 205–235.

Boneva, B. S., & Frieze, I. H. (2001). Toward a concept of a migrant personality. *Journal of Social Issues, 57,* 477–491.

Bonham, V. L., Warshauer-Baker, E., & Collins, F. S. (2005). Race and ethnicity in the genome era: The complexity of the constructs. *American Psychologist, 60*(1), 9–15.

Borkenau, P., & Liebler, A. (1993). Convergence of stranger ratings of personality and intelligence with self-ratings, partner ratings, and measured intelligence. *Journal of Personality and Social Psychology, 65,* 546–553.

Borkenau, P., Riemann, R., Angleitner, A., & Spinath, F. M. (2001). Genetic and environmental influences on observed personality: Evidence from the German Observational Study of Adult Twins. *Journal of Personality and Social Psychology, 80*(4), 655–668.

Borroni, P., & Baldissera, F. (2008). Activation of motor pathways during observation and execution of hand movements. *Social Neuroscience, 3,* 276–288.

Borys, S., & Perlman, D. (1985). Gender differences in loneliness. *Personality and Social Psychology Bulletin, 11*(1), 63–74.

Bottome, P. (1957). *Alfred Adler: A portrait from life.* New York: Vanguard.

Bouchard, T. J. (1999). Genes, environment, and personality. In S. J. Ceci & W. M. Williams (Eds.), *The nature–nurture debate: The essential readings* (pp. 97–103). Malden, MA: Blackwell.

Bouchard, T. J., & McGue, M. (2003). Genetic and environmental influences on human psychological differences. *Journal of Neurobiology, 54,* 4–45.

Bouchard, T. J., Jr. (2004). Genetic influence on human psychological traits: A survey. *Current Direction in Psychological Science, 13,* 148–151.

Bouchard, T. J., Lykken, D. T., McGue, M., & Segal, N. L. (1990). Sources of human psychological differences: The Minnesota study of twins reared apart. *Science, 250*(4978), 223–228.

Bowlby, J. (1969). *Attachment and loss.* New York: Basic Books.

Bowman, P. J., & Howard, C. (1985). Race-related socialization, motivation, and academic achievement: A study of black youths in three-generation families. *Journal of the American Academy of Child Psychiatry, 24,* 134–141.

Box–reared babies. (1954, February 22). [Review of the book *Walden Two*]. *Time.*

Boyce, C. J., Brown, G. D. A., & Moore, S. C. (2010). Money and happiness: Rank of income, not income, affects life satisfaction. *Psychological Science, 21,* 471–475.

Brackett, M. A., Rivers, S. E., Shiffman, S., Lerner, N., & Salovey, P. (2006). Relating emotional abilities to social functioning: A comparison of self-report and performance measures of emotional intelligence. *Journal of Personality and Social Psychology, 91*(4), 780–795.

Brain, P. F. (Ed.). (1986). *Alcohol and aggression.* London: Croom Helm.

Breazeal, C. (2003). Toward sociable robots. *Robotics and Autonomous Systems, 42,* 167–175.

Brennan, K. A., & Shaver, P. R. (1995). Dimensions of adult attachment, affect regulation, and romantic relationship functioning. *Personality and Social Psychology Bulletin, 21*(3), 267–283.

Brenner, C. (1994). The mind as conflict and compromise formation. *Journal of Clinical Psychoanalysis, 3,* 473–488.

Breuer, J., & Freud, S. (1957). *Studies on hysteria.* New York: Basic Books.

Briggs, S. R., & Cheek, J. M. (1988). On the nature of self-monitoring: Problems with assessment, problems with validity. *Journal of Personality and Social Psychology, 54,* 663–678.

Britt, T. A., & Shepperd, J. A. (1999). Trait relevance and trait assessment. *Personality and Social Psychology Review, 3*(2), 108–122.

Brome, V. (1981). *Jung: Man and myth.* New York: Atheneum Books.

Broverman, I. K., Vogel, S. R., Broverman, D. M., Clarkson, F. E., & Rosekrantz, P. S. (1972). Sex-role stereotypes: A current appraisal. *Journal of Social Issues, 28,* 59–78.

Brown, P., & Levinson, S. C. (1987). *Politeness: Some universals in language usage.* Cambridge, UK: Cambridge University Press.

Brown, R. (1965). *Social psychology.* New York: Free Press.

Brown, R. (1970). *Psycholinguistics: Selected papers by Roger Brown.* New York: Free Press.

Brown, R. I. (1986). Arousal and sensation-seeking components in the general explanation of gambling and gambling addictions. *International Journal of the Addictions, 21*(9–10), 1001–1016.

Brown, R. P., & Pinel, E. C. (2003). Stigma on my mind: Individual differences in the experience of stereotype threat. *Journal of Experimental Social Psychology, 39*(6), 626–633.

Browning, D. S. (1987). *Religious thought and the modern psychologies.* Philadelphia: Fortress Press.

Brumbaugh, C. C., & Fraley, R. C. (2007). Transference of attachment patterns: How important relationships influence feelings toward novel people. *Personal Relationships, 14,* 513–530.

Bruner, J. S., Goodnow, J. J., & Austin, G. A. (1956). *A study of thinking.* New York: Wiley.

Brunstein, J. C. & Heckhausen, H. (2008). Achievement motivation. In J. Heckhausen & H. Heckhausen (Eds), *Motivation and action* (2nd ed.), (pp. 137–183). New York: Cambridge University Press.

Buber, M. (1937). *I and thou* (R. G. Smith, Trans.). Edinburgh: T. & T. Clark.

Buck, R. (1979). Individual differences in nonverbal sending accuracy and electrodermal responding: The externalizing-internalizing dimension. In R. Rosenthal (Ed.), *Skill in nonverbal communication* (pp. 140–170). Cambridge, MA: Oelgeschlager, Gunn, & Hain.

Buck, R. (1984). *The communication of emotion.* New York: Guilford Press.

Buhrich, N., Bailey, J. M., & Martin, N. G. (1991). Sexual orientation, sexual identity, and sex-dimorphic behaviors in male twins. *Behavior Genetics, 21,* 75–96.

Bullock, A. (1962). *Hitler, a study in tyranny* (Rev. ed.). Harmondsworth, UK: Penguin.

Burns, G. (1976). *Living it up.* New York: Putnam.

Burnstein, E., Crandall, C., & Kitayama, S. (1994). Some neo-Darwinian decision rules for altruism: Weighing cues for inclusive fitness as a function of the biological importance of the decision. *Journal of Personality and Social Psychology, 67,* 773–789.

Burwick, S., & Knapp, R. R. (1991). Advances in research using the Personal Orientation Inventory. *Journal of Social Behavior and Personality, 6,* 311–320.

Busato, V. V., Prins, F. J., Elshout, J. J., & Hamaker, C. (1999). The relation between learning styles, the Big Five personality traits and achievement motivation in higher education. *Personality and Individual Differences, 26,* 129–140.

Buss, A. H., & Plomin, R. (1984). *Temperament: Early developing personality traits.* Hillsdale, NJ: Erlbaum.

Buss, D. M. (1989). Sex differences in human mate preferences: Evolutionary hypotheses tested in 37 cultures. *Behavioral and Brain Sciences, 12*(1), 1–49.

Buss, D. M. (1990). Toward a biologically informed psychology of personality. *Journal of Personality, 58,* 1–16.

Buss, D. M. (1991). Evolutionary personality psychology. *Annual Review of Psychology, 42,* 459–492.

Buss, D. M. (1994). *The evolution of desire: Strategies of human mating.* New York: Basic Books.

Buss, D. M. (1995a). Evolutionary psychology: A new paradigm for psychological science. *Psychological Inquiry, 6,* 1–30.

Buss, D. M. (1995b). Psychological sex differences: Origins through sexual selection. *American Psychologist, 50,* 164–168.

Buss, D. M. (1999). *Evolutionary psychology: The new science of the mind.* Boston: Allyn & Bacon.

Buss, D. M. (2003). *Evolutionary psychology: The new science of the mind* (2nd ed.). Boston: Allyn & Bacon.

Buss, D. M. (2007). The evolution of human mating. *Acta Psychologica Sinica, 39*(3), 502–512.

Buss, D. M. (2009). How can evolutionary psychology successfully explain personality and individual differences? *Perspectives on Psychological Science, 4,* 359–366.

Buss, D. M., & Angleitner, A. (1989). Mate selection preferences in Germany and the United States. *Personality and Individual Differences, 10*(12), 1269–1280.

Buss, D. M., & Craik, K. H. (1983). The act frequency approach to personality. *Psychological Review, 90,* 105–126.

Buss, D. M., & Schmitt, D. P. (1993). Sexual Strategies Theory: An evolutionary perspective on human mating. *Psychological Review, 100*(2), 204–232.

Buss, D. M., Larsen, R. J., Westen, D., & Semmelroth, J. (1992). Sex differences in jealousy: Evolution, physiology, and psychology. *Psychological Science, 3,* 251–255.

Buss, D. M., Haselton, M. G., Shackelford, T. K., Bleske, A. L., & Wakefield, J. C. (1998). Adaptations, exaptations, and spandrels. *American Psychologist, 53,* 533–548.

Butcher, J. N. (1990). *MMPI-2 in psychological treatment.* New York: Oxford University Press.

Buunk, B. P., Dijkstra, P., Kenrick, D. T., & Warntjes, A. (2001). Age preferences for mates as related to gender, own age, and involvement level. *Evolution & Human Behavior, 22,* 241–250.

Bylsma, W. H., & Major, B. (1994). Social comparisons and contentment: Exploring the psychological costs of the gender wage gap. *Psychology of Women Quarterly, 18*(2), 241–249.

Cacioppo, J. T., & Patrick, W. (2008). Loneliness: Human nature and the need for social connection. New York: W. W. Norton & Co.

Cacioppo, J. T., Berntson, G. G., Sheridan, J. F., & McClintock, M. K. (2000). Multilevel integrative analyses of human behavior: Social neuroscience and the complementing nature of social and biological approaches. *Psychological Bulletin, 126*(6), 829–843.

Cacioppo, J. T., Crites, S. L., Berntson, G. G., & Coles, M. G. (1993). If attitudes affect how stimuli are processed, should they not affect the event-related brain potential? *Psychological Science, 4,* 108–112.

Campbell, D. T. (1960). Recommendations for the APA test standards regarding construct, trait, and discriminant validity. *American Psychologist, 15,* 546–553.

Campbell, D. T. (1988). *Methodology and epistemology for social science: Selected papers* (E. S. Overman, Ed.). Chicago: University of Chicago Press.

Campbell, D. T., & Fiske, D. W. (1959). Convergent and discriminant validation by the multitrait-multimethod matrix. *Psychological Bulletin, 56,* 81–105.

Campbell, D. T., & Stanley, J. C. (1963). *Experimental and quasi-experimental designs for research.* Chicago: Rand McNally.

Campbell, J. M., Amerikaner, M., Swank, P. R., & Vincent, K. (1989). The relationship between the Hardiness Test and the Personal Orientation Inventory. *Journal of Research in Personality, 23,* 373–380.

Camras, L. (1982). Ethological approaches to nonverbal communication. In R. S. Feldman (Ed.), *Development of nonverbal behavior in children* (pp. 3–28). New York: Springer-Verlag.

Canli, T. (Ed.). (2006). *Biology of personality and individual differences.* New York: Guilford Press.

Canli, T., Zhao, Z., Desmond, J. E., Kang, E., Gross, J., & Gabrieli, J. D. E. (2001). An fMRI study of personality influences on brain reactivity to emotional stimuli. *Behavioral Neuroscience, 115*(1), 33–42.

Cantor, N. (1994). Life task problem solving: Situational affordances and personal needs. *Personality and Social Psychology Bulletin, 20*(3), 235–243.

Cantor, N., & Kihlstrom, J. F. (1987). *Personality and social intelligence.* Englewood Cliffs, NJ: Prentice-Hall.

Cantor, N., Norem, J. K., Niedenthal, P. M., Langston, C. A., & Brower, A. M. (1987). Life tasks, self-concept ideals, and cognitive strategies in a life transition [Special issue]. *Journal of Personality and Social Psychology, 53*(6), 1178–1191.

Carlson, R. (1980). Studies of Jungian typology: Vol. 2. Representations of the personal world. *Journal of Personality and Social Psychology, 38*, 801–810.

Carney, D. R., Colvin, C. R., & Hall, J. A. (2007). A thin slice perspective on the accuracy of first impressions. *Journal of Research in Personality, 41*, 1054–1072.

Carroll, K. M., & Rounsaville, B. J. (2007). A perfect platform: Combining contingency management with medications for drug abuse. *American Journal of Drug and Alcohol Abuse, 33*(3), 343–365.

Carter, C. S., Krener, P., Chaderjian, M., Northcutt, C., & Wolfe, V. (1995). Asymmetrical visual-spatial attentional performance in ADHD: Evidence for a right hemispheric deficit. *Biological Psychiatry, 37*(11), 789–797.

Carver, C. S., & Connor-Smith, J. (2010). Personality and coping. *Annual Review of Psychology, 61*, 679–704.

Carver, C. S., & Scheier, M. F. (1981). *Attention and self-regulation: A control-theory approach to human behavior.* New York: Springer-Verlag.

Carver, C. S., & Scheier, M. F. (1990). Principles of self-regulation: Action and emotion. In E. T. Higgins & R. M. Sorrentino (Eds.), *Handbook of motivation and cognition: Foundations of social behavior* (Vol. 2, pp. 3–52). New York: Guilford Press.

Carver, C. S., Johnson, S. L., & Joormann, J. (2008). Serotonergic function, two-mode models of self-regulation, and vulnerability to depression: What depression has in common with impulsive aggression. *Psychological Bulletin, 134*, 912–943.

Carver, C. S., Johnson, S. L., & Joormann, J. (2009). Two-mode models of self-regulation as a tool for conceptualizing effects of the serotonin system in normal behavior and diverse disorders. *Current Directions in Psychological Science, 18*, 195–199.

Carver, C. S., Scheier, M. F., & Segerstrom, S. C. (2010). Optimism. *Clinical Psychology Review, 30*, 879–889.

Cash, T. F., Mikulka, P. J., & Brown, T. A. (1989). Validity of Millon's computerized interpretation system for the MCMI: Comment on Moreland and Onstad. *Journal of Consulting and Clinical Psychology, 57*(2), 311–312.

Caspi, A. (2000). The child is father of the man: Personality continuities from childhood to adulthood. *Journal of Personality and Social Psychology, 78*(1), 158–172.

Caspi, A., & Bem, D. J. (1990). Personality continuity and change across the life course. In L. A. Pervin (Ed.), *Handbook of personality: Theory and research* (pp. 549–575). New York: Guilford Press.

Caspi, A., & Roberts, B. W. (2001). Personality development across the life course: The argument for change and continuity. *Psychological Inquiry, 12*, 49–66.

Caspi, A., & Silva, P. A. (1995). Temperamental qualities at age three predict personality traits in young adulthood: Longitudinal evidence from a birth cohort. *Child Development, 66*, 486–498.

Caspi, A., Bem, D. J., & Elder, G. H. (1989). Continuities and consequences of interactional styles across the life course [Special issue: Long-term stability and change in personality]. *Journal of Personality, 57*, 375–406.

Caspi, A., Roberts, B. W. & Shiner, R. L. (2005). Personality development: Stability and change. *Annual Review of Psychology, 56*, 453–484.

Caspi, A., Sugden, K., Moffitt, T. E., Mill, J., Taylor, A., Craig, I. W., et al. (2003). Influence of life stress on depression: Moderation by a polymorphism in the 5-HTT gene. *Science, 301*, 386–389.

Catania, C., & Harnad, S. (Eds.). (1988). *The selection of behavior: The operant behaviorism of B. F. Skinner: Comments and consequences.* New York: Cambridge University Press.

Cattell, R. B. (1966). *The scientific analysis of personality.* Chicago: Aldine.

Cattell, R. B. (1990). Advances in Cattellian personality theory. In L. A. Pervin (Ed.), *Handbook of personality: Theory and research* (pp. 101–110). New York: Guilford Press.

Cervone, D. (2004). The architecture of personality. *Psychological Review. 111*(1), 183–204.

Champagne, F. A. (2009). Nurturing nature: Social experiences and the brain. *Journal of Neuroendocrinology, 21*, 867–868.

Champagne, F. A., & Mashoodh, R. (2009). Genes in context: Gene-environment interplay and the origins of individual differences in behavior. *Current Directions in Psychological Science, 18*, 127–131.

Chang, E. C., Asakawa, K., & Sanna, L. J. (2001). Cultural variations in optimistic and pessimistic bias: Do Easterners really expect the worst and Westerners really expect the best when predicting life events? *Journal of Personality and Social Psychology, 81*, 476–491.

Chapman, A. H. (1976). *Harry Stack Sullivan: His life and his work.* New York: Putnam.

Charles, S. T., & Carstensen, L. L. (2008). Unpleasant situations elicit different emotional responses in younger and older adults. *Psychology and Aging, 23*, 495–504.

Charles, S. T., & Piazza, J. R. (2009). Age differences in affective well-being: Context matters. *Social and Personality Psychology Compass, 3*, 711–724.

Chartrand, T. L., Maddux, W. W., & Lakin, J. L. (2005). Beyond the perception-behavior link: The ubiquitous utility and motivational moderators of nonconscious mimicry. In R. R. Hassin, J. S. Uleman, & J. A. Bargh (Eds.), *The new unconscious* (pp. 334–361). New York: Oxford University Press.

Chassin, L., Rogosch, F., & Barrera, M. (1991). Substance use and symptomatology among adolescent children of alcoholics. *Journal of Abnormal Psychology, 100*, 449–463.

Chassin, L., Presson, C. C., Sherman, S. J., & Edwards, D. A. (1991). Four pathways to young-adult smoking status: Adolescent social-psychological antecedents in a midwestern community sample. *Health Psychology, 10*, 409–418.

Chassin, L., Presson, C. C., Sherman, S. J., Corty, E., & Olshavsky, R. W. (1984). Predicting the onset of cigarette smoking in adolescents: A longitudinal study. *Journal of Applied Social Psychology, 14*, 224–243.

Cheek, J. M. (1989). *Conquering shyness: The battle anyone can win.* New York: Putnam.

Cheek, J. M., & Melchior, L. A. (1990). Shyness, self-esteem, and self-consciousness. In H. Leitenberg (Ed.), *Handbook of social and evaluation anxiety* (pp. 47–82). New York: Plenum Press.

Chen, Z.-Y., Jing, D., Bath, K. G., Ieraci, A., Khan, T., Siao, C.-J., et al. (2006). Genetic variant BDNF (Val66Met) polymorphism alters anxiety-related behavior. *Science, 314*, 140–143.

Chesney, M. A., & Rosenman, R. H. (Eds.). (1985). *Anger and hostility in cardiovascular and behavioral disorders.* Washington, DC: Hemisphere.

Chesney, M. A., Eagleston, J. R., & Rosenman, R. H. (1980). The Type A structured interview. *Journal of Behavioral Assessment, 2*, 255–272.

Chipuer, H. M., Plomin, R., Pedersen, N. L., McClearn, G. E., & Nesselroade, J. (1993). Genetic influence on family environment: The role of personality. *Developmental Psychology, 29*, 110–118.

Chodorow, N. J. (1999a). *The power of feelings: Personal meaning in psychoanalysis, gender, and culture.* New Haven, CT: Yale University Press.

Chodorow, N. J. (1999b). Toward a relational individualism: The mediation of self through psychoanalysis. In S. A. Mitchell & L. Aron (Eds.), *Relational psychoanalysis: The emergence of a tradition.* Relational perspectives book series (Vol. 14, pp. 109–130). Hillsdale, NJ: Analytic Press.

Chomsky, N. (1973). *For reasons of state.* New York: Pantheon.

Choy, Y., Fyer, A. J., & Lipsitz, J. D. (2007). Treatment of specific phobia in adults. *Clinical Psychology Review, 27*(3), 266–286.

Chua-Eoan, H. (1997, April 7). Imprisoned by his own passions. *Time, 149*, 40–43.

Church, A. T. (2009). Prospects for an integrated trait and cultural psychology. *European Journal of Personality, 23*, 153–182.

Church, A. T., Katigbak, M. S., Miramontes, L. G., del Prado, A. M., & Cabrera, H. F. (2007). Culture and the behavioural manifestations of traits: An application of the act frequency approach. *European Journal of Personality, 21*(4), 389–417.

Clapper, R. L., Martin, C. S., & Clifford, P. R. (1994). Personality, social environment, and past behavior as predictors of late adolescent alcohol use. *Journal of Substance Abuse, 6*(3), 305–313.

Clark, L. A. (2009). Stability and change in personality disorder. *Current Directions in Psychological Science, 18*, 27–31.

Clark, L. A., & Halford, G. S. (1983). Does cognitive style account for cultural differences in scholastic achievement? *Journal of Cross-Cultural Psychology, 14*(3), 279–296.

Clifford, J. (2001, August 11). Would you let your baby be branded? *The San Diego Union Tribune,* p. E-1.

Cloninger, C. R. (1998). The genetics and psychobiology of the seven-factor model of personality. In K. R. Silk (Ed.), *Biology of personality disorders* (pp. 63–92). Washington, DC: American Psychiatric Press.

Cohen, A. B. (2009). Many forms of culture. *American Psychologist, 64*, 194–204.

Cohen, A. B., & Hill, P. C. (2007). Religion as culture: Religious individualism and collectivism among American Catholics, Jews, and Protestants. *Journal of Personality, 75*, 709–742.

Cohen, A. B., & Rankin, A. (2004). Religion and the morality of positive mentality. *Basic & Applied Social Psychology, 26*, 45–57.

Cohen, J., Nuttin, J., & Maslow, A. (1968). The psychology of man: Today. *Psychological Scene, 2*, 5–16.

Cohen, J. D., & Schooler, J. W. (Eds.). (1997). *Scientific approaches to consciousness.* Mahwah, NJ: Erlbaum.

Cohn, M. A., Fredrickson, B. L., Brown, S. L., Mikels, J. A., & Conway, A. M. (2009). Happiness unpacked: Positive emotions increase life satisfaction by building resilience. *Emotion, 9*, 361–368.

Coles, R. (1970). *Erik Erikson: The growth of his work.* Boston: Little, Brown.

Collings, R. D. (2001). An examination of vigilance and behavior inhibition deficits related to Attention-Deficit/Hyperactivity Disorder Inattentive and Combined types (Doctorial dissertation, University of California Riverside, 2001).

Commons, M. L., Nevin, J. A., & Davison, M. C. (1991). *Signal detection: Mechanisms, models and applications.* Hillsdale, NJ: Erlbaum.

Conley, J. J. (1984). Longitudinal consistency of adult personality: Self-reported psychological characteristics across 45 years. *Journal of Personality and Social Psychology, 47*(6), 1325–1333.

Connell, R. W. (1992). A very straight gay: Masculinity, homosexual experience, and the dynamics of gender. *American Sociological Review, 57*, 735–751.

Conrad, K. M., Flay, B. R., & Hill, D. (1992). Why children start smoking cigarettes: Predictors of onset. *British Journal of Addiction, 87*, 1711–1724.

Contreras, R., Hendrick, S. S., & Hendrick, C. (1996). Perspectives on marital love and satisfaction in Mexican American and Anglo-American couples. *Journal of Counseling and Development, 74*(4), 408–415.

Conway, M. A. (Ed.). (1996). *False and recovered memories.* Oxford, UK: Oxford University Press.

Cook-Gumperz, J., & Szymanski, M. (2001). Classroom "families": Cooperating or competing: Girls' and boys' interactional styles in a bilingual classroom. *Research on Language & Social Interaction, 34*(1), 107–130.

Cooper, M. L. (2010). Toward a person × situation model of sexual risk-taking behaviors: Illuminating the conditional effects of traits across sexual situations and relationship contexts. *Journal of Personality and Social Psychology, 98*, 319–341.

Cooper, M. L., Agocha, V. B., & Sheldon, M. S. (2000). A motivational perspective on risky behaviors: The role of personality and affect regulatory processes. *Journal of Personality, 68*(6), 1059–1088.

Corr, P. J. (2002). J. A. Gray's reinforcement sensitivity theory: Tests of the joins subsystems hypothesis of anxiety and impulsivity. *Personality and Individual Differences, 33*, 511–532.

Corr, P. J. (Ed.). (2008). *The reinforcement sensitivity theory of personality.* New York: Cambridge University Press.

Cortina, L. M. (2001). Assessing sexual harassment among Latinas: Development of an instrument. *Cultural Diversity & Ethnic Minority Psychology, 7*(2), 164–181.

Costa, P. T., Jr., & McCrae, R. R. (1987a). On the need for longitudinal evidence and multiple measures in behavioral-genetic studies of adult personality. *Behavioral & Brain Sciences, 10*, 22–23.

Costa, P. T., Jr., & McCrae, R. R. (1987b). Role of neuroticism in the perception and presentation of chest pain symptoms and coronary artery disease. In J. W. Elias & P. H. Marshall (Eds.), *Cardiovascular disease and behavior* (pp. 39–66). Washington, DC: Hemisphere.

Costa, P. T., Jr., & McCrae, R. R. (1992a). Four ways five factors are basic. *Personality & Individual Differences, 13*, 653–665.

Costa, P. T., Jr., & McCrae, R. R. (1992b). Normal personality assessment in clinical practice: The NEO Personality Inventory. *Psychological Assessment, 4*, 5–13.

Costa, P. T., Jr., & McCrae, R. R. (1994). Set like plaster: Evidence for the stability of adult personality. In T. F. Heatherton

& J. L. Weinberger (Eds.), *Can personality change?* (pp. 21–40). Washington, DC: American Psychological Association.

Costa, P. T., Jr., & McCrae, R. R. (1995a). Primary traits of Eysenck's P-E-N system: Three- and five-factor solutions. *Journal of Personality and Social Psychology, 69*(2), 308–317.

Costa, P. T., Jr., & McCrae, R. R. (1995b). Solid ground in the wetlands of personality: A reply to Block. *Psychological Bulletin, 117*(2), 216–220.

Costa, P. T., Jr., & McCrae, R. R. (2006). Trait and factor theories. In J. C. Thomas, D. L. Segal, & M. Hersen (Eds.), *Comprehensive handbook of personality and psychopathology: Vol. 1. Personality and everyday functioning* (pp. 96–114). Hoboken, NJ: Wiley.

Costa, P. T., Jr., Herbst, J. H, McCrae, R. R., Samuels, J., & Ozer, D. J. (2002). The replicability and utility of three personality types. *European Journal of Personality, 16*, S73–S87.

Costa, P. T., Jr., Zonderman, A. B., McCrae, R. R., Cornoni-Huntley, J., Locke, B. Z., & Barbano, H. E. (1987). Longitudinal analysis of psychological well-being in a national sample: Stability of means levels. *Journal of Gerontology, 42*(1), 50–55.

Coyne, J. C., & Whiffen, V. E. (1995). Issues in personality as diathesis for depression: The case of sociotropy–dependency and autonomy–self-criticism. *Psychological Bulletin, 118*(3), 358–378.

Craig, R. J. (Ed.) (1993). *The Millon Clinical Multiaxial Inventory: A clinical research information synthesis.* Hillsdale, NJ: Erlbaum.

Craik, K., Hogan, R., & Wolfe, R. N. (Eds.). (1993). *Fifty years of personality psychology.* New York: Plenum Press.

Crews, F. (1996). Forward to 1896? Commentary on papers by Harris and Davies. *Psychoanalytic Dialogues, 6*(2), 231–250.

Crichton, M. (1994). *Disclosure.* New York: Alfred A. Knopf.

Crider, A., & Lunn, R. (1971). Electrodermal lability as a personality dimension. *Journal of Experimental Research in Personality, 5*, 145–150.

Crocker, J., & Knight, K. M. (2005). Contingencies of self-worth. *Current Directions in Psychological Science, 14*, 200–203.

Crockett, L. (1994). *The Turing test and the frame problem: AI's mistaken understanding of intelligence.* Norwood, NJ: Ablex.

Cross, W. E., Jr., & Vandiver, B. J. (2001). Nigrescence theory and measurement: Introducing the Cross Racial Identity Scale (CRIS). In J. G. Ponterotto, J. M. Casas, L. A. Suzuki, & C. M. Alexander (Eds.), *Handbook of multicultural counseling* (2nd ed., pp. 371–393). Thousand Oaks, CA: Sage.

Cross-National Collaborative Group. (1992). The changing rate of major depression: Cross-national comparisons. *Journal of the American Medical Association, 268*, 3098–3105.

Crowell, S. E., Beauchaine, T. P., & Linehan, M, M. (2009). A biosocial developmental model of borderline personality: Elaborating and extending Linehan's theory. *Psychological Bulletin, 135*, 495–510.

Csikszentmihalyi, M. (1996). *Creativity: Flow and the psychology of discovery and invention.* New York: HarperCollins.

Csikszentmihalyi, M. (2000). *Beyond boredom and anxiety.* San Francisco: Jossey-Bass.

Csikszentmihalyi, M., & Larson, R. (1984). *Being adolescent: Conflict and growth in the teenage years.* New York: Basic Books.

Cunningham, M. R. (1977). Personality and the structure of the nonverbal communication of emotion. *Journal of Personality, 45*, 564–584.

Cyders, M. A., & Smith, G. T. (2008). Emotion-based dispositions to rash action: Positive and negative urgency. *Psychological Bulletin, 134*, 807–828.

Dabbs, J. M., Jr. (1993). Salivary testosterone measurements in behavioral studies. In D. Malamud & L. A. Tabak (Eds.), *Annals of the New York Academy of Sciences: Vol. 694. Saliva as a diagnostic fluid* (pp. 177–183). New York: New York Academy of Sciences.

Dabbs, J. M., Jr., Karpas, A. E., Dyomina, N., Juechter, J., & Roberts, A. (2002). Experimental raising or lowering of testosterone level affects mood in normal men and women. *Social Behavior and Personality, 30*(8), 795–806.

Daly, M., & Wilson, M. (1988a). Evolutionary social psychology and family homicide. *Science, 242*, 519–524.

Daly, M., & Wilson, M. (1988b). *Homicide.* Hawthorne, NY: Aldine.

Daly, M., & Wilson, M. (1998). *The truth about Cinderella: A Darwinian view of parental love.* New Haven, CT: Yale University Press.

Daly, M., & Wilson, M. (2005a). The 'Cinderella effect' is no fairy tale: Comment. *Trends in Cognitive Sciences, 9*, 507–508.

Daly, M., & Wilson, M. (2005b). Human behavior as animal behavior. In J. J. Bolhuis & L.-A. Giraldeau (Eds.), *The behavior of animals: Mechanisms, function, and evolution* (pp. 393–408). Malden, MA: Blackwell.

Daly, M., Wilson, M. I., & Weghorst, S. J. (1982). Male sexual jealousy. *Ethology and Sociobiology, 3*(1), 11–27.

Dana, R. H. (Ed.) (2000). *Handbook of cross-cultural and multicultural personality assessment.* Mahwah, NJ: Erlbaum.

Daniel, D. (1997, April 14). The beginning of the journey. *Newsweek, 129*, 36–37.

Dapretto, M., Davies, M. S., & Pfeifer, J. H. (2006). Understanding emotions in others: Mirror neuron dysfunction in children with autism spectrum disorders. *Nature Neuroscience, 9*(1), 28–30.

Darwin, C. (1859). *The origin of species by means of natural selection: or, The preservation of favored races in the struggle for life.* London: J. Murray.

Davidson, E. (1977). *The making of Adolf Hitler.* New York: Macmillan.

Davidson, R. J. (2004). Well-being and affective style: Neural substrates and biobehavioural correlates. *Philosophical Transactions of the Royal Society (London), 359*, 1395–1411.

Davidson, R. J., & Fox, N. A. (1989). Frontal brain asymmetry predicts infants' response to maternal separation. *Journal of Abnormal Psychology, 98*(2), 127–131.

Davis, C., Patte, K., Levitan, R., Reid, C., Tweed, S. & Curtis, C. (2007). From motivation to behaviour: A model of reward sensitivity, overeating, and food preferences in the risk profile for obesity. *Appetite, 48*(1), 12–19.

Dawes, R. M. (1998). Standards for psychotherapy. In H. S. Friedman (Ed.), *Encyclopedia of mental health* (Vol. 3, 589–597). San Diego, CA: Academic Press.

de Rivera, J. (Ed.). (1976). *Field theory as human-science: Contributions of Lewin's Berlin group.* New York: Gardner Press.

de Waal, F. B. M. (1996). *Good natured: The origins of right and wrong in humans and other animals.* Cambridge, MA: Harvard University Press.

de Waal, F. B. M. (2001a). *The ape and the sushi master: Cultural reflections of a primatologist.* New York: Basic Books.

de Waal, F. B. M. (Ed.). (2001b). *Tree of origin: What primate behavior can tell us about human social evolution.* Cambridge, MA: Harvard University Press.

Deaux, K. (2006). To be an immigrant. New York: Russell Sage Foundation.

Deaux, K., & Lewis, L. (1984). Structure of gender stereotypes: Interrelationships among components and gender label. *Journal of Personality and Social Psychology, 46,* 991–1004.

Deaux, K., & Major, B. (1987). Putting gender into context: An interactive model of gender-related behavior. *Psychological Review, 94,* 369–389.

DeGiustino, D. (1975). *The conquest of mind: Phrenology and Victorian social thought.* Totowa, NJ: Rowman & Littlefield.

Dell, G. S. (1995). Speaking and misspeaking. In L. Gleitman & M. Liberman (Eds.), *Language: An invitation to cognitive science* (Vol. 1, 2nd ed., pp. 183–208). Cambridge, MA: MIT Press.

DeNeve, K. M., & Cooper, H. (1998). The happy personality: A meta-analysis of 137 personality traits and subjective well-being. *Psychological Bulletin, 124*(2), 197–229.

Dennett, D. C. (2003). Making ourselves at home in our machines: The illusion of conscious will. *Journal of Mathematical Psychology, 47,* 101–104.

Denollet, J. (2000). Type D personality: A potential risk factor defined. *Journal of Psychosomatic Research, 49,* 255–266.

DePaulo, B. M., & Friedman, H. S. (1998). Nonverbal communication. In D. T. Gilbert, S. T. Fiske, & G. Lindzey (Eds.), *The handbook of social psychology* (Vol. 2, 4th ed., pp. 3–40). Boston: McGraw-Hill.

DePaulo, B. M., Blank, A. L., Swain, G. W., & Hairfield, J. G. (1992). Expressiveness and expressive control. *Personality and Social Psychology Bulletin, 18,* 276–285.

Derlega, V. J., Winstead, B. A., & Jones, W. H. (1991). *Personality: Contemporary theory and research.* Chicago: Nelson-Hall.

Descartes, R. (1961). *Essential works* (R. Blair, Trans.) New York: Bantam.

DeSteno, D., & Salovey, P. (1996). Evolutionary origins of sex differences in jealousy? Questioning the "fitness" of the model. *Psychological Science, 7,* 367–372.

Devos, T., & Banaji, M. R. (2003). Implicit self and identity. *Annals of the New York Academy of Sciences, 1001,* 177–211.

DeWall, C. N., Twenge, J. M., Gitter, S. A., & Baumeister, R. F. (2009). It's the thought that counts: The role of hostile cognition in shaping aggressive responses to social exclusion. *Journal of Personality and Social Psychology, 96,* 45–59.

Diamond, L. M. (2008). Female bisexuality from adolescence to adulthood: Results from a 10-year longitudinal study. *Developmental Psychology, 44,* 5–14.

Diener, C. I., & Dweck, C. S. (1980). An analysis of learned helplessness: The processing of success. *Journal of Personality and Social Psychology, 39*(5), 940–952.

Diener, E. (2000). Subjective well-being: The science of happiness and a proposal for a national index. *American Psychologist, 55*(1), 34–43.

Diener, E., & Seligman, M. E. P. (2004). Beyond money: Toward an economy of well-being. *Psychological Science in the Public Interest, 5,* 1–31.

Diener, E., Lucas, R., & Scollon, C. N. (2006). Beyond the hedonic treadmill: Revising the adaptation theory of well-being. *American Psychologist, 61,* 305–314.

Dijksterhuis, A., & Nordgren, L. F. (2006). A theory of unconscious thought. *Perspectives on Psychological Science, 1*(2) 95–109.

DiLalla, D. L. (1998). Genetic contributors to mental health. In H. S. Friedman (Ed.), *Encyclopedia of mental health* (Vol. 2, pp. 277–287). San Diego, CA: Academic Press.

Dion, K. K. (1972). Physical attractiveness and evaluation of children's transgressions. *Journal of Personality and Social Psychology, 24,* 207–213.

Dion, K. K. (1973). Young children's stereotyping of facial attractiveness. *Developmental Psychology, 9,* 183–188.

Dion, K. L., & Dion, K. K. (1993). Gender and ethnocultural comparisons in styles of love [Special issue]. *Psychology of Women Quarterly, 17*(4), 463–473.

Doi, T. (1981). *The Anatomy of Dependence: The Key Analysis of Japanese Behavior.* English trans. John Bester (2nd ed.). Tokyo: Kodansha International.

Dole, A. A. (1995). Why not drop race as a term? *American Psychologist, 50*(1), 40.

Dollard, J., & Miller, N. E. (1950). *Personality and psychotherapy: An analysis in terms of learning, thinking, and culture.* New York: McGraw-Hill.

Dollard, J., Miller, N. E., Doob, L. W., Mowrer, O. H., & Sears, R. R. (1939). *Frustration and aggression.* New Haven, CT: Yale University Press.

Donohew, L., Zimmerman, R., Cupp, P. S., Novak, S., Colon, S., & Abell, R. (2000). Sensation seeking, impulsive decision-making, and risky sex: Implications for risk-taking and design of interventions. *Personality and Individual Differences, 28*(6), 1079–1091.

Donohue, M. V. (1995). A study of the development of traits of entry-level occupational therapy students. *American Journal of Occupational Therapy, 49*(7), 703–709.

Doob, L. W. (1958). Behavior and grammatical style. *Journal of Abnormal and Social Psychology, 56,* 398–401.

Douglas, C. (1993). *Translate this darkness: The life of Christiana Morgan.* New York: Simon & Schuster,

Douglas, J. E. (1995). *Mindhunter: Inside the FBI's elite serial crime unit.* (J. Douglas & M. Olshaker, Eds.). New York: Scribner.

Dreher, J.-C., Schmidt, P. J., Kohn, P., Furman, D., Rubinow, D., & Berman, K. F. (2007). Menstrual cycle phase modulates reward-related neural function in women. *PNAS Proceedings of the National Academy of Sciences of the United States of America, 104*(7), 2465–2470.

Driver-Dunckley, E., Samanta, J., & Stacy, M. (2003). Pathological gambling associated with dopamine agonist therapy in Parkinson's disease. *Neurology, 61,* 422–423.

Dubey, S. N. (1987). Personality characteristics of the socioculturally deprived class. *Perspectives in Psychological Researches, 10*(2), 51–53.

DuBois, W. E. B. (1969). *The souls of black folk.* New York: Signet.

Duhigg, C. (2009, May 17). Your credit-card company wants to get to know you. *New York Times Magazine.* Retrieved from http://www.nytimes.com

Dunbar, Flanders. (1947). *Mind and body: Psychosomatic medicine.* New York: Random House.

Duncan, L. E., & Stewart, A. J. (2007). Personal political salience: The role of personality in collective identity and action. *Political Psychology, 28,* 143–164.

Dunn, J., & Plomin, R. (1990). *Separate lives: Why siblings are so different.* New York: Basic Books.

Dweck, C. (2006). *Mindset: The new psychology of success.* New York: Random House.

Dweck, C. S., Higgins, E. T., & Grant-Pillow, H. (2003). Self-systems give unique meaning to self variables. In M. R. Leary (Ed.), *Handbook of self and identity* (pp. 239–252). New York: Guilford Press.

Dworkin, A. (1981). *Pornography: Men possessing women.* New York: Perigee Books/G. Putnam.

Eagly, A. H. (1978). Sex differences in influenceability. *Psychological Bulletin, 85,* 86–116.

Eagly, A. H. (1987). *Sex differences in social behavior: A social-role interpretation.* Hillsdale, NJ: Erlbaum.

Eagly, A. H. (1995). The science and politics of comparing women and men. *American Psychologist, 50*(3), 145–158.

Eagly, A. H., & Carli, L. L. (1981). Sex of researchers and sex-typed communications as determinants of sex differences in influenceability: A meta-analysis of social influence studies. *Psychological Bulletin, 90,* 1–20.

Eagly, A. H., & Carli, L. L. (2007). Women and the labyrinth of leadership. *Harvard Business Review, 85*(9), 62.

Eagly, A. H., & Crowley, M. (1986). Gender and helping behavior: A meta-analytic review of the social psychological literature. *Psychological Bulletin, 100*(3), 283–308.

Eagly, A. H., & Johnson, B. T. (1990). Gender and leadership style: A meta-analysis. *Psychological Bulletin, 108*(2), 233–256.

Eagly, A. H., & Steffen, V. J. (1986). Gender and aggressive behavior: A meta-analytic review of the social psychological literature. *Psychological Bulletin, 100*(3), 309–330.

Eagly, A. H., Karau, S. J., & Makhijani, M. G. (1995). Gender and the effectiveness of leaders: A meta-analysis. *Psychological Bulletin, 117*(1), 125–145.

Eagly, A. H., Makhijani, M. G., & Klonsky, B. G. (1992). Gender and the evaluation of leaders: A meta-analysis. *Psychological Bulletin, 111*(1), 3–22.

Efron, R. (1990). *The decline and fall of hemispheric specialization.* Hillsdale, NJ: Erlbaum.

Ehrlich, P., & Feldman, M. W. (2007). Genes, environments & behaviors. *Daedalus, 136*(2), 5–12.

Ehrlichman, H., & Eichenstein, R. (1992). Private wishes: Gender similarities and differences. *Sex Roles, 26,* 399–422.

Eibl-Eibesfeldt, I. (1971). *Love and hate: The natural history of basic behaviour patterns* (G. Strachan, Trans.). London: Methuen.

Eibl-Eibesfeldt, I. (1972). Similarities and differences between cultures in expressive movements. In R. Hinde (Ed.), *Non-verbal communication.* Cambridge, UK: Cambridge University Press.

Eibl-Eibesfeldt, I. (1979). *The biology of peace and war: Men, animals, and aggression* (E. Mosbacher, Trans.). New York: Viking Press.

Eisenberger, N. I., Gable, S. L., & Lieberman, M. D. (2007). fMRI responses relate to differences in real-world social experience. *Emotion, 7,* 745–754.

Eisenberger, N. I., Lieberman, M. D., & Satpute, A. B. (2005). Personality from a controlled processing perspective: An fMRI study of neuroticism, extraversion, and self-consciousness. *Cognitive, Affective, and Behavioral Neuroscience, 5,* 169–181.

Eisenman, R. (1995). Why psychologists should study race. *American Psychologist, 50*(1), 42–43.

Ekman, P. (1973). Cross-cultural studies of facial expression. In P. Ekman (Ed.), *Darwin and facial expression.* New York: Academic Press.

Ekman, P., Friesen, W. V., & Hager, J. C. (2002). *Facial action coding system.* Salt Lake City: Research Nexus.

Elder, G. H., Jr., & Caspi, A. (1988). Human development and social change: An emerging perspective on the life course. In N. Bolger, A. Caspi, G. Downey, & M. Moorehouse (Eds.), *Persons in context: Developmental processes. Human development in cultural and historical contexts* (pp. 77–113). New York: Cambridge University Press.

Eliot, G. (1859). *Adam Bede.* New York: Harper & Brothers.

Elliot, A. J., Sheldon, K. M., & Church, M. A. (1997). Avoidance personal goals and subjective well-being. *Personality and Social Psychology Bulletin, 23,* 915–927.

Elliott, E. S., & Dweck, C. S. (1988). Goals: An approach to motivation and achievement. *Journal of Personality and Social Psychology, 54*(1), 5–12.

Ellis, A., & Harper, R. A. (1975). *A new guide to rational living.* Hollywood, CA: Wilshire Books.

Ellis, H. (1913). *Analysis of the sexual impulse, love, and pain* (2nd ed.). Philadelphia: F. A. Davis.

Ellis, H. (1936). *Studies in the psychology of sex.* New York: Random House. (Original work published 1899)

Else-Quest, N. M., Hyde, J. S., & Linn, M. C. (2010). Cross-national patterns of gender differences in mathematics: A meta-analysis. *Psychological Bulletin, 136,* 103–127.

Else-Quest, N. M., Hyde, J. S., Goldsmith, H. H., & Van Hulle, C. A. (2006). Gender differences in temperament: A meta-analysis. *Psychological Bulletin, 132,* 33–72.

Emde, R. N., Plomin, R., Robinson, J., Corley, R., DeFries, J., Fulker, D. W., et al. (1992). Temperament, emotion, and cognition at fourteen months: The MacArthur Longitudinal Twin Study. *Child Development, 63*(6), 1437–1455.

Emmelkamp, P. M. G., Krijn, M., Hulsbosch, L., de Vries, S., Schuemie, M. J., & van der Mast, C. A. P. G. (2002). Virtual reality treatment versus exposure in vivo: A comparative evaluation in acrophobia. *Behaviour Research & Therapy, 40,* 25–32.

Emmons, R. A. (1986). Personal strivings: An approach to personality and subjective well-being. *Journal of Personality and Social Psychology, 51,* 1058–1068.

Emmons, R. A. (1992). The repressive personality and social support. In H. S. Friedman (Ed.), *Hostility, coping, & health* (pp. 141–150). Washington, DC: American Psychological Association.

Engler, B. (1991). *Personality theories: An introduction* (3rd ed.). Boston: Houghton Mifflin.

Epstein, S. (1983). Aggregation and beyond: Some basic issues on the prediction of behavior. *Journal of Personality, 51,* 360–392.

Erdelyi, M. H. (1996). *The recovery of unconscious memories: Hypermnesia and reminiscence.* Chicago: University of Chicago Press.

Erdelyi, M. H. (2006). The unified theory of repression. *Behavioral and Brain Sciences, 29,* 499–511.

Erikson, E. H. (1950). *Childhood and society.* New York: Norton.

Erikson, E. H. (1958). *Young man Luther: A study in psycho-analysis and history.* New York: Norton.

Erikson, E. H. (1963). *Childhood and society* (2nd ed.). New York: Norton.

Erikson, E. H. (1969). *Gandhi's truth: On the origins of militant nonviolence.* New York: Norton.

Erikson, E. H. (Ed.). (1978). *Adulthood.* New York: Norton.

Evidence found for a possible aggression gene [Research News]. (1993). *Science, 260,* 1722–1723.

Exline, R. V. (1972). Visual interaction: The glances of power and preference. *Nebraska Symposium on Motivation, 19,* 163–206.

Exline, R. V., Ellyson, S. L., & Long, B. (1975). Visual behavior as an aspect of power role relationships. In P. Pliner, L. Krames, & T. Alloway (Eds.), *Nonverbal communication of aggression* (pp. 21–52). New York: Plenum Press.

Exner, J. (1986). *The Rorschach: A comprehensive system* (2nd ed.). New York: Wiley.

Eysenck, H. J. (1967). *The biological basis of personality.* Springfield, IL: Charles C Thomas.

Eysenck, H. J. (1990). Biological dimensions of personality. In L. A. Pervin (Ed.), *Handbook of personality: Theory and research* (pp. 244–276). New York: Guilford Press.

Eysenck, H. J. (1992). Four ways five factors are not basic. *Personality and Individual Differences, 13*(6) 667–673.

Eysenck, H. J. (1994). The Big Five or giant three: Criteria for a paradigm. In C. F. Halverson, Jr., G. A. Kohnstamm, & R. P. Martin (Eds.), *The developing structure of temperament and personality from infancy to adulthood* (pp. 37–51). Hillsdale, NJ: Erlbaum.

Eysenck, H. J., & Eysenck, M. W. (1985). *Personality and individual differences: A natural science approach.* New York: Plenum Press.

Eysenck, H. J., & Rachman, S. (1965). *The causes and cures of neurosis.* San Diego, CA: Robert R. Knapp.

Fagala, G. E., & Wigg, C. L. (1992). Psychiatric manifestations of mercury poisoning. *Journal of the American Academy of Child and Adolescent Psychiatry, 31*(2), 306–311.

Fairbanks, L. A. (2001). Individual differences in response to a stranger: Social impulsivity as a dimension of temperament in vervet monkeys (Cercopithecus aethiops sabaeus). *Journal of Comparative Psychology, 115*(1), 22–28.

Fairbanks, L. A., Melega, W. P., Jorgensen, M. J., & Kaplan, J. R. (2001). Social impulsivity inversely associated with CSF 5-HIAA and fluoxetine exposure in vervet monkeys. *Neuropsychopharmacology, 24*(4), 370–378.

Fancher, R. E. (1995). The bell curve on separated twins. *Alberta Journal of Educational Research, 41*(3), 265–270.

Fanon, F. (1967). *Black skin, white masks* (C. L. Markmann, Trans.). New York: Grove Press. (Original work published 1952 as *Peau noire, masques blancs*)

Farde, L., Gustavsson, J. P., & Jonsson, E. (1997, February 13). D2 dopamine receptors and personality traits [Letter]. *Nature, 385,* 590.

Fausto-Sterling, A. (1985). *Myths of gender: Biological theories about women and men.* New York: Basic Books.

Fazio, R., Jackson, J. R., Dunton, B., & Williams, C. J. (1995). Variability in automatic activation as an unobtrusive measure of racial attitudes: A bona fide pipeline? *Journal of Personality and Social Psychology, 69,* 1013–1027.

Fehr, B., & Russell, J. A. (1991). The concept of love viewed from a prototype perspective. *Journal of Personality and Social Psychology, 60*(3), 425–438.

Feingold, A. (1994). Gender differences in personality: A meta-analysis. *Psychological Bulletin, 116*(3), 429–456.

Feingold, A. (1995). The additive effects of differences in central tendency and variability are important in comparisons between groups. *American Psychologist, 50*(1), 5–13.

Fernandez, E., & Turk, D. C. (1995). The scope and significance of anger in the experience of chronic pain. *Pain, 61,* 165–175.

Feshbach, N. D., & Feshbach, S. (1969). The relationship between empathy and aggression in two age groups. *Developmental Psychology, 1,* 102–107.

Feshbach, N. D., & Feshbach, S. (1982). Empathy training and the regulation of aggression: Potentialities and limitations. *Academic Psychology Bulletin, 4,* 399–413.

Feshbach, S. (1971). Dynamics and morality of violence and aggression: Some psychological considerations. *American Psychologist, 26,* 281–292.

Feshbach, S. (1984). The catharsis hypothesis, aggressive drive, and the reduction of aggression. *Aggressive Behavior, 10,* 91–101.

Findley, M. J., & Cooper, H. M. (1983). Locus of control and academic achievement: A literature review. *Journal of Personality and Social Psychology, 44,* 419–427.

Firestone, S. (1970). *The dialectic of sex: The case for feminist revolution.* New York: William Morrow.

Fischer, A. H. (1993). Sex differences in emotionality: Fact or stereotype? *Feminism & Psychology, 3,* 303–318.

Fisher, B. C. (1998). *Attention deficit disorder misdiagnosis: Approaching ADD from a brain-behavior/neuropsychological perspective for assessment and treatment.* Boca Raton, FL: CRC Press.

Fisher, H. (2006). The drive to love: the neural mechanism for mate selection. In R. J. Sternberg & K. Weis (Eds.), *The new psychology of love* (pp. 87–115). New Haven, CT: Yale University Press.

Fisher, M., & Pressley, S. A. (1997, March 29). Crisis of sexuality launched strange journey. *Washington Post,* p. A1.

Fisher, S., & Greenberg, R. P. (1996). *Freud scientifically reappraised: Testing the theories and therapy.* New York: Wiley.

Fiske, D. W. (1971). *Measuring the concepts of personality.* Chicago: Aldine.

Fivush, R., & Nelson, K. (2004). Culture and language in the emergence of autobiographical memory. *Psychological Science, 15,* 573–577.

Flannery, D. J., Vazsonyi, A. T., & Waldman, I. D. (Eds.). (2007). *The Cambridge handbook of violent behavior and aggression.* Oxford, UK: Cambridge University Press.

Flannery, W. P., Reise, S. P., & Widaman, K. F. (1995). An item response theory analysis of the general and academic scales of the Self-Description Questionnaire II. *Journal of Research in Personality, 29*(2), 168–188.

Fleeson, W. (2004). Moving beyond the person-situation debate. *Current Directions in Psychological Science, 13,* 83–87.

Fontaine, K. R. (1994). Personality correlates of sexual risk-taking among men. *Personality and Individual Differences, 17*(5), 693–694.

Ford, C. S., & Beach, F. A. (1951). *Patterns of sexual behavior.* New York: Harper & Paul B. Hoeber.

Forsyth, D. R., Lawrence, N. K., Burnette, J. L., & Baumeister, R. R. (2007). Attempting to improve the academic performance of struggling college students by bolstering their self-esteem: An intervention that backfired. *Journal of Social & Clinical Psychology, 26*(4), 447–459.

Fowler, J. H., Baker, L. A., & Dawes, C. T. (2008). Genetic variation in political participation. *The American Political Science Review, 102*, 233–248.

Fox, N. A., Henderson, H. A., Marshall, P. J., Nichols, K. E., & Ghera, M. M. (2005). Behavioral inhibition: Linking biology and behavior within a developmental framework. *Annual Review of Psychology, 56*, 235–262.

Frank, A. (1952). *The diary of a young girl* (B. M. Mooyaart, Trans.; Eleanor Roosevelt, Intro.). Garden City, NY: Doubleday.

Franken, I. H. A., Muris, P., & Georgieva, I. (2006). Gray's model of personality and addiction. *Addictive Behaviors, 31*(3), 399–403.

Frankl, V. E. (1962). *Man's search for meaning: An introduction to logotherapy* (Rev. ed.; I. Lasch, Trans.). Boston: Beacon Press.

Frankl, V. E. (1984). *Man's search for meaning* (Rev. and updated.) New York: Washington Square Press.

Franklin, B. (1906). *The autobiography of Benjamin Franklin, with illustrations.* Boston: Houghton Mifflin.

Fraser, G. E., Beeson, W. L., & Phillips, R. L. (1991). Diet and lung cancer in California Seventh-day Adventists. *American Journal of Epidemiology, 133*, 683–693.

Fraser, S. (Ed.). (1995). *The Bell Curve wars: Race, intelligence, and the future of America.* New York: Basic Books.

Fredrickson, B. L. (2001). The role of positive emotions in positive psychology: The broaden-and-build theory of positive emotions. *American Psychologist, 56*(3), 218–226.

Freedman, M. B., Ossorio, A. G., & Coffey, H. S. (1951). The interpersonal dimension of personality. *Journal of Personality, 20*, 143–161.

Freitas-Ferrari, M. C., Hallak, J. E. C., Trzesniak, C., Filho, A. S., Machado-de-Sousa, J. P., Chagas, M. H. N., Nardi, A. E., & Crippa, J. A. S. (2010). Neuroimaging in social anxiety disorder: A systematic review of the literature. *Progress in Neuro-Psychopharmacology & Biological Psychiatry, 34*, 565–580.

Freud, A. (1942). *The ego and the mechanisms of defense* (C. Baines, Trans.). London: Hogarth Press.

Freud, A. (1981). *The writings of Anna Freud.* New York: International Universities Press.

Freud, S. (1908). Character and anal eroticism. In *Collected papers* (Vol. 3). London: Hogarth Press.

Freud, S. (1913). *The interpretation of dreams* (3rd ed.; A. A. Brill, Trans.). New York: Macmillan.

Freud, S. (1917). *Psychopathology of everyday life* (A. A. Brill, Trans.). New York: Macmillan.

Freud, S. (1924a). *A general introduction to psychoanalysis* (J. Riviere, Trans.). New York: Washington Square Press. (Original work published 1917)

Freud, S. (1924b). *Collected papers* (Trans.). London: Hogarth Press.

Freud, S. (1947). *Leonardo da Vinci: A study in psychosexuality.* New York: Random House.

Freud, S. (1952). *Totem and taboo: Some points of agreement between the mental lives of savages and neurotics.* (J. Strachey, Trans.) New York: Norton.

Freud, S. (1963a). Introductory lectures on psychoanalysis. In J. Strachey (Ed. & Trans.), *The standard edition of the complete psychological works of Sigmund Freud* (Vol. 16). London: Hogarth Press. (Original work published 1916–1917)

Freud, S. (1963b). *Three case histories: The "Wolf Man," the "Rat Man," and the psychotic Doctor Schreber.* (P. Reiff, Ed.). New York: Macmillan.

Freud, S. (1966a). Character and anal eroticism. In J. Strachey (Ed. & Trans.), *The standard edition of the complete psychological works of Sigmund Freud*, (Vol. 9). London: Hogarth Press. (Original work published 1908)

Freud, S. (1966b). *On the history of the psycho-analytic movement.* New York: Norton.

Freud, S. (1967). Analysis of a phobia in a five-year-old boy. In J. Strachey (Ed. & Trans.), *The standard edition of the complete psychological works of Sigmund Freud* (Vol. 10). London: Hogarth Press. (Original work published 1909)

Friedan, B. (1963). *The feminine mystique.* New York: Norton.

Friedman, H. S. (1979). The concept of skill in nonverbal communication: Implications for understanding social interaction. In R. Rosenthal (Ed.), *Skill in nonverbal communication* (pp. 2–27). Cambridge, MA: Oelgeschlager, Gunn, & Hain.

Friedman, H. S. (2000a). Long-term relations of personality and health: Dynamism, mechanisms, tropisms. *Journal of Personality, 68*(6), 1089–1107.

Friedman, H. S. (2000b). *The self-healing personality: Why some people achieve health and others succumb to illness.* Lincoln, NE: iUniverse (www.iuniverse.com).

Friedman, H. S. (2001). Paradoxes of nonverbal detection, expression, and responding: Points to PONDER. In J. A. Hall & F. J. Bernieri (Eds.), *Interpersonal sensitivity: Theory and measurement* (pp. 351–362). Mahwah, NJ: Erlbaum.

Friedman, H. S. (2007). Personality, disease, and self-healing. In H. S. Friedman & R. C. Silver (Eds.), *Foundations of health psychology* (pp. 172–199). New York: Oxford University Press.

Friedman, H. S. (2008). The multiple linkages of personality and disease. *Brain, Behavior, and Immunity, 22*, 668–675.

Friedman, H. S., & Booth-Kewley, S. (1987a). "The disease-prone personality": A meta-analytic view of the construct. *American Psychologist, 42*, 539–555.

Friedman, H. S., & Booth-Kewley, S. (1987b). Personality, Type A behavior, and coronary heart disease: The role of emotional expression. *Journal of Personality and Social Psychology, 53*, 783–792.

Friedman, H. S., & Kern, M. L. (2010). Contributions of personality to health psychology. In J. Suls, K. Davidson & R. M. Kaplan (Eds.), *Handbook of Health Psychology and Behavioral Medicine.* New York: Guilford.

Friedman, H. S., & Martin, L. R. (2007). A life-span approach to personality and longevity: The case of conscientiousness. In C. Aldwin, C. Park, & A. Spiro (Eds.), *Handbook of health psychology and aging* (pp. 167–185). New York: Guilford Press.

Friedman, H. S., & Martin, L. R. (2011). *The Longevity Project: Surprising Discoveries for Health and Long Life from the Landmark Eight-Decade Study.* New York: Hudson Street Press.

Friedman, H. S., & Miller-Herringer, T. (1991). Nonverbal display of emotion in public and private: Self-monitoring, personality, and expressive cues. *Journal of Personality and Social Psychology, 61*, 766–775.

Friedman, H. S., & Riggio, R. E. (1981). Effect of individual differences in nonverbal expressiveness on transmission of emotion. *Journal of Nonverbal Behavior, 6,* 96–104.

Friedman, H. S., & VandenBos, G. (1992). Disease-prone and self-healing personalities. *Hospital and Community Psychiatry: A Journal of the American Psychiatric Association, 43,* 1177–1179.

Friedman, H. S., DiMatteo, M. R., & Taranta, A. (1980). A study of the relationship between individual differences in nonverbal expressiveness and factors of personality and social interaction. *Journal of Research in Personality, 14,* 351–364.

Friedman, H. S., Hall, J. A., & Harris, M. J. (1985). Type A behavior, nonverbal expressive style, and health. *Journal of Personality and Social Psychology, 48,* 1299–1315.

Friedman, H. S., Kern, M. L., & Reynolds, C. A. (2010). Personality and health, subjective well-being, and longevity. *Journal of Personality, 78,* 179–216.

Friedman, H. S., Riggio, R. E., & Casella D.F. (1988). Nonverbal skill, personal charisma, and initial attraction. *Personality and Social Psychology Bulletin, 14,* 203–211.

Friedman, H. S., Riggio, R. E., & Segall, D. O. (1980). Personality and the enactment of emotion. *Journal of Nonverbal Behavior, 5,* 35–48.

Friedman, H. S., Prince, L. M., Riggio, R. E., & DiMatteo, M. (1980). Understanding and assessing nonverbal expressiveness: The Affective Communication Test. *Journal of Personality and Social Psychology, 39,* 333–351.

Friedman, H. S., Tucker, J. S., Martin, L. R., Tomlinson-Keasey, C., Schwartz, J. E., Wingard, D. L., et al. (1994). Do non-scientists really live longer? *The Lancet, 343,* 296.

Friedman, H. S., Tucker, J. S., Schwartz, J. E., Tomlinson-Keasey, C., Martin, L. R., Wingard, D. L., & Criqui, M. H. (1995). Psychosocial and behavioral predictors of longevity: The aging and death of the "Termites." *American Psychologist, 50,* 69–78.

Friedman, H. S., Tucker, J. S., Tomlinson-Keasey, C., Schwartz, J. E., Wingard, D. L., & Criqui, M. H. (1993). Does childhood personality predict longevity? *Journal of Personality and Social Psychology, 65,* 176–185.

Friedman, M., & Rosenman, R. H. (1974). *Type A behavior and your heart.* New York: Knopf.

Fromm, E. (1941). *Escape from freedom.* New York: Farrar & Rinehart.

Fromm, E. (1947). *Man for himself: An inquiry into the psychology of ethics.* New York: Rinehart.

Fromm, E. (1956). *The art of loving.* New York: Harper & Row.

Fromm, E. (1973). *The anatomy of human destructiveness.* New York: Fawcett Crest.

Fromm, E., & Maccoby, M. (1970). *Social character in a Mexican village: A sociopsychoanalytic study.* Englewood Cliffs, NJ: Prentice-Hall.

Fuchs, A. H. (1998). Psychology and "The Babe." *Journal of the History of the Behavioral Sciences, 34,* 153–165.

Funder, D. C. (1987). Errors and mistakes: Evaluating the accuracy of social judgment. *Psychological Bulletin, 101,* 75–90.

Funder, D. C. (2001). Personality. *Annual Review of Psychology, 52,* 197–221.

Funder, D. C. (2006). Towards a resolution of the personality triad: Persons, situations, and behaviors. *Journal of Research in Personality, 40,* 21–34.

Funder, D. C., & Colvin, C. R. (1988). Friends and strangers: Acquaintanceship, agreement, and the accuracy of personality judgments. *Journal of Personality and Social Psychology, 55,* 149–158.

Funder, D. C., & Colvin, C. R. (1991). Explorations in behavioral consistency: Properties of persons, situations, and behaviors. *Journal of Personality and Social Psychology, 60*(5), 773–794.

Funder, D. C., & Dobroth, K. M. (1987). Differences between traits: Properties associated with inter-judge agreement. *Journal of Personality and Social Psychology, 52,* 409–418

Funder, D. C., & Fast, L. A. (2010). Personality in social psychology. In S. T. Fiske, D. T. Gilbert, & G. Lindzey (Eds.), *Handbook of social psychology, Vol 1* (5th ed.), (pp. 668–697). Hoboken, NJ: John Wiley & Sons.

Funder, D. C., & Ozer, D. J. (1983). Behavior as a function of the situation. *Journal of Personality and Social Psychology, 44*(1), 107–112.

Funder, D. C., & Sneed, C. D. (1993). Behavioral manifestations of personality: An ecological approach to judgmental accuracy. *Journal of Personality and Social Psychology, 64*(3), 479–490.

Funder, D. C., Furr, R. M., & Colvin, C. R. (2000). The Riverside Behavioral Q-sort: A tool for the description of social behavior. *Journal of Personality, 68,* 451–489.

Funder, D. C., Kolar, D. C., & Blackman, M. C. (1995). Agreement among judges of personality: Interpersonal relations, similarity, and acquaintanceship. *Journal of Personality and Social Psychology, 69*(4), 656–672.

Furnham, A., & Saipe, J. (1993). Personality correlates of convicted drivers. *Personality and Individual Differences, 14*(2), 329–336.

Gadlin, H., & Ingle, G. (1975). Through the one-way mirror: The limits of experimental self-reflection. *American Psychologist, 30,* 1003–1009.

Gaines, S. O., & Reed, E. S. (1995). Prejudice: From Allport to DuBois. *American Psychologist, 50,* 96–103.

Gale, A. (1983). Electroencephalographic studies of extraversion-introversion: A case study in the psychophysiology of individual differences. *Personality & Individual Differences, 4,* 371–380.

Gallaher, P. E. (1992). Individual differences in nonverbal behavior: Dimensions of style. *Journal of Personality and Social Psychology, 63,* 133–145.

Galton, F. (1869). *Hereditary genius: An inquiry into its laws and consequences.* London: Macmillan.

Galton, F. (1907). *Inquiries into human faculty and its development* (2nd ed.). London: J. M. Dent.

Gangestad, S. W. (1989). The evolutionary history of genetic variation: An emerging issue in the behavioral genetic study of personality. In D. M. Buss & N. Cantor (Eds.), *Personality psychology: Recent trends and emerging directions* (pp. 320–332). New York: Springer-Verlag.

Garcia, J., & Koelling, R. A. (1966). Relation of cue to consequence in avoidance learning. *Psychonomic Science, 4*(3), 123–124.

Garcia-Palacios, A., Botella, C., Hoffman, H., & Fabregat, S. (2007). Comparing acceptance and refusal rates of virtual reality exposure vs. in vivo exposure by patients with specific phobias. *CyberPsychology & Behavior, 10*(5), 722–724.

Garcia-Palacios, A., Hoffman, H. G., See, S. K., Tsai, A., & Botella, C. (2001). Redefining therapeutic success with virtual reality exposure therapy. *CyberPsychology & Behavior, 4*(3), 341–348.

Gardner, H. (1983). *Frames of mind.* New York: Basic Books.

Garza, R. T., & Santos, S. J. (1991). Ingroup/outgroup balance and interdependent interethnic behavior. *Journal of Experimental Social Psychology, 127*, 124–137.

Gastil, J. (1990). Generic pronouns and sexist language: The oxymoronic character of masculine generics. *Sex Roles, 23*, 629–643.

Gatewood, J. D., Wills, A., Shetty, S., Xu, J., Arnold, A. P., Burgoyne, P. S., et al. (2006). Sex chromosome complement and gonadal sex influence aggressive and parental behaviors in mice. *Journal of Neuroscience, 26*(8), 2335–2342.

Gay, P. (1988). *Freud: A life for our time.* New York: Norton.

Geary, D. C. (1995). Reflections of evolution and culture in children's cognition: Implications for mathematical development and instruction. *American Psychologist, 50*(1), 24–37.

Gergen, K. (2001). Psychological science in a postmodern context. *American Psychologist, 56*, 803–813.

Gifford, R. (1994). A lens-mapping framework for understanding the encoding and decoding of interpersonal dispositions in nonverbal behavior. *Journal of Personality and Social Psychology, 66*, 398–412.

Gillath, O., Shaver, P. R., Baek, J-M., & Chun, D. S. (2008). Genetic correlates of adult attachment style. *Personality and Social Psychology Bulletin, 34*, 1396–1405.

Glass, D. C., Krakoff, L. R., Contrada, R., Hilton, W. F., Kehoe, K., Mannucci, E. G., et al. (1980). Effect of harassment and competition upon cardiovascular and plasma catecholamine responses in Type A and Type B individuals. *Psychophysiology, 17*, 453–463.

Glick, P., Gottesman, D., & Jolton, J. (1989). The fault is not in the stars: Susceptibility of skeptics and believers in astrology to the Barnum effect. *Personality and Social Psychology Bulletin, 15*(4), 572–583.

Glick, S. D. (Ed.). (1985). *Cerebral lateralization in nonhuman species.* New York: Academic Press.

Goffman, E. (1967). *Interaction ritual: Essays in face-to-face behavior.* Chicago: Aldine.

Goldberg, L. R. (1990). An alternative "description of personality": The Big-Five factor structure. *Journal of Personality and Social Psychology, 59*(6), 1216–1229.

Goldberg, L. R. (2001). Analyses of Digman's child-personality data: Derivation of Big-Five Factor scores from each of six samples. *Journal of Personality, 69*(5), 709–743.

Goldberg, L. R., & Saucier, G. (1995). So what do you propose we use instead? A reply to Block. *Psychological Bulletin, 117*(2), 221–225.

Goldenberg, I., Matheson, K., & Mantler, J. (2006). The assessment of emotional intelligence: A comparison of performance-based and self-report methodologies. *Journal of Personality Assessment, 86*(1), 33–45.

Goldsmith, H. H. (1989). Behavior-genetic approaches to temperament. In G. A. Kohnstamm, J. E. Bates, & M. K. Rothbart (Eds.), *Temperament in childhood* (pp. 111–132). Chichester, UK: Wiley.

Goldstein, A. P., & Segall, M. H. (1983). *Aggression in global perspective.* New York: Pergamon Press.

Goldstein, K. (1963). *The organism, a holistic approach to biology derived from pathological data in man.* (Foreword, K. S. Lashley.) Boston: Beacon Press.

Goleman, D. (1995). *Emotional intelligence.* New York: Bantam.

Goleman, D. (2004). *Destructive emotions: A scientific dialogue with the Dalai Lama.* New York: Bantam Dell.

Goodkind, M. S., Gyurak, A., McCarthy, M., Miller, B. L., & Levenson, R. W. (2010). Emotion regulation deficits in frontotemporal lobar degeneration and Alzheimer's disease. *Psychology and Aging, 25*, 30–37.

Gosling, S. D. (2001). From mice to men: What can we learn about personality from animal research? *Psychological Bulletin, 127*, 45–86.

Gosling, S. D. (2008). Personality in non-human animals. *Social and Personality Psychology Compass, 2*, 985–1001.

Gosling, S. D., & John, O. P. (1999). Personality dimensions in non-human animals: A cross-species review. *Current Directions in Psychological Science, 8*, 269–275.

Gosling, S. D., Kwan, V. S. Y., & John, O. P. (2003). A dog's got personality: A cross-species comparative approach to personality judgments in dogs and humans. *Journal of Personality and Social Psychology, 85*, 1161–1169.

Gottesman, I. I. (1991). *Schizophrenia genesis: The origins of madness.* New York: Freeman.

Gottesman, I. I., & Moldin, S. O. (1998). Genotypes, genes, genesis, and pathogenesis in schizophrenia. In M. F. Lenzenweger & R. H. Dworkin (Eds.), *Origins and development of schizophrenia: Advances in experimental psychopathology* (pp. 5–26). Washington, DC: American Psychological Association.

Gottlieb, B. (1998). Support groups. In H. S. Friedman (Ed.), *Encyclopedia of mental health* (Vol. 3, pp. 635–648). San Diego, CA: Academic Press.

Gottlieb, B. H., & Wachala, E. D. (2007). Cancer support groups: A critical review of empirical studies. *Psycho-Oncology, 16*, 379–400.

Gottlieb, G. (2000). Environmental and behavioral influences on gene activity. *Current Directions in Psychological Science, 9*, 93–97.

Gough, H. G. (1987). *CPI, California Psychological Inventory: Administrator's guide.* Palo Alto, CA: Consulting Psychologists Press.

Gough, H. G., Fox, R. E., & Hall, W. B. (1972). Personality inventory assessment of psychiatric residents. *Journal of Counseling Psychology, 19*(4), 269–274.

Gould, S. J. (1981). *The mismeasure of man.* New York: Norton.

Gould, S. J. (1996). *The mismeasure of man* (2nd ed.). New York: Norton. (Original work published 1981)

Graf, P., Mandler, G., & Squire, L. R. (1984). The information that amnesic patients don't forget. *Journal of Experimental Psychology: Learning, Memory, & Cognition, 10*, 164–178.

Graves, J. L., Jr. (2001). *The emperor's new clothes: Biological theories of race at the millennium.* New Brunswick, NJ: Rutgers University Press.

Gray, J. (1992). *Men are from Mars, women are from Venus: A practical guide for improving communication and getting what you want in your relationships.* New York: HarperCollins.

Gray, J. A. (1987). Perspectives on anxiety and impulsivity: A commentary. *Journal of Research in Personality, 21*, 493–510.

Gray, J. A., & McNaughton, N. (2000). *The neuropsychology of anxiety: An enquiry into the function of the septo-hippocampal system* (2nd ed.). Oxford, UK: Oxford University Press.

Graziano, W. G., & Eisenberg, N. (1997). Agreeableness: A dimension of personality. In R. Hogan, J. Johnson, & S. Briggs (Eds.), *Handbook of personality psychology* (pp. 795–824). San Diego, CA: Academic Press.

Greenbaum, C. W., Auerbach, J. G., & Guttman, R. (1989). Fathers' and mothers' perceptions of temperament in Israeli neonates: Effects of adoption and social class. *Israel Journal of Psychiatry and Related Sciences, 26*(1–2), 85–95.

Greenfield, P. M., Trumbull, E., Keller, H., Rothstein-Fisch, C., Suzuki, L., & Quiroz, B. (2006). Cultural conceptions of learning and development. In P. Winne & P. Alexander (Eds.), *Handbook of Educational Psychology,* 2nd ed. (pp.675–692). Washington, DC: American Psychological Association.

Greenwald, A. G., Banaji, M. R., Rudman, L. A., Farnham, S. D., Nosek, B. A., & Mellott, D. S. (2002). A unified theory of implicit attitudes, stereotypes, self-esteem, and self-concept. *Psychological Review, 109,* 3–25.

Greer, G. (1971). *The female eunuch.* New York: McGraw-Hill.

Gridley, M. C. (2006). Preferred thinking styles of professional fine artists. *Creativity Research Journal, 18*(2), 247–248.

Grunberg, N. E., Klein, L. C., & Brown, K. J. (1998). Psychopharmacology. In H. S. Friedman (Ed.), *Encyclopedia of mental health* (Vol. 3, pp. 335–344). San Diego, CA: Academic Press.

Guay, D. R. P. (2009). Drug treatment of paraphilic and non-paraphilic sexual disorders. *Clinical Therapeutics: The International Peer-Reviewed Journal of Drug Therapy, 31,* 1–31.

Guilford, J. P. (1940). Human abilities. *Psychological Review, 47,* 367–394.

Guilford, J. P. (1959). *Personality.* New York: McGraw-Hill.

Hagell, A., & Jeyarajah-Dent, R. (Eds.) (2006). *Children who commit acts of serious interpersonal violence: Messages for best practice.* London, England: Jessica Kingsley Publishers.

Halberstadt, A. (1991). Family patterns of nonverbal development. In R. S. Feldman & B. Rime (Eds.), *Fundamentals of nonverbal behavior.* Cambridge, UK: Cambridge University Press.

Halberstam, J. (1998). *Female masculinity.* Durham, NC: Duke University Press.

Hall, J. A. (1990). *Nonverbal sex differences: Accuracy of communication and expressive style.* Baltimore: Johns Hopkins University Press.

Hall, J. A. (2006). Women's and men's nonverbal communication: Similarities, differences, stereotypes, and origins. In V. Manusov & M. L. Patterson (Eds.), *The Sage handbook of nonverbal communication* (pp. 201–218). Thousand Oaks, CA: Sage.

Hall, J. A., & Bernieri, F. (Eds.). (2001). *Interpersonal sensitivity: Theory and measurement.* Mahwah, NJ: Erlbaum.

Hall, J. A., & Halberstadt, A. G. (1986). Smiling and gazing. In J. S. Hyde & M. C. Linn (Eds.), *The psychology of gender: Advances through meta-analysis.* Baltimore: Johns Hopkins University Press.

Hall, J. A., & Matsumoto, D. (2004). Gender differences in judgments of multiple emotions from facial expressions. *Emotion, 4*(2), 201–206.

Hall, J. A., & Veccia, E. M. (1990). More "touching" observations: New insights on men, women, and interpersonal touch. *Journal of Personality and Social Psychology, 59,* 1155–1162.

Hall, J. A., Andrzejewski, S. A., Yopchick, J. E. (2009). Psychosocial correlates of interpersonal sensitivity: A meta-analysis. *Journal of Nonverbal Behavior, 33,* 149–180.

Hall, J. A., Bernieri, F. J., & Carney, D. R. (2005). Nonverbal behavior and interpersonal sensitivity. In J. A. Harrigan, R. Rosenthal, & K. Scherer (Eds.), *The new handbook of methods in nonverbal behavior research* (pp. 237–281). New York: Oxford University Press.

Hall, J. A., Friedman, H. S., & Harris, M. J. (1986). Nonverbal cues, the Type A behavior pattern, and coronary heart disease. In P. D. Blanck, R. Buck, & R. Rosenthal (Eds.), *Nonverbal communication in the clinical context* (pp. 144–168). University Park: Pennsylvania State University Press.

Hall, M. H. (1967). An interview with "Mr. Behaviorist": B. F. Skinner. *Psychology Today, 1,* 68–71.

Halpern, D. F. (1992). *Sex differences in cognitive abilities* (2nd ed.). Hillsdale, NJ: Erlbaum.

Halpern, D. F. (2004). A cognitive-process taxonomy for sex differences in cognitive abilities. *Current Directions in Psychological Science, 13,* 135–139.

Halpern, D. F. (2006). Assessing gender gaps in learning and academic achievement. In P. A. Alexander & P. H. Winne (Eds), *Handbook of educational psychology,* (pp. 635–653). Mahwah, NJ: Lawrence Erlbaum Associates.

Halpern, D. F., Benbow, C. P., Geary, D. C., Gur, R. C., Hyde, J. S., & Gernsbacher, M. A. (2007). The science of sex differences in science and mathematics. *Psychological Science in the Public Interest, 8*(1), 1–51.

Hamilton, D. L., & Sherman, J. W. (1994). Stereotypes. In R. S. Wyer, Jr., & T. K. Srull (Eds.), *Handbook of social cognition* (pp. 1–68). Hillsdale, NJ: Erlbaum.

Hamilton, J. A. (1989). Postpartum psychiatric syndromes. *The Psychiatric Clinics of North America, 12*(1), 89–103.

Hammer, A. L. (Ed.). (1996). *MBTI applications: A decade of research on the Myers-Briggs Type Indicator.* Palo Alto, CA: Consulting Psychologists Press.

Hampson, S., & Friedman, H. S. (2008). Personality and health: A life span perspective. In O. P. John, R. W. Robins, & L. A. Pervin (Eds.), *The handbook of personality: Theory and research* (3rd ed.). New York: Guilford Press.

Hampson, S. E., & Goldberg, L. R. (2006). A first large cohort study of personality trait stability over the 40 years between elementary school and midlife. *Journal of Personality and Social Psychology, 91,* 763–779.

Hansen, K. (1983). The anals of history: Unintentional humor from freshman composition. *English Journal, 72.*

Hare, A. P., & Blumberg, H. H. (1988). *Dramaturgical analysis of social interaction.* New York: Praeger.

Hare, B., Plyusnina, I., Ignacio, N., Schepina, O., Stepika, A., Wrangham, R., et al. (2005). Social cognitive evolution in captive foxes is a correlated by-product of experimental domestication. *Current Biology, 15*(3), 226–230.

Hargreaves, D. J. (1987). Psychological theories of sex-role stereotyping. In D. J. Hargreaves & A. M. Colley (Eds.), *The psychology of sex roles* (pp. 27–44). Cambridge, UK: Hemisphere.

Hargreaves, D. J., & Colley, A. M. (Eds.). (1987). *The psychology of sex roles.* Cambridge, UK: Hemisphere.

Hariri, A. R. (2009). The neurobiology of individual differences in complex behavioral traits. *Annual Review of Neuroscience, 32,* 225–247.

Harlow, H. F. (1986). *From learning to love: The selected papers of H. F. Harlow* (Clara Mears Harlow, Ed.). New York: Praeger.

Harlow, H. F., & Mears, C. (1979). *The human model: Primate perspectives.* Washington, DC: V. H. Winston.

Harmon-Jones, E. A., & Harmon-Jones, C. (2007). Anger: Causes and components. In T. A. Cavell & K. T. Malcolm (Eds.), *Anger, aggression and interventions for interpersonal violence* (pp. 99–117). Mahwah, NJ: Erlbaum.

Harris, C. R. (2000). Psychophysiological responses to imagined infidelity: The specific innate modular view of jealousy reconsidered. *Journal of Personality and Social Psychology, 78,* 1082–1091.

Harris, J. R. (1999). *The nurture assumption.* New York: Touchstone.

Harrison, C., & Lester, D. (2000). Learning style and personality type in high school students. *Psychological Reports, 87,* 1022.

Harrison, N. A., Singer, T., Rotshtein, P., Dolan, R. J., & Critchley, H. D. (2006). Pupillary contagion: Central mechanisms engaged in sadness processing. *Social Cognitive and Affective Neuroscience, 1,* 5–17.

Harsch, N., & Neisser, U. (1989). *Substantial and irreversible errors in flashbulb memories of the Challenger explosion.* Poster presented at the meeting of the Psychonomic Society, Atlanta, GA.

Hart, D., Eisenberg, N., & Valiente, C. (2007). Personality change at the intersection of autonomic arousal and stress. *Psychological Science, 18,* 492–497.

Hartmann, H. (1958). *Ego psychology and the problem of adaptation* (D. Rapaport, Trans.). New York: International Universities Press.

Hartshorne, H., & May, M. A. (1928). *Studies in the nature of character* (Vol. 1). New York: Macmillan.

Hassin, R. R., Uleman, J. S., & Bargh, J. A. (Eds.). (2005). *The new unconscious.* New York: Oxford University Press.

Hastorf, A. H., & Cantril, H. (1954). They saw a game: A case study. *Journal of Abnormal and Social Psychology, 49,* 129–134.

Hatfield, E., & Sprecher, S. (1986). Measuring passionate love in intimate relationships. *Journal of Adolescence, 9,* 383–410.

Hawkins, J. D., Catalano, R. F., & Miller, J. Y. (1992). Risk and protective factors for alcohol and other drug problems in adolescence and early adulthood: Implications for substance abuse prevention. *Psychological Bulletin, 112,* 64–105.

Hawkley, L. C., & Cacioppo, J. T. (2007). Aging and loneliness: Downhill quickly? *Current Directions in Psychological Science,16*(4), 187–191.

Haworth, C. M. A., Dale, P. S., & Plomin, R. (2009a). The etiology of science performance: Decreasing heritability and increasing importance of the shared environment from 9 to 12 years of age. *Child Development, 80,* 662–673.

Haworth, C. M. A., Dale, P. S., & Plomin, R. (2009b). Sex differences and science: The etiology of science excellence. *Journal of Child Psychology and Psychiatry, 50,* 1113–1120.

Hazan, C., & Shaver, P. (1987). Romantic love conceptualized as an attachment process. *Journal of Personality and Social Psychology, 52*(3), 511–524.

Healy, M. D., & Ellis, B. J. (2007). Birth order, conscientiousness, and openness to experience: Tests of the family-niche model of personality using a within-family methodology. *Evolution and Human Behavior, 28,* 55–59.

Heath, A. C., Eaves, L. J., & Martin, N. G. (1989). The genetic structure of personality: Multivariate genetic item analysis of the EPQ. *Personality and Individual Differences, 10,* 877–888.

Heatherton, T. F., & Hebl, M. R. (1998). Body image. In H. S. Friedman (Ed.), *Encyclopedia of mental health* (Vol. 1, pp. 257–266). San Diego, CA: Academic Press.

Heidegger, M. (1962). *Being and time* (J. Macquarrie & E. Robinson, Trans.). New York: Harper.

Heim, C., Newport, D. J., Heit, S., Graham, Y. P., Wilcox, M., Bonsall, R., et al. (2000). Pituitary-adrenal and autonomic responses to stress in women after sexual and physical abuse in childhood. *Journal of the American Medical Association, 284,* 592–597.

Heine, S., Lehman, D. R., Markus, H. R., & Kitayama, S. (1999). Is there a universal need for positive self-regard? *Psychological Review, 106,* 766–794.

Helgeson, V. S. (1994). The relation of agency and communion to well-being: Evidence and potential explanations. *Psychological Bulletin, 116,* 412–428.

Heller, D., Watson, D. & Ilies, R (2004). The role of person versus situation in life satisfaction: A critical examination. *Psychological Bulletin, 130,* 574–600.

Helmreich, R. L., Spence, J. T., & Wilhelm, J. A. (1981). A psychometric analysis of the Personal Attributes Questionnaire. *Sex Roles, 7,* 1097–1108.

Helson, R., & Roberts, B. W. (1994). Ego development and personality change in adulthood. *Journal of Personality and Social Psychology, 66*(5), 911–920.

Helson, R., Kwan, V. S. Y., John, O. P., & Jones, C. (2002). The growing evidence of personality change in adulthood: Findings from research with personality inventories. *Journal of Research in Personality, 36,* 287–306.

Helzer, J. E., Robins, L. N., & McEvoy, L. (1987). Post-traumatic stress disorder in the general population. *New England Journal of Medicine, 317,* 1630–1634.

Hendricks, T. J., Fyodorov, D. V., Wegman, L. J., Lelutiu, N. B., Pehek, E. A., Yamamoto, B., et al. (2003). Pet-1 ETS gene plays a critical role in 5-HT neuron development and is required for normal anxiety-like and aggressive behavior. *Neuron, 37,* 233–247.

Henley, N. (1977). *Body politics: Power, sex, and nonverbal communication.* Englewood Cliffs, NJ: Prentice-Hall.

Henrich, J., Heine S., & Norenzayan, A. (2010). *Behavioral and Brain Sciences, 33:* 61–83.

Herbranson, W. T., & Schroeder, J. (2010). Are birds smarter than mathematicians? Pigeons (Columba livia) perform optimally on a version of the Monty Hall Dilemma. *Journal of Comparative Psychology, 124,* 1–13.

Herek, G. M. (2006). Legal recognition of same-sex relationships in the United States: A social science perspective. *American Psychologist, 61*(6), 607–621.

Herman, J. L. (1992). *Trauma and recovery.* New York: Basic Books.

Hermann, M. G. (2005). Saddam Hussein's leadership style. In J. M. Post (Ed.), *The psychological assessment of political leaders: With profiles of Saddam Hussein and Bill Clinton* (pp. 375–386). Ann Arbor: University of Michigan Press.

Hermans, H., Kempen, H., & van Loon, R. (1992). The dialogical self. *American Psychologist, 47*, 23–33.

Herringer, L. G., Miller-Herringer, T., & Lewis, S. C. (2006). Gratitude and thanksgiving. Poster presented at the Western Psychological Association meeting, Palm Springs, CA.

Herrmann, E., Hernández-Lloreda, M. V., Call, J., Hare, B., & Tomasello, M. (2010). The structure of individual differences in the cognitive abilities of children and chimpanzees. *Psychological Science, 21*, 102–110.

Herrnstein, R. J., & Murray, C. A. (1994). *The bell curve: Intelligence and class structure in American life.* New York: Free Press.

Herschberger, S. L. (1998). Homosexuality. In H. S. Friedman (Ed.), *Encyclopedia of mental health* (Vol. 2, pp. 403–420). San Diego, CA: Academic Press.

Hetherington, E. M. (1991). Families, lies, and videotapes. *Journal of Research on Adolescence, 1*, 323–348.

Higgins, E. T. (1999). Self-discrepancy: A theory relating self and affect. In R. F. Baumeister (Ed.), *The self in social psychology* (pp. 150–181). Philadelphia: Taylor & Francis Psychology Press.

Higgins, E. T., & Spiegel, S. (2004). Promotion and prevention strategies for self-regulation: A motivated cognition perspective. In R. F. Baumeister & K. D. Vohs (Eds.), *Handbook of self-regulation: Research, theory and applications* (pp. 171–187). New York: Guilford Press.

Hines, M., & Sandberg, E. C. (1996). Sexual differentiation of cognitive abilities in women exposed to diethylstilbestrol (DES) prenatally. *Hormones & Behavior, 30*, 354–363.

Hobson, P. (1993). The emotional origins of social understanding. *Philosophical Psychology, 6*, 227–249.

Hockett, C. F. (1966). The problem of universals in language. In J. H. Greenberg (Ed.), *Universals of language* (2nd ed.). Cambridge, MA: MIT Press.

Hoeller, K. (Ed.). (1990). *Readings in existential psychology and psychiatry.* Seattle: Review of Psychology and Psychiatry.

Hofstadter, R. (1959). *Social Darwinism in American thought* (Rev. ed.). New York: G. Braziller.

Holleran, S. E., Mehl, M. R., & Levitt, S. (2009). Eavesdropping on social life: The accuracy of stranger ratings of daily behavior from thin slices of natural conversations. *Journal of Research in Personality, 43*, 660–672.

Holmes, J. G., & Cavallo, J. V. (2010). The Atlas of Interpersonal Situations: A theory-driven approach to behavioral signatures. In C. R. Agnew, D. E. Carlston, W. G. Graziano, & J. R. Kelly (Eds.), *Then a miracle occurs: Focusing on behavior in social psychological theory and research,* (pp. 321–341). New York: Oxford University Press.

Hong, R. Y., & Paunonen, S. V. (2009). Personality traits and health-risk behaviours in university students. *European Journal of Personality, 23*, 675–696.

Hong, Y., Benet-Martínez, V., Chiu, C., & Morris, M. (2003). Boundaries of cultural influence: Construct activation as a mechanism for cultural differences in social perception. *Journal of Cross-Cultural Psychology, 34*, 453–464.

Hooker, E. (1956). A preliminary analysis of group behavior of homosexuals. *Journal of Psychology, 42*, 217–225.

Hooker, E. (1993). Reflections of a 40-year exploration: A scientific view on homosexuality. *American Psychologist, 48*, 450–453.

Horner, M. S. (1972). Toward an understanding of achievement-related conflicts in women. *Journal of Social Issues, 28*(2), 157–175.

Horney, K. (1942). *Self-analysis.* New York: Norton.

Horney, K. (1945). *Our inner conflicts: A constructive theory of neurosis.* New York: Norton.

Horney, K. (1950). *Neurosis and human growth.* New York: Norton.

Horney, K. (1968). *Self-analysis.* New York: Norton.

Horney, K. (1980). *The adolescent diaries of Karen Horney.* New York: Basic Books.

Horney, K. (1987). *Final lectures* (D. H. Ingram, Ed.). New York: Norton.

Horney, K. (1991). The goals of analytic therapy [Special issue] (A. Dlaska, Trans.). *American Journal of Psychoanalysis, 51*(3), 219–226.

Horowitz, L. M., Rosenberg, S. E., Baer, B. A., Ureno, G., & Villasenor, V. S. (1988). Inventory of interpersonal problems: Psychometric properties and clinical applications. *Journal of Consulting & Clinical Psychology, 56*(6), 885–892.

Horowitz, M. J. (1998). Psychoanalysis. In H. S. Friedman (Ed.), *Encyclopedia of mental health* (Vol. 3, pp. 299–313). San Diego, CA: Academic Press.

House, J. S. (1990). Social structure and personality. In M. Rosenberg & R. H. Turner (Eds.), *Social psychology: Sociological perspectives* (pp. 525–561). New Brunswick, NJ: Transaction.

Howells, K. (1987). Sex roles and sexual behavior. In D. J. Hargreaves & A. M. Colley (Eds.), *The psychology of sex roles* (pp. 268–286). Cambridge, UK: Hemisphere.

Hrdy, S. B. (1999). *Mother nature: A history of mothers, infants, and natural selection.* New York: Pantheon Press.

Hubbs-Tait, L., Nation, J. R., Krebs, N. F., & Bellinger, D. C. (2005). Neurotoxicants, micronutrients, and social environments: Individual and combined effects on children's development. *Psychological Science in the Public Interest, 6*(3), 67–121.

Huesmann, L. R., Eron, L. D., & Yarmel, P. W. (1987). Intellectual functioning and aggression. *Journal of Personality and Social Psychology, 52*(1), 232–240.

Hugdahl, K., & Davidson, R. J. (Eds.). (2003). *The asymmetrical brain.* Cambridge, MA: MIT Press.

Hull, C. L. (1940). *Mathematico-deductive theory of rote learning.* New Haven, CT: Yale University Press.

Hull, C. L. (1943). *Principles of behavior: An introduction to behavior theory.* New York: D. Appleton-Century.

Hunter, J. A., Figueredo, A. J., & Malamuth, N. M. (2010). Developmental pathways into social and sexual deviance. *Journal of Family Violence, 25*, 141–148.

Hunyady, O., Josephs, L., & Jost, J. T. (2008). Priming the primal scene: Betrayal trauma, narcissism, and attitudes toward sexual infidelity. *Self & Identity, 7*, 278–294.

Huston, T. L., Niehuis, S., & Smith, S. E. (2001). The early roots of conjugal distress and divorce. *Current Directions in Psychological Science, 10*, 116–119.

Hyde, J. S. (1986a). Gender differences in aggression. In J. S. Hyde & M. C. Linn (Eds.), *The psychology of gender: Advances through meta-analysis.* Baltimore: Johns Hopkins University Press.

Hyde, J. S. (1986b). Introduction: Meta-analysis and the psychology of gender. In J. S. Hyde & M. C. Linn (Eds.), *The psychology of gender: Advances through meta-analysis.* Baltimore: Johns Hopkins University Press.

Hyde, J. S. (1991). *Half the human experience: The psychology of women* (4th ed.). Lexington, MA: D. C. Heath.

Hyde, J. S. (2007). New directions in the study of gender similarities and differences. *Current Directions in Psychological Science, 16*(5), 259–263.

Hyde, J. S., & Frost, L. A (1993). Meta-analysis in the psychology of women. In F. L. Denmark, & M A. Paludi (Eds.), *Psychology of women: A handbook of issues and theories* (pp. 67–103). Westport, CT: Greenwood Press.

Hyde, J. S., & Linn, M. C. (1986). *The psychology of gender: Advances through meta-analysis.* Baltimore: Johns Hopkins University Press.

Hyde, J. S., Lindberg, S. M., Linn, M. C., Ellis, A. B., & Williams, C. C. (2008). Gender similarities characterize math performance. *Science, 321,* 494–495.

Iacoboni, M. (2009). Imitation, Empathy, and Mirror Neurons. *Annual Review of Psychology, 60,* 653–670.

Ickes, W., Gesn, P. R., & Graham, T. (2000). Gender differences in empathic accuracy: Differential ability or differential motivation? *Personal Relationships, 7,* 95–109.

Ickes, W., Snyder, M., & Garcia, S. (1997). Personality influences on the choice of situations. In R. Hogan, J. A. Johnson, & S. Briggs (Eds.), *Handbook of personality psychology* (pp. 165–195). San Diego, CA: Academic Press.

Inglehart, R., Foa, R., Peterson, C., & Welzel, C. (2008). Development, freedom, and rising happiness: A global perspective (1981–2007). *Perspectives on Psychological Science, 3,* 264–285.

Ingram, R. E., & Scher, C. (1998). Depression. In H. S. Friedman (Ed.), *Encyclopedia of mental health* (Vol. 1, pp. 723–732). San Diego, CA: Academic Press.

International Conference on Carcinogenesis and Risk Assessment. (1996). Genetics and cancer susceptibility: Implications for risk assessment. *Proceedings of the Eighth International Conference on Carcinogenesis and Risk Assessment.* New York: Wiley-Liss.

International Personality Item Pool. (2001). A Scientific Collaboratory for the Development of Advanced Measures of Personality Traits and Other Individual Differences (http://ipip.ori.org/).

Isaacowitz, D. M. (2006). Motivated gaze: The view from the gazer. *Current Directions in Psychological Science, 15,* 68–72.

It Didn't Work (1952, June 30). *Time.*

Izard, C. E. (1971). *The face of emotion.* New York: Appleton-Century-Crofts.

Izard, C. E. (1992). Basic emotions, relations among emotions, and emotion-cognition relations. *Psychological Review, 99,* 561–565.

Izard, C. E., Fine, S., Schultz, D., Mostow, A., Ackerman, B., & Youngstrom, E. (2001). Emotion knowledge as a predictor of social behavior and academic competence in children at risk. *Psychological Science, 12,* 18–23.

Jacklin, C. N., Wilcox, K. T., & Maccoby, E. E. (1988). Neonatal sex-steroid hormones and intellectual abilities at six years. *Developmental Psychobiology, 21*(6), 567–574.

Jackson, C. J. (2003). Gray's Reinforcement Sensitivity Theory: A psychometric critique. *Personality and Individual Differences, 34,* 533–544.

Jackson, D. N., & Messick, S. (Eds.). (1967). *Problems in human assessment.* Huntington, NY: R. E. Krieger.

Jackson, J. J., Bogg, T., Walton, K. E., Wood, D., Harms, P. D., Lodi-Smith, J., Edmonds, G. W., & Roberts, B. W. (2009). Not all conscientiousness scales change alike: A multimethod, multisample study of age differences in the facets of conscientiousness. *Journal of Personality and Social Psychology, 96,* 446–459.

Jaeger, J. (1992). "Not by the chair of my hinny hin hin": Some general properties of slips of the tongue in young children. *Journal of Child Language, 19,* 335–366.

Jaffee, S. R., & Price, T. S. (2007). Gene–environment correlations: A review of the evidence and implications for prevention of mental illness. *Molecular Psychiatry, 12,* 432–442.

Jaffee, S. R., Caspi, A., Moffitt, T. E., Polo-Tomás, M., & Taylor, A. (2007). Individual, family, and neighborhood factors distinguish resilient from non-resilient maltreated children: A cumulative stressors model. *Child Abuse & Neglect, 31*(3), 231–253.

Jaffee, S. R., Caspi, A., Moffitt, T. E., Dodge, K. A., Rutter, M., Taylor, A., et al. (2005). Nature 3 Nurture: Genetic vulnerabilities interact with physical maltreatment to promote behavior problems. *Development and Psychopathology, 17,* 67–84.

James, W. (1890). *Principles of psychology.* New York: Henry Holt.

Janet, P. (1907). *The major symptoms of hysteria: Fifteen lectures given in the Medical School of Harvard University.* New York: Macmillan.

Jaycox, L., & Foa, E. B. (1998). Posttraumatic stress. In H. S. Friedman (Ed.), *Encyclopedia of mental health* (Vol. 3, pp. 209–218). San Diego, CA: Academic Press.

Jellinek, M. S., & Slovik, L. S. (1981). Current concepts in psychiatry. Divorce: Impact on children. *New England Journal of Medicine, 305*(10), 557–560.

Jensen, A. R. (1995). Psychological research on race differences. *American Psychologist, 50*(1), 41–42.

Jensen, M. R. (1987). Psychobiological factors predicting the course of breast cancer. *Journal of Personality, 55,* 317–342.

John, O. P. (1990). The "Big Five" factor taxonomy: Dimensions of personality in the natural language and in questionnaires. In L. A. Pervin (Ed.), *Handbook of personality: Theory and research* (pp. 66–100). New York: Guilford Press.

John, O. P., Robins, R. W., & Pervin, L. A. (Eds.). (2008). *Handbook of personality: Theory and research* (3rd ed.). New York: Guilford Press.

Johnson, S. C., Dweck, C. S., & Chen, F. S. (2007). Evidence for infants' internal working models of attachment. *Psychological Science 18*(6), 501–502.

Johnson, W., & Krueger, R. F. (2006). How money buys happiness: Genetic and environmental processes linking finances and life satisfaction. *Journal of Personality and Social Psychology, 90*(4), 680–691.

Johnson, W., Turkheimer, E., Gottesman, I. I., & Bouchard, T. J., Jr. (2009). Beyond heritability: Twin studies in behavioral research. *Current Directions in Psychological Science, 18,* 217–220.

Johnstone, B., & Bean, J. M. (1997). Self-expression and linguistic variation. *Language in Society, 26,* 221–246.

Jolly, A. (2004). Evolutionary biology: The wide spectrum of sex and gender. *Science, 304,* 965–966.

Jones, E. (1953). *The life and work of Sigmund Freud*. New York: Basic Books.

Jones, E. E., & Nisbett, R. E. (1987). The actor and the observer: Divergent perceptions of the causes of behavior. In E. E. Jones, D. E. Kanouse, H. H. Kelley, R. E. Nisbett, S. Valins, & B. Weiner (Eds.), *Attribution: Perceiving the causes of behavior* (pp. 79–94). Hillsdale, NJ: Erlbaum.

Jones, M. C. (1924). The elimination of children's fears. *Journal of Experimental Psychology, 7*, 383–390.

Joseph, J. E., Liu, X., Jiang, Y., Lynam, D., & Kelly, T. H. (2009). Neural correlates of emotional reactivity in sensation seeking. *Psychological Science, 20*, 215–223.

Jost, J. T. (2006). The end of the end of ideology. *American Psychologist, 61*(7), 651–670.

Jost, J. T. (2009). "Elective affinities": On the psychological bases of left–right differences. *Psychological Inquiry, 20*, 129–141.

Jost, J. T., Glaser, J., Kruglanski, A. W., & Sulloway, F. J. (2003). Political conservatism as motivated social cognition. *Psychological Bulletin, 129*(3), 339–375.

Jung, C. G. (1910). The Association Method. *American Journal of Psychology, 31*, 219–269.

Jung, C. G. (1924). *Psychological types*. New York: Harcourt Brace.

Jung, C. G. (1933). *Modern man in search of a soul*. New York: Harcourt, Brace.

Jung, C. G. (1959). Psychological aspects of the mother archetype. In *Collected works of C. G. Jung* (Vol. 9, Part I). Princeton, NJ: Princeton University Press.

Jung, C. G. (1961a). *Memories, dreams, reflections* (A. Jaffe, Ed.). New York: Pantheon.

Jung, C. G. (1961b). On psychological understanding. In *Collected Works* (Vol. 3). New York: Pantheon.

Jung, C. G. (1961c). The psychogenesis of mental disease. In *Collected Works* (Vol. 3). New York: Pantheon.

Jung, C. G. (1967). Psychological types. In *Collected works of C. G. Jung* (Vol. 6). Princeton, NJ: Princeton University Press. (Original work published 1921)

Jung, C. G. (1968). *Analytical psychology: Its theory and practice*. New York: Pantheon.

Jung, C. G. (1990). *The basic writings of C. G. Jung* (R. F. C. Hull, Trans.). Princeton, NJ: Princeton University Press.

Jung, C. G. (2009). *The red book = Liber novus*. Edited by S. Shamdasani; preface by U. Hoerni; translated by M. Kyburz, J. Peck, & S. Shamdasani. New York: W. W. Norton.

Kagan, J., & Moss, H. A. (1962). *From birth to maturity*. New York: Wiley.

Kagan, J., & Snidman, N. (2004). *The long shadow of temperament*. Cambridge, MA: Belknap Press.

Kagan, J., Snidman, N., & Arcus, D. (1995). The role of temperament in social development. In G. P. Chrousos, R. McCarty, K. Pacak, G. Cizza, E. Sternberg, P. W. Gold, et al. (Eds.), *Stress: Basic mechanisms and clinical implications: Vol. 771. Annals of the New York Academy of Sciences* (pp. 485–490). New York: New York Academy of Sciences.

Kagan, J., Reznick, J. S., Snidman, N., Gibbons, J., & Johnson, M. O. (1988). Childhood derivatives of inhibition and lack of inhibition to the unfamiliar. *Child Development, 59*, 1580–1589.

Kagan, S., & Madsen, M. C. (1972). Experimental analyses of cooperation and competition of Anglo-American and Mexican children. *Developmental Psychology, 6*(1), 49–59.

Kagan, S., & Zahn, B. L. (1975). Field dependence and the school achievement gap between Anglo-American and Mexican-American children. *Journal of Educational Psychology, 67*(5), 643–650.

Kamarck, T. W., & Jennings, J. R. (1991). Biobehavioral factors in sudden cardiac death. *Psychological Bulletin, 109*, 42–75.

Kanagawa, C., Cross, S. E., & Markus, H. R. (2001). "Who am I?" The cultural psychology of the conceptual self. *Personality and Social Psychology Bulletin, 27*(1), 90–103.

Kaplan, H. S. (1983). *The evaluation of sexual disorders: Psychological and medical aspects*. New York: Brunner/Mazel.

Kaplan, J. T., & Iacoboni, M. (2006). Getting a grip on other minds: Mirror neurons, intention understanding, and cognitive empathy. *Social Neuroscience, 1*, 175–183.

Katz, D., & Braly, K. (1933). Racial stereotypes of one hundred college students. *Journal of Abnormal & Social Psychology, 28*, 280–290.

Kazdin, A. E. (2005). Child, parent, and family based treatment of aggressive and antisocial child behavior. In E. D. Hibbs & P. S. Jensen (Eds.), *Psychosocial treatments for child and adolescent disorders: Empirically based strategies for clinical practice* (2nd ed., pp. 445–476). Washington, DC: American Psychological Association.

Kelley, H. H., Holmes, J. G., Kerr, N. L., Reis, H. T., Rusbult, C. E., & Van Lange, P. A. M. (2003). *An atlas of interpersonal situations*. New York: Cambridge University Press.

Kelly, G. A. (1955). *The psychology of personal constructs: A theory of personality*. New York: Norton.

Kelly, G. A. (1963). *A theory of personality: The psychology of personal constructs*. New York: Norton.

Kelly, O. E. (1979). *Until tomorrow comes*. New York: Everest House.

Keltikangas-Jarvinen, L., & Terav, T. (1996). Social decision-making strategies in individualist and collectivist cultures: A comparison of Finnish and Estonian adolescents. *Journal of Cross-Cultural Psychology, 27*, 714–732.

Kemeny, M. E. (2007). Psychoneuroimmunology. In H. S. Friedman & R. C. Silver (Eds.), *Foundations of health psychology* (pp. 92–116). New York: Oxford University Press.

Kendler, K. S., & Baker, J. H. (2006). Genetic influences on measures of the environment: A systematic review. *Psychological Medicine, 37*, 615–626.

Kenny, D. A., Horner, C., Kashy, D. A., & Chu, L. C. (1992). Consensus at zero acquaintance: Replication, behavioral cues, and stability. *Journal of Personality and Social Psychology, 62*(1), 88–97.

Kenrick, D. T. (2006). A dynamical evolutionary view of love. In R. J. Sternberg & K. Weis (Eds.), *The new psychology of love* (pp. 15–34). New Haven, CT: Yale University Press.

Kenrick, D. T., & Funder, D. C. (1988). Profiting from controversy: Lessons from the person–situation debate. *American Psychologist, 43*, 23–34.

Kenrick, D. T., Neuberg, S. L., Zierk, K. L., & Krones, J. M. (1994). Evolution and social cognition: Contrast effects as a function of sex, dominance, and physical attractiveness. *Personality and Social Psychology Bulletin, 20,* 210–217.

Kern, C. H., Stanwood, G. D., & Smith, D. R. (2010). Preweaning manganese exposure causes hyperactivity, disinhibition, and spatial learning and memory deficits associated with altered dopamine receptor and transporter levels. *Synapse, 64,* 363–378.

Kern, M. L., & Friedman, H. S. (2008). Do conscientious individuals live longer? A quantitative review. *Health Psychology, 27,* 505–512.

Kern, M. L., Martin, L. R., & Friedman, H. S. (2010, January). Personality and longevity across seven decades. Poster presented at the 11th Annual Meeting of the Society of Personality and Social Psychology, Las Vegas, NV.

Kernberg, O. F. (1984). *Object-relations theory and clinical psychoanalysis.* New York: J. Aronson.

Kernis, M. H., Brown, A. C., & Brody, G. H. (2000). Fragile self-esteem in children and its associations with perceived patterns of parent–child communication. *Journal of Personality, 68,* 225–252.

Key, S. (1995). The definition of race. *American Psychologist, 50*(1), 43–44.

Keysers, C., & Fadiga, L. (2008). The mirror neuron system: New frontiers. *Social Neuroscience, 3,* 193–198.

Kihlstrom, J. F. (1987). The cognitive unconscious. *Science, 237,* 1445–1452.

Kihlstrom, J. F. (1998). Hypnosis and the psychological unconscious. In H. S. Friedman (Ed.), *Encyclopedia of mental health* (Vol. 2, pp. 467–487). San Diego, CA: Academic Press.

Kihlstrom, J. F., & Barnhardt, T. M. (1993). The self-regulation of memory: For better and for worse, with and without hypnosis. In D. M. Wegner & J. W. Pennebaker (Eds.), *Handbook of mental control* (pp. 88–125). Englewood Cliffs, NJ: Prentice-Hall.

Kihlstrom, J. F., & Glisky, E. L. (1998). Amnesia. In H. S. Friedman (Ed.), *Encyclopedia of mental health* (Vol. 1, pp. 83–93). San Diego, CA: Academic Press.

Kim, H. S., Sherman, D. K., & Taylor, S. E. (2008). Culture and social support. *American Psychologist, 63,* 518–526.

Kim, S. H., Hwang, J. H., Park, H. S., & Kim, S. E. (2008). Resting brain metabolic correlates of neuroticism and extraversion in young men. *NeuroReport: For Rapid Communication of Neuroscience Research, 19,* 883–886.

King, A. (2000). Situated cognition. In A. Kazdin (Ed.), *Encyclopedia of psychology* (Vol. 7, pp. 289–291). New York: Oxford University Press.

King, J. E., & Landau, V. (2003). Can chimpanzee (Pan troglodytes) happiness be estimated by human raters? *Journal of Research in Personality, 37,* 1–15.

Kinsey, A. C., Pomeroy, W. B., & Martin, C. E. (1948). *Sexual behavior in the human male.* Philadelphia: W. B. Saunders.

Kircher, T. T. J., Senior, C., Phillips, M. L., Benson, P. J., Bullmore, E. T., Brammer, M., et al. (2000). Towards a functional neuroanatomy of self-processing: Effects of faces and words. *Cognitive Brain Research, 10,* 133–144.

Kirk, H. L. (1974). *Pablo Casals: A biography.* New York: Holt, Rinehart & Winston.

Kirsch, L. G., & Becker, J. V. (2007). Emotional deficits in psychopathy and sexual sadism: Implications for violent and sadistic behavior. *Clinical Psychology Review, 27,* 904–922.

Kitayama, S., & Markus, H. R. (1999). Yin and Yang of the Japanese self: The cultural psychology of personality coherence. In D. Cervone & Y. Shoda (Eds.), *The coherence of personality: Social-cognitive bases of consistency, variability, and organization* (pp. 242–302). New York: Guilford Press.

Kitayama, S., Markus, H. R., & Matsumoto, H. (1995). Culture, self, and emotion: A cultural perspective on "self-conscious" emotions. In J. P. Tangney & K. W. Fischer (Eds.), *Self-conscious emotions: The psychology of shame, guilt, embarrassment, and pride* (pp. 439–464). New York: Guilford Press.

Klein, M. (1975). *The writings of Melanie Klein.* London: Hogarth Press.

Klein, T. A., Neumann, J., Reuter, M., Hennig, J., von Cramon, D., & Ullsperger, M. (2007). Genetically determined differences in learning from errors. *Science, 318*(5856), 1642–1645.

Klineberg, O. (1935). *Race differences.* New York: Harper.

Kluckhohn, C. (1953). *Personality in nature, society, and culture.* New York: Alfred A. Knopf.

Knickmeyer, R. C., & Baron-Cohen, S. (2006). Fetal testosterone and sex differences. *Early Human Development, 82*(12), 755–760.

Knight, R. G., & Longmore, B. E. (1994). *Clinical neuropsychology of alcoholism.* New York: Psychology Press.

Kobasa, S. C. (1979). Stressful life events, personality, and health: An inquiry into hardiness. *Journal of Personality and Social Psychology, 37,* 1–11.

Kober, H., Kross, E. F., Mischel, W., Hart, C. L., & Ochsner, K. N. (2010). Regulation of craving by cognitive strategies in cigarette smokers. *Drug and Alcohol Dependence, 106,* 52–55.

Koestler, A. (1967). *The ghost in the machine.* London: Hutchinson.

Kohler, W. (1947). *Gestalt psychology: An introduction to new concepts in modern psychology.* New York: Liveright.

Kohn, M. L. (1999). Social structure and personality under conditions of apparent social stability and radical social change. In A. Jasinska-Kania, M. L. Kohn, & K. Slomczynski (Eds.), *Power and social structure: Essays in honor of Wodzimierz Wesoowski* (pp. 59–69). Warsaw, Poland: University of Warsaw Press.

Kohut, H. (1971). *The analysis of the self: A systematic approach to the psychoanalytic treatment of narcissistic personality disorders.* New York: International Universities Press.

Koss, M. P., & Harvey, M. R. (1991). *The rape victim: Clinical and community interventions* (2nd ed.). Newbury Park, CA: Sage.

Kouider, S., & Dupoux, E. (2005). Subliminal speech priming. *Psychological Science, 16*(8), 617–625.

Krafft-Ebing, R. von (1965). *Psychopathia sexualis: A medicoforensic study.* (H. E. Wedeck, Trans.) New York: Putnam. (Original work published 1886).

Krahe, B. (1990). *Situation cognition and coherence in personality.* New York: Cambridge University Press.

Kramer, P. D. (1993). *Listening to Prozac.* New York: Viking.

Kretschmer, E. (1925). *Physique and character: An investigation of the nature of constitution and of the theory of temperament.* New York: Harcourt, Brace.

Kretschmer, E. (1934). *Medizinische psychologie* [Medical psychology]. Translated with an introduction by E. B. Strauss. London: Oxford University Press.

Krishnan, P. (1995). *The Bell Curve:* Some statistical concerns [Special issue]. *Alberta Journal of Educational Research, 41*(3), 274–276.

Kroll, J. (2001). Borderline personality disorder. In H. S. Friedman (Ed.), *The disorders* (pp. 107–116). San Diego, CA: Academic Press.

Kruglanski, A. W. (2004). *The psychology of closed-mindedness.* New York: Psychology Press.

Kruglanski, A. W., Pierro, A., Mannetti, L., & De Grada, E. (2006). Groups as epistemic providers: Need for closure and the unfolding of group-centrism. *Psychological Review, 113,* 84–100.

Kuepper, Y., Alexander, N., Osinsky, R., Mueller, E. Schmitz, A., Netter, P., & Hennig, J. (2010). Aggression—Interactions of serotonin and testosterone in healthy men and women. *Behavioural Brain Research, 206,* 93–100.

Kuhn, T. S. (1962). *The structure of scientific revolutions.* Chicago: University of Chicago Press.

Kumari, V., Ffytche, D. H., Williams, S. C. R., & Gray, J. A. (2004). Personality predicts brain responses to cognitive demands. *The Journal of Neuroscience, 24,* 10636–10641.

Ladd, C. O., Owens, M. J., & Nemeroff, C. B. (1996). Persistent changes in corticotropin-releasing factor neuronal systems induced by maternal deprivation. *Endocrinology, 137,* 1212–1218.

LaFrance, M., & Mayo, C. (1976). Racial differences in gaze behavior during conversations: Two systematic observational studies. *Journal of Personality and Social Psychology, 33,* 547–552.

Lagerspetz, K. M. J., & Bjorkqvist, K. (1994). Indirect aggression in boys and girls. In L. R. Huesmann (Ed.), *Aggressive behavior: Current perspectives. Plenum series in social/clinical psychology* (pp. 131–150). New York: Plenum Press.

Lahey, B., Moffitt, T. E., & Caspi, A. (Eds.). (2003). *Causes of conduct disorder and juvenile delinquency.* New York: Guilford Press.

Långström, N., Rahman, Q., Carlström, E., & Lichtenstein, P. (2010). Genetic and environmental effects on same-sex sexual behavior: A population study of twins in Sweden. *Archives of Sexual Behavior, 39,* 75–80.

Larrance, D. T., & Zuckerman, M. (1981). Facial attractiveness and vocal likeability as determinants of nonverbal sending skills. *Journal of Personality, 49,* 349–362.

Larsen, R. J. (1989). A process approach to personality. In D. M. Buss & N. Cantor (Eds.), *Personality psychology: Recent trends and emerging directions* (pp. 177–193). New York: Springer-Verlag.

Lecci, L., & Johnson, J. D. (2008). Black antiwhite attitudes: The influence of racial identity and the Big Five. *Personality and Individual Differences, 44,* 182–192.

Lee, K. M., Peng, W., Jin, S-A., & Yan, C. (2006). Can robots manifest personality?: An empirical test of personality recognition, social responses, and social presence in human–robot interaction. *Journal of Communication, 56*(4), 754–772.

Letters: Debating sexual selection and mating strategies. (2006). *Science, 312,* 689–697.

Leue, A., & Beauducel, A. (2008). A meta-analysis of Reinforcement Sensitivity Theory: On performance parameters in reinforcement tasks. *Personality and Social Psychology Review, 12,* 353–369.

LeVay, S. (1991). A difference in hypothalamic structure between heterosexual and homosexual men. *Science, 253,* 1034–1037.

LeVay, S. (1993). *The sexual brain.* Cambridge, MA: MIT Press.

Levenson, H. (1981). Differentiating among internality, powerful others, and chance. In H. Lefcourt (Ed.), *Research with the locus of control concept.* New York: Academic Press.

Levesque, M. J., & Kenny, D. A. (1993). Accuracy of behavioral predictions at zero acquaintance: A social relations analysis. *Journal of Personality and Social Psychology, 65,* 1178–1187.

Levine, R., Sato, S., Hashimoto, T., & Verma, J. (1995). Love and marriage in eleven cultures. *Journal of Cross-Cultural Psychology, 26*(5), 554–571.

Lewin, K. (1935). *A dynamic theory of personality: Selected papers* (D. K. Adams & K. E. Zener, Trans.). New York: McGraw-Hill.

Lewin, K. (1947). Group decision and social change. In T. M. Newcomb & E. L. Hartley (Eds.), *Readings in social psychology* (pp. 330–344). New York: Henry Holt.

Lewin, K., Lippitt, R., & White, R. K. (1939). Patterns of aggressive behavior in experimentally created "social climates." *Journal of Social Psychology, 10,* 271–299.

Lewis, C. (1987). Early sex-role socialization. In D. J. Hargreaves & A. M. Colley (Eds.), *The psychology of sex roles* (pp. 95–117). Cambridge, UK: Hemisphere.

Lewis, C. A. (1996). Examining the specificity of the orality-depression link: Anal personality traits and depressive symptoms. *Journal of Psychology, 130,* 221–223.

Lieberman, M. D., & Cunningham, W. A. (2009). Type I and Type II error concerns in fMRI research: Re-balancing the scale. *Social Cognitive and Affective Neuroscience, 4,* 423–428.

Liem, E. B., Joiner, T. V., Tsueda, K., & Sessler, D. I. (2005). Increased sensitivity to thermal pain and reduced subcutaneous lidocaine efficacy in redheads. *Anesthesiology, 102,* 509–514.

Lifton, R. J. (1986). *The Nazi doctors: Medical killing and the psychology of genocide.* New York: Basic Books.

Lilienfeld, S. O., Wood, J. M., & Garb, H. N. (2000). The scientific status of projective techniques. *Psychological Science in the Public Interest, 1,* 27–66.

Lindzey, G. (1961). *Projective techniques and cross-cultural research.* New York: Appleton-Century-Crofts.

Linehan, M. M. (2000). The empirical basis of dialectical behavior therapy: Development of new treatments versus evaluation of existing treatments. *Clinical Psychology: Science & Practice, 7,* 113–119.

Linton, R. (1945). *The cultural background of personality.* New York: Appleton-Century.

Lippa, R. A., Martin, L. R., & Friedman, H. S. (2000). Gender-related individual differences and mortality in the Terman longitudinal study: Is masculinity hazardous to your health? *Personality and Social Psychology Bulletin, 26,* 1560–1570.

Lips, H. M., & Colwill, N. L. (1978). *The psychology of sex differences.* Englewood Cliffs, NJ: Prentice-Hall.

Little, B. R. (1993). Personal projects and the distributed self: Aspects of a conative psychology. In J. M. Suls (Ed.), *The self in social perspective* (pp. 157–185). Hillsdale, NJ: Erlbaum.

Little, B. R., Salmela-Aro, K., & Phillips, S. D. (Eds.). (2007). *Personal project pursuit: Goals, action, and human flourishing.* Mahwah, NJ: Erlbaum.

Liu, M., & Cohn, B. (1993, May 17). The reluctant star. *Newsweek,* 42.

LoBue, V., & DeLoache, J. S. (2010). Superior detection of threat-relevant stimuli in infancy. *Developmental Science, 13,* 221–228.

Lochman, J. E., & Dodge, K. A. (1994). Social-cognitive processes of severely violent, moderately aggressive, and nonaggressive boys. *Journal of Consulting and Clinical Psychology, 62*(2), 366–374.

Locke, J. (1964). *An essay concerning human understanding* (A. D. Woozley, Ed.). Cleveland: Meridian Books, 1964. (Original work published 1690)

Lodi-Smith, J., & Roberts, B. W. (2007). Social investment and personality: A meta-analysis of the relationship of personality traits to investment in work, family, religion, and volunteerism. *Personality and Social Psychology Review, 11,* 1–19.

Lodi-Smith, J., Geise, A. C., Roberts, B. W., & Robins, R. W. (2009). Narrating personality change. *Journal of Personality and Social Psychology, 96,* 679–689.

Loehlin, J. C. (1992). *Genes and environment in personality development.* Newbury Park, CA: Sage.

Loevinger, J. (1987). *Paradigms of personality.* New York: W. H. Freeman. (See pages 93–120, The psychometric approach: Traits.)

Loevinger, J. (1996). The meaning and measurement of ego development. *American Psychologist, 21,* 195–206.

Loevinger, J. (1997). Stages of personality development. In R. Hogan, J. A. Johnson, & S. R. Briggs (Eds.), *Handbook of personality psychology* (pp. 199–208). San Diego, CA: Academic Press.

Loevinger, J., Cohn, L. D., Bonneville, L. P., Redmore, C. D., Streich, D. D., & Sargent, M. (1985). Ego development in college. *Journal of Personality and Social Psychology, 48,* 947–962.

Loewald, H. W. (1988). *Sublimation: Inquiries into theoretical psychoanalysis.* New Haven, CT: Yale University Press.

Loftus, E. F. (2004). Memories of things unseen. *Current Directions in Psychological Science, 13,* 145–149.

Loftus, E. F., & Davis, D. (2006). Recovered memories. *Annual Review of Clinical Psychology, 2,* 469–498.

Loftus, E. F., & Ketcham, K. (1991). *Witness for the defense: The accused, the eyewitness, and the expert who puts memory on trial.* New York: St. Martin's Press.

Lonner, W. J., & Berry, J. W. (Eds.). (1986). *Field methods in cross-cultural research.* Beverly Hills, CA: Sage.

Lord, C. G. (1982). Predicting behavioral consistency from an individual's perception of situational similarities. *Journal of Personality and Social Psychology, 42,* 1076–1088.

Lorenz, K. (1937). The companion in the bird's world. *Auk, 54,* 245–273.

Lorenz, K. (1967). *On aggression* (M. Kerr, Trans.). Toronto: Bantam Books.

Lown, B. (1987). Sudden cardiac death. *Circulation, 76*(Suppl. 1), 186–196.

Lown, B. (1988). Reflections on sudden cardiac death: Brain and heart. *Transactions and Studies of the College of Physicians of Philadelphia, 10*(1–4), 63–80.

Lowrey, R. (1973). *A. H. Maslow: An intellectual portrait.* Monterey, CA: Brooks Cole.

Lucas, R. E. (2007). Long-term disability is associated with lasting changes in subjective well-being: Evidence from two nationally representative longitudinal studies. *Journal of Personality and Social Psychology, 92*(4), 717–730.

Lucas, R. E., & Diener, E. (2001). Understanding extraverts' enjoyment of social situations: The importance of pleasantness. *Journal of Personality and Social Psychology, 81*(2), 343–356.

Lüdtke, O., Trautwein, U., & Husemann, N. (2009). Goal and personality trait development in a transitional period: Assessing change and stability in personality development. *Personality and Social Psychology Bulletin, 35,* 428–441.

Lyon, D., & Greenberg, J. (1991). Evidence of codependency in women with an alcoholic parent: Helping out Mr. Wrong. *Journal of Personality and Social Psychology, 61,* 435–439.

Lyubomirsky, S. (2001). Why are some people happier than others? The role of cognitive and motivational processes in well-being. *American Psychologist, 56,* 239–249.

Lyubomirsky, S., & Ross, L. (1999). Changes in attractiveness of elected, rejected, and precluded alternatives: A comparison of happy and unhappy individuals. *Journal of Personality and Social Psychology, 76*(6), 988–1007.

Lyubomirsky, S., King, L. A., & Diener, E. (2005). The benefits of frequent positive affect. *Psychological Bulletin, 131,* 803–855.

Lyubomirsky, S., Sousa, L., & Dickerhoof, R. (2006). The costs and benefits of writing, talking, and thinking about life's triumphs and defeats. *Journal of Personality and Social Psychology, 90*(4), 692–708.

Maccoby, E. E., & Jacklin, C. N. (1974). *The psychology of sex differences.* Stanford, CA: Stanford University Press.

MacDonald, K. (1995). Evolution, the five-factor model, and levels of personality. *Journal of Personality, 63,* 525–567.

MacDonald, K., & MacDonald, T. M. (2010). The peptide that binds: A systematic review of oxycotin and its prosocial effects in humans. *Harvard Review of Psychiatry, 18,* 1–21.

MacSweeney, E. (2007). Reluctant Romeo. *Vogue, 197*(2), 232–237.

Maddahian, E., Newcomb, M. D., & Bentler, P. M. (1986). Adolescents' substance use: Impact of ethnicity, income, and availability. *Advances in Alcohol & Substance Abuse, 5,* 63–78.

Maddi, S. R. (1970). Alfred Adler and the fulfillment model of personality theorizing. *Journal of Individual Psychology, 26,* 153–160.

Maddi, S. R., & Kobasa, S. C. (1984). *The hardy executive.* Chicago: Dorsey.

Madigan, S., & O'Hara, R. (1992). Initial recall, reminiscence, and hypermnesia. *Journal of Experimental Psychology: Learning, Memory, & Cognition, 19,* 421–425.

Magnus, K., Diener, E., Fujita, F., & Payot, W. (1993). Extraversion and neuroticism as predictors of objective life events: A longitudinal analysis. *Journal of Personality and Social Psychology, 65,* 1046–1053.

Magnusson, D. (1990). Personality development from an interactional perspective. In L. A. Pervin (Ed.), *Handbook of personality: Theory and research* (pp. 193–222). New York: Guilford Press.

Magnusson, D., & Endler, N. S. (Eds.). (1997). *Personality at the crossroads: Current issues in interactional psychology.* Hillsdale, NJ: Erlbaum.

Mahler, M. S. (1979). *Infantile psychosis and early contributions.* New York: J. Aronson.

Major, B. (1993). Gender, entitlement, and the distribution of family labor. *Journal of Social Issues, 49*(3), 141–159.

Major, B., Schmidlin, A. M., & Williams, L. (1990). Gender patterns in social touch: The impact of setting and age. *Journal of Personality and Social Psychology, 58*(4), 634–643.

Malamuth, N. M. (1986). Predictors of naturalistic sexual aggression. *Journal of Personality and Social Psychology, 50*(5), 953–962.

Malamuth, N. M. (1989). The Attraction to Sexual Aggression scale: II. *Journal of Sex Research, 26*(3), 324–354.

Malamuth, N. M., Huppin, M., & Paul, B. (2005). Sexual coercion. In D. M. Buss (Ed.), *The handbook of evolutionary psychology*, (pp. 394-418). Hoboken, NJ: John Wiley

Mansfield, E. D., & McAdams, D. P. (1996). Generativity and themes of agency and communion in adult autobiography. *Personality and Social Psychology Bulletin, 22*, 721–731.

Manstead, A. (1991). Expressiveness as an individual difference. In R. S. Feldman & B. Rime (Eds.), *Fundamentals of nonverbal behavior*. Cambridge, UK: Cambridge University Press.

Manusov, V., & Patterson, M. L. (Eds.) (2006). *The Sage handbook of nonverbal communication*. Thousand Oaks, CA: Sage Publications, Inc.

Marcus, D. K., Fulton, J. J., & Clarke, E. J. (2010). Lead and conduct problems: A meta-analysis. *Journal of Clinical Child and Adolescent Psychology, 39*, 234–241.

Marcus-Newhall, A., Pedersen, W. C., Carlson, M., & Miller, N. (2000). Displaced aggression is alive and well: A meta-analytic review. *Journal of Personality and Social Psychology, 78*, 670–689.

Marín G., & Marín, B. (1991). *Research with Hispanic populations*. Newbury Park, CA: Sage.

Markey, P. M., & Markey, C. N. (2010). Vulnerability to violent video games: A review and integration of personality research. *Review of General Psychology, 14*, 82–91.

Markus, H. R., & Kitayama, S. (1991). Culture and the self: Implications for cognition, emotion, and motivation. *Psychological Review, 98*, 224–253.

Markus, H. R., & Ruvolo, A. (1989). Possible selves: Personalized representations of goals. In L. A. Pervin (Ed.), *Goal concepts in personality and social psychology* (pp. 211–241). Hillsdale, NJ: Erlbaum.

Marsh, A. A., Elfenbein, H. A., & Ambady, N. (2003). Nonverbal "accents": Cultural differences in facial expressions of emotion. *Psychological Science, 14*, 373–376.

Martin, C. L., Ruble, D. N., & Szkrybalo, J. (2002). Cognitive theories of early gender development. *Psychological Bulletin, 128*(6), 903–933.

Martin, J. H., Montgomery, R. L., & Saphian, D. (2006). Personality, achievement test scores, and high school percentile as predictors of academic performance across four years of coursework. *Journal of Research in Personality, 40*, 424–431.

Martin, L. R., Friedman, H. S., & Schwartz, J. E. (2007). Personality and mortality risk across the lifespan: The importance of conscientiousness as a biopsychosocial attribute. *Health Psychology, 26*(4), 428–436.

Martin, L. R., Friedman, H. S., Tucker, J. S., Schwartz, J. E., Criqui, M. H., Wingard, D. L., et al. (1995). An archival prospective study of mental health and longevity. *Health Psychology, 14*, 381–387.

Martin, L. R., Friedman, H. S., Tucker, J. S., Tomlinson-Keasey, C., Criqui, M. H., & Schwartz, J. E. (2002). A life course perspective on childhood cheerfulness and its relation to mortality risk. *Personality and Social Psychology Bulletin, 28*, 1155–1165.

Marx, K. (1872). *Das kapital: Kritik der politischen oekonomic*. Hamburg, Germany: O. Meissner.

Maslow, A. H. (1942). Self-esteem (dominance-feeling) and sexuality in women. *Journal of Social Psychology, 16*, 259–294.

Maslow, A. H. (1968). *Toward a psychology of being* (2nd ed.). Princeton, NJ: Van Nostrand.

Maslow, A. H. (1970). *Motivation and personality*. New York: Harper & Row.

Maslow, A. H. (1982). *The journals of Abraham Maslow*, edited by Richard J. Lowry for the International Study Project, Inc.; in cooperation with Bertha G. Maslow; abridged by Jonathan Freedman. Lexington, MA: Lewis.

Maslow, A. H. (1987). *Motivation and personality* (3rd ed.). New York: Harper & Row.

Masson, J. (1984). *The assault on truth: Freud's suppression of the seduction theory*. New York: Farrar, Strauss, & Giroux.

Masters, W. H., & Johnson, V. E. (1966). *Human sexual response*. Boston: Little, Brown.

Matarazzo, J. D. (1992). Psychological testing and assessment in the 21st century. *American Psychologist, 8*, 1007–1018.

Mathews, A., & MacLeod, C. (1986). Discrimination of threat cues without awareness in anxiety states. *Journal of Abnormal Psychology, 95*, 131–138.

Matsumoto, D. R. (1996). *Culture and psychology*. Pacific Grove, CA: Brooks/Cole.

Maxwell, J. S., & Davidson, R. J. (2007). Emotion as motion: Asymmetries in approach and avoidant actions. *Psychological Science, 18*, 1113–1119.

May, R. (1969). *Love and will*. New York: Norton.

May, R. (1972). *Power and innocence*. New York: Norton.

May, R. (1977). *The meaning of anxiety* (Rev. ed.). New York: Norton.

Mayr, E. (1991). *One long argument: Charles Darwin and the genesis of modern evolutionary thought*. Cambridge, MA: Harvard University Press.

Mazaheri, A., Coffey-Corina, S., Mangun, G. R., Bekker, E. M., Berry, A. S., & Corbett, B. A. (2010). Functional disconnection of frontal cortex and visual cortex in attention-deficit/hyperactivity disorder. *Biological Psychiatry, 67*, 617–623.

McAdams, D. P. (1988). Biography, narrative, and lives: An introduction. *Journal of Personality, 56*, 1–18.

McAdams, D. P. (1991). Self and story. In D. J. Ozer, J. M. Healy Jr., & A. J. Stewart (Eds.), *Perspectives in personality* (pp. 133–159). London: Jessica Kingsley Publishers.

McAdams, D. P. (2009). The moral personality. In D. Narvaez & D. K. Lapsley (Eds,), *Personality, identity, and character: Explorations in moral psychology*, (pp. 11–29). New York: Cambridge University Press.

McAdams, D. P., & Olson, B. D. (2010). Personality development: Continuity and change over the life course. *Annual Review of Psychology, 61*, 517–542.

McBride, C. M., Bowen, D., Brody, L. C., Condit, C. M., Croyle, R. T., Gwinn, M., Khoury, M. J., Koehly, L. M., Korf, B. R., Marteau, T. M., McLeroy, K., Patrick, K., & Valente, T. W. (2010). Future health applications of genomics: priorities for communication, behavioral, and social sciences research. *American Journal of Preventive Medicine, 38*, 556–565.

McCartney, K., Harris, M. J., & Bernieri, F. (1990). Growing up and growing apart: A developmental meta-analysis of twin studies. *Psychological Bulletin, 107*, 226–237.

McClelland, D. C. (1961). *The achieving society*. Princeton, NJ: Van Nostrand.

McClelland, D. C. (1984). *Motives, personality, and society*. New York: Praeger.

McClelland, D. C., Atkinson, J. W., Clark, R. A., & Lowell, E. L. (1953). *The achievement motive*. New York: Irvington.

McClintock, M. K., & Herdt, G. (1996). Rethinking puberty: The development of sexual attraction. *Current Directions in Psychological Science, 5*, 178–186.

McConnell, A. R., & Fazio, R. H. (1996). Women as men and people: Effects of gender-marked language. *Personality and Social Psychology Bulletin, 22*, 1004–1013.

McCrae, R. R., & Costa, P. T., Jr. (1985). Updating Norman's "adequacy taxonomy": Intelligence and personality dimensions in natural language and in questionnaires. *Journal of Personality and Social Psychology, 49*, 710–721.

McCrae, R. R., & Costa, P. T., Jr. (1987). Validation of the five-factor model of personality across instruments and observers. *Journal of Personality and Social Psychology, 52*, 81–90.

McCrae, R. R., & Costa, P. T., Jr. (1989). Reinterpreting the Myers-Briggs Type Indicator from the perspective of the five-factor model of personality. *Journal of Personality, 57*, 17–40.

McCrae, R. R., & Costa, P. T., Jr. (1990). *Personality in adulthood*. New York: Guilford Press.

McCrae, R. R., & Costa, P. T., Jr. (1997a). Conceptions and correlates of openness to experience. In R. Hogan, J. Johnson, & S. Briggs (Eds.), *Handbook of personality psychology* (pp. 825–847). San Diego, CA: Academic Press.

McCrae, R. R., & Costa, P. T., Jr. (1997b). Personality trait structure as a human universal. *American Psychologist, 52*, 509–516.

McCrae, R. R., & Costa, P. T., Jr. (2008). The five-factor theory of personality. In O. P. John, R. W. Robins, & L. A. Pervin (Eds.), *Handbook of personality: Theory and research* (3rd ed.), (pp. 159–181). New York: Guilford Press.

McCrae, R. R., & John, O. P. (1992). An introduction to the five-factor model and its applications [Special issue]. *Journal of Personality, 60*, 175–215.

McCrae, R. R., & Terracciano, A. (2006). National character and personality. *Current Directions in Psychological Science, 15*, 156–161.

McCrae, R. R., Terracciano, A., Costa, P. T., Jr., & Ozer, D. J. (2006). Person-factors in the California adult Q-set: Closing the door on personality trait types? *European Journal of Personality, 20*, 29–44.

McCrae, R. R., Costa, P. T., Jr, Martin, T. A, Oryol, V. E., Rukavishnikov, A. A., Senin, I. G., et al. (2004). Consensual validation of personality traits across cultures. *Journal of Research in Personality, 38*, 181–201.

McCullough, M. E. & Willoughby, B. L. B. (2009). Religion, self-regulation, and self-control: Associations, explanations, and implications. *Psychological Bulletin, 135*, 69–93.

McCullough, M. E., Bono, G., & Root, L. M. (2005). Religion and forgiveness. In R. F. Paloutzian & C. L. Park (Eds.), *Handbook of the psychology of religion and spirituality* (pp. 394–411). New York: Guilford Press.

McCullough, M. E., Tsang, J., & Emmons, R. A. (2004). Gratitude in intermediate affective terrain: Links of grateful moods to individual differences and daily emotional experience. *Journal of Personality and Social Psychology, 86*, 295–309.

McCullough, M. E., Bellah, C. G., Kilpatrick, S. D., & Johnson, J. L. (2001). Vengefulness: Relationships with forgiveness, rumination, well-being, and the Big Five. *Personality and Social Psychology Bulletin, 27*, 601–610.

McCullough, M. E., Friedman, H. S., Enders, C. K., & Martin, L. R. (2009). Does devoutness delay death? Psychological investment in religion and its association with longevity in the Terman sample. *Journal of Personality and Social Psychology, 97*, 866–882.

McDonald, K. L., Bowker, J. C., Rubin, K. H., Laursen, B., & Duchene, M. S. (2010). Interactions between rejection sensitivity and supportive relationships in the prediction of adolescents' internalizing difficulties. *Journal of Youth and Adolescence, 39*, 563–574.

McDougall, W. (1908). *Introduction to social psychology*. London: Methuen.

McGregor, I., McAdams, D. P., & Little, B. R. (2006). Personal projects, life stories, and happiness: On being true to traits. *Journal of Research in Personality, 40*(5), 551–572.

McGue, M., & Lykken, D. T. (1992). Genetic influence on risk of divorce. *Psychological Science, 3*, 368–373.

McLaughlin, M., & Lester, D. (1997). Brain hemisphere dominance and personality. *Perceptual & Motor Skills, 85*(3, Pt. 1), 786.

McMahon, R. C., & Richards, S. K. (1996). Profile patterns, consistency and change in the Millon Clinical Multiaxial Inventory-II in cocaine abusers. *Journal of Clinical Psychology, 52*, 75–79.

Mead, G. H. (1968). *George Herbert Mead: Essays on his social philosophy* (J. W. Petras, Intro.). New York: Teachers College Press.

Mead, M. (1929). *Coming of age in Samoa: A psychological study of primitive youth for Western civilisation* (F. Boas, Foreword). London: Jonathan Cape.

Mead, M. (1935). *Sex and temperament in three primitive societies*. New York: William Morrow.

Mead, M. (1939). *From the South Seas; Studies of adolescence and sex in primitive societies*. New York: William Morrow.

Mead, M. (1954). Cultural discontinuities and personality transformation. *Journal of Social Issues*, Suppl. No. 8, 3–16.

Mead, M. (1963). *Sex and temperament in three primitive societies*. New York: Morrow. (Original work published 1935)

Mechanic, D. (1968). *Medical sociology: A selective view*. New York: Free Press.

Mehrabian, A. (1969). Significance of posture and position in the communication of attitude and status relationships. *Psychological Bulletin, 71*, 359–372.

Melburg, V., & Tedeschi, J. T. (1989). Displaced aggression: Frustration or impression management? *European Journal of Social Psychology, 19*, 139–145.

Mencius. (1898). *The four books; or, The Chinese classics in English compiled from previous works*. Hong Kong: Man Yu Tong.

Menninger, K. A., & Menninger, W. C. (1936). Psychoanalytic observations in cardiac disorders. *American Heart Journal, 11*, 1–12.

Menza, M. A., Forman, N. E., Goldstein, H. S., & Golbe, L. I. (1990). Parkinson's disease, personality, and dopamine. *Journal of Neuropsychiatry and Clinical Neurosciences, 2*, 282–287.

Mercer, J. R. (1979). In defense of racially and culturally non-discriminatory assessment. *School Psychology Review, 8,* 89–115.

Meyer, R. C., Wolverton, D., & Deitsch, S. E. (1998). Antisocial personality disorder. In H. S. Friedman (Ed.), *Encyclopedia of mental health* (Vol. 1, pp. 119–128). San Diego, CA: Academic Press.

Meyer-Bahlburg, H. F. L., Ehrhardt, A. A., Rosen, L. R., & Gruen, R. S. (1995). Prenatal estrogens and the development of homosexual orientation. *Developmental Psychology, 31*(1), 12–21.

Milgram, S. (1974). *Obedience to authority.* New York: Harper & Row.

Miller, B. (2001, May). *Pick's disease.* Paper presented at American Academy of Neurology, Philadelphia.

Miller, H. L., & Siegel, P. S. (1972). *Loving: A psychological approach.* New York: Wiley.

Miller, N. E., & Dollard, J. (1941). *Social learning and imitation.* New Haven, CT: Yale University Press.

Miller, N., Pedersen, W. C., Earleywine, M., & Pollock, V. E. (2003). A theoretical model of triggered displaced aggression. *Personality and Social Psychology Review, 7,* 75–97.

Millett, K. (1974). *Flying.* New York: Knopf.

Millon, T. (Ed.). (1997). *The Millon inventories: Clinical and personality assessment.* New York: Guilford Press.

Milner, B. (1962). Les troubles de la memoire accompagnant des lesions hippocampiques bilaterales. In P. Passonant (Ed.), *Physiologie de l'hippocampique.* Paris: Centre National de la Recherche Scientifique.

Mischel, W. (1968). *Personality and assessment.* New York: Wiley.

Mischel, W. (1973). Toward a cognitive social learning reconceptualization of personality. *Psychological Review, 80,* 252–283.

Mischel, W. (1977). On the future of personality assessment. *American Psychologist, 32,* 246–254.

Mischel, W. (1990). Personality dispositions visited and revisited: A view after three decades. In L. A. Pervin (Ed.), *Handbook of personality: Theory and research.* New York: Guilford Press.

Mischel, W. (2007). Walter Mischel. In G. Lindzey & W. M. Runyan (Eds.), *A history of psychology in autobiography* (Vol. 9, pp. 229–267). Washington, DC: American Psychological Association.

Mischel, W., & Shoda, Y. (1995). A cognitive-affective system theory of personality: Reconceptualizing situations, dispositions, dynamics, and invariance in personality structure. *Psychological Review, 102,* 246–268.

Mishnah, Torah, Hilchot Teshuva, 5.1.

Mitchell, S. A. (2000). *Relationality: From attachment to intersubjectivity.* Hillsdale, NJ: Analytic Press.

Moffitt, T. E. (2005). The new look of behavioral genetics in developmental psychopathology: Gene-environment interplay in antisocial behaviors. *Psychological Bulletin, 131,* 533–554.

Moir, A., & Jessel, D. (1991). *Brain sex: The real difference between men & women.* London: Mandarin.

Moore, T., & Merikle, P. (1991). *In the mind's eye: Enhancing human performance.* Washington, DC: National Academy Press.

Morawski, J. G. (1985). The measurement of masculinity and femininity: Engendering categorical realities [Special issue]. *Journal of Personality, 53*(2), 196–223.

Morehouse, R. E., Farley, F. H., & Youngquist, J. V. (1990). Type T personality and the Jungian classification system. *Journal of Personality Assessment, 54,* 231–235.

Moreland, K. L., Eyde, L. D., Robertson, G. J., Primoff, E. S., & Most, R. B. (1995). Assessment of test user qualifications: A research-based measurement procedure. *American Psychologist, 50*(1), 14–23.

Morell, V. (1993). Evidence found for a possible "aggression gene." *Science, 260* (5115), 1722–1723.

Morewedge, C. K., & Norton, M. I. (2009). When dreaming is believing: The (motivated) interpretation of dreams. *Journal of Personality and Social Psychology, 96,* 249–264.

Morf, C. C., & Horvath, S. (2010). Self-regulation processes and their signatures: Dynamics of the self-system. In R. H. Hoyle (Ed.), *Handbook of personality and self-regulation,* (pp. 117–144). Malden, MA: Wiley-Blackwell.

Morgan, J. P. (Ed.). (2006). *Perspectives on the psychology of aggression.* Hauppauge, NY: Nova Science.

Morling, B., & Lamoreaux, M. (2008). Measuring culture outside the head: A meta-analysis of individualism-collectivism in cultural products. *Personality and Social Psychology Review, 12,* 199–221.

Mowrer, O. H., & Mowrer, W. A. (1938). Enuresis: A method for its study and treatment. *American Journal of Orthopsychiatry, 8,* 436–459.

Mroczek, D. K., & Spiro, A. III. (2003). Modeling intraindividual change in personality traits: Findings from the Normative Aging Study. *Journal of Gerontology: Psychological Sciences, 58B*(3), P153–P165.

Mroczek, D. K., & Spiro, A. III. (2005). Change in life satisfaction during adulthood: Findings from the VA normative aging study. *Journal of Personality and Social Psychology, 88,* 189–202.

Murphy, G. (1949). *Historical introduction to modern psychology.* (Rev. ed.). New York: Harcourt, Brace.

Murray, H. A. (1938). *Explorations in personality: A clinical and experimental study of fifty men of college age, by the workers at the Harvard Psychological Clinic.* New York: Oxford University Press.

Murray, H. A. (1943). *Analysis of the personality of Adolph Hitler.* Office of Strategic Services (OSS) Confidential Report. Ithaca, NY: Cornell University Law Library.

Murray, H. A. (1948). *Assessment of men.* New York: Rinehart.

Murray, H. A. (1962). *Explorations in personality.* New York: Science Editions.

Murray, S. O. (1996). *American gay.* Chicago: University of Chicago Press.

Murtha, T. C., Kanfer, R., & Ackerman, P. L. (1996). Toward an interactionist taxonomy of personality and situations: An integrative situational-dispositional representation of personality traits. *Journal of Personality and Social Psychology, 71,* 193–207.

Mussell, M. P., & Mitchell, J. E. (1998). Anorexia nervosa and bulimia nervosa. In H. S. Friedman (Ed.), *Encyclopedia of mental health* (Vol. 1, pp. 111–118). San Diego, CA: Academic Press.

Myers, D. G. (2000). *The American paradox: Spiritual hunger in an age of plenty.* New Haven, CT: Yale University Press.

Myers, I. B. (1962). *The Myers-Briggs Type Indicator.* Princeton, NJ: Educational Testing Service.

Myers, I. B., & McCaulley, M. H. (1985). *Manual, a guide to the development and use of the Myers-Briggs Type Indicator* (R. Most, Ed.). Palo Alto, CA: Consulting Psychologists Press.

Myrdal, G. (1944). *An American dilemma: The Negro problem and modern democracy.* New York, London: Harper & Brothers.

Nabokov, V. (1973). *Strong opinions.* New York: McGraw-Hill., (p. 66).

Nakamura, J., & Csikszentmihalyi, M. (2009). Flow theory and research. In C. R. Snyder & S. J. Lopez (Eds.), *Oxford handbook of positive psychology* (2nd ed.), (pp. 195–206). New York: Oxford University Press.

Nakano, K. (1990). Effects of two self-control procedures on modifying Type A behavior. *Journal of Clinical Psychology, 46*(5), 652–657.

Napier, J. L., & Jost, J. T. (2008). Why are conservatives happier than liberals? *Psychological Science, 19*, 565–572.

National Institutes of Health. (1998). Diagnosis and Treatment of Attention-Deficit/Hyperactivity Disorder. *Consensus Statement, 16*(2), 1–37.

Needleman, H. L., & Bellinger, D. (1991). The health effects of low level exposure to lead. *Annual Review of Public Health, 12*, 111–140.

Nelson, K. (1993). The psychological and social origins of autobiographical memory. *Psychological Science, 4*, 7–14.

Nesse, R. M. (1990). The evolutionary functions of repression and the ego defenses. *Journal of the American Academy of Psychoanalysis, 18*, 260–285.

Neubauer, P. B. (1994). The role of displacement in psychoanalysis. *Psychoanalytic Study of the Child, 49*, 107–119.

Newcomb, M. D., Maddahian, E., & Bentler, P. M. (1986). Risk factors for drug use among adolescents: Concurrent and longitudinal analyses. *American Journal of Public Health, 76*, 525–531.

Newcombe, N. S., Drummey, A. B., Fox, N. A., Lie, E., & Ottinger-Alberts, W. (2000). Remembering early childhood: How much, how, and why (or why not). *Current Directions in Psychological Science, 9*(2), 55–58.

Newman, L. S., Duff, K. J., & Baumeister, R. F. (1997). A new look at defensive projection: Thought suppression, accessibility, and biased person perception. *Journal of Personality and Social Psychology, 72*, 980–1001.

Nicholson, J. (1993). *Men and women: How different are they?* Oxford, UK: Oxford University Press.

Nisbett, R. E. (2003). *The geography of thought.* New York: Free Press.

Nisbett, R. E. (2009). *Intelligence and how to get it: Why schools and cultures count.* New York: W. W. Norton & Co.

Nisbett, R. E., & Cohen, D. (1996). *Culture of honor: The psychology of violence in the South.* Boulder, CO: Westview Press.

Noel, J. G., Forsyth, D. R., & Kelley, K. N. (1987). Improving the performance of failing students by overcoming their self-serving attributional biases. *Basic & Applied Social Psychology, 8*, 151–162.

Norem, J. K. (1989). Cognitive strategies as personality: Effectiveness, specificity, flexibility, and change. In D. M. Buss & N. Cantor (Eds.), *Personality psychology: Recent trends and emerging directions* (pp. 45–60). New York: Springer-Verlag.

Norem, J. K. (2008). Defensive pessimism, anxiety, and the complexity of evaluating self-regulation. *Social and Personality Psychology Compass, 2*, 121–134.

Norem, J. K., & Cantor, N. (1986). Defensive pessimism: Harnessing anxiety as motivation. *Journal of Personality and Social Psychology, 51*(6), 1208–1217.

Norem, J. K., & Smith, S. (2006). Defensive pessimism: Positive past, anxious present, and pessimistic future. In L. J. Sanna & E. C. Chang, *Judgments over time: The interplay of thoughts, feelings, and behaviors* (pp. 34–46). New York: Oxford University Press.

Norenzayan, A., & Lee, A. (2010). It was meant to happen: Explaining cultural variations in fate attributions. *Journal of Personality and Social Psychology, 98*, 702–720.

Norman, C. C., & Aron, A. (2003). Aspects of possible self that predict motivation to achieve or avoid it. *Journal of Experimental Social Psychology, 39*, 500–507.

Norman, W. T. (1963). Toward an adequate taxonomy of personality attributes: Replicated factor structure in peer nomination personality ratings. *Journal of Abnormal and Social Psychology, 66*(6), 574–583.

Norman, W. T., & Goldberg, L. R. (1966). Raters, ratees, and randomness in personality structure. *Journal of Personality and Social Psychology, 4*(6), 681–691.

North, M. M., North, S. M., & Coble, J. R. (1998). Virtual reality therapy: An effective treatment for phobias. *Studies in Health Technology and Informatics, 58*, 112–119.

Nsamenang, A. B. (2004). *Cultures of human development and education: Challenge to growing up African.* Hauppauge, NY: Nova Science.

Nyborg, H. (Ed.). (1997). *The scientific study of human nature: Tribute to Hans J. Eysenck at eighty.* New York: Elsevier Science.

O'Carroll, R. E., Masterton, G., Dougall, N., & Ebmeier, K. P. (1995). The neuropsychiatric sequelae of mercury poisoning: The Mad Hatter's disease revisited. *British Journal of Psychiatry, 167*(1), 95–98.

O'Connor, M. C., & Paunonen, S. V. (2007). Big Five personality predictors of post-secondary academic performance. *Personality and Individual Differences, 43*, 971–990.

O'Driscoll, P. (2006, November 6). Pastor: "I am a deceiver and a liar." *USA Today.*

O'Hara, M. W. (1995). Postpartum depression. In L. B. Alloy (Ed.), *Series in Psychopathology* (pp. 1–27). New York: Springer-Verlag.

Oakes, L. M., Ross-Sheehy, S., & Luck, S. J. (2006). Rapid development of feature binding in visual short term memory. *Psychological Science, 17*(9), 781–787.

Oakley, A. (1972). *Sex, gender and society.* New York: Harper & Row.

Oberman, L. M., & Ramachandran, V. S. (2008). Preliminary evidence for deficits in multisensory integration in autism spectrum disorders: The mirror neuron hypothesis. *Social Neuroscience, 3*, 348–355.

Odgers, C. L., Moffitt, T. E., Broadbent, J. M., Dickson, N., Hancox, R. J., Harrington, H., Poulton, R., Sears, M. R., Thomson, W. M., & Caspi, A. (2008). Female and male antisocial trajectories: From childhood origins to adult outcomes. *Development and Psychopathology, 20*, 673–716.

Ohman, A., & Mineka, S. (2003). The malicious serpent: Snakes as a prototypical stimulus for an evolved module of fear. *Current Directions in Psychological Science, 12*, 5–8.

Olson, J. M., Vernon, P. A., Harris, J. A., & Jang, K. L. (2001). The heritability of attitudes: A study of twins. *Journal of Personality and Social Psychology, 80*(6), 845–860.

Omoto, A. M., & Snyder, M. (1995). Sustained helping without obligation: Motivation, longevity of service, and perceived attitude change among AIDS volunteers. *Journal of Personality and Social Psychology, 68,* 671–686.

Online Mendelian Inheritance in Man: National Center for Biotechnology Information, National Library of Medicine (Bethesda, MD), www.ncbi.nlm.nih.gov/omim.

Oren, D. A. (1985). *Joining the club: A history of Jews and Yale.* New Haven, CT: Yale University Press.

Orgler, H. (1963). *Alfred Adler: The man and his work.* New York: Capricorn.

Orwell, G. (1949). *1984.* New York: Harcourt Brace.

Ostrov, J. M., & Godleski, S. A. (2010). Toward an integrated gender-linked model of aggression subtypes in early and middle childhood. *Psychological Review, 117,* 233–242.

Otten, C. M. (1985). Genetic effects on male and female development and on the sex ratio. In R. L. Hall (Ed.), *Male–female differences: A biocultural perspective.* New York: Praeger.

Overmier, J. B., & Seligman, M. E. (1967). Effects of inescapable shock upon subsequent escape and avoidance responding. *Journal of Comparative and Physiological Psychology, 63,* 28–33.

Owens, J., Bower, G. H., & Black, J. B. (1979). The "soap opera" effect in story recall. *Memory and Cognition, 7,* 185–191.

Ozer, D. J. (1986). *Consistency in personality: A methodological framework.* New York: Springer-Verlag.

Ozer, D. J. (1993). The Q-sort method and the study of personality development. In D. C. Funder, R. D. Parke, C. Tomlinson-Keasey, & K. Widaman (Eds.), *Studying lives through time: Personality and development* (pp. 147–168). Washington, DC: American Psychological Association.

Ozer, D. J., & Benet-Martínez, V. (2006). Personality and the prediction of consequential outcomes. *Annual Review of Psychology, 57,* 401–421.

Palmer, J. P. (Ed.). (1996). *Prediction, prevention, and genetic counseling in IDDM.* New York: Wiley.

Panksepp, J. (1991). Affective neuroscience: A conceptual framework for the neurobiological study of emotions. In K. Strongman (Ed.), *International reviews of studies in emotions* (pp. 59–99). New York: Wiley.

Parker, E. S., & Noble, E. P. (1977). Alcohol consumption and cognitive functioning in social drinkers. *Journal of Studies on Alcohol, 38*(7), 1224–1232.

Parsons, J. E. (1980). Psychosexual neutrality: Is anatomy destiny? In J. E. Parsons (Ed.), *The psychobiology of sex differences and sex roles.* Cambridge, UK: Hemisphere.

Parsons, T. D., & Rizzo, A. A. (2008). Affective outcomes of virtual reality exposure therapy for anxiety and specific phobias: A meta-analysis. *Journal of Behavior Therapy and Experimental Psychiatry, 39,* 250–261.

Pascal, B. (1961). *Pensées.* Paris: Garnier Frères. (Original work published 1670)

Passini, F., & Norman, W. (1966). A universal conception of personality structure? *Journal of Personality and Social Psychology, 4,* 44–49.

Paulhus, D. L., Trapnell, P. D., & Chen, D. (1999). Birth order effects on personality and achievement within families. *Psychological Science, 10*(6), 482–488.

Pavlov, I. P. (1927). *Conditioned reflexes: An investigation of the physiological activity of the cerebral cortex.* Oxford, UK: Oxford University Press.

Payer, L. (1966). *Medicine and culture: Varieties of treatment in the United States, England, West Germany, and France.* New York: Henry Holt.

Pearce, J. (1985). Harry Stack Sullivan: Theory and practice. *American Journal of Social Psychiatry, 5*(4), 5–13.

Pearson, P. R., Lankshear, D. W., & Francis, L. J. (1989). Personality and social class among eleven-year-old children. *Educational Studies, 15*(2), 107–113.

Pedersen, N. L., Plomin, R., McClearn, G. E., & Friberg, L. (1988). Neuroticism, extraversion, and related traits in adult twins reared apart and reared together. *Journal of Personality and Social Psychology, 55,* 950–957.

Pederson, A. K., King, J. E., & Landau, V. I. (2005). Chimpanzee (Pan troglodytes) personality predicts behavior. *Journal of Research in Personality, 39,* 534–549.

Pederson, D. R., Moran, G., Sitko, C., Campbell, K., Ghesquire, K., & Acton, H. (1990). Maternal sensitivity and the security of infant–mother attachment: A Q-sort study. *Child Development, 61,* 1974–1983.

Penke, L., & Asendorpf, J. B. (2008). Evidence for conditional sex differences in emotional but not in sexual jealousy at the automatic level of cognitive processing. *European Journal of Personality, 22,* 3–30.

Pennebaker, J. W. (1982). *The psychology of physical symptoms.* New York: Springer-Verlag.

Pennebaker, J. W. (1990). *Opening up: The healing power of confiding in others.* New York: William Morrow.

Pennebaker, J. W., & Chung, C. K. (2007). Expressive writing, emotional upheavals, and health. In H. S. Friedman & R. C. Silver (Eds.), *Foundations of health psychology* (pp. 263–284). New York: Oxford University Press.

Pennebaker, J. W., & Graybeal, A. (2001). Patterns of natural language use: Disclosure, personality, and social integration. *Current Directions in Psychological Science, 10*(3), 90–93.

Pennebaker, J. W., & Keough, K. A. (1999). Revealing, organizing, and reorganizing the self in response to stress and emotion. In R. J. Contrada & R. D. Ashmore (Eds.), *Self, social identity, and physical health: Interdisciplinary explorations* (pp. 101–121). New York: Oxford University Press.

Pennebaker, J. W., & Lay, T. C. (2002). Language use and personality during crises: Analyses of Mayor Rudolph Giuliani's press conferences. *Journal of Research in Personality, 36,* 271–282.

Pennebaker, J. W., & Seagal, J. D. (1999). Forming a story: The health benefits of narrative. *Journal of Clinical Psychology, 55*(10), 1243–1254.

Pennebaker, J. W., & Stone, L. D. (2003). Words of wisdom: Language use over the life span. *Journal of Personality and Social Psychology, 85*(2), 291–301.

Pennebaker, J. W., Burnam, M. A., Schaeffer, M. A., & Harper, D. C. (1997). Lack of control as a determinant of perceived physical symptoms. *Journal of Personality and Social Psychology, 35,* 167–174.

Peplau, L. A., & Caldwell, M. A. (1978). Loneliness: A cognitive analysis. *Essence, 2*(4), 207–220.

Peplau, L. A., & Perlman, D. (Eds.). (1982). *Loneliness: A sourcebook of current theory, research, and therapy.* New York: Wiley Interscience.

Perlman, D., & Joshi, P. (1987). The revelation of loneliness. *Journal of Social Behavior and Personality, 2* (2, Pt. 2), 63–76.

Perlman, D., & Peplau, L. A. (1998). Loneliness. In H. S. Friedman (Ed.), *Encyclopedia of mental health* (Vol. 2, pp. 571–581). San Diego, CA: Academic Press.

Perlman, D., Gerson, A. C., & Spinner, B. (1978). Loneliness among senior citizens: An empirical report. *Essence, 2*(4), 239–248.

Perls, F. S., Hefferline, R., & Goodman, P. (1951). *Gestalt therapy: Excitement and growth in human personality.* New York: Julian Press.

Perry, H. S. (1982). *Psychiatrist of America: The life of Harry Stack Sullivan.* Cambridge, MA: Belknap Press.

Perry, R. J., & Miller, B. L. (2001). Behavior and treatment in frontotemporal dementia. *Neurology, 56* (Suppl. 4), S46–S51.

Persky, H. (1987). *Psychoendocrinology of human sexual behavior.* New York: Praeger.

Persky, V., Kempthorne-Rawson, J., & Shekelle, R. (1987). Personality and risk of cancer: 20-year follow-up of the Western Electric Study. *Psychosomatic Medicine, 49*(5), 435–449.

Pervin, L. A. (Ed.). (1990). *Handbook of personality: Theory and research.* New York: Guilford Press.

Peterman, A. H., & Lecci, L. (2007). Personal projects in health and illness. In B. R. Little, K. Salmela-Aro, & S. D. Phillips (Eds.), *Personal project pursuit: Goals, action, and human flourishing* (pp. 329–353). Mahwah, NJ: Erlbaum.

Peterson, C., & Barrett, L. C. (1987). Explanatory style and academic performance among university freshmen. *Journal of Personality and Social Psychology, 53,* 603–607.

Peterson, C., & Park, N. (2009). Increasing happiness in lasting ways. *The Psychologist, 22,* 304–307.

Peterson, C., & Seligman, M. E. P. (1987). Explanatory style and illness. *Journal of Personality, 55,* 237–265.

Peterson, C., Seligman, M. E. P., & Vaillant, G. E. (1988). Pessimistic explanatory style is a risk factor for physical illness: A thirty-five year longitudinal study. *Journal of Personality and Social Psychology, 55*(1), 23–27.

Peterson, R. (1978). Review of the Rorschach. In O. Buros (Ed.), *The eighth mental measurements yearbook.* Hyland Park, NJ: Gryphon.

Petrinovich, L. F. (1995). *Human evolution, reproduction, and morality.* New York: Plenum Press.

Pettigrew, T. (1958). Personality and sociocultural factors in intergroup attitudes: A cross-national comparison. *Journal of Conflict Resolution, 2,* 29–42.

Pew Research Center. (2006). *Are we happy yet?* [Social Trends Report]. Washington, DC: Pew Research Center.

Pezdek, K., & Banks, W. P. (Eds.). (1996). *The recovered memory/false memory debate.* San Diego, CA: Academic Press.

Phillips, D. P., Van Voorhees, C. A., & Ruth, T. E. (1992). The birthday: Lifeline or deadline? *Psychosomatic Medicine, 54*(5), 532–542.

Phinney, J. S. (1993). A three stage model of ethnic identity development in adolescence. In M. E. Bernal & G. P. Knight (Eds.), *Ethnic identity: Formation and transmission among Hispanics and other minorities* (pp. 61–79). New York: State University of New York Press.

Phinney, J. S. (1996). When we talk about American ethnic groups, what do we mean? *American Psychologist, 51*(9), 918–927.

Phinney, J. S. (2003). Ethnic identity and acculturation. In K. Chun, P. Ball, & Marin, G. (Eds.), *Acculturation: Advances in theory, measurement, and applied research* (pp. 63–81). Washington, DC: American Psychological Association.

Piaget, J. (1952). *The origins of intelligence in children.* New York: International University Press.

Pickering, A. D. (1997). The conceptual nervous system and personality: From Pavlov to neural networks. *European Psychologist, 2*(2), 139–163.

Pickering, A. D., & Gray, J. A. (1999). The neuroscience of personality. In L. A. Pervin & O. P. John (Eds.), *The handbook of personality* (2nd ed.). New York: Guilford Press.

Pietrzak, J., Downey, G., & Ayduk, O. (2005). Rejection sensitivity as an interpersonal vulnerability. In M. W. Baldwin (Ed.), *Interpersonal cognition* (pp. 62–84). New York: Guilford Press.

Pillemer, D. B., & White, S. (1989). Childhood events recalled by children and adults. In H. W. Reese (Ed.), *Advances in child development and behavior* (Vol. 21, pp. 297–340). New York: Academic Press.

Pinizzotto, A. J., & Finkel, N. J. (1990). Criminal personality profiling. *Law and Human Behavior, 14,* 215–233.

Plaks, J. E., Stroessner, S. J., Dweck, C. S., & Sherman, J. W. (2001). Person theories and attention allocation: Preferences for stereotypic versus counterstereotypic information. *Journal of Personality and Social Psychology, 80*(6), 876–893.

Plomin, R. (2001). Genetics and behaviour. *Psychologist, 14*(3), 134–139.

Plomin, R., & Crabbe, J. (2000). DNA. *Psychological Bulletin, 126*(6), 806–828.

Plomin, R., & McGuffin, P. (2003). Psychopathology in the postgenomic era. *Annual Review of Psychology, 54,* 205–228.

Plomin, R., & Neiderhiser, J. M. (1992). Genetics and experience. *Current Directions in Psychological Science, 1*(5), 160–163.

Plomin, R., & Nesselroade, J. R. (1990). Behavioral genetics and personality change. *Journal of Personality, 58,* 191–220.

Plomin, R., Haworth, C. M., & Davis, O. S. (2009). Common disorders are quantitative traits. *National Review of Genetics, 10,* 872–878.

Plutchik, R., & Conte, H. R. (1997). *Circumplex models of personality and emotions.* Washington, DC: American Psychological Association.

Pogrebin, L. C. (1983). *Family politics: Love and power on an intimate frontier.* New York: McGraw-Hill.

Porter, C. A., & Suedfeld, P. (1981). Integrative complexity in the correspondence of literary figures: Effects of personal and societal stress. *Journal of Personality and Social Psychology, 40,* 321–330.

Post, J. M. (2007). *The mind of the terrorist: The psychology of terrorism from the IRA to al-Qaeda.* New York: Palgrave Macmillan.

Pressman, S., & Cohen, S. (2005). Does positive affect influence health? *Psychological Bulletin, 131*, 925–971.

Prince, R. J., & Guastello, S. J. (1990). The Barnum effect in a computerized Rorschach interpretation system. *Journal of Psychology, 124*(2), 217–222.

Proffitt, D. R. (2006). Embodied perception and the economy of action. *Perspectives on Psychological Science, 1*(2), 110–122.

Psyche in 3-D. (1960, March 28). *Time, 75*(13).

Putnam, R. D. (2000). *Bowling alone: The collapse and revival of American community.* New York: Simon & Schuster.

Quay, H. C. (1997). Inhibition and attention-deficit/hyperactivity disorder. *Journal of Abnormal Child Psychology, 25*(1), 7–13.

Quinn, S. (1987). *A mind of her own: The life of Karen Horney.* New York: Simon & Schuster.

Rahman, Q., & Hull, M. S. (2005). An empirical test of the kin selection hypothesis for male homosexuality. *Archives of Sexual Behavior, 34*, 461–467.

Ramirez, J. M. (2003). Hormones and aggression in childhood and adolescence. *Aggression and Violent Behavior, 8*(6), 621–644.

Ramírez-Esparza, N., Gosling, S. D., Benet-Martínez, V., Potter, J. P., & Pennebaker, J. W. (2006). Do bilinguals have two personalities? A special case of cultural frame switching. *Journal of Research in Personality, 40*(2), 99–120.

Rauch, A., & Frese, M. (2007). Born to be an entrepreneur? Revisiting the personality approach to entrepreneurship. In J. R. Baum, M. Frese, & R. A. Baron (Eds.), *The psychology of entrepreneurship* (pp. 41–65). Mahwah, NJ: Erlbaum.

Rausch, M. L. (1977). Paradox, levels, and junctions in person–situation systems. In D. Magnusson & S. S. Endler (Eds.), *Personality at the crossroads* (pp. 287–303). Hillsdale, NJ: Erlbaum.

Raven, J. C. (1938). *Progressive matrices.* London: Lewis.

Read, S. J., & Miller, L. C. (2002). Virtual personalities: A neural network model of personality. *Personality and Social Psychology Review, 6*, 357–369.

Read, S. J., Monroe, B. M., Brownstein, A. L., Yang, Y., Chopra, G., & Miller, L. C. (2010). A neural network model of the structure and dynamics of human personality. *Psychological Review, 117*, 61–92.

Reicher, S., Spears, R., & Postmes, T. (1995). A social identity model of deindividuation phenomena. *European Review of Social Psychology, 6*, 161–198.

Reiss, D. (1997). Mechanisms linking genetic and social influences in adolescent development. *Current Directions in Psychological Science, 6*, 100–105.

Rentfrow, P. J., & Gosling, S. D. (2003). The Do-Re-Mi's of everyday life: Examining the structure and personality correlates of music preferences. *Journal of Personality and Social Psychology, 84*, 1236–1256.

Rentfrow, P. J., & Gosling, S. D. (2006). Message in a ballad: The role of music preferences in interpersonal perception. *Psychological Science, 17*(3), 236–242.

Rentfrow, P. J., Gosling, S. D., & Potter, J. (2008). A theory of the emergence, persistence, and expression of geographic variation in psychological characteristics. *Perspectives on Psychological Science, 3*, 339–369.

Richardson, D. S., & Hammock, G. S. (2007). Social context of human aggression: Are we paying too much attention to gender? *Aggression and Violent Behavior, 12*(4), 417–426.

Richmond, J., & Nelson, C. A. (2007). Accounting for change in declarative memory: A cognitive neuroscience perspective. *Developmental Review, 27*(3), 349–373.

Rieger, G., Chivers, M. L., & Bailey, J. M. (2005). Sexual arousal patterns of bisexual men. *Psychological Science 16*(8), 579–584.

Riggio, R. E. (1986). Assessment of basic social skills. *Journal of Personality and Social Psychology, 51*, 649–660.

Riggio, R. E. (1992). Social interaction skills and nonverbal behavior. In R. S. Feldman (Ed.), *Applications of nonverbal behavioral theories and research* (pp. 3–30). Hillsdale, NJ: Erlbaum.

Riggio, R. E., & Friedman, H. S. (1986). Impression formation: The role of expressive behavior. *Journal of Personality and Social Psychology, 50*, 421–427.

Riggio, R. E., & Reichard, R. J. (2008). The emotional and social intelligences of effective leadership: An emotional and social skill approach. *Journal of Managerial Psychology, 23*, 169–185.

Rippl, S., & Boehnke, K. (1995). Authoritarianism: Adolescents from East and West Germany and the United States compared. In J. Youniss (Ed.), *After the wall: Family adaptations in East and West Germany* (pp. 57–70). San Francisco: Jossey-Bass.

Riva, G., Raspelli, S., Algeri, D., Pallavicini, F., Gorini, A., Wiederhold, B. K., & Gaggioli, A. (2010). Interreality in practice: Bridging virtual and real worlds in the treatment of posttraumatic stress disorders. *Cyberpsychology, Behavior, and Social Networking, 13*, 55–65.

Rizzolatti, G., & Craighero, L. (2004). The mirror-neuron system. *Annual Review of Neuroscience, 27*, 169–192.

Roberson, L., & Kulik, C. T. (2007). Stereotype threat at work. *The Academy of Management Perspectives, 21*, 24–40.

Roberts, B. W., & Caspi, A. (2001). Personality development and the person–situation debate: It's déjà vu all over again. *Psychological Inquiry, 12*(2), 104–109.

Roberts, B. W., & Caspi, A. (2003). The cumulative continuity model of personality development: Striking a balance between continuity and change in personality traits across the life course. In R. M. Staudinger & U. Lindenberger (Eds.), *Understanding human development: Lifespan psychology in exchange with other disciplines* (pp. 183–214). Dordrecht, NL: Kluwer Academic.

Roberts, B. W., & DelVecchio, W. F. (2000). The rank-order consistency of personality traits from childhood to old age: A quantitative review of longitudinal studies. *Psychological Bulletin, 126*(1), 3–25.

Roberts, B. W., & Mroczek, D. (2008). Personality trait change in adulthood. *Current Directions in Psychological Science, 17*, 31–35.

Roberts, B. W., Walton, K. E., & Viechtbauer, W. (2006). Patterns of mean-level change in personality traits across the life course: A meta-analysis of longitudinal studies. *Psychological Bulletin, 132*, 1–25.

Roberts, B. W., Kuncel, N. R., Shiner, R., Caspi, A., & Goldberg, L. R. (2007). The power of personality: The comparative validity of personality traits, socioeconomic status, and cognitive ability for predicting important life outcomes. *Perspectives on Psychological Science, 2*(4), 313–345.

Roberts, R. E., Deleger, S., Strawbridge, W. J., & Kaplan, G. A. (2003). Prospective association between obesity and depression: Evidence from the Alameda County Study. *International Journal of Obesity and Related Metabolic Disorders, 27,* 514–521.

Roberts, R. E., Strawbridge, W. J., Deleger, S., & Kaplan, G. A. (2002). Are the fat more jolly? *Annals of Behavioral Medicine, 24,* 169–180.

Robins, R. W., Fraley, R. C., & Krueger R. F. (Eds.). (2007). *Handbook of research methods in personality psychology.* New York: Guilford.

Robins, R. W., Fraley, R. C., Roberts, B. W., & Trzesniewski, K. H. (2001). A longitudinal study of personality change in young adulthood. *Journal of Personality, 69,* 617–640.

Robinson, F. G. (1992). *Love's story told: A life of Henry A. Murray.* Cambridge, MA: Harvard University Press.

Roccas, S., Sagiv, L., Schwartz, S. H., & Knafo, A. (2002). Basic values and the five factor model of personality traits. *Personality and Social Psychology Bulletin, 28,* 789–801.

Roemer, L., Litz, B. T., Orsillo, S. M., & Wagner, A. W. (2001). A preliminary investigation of the role of strategic withholding of emotions in PTSD. *Journal of Traumatic Stress, 14*(1), 149–156.

Rogers, C. R. (1951). *Client-centered therapy: Its current practice, implications, and theory.* Boston: Houghton Mifflin.

Rogers, C. R. (1961). *On becoming a person: A therapist's view of psychotherapy.* Boston: Houghton Mifflin.

Rogers, C. R., & Dymond, R. F. (Eds.). (1954). *Psychotherapy and personality change; Coordinated research studies in the client-centered approach.* Chicago: University of Chicago Press.

Rogers, C. R., & Stevens, B. (1967). *Person to person: The problem of being human.* New York: Simon & Schuster.

Romero-Canyas, R., & Downey, G. (2005). Rejection sensitivity as a predictor of affective and behavioral responses to interpersonal stress: A defensive motivational system. In K. D. Williams, J. P. Forgas, & W. von Hippel (Eds.), *The social outcast: Ostracism, social exclusion, rejection, and bullying* (pp. 131–154). New York: Psychology Press.

Rook, K. S. (1988). Toward a more differentiated view of loneliness. In S. Duck, D. F. Hay, S. E. Hobfoll, W. Ickes, & B. M. Montgomery (Eds.), *Handbook of personal relationships: Theory, research and interventions* (pp. 571–589). Chichester, UK: Wiley.

Rook, K. S. (1991). Facilitating friendship formation in late life: Puzzles and challenges. *American Journal of Community Psychology, 19,* 103–110.

Rose, R. J., Koskenvuo, M., Kaprio, J., Sarna, S., & Langinvainio, H. (1988). Shared genes, shared experiences, and similarity of personality. *Journal of Personality and Social Psychology, 54,* 161–171.

Rosenman, R. H. (1978). Role of Type A behavior pattern in the pathogenesis of ischemic heart disease, and modification for prevention. *Advances in Cardiology, 25,* 35–46.

Rosenthal, R. (Ed.). (1979). *Skill in nonverbal communication: Individual differences.* Cambridge, MA: Oelgeschlager, Gunn & Hain.

Rosenthal, R., & Rosnow, R. L. (1991). *Essentials of behavioral research: Methods and data analysis* (2nd ed.). New York: McGraw-Hill.

Ross, L., & Nisbett, R. E. (1991). *The person and the situation: Perspectives of social psychology.* New York: McGraw-Hill.

Rothbart, M. K. (1981). Measurement of temperament in infancy. *Child Development, 52,* 569–578.

Rotter, J. B. (1954). *Social learning and clinical psychology.* Englewood Cliffs, NJ: Prentice-Hall.

Rotter, J. B. (1966). Generalized expectancies for internal versus external control of reinforcement. *Psychological Monographs, 80*(1, Whole No. 609).

Rotter, J. B. (1980). Interpersonal trust, trustworthiness, and gullibility. *American Psychologist, 35*(1), 1–7.

Rotter, J. B. (1982). *The development and applications of social learning theory: Selected papers.* New York: Praeger.

Rotter, J. B., Chance, J. E., & Phares, E. J. (Eds.). (1972). *Applications of a social learning theory of personality.* New York: Holt, Rinehart & Winston.

Rottnek, M. (Ed.). (1999). *Sissies and tomboys: Gender nonconformity and homosexual childhood.* New York: New York University Press.

Rubin, Z. (1973). *Liking and loving: An invitation to social psychology.* New York: Holt, Rinehart & Winston.

Rumelhart, D. E. (1980). Schemata: The building blocks of cognition. In R. Spiro, B. Bruce, & W. Brewer (Eds.), *Theoretical issues in reading comprehension.* Hillsdale, NJ: Erlbaum.

Rushton, J. P. (1995). Construct validity, censorship, and the genetics of race. *American Psychologist, 50*(1), 40–41.

Rutter, M., & Silberg, J. (2002). Gene-environment interplay in relation to emotional and behavioral disturbance. *Annual Review of Psychology, 53,* 463–490.

Rychlak, J. F. (1997). *In defense of human consciousness.* Washington, DC: American Psychological Association.

Sabatelli, R. M., & Rubin, M. (1986). Nonverbal expressiveness and physical attractiveness as mediators of interpersonal perceptions. *Journal of Nonverbal Behavior, 10,* 120–133.

Saegert, S. C., Adler, N. E., Bullock, H. E., Cauce, A. M., Liu, W. M., & Wyche, K. F. (2007). *Report of the APA task force on socioeconomic status.* Washington, DC: American Psychological Association.

Saenger, P. (1996). Current concepts: Turner's syndrome. *New England Journal of Medicine, 335*(23), 1749–1754.

Sagan, C. (1996). *The demon-haunted world: Science as a candle in the dark.* New York: Random House.

Sahakian, W. S. (Ed.). (1968). *History of psychology: A sourcebook in systematic psychology.* Itasca, IL: F. E. Peacock.

Salinger, J. D. (1951). *The catcher in the rye.* Boston: Little, Brown.

Salovey, P., & Grewal, D. (2005). The science of emotional intelligence. *Current Directions in Psychological Science, 14*(6), 281–285.

Sapir, E. (1956). *Culture, language and personality.* Berkeley: University of California Press.

Sartre, J. P. (1956). *Being and nothingness: A phenomenological essay on ontology* (H. E. Barnes, Trans.). New York: Washington Square Press.

Saudino, K. J. (1997). Moving beyond the heritability question: New directions in behavioral genetic studies of personality. *Current Directions in Psychological Science, 6,* 86–90.

Saudino, K. J., Pedersen, N. L., Lichtenstein, P., & McClearn, G. E. (1997). Can personality explain genetic influences on life events? *Journal of Personality and Social Psychology, 72,* 196–206.

Saul, S. (2007, March 15). F.D.A. warns of sleeping pills' strange effects. *New York Times.*

Savic, I., Berglund, H., & Lindström, P. (2005). Brain response to putative pheromones in homosexual men. *Proceedings of the National Academy of Sciences of the United States of America, 102*(20), 7356–7361.

Scarr, S., & McCartney, K. (1990). How people make their own environments: A theory of genotype to environment effects. *Child Development, 54,* 424–435.

Schacter, D. L. (1987). Implicit memory: History and current status. *Journal of Experimental Psychology: Learning, Memory, and Cognition, 13,* 501–518.

Schacter, D. L. (1992). Understanding implicit memory: A cognitive neuroscience approach. *American Psychologist, 47,* 559–569.

Schapiro, B. A. (2007). Who's afraid of being kicked off the island? In R. J. Gerrig (Ed.), *The psychology of Survivor: Leading psychologists take an unauthorized look at the most elaborate psychological experiment ever conducted . . . Survivor!,* (pp. 3–14). Dallas, TX: BenBella Books.

Scheier, M. F., & Carver, C. S. (1985). Optimism, coping, and health: Assessment and implications of generalized outcome expectancies. *Health Psychology, 4,* 219–247.

Scheier, M. F., & Carver, C. S. (1988). A model of behavioral self-regulation. In L. Berkowitz (Ed.), *Advances in Experimental Social Psychology* (Vol. 21, pp. 303–346). New York: Academic Press.

Scherer, K. R. (1978). Personality inference from voice quality: The loud voice of extroversion. *European Journal of Social Psychology, 8,* 467–487.

Scherer, K. R. (1982). Methods of research on vocal communication: Paradigms and parameters. In K. R. Scherer & P. Ekman (Eds.), *Handbook of methods in nonverbal behavior research* (pp. 136–198). Cambridge, UK: Cambridge University Press.

Schiffman, J., & Walker, E. (1998). Schizophrenia. In H. S. Friedman (Ed.), *Encyclopedia of mental health* (Vol. 3, pp. 399–410). San Diego, CA: Academic Press.

Schmitt, D. P., Realo, A., Voracek, M., & Allik, J. (2008). Why can't a man be more like a woman? Sex differences in Big Five personality traits across 55 cultures. *Journal of Personality and Social Psychology, 94,* 168–182.

Schober, J. M., Kuhn, P. J., Kovacs, P. G., Earle, J. H., Byrne, P. M., & Fries, R. A. (2005). Leuprolide acetate suppresses pedophilic urges and arousability. *Archives of Sexual Behavior, 34,* 691–705.

Schultheiss, O. C., Kordik, A., Kullmann, J. S., Rawolle, M., & Rösch, A. G. (2009). Motivation as a natural linchpin between person and situation. *Journal of Research in Personality, 43,* 268–269.

Schuster, B., Försterling, F., & Weiner, B. (1989). Perceiving the causes of success and failure: A cross-cultural examination of attributional concepts. *Journal of Cross-Cultural Psychology, 20*(2), 191–213.

Schwartz, C. E., Kunwar, P. S., Greve, D. N., Moran, L. R., Viner, J. C., Covino, J. M., Kagan, J., Stewart, S. E., Snidman, N. C., Vangel, M. G., & Wallace, S. R. (2010). Structural differences in adult orbital and ventromedial prefrontal cortex predicted by infant temperament at 4 months of age. *Archives of General Psychiatry, 67,* 78–84.

Schwartz, J. E., Friedman, H. S., Tucker, J. S., Tomlinson-Keasey, C., Wingard, D. L., & Criqui, M. H. (1995). Sociodemographic and psychosocial factors in childhood as predictors of adult mortality. *American Journal of Public Health, 85*(9), 1237–1245.

Scott, S. G., & Bruce, R. A. (1995). Decision-making style: The development and assessment of a new measure. *Educational and Psychological Measurement, 55,* 818–831.

Seal, D. W., & Agostinelli, G. (1994). Individual differences associated with high-risk sexual behaviour: Implications for intervention programmes. *AIDS Care, 6*(4), 393–397.

Sears, R. R. (1951). A theoretical framework for personality and social behavior. *American Psychologist, 6,* 476–483.

Sears, R. R., Maccoby, E. E., & Levin, H. (1957). *Patterns of child rearing.* Evanston, IL: Row, Peterson.

Sears, R. R., Rau, L., & Alpert, R. (1966). *Identification and child rearing.* Stanford, CA: Stanford University Press.

Sears, R. R., Whiting, J. W. M., Nowlis, V., & Sears, P. S. (1953). Some child-rearing antecedents of aggression and dependency in young children. *Genetic Psychology Monographs, 47,* 135–234.

Seem, S. R., & Clark, M. D. (2006). Healthy women, healthy men, and healthy adults: An evaluation of gender role stereotypes in the twenty-first century. *Sex Roles, 55,* 247–258.

Segal, N. L. (1999). *Entwined lives: Twins and what they tell us about human behavior.* New York: Dutton/Penguin Books.

Segall, M. H., Dasen, P. R., Berry, J. W., & Poortinga, Y. H. (1990). *Human behavior in global perspective: An introduction to cross-cultural psychology.* New York: Pergamon Press.

Seldin, D. R. , Friedman, H. S., & Martin, L. R. (2002). Sexual activity as a predictor of life-span mortality risk. *Personality and Individual Differences, 12,* 409–426.

Seligman, M. E. P. (1975). *Helplessness: On depression, development, and death.* San Francisco: Freeman.

Seligman, M. E. P. (2006). *Learned optimism.* New York: Vintage Books.

Seligman, M. E. P., & Csikszentmihalyi, M. (2000). Positive psychology: An introduction. *American Psychologist, 55*(1), 5–14.

Seligman, M. E. P., Reivich, K., Jaycox, L., & Gillham, J. (1995). *The optimistic child.* Boston: Houghton Mifflin.

Seo, D., Patrick, C. J., & Kennealy, P. J. (2008). Role of serotonin and dopamine system interactions in the neurobiology of impulsive aggression and its comorbidity with other clinical disorders. *Aggression and Violent Behavior, 13,* 383–395.

Serin, R. C., & Kuriychuk, M. (1994). Social and cognitive processing deficits in violent offenders: Implications for treatment. *International Journal of Law and Psychiatry, 17*(4), 431–441.

Seyfried, L. S., & Marcus, S. M. (2003). Postpartum mood disorders. *International Review of Psychiatry, 15*(3), 231–242.

Shapiro, J. R., & Neuberg, S. L. (2007). From stereotype threat to stereotype threats: Implications of a multi-threat framework for causes, moderators, mediators, consequences, and interventions. *Personality and Social Psychology Review, 11,* 107–130.

Sharp, A. H., & Ross, C. A. (1996). Neurobiology of Huntington's disease. *Neurobiological Disease, 3*(1), 3–15.

Shaver, P. R., & Mikulincer, M. (2005). Attachment theory and research: Resurrection of the psychodynamic approach to personality. *Journal of Research in Personality, 39*(1), 22–45.

Shaver, P. R., Collins, N., & Clark, C. L. (1996). Attachment styles and internal working models of self and relationship partners. In G. J. O. Fletcher & J. Fitness (Eds.), *Knowledge structures in close relationships: A social psychological approach* (pp. 25–61). Mahwah, NJ: Erlbaum.

Shaver, P., & Hendrick, C. (Eds.). (1987). *Sex and gender.* Newbury Park, CA: Sage.

Shaw, D. S., Emery, R. E., & Tuer, M. D. (1993). Parental functioning and children's adjustment in families of divorce: A prospective study. *Journal of Abnormal Child Psychology, 21,* 119–134.

Sheldon, K. M., Elliot, A. J., Kim, Y., & Kasser, T. (2001). What is satisfying about satisfying events? Testing 10 candidate psychological needs. *Journal of Personality and Social Psychology, 80*(2), 325–339.

Sheldon, W. H., & Stevens, S. S. (1942). *The varieties of temperament: A psychology of constitutional differences* (4th ed.). New York: Harper.

Shelton, J. N., & Sellers, R. M. (2000). Situational stability and variability in African American racial identity. *Journal of Black Psychology, 26,* 27–50.

Shibasaki, M., & Kawai, N. (2009). Rapid detection of snakes by Japanese monkeys (Macaca fuscata): An evolutionarily predisposed visual system. *Journal of Comparative Psychology, 123,* 131–135.

Shibley-Hyde, J., & Durik, A. M. (2000, May). Gender differences in erotic plasticity—evolutionary or sociocultural forces? Comment on Baumeister (2000). *Psychological Bulletin, 126*(3), 375–379.

Shields, S. A. (1975). Darwinism and the psychology of women: A study in social myth. *American Psychologist, 30*(7), 181–195.

Shimizu, M., & Pelham, B. W. (2008). Postponing a date with the Grim Reaper: Ceremonial events and mortality. *Basic and Applied Social Psychology, 30,* 36–45.

Shiner, R. L., Masten, A. S., & Roberts, J. M. (2003). Childhood personality foreshadows adult personality and life outcomes two decades later. *Journal of Personality, 71,* 1145–1170.

Shoda, Y., Mischel, W., & Wright, J. C. (1994). Intraindividual stability in the organization and patterning of behavior: Incorporating psychological situations into the idiographic analysis of personality. *Journal of Personality and Social Psychology, 67*(4), 674–687.

Shonkoff, J. P., Boyce, W. T., and McEwen, B. S. (2009). Neuroscience, molecular biology, and the childhood roots of health disparities: Building a new framework for health promotion and disease prevention. *Journal of the American Medical Association, 301,* 2252–2259.

Shore, B. (1996). *Culture in mind: Cognition, culture, and the problem of meaning.* New York: Oxford University Press.

Shostrom, E. L. (1974). *Manual for the Personal Orientation Inventory.* San Diego, CA: EdITS/Educational and Industrial Testing Service.

Shweder, R. A. (1990). In defense of moral realism: Reply to Gabennesch. *Child Development, 61,* 2060–2067.

Shweder, R. A., & Sullivan, M. A. (1990). The semiotic subject of cultural psychology. In L. A. Pervin (Ed.), *Handbook of personality: Theory and research* (pp. 399–416). New York: Guilford Press.

Sibley, C. G., & Duckitt, J. (2008). Personality and prejudice: A meta-analysis and theoretical review. *Personality and Social Psychology Review, 12,* 248–279.

Siegel, L. S. (1995). Does the IQ god exist? [Special issue]. *Alberta Journal of Educational Research, 41*(3), 283–288.

Siegler, R. S. (2000). Unconscious insights. *Current Directions in Psychological Science, 9*(3), 79–83.

Silverberg, J., & Gray, J. P. (Eds.). (1992). *Aggression and peacefulness in humans and other primates.* New York: Oxford University Press.

Silverman, K., Svikis, D., Robles, E., Stitzer, M. L., & Bigelow, G. E. (2001). A reinforcement-based Therapeutic Workplace for the treatment of drug abuse: Six-month abstinence outcomes. *Experimental & Clinical Psychopharmacology, 9*(1), 14–23.

Simonton, D. K. (1994). *Greatness: Who makes history and why.* New York: Guilford Press.

Simpson, J. A., & Gangestad, S. W. (1991). Personality and sexuality: Empirical relations and an integrative theoretical model. In K. McKinney & S. Sprecher (Eds.), *Sexuality in close relationships* (pp. 71–92). Hillsdale, NJ: Erlbaum.

Simpson, J. A., & Kenrick, D. T. (Eds.). (1997). *Evolutionary social psychology.* Mahwah, NJ: Erlbaum.

Simpson, J. A., Ickes, W., & Blackstone, T. (1995). When the head protects the heart: Empathic accuracy in dating relationships. *Journal of Personality and Social Psychology, 69,* 629–641.

Skinner, B. F. (1938). *The behavior of organisms: An experimental analysis.* New York: Appleton-Century-Crofts.

Skinner, B. F. (1948). *Walden Two.* New York: Macmillan.

Skinner, B. F. (1957). *Verbal behavior.* Englewood Cliffs, NJ: Prentice-Hall.

Skinner, B. F. (1971). *Beyond freedom and dignity.* New York: Knopf.

Skinner, B. F. (1974). *About behaviorism.* New York: Knopf.

Smedley, A., & Smedley, B. D. (2005). Race as biology is fiction, racism as a social problem is real. *American Psychologist, 60*(1), 16–26.

Smillie, L. D., Pickering, A. D., & Jackson, C. J. (2006). The new reinforcement sensitivity theory: Implications for personality measurement. *Personality and Social Psychology Review, 10*(4), 320–335.

Smith, C. P. (1992). Reliability issues. In C. P. Smith, J. W. Atkinson, D. C. McClelland, & J. Veroff (Eds.), *Motivation and personality: Handbook of thematic content analysis* (pp. 126–139). New York: Cambridge University Press.

Smith, C. P., Atkinson, J. W., McClelland, D. C., & Veroff, J. (Eds.). (1992). *Motivation and personality: Handbook of thematic content analysis.* Cambridge, UK: Cambridge University Press.

Smith, E. R., & Semin, G. R. (2004, 2007). Socially situated cognition: Cognition in its social context. *Advances in Experimental Social Psychology, 36,* 53–117.

Smith, E. R., & Semin, G. R. (2007). Situated social cognition. *Current Directions in Psychological Science, 16,* 132–135.

Smith, J. D. (1988). *Psychological profiles of conjoined twins: Heredity, environment, and identity.* New York: Praeger.

Smith, J. W., Frawley, P. J., & Polissar, N. L. (1997). Six- and twelve-month abstinence rates in inpatient alcoholics treated with either faradic aversion or chemical aversion compared with matched inpatients from a treatment registry. *Journal of Addictive Diseases, 16*(1), 5–24.

Smith, T. W., & Gallo, L. C. (2001). Personality traits as risk factors for physical illness. In A. Baum, T. Revenson, & J. Singer (Eds.), *Handbook of health psychology* (pp. 139–172). Hillsdale, NJ: Erlbaum.

Snodgrass, M. A. (1987). The relationships of differential loneliness, intimacy, and characterological attributional style to duration of loneliness. *Journal of Social Behavior and Personality, 2,* 173–186.

Snyder, C. R., Shenkel, R. J., & Lowery, C. R. (1977). Acceptance of personality interpretations: The "Barnum effect" and beyond. *Journal of Consulting & Clinical Psychology, 45*(1), 104–114.

Snyder, C. R., Shorey, H. S., Cheavens, J., Pulvers, K. M., Adams, V. H., & Wiklund, C. (2002). Hope and academic success in college. *Journal of Educational Psychology, 94*(4), 820–826.

Snyder, D. K., Wills, R. M., & Grady-Fletcher, A. (1991). Long-term effectiveness of behavioral versus insight-oriented marital therapy: A 4-year follow-up study. *Journal of Consulting & Clinical Psychology, 59,* 138–141.

Snyder, M. (1974). Self-monitoring of expressive behavior. *Journal of Personality and Social Psychology, 30*(4), 526–537.

Snyder, M. (1987). *Public appearances, private realities: The psychology of self-monitoring.* New York: Freeman.

Snyder, M., & Klein, O. (2005). Construing and constructing others: On the reality and the generality of the behavioral confirmation scenario. *Interaction Studies, 6,* 53–67.

Sommer, R. (1969). *Personal space: The behavioral basis of design.* Englewood Cliffs, NJ: Prentice-Hall.

Sommer, R. (1971). *Design awareness.* San Francisco, CA: Rinehart Press.

Sontag, S. (1978). *Illness as metaphor.* New York: Farrar, Straus, and Giroux.

Sorrentino, R. M., & Roney, C. J. R. (2000). *The uncertain mind: Individual differences in facing the unknown.* New York: Psychology Press.

Spearman, C. (1925). The new psychology of "shape." *British Journal of Psychology, 15,* 211–225.

Srivastava, S., John, O. P., Gosling, S. D., & Potter, J. (2003). Development of personality in adulthood: Set like plaster or persistent change? *Journal of Personality and Social Psychology, 84,* 1041–1053.

Sroufe, L. A., & Fleeson, W. (1986). Attachment and the construction of relationships. In W. W. Hartup & Z. Rubin (Eds.), *Relationships and development.* Hillsdale, NJ: Erlbaum.

Srull, T. K., & Wyer, R. S., Jr. (1989). Person memory and judgment. *Psychological Review, 96,* 58–83.

Stabler, B., Surwit, R. S., Lane, J. D., Morris, M. A., Litton, J., & Feinglos, M. N. (1987). Type A behavior and blood glucose control in diabetic children. *Psychosomatic Medicine, 49,* 313–316.

Stagner, R. (1937). *Psychology of personality.* New York: McGraw-Hill.

Staudinger, U. M. (2008). A psychology of wisdom: History and recent developments. *Research in Human Development, 5,* 107–120.

Staudinger, U. M., Lopez, D. F., & Baltes, P. B. (1997). The psychometric location of wisdom-related performance. *Personality and Social Psychology Bulletin, 23,* 1200–1214.

Steele, C. M. (1997). A threat in the air: How stereotypes shape intellectual identity and performance. *American Psychologist, 52,* 613–629.

Stein, D. J., & Vythilingum, B. (2009). Love and attachment: The psychobiology of social bonding. *CNS Spectrums, 14*(5), 239–242.

Stelmack, R. M., & Pivik, R. T. (1996). Extraversion and the effect of exercise on spinal motoneuronal excitability. *Personality & Individual Differences, 21,* 69–76.

Sternberg, R. J., & Barnes, M. L. (Eds.). (1988). *The psychology of love.* New Haven, CT: Yale University Press.

Sternberg, R. J., & Grigorenko, E. L. (1997). Are cognitive styles still in style? *American Psychologist, 52*(7), 700–712.

Sternberg, R. J., & Zhang, L.-F. (Eds.). (2001). *Perspectives on thinking, learning, and cognitive styles.* Mahwah, NJ: Erlbaum.

Stigler, J. W., Shweder, R. A., & Herdt, G. (Eds.). (1990). *Cultural psychology: Essays on comparative human development.* New York: Cambridge University Press.

Stillman, T. F., Baumeister, R. F., Lambert, N. M., Crescioni, A. W., DeWall, C. N., & Fincham, F. D. (2009). Alone and without purpose: Life loses meaning following social exclusion. *Journal of Experimental Social Psychology, 45,* 686–694.

Stirman, S. W., & Pennebaker, J. W. (2001). Word use in the poetry of suicidal and nonsuicidal poets. *Psychosomatic Medicine, 63*(4), 517–522.

Stockard, J., & Johnson, M. M. (1992). *Sex and gender in society* (2nd ed.). Englewood Cliffs, NJ: Prentice-Hall.

Stoff, D. M., & Cairns, R. B. (Eds.). (1996). *Aggression and violence: Genetic, neurobiological, and biosocial perspectives.* Mahwah, NJ: Erlbaum.

Stone, A. A., Kessler, R. C., & Haythornthwaite, J. A. (1991). Measuring daily events and experiences: Decisions for the researcher [Special issue]. *Journal of Personality, 59*(3), 575–607.

Storms, M. D. (1981). A theory of erotic orientation development. *Psychological Review, 88,* 340–353.

Strachan, E., Pyszczynski, T., Greenberg, J., & Solomon, S. (2001). Coping with the inevitability of death: Terror management and mismanagement. In C. R. Snyder (Ed.), *Coping with stress: Effective people and processes* (pp. 114–136). New York: Oxford University Press.

Strathearn, L., Li, J., Fonagy, P., & Montague, P. R. (2008). What's in a smile? Maternal brain responses to infant facial cues. *Pediatrics, 122*(1), 40–51.

Strauss, N. (2006, November 30). The man behind the mustache. *Rolling Stone, 1014,* 58–70.

Strelau, J., & Eysenck, H. J. (Eds.). (1987). *Personality dimensions and arousal.* New York: Plenum Press.

Strube, M. J. (1989). Evidence for the type in Type A behavior: A taxometric analysis. *Journal of Personality and Social Psychology, 56,* 972–987.

Suddath, R. L., Christison, G. W., Torrey, E. F., & Casanova, M. F. (1990). Anatomical abnormalities in the brains of monozygotic twins discordant for schizophrenia. *New England Journal of Medicine, 322*(12), 789–794.

Suinn, R. M. (1995). Schizophrenia and bipolar disorder: Origins and influences. *Behavior Therapy, 26*, 557–571.

Sullins, E. S. (1989). Perceptual salience as a function of nonverbal expressiveness. *Personality and Social Psychology Bulletin, 15*, 584–595.

Sullivan, H. S. (1953). *The interpersonal theory of psychiatry.* New York: Norton.

Sullivan, K. T., & Christensen, A. (1998). Couples therapy. In H. S. Friedman (Ed.), *Encyclopedia of mental health* (Vol. 1, pp. 595–606). San Diego, CA: Academic Press.

Sulloway, F. J. (1996). *Born to rebel: Birth order, family dynamics, and creative lives.* New York: Pantheon.

Suls, J., & Bunde, J. (2005). Anger, anxiety, and depression as risk factors for cardiovascular disease: The problems and implications of overlapping affective dispositions. *Psychological Bulletin, 131*(2), 260–300.

Sulston, J., & Ferry, G. (2002). *The common thread: A story of science, politics, ethics, and the human genome.* Washington, DC: National Academic Press.

Suomi, S. J. (2003). Gene-environment interactions and the neurobiology of social conflict. *Annals of the New York Academy of Sciences, 1008*, 132–139.

Surtees, P., Wainwright, N., Luben, R., Khaw, K. T., & Day, N. (2003). Sense of coherence and mortality in men and women in the EPIC-Norfolk United Kingdom prospective cohort study. *American Journal of Epidemiology, 158*, 1202–1209.

Swann, W. B., & Read, S. J. (1981). Acquiring self-knowledge: The search for feedback that fits. *Journal of Personality and Social Psychology, 41*(6), 1119–1128.

Swann, W. B., & Seyle, C. (2005). Personality psychology's comeback and its emerging symbiosis with social psychology. *Personality and Social Psychology Bulletin, 31*, 155–165.

Swanson, J. M., Posner, M. I., Cantwell, D., Wigal, S., Crinella, F., Filipek, P., et al. (1998). Attention-deficit/hyperactivity disorder: Symptom domains, cognitive processes, and neural networks. In R. Parasuraman (Ed.), *The attentive brain* (pp. 445–460). Cambridge, MA: MIT Press.

Tangney, J. P., & Fischer, K. W. (Eds.). (1995). *Self-conscious emotions: The psychology of shame, guilt, embarrassment, and pride.* New York: Guilford Press.

Tangney, J. P., Wagner, P. E., Hill-Barlow, D., & Marschall, D. E. (1996). Relation of shame and guilt to constructive versus destructive responses to anger across the lifespan. *Journal of Personality and Social Psychology, 70*(4), 797–809.

Tavris, C. (1992). *The mismeasure of woman.* New York: Simon & Schuster.

Taylor, S. E. (2006). Tend and befriend: Biobehavioral bases of affiliation under stress. *Current Directions in Psychological Science, 15*, 273–277.

Taylor, S. E. (2010). Health. In S. T. Fiske, D. T. Gilbert, & G. Lindzey, (Eds.), *Handbook of social psychology, Vol 1* (5th ed.), (pp. 698–723). Hoboken, NJ: John Wiley.

Taylor, S. E., & Crocker, J. (1981). Schematic bases of social information processing. In E. T. Higgins, C. P. Herman,

& M. P. Zanna (Eds.), *Social cognition: The Ontario symposium* (Vol. 1). Hillsdale, NJ: Erlbaum.

Taylor, S. E., & Gonzaga, G. C. (2007). Affiliative responses to stress: A social neuroscience model. In E. Harmon-Jones & P. Winkielman (Eds.), *Social neuroscience: Integrating biological and psychological explanations of social behavior* (pp. 454–473). New York: Guilford Press.

Taylor, S. E., Welch, W. T., Kim, H. S., & Sherman, D. K. (2007). Cultural differences in the impact of social support on psychological and biological stress responses. *Psychological Science, 18*, 831–837.

Taylor, S. E., Kemeny, M. E., Reed, G. M., Bower, J. E., & Gruenewald, T. L. (2000). Psychological resources, positive illusions, and health. *American Psychologist, 55*(1), 99–109.

Taylor, S. E., Lewis, B. P., Gruenewald, T. L., Gurung, R. A. R., Updegraff, J. A., & Klein, L. C. (2002). Sex differences in biobehavioral responses to threat: Reply to Geary and Flinn (2002). *Psychological Review, 109*(4), 751–753.

Temoshok, L. (1998). HIV and AIDS. In H. S. Friedman (Ed.), *Encyclopedia of mental health* (Vol. 2, pp. 375–392). San Diego, CA: Academic Press.

Tennant, C. (1988). Parental loss in childhood: Its effect in adult life. *Archives of General Psychiatry, 45*, 1045–1050.

Tennen, H., & Affleck, G. (1987). The costs and benefits of optimistic explanations and dispositional optimism. *Journal of Personality, 55*, 377–393.

Terman, L. M. (1917). The intelligence quotient of Francis Galton in childhood. *American Journal of Psychology, 28*, 208–215.

Terman, L. M. (1921). *Suggestions for the education and training of gifted children.* Stanford, CA: Stanford University Press.

Terman, L. M. (1954). Scientists and nonscientists in a group of 800 gifted men. *Psychological Monographs, 68*, No. 7.

Terman, L. M., & Oden, M. H. (1947). *The gifted child grows up: Twenty-five years' follow-up of a superior group.* Stanford, CA: Stanford University Press.

Terracciano, A., & Costa, P. T., Jr. (2004). Smoking and the five-factor model of personality. *Addiction, 99*, 472–481.

Terracciano, A., Costa, P. T., Jr., & McCrae, R. R. (2006). Personality plasticity after age 30. *Personality and Social Psychology Bulletin, 32*, 999–1009.

Tett, R. P., & Guterman, H. A. (2000). Situation trait relevance, trait expression, and cross-situational consistency: Testing a principle of trait activation. *Journal of Research in Personality, 34*(4), 397–423.

Thomas, A., Chess, S., & Korn, S. J. (1982). The reality of difficult temperament. *Merrill-Palmer Quarterly, 28*, 1–20.

Thompson, C. (2010, June 14) What is I.B.M.'s Watson? *New York Times.* Retrieved from http://www.nytimes.com

Thoreau, H. D. (1854). *Walden: or, Life in the woods.* Boston: Ticknor and Fields.

Thorne, A. (1987). The press of personality: A study of conversations between introverts and extraverts. *Journal of Personality and Social Psychology, 53*, 718–726.

Tickle-Degnen, L., & Lyons, K. D. (2004). Practitioners' impressions of patients with Parkinson's disease: The social ecology of the expressive mask. *Social Science & Medicine, 58*, 603–614.

Tomasello, M. (2000). Culture and cognitive development. *Current Directions in Psychological Science, 9*(2), 37–40.

Tooby, J., Cosmides, L., & Barrett, H. C. (2003). The second law of thermodynamics is the first law of psychology: Evolutionary developmental psychology and the theory of tandem, coordinated inheritances. *Psychological Bulletin, 129*(6), 858–865.

Torestad, B., Magnusson, D., & Olah, A. (1990). Coping, control, and experience of anxiety: An interactional perspective. *Anxiety Research, 3*(1), 1–16.

Trentacosta, C. J., & Izard, C. E. (2007). Kindergarten children's emotion competence as a predictor of their academic competence in first grade. *Emotion, 7*(1), 77–88.

Triandis, H. C. (1989). The self and social behavior in differing cultural contexts. *Psychological Review, 96*(3), 506–520.

Triandis, H. C. (1994). *Culture and social behavior.* New York: McGraw-Hill.

Triandis, H. C. (1995). *Individualism and collectivism.* Boulder, CO: Westview Press.

Triandis, H. C., & Suh, E. M. (2002). Cultural influences on personality. *Annual Review of Psychology, 53*, 133–160.

Triandis, H. C., & Trafimow, D. (2001). Cross-national prevalence of collectivism. In C. Sedikides & M. B. Brewer (Eds.), *Individual self, relational self, collective self* (pp. 259–276). Philadelphia: Psychology Press/Taylor & Francis.

Triesman, A. M. (1964). Selective attention in man. *British Medical Bulletin, 20*, 12–16.

Trivers, R. L. (1996). Parental investment and sexual selection. In L. D. Houck & L. C. Drickamer (Eds.), *Foundations of animal behavior: Classic papers with commentaries* (pp. 795–838). Chicago: University of Chicago Press.

Trzesniewski, K. H., Donnellan, M. B., & Robins, R. W. (2003). Stability of self-esteem across the lifespan. *Journal of Personality and Social Psychology, 84*, 205–220.

Tsuang, M. T., Bar, J. L., Harley, R. M., & Lyons, M. J. (2001). The Harvard Twin Study of Substance Abuse: What we have learned. *Harvard Review of Psychiatry, 9*, 267–279.

Tucker, J. M., Friedman, H. S., Tomlinson-Keasey, C., Schwartz, J. E., Wingard, D. L., & Criqui, M. H. (1995). Childhood psychosocial predictors of adulthood smoking, alcohol consumption, and physical activity. *Journal of Applied Social Psychology, 25*, 1884–1899.

Tucker, L. A. (1983). Muscular strength and mental health. *Journal of Personality and Social Psychology, 45*, 1355–1360.

Tulving, E., & Osler, S. (1968). Effectiveness of retrieval cues in memory for words. *Journal of Experimental Psychology, 77*, 593–601.

Turkheimer, E., & Waldron, M. (2000). Nonshared environment: A theoretical, methodological, and quantitative review. *Psychological Bulletin, 126*(1), 78–108.

Twenge, J. M. (2000). The age of anxiety? The birth cohort change in anxiety and neuroticism, 1952–1993. *Journal of Personality and Social Psychology, 79*(6), 1007–1021.

Twenge, J. M. (2001). Birth cohort changes in extraversion: A cross-temporal meta-analysis, 1966–1993. *Personality & Individual Differences, 30*(5), 735–748.

Twenge, J. M. (2002). Birth cohort, social change, and personality: The interplay of dysphoria and individualism in the 20th century. In D. Cervone & W. Mischel (Eds.), *Advances in personality science* (pp. 196–218). New York: Guilford Press.

Twenge, J. M. (2006). *Generation Me: Why today's young Americans are more confident, assertive, entitled—and more miserable than ever before.* New York: Free Press.

Twenge, J. M., & Campbell, W. K. (2003). "Isn't it fun to get the respect that we're going to deserve?" Narcissism, social rejection, and aggression. *Personality and Social Psychology Bulletin, 29*, 261–272.

Twenge, J. M., & Campbell, W. K. (2009). *The narcissism epidemic: Living in the age of enlightenment.* New York: Free Press.

Twenge, J. M., Zhang, L., & Im, C. (2004). It's beyond my control: A cross-temporal meta-analysis of increasing externality in locus of control, 1960–2002. *Personality and Social Psychology Review, 8*, 308–319.

Twenge, J. M., Gentile, B., DeWall, C. N., Ma, D., Lacefield, K., & Schurtz, D. R. (2010). Birth cohort increases in psychopathology among young Americans, 1938–2007: A cross-temporal meta-analysis of the MMPI. *Clinical Psychology Review, 30*, 145–154.

Ulrich, R. E., Stachnik, T. J., & Stainton, N. R. (1963). Student acceptance of generalized personality interpretations. *Psychological Reports, 13*, 831–834.

Uttal, W. R. (2000). *The war between mentalism and behaviorism.* Mahwah, NJ: Erlbaum.

Vaidya, C. J., Austin, G., Kirkorian, G., Ridlehuber, H. W., Desmond, J. E., Glover, G. H., et al. (1998, November 24). Selective effects of methylphenidate in attention deficit hyperactivity disorder: A functional magnetic resonance study. *Proceedings of the National Academy of Sciences, 95*(24).

Vaillant, G. E. (Ed.). (1986). *Empirical studies of ego mechanisms of defense.* Washington, DC: American Psychiatric Press.

Vaillant, G. E. (2002). *Aging well: Surprising guideposts to a happier life from the landmark Harvard study of adult development.* Boston: Little, Brown.

Vaillant, G. E. (2007). Aging well. *The American Journal of Geriatric Psychiatry, 15*, 181–183.

Vaillant, G. E., Bond, M., & Vaillant, C. O. (1986). An empirically validated hierarchy of defense mechanisms. *Archives of General Psychiatry, 43*(8), 786–794.

van der Noll, J., Poppe, E., & Verkuyten, M. (2010). Political tolerance and prejudice: Differential reactions toward Muslims in the Netherlands. *Basic and Applied Social Psychology, 32*, 46–56.

Van Deusen-Phillips, S. B., Goldin-Meadow, S., & Miller, P. J. (2001). Enacting stories, seeing worlds: Similarities and differences in the cross-cultural narrative development of linguistically isolated deaf children. *Human Development, 44*(6), 311–336.

Van Heck, G. L. (1997). Personality and physical health: Toward an ecological approach to health-related personality research. *European Journal of Personality, 11*, 415–443.

Vandenberg, B. (1991). Is epistemology enough? An existential consideration of development. *American Psychologist, 46*(12), 1278–1286.

Vandiver, B. J., Cross, W. E., Jr., Worrell, F. C., & Fhagen-Smith, P. E. (2002). Validating the Cross Racial Identity Scale. *Journal of Counseling Psychology, 49*, 71–85.

Vasey, P. L., & VanderLaan, D. P. (2010). An adaptive cognitive dissociation between willingness to help kin and nonkin in Samoan Fa'afafine. *Psychological Science, 21*, 292–297.

Vazire, S. (2006). Informant reports: A cheap, fast, and easy method for personality assessment. *Journal of Research in Personality, 40*, 472–481.

Vega, V., & Malamuth, N. M. (2007). Predicting sexual aggression: The role of pornography in the context of general and specific risk factors. *Aggressive Behavior, 33*(2), 104–117.

Vohs, K. D., Mead, N. L., & Goode, M. R. (2006). The psychological consequences of money. *Science, 314*, 1154–1156.

Volkow, N. D., Wang, G.-J., Fowler, J. S., & Ding, Y.-S. (2005). Imaging the effects of methylphenidate on brain dopamine: New model on its therapeutic actions for attention-deficit/hyperactivity disorder. *Biological Psychiatry, 57*(11), 1410–1415.

Volkow, N. D., Wang, G.-J., Fowler, J. S., Logan, J., Gerasimov, M., Maynard, L., et al. (2001). Therapeutic doses of oral methylphenidate significantly increase extracellular dopamine in the human brain. *Journal of Neuroscience, 21*(2), RC121, 1–5.

Vollrath, M. E., & Torgersen, S. (2008). Personality types and risky health behaviors in Norwegian students. *Scandinavian Journal of Psychology, 49*, 287–292.

von Helmholtz, H. L. F. (1925). *Handbuch der physiologischen optik* (Vol. 3). Liepzig. In J. P. C. Southall (Trans.), *Helmholtz's Treatise on Physiological Optics* (Vol. 3). Rochester, NY: Optical Society of America. (Original work published 1866)

Wagerman, S. A., & Funder, D. C. (2007). Acquaintance reports of personality and academic achievement: A case for conscientiousness. *Journal of Research in Personality, 41*, 221–229.

Wahlsten, D. (1995). Increasing the raw intelligence of a nation is constrained by ignorance, not its citizens' genes [Special issue]. *Alberta Journal of Educational Research, 41*(3), 257–264.

Waller, N. G., Kojetin, B. A., Bouchard, T. J., & Lykken, D. T. (1990). Genetic and environmental influences on religious interests, attitudes, and values: A study of twins reared apart and together. *Psychological Science, 1*, 138–142.

Wan, W. W. N., Luk, C.-L., & Lai, J. C. L. (2000). Personality correlates of loving styles among Chinese students in Hong Kong. *Personality & Individual Differences, 29*, 169–175.

Warrington, E. K., & Weiskrantz, L. (1978). Further analysis of the prior learning effect in amnesic patients. *Neuropsychologia, 16*, 169–176.

Wason, P. C., & Johnson-Laird, P. N. (1972). *Psychology of reasoning: Structure and content.* Cambridge, MA: Harvard University Press.

Watson, D. (1989). Strangers' ratings of five robust personality factors: Evidence of a surprising convergence with self-report. *Journal of Personality and Social Psychology, 57*, 120–128.

Watson, D. (2000). *Mood and temperament.* New York: Guilford Press.

Watson, J. B. (1914). *Behavior.* New York: Holt, Rinehart & Winston.

Watson, J. B. (1919). *Psychology from the standpoint of a behaviorist.* London: Routledge/Thoemmes Press.

Watson, J. B. (1924). *Behaviorism.* New York: People's Institute Press.

Watson, J. B., & Rayner, R. (1920). Conditioned emotional reactions. *Journal of Experimental Psychology, 3*, 1–14.

Watts, A. (1961, April 21). Eager exponent of Zen. *Life Magazine*, p. 21.

Way, B. M., Taylor, S. E., & Eisenberger, N. I. (2009). Variation in the µ-opioid receptor gene (OPRM1) is associated with dispositional and neural sensitivity to social rejection. *PNAS Proceedings of the National Academy of Sciences of the United States of America, 106*, 15079-15084.

Webb, J. A., Baer, P. E., McLaughlin, R. J., McKelvey, R. S., & Caid, C. D. (1991). Risk factors and their relation to initiation of alcohol use among early adolescents. *Journal of the American Academy of Child & Adolescent Psychiatry, 30*, 563–568.

Weber, M. (2001). *The Protestant ethic and the spirit of capitalism* (T. Parsons, Trans.). London: Routledge. (Original work published 1930)

Wegner, D. M. (1994). Ironic processes of mental control. *Psychological Review, 101*, 34–52.

Wegner, D. M. (2002). *The illusion of conscious will.* Cambridge, MA: MIT Press.

Wegner, D. M. (2003). The mind's best trick: How we experience conscious will. *Trends in Cognitive Sciences, 7*(2), 65–69.

Wegner, D. M., & Erskine, J. A. K. (2003). Voluntary involuntariness: Thought suppression and the regulation of the experience of will. *Consciousness & Cognition: An International Journal, 12*, 684–694.

Wegner, D. M., Wenzlaff, R. M., & Kozak, M. (2004). Dream Rebound. *Psychological Science, 15*, 232–236.

Weiner, B. (1985). An attributional theory of achievement motivation and emotion. *Psychological Review, 92*(4), 548–573.

Weininger, O. (1996). *Being and not being: Clinical applications of the death instinct.* Madison, CT: International Universities Press.

Weinstein, N. (1984). Why it won't happen to me: Perceptions of risk factors and susceptibility. *Health Psychology, 3*, 431–457.

Weiss, A. S. (1991). The measurement of self-actualization: The quest for the test may be as challenging as the search for the self. *Journal of Social Behavior and Personality, 6*, 265–290.

Weiss, A., & Costa, P. T., Jr. (2005). Domain and facet personality predictors of all-cause mortality among Medicare patients aged 65 to 100. *Psychosomatic Medicine, 67*, 724–733.

Westen, D. (1998). The scientific legacy of Sigmund Freud: Toward a psychodynamically informed psychological science. *Psychological Bulletin, 124*(3), 333–371.

Westen, D., & Rosenthal, R. (2003). Quantifying construct validity: Two simple measures. *Journal of Personality and Social Psychology, 84*, 608–618.

Whalen, R. E., Geary, D. C., & Johnson, F. (1990). Models of sexuality. In D. P. McWhirter, S. A. Sanders, & J. M. Reinisch (Eds.), *Homosexuality/heterosexuality: Concepts of sexual orientation* (The Kinsey Institute Series, Vol. 2). New York: Oxford University Press.

Whitbourne, S. K., Zuschlag, M. K., Elliot, L. B., & Waterman, A. S. (1992). Psychosocial development in adulthood:

A 22-year sequential study. *Journal of Personality and Social Psychology, 63,* 260–271.

White, R. W. (1959). Motivation reconsidered: The concept of competence. *Psychological Review, 66,* 297–333.

Whiting, B. B., & Edwards, C. P. (1988). *Children of different worlds: The formation of social behavior.* Cambridge, MA: Harvard University Press.

Whiting, B. B., & Whiting, J. W. (1975). *Children of six cultures: A psychocultural analysis.* Cambridge, MA: Harvard University Press.

Whitman, W. (1871). *Democratic vistas.* New York: J. S. Redfield.

Whitney, K., Sagrestano, L. M., & Maslach, C. (1994). Establishing the social impact of individuation. *Journal of Personality and Social Psychology, 66,* 1140–1153.

Whitson, E. R., & Olczak, P. V. (1991). The use of the POI in clinical situations: An evaluation. *Journal of Social Behavior and Personality, 6,* 291–310.

Wiederhold, B. K., & Wiederhold, M. D. (Eds.). (2005). *Virtual reality therapy for anxiety disorders: Advances in evaluation and treatment.* Washington, DC: American Psychological Association.

Williams, M. D., & Hollan, J. D. (1982). The process of retrieval from very long-term memory. *Cognitive Science, 5,* 87–119.

Wilson, E. O. (1975). *Sociobiology: The new synthesis.* Cambridge, MA: Belknap Press.

Wilson, R. S., Mendes de Leon, C. F., Bienias, J. L., Evans, D. A., & Bennett, D. A. (2004). Personality and mortality in old age. *The Journals of Gerontology Series B: Psychological Sciences and Social Sciences, 59,* P110–P116.

Wilson, T. D. (2002). *Strangers to ourselves: Discovering the adaptive unconscious.* Cambridge, MA: Belknap Press.

Wilt, J., & Revelle, W. (2009). Extraversion. In M. R. Leary & R. H. Hoyle (Eds.), *Handbook of individual differences in social behavior,* (pp. 27–45). New York: Guilford Press.

Windholz, G. (1991). I. P. Pavlov as a youth. *Integrative Physiological and Behavioral Science, 26,* 51–67.

Winkielman, P., & Berridge, K. (2004). Unconscious emotion. *Current Directions in Psychological Science, 13,* 120–123.

Winter, D. G. (1973). *The power motive.* New York: Free Press.

Winter, D. G. (1987). Leader appeal, leader performance, and the motive profiles of leaders and followers: A study of American presidents and elections. *Journal of Personality and Social Psychology, 52,* 196–202.

Winter, D. G. (1992). Power motivation revisited. In C. P. Smith, J. W. Atkinson, D. C. McClelland, & J. Veroff (Eds.), *Motivation and personality: Handbook of thematic content analysis* (pp. 301–310). New York: Cambridge University Press.

Winter, D. G. (1993). Power, affiliation, and war: Three tests of a motivational model. *Journal of Personality and Social Psychology, 65,* 532–545.

Winter, D. G. (1994). Presidential psychology and governing styles: A comparative psychological analysis of the 1992 presidential candidates. In S. A. Renshon (Ed.), *The Clinton presidency: Campaigning, governing, and the psychology of leadership* (pp. 113–134). Boulder, CO: Westview Press.

Winter, D. G. (2001). Measuring Bush's motives. *ISPP News: International Society of Political Psychology, 12*(1), 9.

Witkin, H. A. (1949). Perception of body position and of the position of the visual field. *Psychological Monographs, 63* (7, Whole No. 302).

Witkin, H. A., & Berry, J. N. (1975). Psychological differentiation in cross-cultural perspective. *Journal of Cross-Cultural Psychology, 6,* 4–87.

Witkin, H. A., & Goodenough, D. R. (1977). Field dependence and interpersonal behavior. *Psychological Bulletin, 84,* 661–689.

Woike, B. (2001). Working with free response data: Let's not give up hope. *Psychological Inquiry, 12,* 157–159.

Wolpe, J., & Plaud, J. J. (1997). Pavlov's contributions to behavior therapy: The obvious and the not so obvious. *American Psychologist, 52,* 966–972.

Wood, J. M., Nezworski, M. T., Lilienfeld, S. O., & Garb, H. N. (2003). *What's wrong with the Rorschach?* San Francisco: Jossey-Bass.

Wood, P. B., Cochran, J. K., Pfefferbaum, B., & Arneklev, B. J. (1995). Sensation-seeking and delinquent substance use: An extension of learning theory. *Journal of Drug Issues, 25*(1), 173–193.

Wood, R., & Bandura, A. (1989). Impact of conceptions of ability on self-regulatory mechanisms and complex decision making. *Journal of Personality and Social Psychology, 56*(3), 407–415.

Wood, W., & Eagly, A. H. (2000). A call to recognize the breadth of evolutionary perspectives: Sociocultural theories and evolutionary psychology. *Psychological Inquiry, 11,* 52–55.

Wood, W., & Eagly, A. H. (2010). Gender. In S. T. Fiske, D. T. Gilbert, & G. Lindzey (Eds.), *Handbook of social psychology,* Vol 1 (5th ed.), (pp. 629–667). Hoboken, NJ: John Wiley & Sons.

Wood-Sherif, C. (1980). A social psychological perspective on the menstrual cycle. In J. E. Parsons (Ed.), *The psychobiology of sex differences and sex roles.* Cambridge, UK: Hemisphere.

Woodworth, R. S. (1919). *Personal data sheet.* Chicago: Stoelting.

Woodworth, R. S. (1934). *Psychology* (3rd ed.). New York: Henry Holt.

Wortman, C. B., & Silver, R. C. (1991). The myths of coping with loss. In A. Monat & R. S. Lazarus (Eds.), *Stress and coping: An anthology* (3rd ed.). New York: Columbia University Press.

Wyatt, W. (1981). *To the point.* London: Weidenfeld and Nicolson.

Yates, T. M. (2004). The developmental psychopathology of self-injurious behavior: Compensatory regulation in posttraumatic adaptation. *Clinical Psychology Review, 24,* 35–74.

Yee, A. H., Fairchild, H. H., Weizmann, F., & Wyatt, G. E. (1993). Addressing psychology's problem with race. *American Psychologist, 48,* 1132–1140.

Yerkes, R. M. (Ed.). (1921). *Psychological examining in the United States Army. Memoirs of the National Academy of Sciences.* Washington, DC: U.S. Government Printing Office.

Yoon, C. K. (2000, October 17). Scientist at work: Joan Roughgarden, a theorist with personal experience of the divide between the sexes. *New York Times.*

Young, S. M., & Pinsky, D. (2006). Narcissism and celebrity. *Journal of Research in Personality, 40,* 463–471.

Young-Bruehl, E. (1988). *Anna Freud: A biography.* New York: Summit.

Yuill, N., & Lyon, J. (2007). Selective difficulty in recognising facial expressions of emotion in boys with ADHD: General performance impairments or specific problems in social cognition? *European Child & Adolescent Psychiatry, 16*(6), 398–404.

Zawadzki, B., & Strelau, J. (2010). Structure of personality: Search for a general factor viewed from a temperament perspective. *Personality and Individual Differences, 49,* 77–82.

Zelenski, J. M., & Larsen, R. J. (2000). The distribution of basic emotions in everyday life: A state and trait perspective from experience sampling data. *Journal of Research in Personality, 34*(2), 178–197.

Zhao, H., & Seibert, S. E. (2006). The Big Five personality dimensions and entrepreneurial status: A meta-analytical review. *Journal of Applied Psychology, 91*(2), 259–271.

Zhao, Y., Zhao, Y., & Song, I. (2009). Predicting new customers' risk type in the credit card market. *Journal of Marketing Research, 46,* 506–517.

Zill, N., Morrison, D. R., & Coiro, M. J. (1993). Long-term effects of parental divorce on parent-child relationships, adjustment, and achievement in young adulthood. *Journal of Family Psychology, 7,* 91–103.

Zivin, G. (1982). Watching the sands shift: Conceptualizing development of nonverbal mastery. In R. S. Feldman (Ed.), *Development of nonverbal behavior in children* (pp. 63–98). New York: Springer-Verlag.

Zori, R. T., Hendrickson, J., Woolven, S., & Whidden, E. M. (1992). Angelman syndrome: Clinical profile. *Journal of Child Neurology, 7,* 270–280.

Zuckerman, M. (Ed.). (1979). *Sensation seeking: Beyond the optimal level of arousal.* Hillsdale, NJ: Erlbaum.

Zuckerman, M. (Ed.). (1983a). *Biological bases of sensation seeking, impulsivity, and anxiety.* Hillsdale, NJ: Erlbaum.

Zuckerman, M. (1983b). Sensation seeking and sports. *Personality and Individual Differences, 4*(3), 285–292.

Zuckerman, M. (1999). *Vulnerability to psychopathology: A biosocial model.* Washington, DC: American Psychological Association.

Zuckerman, M. (2007). Sensation seeking. In M. Zuckerman (Ed.), *Sensation seeking and risky behavior* (pp. 3–49). Washington, DC: American Psychological Association.

Zuckerman, M., & Kuhlman, D. M. (2000). Personality and risk-taking: Common biosocial factors. *Journal of Personality, 68*(6), 999–1029.

Zuckerman, M., Joireman, J., Kraft, M., & Kuhlman, D. M. (1999). Where do motivational and emotional traits fit within three factor models of personality? *Personality & Individual Differences, 26*(3), 487–504.

Index